Inventing Autopia

D1263964

The publisher gratefully acknowledges the generous support
of the Lisa See Endowment Fund in Southern California History
of the University of California Press Foundation.

Inventing Autopia

Dreams and Visions of the Modern
Metropolis in Jazz Age Los Angeles

Jeremiah B. C. Axelrod

UNIVERSITY OF CALIFORNIA PRESS
Berkeley   Los Angeles   London

University of California Press, one of the most distinguished university presses in the United States, enriches lives around the world by advancing scholarship in the humanities, social sciences, and natural sciences. Its activities are supported by the UC Press Foundation and by philanthropic contributions from individuals and institutions. For more information, visit www.ucpress.edu.

University of California Press
Berkeley and Los Angeles, California

University of California Press, Ltd.
London, England

Library of Congress Cataloging-in-Publication Data
Axelrod, Jeremiah B. C.
    Inventing autopia : dreams and visions of the modern metropolis in jazz age Los Angeles / Jeremiah B. C. Axelrod.
        p.   cm.
    Includes bibliographical references and index.
    ISBN: 978-0-520-25284-4 (cloth : alk. paper)
    ISBN: 978-0-520-25285-1 (pbk. : alk. paper)
    1. Urbanization—California—Los Angeles Metropolitan Area—History—20th century.   2. City planning—California—Los Angeles Metropolitan Area—History—20th century.   3. Regional planning—California—Los Angeles Metropolitan Area—History—20th century. 4. Sociology, Urban—California—Los Angeles Metropolitan Area—History—20th century.   5. Los Angeles Metropolitan Area (Calif.)—Social conditions—20th century.   I.   Title.
HT384.U52L672   2009
307.1'416097949409042—dc22   2008025400

Manufactured in the United States of America
18   17   16   15   14   13   12   11   10   09
10   9   8   7   6   5   4   3   2   1

This book is printed on Natures Book, which contains 50% post-consumer waste and meets the minimum requirements of ANSI/NISO Z39.48–1992 (R 1997) (Permanence of Paper).

To
the memory of
Edna Borenstein
and
Bernard Axelrod
and
Kathryn O'Rourke

CONTENTS

List of Illustrations   *ix*
Acknowledgments   *xi*

Introduction. Looking toward Autopia   *1*
Prologue. A City That Does Not Move   *14*
1. "Los Angeles Is Not the City It Could Have Been"   *20*
2. Paradise Misplaced   *62*
3. Imagining the Metropolis in a Modern Age   *114*
4. Modern Los Angeles   *164*
5. Metropolis at a Crossroads   *210*
6. Gardens and Cities   *242*
Epilogue. A City That Moves   *288*
Conclusion. "To Dream Dreams and See Visions"   *310*

Notes   *325*
Bibliography   *377*
Index   *395*

ILLUSTRATIONS

1. The sprawling megalopolis   *15*
2. The *Los Angeles Times'* judgment on the parking ban   *18*
3. Gordon Whitnall   *25*
4. Downtown Los Angeles, 1919   *42*
5. Burgess model of concentric city growth   *45*
6. Garden city plan   *52*
7. Garden city and environs   *53*
8. Relation of garden cities to one another   *55*
9. Demonstration of the need for city planning   *60*
10. A victim of the parking ban   *66*
11. Clara Kimball Young   *67*
12. "Miss L.A." attacks parking ban   *69*
13. "More Rerouting"   *72*
14. "The claim-jumper"   *76*
15. Traffic mayhem as entertainment   *80*
16. The chaos of migration   *83*
17. "The modern Tower of Babel"   *84*
18. Wilshire Boulevard extension plans   *103*
19. Chicago's Loop, 1930s   *118*
20. New York's skyline, 1915   *125*
21. The Equitable Building   *128*
22. Ferriss and Corbett's multilevel streets   *139*
23. King's dream of New York, 1908 and 1911   *143*
24. "Visionary City"   *145*

25. Pasadena property values exhibit   *153*
26. View of a vertical Los Angeles   *165*
27. Lloyd Wright tower plan   *166*
28. Vertical sublime dreams for Los Angeles   *171*
29. Hollywood subway   *178*
30. Pacific Electric subway plan   *179*
31. "Make Wilshire Blvd. the Fifth Ave. of the *West*"   *186*
32. "Keep the 'L' out of Los Angeles"   *189*
33. "Even California sun would balk at this"   *190*
34. Los Angeles Chinatown, before and after   *196*
35. Skyscraper poetry and "Top Heavy"   *205*
36. Wilshire Boulevard   *215*
37. "Hypothetical lines of communication"   *219*
38. Merritt Parkway bridge   *255*
39. Taconic Parkway   *256*
40. Reconstructing nature   *257*
41. Parkway landscaping   *259*
42. Los Angeles Parkway plan   *277*
43. Parkway construction diagram   *281*
44. An ideal parkway envisioned in the Olmsted/Bartholomew plan   *283*
45. Ramona Gardens community commons   *291*
46. Ideal map from ". . . And Now We Plan"   *293*
47. Detail of model community diagram   *294*
48. Automobile Club motorway proposals   *298–99*
49. Vertical sublime fantasia   *300*
50. Automobile Club vision of urban elevated motorway   *301*
51. Arroyo Seco Parkway   *302*
52. Cahuenga Freeway   *303*
53. Futurama arcaded street scene   *305*
54. ". . . Now We Plan" theatrical set   *307*
55. ". . . Now We Plan" exhibit space   *308*

ACKNOWLEDGMENTS

Academia often fosters the precious illusion of monastic individual scholarship, but this book would never have come into existence without the contributions of many generous colleagues and mentors. At the University of California, Irvine, Alice Fahs and Jon Wiener provided me with valuable insights pertaining to this text and the ideas contained therein, afforded me much moral support and practical advice, and have always proven to be the most gentle stewards of the profession's best traditions and values. Other faculty at the university have rendered valuable support and advice throughout my graduate career, including, to name merely a few, Karen Merrill, Dave Bruce, Mark Poster, Mike Johnson, Anne Friedberg, and Linda Williams.

In addition to those at the University of California, a number of other scholars and kind souls have contributed to this volume. Fellow historians of California and modern urbanism, such as Jon Mochizuki, John Schwetman, Greg Hise, William Deverell, Mike Davis, Kevin Starr, and particularly Kyle Julien and John Ganim, have provided both personal encouragement and inspiring models of serious scholarship on the region. Similarly, George Lipsitz has always been a wonderful inspiration and teacher. Lynn Dumenil and the faculty and students at Occidental College have helped sustain and foster my understanding and enjoyment of Los Angeles, its people, and its cultures. My gratitude also goes to the other educators who have taught me so much, particularly the late Marjorie Herring in Riverside, as well as Shanti Singham, Mark Reinhardt, and, in fond memory, S. Paige Baty in Williamstown.

The staff at Special Collections in the Young Library at the University of California, Los Angeles; the Bancroft Library at Berkeley; the Carl A. Kroch Library at Cornell; and the Regional History Library at the University of Southern California, as well as everyone at the Los Angeles Public Library, have all been extremely supportive of this research project. I would also like to thank the wonderful folks at UC Press for their extraordinary work on this book, particularly Niels Hooper, Rachel Lockman, Laura Harger, and Elizabeth Berg.

Lastly, I would like to thank my family, who have always been the center of my life: Ron, Laura, Mort, Greg, and Max Borenstein and Melissa and David Axelrod. I owe the greatest debt of all to my parents, who have always provided unflagging encouragement, gentle understanding, and profound intelligence. This is merely one in a long line of reciprocal acknowledgments—a treasured tradition the continuation of which I anticipate eagerly. This book is dedicated to the perpetual memory of my heroic grandfather Bernard Axelrod, my role model and grandmother Edna Borenstein, and my dear friend, who helped so much with this manuscript, Kathryn O'Rourke.

Introduction

Looking toward Autopia

This book is about the relationships between imagination and place, between the ways people see urban landscapes and the ways they extrapolate these images into imagined or desired futures. Although it traces conceptions of a single city over a relatively short period of time—greater Los Angeles during the Jazz Age—it relates that particular place to its contemporaries among exemplary American metropolises and illuminates processes of thinking about space and social organization that have characterized a great deal of urban social thought in the twentieth century.

In the course of examining some of the principal ways Angelenos envisioned their city's future during the 1920s, this book presents an overview of how Southern California was organized in the pivotal period of its most explosive growth, and particularly how certain groups of experts understood that structure. It endeavors, in other words, to map onto the city's imagined future topography some of the critical understandings of power and social organization structuring contemporary knowledge of the metropolis, and especially the common sense awareness Angelenos had of the seemingly rigid systems of race, gender, and class that were at the time so evident and important to locals, and which circulated so widely through the city's influential cultural representations. It also shows how some Angelenos revised their imagining of the city's ideal future in response to social changes over the decade that seemed to threaten the visibility of these critical alignments.

In a larger sense, though, this work seeks to examine how urbanites in a given place imagine their metropolitan landscapes and how their own shared experiences of a particular urban form shape the way they go about imagining the sort of place their city should ideally be. How Angelenos perceived their metropolis—and those lines of power that so sharply defined its internal ideological boundaries and spaces—played a large part in determining how those citizens went about envisioning their city's future character.

As a work about urban vision and envisioning, this book focuses on efforts to read greater Los Angeles in the 1920s, to make sense of its spaces and to comprehend its real and ideal topographies. The relationship between lived and imagined spaces emerges here as a primary object of analysis, but if the ideal metropolis at times seems to overshadow the real, actual, or existing city in this study, that is intentional—such a relatively brief work can reference and extend, but should not seek to replicate or retread, the ground covered by the social historiography of the region that has emerged in the last thirty years—and perhaps fitting. Indeed, in its fascination with the power of imagined urban templates, this treatise merely echoes the efforts of Angelenos during the era, who were similarly concerned with the metropolis's representational images.

And in this respect Angelenos were not alone, for Los Angeles had emerged by the beginning of the 1920s as one of the world's most frequently portrayed cities. Images of its landscapes traveled widely and rapidly, circulated by an enormous real estate and tourism marketing combine, which effectively turned boosterism into an industrial process. More subtle but no less alluring and pervasive were the depictions of the region projected by motion pictures, as the characteristic landscapes of Southern California appeared behind the action of a striking portion of the world's film output.

Nevertheless, even enhanced by the city's most powerful representational machinery, the face of Los Angeles remained fuzzy to many spectators. In fact, despite this exposure, Los Angeles was an extraordinarily difficult place to grasp. In film and advertising, it was betokened by such generic images as the majestic *Washingtonia-robusta* palm and endless rows of citrus groves, rustic bungalows, and sun-drenched beaches, and yet, although each of these signs became easily recognizable as characteristic of the place, none identified it in any specific or definitive way. Before the existence of such iconic local landmarks as the freeway interchanges or even city hall, the growing metropolis persisted in the public imagination more as a collection of romantic but generic sets and locations than as a real, concrete place. Just as, in so many movies, Los Angeles's modest downtown buildings stood in for the towers of any midsize American city of the era and its suburban fields as the ranges of countless Westerns, just about any given image of this exemplary city could represent the entirety without being recognizable as any place in particular. As a matter of fact, out of this flood of images, very few characterized any actual identifiable sites in a metropolis almost utterly lacking in synecdochic markers. No other city in the era was so recognizable to so many people without any specific part of it being recognizable to just about anyone.

In its historiography too, Southern California in the Jazz Age sometimes seems a community out of focus, torn and twisted out of recognizable shape by a cluster of cultural, social, and demographic temblors that all seemed to hit at once in the 1920s. In fact, the particular character of Los Angeles's emergence as a major metropolis—its rise was not merely sudden but was accompanied by a host of social developments, such as the rise of the automobile, extensive suburbanization, internal migrations, and the consolidation of a mass media market—often appears inseparable from the other changes of the era. At times, the uncertainties about Southern California have simply been attributed to the dominance of these new forms within the region's culture or, even more frequently, to the mystifying upheavals of rapid growth itself, as if the speed and scale of Los Angeles's change in relative status among cities could explain away its peculiarities. Significantly, the expansion of the region during the 1920s, often referred to as an "explosion," has at times been taken to imply that Los Angeles's ascendance from small city to metropolis to megalopolis simply and by itself suddenly blasted all received assumptions about urban form and culture into the air, leaving the scattered pieces to fall willy-nilly into a new sort of urbanity. And in this historiography, as in the cultural representations of the time, aspects of the perceived landscapes of Jazz Age Los Angeles remain recognizable in fragments but are chaotic and utterly incomprehensible taken as a whole.

What is most surprising about this refracted image of Los Angeles is that, if the city of the 1920s has so often appeared jumbled or incoherent to outsiders gauging it from great geographical or temporal remove, it began the decade looking remarkably ordinary and comprehensible to local observers. It was a small enough city to be well understood by most of its longtime residents. It was also a place structured along social and economic lines that were fairly conventional for its era. Furthermore, after a tumultuous decade defined by battles between radicals and reactionaries, it seemed clear by 1920 that the reactionaries had in fact won and that the city would for the moment remain socially quiescent enough for its entrenched business and social elites to focus more on visions of municipal progress than on threats of wrenching change. Among the city's emerging professional civil service— a curiously mixed group of local capitalist boosters fixated on growth and technocratic quasi-socialists more interested in Progressive reform than social revolution, who collectively play a large part in this book—the city's prospects seemed both easily controllable and eminently predictable. Their goals centered around Los Angeles's structural order and efficiency, and their ambitions were great. Consequently, for those charged with perceiving the metropolis's future, the coming decade seemed to promise not vast and dramatic dislocation and disorientation but rather a great potential for increased clarity of social and topographical organization. At the beginning of the 1920s, local visions of both present and future Los Angeles stood in sharp contrast to the tumultuous, confused, and even strangely disembodied city, which, by the end of the decade, fired the imagination of both casual contemporary observers and successive generations of serious historians. How these confident and even complacent local visions of Southern California radically changed in the course of the 1920s is the primary subject of the chapters that follow.

MAKING SENSE OF THE CITY

Before embarking on this analysis, however, we should pause to make explicit the theoretical methodology that structures the arguments to come. At the most basic level, this book is concerned with how urbanites make sense of their surroundings and how confident they are in their ability to do so. Consciousness of basic urban comprehensibility is, in essence, the prism that focuses the diverse sorts of urban visions discussed here. Urban planner and theorist Kevin Lynch offered in 1960 what remains the most systematic basis for conceptualizing this comprehension of lived environments. In his influential *The Image of the City*, Lynch directs us to attend to the way locals "read" their urban surroundings, how they orient themselves within the vast array of disparate topographical and architectural elements within a modern city. He calls the ability of citizens to make sense of their town that place's "legibility."

Basing his work on a series of social scientific studies he undertook with Gyorgy Kepes at MIT, Lynch identifies five basic perceptual tools—or, as he puts it, "types of elements"—that help urbanites make sense of their cities: paths, edges, districts, nodes, and landmarks.[1] These five elements allow urbanites, Lynch argues, to understand their surroundings and to organize the city into a meaningful set of relationships. These elements thus represent generic ways of ordering unique and diverse urban features—streets, buildings, parks, fences, and so on—into categories of similarity and difference that can effectively transform a chaotic landscape into a legible array of simple, definitely located signs.

Although this explanation of how urbanites form readable "words" or "phrases" out of a discontinuous urban topography is both powerful and flexible, it tends to hang up on an inherent contradiction in the typology itself. This difficulty arises most clearly in his extended and detailed discussion of paths, the component that receives pride of place among the urban elements described in *The Image of the City*. "Paths," Lynch states, "are the channels along which the observer customarily, occasionally, or potentially moves. . . . People observe the city while moving through it, and along these paths the other environmental elements are arranged and related."[2] By this definition, it appears that the path is some sort of master subcategory: a path can contain and reference, even order and "arrange," the other four elements but generally cannot be referenced as such by them. This fact creates an incongruity within the list of categories presented; the path sticks out, as it were, from the collection of elements as might the name of a forest from a list of trees.

Lynch repeatedly attempts to resolve this conflict by referencing paths as if they were simply given streets and not collocations of other elements. In defining *path*, for instance, Lynch explains that "concentration of special use or activity along a street may give it prominence in the minds of observers. Washington Street is the outstanding Boston example: subjects consistently associated it with shopping and theatres."[3] If a path is reduced to an existing linear street, as it is in this quotation (and many others in the section on paths), then it is effectively merely a fixed object, and thus can be referenced in the definitions of other elements (e.g., a district could be bounded by that path on one side, as a perceptible barrier [an edge], or that district could be defined by its proximity to that street—which could, for example, run right through the district—just as it could be to a nearby building [a landmark]. Houston Street in Manhattan expresses the first relation to SoHo, just as Ventura Boulevard would to the San Fernando Valley). Clearly, though, the path, if understood fully as a serial arrangement of space that can, in fact, incorporate many different streets into its itinerary, cannot be so easily compressed into a single urban avenue.

This confusion in Lynch's definition of the path is not incidental or the result of an insufficiently rigorous choice of categorizational criteria, but instead reflects a far more substantial cleavage in the ways urbanites orient themselves, in the ways they read their cities. Are *The Image of the City*'s categories merely linear reference points, or are they, as often seems the case in his case studies, entirely different ways of organizing urban space? If paths are merely individual streets that serve to divide up a city, they are in actuality little more than boundaries (what he in other cases terms "edges") between his "districts" or "landmarks" or "nodes," which serve as stable and identifiable markers in an otherwise indiscriminate and homogeneous cityscape. If, however, one treats these paths as not simply demarcated thoroughfares but collections of repeatable or representative itineraries, serial collections of urban elements ordered not by absolute geographical proximity but by contingent experience in temporal or experiential sequence, then these paths describe an entirely different notion of urban navigation. The city is not composed merely of significant reference points whose importance arises from a self-evident distinctiveness, and which would remain significant no matter where one was in the city (so long as the markers remained visible) and no matter where one wished to go; rather it is a field of myriad possible routes, where individual urban elements only assume significance in the context of those other points that should logically come before them or after them in the process of moving through the city. In other words, the city exists either as an absolute and timeless collection of relatively hierarchical objects (some being inherently more distinctive or navigationally useful than others) or as a vast array of contingent waypoints, the significance of which varies depending on the other points drawn into relation to them by the movement of the observer through the fabric of the city.

The first mode of urban perception is timeless and abstract; it corresponds to what French theorist Michel de Certeau characterizes as the map. The second mode structures the city serially, over time, in a manner de Certeau identifies with routes or itineraries (and more generally, with narration itself, such as in any story with a plot).[4] The map conceives of a landscape omnisciently, as it were, taking in the whole thing at once and establishing natural, fixed relationships between all identified elements. Particular landmarks, in this way of understanding urban space, always remain significant. These urban elements persist indefinitely with a clear hierarchy of importance (and this pattern remains fixed as long as elements are neither added nor subtracted physically from the cityscape). The route, on the other hand, establishes the relative importance of elements in the city by reference not to an abstract absolute relationship but in terms of the particular starting and ending points of the individual trip. Different journeys through the urban fabric, even over much the same ground, would potentially find entirely different points of significance along the way, selecting certain objects as landmarks (for this particular route) that could very well be ignored as insignificant if passed on a different trip. The operative hierarchy of signification here is constantly shifting, situational, all without a single atom of the built environment changing.

The contrast between these two systems of spatial reference—between map and route, between fixed reckoning point and path—will play an important role in the larger arguments to come. For the time being, though, it is worth keeping in mind that many of the actors in the next chapters tend to read the city in a rigidly "map-like" way. Experts in urban planning and envisioning hold to conceptions of urban space that, however diverse in form, often appear fixed, diagrammatic, and abstracted. This epistemological inflexibility has repercussions in the choices people in Jazz Age Southern California made, and it even determined in large measure the field of choices they were capable of imagining in the first place.

LENSES FOR READING A CITY: AN IDEOLOGICAL
UNDERSTANDING OF URBAN EPISTEMOLOGY

Though this work is indebted to Kevin Lynch's concept of legibility, I would like to offer a more contingent, contextual understanding of the ways this comprehension operates within a community. This book suggests that Lynch's five categories should be considered not so much as material, concrete things (buildings [landmark], rivers [edge], intersections or business clusters [node], neighborhoods [district], or especially major thoroughfares [path]), as Lynch usually does, but as more general means of making sense of a given environment. These "elements" are better conceived as produced objects of knowledge instead of universal, preexisting terrain features to be cited through the organizational logic of the map or the route. In reality, they are not timeless or inherent but rather contingent and contextual. Their significance—their very existence as discrete and worthy of note—relies less on their architectural distinctiveness or relation to other urban elements than on the way the observer "reads" the cityscape as a whole. These categorized urban elements, then, are not merely neutral and transcendent categories but instead elements in constitutive lenses for viewing—or reading—the city, and for making meaning from it.

Before one looks in a city for features that might impart meaning, then, one should first ask what larger urban epistemologies—what means of making sense of an environment—might shape a particular viewer's gaze. It is this more comprehensive mode of knowing the city that determines in large part which aspects of a given built environment seem important in the first place, and it is this epistemology that controls how an observer relates these perceived elements to each other. In essence, these epistemologies, these lenses, might even be considered ideological, in a Gramscian sense: they comprise common sense systems of meaning that shape and influence how people go about ordering the hierarchy of a place, identifying significant sites (as landmarks, edges, districts, etc.), and indeed, choosing what objects are worthy of note. Such features cannot, therefore, be thought of as self-evident or preexisting topographical features, or even as emplaced relationships arising from the contrast or continuity between such features, but instead are entirely immersive ways of knowing a given set of spaces.

Urban observers, then, are not free to pick and choose among the vast array of objects in the built environment in seeking to locate themselves. Instead, certain sorts of objects naturally stand out to observers looking at the city one way, while they are utterly unremarkable to those reading the same environment through different lenses. In our two umbrella examples cited above, a maplike way of seeing a city will privilege one set of urban objects, while a route-based epistemology will likely select an entirely different (and probably less easily generalizable) collection of features. The ability to be read properly—legibility—thus cannot inhere in the landscape itself, as Lynch rigidly assumes, but resides in the eyes of the beholders.

To understand this critical difference in notions of legibility, we should briefly return to Lynch's survey methodology. He had undertaken his study, he explains in a later article, "Reconsidering *The Image of the City*," to encourage planners to attend to the ways actual users of cities make sense of them. This certainly was laudable. Yet he had done so, as he says, looking for patterns, and that had led him to ignore "observer variation," or the differences in how different sorts of urbanites go about interpreting their surroundings.[5] Even more problematic, I would suggest, were Lynch's choice of metaphor and the implications he drew, perhaps unconsciously, from that important selection. *The Image of the City* views the city as a text that can be read, and thus implicitly bases its understanding of legibility on notions of reading and literacy that were dominant when the book was published. He assumed that a single coherent text (in this case, of course, a given city) transmits definite and fixed messages to a receptive reader (the urban observer) in a simple and direct manner. Thus, he believed that the reports of his readers (survey respondents), in aggregate, would accurately summarize what the city itself had to say. By interviewing fluent readers about their understanding of the city, in other words, Lynch hoped to reconstruct the plot of their common text.[6] Now, if we assume, as most scholars have tended to do in the past forty years, that the relationship between reader and text is considerably more complex than a simple mimetic transmission of information, it becomes far more difficult to trace the definite and objective contours of the text merely by talking to readers. Not only do observers' accounts vary, as Lynch now acknowledges, depending upon their class, race, gender, or other identity positions, but the reconstructed account may better reflect the reading strategies, or ideologies, of the observers than the plot of the original source text. Instead of discovering inherently significant facts about a given cityscape, then, Lynch's survey may have uncovered one particular, ideologically shaped interpretation of that topography. And that one ideology might in fact be shared among a variety of respondents (particularly when they are all of roughly similar demographic backgrounds, as Lynch confesses) merely testifies to the ability of ideology to implicate itself into people's "common sense" once it has achieved hegemony.[7] These shared readings, which might correspond to what Lynch calls "public images" of a city,[8] reflect a particular, and particularly contingent, urban epistemology, but do not necessarily say anything at all about the actual physical built environment of a city in the abstract.

Since, as Lynch himself implies, one mode of reading a city can potentially achieve dominance in a particular place during a particular period of time, urban observers will never be simply left on their own to freely derive individual systems of urban orientation. Most frequently, one mindset—a master urban epistemology, or way of reading a city—will become dominant. Henceforth, most citizens, or at least those sufficiently familiar with the city and its culture to "know their way around" the landscape with some degree of fluency, will share a set of epistemological priorities and techniques (which, at the most practical level, can be used in giving comprehensible directions to total strangers).

To this entire citizenry, then, certain ways of viewing the city, or even cities in the abstract, seem natural. The hegemonic urban epistemology draws their attention to certain relationships and features in a city (tall buildings, say, in a community that relies on an urban epistemology that privileges this sort of landmark as an orientation tool), while ignoring others (such as localized districts) that might seem both useful and important to a confused visitor from a city where a different set of urban epistemologies dominates. In fact, bewildered hypothetical district-minded tourists would, logically, be looking to find neighborhood boundaries and distinctive local characteristics (architectural, demographic, etc.) to orient themselves but would only be offered direction around town by locals in relation to visible landmarks. For those locals unaware of the importance the visitor places on neighborhoods as means of navigation, urban districts might be entirely insignificant for finding one's way around town, or would matter only in relationship to the truly significant objects around which they are arrayed (i.e., the part of town between two particularly noteworthy towers, or those residential areas directly north of the clustered skyscrapers). In any case, there would be an inherent incommensurability in conceptions of basic urban organization, which would make it extremely frustrating to ask or give directions. Those capable of properly reading the city in the dominant way would have a very difficult time indeed telling that story to someone literate in an entirely different navigational rhetoric.[9]

MAKING MEANING FROM URBAN TOPOGRAPHY

Beyond these problems of basic communication, though, are there other implications arising from the dominance of one or another mode of urban epistemology in a given city? This book argues that there are. It suggests that one's dominant way of making sense of a cityscape emphasizes particular elements of that landscape as significant and worthy of note, while suppressing others as insignificant or even invisible. Modes of urban perception produced a powerful and influential aesthetics of urban form. Those objects singled out for significance by a given way of reading a city also gain a tangible sacral value—their manifest importance clings to them like an aura, reflecting the exemplary position they play in dominant local systems of signification. They may even seem beautiful. In cities organized according to a panoramic urban epistemology that privileges a fixed elevated observational perspective, such as New York City during the 1920s, the tall building took on immense cultural weight. These skyscrapers were not merely useful as landmarks within a system of urban location; they were actively awe-inspiring. They transcended their mere physical forms, as impressive as these might be, to evoke powerful and heretofore inexplicable emotions and sensations in their admirers. The language used to describe this ideological supplement to their ordinary appearance was that of the sublime; their descriptions frequently evoked almost mystical or even religious connotations from these artifices of steel, concrete, and glass. This ability of urban epistemology to influence the shared aesthetic values of a populace and to manipulate powerful related conceptions of modernity, progress, and efficiency testifies to the cultural power of these seemingly abstract ways of making sense of a city.

Similarly, these systems of perception subtly influenced a host of more concrete anxieties in Southern California. Observers of greater Los Angeles during the course of the tumultuous 1920s often judged the city by its apparent comprehensibility, order, and clarity—in other words, by its legibility. These urbanites regularly attached great significance to their ability to easily and accurately make sense of the growing region. Here, legibility not only implied a way of parsing the topography but once more related that perceived topographical order to a range of important urban evaluations that on the surface appeared entirely unrelated. This study delves into an aspect of the image of a city that Lynch left open in his work. Beyond his five elements, Lynch offers three primary, overarching "components" of urban perception: identity, structure, and meaning.[10] The process of identifying the five types of urban elements and placing them into coherent structural relationships with each other allows urbanites to find meaning in the cityscapes around them. *The Image of the City* explicitly restricts its analysis to the first two components.

Like Lynch's book, this work does not purport to trace the way millions of individual citizens comprehend particular and personal urban meanings—to recount, in a sort of archaeology, what Michel de Certeau calls the myriad "spatial stories" that have echoed though a city.[11] This work does suggest, though, that these meanings are produced from the ability of a given urban epistemology to make sense efficiently of a given cityscape, that these meanings can be shared in a citizenry's "common sense," and that these hegemonic common meanings are often circulated through and modified in popular mass discourse. This book seeks to track and analyze a number of these larger discourses.

This study, therefore, works from the assumption that modes of perception determine to a great degree not merely the city's perceived topographical features and the relations between part and whole, but the actual situation of identified urban elements within the social and cultural machinery of the community. This book further argues that the implications of this cultural production extend far beyond relatively abstract and technical direct discussions of urban form. They often feed or spill over into shared discourses on a range of vital civic matters, including debates over and understandings of public space and community, as well as contributing to the always contested dynamics of race, ethnicity, class, gender, and other important axes of power in a city. Particular alignments within systems of urban comprehension, then, can strongly influence residents' positions in these matrices of social signification, bringing particular individuals or groups into visibility or insignificance just as surely as they do for a building or a roadway.

These discourses, I suggest, can also operate reciprocally, translating debates about race or class, for instance, into discussions of urban space. This book traces in some detail, within the context of Jazz Age Los Angeles, a few of the ways this transference can occur. Often, through the course of the 1920s, space in Southern California was racialized, and often Angelenos judged the comprehensibility of the larger metropolis by the relative clarity of the lines of segregation inscribed there. Urban legibility in greater Los Angeles was throughout this period always bound up in matters of demographic demarcation and identification. This was quite simply the basis of clear urban order for many Angelenos, as for many other Americans in an era when racial lines ran particularly deep. These alignments of racial comprehension and larger urban form within Los Angeles structured many debates relating to the character of the city itself.

A CRISIS IN URBAN LEGIBILITY

Never thought that I would lose myself in Los Angeles, but I sure did this morning. My automobile was out of order and I took a streetcar. It looked all right and ran all right but it never got me to where I wanted to go. No more streetcars for me. I take an automobile or I walk.

LOS ANGELES CHIEF OF POLICE GEORGE HOME, ON THE DAY OF
THE GREAT STREETCAR REROUTING OF 1920, QUOTED IN HENSTELL,
SUNSHINE AND WEALTH (23–24)

What happens when these constitutive epistemological techniques no longer appropriately make sense of the changing metropolis, when the very lines of demarcation that structure vital human relations into vivid topographical clarity begin to erode? The result is an epistemological emergency, and this is precisely what struck Southern California during this blurry and confused period of its greatest proportional growth. If they could not easily read the city, Angelenos assumed there was something wrong with its development. Worse, by the later years of the decade, many urbanites looking at Southern California saw only chaos and disorder in the urban landscape. The anxiety that was produced and circulated through local discourse fed into what I call here a crisis in urban legibility within Jazz Age Los Angeles.

In a sense, then, this work takes as its starting point Lynch's almost casual observation that "the very word 'lost' in our language means much more than simple geographical uncertainty; it carries overtones of utter disaster."[12] Through the course of the 1920s in Southern California, more and more Angelenos began to feel "lost" in their own town. Residents, once so confidently able to make sense of their city, began during the 1920s to become disoriented. This should not be taken literally to mean that, like the police chief quoted in the epigraph above, Angelenos regularly lost their bearings while moving about the city, although that certainly must have happened quite a bit in such a rapidly expanding built environment. Instead, it seems to have become increasingly difficult, even for local experts in city planning, to compactly conceive and represent the entire city, even in abstracted diagrammatic form.

Nevertheless, that confusion, that rupture in urban comprehension, did not leave citizens powerless or mute, unable to derive any meaning from their surroundings. On the contrary, although this breakdown in legibility produced a great deal of anomie and even anger, it also spurred a vital and contentious discourse on the city—a stream of opinion and interpretation that was vividly and energetically expressed and circulated by urbanites in civic debate, popular culture, and even scientific investigation—which itself helped urbanites to make sense of their urban landscapes. In other words, not only can familiarity with a city's landmarks and structure allow residents to attach meanings to urban sites, but the confusion and disorientation produced by profound urban dislocation can elicit shared understandings of place. This book interprets these broadly circulated meanings by correlating the dramatic social changes of the era with Angelenos' ability to make sense of urban topography. The chapters that follow, then, integrate a number of the critical transformations historians identify in the city during that period by interpreting them in terms of the threat they posed to legibility of the metropolis for those who lived there. Beyond this connection, this study suggests that the emergent crisis in urban legibility played a large part in determining how some Angelenos, particularly those planning experts charged with maintaining the proper structural order of the metropolis, reacted to the social changes around them.

In probing a few of the characteristic and powerful ways that urban legibility affects how people, and particularly professionals in urban observation, imagine the proper functional relationships and geographical structures of a particular urban area, this study suggests that the very attempt to perceive the city in clear, diagrammatic terms—through a particular epistemological lens—played a large part in constraining how the future of greater Los Angeles could be imagined during the Jazz Age. Specifically, the chapters that follow argue that professional urban planners, through their disciplinary obsession with seeing the cityscape clearly as a set of functional relationships rendered according to the logic of the abstracted survey map, were driven to force the developing urban fabric to conform physically to a particular ideal of clarity and order. As greater Los Angeles deviated, almost inevitably, from that schematic form in more and more dramatic ways—such that vast portions of the city no longer seemed legible through the epistemological lenses to which planners were devoted—these experts began to react ever more strongly to the chaos they saw before them. Throughout the 1920s, the manifest and growing illegibility of the city drove planners to radical imaginings of urban reconstruction in order to repair the visible disorientation before them—a confusion, or epistemological crisis, that had as much to do with the instruments with which these urban observers preferred to view the city as with the actual physical shape, no matter how novel, of the metropolis itself.

In Jazz Age Southern California, moreover, urban priorities were often viewed by city leaders in purely structural terms, not human or social ones. The city appeared not as an amalgamation of diverse individuals and human communities, but as an autonomous mechanism, or being, in and of itself. The half-million or more Angelenos seemed, in comparison with this larger structural order, to be absolutely chaotic, random, and irrational in their movements. This impression may explain why citizens so often appear in planning discourse only through analysis of jumbled traffic patterns, for transit was the only manifestation of these millions of daily human activities and movements that was visible through these abstracted lenses. Vexing human problems, as a consequence, were frequently subsumed into "larger" urban structural crises, which could be more easily observed, comprehended, and treated by experts. This logic explains why persistent and serious social conflicts and dislocations were played out in 1920s Los Angeles through recurrent panics over the threat of blight within the city, urban sprawl, and especially, automobile traffic.

For the most part, instead of exploring new techniques of perceiving or reading the illegible topography of the expanding metropolis, these planners posited more and more radical—or reactionary—plans to remake the city in such a way that it could once more be clearly and sharply seen by traditional means. This obsessive epistemological inflexibility led planners not only to depart from the reigning cultural visions of modern urbanity but eventually to break with the urban booster elites upon whose support they so profoundly depended. Ultimately, city planning and envisioning in Southern California were driven as much by the desire to bring the metropolis into a particular epistemological focus as by notions of "the good life" or of the efficient and proper operation of the city.

Visuality obsessed urban observers of Los Angeles in the 1920s. The demands of clear, discriminating vision determined to a surprising degree the ideal form of the future metropolis. Clear urban legibility—manifesting itself only through a particular sort of visual clarity and order—became the primary criterion for future city planning in Los Angeles. Conversely, certain urban spatial arrangements, imagined in abstracted and diagrammatic form, garnered particular favor among local planners largely because they were so clearly comprehensible on paper. These envisioned urban configurations were assumed to naturally determine efficient and harmonious social relations among human inhabitants principally because the city form appeared efficient and harmonious. Desirable social order was assumed to inhere in certain urban spatial orders. A legible city must, it was assumed, be a humane and livable place. The form would guarantee the function, and the ready comprehensibility of the chosen form (or, in other words, its appropriateness and adaptation to a particular urban epistemic lens) would clearly illustrate its proper functional operation.

At its essence, then, this book is concerned both with the ways people see urban environments and, more fundamentally, how they routinely remake those environments to see them more clearly or to make them conform to imagined urban archetypes. To this end, the chapters that follow trace an epistemological metadiscourse on visuality, a series of urban envisionings that express the running conversation between experts, elites, and ordinary urbanites about how the image of the city bears on residents' ability to make sense of their community. They trace the fragmentation of preexisting systems of urban legibility not merely in terms of what was lost or how people responded to that loss, but also in terms of how they revealed this epistemic process in their diagnoses and envisioned cures. The ways urban dwellers attempted to understand and repair the breakdown of urban comprehensibility say a great deal about how these people produced meaning from the metropolitan landscape. Clearly, in Jazz Age Los Angeles, the imagined face of the metropolis echoed through popular consciousness. Ultimately, as everyone in Hollywood already knew, image really was everything.

Prologue

A City That Does Not Move

In the early years of the twentieth century, Los Angeles was a medium-sized city of around one hundred thousand residents. It was typical of towns of its type in that the city was structured around a thriving downtown centered not far from where the original Plaza had first established El Pueblo de Nuestra Señora La Reina de Los Angeles in 1781. The city's chief claims to fame—the pillars on which its hopes of future growth were seen to rest—were its balmy "Mediterranean" climate, with clear, orange-scented breezes, and its extensive interurban rail system, the largest in the world at the time. With an economy built on citrus, sales of cheap subdivided land, and tourism (the latter two facilitated by the local rail system), the region's boosters saw a bright future in Los Angeles for a new sort of livable metropolis. Around its bustling downtown (already a thriving western commercial center), Los Angeles would expand to fill its ample valleys with pleasant bungalows and quiet residential neighborhoods, and in the process avoid the urban problems that vexed so much of early twentieth-century America.

A half-century later, Los Angeles had become synonymous with "sprawl," a "devouring monster" that had come to engulf the entire Southern Californian region (see figure 1). As U.S. undersecretary of the interior James Carr (a third-generation Californian) put it at the time, "In a single generation we have almost ruined the superb Mediterranean climate of Southern California. . . . Cities slobber over into the countryside, cluttered with billboards, spawning sleazy developments that have brought new, ugly words to our California lexicon—slurbs and slurburbia."[1] The paradise of the 1910s and 1920s had turned into an urban inferno:

> Millions have poured into the new promised land over the past several years, seeking a better place to live and a better place to raise a family—a vine-covered cottage on a

FIGURE 1. "Atom-bomb the place and start all over": the sprawling megalopolis. Dan
Fowler, "Los Angeles: The World's Worst Growing Pains," *Look* 20, no. 5 (6 March 1956):
21. Look Magazine Collection, Library of Congress, Prints and Photographs Division.

few acres, a near-perfect climate, a convertible and a fabulous playground of mountains, desert and a seashore. What do they have instead? Sunshine and sweeping vistas
obscured by smog that burns the eyes and chokes the lungs. The few acres shoved aside
by row on row of tract houses on 50-foot lots. A traffic mess that transforms once-
quiet neighborhoods into bedlam, makes getting to work a nerve-frazzling experience and takes most of the pleasure out of mountains, desert and seashore.[2]

By 1956 *Look* magazine was giving teasing endorsement to a suggestion by "a University of California authority on city planning" that "the only solution to this mess
is to atom-bomb the place and start all over."[3] Los Angeles had already effectively
ceased to exist as a human settlement, according to one congressman; it was "not
a city at all, but a highway parking lot, bordered by a few buildings."[4]

Why did Los Angeles choose this strange future? Why did civic leaders, so manifestly committed early on to boosterism and the dream of establishing the premier western metropolis, turn away not only from the idyllic past but also from all the obvious models of urbanism of the first half of the century? Why did Los Angeles's elites let their proud downtown lose its grip on the region's economy and culture, abdicating to suburban enclaves and distant satellite communities? Why did Los Angeles spurn the most potent symbol of aspiring urbanism and community pride in the first part of the century—the skyscraper (banned in Los Angeles between 1905 and 1957 by a rigorous thirteen-story height limit ordinance)[5]—and neglect its renowned streetcar system? Why did this city so dedicated to growth and power totally reject plans for the sort of rapid transit construction—elevated railways and subterranean subways—that other cities felt was essential to their status as modern cities, preferring a "traffic nightmare" where "the center of the city is a solid mass of stalled, immovable, horn-blowing vehicles"?[6] Finally, why did the city pin all hopes for salvation in the years after World War II on a freeway system, the very technology that seemed to doom the region to becoming a desert of asphalt and concrete?

In large measure, the critical decisions to be made in shaping Los Angeles as an automotive metropolis in the second half of the twentieth century were made before the onset of World War II. Further, although it was at this point that planners for the region committed the city's resources to an extensive plan for automotive freeways, a number of the more dramatic changes in the topography and structure of the city had begun over the course of the previous two decades.

One could be even more specific and say that it all started quite innocuously one day in April 1920, when civic leaders met to debate one of the most ordinary and unexceptional of everyday urban problems: downtown traffic congestion.

A CITY AT THE CROSSROADS

By five o'clock on a hazy afternoon in early April 1920, downtown Los Angeles was a jumble. As the central banking, retail, and management core of a thriving metropolis containing almost six hundred thousand people within its city limits,[7] the downtown area, constricted to about three hundred square blocks, anchored the city's economy and concentrated its capital—and, it seemed by 5 P.M., much of its labor. Indeed, the crush to catch the interurban trains had become a daily trial for the more than half a million workers who, like many of their white-collar contemporaries in early twentieth-century urban America, took the street railway to and from work downtown.[8] Further complicating matters, the trains ran late. As a matter of fact, thanks to the traffic caused by the crush of automobiles parked on too narrow streets not designed for such a crush,[9] the downtown lines often ran forty-five to sixty minutes behind during rush hour. The snarl of cars, interurbans, and pedestrians brought the downtown—as business hub of the city, as well as the hub of the railway system—to a standstill. By this time, business—especially the downtown department stores that dominated commerce in the city—was beginning to suffer from the congestion. Shoppers were hesitant to take the interurban train the short distance from their residential districts and nearby bedroom communities to downtown for fear of being caught in the gridlock. Automobiles were even more impractical as a mode of transportation, as the main streets of the city leading downtown were uniformly congested all along their narrow roadways.

With foresight, the elites firmly established at the core of this metropolis directed the city to appoint a planning commission to design a workable solution to these traffic problems and to manage the growth of the city as a whole. As their most urgent goal, the planning experts were charged with finding a way to make the urban rail system run punctually and smoothly again, as the entire city's transportation network was snarled by congestion and delays at its downtown hub. By mid-April the commission—fully backed by the downtown banking and retail interests—recommended what appeared to be an eminently sensible and prudent plan of reform, which the city council, also dominated by those downtown interests, promptly put into force. The city would immediately institute a ban on automobile parking downtown. No cars would be allowed to park during business hours; the automobile, with its attendant gridlock and interference with light rail operation, would be effectively banished from the heart of the city. This plan was widely considered a triumph of Progressive Era rational planning, efficiently designed and implemented by the most prominent experts in the Beaux-Arts tradition. Indeed, the experts seemed to have proved their worth: the day after the plan was instituted, the trains ran on time for the first time in years. Thursday, 22 April 1920, was the dawning of a new era of control over urban automotive congestion: cars would be properly subordinated to the needs of the centralized city and of its centralized rail transportation system.

Two days later, 24 April 1920, at two in the afternoon, tens of thousands of enraged urbanites, urged on by public speakers and led by "grand marshal" Clara Kimball Young, a prominent film star of the time, descended on downtown in their cars, deliberately clogging the streets to protest the parking ban. The police department, which had confidently printed up an extra five thousand parking tickets in preparation for parking ban enforcement, was overwhelmed. Within a week, the city council had withdrawn the downtown parking ban, the captains of local commerce having seen their retail business decline by a quarter (see figure 2).

Within ten years, the downtown retail interests had been crippled, the city's major department stores and movie palaces increasingly scattered to distant locations along broad boulevards that had displaced the city center as economic sites. Likewise, the concentrations of industrial wealth and capital had moved to a variety of locations throughout the increasingly decentralized region. Within twenty years, the interurban system—the most extensive and wide-reaching in the world, with

No-Parking Law Proves Motor Cars Absolutely Essential.

FIGURE 2. The *Los Angeles Times* renders its final judgment on the parking ban, 25 April 1920.

over a thousand miles of track[10]—was in serious decline. The downtown had become a New Deal social problem, with scattered programs for redevelopment and public housing mired in political resistance—victim to a public that had apparently turned its attention and its loyalties fully to its own localized residential and commercial enclaves, which were spreading farther and farther from the city center. By the onset of World War II, Los Angeles had been transformed from a small, if ambitiously spread out, city physically structured by and built around an electric rail system, as was the American norm, to an increasingly decentralized metropolis committed unequivocally to the private automobile. In those two decades, the region had become a megalopolis of nearly six million inhabitants, featuring a topography of dispersed industrial, residential, and commercial sites spread over hundreds of square miles and fifty separate cities. The formerly sleepy suburbs were now speckled with heavy manufacturing and other industry, cut off entirely from any material connection to the urban core. And the automobiles ruled over all; the cars glided across this strange landscape[11]—no longer exactly urban, certainly not suburban in any traditional sense—at speeds up to fifty miles per hour along new broad, six- and eight-lane dedicated concrete and asphalt strips that cut straight through the old neighborhoods, barrios, and ghettoes of the city. Throughout the region, plans were underway for the construction of dozens of similar automotive transportation corridors, which would further rearrange even the most peripheral social spaces and cultural patterns of the sprawling megalopolis. Los Angeles had deferred all plans to "save" the rail system in favor of a new plan dedicated wholly to the freeway—a radically new technological device—as the region's primary "mass transportation" system of tomorrow. The traditional medium-sized city of 1920, with its bustling downtown commercial district and extensive light rail network, structurally on a par with Cleveland or Detroit, was a distant nostalgic past, not unlike the original Spanish pueblo or the scattered missions. By the time all major civic construction projects in Los Angeles were temporarily frozen as part of the wartime production footing that was already in place many months before the bombing of Pearl Harbor, Los Angeles had committed its future to the freeway.

1

"Los Angeles Is Not the City It Could Have Been"

How could a minor civic ordinance like a business-hours ban on downtown parking have such a dramatic effect on the future of a growing metropolis? The answer has roots that fan out far beyond the hundred square blocks of downtown Los Angeles and extend much deeper than those few weeks in 1920. Indeed, in retrospect it is clear that the parking ban was merely a sign heralding a series of transformations that shaped the city Los Angeles would become in the twentieth century. Furthermore, it is clear that the failure of the parking restrictions was but a shadow of a far more profound failure of urban vision and planning, for Los Angeles by 1940 was not the kind of city it was intended to be.

Several prominent urban historians have suggested over the last fifteen years that Los Angeles was, in fact, largely unplanned. David Gebhard and Harriette von Breton, Martin Wachs, Mark Foster, Scott Bottles, and Robert Fogelson all essentially agree that city planners failed to make much of a difference in the transformation of the city during what all say was a critical period in the city's formation.[1] As Fogelson puts it in his landmark 1967 study, *Fragmented Metropolis,* "The planners succeeded only where their goals corresponded with those of the developers, and planning, instead of guiding private development, merely sanctioned it."[2] Greg Hise takes to heart this assessment to such a degree that he devotes the extensive research in his *Magnetic Los Angeles* for the most part not to a study of official city planners but to private subdividers—whom he refers to as "community builders."[3] These were the people doing real planning work, in Hise's view.[4] Similarly, architectural historians David Gebhard and Harriette von Breton lament that, in the period between the establishment of the Los Angeles City Planning Commission in 1920 and the beginning of World War II in late 1941, city and county planners were largely fixated on a losing battle with congestion. Summing up the state of the city's urban planning in the years before the Second World War in *Los Angeles in the Thirties,* Gebhard and von Breton conclude that "a careful reading of the published histories of planning and the planning profession in L.A. gives the distinct impression that the task of the planner was to bureaucratize and codify that which existed. Only in the planning and design of freeways . . . did the work of the planners run neck and neck with that of the real world."[5] Planners, in this view, far from being dreamers, were fundamentally conservative even when they were able to attend to anything aside from traffic.

This grim assessment is curiously mirrored by the writings of Los Angeles's planners themselves at the end of this period. Writing in 1941, Charles Clark, who was at the time the chief land planning consultant for the Federal Housing Administration for the western states and territories, as well as being a long-time Los Angeles planner, declared that it was not planners but private "subdividers [who] are largely responsible for the pattern of present day Los Angeles."[6] The outcome of this chaotic lack of central planning was, in his considered opinion, dire. Under the heading "Planning Deficiencies," Clark produced a serious indictment of a city he saw as rotten at its core: "Los Angeles would not like to be called a 'bad apple,' yet this term is suitable. The healthy skin of an apple may conceal decay."[7] All this was due to a lack of professional planning: "The unplanned and uncontrolled subdivision of land can and has blocked traffic circulation, created slums through land crowding, and has caused terrific assessment burdens through necessary condemnation for rights-of-way which should have been considered in subdivision design."[8] The consensus of Los Angeles's planners on the eve of the Second World War is probably best summed up by L. Demming Tilton in his chapter of *Los Angeles: Preface to a Master Plan* titled simply "The Master Plan":

> The city-dweller steels himself with difficulty against the various types of irritations encountered in a badly organized urban area. He suffers from the noise and fumes of heavy traffic, the friction and conflicts of congested dwellings and residential areas. He views with shame the profuse and garish displays of commercialism, the unkempt vacant land along main arteries, the sordid slums. He misses the positive values in convenient, soothing rest spots, in spacious tree-bordered plazas, inspiring vistas, wide, well-planned scenic drives, impressive architectural compositions. Los Angeles is not the city it could have been, because no agency was responsible in its earlier days for the production of the plans and specifications from which a truly great metropolitan center could have been built.[9]

This failure echoes through commentary about Southern California. Dan Fowler, writing in *Look* fifteen years later, surmised regretfully that "Los Angeles could have been one of the beautiful cities of the world. It pioneered in planning for good living. The fact that it is no longer the beautiful city it was can be blamed partly on the fly-by-night developer and what he did to planning and zoning laws."[10]

DREAMS AND VISIONS

If it is true that city planning in Los Angeles was a failure, it was not in fact for lack of commitment by official city planners. Long before the parking ban, Los Angeles was a city taken with the idea of planning for tomorrow. As a city deeply invested in its own future, boosterish Los Angeles was, particularly in the first decades of the century, engrossed in envisioning itself as a great western metropolis to rival—and eventually replace—San Francisco.

Sometimes it seems, as Kevin Starr paints in his reverential multivolume history of California, the city is itself hardly more than a hopeful dream. It is a series of possibilities or, rather, the very spirit of possibility. For Starr, Los Angeles is less a place than a muse. Somewhat more critically, Mike Davis begins *City of Quartz* by exploring some of the more dreamy utopian possibilities of Southern California, ranging from the socialist high desert commune of Llano del Rio to the vanished hopes of corporate paternalism in working-class Fontana. For Davis, Los Angeles has always been a battleground between divergent utopias, from lush Mediterranean Progressive Era paradise to proving ground for a hostile and paranoid future corporate metropolis bitterly divided along lines of race and class. These potential envisioned cities ultimately partake of this grand tradition of Los Angeles futurism, its ideology and architecture echoing endlessly between competing "sunshine" boosterism and critical "noir" discourses. Like Starr's *Inventing the Dream, Material Dreams,* and *Endangered Dreams, City of Quartz* is engaged in, as its subtitle proclaims, "Excavating the Future in Los Angeles." Whether lost futures of social justice or enduring dreams of material prosperity and individual freedom, these histories have contributed to the long discourse of envisioning possible tomorrows through the lens of Los Angeles.[11]

In the first decades of the century, attempts to prepare for the future led Los Angeles's city leaders to pay careful attention to planning the city. As early as 1907, booster and social worker Dana Bartlett pictured Southern California as "the better city" (in his book of that title), arguing that "this City of the Angeles can be among the first to realize the world's dream of the City Beautiful."[12] Bartlett had early on called for "a comprehensive plan of beautifying buildings covering not only the present city, but reaching far out into the suburbs."[13] This plan would ideally be formulated by members of "a new profession—that of the city architect, beauty expert, or civic decorator—a profession so unique that the title has not yet become fixed."[14]

Soon thereafter, Charles Mulford Robinson more formally answered the call, bringing a new discipline—now called "city planning"—to Southern California with a potential master plan for Los Angeles.[15] His envisioned future was consistent with long-cherished local notions of the region's destiny. He saw the city as a Mediterranean paradise. Projecting into the future the synthetic past the region's boosters had been promoting for years, Robinson's city would revel in its spread-out shape, with wide boulevards, abundant sunlight, and plentiful parks and open space to better present "the natural splendor of the city's environs."[16] The formal report, titled simply *Los Angeles, California: The City Beautiful,* emphasized the opportunities of the city's topography and climate, not just as a natural amenity but as a matter of practical business. His suggested improvements, Robinson reminded boosterish Angelenos, were intended to ensure "that tourists will not pass through Los Angeles. They will stay here, in a real 'Paris of America'—a summer city, when the East is swept by wind and snow; and they will find a gay outdoor life where other cities are stamped with the grime and rush or an earnestness that knows not how to play."[17] Careful planning could demonstrate to the world that Los Angeles was a city in harmony with its surroundings, fully delivering on its booster promises.

What might seem a bit odd about this "city beautiful" plan in this context, though, is its continual emphasis on road improvements over more obvious amenities. After routine discussions of a proposed unified railroad terminal and a new civic center (standard features of city plans of the era),[18] the remainder of the Robinson report chiefly discusses an elaborate boulevard system for the metropolis. In fact, this is the element of the report that has received the most praise from historians. Indeed, as Mansel Blackford describes it in *The Lost Dream,* in Robinson's plan "boulevards would spread out to connect parks as 'links in the chain' throughout Los Angeles."[19] In Robinson's Haussmannesque plan, grand boulevards would be stately monuments in their own right, serving by their peripheral plantings (about which Robinson's report has a great deal to say) and their demarcated terminal points to clarify and order the metropolitan fabric, as well as a real tool to knit together the already overgrown city.[20] As a consequence of this forward-thinking planning, Southern California would be "one city from the mountains to the sea," in the oft-quoted words of one nineteenth-century Californio rancher[21]—a city beautiful on a grand regional scale.

How, though, could a system of boulevards lead visitors and natives alike to the "outdoor life" of the region? One clear answer is that these roads would link the city's existing parks and open spaces, rendering them accessible to all. Yet it is critical to remember that, even in Southern California, most people still did not have access to automobiles in 1907. The call for public pleasure boulevards, then, was no populist plea. In fact, many times Robinson's boulevards directly conflict with the ordinary needs of the masses of Angelenos: "In Los Angeles, there is now no boulevard system whatever, and in attempting to create one there is the almost constant obstacle of a double car track on every street of considerable breadth and easy grade."[22] The city's primary transportation infrastructure, with its common streetcars and interurbans, remains little but a disfigurement in this city beautiful scheme. No, this is a plan directed to appeal to a narrow urban elite, and it is a nostalgic appeal at that. These boulevards are envisioned in Robinson's plan as surrey trails, seldom wider than fifty feet,[23] intended as public spaces but hardly accessible to the majority of Angelenos. Instead, the city's high society could take pleasure, under Robinson's proposed improvements, in pleasure drives—either by horse carriage or (for the more adventurous) by horseless carriage—between downtown and ritzy Pasadena, and in sunny afternoons spent observing stately street traffic: "As it [the proposed renovated Figueroa Street] would carry a ceaseless stream of carriage travel, it would necessarily become a show drive, and I would have seats at intervals along the wide side parking, in furtherance of the purpose to facilitate the city's outdoor life."[24] This phase of city planning was an elite pastime, a civic improvement that paired aesthetics with real estate values, open space with courtly leisure, and public sites with the civic pride of a prosperous commercial class.

Robinson's plan was also somewhat grandiose; it was ambitious and expensive. Although it was generally viewed positively, city leaders were not prepared to commit in 1907 to a single comprehensive future vision—even one that promised to make Los Angeles the "Paris of America." Consequently, Robinson's plan never resulted in action.[25] It remained significant, however, as part of an ongoing discourse about the proper way to plan the metropolis of the future, and elements of it found their way into many later plans for the city. Robinson's vision of a city that aimed "not to be simply big; but to be beautiful as well" echoed, although in different terms, Bartlett's call for Los Angeles to become not just a bigger but a better, more moral and godly city.[26] But whether interested in moral uplift or civic pride, these influential early proponents of planning did not succeed in their stated goal of putting planning at the heart of local decision making.

The institutionalization of city planning in Los Angeles came from quite another quarter. In April 1914, a full five years after the publication of Robinson's plan, a number of Progressive civic organizations—including, notably, the publishers of the left-leaning local Progressive weekly, *The California Outlook*—arranged to import from New York an elaborate city planning exhibit. The purpose of this display was to impress upon Angelenos the practical importance of planning for all citizens. As the director of the exhibit put it in an article in the *Outlook*, "The city planning exhibition is not a merely technical presentation of the problems relating to city building. It is an intensely human proposition, it is an aid toward the making over of a city for the people, to give them a better as well as more economic place in which to live and work and play. City planning is not a device merely to beautify. It is not for the rich. . . . City planning is for the average man and we must build our city for the average man."[27]

Given the populist associations of this sort of central planning, it should come as no surprise that "Gordon Whitnall, a young and articulate secretary of the local Socialist Party, assisted in setting up the exhibit" (see figure 3).[28] This exhibit proved quite influential among ordinary Angelenos, as well as city officials. Equally im-

FIGURE 3. Los Angeles planning director Gordon Whitnall, 1930.
From Board of City Planning Commissioners, *Annual Report* (Los
Angeles: Board of City Planning Commissioners, 1930).

portant for the development of the city planning profession in Southern California, though, was Whitnall's more practical political contributions. As Robert Lee Williams, who interviewed Whitnall before his death, recounts in "The City Planning Movement in Los Angeles, 1900–1920," "Whitnall had come to the Southland from the city of Milwaukee where he had been active in the reform politics of the Social Democratic Party."[29] After arriving in Southern California in 1910, he continued his radical political work by assisting in the election of Socialist candidate Fredrick C. Wheeler to the Los Angeles City Council in 1913. As Socialist Party secretary, Whitnall had drafted a platform upon which Wheeler was obligated by his party bylaws to legislate if elected. The primary plank of that platform was a call for a formal, professionalized city planning commission. In April 1914, shortly after the planning exhibit was installed at the Bronson Building in downtown Los Angeles, Wheeler dutifully submitted to the council Whitnall's formal resolution for the establishment of a city planning commission. Although the resolution did not pass the city council at this time, Whitnall used the publicity generated by the deliberations, as well as the enthusiasm surrounding the planning exhibit, to call for a public meeting, which culminated in the formation of a quasi-official City Planning Association, with Whitnall as its executive-secretary.[30]

This body was the first formal city planning agency for Los Angeles. Over the course of the 1910s, the association gathered together many of the men who would later serve as professional planners in Southern California, including Whitnall, George Damon, and Hugh Pomeroy, among several others. As they came to share a common language of city planning—they were initially drawn from a diverse array of professions—they began to consider themselves professionals in the new field of expert city planning. During this period, these planners consolidated many of the notions of a future metropolis—some of which were quite radical—that would preoccupy planning discourse throughout the subsequent decade.

After a six-year delay, part of which was attributable to the war, the city council formally recognized the status of this long-coalescing local planning community in April 1920 by establishing an official City Planning Commission, with Whitnall as its head. With its new status, this commission at once set itself as the center of future utopian envisioning for the city; along with its offshoot, the County Regional Planning Commission, the new city agency would assume the mantle of planning the metropolis over the following decades. It would operate "as a coordinating medium thru which all agencies . . . which contribute to the physical development of the community shall be focused in a single attack upon the task of building the city of tomorrow."[31] As Gordon Whitnall, the city's chief planner and chairman of the commission, put it to the city council in July 1920, "Right from the start, we must understand that we are not the conservative branch of City Government. We are the ones who should 'Dream dreams and see Visions'—visions of the better City to be."[32]

THE CITY ENVISIONED

Whitnall's statement was significant. It indicated that city planners would henceforth claim authority over and formal sanction for imagining Los Angeles's future—a claim that would not go entirely uncontested. The City Planning Commission would have an official monopoly on envisioning the shape that the city of the future would take. Whitnall put it bluntly a few years after the establishment of the commission: "Weary with educating successive political administrations, we went with our message to the schools, the women's clubs, the civic bodies and commercial organizations, until today there is not a man in the city council, and there is not a future city council which will oppose the work of the city plan commission."[33] This sort of hubris was generally consistent with the norms of the profession of city planning in the era. As a new discipline struggling for legitimacy, city planning had to continually redefine and reiterate its mandate and its domain of action. Planners sought to both establish their authorship rights to and actually manipulate the city by means of a particular methodology. As a consequence, the ends and the means of the new science of city planning were intertwined. Whitnall's claim to authority over the city's utopian destiny—"the better city to be"[34]—was based firmly on the planner's ability to see: to "Dream dreams and see Visions." The visionary planner would both prophesy the future of the city and acutely observe the present condition of the metropolis. This supposedly unique ability to see the city in its entirety, as a whole, and to thus better forecast its future development, was the main scientific claim of the new profession of city planning.

Whereas previous generations of planners and moral reformers—mostly amateurs and often middle-class women, quasi-aristocratic male dilettantes like Charles Mulford Robinson, or, like Dana Bartlett, clergymen—had sought to upgrade the urban social environment to improve the city's residents, the men of the new professional discipline of city planning were concerned with the city itself. The earlier reformers had seen the city largely as a collection of human environments that mirrored social relationships and fostered individuals' moral character: "So, the improvers believed, the essence of every social problem was part of the fabric of the city and embodied within it; all varieties of social, physical, and spiritual disorders— crime, saloons, decline of the birthrate, physical fatigue, a steady deterioration of mind and body—developed out of the chaos and physical disarray of the urban form. This disorder was a "contaminating poison," recruiting members of the lowest grade of humanity."[35] Moral reformers would only effect urban change as a means of affecting urban residents. Their ultimate aim was to improve the citizens. Consequently, in the view of the new professional planners, this earlier generation of reformers offered piecemeal solutions and partial, situational remedies. Their direct architectural and personal interventions were not addressed to the structural problems of the city taken as a whole.

In contrast, as M. Christine Boyer argues in *Dreaming the Rational City*, the profession of city planning was largely unconcerned with moral uplift or with individual human beings and their immediate environments. City planning took the total city as its object of knowledge and sought to turn that knowledge into a set of precise techniques for manipulating the city in accordance with "an ideal: the city as a perfectly disciplined spatial order."[36] Specifically, these planners saw the city as a coherent, self-contained, autonomous system—a network of functions, processes, and flows that operated according to an identifiable logical order. In this view, the city was primarily something organic. It was no longer a place or a collection of environments; it was an entity in its own right. It therefore followed that the job of the planner was twofold: first, to properly observe the city as a whole, and second, to correct any disruptions in the proper functioning of this organism. Here, the city planner operated in a manner analogous to a doctor, first diagnosing the patient, and then directly intervening in his or her body. In claiming the city as a discrete and autonomous domain of professional scientific expertise, city planners were both establishing authority over their object of study, after the manner of so many other movements for professional disciplinary control during the era of Progressivism, and legitimating their precise disciplinary methodology. Consequently, as Boyer notes, city planning staked its professional stature on a fundamental reorientation of the meaning of the city. In less than twenty years, between the 1890s and 1910s, the entire language of urban observation had changed: "Between the terms *instinct*, *upliftance, harmony* and those of *organic unity, expert, control,* a radical realignment of discourse had occurred."[37]

    In dealing with the urban organism, the planners' goals were simple; they followed inevitably from the chosen metaphor. They would be primarily concerned with the readily identifiable organic processes of their patient: flows and circulation, respiration and congestion, "cancers" and "blight," growth and "development." Those specific urban forms that could be easily identified and diagnosed through the focused lens of this organic metaphor would now be subject to the attentions of urban planning and redevelopment. This discourse did not merely direct the planners' clinical gaze; it compelled these planners to view any urban forms inconsistent with the imaginary ideal of the "healthy" body as necessarily problematic. The organic metaphor led planners to see certain urban forms as *by definition* unhealthy for the urban patient.[38] Ethically, the organic metaphor compelled the planner to take action, to accept the responsibility and treat the patient. The stakes were high: if proper action was not swiftly taken, the patient's condition would likely deteriorate to a critical point. Eventually, the patient could die. Radical surgery upon the body of the city was not only preferable, therefore, but necessary. To do otherwise would be to risk utter planning malpractice. Large-scale, drastic solutions—urban surgery—would henceforth be within the mandate of the planner.

    Of course, such drastic measures would not always be necessary. Furthermore, in the 1910s and most of the 1920s, the new profession of city planning lacked the power to perform such radical surgery. Consequently, planners hoped to correct problems before they turned life-threatening. Preventive medicine would be more consistent with planners' claims to be able to not only treat urban problems but to predict—and thus work to forestall—future crises. Indeed, central to the critical planning project of seeing the city as a whole was an overriding concern with diagnostics and proper observation. Planners sought above all to make the city comprehensible—to subject the urban organism to careful and precise analysis. Legibility was the profession's first principle. As a result, the planner began treating the urban body by making a precise diagnosis. The planner had to observe his object of study in minute detail and comprehensively. The microscopic concern with the city's myriad cellular structures had to be tempered, always, with the macroscopic mission to view the city as an organic unity. "The act of city planning required a new totalization: a network of special investigations penetrating the conditions" of the urban body.[39] To this end, city planners devised critical technologies that allowed them to speculate with greater precision on their urban patients. These tools determined how planners would make sense of the city.

Planners created observational "machinery [that] would . . . give rise to a body of detailed knowledge about the city and a set of ideal urban observatories that would constantly survey and correct its form."[40] To derive this knowledge and to properly position future probes, planners required systematic urban data. Consequently, chief among these new technologies of observation was the professional urban survey. The survey would be both minute and comprehensive. It would divide the city into comprehensible bits, while deriving extensive information about the relations between these elements. By digesting the organic whole of the city, the discipline of planning would in turn discipline the city itself:

> Above all else disciplinary space is cellular; its purpose is to be able to separate or break up confusing overlaps, to fix peripatetic land uses, to set up more useful communications among the parts of the city. This first operation required a survey that organized a multitude of activities and distributed them into cellular spaces. . . . In turn the surface of the city was carved up into a series of distinct entities: an exhaustive survey of all the visible aspects of squares, parks, buildings, sewers, conduit pipes, poles and wires, railways, streets, waterways, reservoirs—in short, every piece of land, building, and improvement, both public and private.[41]

The city planner would use the survey to track and locate each cell in the larger organism. Furthermore, the planner would then be able to sort the elements into comprehensible reductionist categories (e.g., multifamily residence, small commercial installation, city park, and so on). Thus, planners could produce a detailed tabulated urban index—a typology of an urban topography, bringing the endless detail under some measure of conceptual order.[42] Through the survey, the city was transformed from organic undifferentiated mass into component parts. The specific objects that planners could quantify became, collectively, the basic elements of an urban environment. All else was irrelevant and was effectively rendered invisible. Further, everything observable in a city could, by definition, potentially be controlled and regulated by planners. The survey thus combined the appearance of omniscience with that of omnipotence.

These surveys were important diagnostic tools, but they effected an epistemic splintering of the city if taken on their own. Although the survey unified the urban landscape through its classifying categorization, in raw form it reduced the city to a series of isolated and, as it were, disembodied tabulations. The city appeared in the survey as an abstract series of quantitative data, figures that did not fully convey or represent the dense fabric of neighborhoods, communities, spatial proximities, cultural patterns, and the like. The task of reconciling this fragmented urban diagnosis with the dreamed and envisioned ideal, unified, organic city required something beyond the diagnostic survey. Consequently, the survey was matched with another critical technology of urban observation in the planners' toolbox: the comprehensive plan and map. After observing the city in detail and thereby diagnosing its ills and weaknesses, the planner once more drew back to view the city as a whole. After compiling the intricate data, planners then reassembled the survey data into a unifying representation of the city. As Boyer puts it, "All of these data that survey the life, labor, and leisure conditions of the people . . . must be territorially represented through a city plan."[43] This survey data must be transferred to a spatial representation to provide a visual picture of the urban organism: "This vast array of information should be displayed upon a series of maps: maps of the location and distribution of foreign quarters, residential areas, workers' neighborhoods; maps pinpointing the location of churches, saloons, schools, vice resorts, red-light districts; maps depicting the congested areas; the location of proposed new street systems; historical maps describing past growth patterns—maps, in short, that established the relationship of each parcel of land to another and then to the whole."[44] In this way, by way of precise scientific surveys, the city is gradually abstracted and transformed into a map, a rational cartography that can then be manipulated as a whole rather than an array of unique places and neighborhoods.

These maps would show all the impurities in the urban organism in relation to the city's vital organs and major arteries. Any malformed structures, inappropriate land use, or other unhealthy urban forms that impeded the proper operation of the urban body would clearly emerge from these diagnostic images. Such blights would stick out like a sore thumb. Consequently, these maps would, as products of the planners' organicist discourse, positively isolate problematic areas that might at some point require treatment. These surveyed and mapped forms that manifestly "were out of place" or "did not belong" thus declared their own excision. So it was that planners produced corresponding series of new, predictive maps representing the envisioned appearance of the future city after being corrected and purified by professionals. Here the planner could produce an imaginary postoperative, "virtual" city at the same level of precision and detail as their depictions of the existing flawed metropolis. Planning experts would not only foretell the future of the city, they would depict it graphically, vividly. Utopia and diagnostic would intertwine, lending the credibility of the scientific survey to the planners' comprehensive plans and an aura of prophecy to the survey (as the "before" picture juxtaposed to the ideal "after" picture). Both representations, in their mutual reinforcement, would manifest the apparent solidity and authority of precise representation. The original diagnostic and new ideal maps could thus be easily compared, and in the juxtaposition, the promise of the planners' methodology would be clearly demonstrated. The comprehensive plan would make use of the artifice of the technical map to both represent the dysfunctional present city and project the proper, healthy city of the future. In both forms, however, this representation would not merely present the urban area—in its infinite complexity and diversity—as it appeared to the untrained naked eye, but would refract it through the logic of the planners' invented categorization. This representation would make the city fully legible, but only to the planner's trained eye.

Together, the reciprocal survey and map formed the primary lens that expert planners of the Progressive Era used to see, and read, their cities. What was visible through these media would henceforth be manipulable, and what was not would not be. Inevitably, planners would judge the existing city by comparison with their ideal maps. The spatial logic of the map determined how planners evaluated the observed, parsed city. This visual bias made planners look unfavorably upon any mapped urban configuration that appeared unbalanced, asymmetrical, or simply untidy. In contrast, parallelism, regular alignment, and proportionality defined the aesthetics of urban form represented in this abstract, diagrammatic manner. For planning professionals, clear order on a map self-evidently demonstrated proper functional relationships on the ground. Symmetry and balance reflected urban health, while chaotic mapped topographies implied blight and confusion. The visual logic of planning took schematic structural clarity for proper form, and valued form above all else.

A LEGIBLE METROPOLIS

Fortunately for the new city planners, this sort of categorization—the application of social criteria, invented commonality, and ideological signification to the surface of the metropolis—was a familiar part of nineteenth- and early twentieth-century urban life. Everyday city experience, as theorists such as Michel de Certeau and George Lipsitz have argued, evokes a complex and sophisticated network of meanings in ordinary urban sites.[45] Long before the advent of expert planning, there already existed in the minds of urbanites complex and sophisticated ways of knowing the city.

American cities of the first decades of the twentieth century were organized in ways that made them fairly comprehensible to their denizens (who were, in turn, well educated in the ways of understanding this structure). In Los Angeles, for instance, an array of technologies and devices of urban demarcation, common to most similar cities, was guaranteed to make the city fully legible to resident and expert planner alike. Many of these techniques ordinarily went unquestioned—if not unobserved—by locals. They operated on a comprehensive scale and reflected the dominant order of a hierarchical culture. Consequently, their specific manifestations were naturalized and taken for granted. In fact, these subtle alignments of race, gender, and neighborhood were so obviously normalized that they entered what Antonio Gramsci has termed a people's "philosophy of common sense, which is the 'philosophy of non-philosophers,' or in other words the conception of the world which is uncritically absorbed by the various social and cultural environments in which the moral individuality of the average man [sic] is developed."[46] The clearly defined categories of social hierarchy are, in a sense, so obvious to the residents of the city as to appear entirely natural. The policing of these common sense social and ideological categories effectively renders them invisible as such. Yet all served to reiterate unmistakably both social bounds and urban boundaries—borders the precise locations of which all urban residents were implicitly, even subconsciously, aware. The arrangements of public and private space within the metropolis cohesively reproduced structures of power in the city and in the larger culture. Topography and demographics converged, interpellating ordinary residents into the urban fabric, rendering the city clearly demarcated. Social order reinforced urban order. Of course, this common sense way of knowing the city was connected to common ways of understanding the larger society and culture. The logic of the city reflected broad ideological configurations brought down to earth.

Planners' categorization and mapping did not just impose an artificial order and logic on a virgin city; the experts often merely picked up and transcribed existing social segmentation and hierarchy. The text of the city was being written long before the planners applied their own technologies of scientific observation and manipulation to it. The machinations of the planners did, however, work to force the city into more rigid structural clarity, turning contingent formations into essential order. The fluid, ever-changing configurations of human environments turned, on a map or in a table of data, into solid and permanent empirical "fact." Moreover, professional observers' surveys and analyses performed another function: they provided a lasting representation of a comprehensible 1920s Los Angeles. Indeed, categorizational logic inscribed in numerous surveys and comprehensive plans serves as a useful conceptual archaeology of the city in that era. These snapshots are blurry, distorted, partial, and biased, but they transmit clearly Los Angeles as it was understood by experts during the period. They transmit something of the methodology of the planners—the specific ways these professionals went about seeing the city.

Perhaps most visible to planners was the social layout of their metropolis. Through familiar naturalized categories of identity—race, class, and gender, as well as locality—urban observers could have confidence in their ability to properly read the city. These social classifications were included beside topographical and architectural ones as perceptible and manipulable elements of urban form. Alignments of racial settlement appeared beside other necessary infrastructures—sewer lines, water mains, electrical grids, streetcar lines—on the experts' cherished maps and surveys. Given this importance, planners took especial care, when tracing these manifestations of identity through their various surveys over the years, to be precise about the locations and arrangements of racial and ethnic minority groups. Demographics and ideological common sense came together in the array of census data, academic sociological studies, city planning maps and surveys, and the like produced during the period. These documents revealed Los Angeles as a city rigidly divided in alignment with racial categories of identity. Consequently, the city was, in the eyes of its planners, an exceptionally well-ordered, clean, and properly segregated metropolis.

Many of the city's residents seemed to appreciate this segregating order; it was one of Southern California's paramount virtues, according to some boosters. Dana Bartlett, for instance, saw Los Angeles as a "Better City" than many of its eastern counterparts precisely because it was free of the confusion and promiscuous mixing of those tenement-bound metropolises: "Another reason why Los Angeles is to be not only a greater but a better city, is found in the fact that it is largely an American city. The majority of its citizens are of American birth."[47] The homogeneous population was a trademark of Southern California in an era of large-scale foreign immigration and internal migration. Some Angelenos worked particularly hard to keep their city this way, innovating legal and quasi-legal means of maintaining the purity of their neighborhoods. Even if the population could not maintain its extreme demographic homogeneity as the city grew, it could—and did—clearly designate the boundaries between ethnic groups, thus enforcing a kind of spatial purity. As a result, by 1920, Los Angeles was segregated into subcommunities exhibiting an extraordinarily high degree of racial uniformity. African Americans, for instance, who accounted for 3.1 percent of the city's population in 1930,[48] were primarily locked into a handful of well-defined areas in the city:

> There were four separate and distinct black neighborhoods close to the center of the city. The largest was the South Central Avenue district, immediately south of the City Hall location. Second in size was the Temple Street district, located just northwest of the business district. Third largest was the relatively high-class Jefferson district, which was southwest of the downtown area, clearly separated from the Central Avenue district. Smallest of the four distinctly black neighborhoods was the Evergreen district, to the southeast of the central area. The fact that all four of the black neighborhoods were located entirely within three miles of the City Hall points out their highly centralized nature.[49]

As Mark Foster observes in "The Decentralization of Los Angeles in the 1920's": "In 1920 Los Angeles had twelve state assembly districts; the most heavily black district contained 40.1 per cent of the city's blacks."[50] By the end of the decade, a single district held 70 percent of the African Americans in Los Angeles.[51] J. Max Bond's "The Negro in Los Angeles," one of a series of detailed sociological surveys undertaken at the University of Southern California under the direction of the eminent Emory Bogardus during the 1920s and 1930s, reveals the claustrophobia of segregation through the eyes of "one of the old settlers" of the teens: "We were encircled by invisible walls of steel. The whites surrounded us and made it impossible to go beyond these walls."[52] The city's racial boundaries were not faint cultural traces; they were tangible and seemingly insurmountable barriers. The categorizational logic of the planners ensured that the city's manifest demarcations were understood in no uncertain terms.

The outlying districts of the region were even more "well-ordered." African Americans "constituted only 0.8 per cent of Los Angeles County's population, exclusive of the city."[53] In fact, "even though many whites settled in the city during the 1920's, a higher proportion of the white newcomers to Los Angeles County settled in the outlying suburbs. . . . In 1930 many of the larger suburbs were practically devoid of minority group residents, a development deliberately designed by the whites who resided there."[54] If the city proper was strictly segregated between black and white, the suburbs were active markers of segregation. They did not contain segregated neighborhoods so much as they were themselves—on a grand scale—segregated neighborhoods. "Many jurisdictions routinely enforced Jim Crow patterns. Glendale, for example, boasted that 'no Negro ever sleeps overnight in our city.'"[55] Further, "though Glendale boasted of its lack of blacks, other suburbs were almost exclusively white. In 1930 South Gate's population was 98.8 per cent white; Glendale 98.3; Huntington Park, 98.2; Long Beach, 98.0; Inglewood, 97.8; Alhambra, 97.7 and Beverly Hills, 96.3. Of the ten largest suburbs in the metropolitan area in 1930, Pasadena contained the lowest percentage of whites with 90.9."[56] These suburbs were lily-white districts of the metropolis. These zones were explicitly set off, in the common sense human topography and racial ideology of the region, from the districts of minority group concentration, such as Central Avenue.[57]

Although Los Angeles was fairly typical of cities of the era in the strict segregation of African Americans (if a particularly extreme example), the city's system of racial division was not exclusively bipolar. Southern California was home to similarly extensive populations of other racial groups—specifically, Japanese Americans, Mexican Americans, and a smaller number of Native Americans, Chinese Americans, and Filipino Americans. Each minority group was confined to specific urban zones, often by clear messages, such as a sign erected at Rose Hills Cemetery that read, "Japs, don't let the sun set on you here: KEEP MOVING—this is Rose Hill."[58] The segregation of Mexican Americans was particularly onerous, as it confined them to the most densely overcrowded parts of the city. Even those residing outside Los Angeles proper were confined to very limited areas:

Roughly 70,000 Mexicans lived outside of the city in the county. However, most of them were highly concentrated; of that number, 45,000 lived in Maravilla Park, a district located only three miles from City Hall at its farthest extremity. Thus, most of the Mexicans in the county lived in one clearly defined neighborhood just east of downtown Los Angeles, which straddled the city limits. A 1931 study revealed that while significant clusters of Mexicans lived in a number of the outlying suburbs, they were strictly segregated and lived in extreme poverty. The Mexicans in the city itself were also highly concentrated. Though most of the city's Mexicans lived just east of the downtown area, there was a somewhat smaller concentration of Mexicans south of the downtown area; as evidence of its proximity to the center of Los Angeles, its most remote point was only a mile and half from City Hall.[59]

Clearly, these racial and ethnic minorities lived in a very restricted range of places. Their patterns of residence were not random or coincidental: the racial identity of a community determined its location in Southern California. Furthermore, as Mark Foster notes in listing the locations of these minority communities, most of these discrete ethnic neighborhoods were located in the older, more central parts of the metropolis. For instance, "almost all of Los Angeles' Chinese lived in the Chinatown district, which was in the shadow of City Hall on North Broadway. A large concentration of Japanese resided in the 'Little Tokyo' district on East First Street, which was even closer to City Hall. Neither district extended more than a mile from that location."[60]

In general, "by the end of the 1920's, the bulk of Los Angeles' Oriental population, like the Mexicans and the blacks, was heavily concentrated close to the center of the city."[61] This centralization of minority communities more broadly defined the central city as a place of chaotic, densely juxtaposed racial groups, and the suburbs and outlying districts as homogeneously white. Yet even this was not so simple. Although the region was peculiar in its era for its low proportion of foreign-born European Americans, there did exist distinctions among whites that also led to residential segregation.[62]

Finally, a further, almost ubiquitous, segregation common to Los Angeles and most American cities was the division along class lines. The distance between the mansions of Pasadena and the farmworkers' barrio in nearby El Monte was measured not just in ethnicity or geography but in class as well. More generally, the fundamental spatial class distinction prevailing in the era was between suburb and city. Like other concentric metropolises, Los Angeles defined its suburban areas as places of refuge and escape from the toil, confusion, and labor of the city itself. The interurban train every day shuttled male white-collar managers out of the urbanized areas and into bucolic and remote bedroom communities. Although these satellite cities were beyond the workaday experience of many urbanites, the relative accessibility of the suburbs in Southern California was central to the booster promise of an affluent lifestyle. Additionally, the increasing infusion of the region's population into these outlying areas during the 1910s, with the consequent expansion of the interurban system, demonstrates the ideological appeal of middle-class modes of life for residents of Southern California. The suburbs were attractive precisely because they clearly represented zones of enhanced economic status; their growth came in direct relation to the increasing social segregation and racial congestion of the more central parts of the city. Thus class relationships interwove with racial and gender dichotomies, further distinguishing among already significantly differentiated people and the places with which they were associated.

These types of segregation helped define the city into clear categories of identity that everyone could recognize and experts could identify as definitively as the street grid.[63] They erected strict boundaries that served, in effect, to lend order to the chaos of a growing metropolis. Of course, unlike the other mapped elements of urban topography, these social demarcations had to be constantly policed and reinforced, and the vigor with which some Angelenos went about doing just that reveals much about the importance they placed upon the racial legibility of their city. In "keep the neighborhood White" drives, the perceived importance of urban boundaries unmistakably reveals itself.[64] Over the course of the first decades of the century, Los Angeles introduced a number of sophisticated new technologies of spatial separation and racial distancing. One of the most effective of these new techniques was the homeowners association—the first homeowners association was the Los Feliz Improvement Association, formed in 1916—whereby neighborhoods could, in effect, regulate their own racial purity: "In the 1920s these associations, relying on restrictive deed covenants, helped realtors and developers keep upscale white neighborhoods segregated, successfully blocking African Americans and Asians from 95 percent of available housing."[65] Restrictive covenants were designed to protect the clear racial legibility of urban spaces. They were an intrinsic part of the city's fundamental structure. By the 1920s, such deed restrictions were almost universal, particularly in the suburbs, as Foster observes: "In the outlying sections of metropolitan Los Angeles, most of the homes were very new. Since many of the new homes had only recently been placed under long term racial restrictions, there were few opportunities for minority group residents to penetrate those areas. Not only did the courts uphold the legality of such racial restrictions, but they even made some of them retroactive. In 1928 the state Supreme Court ruled that blacks had to vacate certain portions of West Los Angeles where they had owned property for years!"[66] The same sorts of demographic categories that the expert planners perceived and used in their surveys were reaffirmed into law by the courts and defended in court by the residents. The racial categorization of Southern California urban spaces rested on firm foundations of legitimacy. The segregation of the city was legally binding and officially valid; the streets of the city were not merely conduits for traffic, they were important delineators of identity and ideology.

Even districts without formal neighborhood associations (and without deed restrictions written into the law) relied on similar, if more informal, schemes of enforcing their own homogeneity. Ordinary neighborhoods devised mechanisms of clearly delineating themselves within the fabric of Southern California, as surveys undertaken during the era reveal. One such study, an extremely sophisticated project undertaken by University of Southern California sociologist Bessie McClenahan, titled "The Changing Urban Neighborhood," traces the means of racial exclusion and the complex motivations underlying this sort of racism. McClenahan observes—at first hand—the constitution of a new community organization dedicated to the racial homogeneity of a particular neighborhood. At its initial meeting on 19 July 1922, McClenahan notes, the Anti-African Housing Association resolved a pact among its members: "At the meeting an informal agreement was drawn up and signed by eight persons which read as follows: 'It is hereby agreed by the undersigned property owners not to sell or agree to sell any property owned by us in the streets between Vermont Avenue and Budlong Avenue to people other than the Caucasian race.'"[67] Such ad hoc acts of boundary definition and reinforcement complemented broader markers of racial segregation that showed up on a planner's map as a definite line.

These boundaries are no less ordinary and familiar to Angelenos, regardless of specific identity. In fact, members of minority groups understood the importance and power of these delineations at least as well as did middle-class whites. Yet the consequences for whites of violating these boundaries during this period were disorientation and confusion, and perhaps the shame of getting lost in one's own town. For members of other racial and class groups, the stakes could be considerably higher. Police harassment and arrest—not to mention vigilante civilian actions—ensured that these urban boundaries remained sacrosanct. Common sense clearly informed all residents of the City of Angels—at least in rough outlines—of the racial topography of their city.

Race and class were not the only systems of common sense boundaries that operated in Los Angeles in the 1920s. In fact, they may not even be the most pervasive. That distinction probably belongs to divisions of gender, often so much a part of our own common sense as to remain invisible even today. The particular structure of gender ideology operating during the period, in Southern California and elsewhere in urban America, extended from the arrangement of large urban forms down to the structure of the predominant single-family home. Margaret Marsh describes in her *Suburban Lives* how growing trends during the late nineteenth century toward suburbia (trends so evident in early twentieth-century Los Angeles) led to new structures of domestic gender ideology as well as home architectural layout. The divisions between rooms in the house—between public rooms (the parlor and dining room; later, the "living room") and private rooms (particularly separate bedrooms)—mirrored gendered public/private distinctions developing, to an extent, throughout the nineteenth century among bourgeois families.[68] These large-scale social trends, amplifying distinctions between home and outside world, resulted in a particular formulation of the architecture of gender in the early twentieth-century suburb. The diurnal circulation of working men from suburban retreat to urban business district (by way of the interurban railroad) reinforced the strict segregation between private and public that separated not only home from community but suburb from city. In this way, one can trace a chain of analogies or ratios ranging from the macroscopic (public) down to the microscopic (private): Downtown : Neighborhood :: Street : House :: Living Room : Bedroom. In this system of gender rationality, suburban women tended to be segregated toward the private end of the continuum, while men moved within what was perceived to be a "public sphere."[69] Even within the larger public world of the city, gender marked the topography; as Harry Carr observed in the mid-1930s, "As nearly as any one could arrange the character of the town, Broadway is a women's street and Spring Street is a man's street."[70]

The divisions in the suburb mirror those between suburb and city and between women and men. Concomitant with this move toward gender segregation, specifically among the middle classes, was an ideological prescription for the separation of women from labor markets: women's labor was ideally dedicated to her family.[71] Likewise, as we have seen, the home served as a retreat and refuge for bourgeois men. Their labor was confined to the commercial city—the suburb ideally remained for them a place of repose. The properly gendered division of labor reinforced the properly gendered division of space. Both buttressed the properly gendered and well-adjusted family (which in turn supported the moral development of the larger society—and so the logic goes, ad infinitum). Consequently, clear distinctions between suburban neighborhood and central city, such as those of interest to city planners, necessarily evoked in the common sense of the 1920s a whole range of desirable social arrangements, implicating labor, architecture, and even transportation in this complex system of gender and urban topography. The interdependence of these ideological signifiers in the era appeared self-evident to such urban observers as Los Angeles's Dana Bartlett:

> The laying out of new subdivisions far out beyond the city limits, makes cheap and desirable home sites, obtainable for a multitude of working men, where they are able to build cheap bungalows or California houses, or at least to erect tents. "The Family Unit," the desire of the sociologist, can be recovered, when by rapid transit, giving a fare of from five to seven cents for a thirty minutes' ride, the working man can be induced to locate with his family far from the noisy city. No work for civic betterment is worth more than this.[72]

In Bartlett's view, the clearer the dichotomy between suburb and city, home and neighborhood, woman and man, the better the metropolis.

The stark contrast between suburb and city underwrote a complex of ideological understandings of urban topography. Professional planning of urban space, social segregation, civic boosterism, economic distinctions, and gender norms were all intimately interconnected in the common sense of the period. Once again, ordinary urban dwellers subconsciously picked up on a wide range of ideological signs in their progress through the city. Although the specific meanings of these boundaries differed for women and men of different racial, class, regional, or other identities, consciousness of the demarcations was a trait common to all.

Finally, perhaps the most familiar way urbanites were able to read their city was in terms of immediate locality. If one lived in the city, one *belonged* to a specific neighborhood. That district of the city was one's true social world. Indeed, in the neighborhood a relatively close-knit community could form, linking residents through their common association based on proximity, shared communal memories, and homogeneous demographics. Neighborhood defined the everyday limits of the urbanite's familiar space, locating the precise coordinates of home territory. Within Los Angeles, then, residential districts—and the streets that bounded them—conveyed additional patterns of significance, inscribing still further layers of signification onto the metropolis. Once more, markers of public and private space served to locate local residents in familiar and unfamiliar regions. In this way, common urban spaces, such as a downtown commercial district or a neighborhood park, evoked a range of meanings. It is in the difference between quasi-"private" neighborhood sites and more "public" municipal areas that understandings of the domain of appropriate political and communal action were rooted. For most locals, patterns of familiarity and association set one's neighborhood off from formal civic spaces. The demarcation of urban spaces in Los Angeles, as in most American metropolises of the age, was a thorough and pervasive process. The lines on planners' maps, derived from exhaustive scientific surveys, often merely reflected the existing delineation of space perceived every day by Angelenos as they went about their lives.

In a whole array of ways, segregation was important to Los Angeles in this period; clearly visible demarcations between spaces—ethnic, racial, gendered, economic, public and private—were central to Angelenos' perception of their city. At times, the maintenance of these stable boundaries seems more important than the specificities of the places so clearly marked by them. Professional understanding of the city depended upon an array of clearly legible boundaries and distinctions that made urban space, and the city as a whole, clearly comprehensible. Traditional cities— such as Los Angeles was in those years—were rigidly segmented and sharply delineated. Much political energy and psychosocial activity went into maintaining and policing these distinctions. In large measure, these common sense boundaries are what made the increasingly diverse metropolis understandable and legible to its own residents (even as many chafed under—and actively resisted—the implications of this segregation). Whatever other social ends this demarcation served, the urban knowledge derived from it allowed ordinary urbanites—black, white, native, immigrant, Asian, Latino, male, female, rich, poor—to read clearly the signs of the city's ideological structure.

As I have indicated, it was the principal mission of the new ranks of expert professional scientific planners not only to recognize and to record these social traces upon the urban form but to preserve them. These segregations and associations were the essence of civic order; they were important technologies for the production of clear and comprehensible urban legibility. These common sense markers of urban space were boundaries that planners treated as no less essential and vital than those between commercial zones and residential zones, between city land and private property.[73] For residents and planners of the Progressive American city, urban distinctions—social, demographic, and topographic—were intertwined and interdependent. Efficient human environments were properly arranged and clearly segregated. Although specific boundaries could be questioned and manipulated, the existence of these divisions was largely taken for granted.[74] The boundaries were essential to the logic of the city. They made the urban landscape comprehensible, lending the city its legibility and order.

It was precisely this promise of legibility that undergirded all the various technologies of urban perception and regulation discussed here, from restrictive covenant and block agreement to scientific survey and city plan. Crucially, these technologies were all fundamentally compatible with the central task of making the heterogeneous city comprehensible to city planners and amenable to their ministrations—planning professionals were particularly quick to pick up on and to make use of already existing ideological urban categories and delineations. Proper perception and manipulation of the mechanisms of segregation were the fundamental supports of the planners' claim to comprehensive vision. The planners therefore promised to bring increased legibility to a potentially chaotic urban environment, both methodologically (through their technologies of observation) and empirically (through their efforts at urban restructuring and healing). Implicitly, they also promised to maintain structural hierarchies of identity in a rapidly growing and evolving metropolis. Therefore, what the planners of 1920 sought to accomplish in Los Angeles—to bring the city into focus and to make it clearly comprehensible—was part of a larger project of envisioning urbanity throughout the nation, as well as being deeply relevant to the specific situation of twentieth-century Southern California. Ultimately, what was at stake in this desire to view the city comprehensively and clearly was the very meaning of urbanism in a modern age. Through various contestations of this meaning, questions of Los Angeles's urban legibility would reassert themselves repeatedly in the years to come.

With powerful tools to reveal the city's social and topographical boundaries and elements, city planners took upon themselves the heavy responsibility of maintaining the region's legibility. As the city's comprehensibility depended upon the clear segregation of urban elements (districts, traffic streams, and people), planners hoped to use their critical technologies of urban observation—such as the scientific quantitative survey and the comprehensive map—to help them maintain and solidify those important boundaries within a shifting physical topography. This task they saw as necessarily "progressive," although it was in many ways reactionary. Nevertheless, these men were heirs to a long booster tradition, and they sought to plan the growth of their emerging metropolis to make it a greater and even, as they saw it, a "better city." In the process, Los Angeles's expert scientific planners even hoped to use their powers of observation (or prophecy) to prepare the future of the American city, with Southern California as a utopia of future possibility.

TRAFFIC AND URBAN VISIBILITY

Given these lofty ambitions and powerful techniques of urban observation, many historians have found it ironic that the first act of Los Angeles's new City Planning Commission was the disastrous 1920 downtown parking ban. Crucially, from the moment this parking ban was put into force that November to such calamitous effect, Los Angeles's planners were forced to devote the vast majority of their efforts to a rearguard action against traffic problems (see figure 4). This preoccupation, according to many urban historians of Los Angeles, is the main reason for the reputed failure of city planning in the years between the wars: "The [planning] commissions, for all practical purposes, focused their everyday staff activities on two principal tasks: the rationalization of land subdivision activity in the county, and the provision of adequate streets and highways, primarily through negotiated agreements with the land developers."[75] Both Martin Wachs, in "Autos, Transit, and the Sprawl of Los Angeles," and Mark Foster, first in "The Decentralization of Los Angeles during the 1920's" and later in such articles as "The Model-T, the Hard Sell, and Los Angeles's Urban Growth," argue that planners were incapacitated by the need to constantly regulate traffic conditions. As Foster puts it in his most recent history of that period's urban planning, *From Streetcar to Superhighway*, "About all [planners] had time or energy to do . . . was to gain rights of way out in the country for adequate streets and highways before profit-crazed realtors choked off any such advance planning by laying out thoughtlessly conceived subdivisions. . . . By 1930, a local planner complained that 90 percent of their time was consumed by zoning variance cases and minor street changes; he stated that local planners did some replanning, but little original planning."[76] In their attempts to keep up with ever-increasing traffic loads, these historians argue, planners were essentially unable to do much actual planning. As we have seen, this judgment has reached something of a consensus in recent years.

Nevertheless, it is wrong. Traffic was important for planners, both analytically and strategically. Planners especially emphasized traffic in viewing the city, both

FIGURE 4. Downtown Los Angeles, 1919. Los Angeles Public Library, Security Pacific Collection.

because it easily fit into the favored organic metaphorical rhetoric (flows and circulation, blockages and congestion) and because it was one of the few detectable ways they could relate actual human behavior to the functional realities of the metropolis. The city, they knew from their surveys, consisted of discrete elements in specific locations. They could relate these elements through the visualization tool of the map, but in this way they perceived the relationships between elements only in the abstract, by surmising from physical proximity and theoretical model. They had little opportunity to directly perceive motion in the city—the everyday interconnections, exchanges, and transactions between identified elements. Traffic afforded planners one means of determining these necessary, ubiquitous, but largely invisible everyday relationships. Movements by individuals, as they went about their private business, collectively traced the functional connections between urban sites. Commuting between home and work or on shopping trips would definitively reveal which business areas served which residential tracts, which houses belonged to workers in which businesses, and so forth. These visible traces also showed the routes—or "lines of communication," in planners' terminology—between these elements. Entire streetcar infrastructures, for example, could be surveyed, mapped, and correlated with measured average ridership (especially through flow-volume diagrams) to provide a general sense of human urban movement.

But the real indicator of where people go is given by automobile traffic, as that could be easily measured by traffic counts and parking spaces.[77] Automobiles could be easily counted and traced, and were therefore the closest planners got to individual citizens on an empirical level. Traffic, quite simply, was the detectable trace of human activity in the city, as well as the motion animating the planners' maps. For experts so dependent upon static, snapshot surveys and rigid maps to properly see the bustling metropolis, traffic was a window both onto everyday change and onto the essential functional relationships between solidly identified urban landmarks. Traffic indicated circulation, and circulation indicated the living operation of the metropolis on a daily basis.

In addition to its evident visibility, ordinary road congestion was also perceived early on by planners to be an opportunity for—not an impediment to—effective and ambitious planning, for traffic lay at the heart of what was wrong with the existing metropolis. First, it was clear to planners that traffic congestion energized Angelenos during the 1920s. It was a problem that dominated discourse within the city, prompting extreme measures and a tolerance for radical solutions. Further, it brought together a wide range of public figures into a grand coalition in support of traffic relief. Planners, boosters, and downtown elites all found common cause in this crusade, and the promise of urban planning professionals to treat this chronic malady allowed them much greater authority and power than they might otherwise have been able to claim. Indeed, traffic was for planners the ticket to municipal influence out of proportion to their material status within the city's power structures. The slowness of the streets put the enterprising experts on the fast track to the sort of institutional status that could allow them to act on their ambitions.

Second, Los Angeles's planners recognized early on that traffic was not a momentary inconvenience. Planners brought to this discourse on congestion a holistic and comprehensive vision, and for these experts, traffic was a symptom of important flaws with the city's urban form. It was not merely the understandable side effect of growth or of widespread adoption of the private automobile, but an intrinsic feature of the concentric modern city. Street traffic was caused not by too many cars or by inadequate streets but by fundamentally flawed urban structure: "A city is built up entirely from its traffic routes—suburban, street, railroad, and vehicular. These traffic routes determine the arteries of travel which make our business centers at the most important intersections, and radiate thence out to outlying residence districts. They therefore determine all real estate values. They are the limitation of our convenience in getting about the community and if they are not properly laid out, can cause absolutely the wrong and most harmful development of a city."[78] For Los Angeles's planning experts, street congestion was a symptom of a larger problem, which was intrinsic to the existing metropolis. Growing public furor over traffic jams, though, might allow planners to justify the radical measures they increasingly felt were necessary to correct the structure of the city.

Fundamentally, the planners believed that, despite its much-publicized amenities, Southern California was in trouble. The city's urban problems were ultimately traceable to its conventional organization. In the traditional American urban topography, the central city sat at the core of a concentric orbit of suburban residential areas (see figure 5). As Kenneth Jackson argues in his landmark *Crabgrass Frontier*, although Americans since the 1880s viewed the more rural suburban areas as the most desirable areas for residence, in this period these enclaves were generally only accessible to the middle and upper classes, who, of course, made up only a small proportion of the total urban population. This trend toward middle-class suburbia had been the original impetus for the streetcar and interurban systems of the late nineteenth and early twentieth centuries.

In Los Angeles, however, the Pacific Electric interurban system had encouraged a particularly fragmented urban landscape, as the Mediterranean myth promulgated by generations of boosters had fostered a quasi-rustic lifestyle. Because the Pacific Electric was so intimately bound up in far-flung speculative land ventures, the system had spread a tremendous distance from the outskirts of the city. The PE rolled far further into the orange groves and brush-covered hills than any other comparable traction system. The interurban went where land was cheap, operating at a loss, the better to sell distant land for development and, collaterally, to chain the new residents to the train. Los Angeles tended to have a spotty pattern of settlement as a result, with large gaps in its blanket of residential coverage, which further increased commute times and fragmented the metropolitan area. Now Los Angeles was ringed by increasingly distant layers of single-family, low-density bungalow developments. Further, since development in the region was primarily a phenomenon of the twentieth century and a product of the interurbans, the suburbs housed a disproportionately large segment of the urban population. Consequently, few of Los Angeles's residents were living in high-density downtown dwellings by the early 1920s, and the downtown had never developed as a walking city, as eastern metropolises had. Nevertheless, the planners' surveys soon revealed that the downtown district had a much higher density than other parts of the region—high even compared with more centralized cities—but it was very compact.

The planners almost immediately recognized that Los Angeles was even more of a concentric city than most, and as a result the disadvantages of this urban topography were correspondingly more severe in Los Angeles. Traffic was only the most visible of these urban ailments endemic to the concentric metropolis, but it was serious. By the 1920s, despite the success of the Pacific Electric, many Angelenos were commuting by private automobile. Worse, this trend was particularly intense in the suburbs, where growth was so rapid that even the Pacific Electric often could not keep pace. Increasingly, these new suburbanites were driving downtown every day, and to deal with the new developments, the Pacific Electric had inaugurated motor coach service to supplement its trains in newly built areas. These buses merely added to the inbound commute, as did the hundreds of private jitneys that sprang up dur-

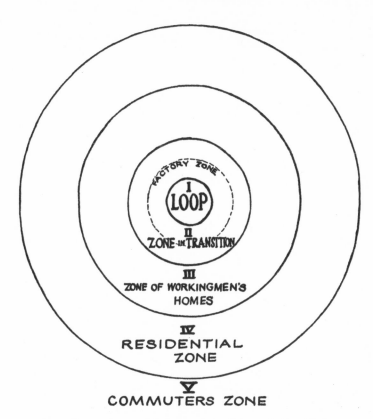

FIGURE 5. The Burgess model of concentric city growth. From Robert Park, Ernest W. Burgess, and Roderick D. McKenzie, *The City* (Chicago: University of Chicago Press, 1925), 51. Courtesy of the University of Chicago Press.

ing the decade to cannibalize the chronically encumbered and tardy streetcars' business. All this traffic was converging on the central business district every workday.

The traffic situation in the existing city was simply untenable. Metaphorically put, as it usually was, the city was suffering from a chronic case of congestive heart failure: circulation around the heart was too restricted to allow the proper operation of that critical organ. The arterial highways connecting downtown with the rapidly expanding suburbs were sclerotic; they no longer provided adequate traffic flow. Given the congested state of these vital conduits, the prognosis for the city was grim. If things were this bad in the city at a bit over half a million people, how severe would the problem be when the population someday approached—as seemed inevitable— a million or more?

The short-term solution was obvious: pressure on the city's circulatory system had to be reduced by increasing the capacity of major arteries. Nevertheless, as the metropolis expanded, the planners foresaw, residential development would move farther and farther into the outskirts, and the Pacific Electric would turn more and more to buses. The load on the arterial regional highways would increase without end. The congestion downtown would increase commensurately, until the commercial and industrial districts at the heart of the city would again begin to fail from lack of proper circulation. No matter how much the planners worked at the arduous task of widening streets, the congestion would intensify, because the number of commuters from the outlying areas would correspondingly increase. The planners, their vision aided by surveys and maps, could clearly see that under extrapolated present conditions, the city would gradually suffocate under the weight of its own expansion. This logic was consistent and had powerful implications. It also directly contradicted the plain common sense of most urbanites in this period. Most American cities, including New York and Chicago, were celebrating their grip over ever-larger urban regions and centering their municipal identities on their towering downtowns. In this respect, then, planners questioned the very essence of urban modernity as it was understood at the time.

In Los Angeles, in contrast to those eastern metropolises, planners seemed willing to take their irreverent conclusions to their logical limits and to directly challenge those widespread notions of modern urbanity. In fact, they were already contemplating dramatic solutions to the problems of centralization as they saw them. And here, once again, planners saw traffic regulation not as an impediment to "real" planning but as its essence. By attending to the effects of the automobile, they would be empowered to effect far more structural change than they might have otherwise been allowed. Endemic concern about urban congestion translated easily into widespread support for road projects.[79] But not only would this need to "modernize" the city's transportation infrastructure allow them far greater scope in rooting out potential urban ailments, it would allow them to shape the city's future. Planners believed that control over the layout of the streets was key to controlling the future growth of the city. Proper, orderly development could be planned in advance through this simple mechanism. As Robert Fogelson observes: "The planners, whose regulatory authority here came from local and state legislation, designated the city's major traffic and the county's regional highway schemes as the bases for subdivision in Los Angeles."[80] Fogelson sees planner interest in such details as subdivision control and road plating as distracting from the larger promise of planning—"In one regulation after another the planners revealed an overriding concern for automobile transport"[81]—but provision for future growth of the urban body was the very focus of advance planning, and the key to this strategy was the planners' control over the street system. In practice, grafting new arteries—the alignment of streets—provided both a useful justification for and an efficient means of urban intervention. Streets constituted the most important element in the city's circulatory system, and as such, they would regulate the flow of goods, resources, and people, and thus prevent congestion throughout the region. This system would be structural as well as circulatory, in that the provision of future streets would shape the development of future subdivisions. By carefully laying out the road grid, the planners would be able to prepare a more efficient and healthy city and to plan—in skeletal and venous outline—the city's future. In the view of the planners, infrastructure was destiny.

But why did planners value so highly the potential to build the future city from scratch? Despite its traffic problems, Los Angeles was clearly already developing into a major American metropolis—it was, judging from its rapid growth, quite an urban success. The reason Los Angeles's planners wished to exert such extraordinary control over the future shape of the city was that they did not in fact wish the metropolis to continue on its current course of development. Planning experts in Los Angeles did indeed have a vision for the city. They seized upon control over the street system and the ordinary suburban subdivisions it anchored as the primary means of achieving that dream precisely because this vision would promise to redefine the meaning of modernity in the urban context. If properly enacted, this design would, they expected, prevent future blight from developing in their city of the future, and if all went according to plan, it would also ameliorate the existing congestion in the built-up parts of the metropolis. It was here that Los Angeles's planners turned into radical utopians and mobilized the booster tradition to envision Southern California as the birthplace of a new model of urbanism. In this aspiration, Los Angeles's planners were on the leading edge of a tide of urban revisionism that was creeping through professional planning circles. Unlike virtually everyone else in this growing traditional centralized city, as well as in contemporary cities, such as New York and Chicago, the apostates of the City Planning Commission felt sure that the continued high-density intensification of the traditional concentric urban-suburban city need no longer be the sole avatar of urban utopianism.

VISIONS OF MODERN URBANITY

A strange ecstatic feeling at such times often possessed me. There flowed through every nerve of my body . . . strains of electricity, giving intense and long continued physical pleasure. . . . The crowded streets—the signs of wealth and prosperity—the bustle—the very confusion and disorder appealed to me, and I was filled with delight.

EBENEZER HOWARD, ON THE EXPERIENCE OF WALKING THE STREETS
OF LONDON, QUOTED IN BUDER, "EBENEZER HOWARD" (398)

In questioning the concentric model of modern urban aspiration, Los Angeles's planners were contemplating the unthinkable. Ever since the late nineteenth century, it had been fixed in the American popular imagination that the city of the future would necessarily be a vertical city—a metropolis of skyscrapers. This city would radiate from a towering central core to take the surrounding countryside under its gaze. Shafts of steel and concrete would puncture the clouds, evincing the industrial age's triumph over gravity and human scale. The skyscraper city reveled in its complexity— it was a mark of increasingly evolved coordination among social functions. This utopian city would become more and more like a machine, and it would reflect society's own advancing mechanization and progress. This was all powerfully evocative for would-be cosmopolitan "moderns" of the early decades of the century. Although we will explore the details of this dominant concentric model of urbanity in much more depth later, it is worth a brief digression to look at one particularly influential expression of the dominant notion of the urban future in order to understand just how unorthodox was the scheme that the planners were contemplating.

This ambitious vision of the modern metropolis was best popularized by Edward Bellamy's immensely successful *Looking Backward: 2000–1887,* published in 1888. In this exemplary urban utopia, Bellamy identified concentration as the essence of modernity. Concentration of wealth, concentration of social power, concentration of resources—these all led to the misery and conflict of the day. Yet *Looking Backward* is by no means a nostalgic book. Bellamy sees in trends toward increasing scale and accumulation not only the sources of society's problems but also the key to their solution. Capitalizing on narratives of progress and social evolution so popular in the age, Bellamy's tract is written as science fiction. It projects its representative gentleman of nineteenth-century Boston—Julian West—113 years into the future. Fittingly for such a progressive tale, this future is a bright one. More than a century of progress has magically brought the forces of concentration to their logical conclusion. Boston, previously a site of "squalor and malodorousness,"[82] has now become a shining city. Waking up in this new twentieth-century Boston, West cannot even be sure he recognizes his hometown: "At my feet lay a great city. Miles of broad streets, shaded by trees and lined with fine buildings, for the most part not in continuous blocks but set in larger or smaller enclosures, stretched in every direction. Every quarter contained large open squares filled with trees, along which statues glistened and fountains flashed in the late-afternoon sun. Public buildings of a colossal size and architectural grandeur unparalleled in my day raised their stately piles on every side. Surely I had never seen this city nor one comparable to it before."[83]

The city exemplifies the productive power of concentration, directed under the coming utopian scheme of social organization to fulfill its promise of abundance and prosperity. The gargantuan metropolis is but the most visible sign of a larger effort to harness the power of ever greater scale to common ends. In many respects this vision was emblematic of a range of mainstream views common by the early years of the century whose shining conclusion *Looking Backward* depicted. Industrial expansion and conglomeration marked the era. Further, modern cities were hosting an intensifying concentration of capital and industrial might during this period, marking this wealth and power by the proliferation of these immense and technically complex skyscrapers. Likewise, censuses indicated an increasing flight of America's population from rural areas to these new dense cities—labor joined capital in ever greater concentration. Urbanity dominated the popular imagination of the future, as these trends toward accumulation and centralization became unmistakable tokens of the modern age.

Yet, by the first decades of this century, against all this manifest progress stood another vision of the modern metropolis. This was a very different conception, which was grounded more in nostalgia for the frontier and the small town than in the promise of dense urban arcologies of the future. It sought to envision the city as self-contained, not cosmopolitan. This was a vision of a decentralized city of lower density and higher comprehensibility. This model of urbanism was essentially rural, even pastoral, in its proclivities. It reflected a rebellion against nineteenth-century trends toward greater urban concentration, and it was deeply invested in a sort of nostalgic futurism. That said, this decentralized vision was, in a new way, strongly utopian, and could also make strong claims to modernity. In its pure form, it promised a new urbanism, in which the new modern city could emerge as a synthesis of town and country.[84] This, its most powerful and influential version, was espoused by the seer/stenographer Ebenezer Howard, one in a grand tradition of British utopian visionaries, in his design for the "garden city."

Howard was truly a dreamer. He had been strongly influenced by Bellamy's utopian novel but had turned against that utopian future's foundational logic. Whereas Bellamy based his prophecy on the modern gospel of concentration, Howard put his faith in decentralization. Whereas Bellamy had seen great potential in the dense modern metropolis, if only organized on a just and rational basis, Howard viewed the great cities of his day as absolutely hopeless. Howard was certainly not antiurban—he found the metropolis of his day stimulating and exciting—but he abhorred the social conditions prevalent in these conurbations. For the working class, Howard thought, the modern metropolis was a modern hell: "Crowded, ill-ventilated, unplanned, unwieldy, unhealthy cities—ulcers on the very face of our beautiful island."[85] His garden city alternative would offer an urban experience set in a verdant landscape. Instead of steel, asphalt, and concrete, this city would revel in wood, stone, and orderly vegetation. In this way, Howard appropriated for his urban vision, or revision, both American frontier ideology of renewal through contact with the land and a more English fascination with the romance of the contemporary landscape garden. Howard's would be a city rooted in a renewing and calmingly benevolent nature.

The garden city was not, though, merely a more pastoral version of that traditional concentric city. It was to be fundamentally different—and the espousing of this difference was Howard's greatest heresy against received planning knowledge. Howard wished to abandon the crowded cities altogether, for their very structure was irretrievably flawed. He wished to overturn the dominant contemporary association of modernity with concentration and density by arguing that the metropolises of his day were wholly inappropriate for the modern world. At their essence, Howard argued in his hugely influential tract, *Garden Cities of To-morrow,* such cities were based on unsound principles:

> These crowded cities have done their work; they were the best which a society largely based on selfishness and rapacity could construct, but they are in the nature of things entirely unadapted for a society in which the social side of our nature is demanding a larger share of recognition—a society where even the very love of self leads us to insist upon a greater regard for the well-being of our fellows. The large cities of today are scarcely better adapted for the expression of the fraternal spirit than would a work on astronomy which taught that the earth was the centre of the universe be capable of adaptation for use in our schools.[86]

Implicitly, Howard here offers himself as the Copernicus of urban doctrine. In his apostatic view, the old concentric cities were as flawed as the Ptolemaic understanding of the solar system. Whereas, in its geocentric folly, the traditional model of urbanism had placed the large metropolis at the heart of the settled region, surrounded by a constellation of suburbs, Howard sought to disrupt and debunk the concentric emphasis on the city by replacing it with an ideal of self-contained towns ordered on a more human scale. As a result, the garden city would be tailored to promote social familiarity and community interaction instead of the alienation and impersonality endemic to the metropolis. As Robert Fishman points out in his study of Howard's ideology, *Urban Utopias in the Twentieth Century,* the difference in scale was "the fundamental principle of the garden city: Radical hopes for a cooperative civilization could be fulfilled only in small communities embedded in a decentralized society."[87]

The garden city was the antidote to the concentration of resources and population that characterized the late nineteenth- and early twentieth-century city. Howard's utopian urbanism envisioned a self-contained commune, open to both common enterprise and small-scale proprietor capitalism.[88] This city could be built in an existing (preferably agricultural) setting and would free the working population from the tyranny of the slum and the tenement. Similarly, this properly proportioned and humane city would liberate its inhabitants from the cold canyon corridors created by towering blocks of skyscrapers. All social interaction would be restored to harmonious balance. Central to this dream of harmony was the city's greenbelt: the integrity of the garden city would be protected by a wide buffer of agricultural land around the verdant city. The garden would both surround the garden city and run through it. Green areas would demarcate parts of the city, as well as marking the city off from its surroundings. In this way, the utopian town would continually expose its inhabitants to the regenerating influence of sunlight, clean air, and abundant foliage. At the same time, and this is crucial, the garden would maintain a comprehensible urban legibility—it would prevent the city from sprawling and clearly demarcate its internal districts. There would be no alienating urban confusion because the city would be constructed on a human scale and limited to that scale by its greenbelt. There would be no social unrest because the city would form a unified community, offering its amenities to all classes—which would be separated from each other only by parks and hedgerows. There would be no traffic and commuting because this would be a walking city, with its residential districts an easy rustic stroll from its industrial and commercial zones. The garden would regulate, buffer, and mediate all social interaction, allowing for a gracious communal order.

These clear separations and connections in Howard's garden city plan were most famously represented in a series of diagrams presented in *Garden Cities of Tomorrow*, which soon achieved the status of icons. These maps graphically revealed the essence of the garden city ideal. The basic circular map of the model garden city represented in compact shorthand the order and balance structuring the functional relationships in the ideal city (see figures 6 and 7). This was more than mere representation, however. Although Howard was quite careful to include a disclaimer that the diagram was intended only as an abstract conceptual model—"N.B. A diagram only. Plan must depend upon site selected"—it was the iconic circular map that came to dominate conceptions of the garden city plan in the years to come.[89]

As with all such maps, the intrinsic functional relationships could only be assumed from proximity, and thus the egalitarian principles that structured Howard's utopia were ignored by subsequent garden city enthusiasts. Only the most general notions of balanced social harmony were perceived by observers; that much, at least, could be inferred by anyone with an interest in planning, merely by examining the symmetry and clarity of the imagined topography. If the detailed descriptions of Howard's prose proved inspiring to dedicated readers, the real proof of the garden city concept seemed to lie in this simple diagram. The map captured the imagination of readers; it graphically presented the (topographical) essence of Howard's utopian vision.[90]

It was critical to Howard's vision of social peace that his city be fully self-contained, with all urban resources integrated into a functional network. Consequently, the garden city would offer on its municipally (and democratically) controlled land both housing and employment. This would not become yet another middle-class suburb, as Robert Fishman observes: "Howard planned the Garden City to be a manufacturing center in which factories would necessarily be close to the homes. In order to separate the residential areas and also to ensure that everyone would be within walking distance of his place of work, Howard put the facto-

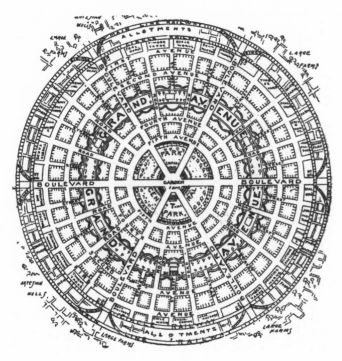

FIGURE 6. Ebenezer Howard's garden city plan, circa 1899.

ries at the periphery of the city."[91] This tight physical association of residence and industry was the hallmark of Howard's vision and its primary claim to utopian urbanism. This model of development would offer, in close proximity, all the most important amenities and social structures of the metropolis, without the endless vertical and horizontal sprawl.

As Lewis Mumford adamantly insisted in his introduction to the most popular mid-twentieth-century edition of *Garden Cities of To-morrow*, this vision offered an ideal way to preserve human proportions in the urban framework: "The Garden City, as Howard defined it, is not a suburb but the antithesis of a suburb: not a more rural retreat, but a more integrated foundation for an effective urban life."[92] The garden city was to be primarily urban; it was a new form of urbanity: "Here again I must utter a warning against those who mistake Howard's programme for one of breaking down the distinction of town and country and turning them into an amorphous suburban mass. . . . For the Garden City, as conceived by Howard, is not a loose indefinite sprawl of individual houses with immense open spaces over the whole landscape: it is rather a compact, rigorously confined urban grouping. . . . He cannot be accused of being an advocate of urban sprawl."[93] Here again Mum-

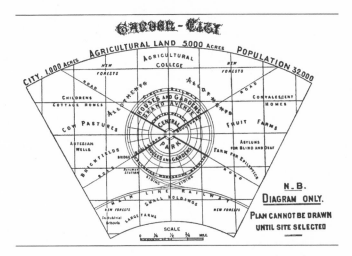

FIGURE 7. A garden city and its environs. From Ebenezer Howard,
Garden Cities of To-morrow (London: Faber and Faber, 1902).

ford is defending Howard's landmark ideal of decentralization against the largely suburban image it had acquired by 1945. It is important to remember that in 1920 decentralization ideology was intimately bound up, for most planners, not so much with Levittowns (still decades in the future) or other suburban developments, but with this new urbanism of Howard's garden city. The garden city was intended to be clearly distinct from both suburban retreats and urban conglomerations. The power of this foundational notion of the small, self-contained, decentralized *city* was undeniable in this age, and it offered a powerful, fully "modern" counterpoint to the skyscraper urbanism then prevalent.

The depth of the cosmopolitanism in his program and the fact that he was not merely advocating a return to small town life are best illustrated in Howard's plan for the final apotheosis of the garden city ideal: the construction of "Social Cities." As Mumford put it, "Not the least part of Howard's conception was his emphasis upon the grouping of garden cities: he realized that the advantages of a single city would be multiplied by the creation of 'town-clusters,' groups or constellations of such cities."[94] *Garden Cities of To-morrow* offered a vision of urban expansion that projected the benefits of the compact community across a vast geographic expanse. Although the individual garden city would be capped at about thirty thousand residents, Howard made provision for future growth:

> I think, feel confident that the people of Garden City will not for a moment permit the beauty of their city to be destroyed by the process of growth. But it may be urged—

if this be true, will not the inhabitants of Garden City in this way be selfishly preventing the growth of their city, and thus preclude many from enjoying its advantages? Certainly not. There is a bright, but overlooked, alternative. The town will grow; but it will grow in accordance with a principle which will result in this—that such growth shall not lessen or destroy, but ever add to its social opportunities, to its beauty, to its convenience.[95]

This growth would not lead to another gargantuan London or New York. It would instead be subordinated to the same mechanism that regulated the garden city itself. The comprehensible proportions of the city would be rigorously maintained.

Garden Cities of To-morrow described the ideal progress and expansion of Howard's utopian city into a larger web of well-ordered communities:

> Garden City is built up. Its population has reached 32,000. How will it grow? It will grow by establishing—under Parliamentary powers probably—another city some little distance beyond its own zone of "country," so that the new town may have a zone of country of its own. I have said "by establishing another city," and, for administrative purposes there would be two cities; but the inhabitant of the one could reach the other in a very few minutes; for rapid transit would be specially provided for, and thus the people of the two towns would in reality represent one community.[96]

Garden Cities of To-morrow envisioned an urban network where countless garden cities could be brought together by an interurban transit system into a sort of decentralized cluster. Each city would maintain its individual identity, jealously protected by its greenswards and zones of functional segregation. Together, these communities would form a composite urbanity, but all practical activity would be confined within each internally.

The carefully structured association of residence and occupation would be preserved by the buffer zones to prevent confusion, while allowing a larger cosmopolitan totality. Here, each city operates as an individual unit, not subordinated by commuting patterns to a larger metropolis. Any hierarchy within this network of garden cities would reflect not a concentric regional dominance but rather a purely symbolic concern for geometrical order and legibility:

> This principle of growth—this principle of always preserving a belt of country round our cities would be ever kept in mind til, in course of time, we should have a cluster of cities . . . so grouped around a Central City that each inhabitant of the whole group, though in one sense living in a town of small size, would be in reality living in, and would enjoy all the advantages of, a great and most beautiful city; and yet all the fresh delights of the country—field, hedgerow, and woodland—not prim parks and gardens merely—would be within very few minutes' walk or ride.[97]

Even this "Central City" would have a strictly limited population (Howard suggests fifty-eight thousand people), and would never exert the domination over its surrounding communities that the concentric metropolis relied upon. The self-

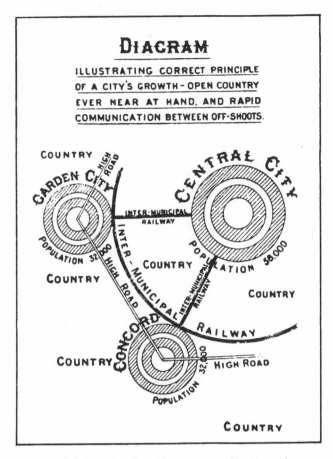

FIGURE 8. Relation of garden cities to one another. From Ebenezer Howard, *Garden Cities of To-morrow* (London: Faber and Faber, 1898).

contained economies of the individual garden cities would be a safeguard to their independence and would free their residents to use the amenities of a somewhat larger urban area without falling victim to congestion and blight. Once more, Howard illustrated his conception with an abstract diagram (see figure 8). The plain geometrical elegance of this sketch of the garden city cluster again testified power-fully, in the eyes of planners, to the natural beauty and efficiency of the underlying model. No existing metropolis, as represented in survey maps, could compare in cleanliness and self-evident order to this ideal.

In its essence, this garden city vision offered a model of distributed urbanity that was expansive without being chaotic. It restructured the nature of the city from an emphasis on concentrated, centralized density to one of decentralized idyllic communalism. Whereas the traditional late nineteenth- and early twentieth-century model of urbanism suggested that continuing population growth would place an increasingly unsustainable burden on the circulatory and managerial systems of the central city, the garden city model seemed to be adapted to indefinite expansion. The cosmopolitan character of the urbanism would only increase with growth, without affecting the circulation or density of the individual modules. While many urban planners and most urbanites assumed that the only response to increasing density was the expansion of the city in another spatial dimension—hence the apparent inevitability of skyscraper urbanism—garden city advocates saw the future in a network of neighborhood-based clusters of a uniformly low density. This was a model of social, as well as urban, progress, as Fishman sums it up:

> Within the city there would be both quiet residential neighborhoods and facilities for a full range of commercial, industrial, and cultural activities. For Howard did not conceive the Garden City as a specialized "satellite town" or "bedroom town" perpetually serving some great metropolis. Rather, he foresaw the great cities of his time shrinking to insignificance as their people desert them for a new way of life in a decentralized society. No longer would a single metropolis dominate a whole region or even a whole nation. Nor would the palatial edifices and giant organization of the big city continue to rule modern society. Instead, the urban population would be distributed among hundreds of Garden Cities whose small scale and diversity of functions embody a world in which the little man has finally won out.[98]

Garden Cities of To-morrow's powerful representation of a decentralized society was tremendously influential in the decades following its publication. Yet the influence of the model did not extend to the full social utopian program. Indeed, the primary impact of the garden city idea was not as a theory of social organization but as a program for town design. Howard's plan was so practical, and so pragmatically expressed, that its utopian social elements were easily separated from its more physical concepts, and the plan, soon stripped of its socialist overtones, proved exceptionally well adapted to the needs of the new planning profession. Sometime planner Mumford put it plainly: "*Garden Cities of To-morrow* has done more than any other single book to guide the modern town planning movement and to alter its objectives."[99] The disciplinary dialect of regional planning—to which Mumford and his contemporaries were deeply committed—was, by the early 1920s, fully invested in the realization of the garden city urban structure. As John L. Thomas explained in a retrospective look at utopian effects on planning ideology, "Even more valuable to twentieth-century planners than their political legacy was the utopians' model of the good society as a composite of city and country."[100] Consequently, by the time British industrialists (the men behind the Cadbury and Lever fortunes) constructed a garden city at Letchworth in the late 1920s, on farmland thirty-five miles outside of London, Howard's urban alternative had already been fully assimilated into the technical expertise of the planners. As Stanley Buder argues in *Visionaries and Planners,* his detailed study of the garden city movement's transformation from social program to architectural doctrine, the garden city's chief legacy was in regional planning: "Letchworth served as a standing example of the modern art or science of town planning. Its lesson, or so supporters contended, was that model communities were greatly superior to those erected by speculative builders. Letchworth's very existence provided a rallying point and a showcase for the emerging profession of town planning."[101]

In the context of the 1920s, this legacy would profoundly shape the imagination of urban planners in Southern California. The garden city program offered the ideal way to fully establish the authority of regional planning in Los Angeles and to construct the region anew. Howard's utopia would at last allow the planners to rescue their patient and in the process make Los Angeles a (garden) city on a hill for twentieth-century urban America.

THE FUTURE GARDEN METROPOLIS

Los Angeles's planners were committed to the goal of freeing Los Angeles from its traditional concentric structure, and in the first thirty years of the twentieth century, the garden city seemed the only realistic way to accomplish this decentralization on a truly regional scale. The first loose association of Angelenos interested in planning called clearly, as far back as 1911, for de-emphasis of the central city in Southern California: "Bad living conditions can be remedied by scattering the population, by a proper distribution of factories, by ruralizing the city and urbanizing the country." The key to all this, they proclaimed in a printed report, was the provision of "industrial villages near factory locations" after the model of contemporary "English Town planning activity, . . . making the industrial village a garden city."[102] Such was the influence of Howard's thought that his envisioned topography stood alone as the only serious thoroughgoing model for planned urban deconcentration in this era.

Although they were seldom entirely explicit in their thinking, many of Southern California's planners gradually became outspoken advocates of radical decentralization. As these experts became more and more convinced through the course of the 1910s of the necessity of wide-ranging metropolitan decentralization, they became more and more fervent in their rejection of the dominant vision of urban modernity. By the 1920s, these professionals began to rail against continued concentration and congestion through frequent publications in planning journals and local newspapers. Likewise, in speeches before a variety of civic organizations, ranging from the influential City Club and various local women's clubs to the chamber of commerce and meetings of the city council, this fairly cohesive cadre of planners outlined their vision of a future Los Angeles of relatively low-density developments arrayed around what some began calling as early as 1911 local "subcenters," which would rival—and eventually replace for most citizens—the singular central business district.[103]

Ultimately, planners hoped that the entire Southern California region could be developed by degrees into a more balanced, harmonious network of self-contained cities, looking to Los Angeles as a cultural resource and civic center, not as the area's exclusive industrial and commercial engine. This was an avowedly urban vision for Southern California but was animated by an entirely new interpretation of urban modernity. This future metropolis would offer all the cosmopolitanism and cultural amenities of the traditional concentric city without the density and congestion. Whereas the dominant model of the modern cosmopolis arrayed its resources vertically, this new form of urbanity would spread its population over a much greater horizontal expanse. This utopian greater Los Angeles of the future, then, would be dedicated to the harmonious and efficient neighborhood, not sacrificed to the all-consuming needs of the congested downtown district.

In retrospect, it is clear what garden city planning promised for Southern California planners, even if they never fully articulated their hopes. First, radical urban decentralization of an existing metropolis might be futuristic and ambitious, but it could be realized without wholesale urban reconstruction or radical incursions on ongoing development. With the wide sweep of land available in the Los Angeles basin, clusters of new garden cities might absorb the vast majority of the expected population influx. Such a plan seemed compatible with the rapid subdivision of land that was already engulfing the area. Decentralizing planners "reasoned that if the region's tracts were effectively regulated prior to development each new parcel would contribute to a more efficient metropolis, coherent community, and attractive landscape."[104] By regulating these new subdivisions and encouraging garden city type development, planners could fairly easily redirect existing trends of far-flung suburbanization toward the construction of autonomous new communities. As Fogelson observes, "[Planners] proposed an alternative of residential dispersal and business decentralization—carefully supervised so as to foster self-sufficient satellite cities instead of sprawling suburban subdivisions."[105] With a bit of careful advance planning, the entire urban network could be reshaped in this manner—long before it began to solidify. Because Los Angeles's core was such a small part of the larger region, there would be far less danger of the city dominating the urban fabric than in an already heavily developed urban region, such as New York or Chicago.

Obviously, given their analytical predilection for visibility, the orderliness of the garden city maps would particularly appeal to Southern Californian expert planners. Here was a deconcentrated form that was clearly manageable on a human scale.

The eye could take in the city at a glance (or at least the diagrams) and make perfect sense of what was seen. Disciplinary reliance on survey and map predisposed Los Angeles planners toward Howard's diagrams. They made a great deal of sense within the system of logic structuring planners' views of the city: the vision was already translated into terms planners could understand and digest. It was extremely legible to them and eminently comprehensible—both in detail and as a whole. Furthermore, this scheme fit planners' priorities for their region. It promised to preserve, in lush greenbelts, much of the bucolic appeal of 1920 Los Angeles, and it offered a way to structure the gradual growth of the vast basin. The fact that the plan was self-contained without relying on concentric growth was a further enticement of the garden city model. Instead of a single circular urban structure arrayed about a central congested core, this map betokened an orderly clustered landscape of walking-scale communities, each properly discrete and well segregated, without chaotic layer upon layer of ever-denser development. Compared to any survey of contemporary Southern California in this period, the advantages of the garden city diagram were clear. The future Los Angeles promised to be equally legible. Chaotic congestion—both of people and of traffic—would diminish without degrading urban comprehensibility. Homogeneous, tight-knit, properly segregated neighborhoods would become the basis of the metropolitan district. Within each community, as within the greater clustered whole, clear lines and hierarchies would be visible to everyone. Cosmopolitanism would not require chaotic and unplanned social mixing. The garden city cluster, essentially a collection of small towns, promised a social order clearly legible to all, as in the small town of the era.

And what was the critical, indispensable element of this decentralization planning? Ironically, it was the very cause of the downtown traffic crises of the early 1920s: the private automobile. The car was the linchpin of the entire garden city aspiration. Fortuitously, the abundance of automobiles that presently clogged the metropolis's arteries would be central to its salvation. Here, the planners' jurisdiction over the street grid would prove crucial. Whereas many historians have bemoaned the fact that local planners were "forced" to cope with the minutiae of urban traffic regulation, the planners themselves most likely considered the growing demand for traffic relief as a welcome sign that the citizenry was beginning to recognize the need for planning solutions to the problems of the congested metropolis (see figure 9).

More directly, domain over the streets was one of the few direct powers planners had at this time, and certainly the most promising. Ideally, their authority over street platting would allow them to map out the future shape of the metropolis, at least in outline. Control over the street system—combined with techniques to fully comprehend and envision the region's development—would allow planners to construct their urban utopia from behind the scenes and within their still limited powers. After all, their vision of garden city decentralization could not realistically contemplate the public ownership of all land, as Howard's did. Instead, planners would

FIGURE 9. Cover of the Progressive *California Outlook* 16, no. 16 (18 April 1914).

have to guide the growth of the region by the arts of encouragement, description, and—most practically—dominion over the skeletal infrastructure of public streets. With a few minor incentives, industry could be encouraged to locate outside of the built-up city, paralleling the ongoing residential subdivisions as they spread across the region, clinging to new networks of roads, sewers, and other utilities.

Private developers and subdividers would continue to do the actual work of buying and selling land, designing and marketing individual projects. The rational material decisions of these many private entrepreneurs, though, would be guided by the invisible hand of the planner's infrastructural design, arraying themselves almost naturally along the lines defined by carefully crafted building codes and regulations. Over time, instead of traditional dependent suburbia, autonomous garden cities would gradually evolve, as if by nature. Finally, completing the circle, this geographical fragmentation, instead of posing a threat to the circulatory health of the metropolis, would relieve a considerable amount of the existing pressure. The traffic woes of the concentric metropolis—which were, of course, underwriting all this radical change—would simply fade away.[106]

For planners in Los Angeles, ultimately, the route to radical urban restructuring on the model of Ebenezer Howard's garden city ideal lay in the pragmatic, technical details of the urban street system, and the vehicle for their ambitions was the transmission of Angelenos' growing concern about traffic. Over the next few years, though, these experts would find their control over that street grid and its jumble of private automobiles to be much more tenuous and uncertain than they had assumed. Indeed, in the 1920s these experts would find that public reaction to the chaos on the city's streets would exert its own influence over the shape of the metropolis to come, complicating the professionals' aspiration to "Dream dreams and see Visions" of "the better city" to come.

2

Paradise Misplaced

Shortly after dusk on an evening in the early spring of 1921, several automobiles sat parked on North Virgil Avenue, in a calm and somewhat secluded neighborhood on what was then the western side of Los Angeles. This was becoming an increasingly common occurrence on cool evenings; young Angelenos sought out such spots for sessions of unhindered petting, far from the eyes of their intrusive parents. Access to their own automobiles offered these youths not just mobility about town—and with it new familiarity with, almost a sense of possession of, the anonymous streets of the growing metropolis—but also virtually total freedom from restrictive moral supervision. In this calm middle-class neighborhood, though, such clusters of parked automobiles seemed out of place—sinister even. Consequently, on the night in question, a middle-aged woman walked from her home at 227 North New Hampshire Street the "several hundred yards" to North Virgil, intent on driving these "'spooners' from the vicinity of her home."[1] When she reached the corner, the woman peered into a parked car, and quite suddenly, "a well-dressed, heavy man seized her by the wrist and dragged her into the machine." Screaming for help, the lady "was thrown to the floor of the automobile." Fortunately, she managed to break "away from the man and leaping over the door of the machine, fled to her home," where her screams had alerted her husband. According to later police reports carried in the local newspapers, "the automobile was at once driven away" as the anxious husband, G. Gordon Whitnall, emerged from the house to investigate. Because, in her panic, "Mrs. Whitnall failed to secure the license number of the machine and on account of the darkness was unable to obtain a good description of her attacker," the police were ultimately unable to identify and apprehend the aggressive and licentious automobilist. The Hollywood division of the LAPD did,

however, "order a special patrol of officers near the Whitnall residence, with orders to allow no parking of automobiles in the neighborhood unless the persons
driving the machines had business in the vicinity." Apparently, this parking ban
succeeded—no further reports of violent parked youths appeared in the local newspapers, and this "attempted kidnapping" of Mrs. Whitnall proved to be an isolated
incident.

"THE TRAFFIC QUESTION HAS BECOME A PROBLEM"

A restrictive parking ban apparently succeeded in maintaining order and peace in
the West Echo Park neighborhood of the city planning chief and his family, but the
rest of the metropolis remained relatively unprotected during these early decades
of automobility. In Los Angeles, incidents such as this one in 1921—and undoubtedly many similar events failed to make it into the major newspapers—had begun
to concern city residents. Gradually, both expert and public discourse about urban
growth began to take the form of a generalized concern about traffic. Aggravating
street congestion and these more threatening incidents combined into a wide public concern with the everyday effects of automobile traffic. Traffic control—central,
as we have seen, to the schemes of planners, who laid out their plats on a grid of
streets and generally tended toward a humoral concern with flows and circulation—
would now emerge as a persistent obsession of the urban populace. Clearly, discourse about automotive congestion was no longer a merely technical concern but
a much broader and much more complicated ideological one. If, for all their hubris,
Southern Californian planners had previously felt themselves to be the magicians
behind the curtain—toiling unseen to shape the long-term development of their
communities in subtle and gradual ways—now they were beginning to recognize
the full cultural weight of their actions. As a consequence of this pervasive discourse,
the public began to share the planners' obsession with seeing the city in terms of
movement and circulation. This way of understanding the city, which only a few
years before had been the esoteric interest of scientific experts, became a common
topic of discussion in the early 1920s. In Southern California during this era, as
planners began to discover, all sorts of urban anxieties and worries—about trans-
gressions of gender boundaries in the city, the increasing disorder of a growing
metropolis, and the perceived social costs of rapid change in Jazz Age modernity—
would be channeled into heated public debates about traffic.

The *Los Angeles Times* kicked off the frenzy, or at least legitimated it, as early as
1910, stating plainly that "the traffic question has become a problem."[2] From this
early point, the major newspapers of the city simply assumed everyone knew that
Los Angeles was plagued by street congestion. Over the next decade, the chronic
problem evolved from one implicating the streetcars—"You couldn't turn a corner
without dodging a Huntington car," local businessman and historian Remy Nadeau

recalled[3]—into one focusing on the automobile. The machine caught up the entire town in its inherent quickness and its seemingly random movement. Southern California's dramatic population expansion and the swiftness of the automobile seemed like twin tokens of disorienting modernity. At times, in fact, the entire boom of 1920s Los Angeles was attributed to the spread of the machine, as if the new technology dictated the changes in urbanity. In actuality, of course, the car lay at the heart of a complicated series of human debates and decisions, often uncoordinated, that ultimately produced this array of profound social shifts. Yet for many urban observers, both in the 1920s and later, especially in Southern California, everything seemed reducible to the car. The auto became a powerful avatar of modernity, but also of social disruption—license and anarchy even. Thus, the automobile and its infrastructure of roads—its entire built environment and the attendant social phenomena (such as traffic, accidents, and even abstract "speed" itself)—assumed privileged positions in debates over the future of modern urbanity.

In the context of the early 1920s, generalized public discourse about urban traffic flourished in Los Angeles in large measure because it provided a convenient locus for the expression of anxiety about a variety of disturbing social developments in the Jazz Age metropolis. The pervasiveness of this discourse explains, at least in part, why Angelenos tested their conflicting notions of the city's future through debate over everyday traffic regulation. By this time, Los Angeles, for all its famed bucolic charm, left many visitors and locals with a predominant impression of upheaval amid the bewildering swirl of a rapidly growing region. One tourist declared with a note of astonishment, "I thought New York was the original Bedlam, but in 'Los' the traffic is like a sack of a city in its confusion."[4] Furthermore, amid the chaos, speed seemed to give way to mere commotion; the bustle of traffic was represented as a pandemonium not of movement but of stagnation. As Mark Foster observes, "The traffic situation in Los Angeles deteriorated steadily throughout the 1920's,"[5] eventually leading many Angelenos, as well as visitors, to compare the gridlock of downtown Los Angeles to that of larger eastern cities. This was one comparison with these older metropolises that Californian boosters were loathe to make. Soon, Los Angeles began to acquire a reputation as a city awash in automotive congestion, its daily business stifled by street traffic.

The manifest inconvenience and confusion conveyed in this traffic discourse was a constant subject of conversation among Angelenos. Yet the public concern with this traffic never directly translated into calls for reevaluating the politics of urban growth in Southern California (as it would in the 1960s and 1970s). Over the 1920s, Angelenos were consistently obsessed with ameliorating the symptoms of urban expansion through countless programs of road widening and law reform and schemes for more efficient automotive flow, rather than trying to deduce and treat the underlying causes.

Perhaps the most interesting example of this sublimation, and the unusual abil-ity of one Angeleno to redirect the anxiety back into the realm of political expres-sion, took place during the famous 1920 downtown parking ban. A coalition of plan-ners and businessmen had attempted to restore order to the downtown streets by restricting automobile traffic. Much to these elites' surprise, however, Angelenos rose up in protest against the regulation. Those opposed to the ban staged a clever publicity campaign that climaxed in a "parade" of nonmoving cars. Demonstrating their "right" to the road, drivers staged something very much resembling a sit-down strike in the central business district. Traffic gridlock was politicized, at least for a day, and congestion suddenly became theater. It seemed as if traffic was the pri-mary medium through which Angelenos could express themselves and—more pointedly—was the only topic about which they had any desire to do so.

Despite the limitations of this narrow discourse, a larger range of social concerns were expressed in that rebellion against the parking ban. Although often dismissed as a figurehead starlet in later accounts, antiban parade leader Clara Kimball Young claimed to speak for a large constituency in her protest against the parking restric-tions (see figures 10 and 11). In effect, she justified her prominent public role by insisting that her legions of local middle-class female fans were being unfairly barred from visiting downtown movie theaters during business hours.[6]

These women's pleas for continued access to the public realm—expressed, Young claimed, through hundreds of pieces of fan mail: "No less than 300 protests have been received this week by Miss Young from admirers, who assert they have been unable to attend matinees at film houses owing to the parking law"[7]—motivated the concerned movie star to claim a place for herself and other women in public urban spaces. Although she did not explicitly profess to speak for the legions of erstwhile female shoppers also attempting to drive to the downtown commercial district, she used the example of the loyal moviegoers—who should properly be her concern—to highlight women's legitimate presence in the crowded business center. The park-ing ban had been almost universally considered an indirect attack on middle-class women's ability to access the downtown district, and Young managed to construct an ad hoc and informal coalition of Angelenos to defend these women's right to the city.[8] She appears to have been fully conscious of the political dimension of her ac-tions, mobilizing other women to aid her efforts, as the Los Angeles Times noted: "She and a committee of Los Angeles women drivers will attempt to visit every merchant in the city today with petitions."[9] According to the papers, the "idea for the parade originated with the film actress, Clara Kimball Young, who called a meeting of mer-chants, who in turn offered support."[10] The movie star had engineered the entire spectacle and had managed to effectively recast the parking regulation as an assault by bureaucrats and businessmen upon the legitimate public activities of the city's middle-class women.[11] By gaining the support of local merchants—who were by

FIGURE 10. Parking ban victim. *Los Angeles Herald*, 10 April 1920, 1:1.

FIGURE 11. Clara Kimball Young, publicity photo, 1916.

this point suffering from what was, in effect, a (female) consumers' boycott of their businesses—Young effectively broke up the coalition behind the parking ban.

The movie star did not at the time publicize, and subsequent historians have not observed, that Young was a substantial business magnate in her own right. She was a spectacularly successful star, who just happened to have a major motion picture opening the weekend of the parking ban parade. While this movie, *For the Soul of Rafael*, was debuting at the downtown Rialto Theater, *Trilby*, another Clara Kimball Young vehicle, was playing on an extended run at the Palace Theater a block away.

Both films received abnormally prominent advertising space in the week running up to the protest. Young's work as "grand marshal" of the parade, then, was part of a larger publicity campaign highlighting her public role in the culture of the metropolis. Newspaper cartoons, primarily published in the *Times*, confirmed her centrality in the traffic discourses of the day by figuring an allegorical "Miss L.A.," looking suspiciously like her, driving away the antiparking ordinance (see figure 12).

Clearly, Young knew how to get noticed in Los Angeles. By turning a measure intended to control and reduce congestion into the largest jam the downtown district had ever seen, she managed to reverse the dynamic of the debate and mobilize omnipresent public anxiety to serve her own ends. By in effect hijacking traffic discourses and associating the regulation with traffic and not its amelioration, Young claimed a voice in the city's affairs as the champion of frustrated drivers. In lending female gender identity to these automobilists, furthermore, Young connected the right of women to venture into public with the right of all drivers to move as they please.

This, without a doubt, was a rhetorical coup. Nonetheless Young accomplished even more in her manipulation of the parking ban protest; she also provided Angelenos with a brief but vivid model of female public activity through her participation in the parade. In effect, the actress's exemplary public role in the parking ban protest focused public attention on and effectively mirrored the less flamboyant everyday activities of her fans. Although the movie star got all the press, she was only one of thousands of female Angelenos who were now venturing quite forthrightly into parts of the metropolis they had previously felt to be foreign.[12]

In the culture of 1920s Southern California, these women's movements through the city ordinarily could only be expressed through the medium of traffic anxiety. Young's parking ban intervention was exceptional; in most cases, Angelenos could not so effectively channel the general concern over traffic. Young accomplished the feat by cleverly uniting two legitimate topics of shared discourse in the culture of Jazz Age Southern California—movies and traffic—in a single representation. Few other Angelenos would have the opportunity or the cultural leverage to pull off such a stunt. Indeed, beyond this one dramatic intervention and outside the narrow spaces of appearance in which she could have such visibility, even Clara Kimball Young's public activities remained largely hidden from most Angelenos, despite the fact that, in addition to her powerful symbolic role, the actress had a powerful economic role in the city. Young was the first woman to head her own motion picture studio and exerted great power within Hollywood circles. Nevertheless, she was able to highlight female Angelenos' expanded roles in public only through the medium of traffic discourse. If it had not been for the parking ban controversy, the middle-class women for whom she claimed to speak would have remained silent. Young's intervention in the protest parade marks an exceptional point when an exemplary public figure managed, if only for a week, to channel public concern over street congestion toward calculated political ends.

FIGURE 12. Edmund W. Gale's "Miss L.A." gets tough. *Los Angeles Times*, 24 April 1920, 2:4.

For most female Angelenos during this period, making bold claims to legitimacy in the public spaces of the metropolis was extraordinarily difficult, and this difficulty reflected the ubiquity of traffic discourse in the urban culture of Southern California. Generally speaking, female mobility in 1920s Los Angeles was most frequently addressed in pervasive and derogatory attacks on women drivers.[13] Women automobilists were said to be careless, distracted, and at the same time self-righteous. They had no proper respect for the rules of the road or for the rights of (male) drivers. The movements of these flappers, in essence, seemed both uncontrolled and willful. One woman affirmed as much in an apology published in *Touring Topics* (the Southern California Automobile Club magazine): "Recent statistics to the contrary notwithstanding, actual experience would seem to prove that we women are, after all, pretty fool drivers."[14] Addressing the rest of the article to women, she wonders if "women lose their heads more easily than men or is it that they just don't know how to drive so well?" Concluding on a note of resignation that "it is probably a combination of both," the female writer admonishes her readers to avoid provoking male drivers whenever possible and, at the least, to experiment in following the rules of the road: "If a man has the right of way let him take it, and watch his look of astonishment and gratitude when you do."[15]

Testimony to the stakes involved in such admissions of incompetence and exhortations of restraint during the period emerges vividly in an article published on the front page of the local section of the *Los Angeles Times* in February 1920: "Capt. James McDowell, head of the police traffic bureau, declared yesterday that the State should pass a law prohibiting women driving automobiles."[16] Thus, within months of the parking ban controversy, the city police contemplated another traffic ban to tame the chaotic streets. Under a thick border, the paper asked, "Shall the woman driver go? Shall the gloved hand be wrenched forcibly from the steering wheel of the modern juggernaut?" The newspaper offered mild support for the radical (and possibly illegal) reform measure, suggesting that "twenty per cent. of the automobile drivers in this city are women, according to the police, and over 30 per cent. of the accident fatalities are due to them." Beyond this statistical evidence for the draconian regulation, the *Times* offered something even more irrefutable: "When quick thinking and instant action are necessary to prevent an accident, well, women are women, Capt. McDowell points out."

Ultimately, what was expressed in the outrage—both internalized and externalized—over the seeming randomness of women's movements was a serious concern that proper gender boundaries were being subverted. By this time, traffic had become a primary way for Angelenos to comment upon profound structural changes in the city. The almost imperceptible erosion of the city's system of gender segregation, represented by the free circulation of (middle-class) women over the public streets of the metropolis—and the concomitant sense among many Angelenos, male and female, that the city's boundaries, both topographical and social, were becoming poorly defined—could only manifest itself in Jazz Age Los Angeles through a pervasive rhetoric of resentment about women as traffic hazards. Historians are correct in interpreting the contemporary public anxiety about women drivers through this lens, for whether fully conscious or not, the city's ubiquitous traffic contained thousands of these individual, invisible middle-class incursions against the existing structure of gender segregation.

TRAFFIC AND URBAN ORDER

The Monday morning papers are regularly filled with accounts of the horrors occasioned by this speed mania and the undertakers make a special provision for an extra rush of business immediately following Sundays and Holidays. Stringent city and State laws limiting the speed per mile of automobiles are broken with a non-chalance that must be the envy of the Bolsheviks.

"SPEED MURDERERS," *LOS ANGELES TIMES*, 8 MARCH 1920

Of course, it was not merely women's mobility that seemed excessively liberated in Jazz Age Los Angeles, and women's subtle subversions of existing structures of segregation were not the only disturbing assaults on the clear order of the metropolis. Los Angeles was, in the words of one visitor to the city, "simply one big jam; people tore and rushed along as fast as gas and electricity could make their motors go. All the pedestrians had a strained look on their faces, as they too rushed along."[17] Here, as in many contemporary accounts, traffic was closely associated with the chaos of the metropolis at large. Indeed, a great deal of traffic discourse noted a perceived confusion, even thoughtlessness, in the movements of Angelenos. Even streetcar traffic was becoming confusing in this era, as the remarks made by the chief of police reported in the introduction indicate. Significantly, interurban companies were forced to reroute their cars (most notably in 1920, but less drastically several times after that) in an attempt to avoid conflict with the throng of automobiles on downtown streets. This reorganization of the urban transportation system disoriented thousands of Angelenos and produced a great deal of frustration and anger (see figure 13). Thanks to the automobiles, even the dependable, fixed streetcar followed unpredictable patterns, fundamentally altering the structure of relative proximities within the metropolis. Thus, although the city's map remained fairly stable, amid all this traffic confusion, residents' actual experience of the city was becoming chaotic and disturbing.[18]

For most Angelenos, of course, the disorientation attending the epochal streetcar reroutings seemed to be an everyday byproduct of private car movements. Automobile traffic, unlike traditional fixed infrastructures such as streetcars, was not easy to make sense of. Although most automobile traffic in concentric Los Angeles

FIGURE 13. The perdition of urban illegibility: Edmund W. Gale's "More Rerouting," *Los Angeles Times*, 11 May 1920, 2:1.

followed predictable radial commuting patterns, which generally reinforced the legible structure of the metropolis as a whole, a considerable amount of the city's traffic seemed random and capricious. Outside observers of this excess of mobility found it extremely disturbing. In a sense, the utter unassimilabilty of these individual movements into the clearly recognizable functional structure of the metropolis made them stand out. Cars seemed to be everywhere, zipping about without rhyme or reason—and this disordered ubiquity was disquieting. The manifold structural transformations in the culture and social order of Jazz Age Los Angeles were too subtle, too subterranean, to be understood as such by most observers at the time. For the most part, the untraceable movements of other Angelenos were inexplicable. It was clear, though, that these perceptible signs of disorder were subversive and dangerous. This perception of the menace inherent in social change may explain why Angelenos became obsessed in the 1920s with traffic violence. In the public culture of the city, apprehension about urban transformation was focused and channeled into traffic anxiety, and that distress expressed itself as a veritable obsession with automobile accidents. By the middle of the 1920s, discourse about this "Saturnalia of death" (as the *Times* frequently termed it) became one of the most common cultural tropes in the city.[19]

All the metropolis's major newspapers made a daily ritual out of reporting collisions. They were singular, dramatic events, they were exceedingly common, and they were deemed inherently newsworthy. For all the more subtle expressions embedded in the traffic mania, the newspapers chiefly fixated on the spectacle of these sensational smash-ups. Because of these accidents, the major newspapers argued, the roads of Los Angeles were becoming deathtraps, making the city's "streets a nightmare for thousands of pedestrians, a graveyard for other drivers and riders."[20] Appearing frequently on the front pages of the city's local news sections, articles about individual collisions were shockingly graphic in their detailed descriptions of the injuries sustained by citizens. One representative piece described the death of "William James Heanski, 7, of Downey," who "suffered a severed artery when he was thrown from his father's lap through the windshield of an automobile in which they were riding when the machine skidded at College and Seventh Streets in Downey. . . . He bled to death before the Downey Hospital was reached. The body was taken to the Thomas L. Miller Undertaking Company in Downey."[21] The power of this tragic and gruesome vignette, one of six deaths fully described in the article, accrues both from the repetition and the mode of description. Victims are always identified in these accounts, their ages and places of residence cited. Such concrete humanizing details—meticulously reported in a factual, almost clinical tone, along with the precise sequence of events of the accident—accentuates both the horror and the exemplary cultural weight of this cause of death. Indeed, traffic mortality received coverage in local papers where ordinary assaults and deaths, with the exception of heinous crimes committed against the well-off or well-known, did not. Combined with these personalized accounts were more abstract statistics conveying the larger cost of traffic to the city. Marked off in heavy leading, much like tabulations of casualties in a major war, a grim count of the local "death toll" from crashes appeared daily. These prominently demarcated boxes, like the detailed and graphic articles accompanying them, testified to the cultural commotion that attended the discussion of traffic accidents.[22]

The human effects of these collisions were certainly tragic and shocking, but perhaps the intensity of the expression reflects the cultural weight of larger concerns embedded in the discourse more than the impact of the accidents. Often it seems as if these collisions are vehicles for the transmission of commentary about the city. Each day's extensive crash report, often described in grisly detail on the front page, under the morbid black death-toll box, had a larger theme. Sometimes it involved threats to the community (how the crowded streetcar was cut off or collided into by the hot-rodding, individualist motorist); at other times the article focused on the hazards of modernization (how the plodding, stately trolley—and often its elderly operator—could not keep pace with darting automobiles in the bustling modern metropolis, and the fatal results of this clash between preterite and modern). In other cases, the accident report exposed otherwise invisible anxieties brought about by Jazz Age social changes, reflecting the need for commuters to travel ever farther to reach work from their homes in the outskirts, the consequent breakdown in Angelenos' connection with their neighborhoods, or even a simple case of getting lost in the tangle of streets. Nevertheless, these broad concerns were only discussed tangentially in print, through the lens of these dramatic accidents.

Here is one example of how cultural transformations we have already discussed played out in newspaper coverage. Ernest C. Johnson complained in the *Times* in 1926 about an accident in which he was tangentially involved. A passenger on a streetcar hit by an errant automobile, Johnson expressed his outrage over the loss of "500 minutes of valuable time . . . because that silly willy woman, whose time was not worth ten cents a day, wanted to impress the world that she owned an auto and as much of the street as she wished to use."[23] The male commuter's venom is clearly directed not only at the delay caused by the accident but at the woman who dared to make use of the public streets during rush hour. Of course, this woman might well have been on her way downtown to do her own work, on her own valuable time. But, as was generally the case in the public concern about women drivers, the labor of the female autoist—either the domestic work of shopping or paid labor— is filtered out of the discourse, leaving only the male commuter's anxiety about the incursions into what he thought was properly his own urban space. This man's anxiety about the subtle changes in gender boundaries taking place around him was given legitimacy of expression because, and only because, he was involved in an accident. His social commentary, as a consequence, was funneled into and filtered through an existing discourse about women drivers. The specific concerns the man may have had, about gender disorder or the relative class positions of himself (as working man) and the woman (as, presumably, upper-class dilettante), are all reduced to a virulent critique of this individual driver.

These regular pieces in the papers allowed some recognition, at least in cartoonish simplicity and personal vignette, of the social costs and conflicts involved in urban modernity. In each case, though, the central action dominated the discourse; ultimately, it was the "carnage" that was the primary concern. Thus, although the press certainly helped focus public interest on the traffic "crisis," it cast the discourse strictly in terms of safety. The appropriate solutions or suggested actions were movements against traffic hazards alone, not agitation for public reform or commentary about the submerged structural urban problems hinted at in the graphic narratives. Traffic thus became the filter through which a range of contemporary social transformations could be publicly expressed, but this filtering limited possible responses to the discussion of traffic safety measures.

More generally, concern about violence against social order was translated through traffic discourse into concern about violence on a personal level. Responsibility for traffic safety was ultimately seen to lie with the individual. It was not long before these accidents began to be posed in terms of the morality tale. The traffic problem appeared not as structure but as culture—or as personal character. The depictions of the speeders became increasingly derisive, characterizing them, as in one article representative of the rhetoric, as "vicious fiends, who regard it as smart and clever to terrorize and risk maiming fellow human beings, blight[ing] their whole lives, if not blotting them out altogether, for the sake of what? A few yards of road, a little getting ahead, a few seconds of time. . . . These people must be drunk with the sense of a little power, a small possession; their minds must be peculiarly warped by the slight elevation to wheels. One can only suppose a previous condition of crawling on their bellies, since the change is obviously so unbalancing."[24] This sort of personalized indictment of the careless driver, and of the society that could produce such creatures, recurred frequently in local popular culture. As a prominent local Presbyterian pastor, Dr. Gusav A. Briegieb, put it in a sermon printed in the Times in 1920, "Human life is made in Los Angeles to be a thing despised and rejected. . . . There is the mania in our high tension life for speed."[25] Condemning "speed demons and reckless drivers who guide steel-ribbed juggernauts through the city streets without regard for human life," the newspaper concurred in the clergyman's indictment of Angelenos' fallible "human selfishness." Like Mr. Johnson's concern about the woman driver, this traffic discourse posed symptoms of a perceived breakdown in the stable communal order as marks of individual failure, of a moral looseness or laxity.[26]

This anxiety in turn produced the growing popular impression that the city was awash with reckless drivers, each pursuing his or (pointedly) her own private agenda, blind to the world around (see figure 14). As a result, "speed murderers" were "keeping a community in a state of terror," for "when they are abroad in their death cars there are only the quick and the dead in the streets."[27] Twisting its usual booster rhetoric, the Times posed this problem in the language of Southern Californian exceptionalism, proclaiming that "Los Angeles harbors more vicious road hogs than

The Claim-Jumper.

FIGURE 14. City streets as deathtraps, by Edmund W. Gale. *Los Angeles Times,* 9 March 1920, 2:4.

any other city in the country. We in this town have the ghastly distinction of maiming and killing more people in a week through the greed and recklessness of our motorists than most cities record in six months."[28] Public stigmatization alone was proving insufficient, local newspapers argued, to halt the "lust for slaughter": "Denouncing the offenders through the press is not sufficient; for a vulgar brute who holds murder of less consequence than losing some joy-ride wager takes a pride in the notoriety that his reckless driving gives."[29] Instead, the *Times* suggested, "this shameful and brutal condition . . . must be tackled with the same kind of public wrath and reprisal that was meted out to the garroters and bomb throwers and other destroyers of human life."[30]

In the face of this moral panic, a number of Angelenos reacted by forming ad hoc "vigilance committees" to patrol the streets for traffic scofflaws and take direct action against the "reckless murderers."[31] The *Los Angeles Herald* boldly proclaimed that "since 8 o'clock this morning no street has been safe for traffic rule violators" now that teams of "respectable citizens" were on the lookout for lawless drivers.[32] Although the *Times* argued that "public indignation is reaching a point where a vigilance committee would not be condemned by many for taking the law in its own hands and meting out summary punishment to the offenders," the civilians were in fact only empowered to issue warning citations to those offenders they spotted.[33]

More extreme responses to the "murderous speed maniacs" seemed justified, though, given the social costs of traffic mayhem: "We repeat that there are more murders committed every week by automobile maniacs than all other classes of criminals."[34] Indeed, the paper warned, "if a murderous auto driver were to be shot down at the wheel by an indignant pedestrian it must be apparent that it would not be easy to pick a jury that would vote for conviction." This sort of frontier justice received favorable coverage from the *Examiner,* the *Times,* and the *Herald,* and was also strongly endorsed by the increasingly important Automobile Club of Southern California. In fact, the Auto Club rode this wave of fear about reckless driving to establish itself as the primary legitimate organization representing the silent majority of safe and careful drivers on the streets of the Southland. If, as traffic discourse proclaimed, the city streets were becoming killing grounds, "lanes of death,"[35] the Automobile Club would assume the mantle of a moral reform organization dedicated to purifying the city streets and protecting the innocent from the ravages of a dangerous minority of irresponsible motorists.

SCREENING THE CITY THROUGH
THE WINDSHIELD OF THE AUTOMOBILE

What was perhaps most disturbing to the traffic moralists was the fact that so many Angelenos, despite their concern about the death toll, seemed to take a perverse pleasure in the carnage. The obverse of anxiety appeared to be fascination; the local culture industry was awash with images of automotive mayhem. In the 1920s, automobile chases were the subject of many films, especially the increasing number produced in Southern California. In fact, it seemed that Hollywood was taking over the film business purely on the strength of the new style of movies produced there—movies that focused on action, use of diverse outdoor locations, and a strong sense of rapid mobility. By the late 1910s and early 1920s, these films typified the great majority of all cinematic representation. Thanks to this generic dominance, the connection became so strong that many contemporary social observers, at least in Southern California, began to lump the automobile and the cinema together as twin products of a modern world speeding out of control. Commentators moved seamlessly from car to movie in their discussions of urban modernity, often without any conscious transition. The two shared a range of correlated associations in the popular imagination—so much so that each became almost a metaphor for the other.

This interchangeability recurs particularly often in the common discourse linking automobiles, movies, and moral looseness. Cars supposedly allowed the young, particularly, the freedom to go unchaperoned to (unsavory) films, or conversely, the movies encouraged teenagers to drive dangerously. The causality was often conflated, but the negative associations were consistent: one thing led to another. Often, though, all attempt at making a logical narrative connection was abandoned and the linkage merely assumed, as in the following statement from a Los Angeles social worker: "Some kids are given autos and turned loose with them long before they ought, and consequently get into all kinds of mischief; and then in the movies they see the wrong type of life played up, and the desire comes to them to emulate this. They see the crook get away with his dirty deals, and the idea comes to them to try the same."[36] Juvenile delinquency, in such discourse, could be taught and learned. The city, through automotive chaos both experienced and represented, was an incubator of sin and depravity. In the moral panic over traffic in Los Angeles, the public spaces of the city's streets were taken as intrinsically dangerous and unwholesome. The fact that these streets became the setting for countless movies merely reinforced this association.

Moreover, in Los Angeles, the connection was more than mere connotation. Southern California and its cinematic products were often indistinguishable. The industrial product, in this sense, *was* Southern California, or at least the filmed representation of it. The commercial value of the circulation of local images certainly did not escape the attention of Los Angeles's promoters, as many local historians have observed. Cinema advertised the surrounding locale in a way that was attractive to the important real estate business. Leonard and Dale Pitt note that film and real estate essentially shared the same means—circulating representations of the local landscape: "Because movies in the silent era usually were filmed on location, audiences soaked up the city's climate, clean streets, landscaped homes, and sunny beaches, building an early image of a fun-loving, laid-back town."[37] Car chases through the orange groves (i.e., future subdivisions) of Southern California served as a sort of travelogue and real estate tour for moviegoers (i.e., potential purchasers). Here, the pastoral and sunlit background to the main action—so often shown through the windows of speeding camera-laden vehicles—might be the real show. Consequently, it soon became apparent that "the movies had won the fighting alliance of the boosters."[38]

In Los Angeles of the '20s, this influence bought the movie makers remarkable latitude in their production methods. As W. W. Robinson recalls, "Hollywood citizens, in the early days of picture-making, were stopped on the streets to join in mob scenes. Hollywood banks were used for fictional holdups. Thoroughfares were roped off to stage realistic automobile accidents."[39] The cinema became a privileged local industry primarily because it showcased the city in its backgrounds, not only advertising the climate and landscape but implicitly associating the region with the modern technology essential to film production. Further, as Ashleigh Brilliant explains, this technological obsession sprang not only from the filmic process but also from the source of the movies' action. "The automobile became firmly established during the 1920's as one of the standard comic props of the Hollywood film comedy. Audiences never seemed to tire of seeing cars colliding, overturning, falling apart, tumbling over precipices, being squashed by trains, flattened by steam rollers, or, as in one famous sequence of Laurel and Hardy's *Two Tars*, simply pulled to pieces by angry men."[40] Popular productions such as these reflected native public concern with automobility. Indeed, if Southern California had become the primary focus of the filmmakers' lenses, it was wholly within the context of the prevailing local preoccupation with automotive transport.

The twin modern technologies of automobile and cinema subtly framed how most Angelenos perceived their cityscape. Just as early Hollywood cinema developed as an appropriate mirror of this potential garden city—making use of the abundant sunlight, the extensive street system, and the diverse and scattered readymade locations made easily accessible by the automobile—the city began to evolve in response to these cinematic images of itself. Gradually, through the spread of distinctive local programmatic architecture, or what Reyner Banham termed the "Hollywood Baroque," the streets of the city developed what Kevin Starr called the "signature features of the Los Angeles/Hollywood cityscape," namely the predominance of "fantasy" in the built environment.[41] More and more urban elements were conceived as visual markers, their design determined by how they appeared from a moving automobile. From billboards to cul-de-sacs, the metropolis developed according to an aesthetic—and a visual logic—appropriate to the smooth movement of both the automobile and the moving picture camera. So often were these two de-

FIGURE 15. The city is the set for automotive play—or mayhem. Keystone Comedies
publicity still, 1916.

vices linked that many motion pictures of the era take the form, at least in segments,
of ordinary tours or travelogues through the urban topography of Southern California. Long, uninterrupted sequences of represented driving through the streets
of the region punctuated Hollywood films, setting mobile action or differentiating
discrete static locations. This way of viewing early twentieth-century Los Angeles
became synonymous with automobility. In the subtle representational language of
early cinema, the traffic discourses of Los Angeles once more pervaded local—and
now more distant—consciousness.

As the streets of Southern California became "locations" for the region's representational machinery, Angelenos' obsessions were paraded out for public amusement. It is therefore no surprise that the traffic discourse which dominated so much
of the popular consciousness in Greater Los Angeles produced the sorts of filmic
representation for which Mack Sennett's Keystone Cops became famous (see figure 15). Remy Nadeau recounts, "At one of the Vanderbilt Cup automobile races in
Santa Monica the grandstanders were horrified to see a wild car go dashing by drag-
ging a body behind. The attending policemen leaped forward to halt the runaway,
only to be sent flying in all directions. A delighted movie crew, which had set the
whole episode in motion with the runaway car, packed up its equipment and escaped with some magnificent footage."[42] Here the real California police uninten-
tionally performed the ludic role of the mock patrolmen. "God bless the police!"
Sennett later wrote, "they were the first Keystone Cops."[43]

Beyond serving as inspiration and unknowing actors, the LAPD also participated
in the very mockery of public safety against which civilian vigilantes were so vo-

ciferously crusading: "As for the Los Angeles police, they regularly looked the other way when movie police wagons or fire trucks careened through town. Many times whole sections of streets were roped off from public access and wetted down to help movie autos skid crazily past the camera."[44] The roads of the region were carefully prepared for the approving eyes of local and national audiences and, under police supervision, for the playful reenactment of the same sorts of automotive mishaps that were the subject of so much local concern and anxiety.

Furthermore, Los Angeles, under the moniker of Hollywood, was becoming a tourist Mecca—and a destination point for automobile-bound migrants—at least partly because of the advertising images recorded on its streets. These pictures of automotive disaster were ironically drawing more and more cars into the region. And this influx was in turn generating more traffic, more congestion, and ultimately, more collisions—smash-ups that were sometimes themselves caught on camera for eventual circulation to appreciative audiences around the country.

This close association between cinema and automobility in Southern California produced a frenzy of chaotic visuality. Once more, popular images of traffic expressed covert social shifts. The danger and randomness of the action in the frenetic car chases of the silent era transmitted a bit of the confusion locals must have felt in observing their rapidly growing and changing urban landscapes. The anonymous new suburban tracts continually popping up, disappearing, and then reappearing in slightly different form in the background of the shots represented an urban randomness and disorder fully the equal of the automotive capers featured in the foreground. This worked reciprocally, reflecting the filmic elision of car and city. Sensational stunts were merely extrapolations of everyday traffic bedlam, and disruptions in the fabric of the metropolis played themselves out in the seemingly random and destructive movements of Angelenos. Cityscapes backgrounding jump cuts edited together for dramatic, instead of geographical, sequence added to the epistemic chaos. The rapidly expanding city, spiraling farther and farther from its compact downtown core, was becoming increasingly difficult to make sense of as a whole. This illegibility manifested itself ludically in a visual language of uncontrolled movement. Cinema thus reflected what Angelenos were seeing every day but not fully recognizing. It made light of chaos and helped translate anxieties over the social, topographical, and demographic change that urbanites saw all around them into an obsession with sheer movement as a force in itself. This representation was entertainment for many Americans of the Jazz Age; it was that and more for those living through and inspiring these frenetic street scenes. Ultimately, the appearance of the city was itself a motion picture, filled with violence and action but without any discernable plot.

In light of the popular traffic in images of automotive mayhem, it might be fair to ask if the Southern California public was following the newspapers' accident reporting so closely throughout the decade as a result of moral outrage at the may-

hem or from a voyeuristic fixation on the details of the crashes—a chance to vicariously and imaginatively reconstruct the action from the morbid (and often surprisingly detailed) descriptions. This may not be a fair question or opposition, however. Clearly, concern with traffic played itself out in Los Angeles in a variety of
interrelated and even contradictory ways. Indeed, it may be that the ubiquitous public discourse in Los Angeles about traffic safety primed local viewers and movie pro-
ducers for an unnatural interest in automotive stunts. In this sense, a widely shared
obsession with traffic and collisions effectively channeled even the most escapist
entertainment into representation of urban transportation chaos. From the fervent
safety crusades of the local press and the Automobile Club to the viewing public's
fascination with cinematic car chases, much of the culture of Southern California
during the '20s seemed to be a reflection on automobility. The differing interpre-
tations, judgments, and even pleasures associated with the car craze mirrored subterranean local divisions over urban culture, presenting conflicts over the form and
structure of this modern metropolis as consequential details of vehicular transportation. In Southern California, the problem of street traffic once more became
a rhetorical ground where conflicting visions of urbanity and social order vied for
position.

   In retrospect, it seems clear that traffic discourse was in some measure a discourse about urban legibility and urban visibility. It reflected a host of subtle but
growing disruptions in the booming metropolis, where faceless new subdivisions
continually transformed the topography without giving it any definite and distinguishing character. Markers of familiar cityscapes constantly changed or were rendered unrecognizable. Traffic degraded stable perceptions of distance and proximity,
making trips that should logically have been short into interminable scenes of frustration. Conversely, long stretches of open road allowed breakneck movement across
the entire city, associating points in the urban fabric that might seem entirely disconnected on a map. The ability to parse these changing landscapes into comprehensive order was constantly threatened by the very pace of change and the shifting relationships between places—relationships that were themselves modified by
traffic and its effects.[45]

   With this topographical assault upon urban legibility came a corresponding demographic, or social, attack. Los Angeles was being deluged with migrants hailing
from the far reaches of the nation (see figure 16). As this cartoon reveals, Angelenos were struck by their city's sudden cosmopolitanism but also disturbed by its
apparent rootlessness. Anxieties about urban growth, like so much else, were
reflected in traffic discourse, and representations of delinquent automobilists never
failed to mention whether they were newcomers to town. The influx of these yokels
betokened an apparent decline in urban knowledge, in local street smarts. With this
unfamiliarity came a profound ignorance, not just of the specific topography—to
a degree excusable, given the difficulty even seasoned hands were having with its

*"If you stand at the corner of Seventh and Broadway long enough, so they say
sooner or later you'll see a car from your own home town"*

FIGURE 16. The chaos of migration. From Hy Sibley, "Our Cosmopolitan Motor Parade,"
Touring Topics 17, no. 12 (1925): 22. Courtesy of the kind permission of the Automobile
Club of Southern California Archives.

rapid changes—but of fundamental norms of conduct, carriage, and order. This may
explain the turn toward vigilantism. It represented, perhaps, a vain attempt to enforce small-town behavioral restrictions and mores in an increasingly worldly city.
As a consequence of immigration, Los Angeles in the 1920s was a circus of accents,
attitudes, and customs. From the point of view of the recent arrival, this city could
be alienating indeed. Linguistic confusion—not just from accents but from new
landscapes marked by often incomprehensible (and seemingly unpronounceable)
place names—highlighted the feeling of bewilderment. An incomprehensible grid
of streets surrounded an urban core that seemed awash in honking automobiles.
As many cultural representations in the traffic discourse put it, Los Angeles was a
"Babel" of visual confusion, rapid changes, and reckless drivers (see figure 17). The
nascent topographical disorientation presaged the breakdown of normal communal bonds—the metaphorical "common language" of the city—and perhaps the over-
determination of the traffic discourse.

The Modern Tower of Babel

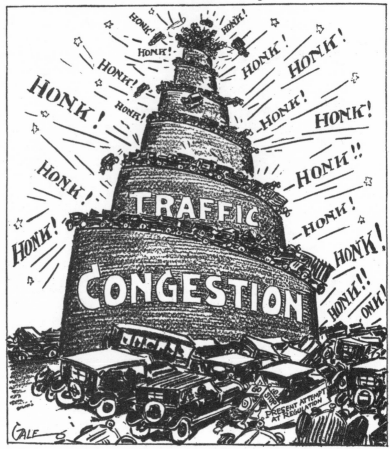

FIGURE 17. Traffic as cacophony. *Los Angeles Times,* 13 December 1923.

CONTROLLING THE METROPOLIS

We are solving our own traffic problem by killing it at its source.

GORDON WHITNALL, "TRAFFIC," *LOS ANGELES TIMES,* 1 JULY 1928

Local planners responded to this concern about traffic conditions with calm assurance that the solution could only come through radical structural change to the metropolis. Southern California's traffic situation was doomed to worsen and its public discourse to become more frenzied, so long as Angelenos continued to depend upon a single, centralized downtown district for so many of their economic and cultural needs. If Los Angeles seemed to be fragmenting under the traffic pressure, the only way to restore metropolitan coherence was to reduce the pressure. The modernization of the metropolitan region—recasting it as a landscape of semi-autonomous garden communities—would free Angelenos from their need to travel across the entire region every day and thus would kill the traffic problem, as Gordon Whitnall put it, "at its source."

As with other urban ailments, the limited direct powers of the planners restricted their response to a program of gradual restructuring through advance planning. Critical to this task was the dependable practice of subdivision control. By guiding the progress of individual real estate developments through such ordinary regulations as those pertaining to permit approval, building codes, street alignment, and the like, the City Planning Commission hoped to encourage the creation of truly autonomous regional subcenters and impede the development of single-use tracts (such as purely residential bedroom subdivisions or large, blighting industrial zones). Localized single-family housing projects and small satellite commercial districts were encouraged in the regulatory process, while proposals for full-scale commuter developments or large contiguous industrial sectors were blocked or delayed. As the city's *Official Subdividers Guide* observed, "A subdivision is not merely a means for marketing land, it is far more, a process in community building."[46] This sort of control was difficult, however. It forced upon planners the burdens of excessive micromanagement, when they would rather be attending to larger regional issues, and it frequently gave rise to irritating minor conflicts with rebellious subdividers. More importantly, basic subdivision control was inherently fragmenting and piecemeal. It was extremely difficult to shape entire cohesive and intradependent communities by such regulatory engineering. The location and general disposition of a particular site was entirely up to land speculators and subdividers; for the most part, planners had no sure way to shape the development of a given parcel of land. The best planners could do to spur the development of desired garden cities was to appropriately align city infrastructure projects—roads, sewers, and other utilities—within already desirable districts.

A serious problem with subdivision controls was that they were so often stymied by real estate speculators, most notably in attempts to establish business developments along public thoroughfares and in the midst of residential districts. These were lucrative spots for commercial and industrial enterprises, but they frequently ended up sabotaging any attempt to construct balanced and self-contained communities. Subdivision control as practiced by the City Planning Commission ultimately was powerless to effectively ban such inappropriate business placement.

Perhaps the worst difficulty with subdivision control, though, was that it was intolerably time-consuming. Regulation was necessarily a gradualist approach in an era of extremely rapid urban expansion. Planners simply could not keep up with the flood of new development. As planning historian Mel Scott recounts with awe, "In 1923, subdividers filed 1,434 maps of new tracts with the county recorder—half again as many as in 1922 and more than twice as many as in 1921."[47] Deluged each month with permit applications and detailed plans for hundreds of diverse projects, the city and regional planning commissions were overwhelmed throughout the decade. "In this era of runaway growth," Scott concludes, the City Planning Commission and its fellow agencies "could barely keep pace with day-to-day demands."[48]

Clearly, what the planners needed was a way to make these burgeoning new subdivisions conform to some larger premeditated blueprint for entire urban districts. Instead of painstakingly dealing with each new subdivision, planning professionals could then be sure that any given area within the metropolis would from the start only draw applications for broadly appropriate sorts of development. In a sense, the solution was there all along, in the form of a series of laws enacted in California during the 1870s to control Chinese American businesses by relegating them to specifically demarcated urban areas or zones. In the intervening years, this sort of zoning legislation had been expanded to regulate more and different types of urban "nuisance." In the 1910s, Los Angeles began instituting new ordinances that applied more positive zoning. The purpose was no longer narrowly to bar specific noxious land uses but to actively promote a range of desired ones. This was quite a change; indeed, these new zoning laws "are now accepted by many urban historians as the beginning of modern zoning in the United States, preceding the better known New York statute by eight years."[49]

Planners succeeded in fully taking control over these zoning ordinances only in the mid-1920s, however, when the City Planning Commission was restructured. Instead of an unwieldy fifty-one-member organization dominated by representatives from a variety of business and civic organizations, the reorganized commission was strictly controlled by professional planners. Among its other duties was the task of implementing a brand-new comprehensive zoning law. This new regulation went far beyond previous legislation, for it was the first in the nation to formally recognize as an enforceable category the residential single-family dwelling, as distinguished not only from commerce and industry but from the residential multifamily dwelling. This new "A" designation sought to turn a booster selling point of the region—its abundance of pleasant bungalows—into law. Despite challenges, the new zoning designation was subsequently upheld by the state courts.[50]

WILSHIRE BOULEVARD:
ZONING FOR URBAN LEGIBILITY

Within months of receiving this enhanced zoning authority, the reformed City Planning Commission was faced with an opportunity to put it to use on an area where ordinary subdivision controls had proved particularly ineffective. This sector, which

extended through the west side of the city along Wilshire Boulevard, was emerging as a primary trouble spot for Los Angeles's garden city planners, as it would remain, in various forms, throughout the decade. Nevertheless, even in the mid-1920s,
the Wilshire corridor looked pretty peaceful. In fact, until the beginning of the
decade, this area was almost entirely undeveloped, as Ralph Hancock observes in
Fabulous Boulevard:

> The only business development of Wilshire Boulevard from Westlake park to Vermont
> Avenue was a single structure at the southeast corner of Vermont and the Boulevard
> containing four storerooms. Then came a long jump to Wilshire and Western Avenue
> where the only business structure was a large market at the northeast corner. From West-
> ern Avenue to La Brea Avenue a few residences and mostly vacant lots made up the
> artery. At La Brea a minor structure containing two small storerooms served the busi-
> ness needs of the district. The next development was a two-store building at the south-
> east corner of Cochran and Wilshire and then a fruit market at Curson and Wilshire.[51]

From the beginning of the decade, planners had fit this corridor—destined, they
were sure, to be a backbone of desirable decentralized western development in the
city—neatly into their own visions of urban modernization. Wilshire was to be a
major thoroughfare devoid of rail transport, thus preventing the road from becoming a mere conduit to the congested downtown district for west side commuters.
Instead, the new boulevard would both connect and insulate from commuting pres-
sures a handful of promising western communities, such as Beverly Hills and West-
wood, which were coming into their own in the western district of the basin.

By the mid-1920s, though, everything had begun to go wrong. Wilshire Boulevard almost immediately began to succumb to the same hazards of local development that plagued so many other parts of the city. Subdividers along the important
thoroughfare were sabotaging all efforts at order by chaotically scattering commercial establishments among the street's existing residences. The brand new boulevard,
not yet even completed, was falling victim to a blight—"ribbon development"—that
had up to that time been an affliction of distant outlying areas. Small retail shops
and gas stations were rapidly springing up all along Wilshire in an attempt to lure
passing commuters. This sort of business development in turn stimulated even more
automobile traffic, which made the thoroughfare an even more desirable location
for small businesses.

It was at this point that the newly reformed City Planning Commission turned
its full attention to Wilshire: this was the opportunity city planners had been looking for to exercise the new zoning authority of the 1925 legislation. Appropriately
enough, experts used the growing traffic along the thoroughfare as a pretext for action. With their new authority, planners promised to control the unseemly commercial growth that was snarling traffic. Thus the Wilshire corridor emerged as the
great test bed for zoning in 1920s Southern California. Planners intended from the

start to do with zoning what they could not with ordinary subdivision controls. Most important, they would now make use of their powerful new specification for single-family residential development to ensure that the widened thoroughfare would be free of offending ribbon development. They did this with enthusiasm, as Richard Longstreth observes: "In contrast to almost every other thoroughfare in the city, Wilshire Boulevard was zoned for residential use only."[52] Zoning could be used to encourage the evolution of the semiautonomous districts planners envisioned. As M. Christine Boyer recounts, "Zoning . . . embodied and exemplified the idea of orderliness in city development; it encouraged the erection of the right building, in the right form, in the right place."[53] With such regulation, the entire west side of the city—already the focus of much real estate speculation—would be made to grow rationally, each localized district arrayed around its own essential facilities. Commuter traffic, with its attendant social effects, could be virtually eliminated, as employment and commerce, on a reasonable and localized scale, would now be provided within a short distance of one's detached home.

    As a planning measure that carried the force of law—that could compel a particular sort of land use—zoning was ambitious. Local planner George Damon clearly expressed his and his colleagues' hopes for the new regulation to their peers at a national planning conference: "As the satellite sub-centers of population become 'city wise,' we can retain the rights of at least half of our citizens to own a little land of their own, only by zoning our residence districts against the intrusion of the factory and the apartment and by opening up additional subdivisions with suitable streets, parkways, boulevards, trading centers and recreational facilities."[54] Damon's discourse, for all its confidence and enthusiasm, reveals the planner's exasperation. By the mid-1920s, Los Angeles was proving more difficult to manage than could have been expected. Confused and conflicting private development schemes constantly threatened the dreams and visions of the professional planner. Zoning perfectly fit this urban context. As much as it promised to work positively, as a means to encourage new garden city development, this was also a technology of prohibition. As Damon makes clear, planners ultimately focused on zoning as a bulwark against improper development. As Sam Bass Warner explains in his classic history of American urbanism, *The Urban Wilderness*, in addition to necessary protestations of its legitimacy under the law, "the typical zoning law" consisted of only two elements: "First, there was a map of the city on which all private land was assigned to a particular area or zone. Second, the restrictions applying to each of these zones were itemized."[55] Although these laws were thought of as tools to promote healthy, desired urban development, at their core, identification and interdiction were the essential functions of all zoning ordinances.

    For Los Angeles's planners, zoning represented an attempt to stabilize the city— to protect the integrity of existing districts from the ravages of improper development, as well as from its principal symptom: traffic congestion. As such, it was also an attempt to impose order, both economic and perceptual, in the city. Instead of merely identifying urban features or encouraging a particular pattern of future development in the city as a whole, this technique could dictate the actual disposition of specific plots of land. "Zoning, the division of the American city into a structure of cells, hierarchically controlled and rearranged,"[56] was essentially an inversion of the professional planning practice of classifying urban typologies, which was central to the planners' larger project of comprehending the city. Now, instead of deriving functional urban use categories from a program of detailed urban observation, an insufficiently differentiated city could have an orderly scheme of land use directly imposed upon it. Whereas the survey was inherently diagnostic, the zoning ordinance was necessarily prescriptive. Zoning did not merely reflect existing patterns of land use, it promoted new, ideal topographies. As such, it represented planners' almost total control over the precise composition of the landscape.

As both a descriptive and a proscriptive practice, zoning offered an antidote to urban illegibility. It was a discipline of categorization (into urban "zones," evidently enough); it was a tool designed specifically to impose clear demarcations of use upon discrete quanta of urban land. Zoning was premised upon the "segregation" of land uses. Like social classes and races in the early twentieth-century metropolis, urban land had to be properly subordinated and separated. As Warner observes, "Everywhere zoning laws interacted with real-estate prices to reinforce segregation by income, national origin, and race within cities."[57] Property, like society, had to be subsumed into a larger structure—a hierarchical, logical, and orderly arrangement of respective elements. Through rigorous zoning, local planners primarily sought to banish the "promiscuous" mixture (again their term) of land uses that had made Wilshire so frustrating and confusing. Only through a detailed and meticulous process of delineation by categorization could urban miscegenation be curbed and properly legible segregation be maintained in the city.

Yet, as a tool for restoring urban legibility, zoning was not so much a conceptual or observational technology as a preemptory, even dictatorial one. Zoning promised to force the city's development to conform to rational schemas of the planners' own derivation. Indeed, zoning fundamentally represented a technology of urban clarification and stabilization; it was a tool to contain the metastasis of inappropriate and chaotic land use and to fix development into rational patterns. The regulatory technology did not merely reveal an epistemic order, it mandated it. In essence, then, zoning was a drastic effort to give the planners police powers to discipline and clarify urban space. It promised to make the existing topography conform to the idealized zoning map. The ideational tool would henceforth dictate to the built environment, imposing upon the unruly city the simple diagrammatic clarity planners had come to expect of the survey map. Zoning essentially gave planners, in the name of proper urban organization and scientific rationality, vast powers over the disposition and use of most urban land. Of course, as far as private property was concerned, zoning was tantamount to martial law. Planners would now be able to dictate density, ultimate use (residential, commercial, or industrial), and social class for each zoned lot. For city officials, zoning was something of a panacea, and it was an end in itself—the promise of total, specific control over the urban form.

For Southern California planners, zoning held out the promise of restoring urban legibility, but it also put professional planners on the defensive. The City Planning Commission would find itself a defender of the (virtual) status quo; from now on, planners would have to fight constantly in the courts, with the city council, and even before the voters to uphold specific zoning decisions—and to protect their cherished maps. Planners intended to use zoning less to radically transform the city than to restore tranquillity to its chaotic streets. It was a drastic response to a structural traffic problem that seemed only to get worse, and at least in the way it applied to the Wilshire corridor, zoning had as much to do in practice with preserving an envisioned shape of the metropolis as with transforming it in some radical way.

Clearly, local planners were already finding that their dreams of garden communities in Southern California would not be realized without opposition. There was more than one vision of urban modernization at play in Los Angeles in the early 1920s, and in the coming debate, planners would soon discover that they were bucking the weight of conventional wisdom and common sense about the proper course of urban growth.

THE POLITICS OF PLANNING
IN TRAFFIC-OBSESSED LOS ANGELES

Of this fluxing, seething maze of private automobiles is the throttling python of traffic made.

E. E. EAST, AUTO CLUB CHIEF TRAFFIC ENGINEER, "THE TRAFFIC SQUEEZE" (21)

Perhaps the strength and vividness of the cultural discourse on traffic reflect the extent to which popular consciousness in Southern California was beginning by the early 1920s to reflect tensions in visions of urban form. Tensions about the structure and character of the modern city flooded through discourse in Los Angeles. In this respect, Southern California was by no means unique. Concern with the automobile, especially its congestion and danger, also preoccupied urbanites in most other large American metropolises during this era of triumphant urbanization. In many eastern cities, though, the predominant vision of the urban future was strikingly vertical. Appropriately, in eastern metropolises, this vision of sublime verticality posed by experts—and enthusiastically consumed by others—offered ready potential solutions to vexing problems of contemporary urban life. These concentric cities possessed powerful ideological and architectural mechanisms for generating and maintaining a clearly legible order, and the private automobile could be readily assimilated into these systems of meaning.

The structural comprehensibility of Los Angeles was in flux during this time period, and the evolving metropolis therefore lacked many of those critical technologies of urban order that would prove so effective back east. As a city grown so recently, and so far removed from more traditional conurbations, Los Angeles had often been touted in its internal discourse as an exceptional place. Angelenos felt they lived in an exciting, different sort of city. This was an urbanity of seemingly endless juxtaposed streets that they could see in the movie houses, a terrain they could directly experience with their meandering automobiles and plodding streetcars. It was also, however, becoming an increasingly confusing place, lacking many of the orienting markers other urbanites relied on. The fact that ambitious local planners had worked for several years to decentralize the metropolis may not have been generally visible to most Angelenos, but these efforts were compounding the confusion as the symbolic and economic significance of the city's downtown district subtly and gradually began to erode.

In an era when the association of modernity and urbanity permeated the popular culture, most citizens were, at least to some degree, invested in questions of city form and structure, especially as those concerns were mediated through obsessions with traffic and boosterish urban expansion. These subjects were not, then, the strict province of experts and city officials. Nevertheless, it was precisely these elites—downtown businessmen as well as professional planners—who felt they had to respond to this widespread concern about traffic. For them, the popular fervor for a cure to the congestion and danger in the city streets represented an opportunity to articulate their own urban agendas. It was thus increasingly through the medium of traffic regulation that divergent groups in the metropolis's power structure sought to advance their own visions of the city's proper future. Traffic control plans in the 1920s, consequently, were never matters of mere technical rationality, but were always embedded in more ambitious and far-reaching conceptions of ideal urban form.

This homogeneous community of local leaders soon discovered that attempts at traffic regulation would reveal significant splits in their ranks. As the decade progressed, consensus about the form of these traffic plans—like the form of the city—began to erode. More subtly, popular concern about traffic frequently forced city leaders to formulate, or merely support, traffic solutions that would not obviously further their own cherished metropolitan visions. The pressure to do something substantial, combined with the abstracting and confusing semiotics of technical discourse on street traffic, oftentimes induced factions to endorse whatever contemporary traffic control proposals seemed readily available and politically feasible. Although at first these men had thought they would be able to handily appropriate the powerful and pervasive traffic discourses to advance their own visions, they would soon find they were as much driven by as driving the traffic frenzy.

In the early years of the decade, Los Angeles elites reacted to the growing traffic problem by adopting, time and again, a simple and uniform policy of containment. The chaos of private automotive transit had to be controlled and limited. Business leaders saw that congestion was stifling commerce, and their reflexive reaction was to push for freezes on automotive use in the affected district. In their view, the automobile was disrupting the proper traditional functioning of the business district. Order had to be restored. Businessmen consequently applied pressure for conservative, even nostalgically reactionary, measures. This was the purpose of parking bans: they were ways to effectively solve the traffic crisis by effectively banishing the automobile from the affected areas. Without so many private cars, the business district would be allowed to resume its proper place in the existing concentric transit networks of streetcars and interurban trains.

This prohibitory impulse lay behind many of the initial responses to the traffic crisis; it was, for instance, what Mrs. Whitnall, and more convincingly the local police, sought to do in the incident described at the beginning of this chapter. Once again, though, the real nexus of elite concern about traffic containment lay in the central business district. Consequently, at the behest of these businessmen, a short-term rush-hour parking ban was briefly reimposed on downtown Los Angeles during the Christmas shopping season of 1921, once more in the face of tremendous opposition.

Given the public resistance to such an avowedly temporary emergency measure, it soon became clear to planners that new thinking was necessary; regulation of automobile movement would neither solve the long-term structural problems of the business district nor prove politically palatable. By the early 1920s, the consensus of downtown businessmen and area planners about the feasibility and desirability of blanket traffic injunctions began to break down. Indeed, the responsibility for enacting such measures properly lay with the Los Angeles Planning Commission and, after 1923, its new metropolitan cousin, the Los Angeles Regional Planning Commission.[58] By the mid-1920s, Southern California's planners had clearly become reluctant to bow again to downtown business demands for further tinkering with localized restrictive ordinances. The planning experts were more and more convinced of the necessity of much more radical structural change for their region than could be accomplished through this sort of reactionary traffic management. They began to believe that simple interdictions on automobile movement would not contain the disruptions to the city brought about by the growing popularity of the private car.

For this reason local planners began to emphasize the power of "good planning"—that is, planning for decentralization—to reduce traffic congestion. Decentralization was sold, both among expert and popular audiences, as traffic relief. These visionaries thus appropriated widespread concern about the effects of the automobile to further their own plans for restructuring the metropolis. They were, however, jeopardizing the ambitions of their fellow elites, who were heavily invested both in the downtown district and in the traditional model of urban growth—and flying in the face of all common sense in the era. Indeed, even the most sun-addled enthusiast would have to admit in 1920 that Los Angeles was really not much of a garden city. If images of orange groves and pleasant detached bungalows dominated most Americans' notions of Southern California, both in the region and farther afield, this impression was the product as much of a marketing fantasy as of the existing landscape. Los Angeles was in many respects more like New York, or especially Chicago, had been at early stages of its development than the Mediterranean agrarian paradise it was advertised to be. This was, despite the rhetoric of the boosters and the dreams of the planners, a traditional concentric city at the beginning of the 1920s, and many Angelenos would probably acknowledge, if forced to, that their city could not forever remain a land of suburban detached homes and rural amenities.

In essence, though, this common sense is precisely what regional planners in Los Angeles denied. Southern California could and would, they believed, remain a land of oranges and bungalows. This heterodox vision clearly contrasted with the era's hegemonic notions of urban development, but more pointedly, if fully known it would have flown in the face of the booster dreams of many of the most influential Angelenos. The substantial businessmen of the metropolis—owners of department stores, cinemas, and small manufacturing concerns, as well as bankers and newspaper editors (always close to their major advertisers)—recognized in Los Angeles the nascent form of the great metropolises of the era. They had firmly established visions of their own city following the course of Chicago or New York, albeit with a milder climate. Further, these elites were almost unanimously based in the existing central business district. Their stores, office buildings, banks, and meeting places were downtown, and there they spent their time working for the future of themselves and their communal institutions. This district was adjacent, not coincidentally, to the offices of city government. So not only did the ideals of massive urban decentralization contradict most Jazz Age notions of modern urbanity, and not only did Los Angeles's expert planners take the notion much farther than the vast majority of their professional peers, but their plans for the city, if made fully explicit, would have surprised and threatened many of Los Angeles's most influential residents.

In effect, there was a powerful tension between opposed urban visions growing in Southern California during the early 1920s, but it was not recognized as such, even by each side's most fervent partisans. A thoroughgoing clustered decentralization program had developed gradually in local planning circles and was not made fully explicit even to potentially sympathetic audiences of expert planners from other cities. Thus, although members of the planning commissions did communicate their decentralizing ambitions to members of the public and to the city's elite through a series of exhibits, lectures (in both governmental and club forums), and publications (reports, memoranda, press releases, and the like), the specifics of their most radical, fundamental repudiations of traditional urban models—and the full implications of their projected replacements—probably remained implicit, suggested, and undeveloped even to most attentive and well-connected Angelenos.

Much of what the planners were going on about must have seemed somewhat academic to civic leaders and businessmen. In ideal circumstances, starting from scratch perhaps, the planners would do away with the concentric modern city form. These experts frequently complained about Los Angeles's urban structure. They alluded to visionary and idealistic schemes for urban reconstruction. They echoed the common assurance that Southern California could be different, better than other parts of the country. Yet it probably never occurred to the movers and shakers in the city that their planning experts actually thought it was possible to put all this into action in a radical, sweeping, unprecedented program of garden city decentralization in their existing city, and to do it in the next few decades. After all, although Los Angeles was certainly destined to grow—and who could predict the form that growth would take?—it was already a well-developed city, structured around a bustling and centralized business district. As a matter of fact, for many of these downtown-oriented elites, the trouble with Los Angeles's business district was not that it was obsolete or unnecessary, but rather that it was too successful, too necessary—and thus too crowded and too gridlocked. For these Angelenos, downtown needed to be rescued from the burdens of its own success, not bypassed altogether.

From the outset of the 1920s, these two influential groups—planners and downtown business leaders—began to subtly diverge in the ways they saw their metropolis. At first merely a difference in emphasis or in confidence about what could reasonably be done, this schism grew over the decade into fundamental conflict about the shape of the city. In this divergence, the aftermath of the parking ban of 1920 was something of a starting point. Simmering, almost subterranean differences between planners (given official status through the formation of the Los Angeles Planning Commission) and city officials had been subsumed in the compromise of that April, which sought to preserve downtown by banishing automotive traffic from the entire district.

The failure of the measure in the face of broad public protest and, eventually, press ridicule, was the first step toward the eventual collapse of the important civic coalition.[59] In retrospect, the parking ban was perhaps the final point when city planners and downtown elites fully understood one another, when both groups worked together to enact the same policies for the same ends. Although in succeeding years the camps would often support the same general policies or civic legislation, from this point onward they did so with divergent rationales. If there was a clear hege-

mony in Los Angeles during the 1920s in favor of urban expansion and development, as many scholars have observed, it was a coalition of convenience, motivated
in different constituencies by different reasons. Beneath all such civic accord of the
'20s lay conflict, sometimes hidden conflict between visions of the city, between
groups who claimed to see the future, and between institutions that sought to control civic policy. What began as little more than a difference in emphasis became,
in a remarkably short time (although during a tumultuous period in Southern California's development), a full-blown clash of urban visions.

This developing conflict, which had been subsumed by the failed compromise
of the parking ban (after which expert planners for the most part gave up on saving the downtown district), reemerged in ever more vindictive and apocalyptic form
throughout the first half of the decade. If the fallout of the failed 1920 parking ban
began to expose these disagreements (if only faintly and only to certain members
of each group), the development and implementation of the Major Traffic Street
Plan from 1922 into the mid-1920s intensified them, and the battle over the Rapid
Transit Plan of 1926 proved something of a final showdown. Still, it was only at the
very end of the decade that planners were willing to put forward a comprehensive
urban restructuring plan. These critical points in the decade crystallized the nascent differences in vision between planners and business elites, making them
clearer to both groups, and set the groups on a collision course.

PUTTING THE AUTOMOBILE
AT THE HEART OF LOS ANGELES

*Southern California, with its delightful climate and natural attractions, to-
gether with the many miles of paved highways radiating throughout the Southwest, with Los Angeles as a center, has become a mecca for motorists.*

AUTOMOBILE CLUB OF SOUTHERN CALIFORNIA, *THE LOS ANGELES
TRAFFIC PROBLEM* (10)

These tensions between Los Angeles's visionaries might have remained quiescent—
and purely theoretical—had it not been for the pervasive traffic discourse circulating in the larger community. The public exerted pressure on city leaders, both
through local popular culture and the news media and through electoral decisions,
for mitigation of the diurnal traffic snarls. And through the succeeding years, this
discourse only intensified as the city grew. Before long, even the most ambitious
boosters were expressing ambivalence at the rate of urban expansion in Southern
California. As Gordon Whitnall, looking back over the first years of the 1920s, later
put it in an address to a national planning conference, "The avalanche of development has been on us in such a degree that we have barely kept our heads above
water."[60] This "random" and "uncontrolled" expansion (a confusion subtly represented perhaps in the planner's mixed metaphors) threatened to overwhelm all ef-

forts at rational urban planning: "In one year alone over 1400 subdivision plans were recorded, most of which we have passed upon."[61] Los Angeles might succumb from the success of its own boosterism.[62]

This flood of new development only added to the existing hysteria over automotive traffic and heightened city leaders' urgency to find solutions, if only temporary ones. Even city planners were beginning to admit that the region was growing so quickly that traffic congestion might gridlock the city altogether before needed structural changes—which would, of course, require a great deal of meticulous planning and patience to reach fruition—could show any noticeable effects. Worse, the region's rapid growth at the beginning of the 1920s was throwing off the careful designs for controlled development that local planners had gestated over the previous decade. As Whitnall complained in 1924, "With our unprecedented increase in population and territorial expansion, we have seen transpire within the period of a few years what usually requires generations to accomplish."[63] Given that Southern California's population expansion would not admit of any stabilizing respite in the years to come—quite the contrary, the 1920s witnessed the largest boom yet in the region's population—planners could only hope to concentrate on their work of regulating new subdivision development. Although planners sought to exploit concern about traffic conditions, they clearly did not wish to bear the burden of dealing with them directly. They felt the still limited resources of their new agencies would be best used in selling their vision of regional planning and managing future peripheral growth.

For their part, the city's business leaders felt that if a traffic ban would not work, something else might. While some of them gestated plans to modernize the city along traditional eastern lines, others contemplated ways of making existing facilities more accessible to cars, such as constructing on-site parking—like their rivals in Pasadena were increasingly doing. In the abstract, decentralization probably did not seem to them so much a threat as a prediction of future marginal trends. Their faith in the continued centrality of the downtown district was resolute. Even if these business elites had been fully aware of the hopes planners invested in decentralization—and it seems, for the most part, they were not—they would certainly have felt such a radical restructuring of the existing metropolis to be impossible. Their primary concern was not some mooted eventual obsolescence of downtown but rather its undue popularity with motorists. Reducing the disruptive congestion, thus freeing their shops for business as usual, was the priority of these Angelenos.

It was this combination of circumstances at the onset of the 1920s—the budding divergences between local planners and (increasingly desperate) downtown elites, the explosive rate of regional growth, and the ubiquitous and somewhat hysterical public discourse on traffic—that made the 1922 proposal by the Automobile Club of Southern California such a watershed. This was a traffic plan that finally exposed the nascent divisions between planners and businessmen and yet, ironically, drove these two groups once more into an uneasy tactical consensus. Without a compelling vision of how to deal with the traffic crisis in the short term, these two groups essentially went along for the ride on a proposal by a third party, which claimed that its efforts were "directed solely toward public benefit."[64] Indeed, *The Los Angeles Traffic Problem* was ostensibly a simple traffic analysis, yet it was the first in a series of significant "surveys" carried out over the next twenty years that were, in actuality, elaborate proposals for action. This report had profound implications for the future of the region, partly through the effects of its suggested actions but also through the way it altered the dynamics of civic influence in Los Angeles. From this point on, no one body would be granted sole authority to "Dream dreams and see Visions" for Southern California.

The Auto Club's plan seemed innocuous enough. It primarily called for a series of road construction projects. As the report summarized, "The improvements shown on this plan may be placed in three groups. First, a broad traffic quadrangle encircling the congested area. Second, diagonal thoroughfares leading from the congested area to the outlying districts. Third, a circulatory system of traffic thoroughfares outside of the congested area."[65]

The call for road rationalization was not new. As early as 1910 the city council had tried to organize commissions toward this end, and it was one of the formal justifications for the formation of the Los Angeles Planning Commission in 1920.[66] But this road plan was a peculiar one. It proposed encircling the "congested area" with new roads, better connecting it to other parts of town, and building new roads entirely outside of this area, but it oddly said very little about what ought to be done to ease traffic within the "congested area" itself. As a matter of fact, the Auto Club proposal seemed to say little about downtown at all. Perhaps a hint of the cause of this strange omission lies in the preface to *The Los Angeles Traffic Problem*, in the telling statement that although "the Club recognized that the City of Los Angeles is the heart of Southern California, . . . its efforts to aid in solving this tremendous problem have been undertaken with a feeling of responsibility not alone to Los Angeles City but to all Southern California."[67] Although the Automobile Club was based in central Los Angeles (at Adams and Figueroa Streets since 1915), it owed its allegiance (and membership) to the entire Southern California region.[68] Further, the organization received its most vocal support from members in those outlying districts least served by the interurbans and consequently most dependent upon the automobile. Certainly, real estate interests in those sections also exerted considerable influence on the club, particularly as new tracts were platted and sold that had no convenient access to existing streetcar lines. It is no surprise that the club in its report primarily called for the construction of new and better roadways, as that had been its main goal for the previous two decades under the aegis of the "Good Roads Movement." Yet these proposals would not have emerged from either the city's existing planning bureaucracy or its interested elites. They represented a new strain of proposals—aimed at making the city safe for automobility—that would have a significant impact upon the traffic debate in Los Angeles.

It was thus at the moment when Los Angeles's regional planners were most committed to—and just beginning to enact—a thorough, radical program of garden city type decentralization through careful subdivision control that they acquiesced to delegating some portion of a major planning task to an interested third party. Likewise, the city's downtown business leaders were so stymied by their traffic conundrum that they were willing to throw their political weight behind a proposal sponsored by an organization that owed as much allegiance to the surrounding counties and suburbs as to Los Angeles itself. In any case, the 1922 Automobile Club plan offered soothing words to both parties, which must have done much to distract from the essence of the proposals. To planners, the plan offered what appeared to be a broadly decentralized vision of the region, focusing attention on helping the central business district by establishing a traffic bypass. One of the Auto Club's experts was a member of the City Planning Commission, and the document specifically advocated increased authority for that agency in subdivision control (while usurping its jurisdiction over traffic regulation). Downtown elites, on the other hand, could easily find statements in the Auto Club's scheme that seemed to directly soothe their own deepest fears. Most notably, the plan closely aligned traffic relief with the goal of reinforcing the centralized structure of the region: "Unless traffic conditions can be improved, it will result in the business district being broadly scattered to outlying points."[69] Moreover, the scheme mentioned, at least in passing, that the current (weak) time restrictions on downtown parking probably ought to be retained. This was certainly not the definitive solution downtown interests were searching for, but it was at least an effort to deal with their most pressing problems.

The Automobile Club's plan was released in August 1922. In December, the Los Angeles Traffic Commission—which, since its founding at the end of the previous year, had been a rather quiescent and unwieldy panel of civic worthies and interested local organizations chartered by the city council to "investigate" the city's traffic snarl—issued its own formal report, specifically endorsing every element of the Auto Club's proposal. This program, titled ambitiously *The Los Angeles Plan*, stated its inspiration up front: "The Automobile Club of Southern California has furnished in their report on traffic problems the basis for the major traffic street plan which is suggested. The Traffic Commission considers this report of the Automobile Club one of the greatest civic contributions ever made to the City of Los Angeles—a noteworthy demonstration of unselfish service, not only to the motoring public, but to the community at large."[70] Not only did the Traffic Commission adopt the Auto Club's blueprint for the city in whole cloth, but this organization henceforth threw itself wholeheartedly into the project of getting the combined plan implemented. To do this, the Los Angeles Traffic Commisssion reinterpreted its mission, transforming itself from an investigative body into a quasi-official pressure group. In this, the Traffic

Commission explicitly undercut the authority of the established City Planning Commission: "The Los Angeles Traffic Commission is founded on an ideal, is unselfishly dedicated to public service, and is unique in its organization and membership. It is dedicated to the solution of traffic problems, cooperating to the fullest extent with the City Planning Commission and other public bodies, and yet occupying a position which, in many cases, cannot be filled by any of them."[71] Here, the new body claimed that it had a purpose distinct from that of the City Planning Commission— it would not merely be an advisory body. Instead, the traffic commissioners reinvented themselves as a product of Progressive Era civil service reform, claiming that "public officials are, by the very nature of their office, prohibited from being participants. They must act in a judicial capacity and it is not appropriate for them to take sides for or against public improvements where there are conflicting interests and divided public opinion. City officials by reason of the position they occupy, are ethically prohibited from initiating such measures."[72] Certainly this was the first the planners had ever heard of such an interdiction against civil servants making specific proposals. Clearly, *The Los Angeles Plan* represented a usurpation of the hard-won authority of local planners to enact their vision of the future city.

The conclusion of this remarkable preface offers a hint of what might have been going on here:

> The Traffic Commission can function as a buffer between the public and the authorities. The Traffic Commission can actively advocate needed public improvements, circulate petitions, secure deeds for streets, solicit funds in accordance with the directions of the Honorable City Council for maintenance of the organization, secure agreements of property owners *and aggressively advocate all measures in the interest of public welfare, looking toward the relief of traffic congestion in the city of Los Angeles, and its immediate vicinity.*[73]

This was from the start an organization that saw itself in political terms, as a pressure group. Was this new Traffic Commission—again, largely comprised of business leaders and city bureaucrats—seizing control of critical planning functions, marginalizing the established experts in planning? Or was this body merely providing political cover, perhaps with the acquiescence of the City Planning Commission, for what might turn out to be a controversial construction program? After all, the head of the Traffic Commission's "Educational Committee" was none other than Harry Chandler, editor-in-chief of the *Los Angeles Times*. Representatives from the *Examiner,* the *Herald,* the *Express,* the (working-class oriented) *Record,* and even the *Hollywood News* were all on the commission. Maybe this body, expert in the art of public relations, was well positioned not only to protect the professional planners from any taint of interest but to actively sell a potentially reluctant populace on the necessary bond issues and enabling legislation. Supporting this more benign interpretation is the fact that the City Planning Commission had two representatives on this body (albeit out of more than one hundred), and one of these was none other than Gordon Whitnall, director of the City Planning Commission and, as we have seen, a leading proponent of garden city decentralization.

The answers to these questions would not begin to emerge until a bit later, when the Traffic Commission began in earnest to work on what would emerge two years later as *A Major Traffic Street Plan*. That 1924 plan would prove to be a pivotal document in the construction of Greater Los Angeles, proving as important as the parking ban of four years earlier in crystallizing and magnifying opposition and conflict in local understandings of the city. The first concrete step of the Traffic Commission, after its initial rush of enthusiasm, was—possibly in recognition that they might be in over their heads—the hiring of a small group of outside consultants: "Early on the commissioners decided to invite a blue-ribbon committee to examine the growing impact of the automobile on the urban environment."[74] As the commission's final report put it a couple of years later, "It was felt . . . that the importance of the subject warranted the employment of experts of national reputation to review the existing plans, making such adjustment and additions as changed conditions dictated, and knitting all into one compact and related whole."[75] This new board comprised Frederick Law Olmsted, Jr., Harland Bartholomew, and Charles Henry Cheney. All three were nationally respected planning experts— "city planners of unquestioned standing,"[76] as the commission put it in the foreword to their landmark 1924 report. The three experts were hand-picked as leading exponents of the regional planning movement. On the surface, at least, this would be a reassuring bunch to local planners. They were, after all, fellow experts and professionals, and all three were well versed in the ideology and rhetoric of urban decentralization.

Despite these encouraging signs, though, after their years of unquestioned rise within the hierarchy of the city, Los Angeles's planners had encountered without a doubt something of a rebuke. Yet, notwithstanding the formation of a rival body of outsiders to oversee the city's road development, there was plenty of room for optimism among the indigenous planning community. The new Traffic Commission clearly did not intend to simply commit the city to a retrograde program dictated solely by downtown interests. Still, the planners' powerful and coherent vision of the future development of Southern California had clearly engendered some powerful opposition. Perhaps the planners saw these obstacles as expected roadblocks, manageable obstacles to their larger ends. Maybe they actually greeted the chance to use a more public planning body as a lightning rod to draw political animosity away from their more important project of subdivision control. And the introduction of prestigious eastern planners must have seemed to ratify their entire project in this remote western outpost. Quite possibly they did not see this new development as a direct threat, since it only pertained to the most thankless areas of the City Planning Commission's authority—in fact, areas that they at times seemed eager to abjure. There is no sign, in public statements or other writings, that the professional planners felt snubbed by the events of 1922. Nevertheless, although the resistance was subtle, it had its effect. An outside body of experts was called in to direct the progress of the Major Traffic Street Plan, a sign of nascent opposition to the planners' hegemony. At the very least, it indicates the shakiness of the planners' position, despite their rapid rise and institutionalization within the city's hierarchy. Clearly, this early challenge to local planners' authority was not an assault on the carefully orchestrated understanding these planners had established in favor of expert planning. Even this attack, if that is what it was, came in the form of a call for more planning, more delegation of civic authority to planning professionals, not as an attack on the profession or its civic influence. Yet importing an outside cadre of planners was clearly, at least in retrospect, an erosion of the power of the Los Angeles Planning Commission. No longer did this body have undivided authority over the city's future form, as it did (at least in theory) for its first few years. Now that power would be formally divided between the City Planning Commission and a new Traffic Commission.

THE 1924 MAJOR TRAFFIC STREET PLAN

The street traffic congestion problem of Los Angeles is exceeded by that of no other city.

LOS ANGELES TRAFFIC COMMISSION, *A MAJOR TRAFFIC STREET PLAN* (9)

Los Angeles's indigenous planners and businessmen must have been surprised by what the Traffic Commission produced. Bartholomew, Olmsted, and Cheney's final report, *A Major Traffic Street Plan for Los Angeles,* when released formally in 1924, called for three distinct projects. The consulting board proposed connecting the suburbs and downtown through a system of wide radial boulevards, aligning a network of "distributor streets" around the central district, and linking outlying regions through interdistrict thoroughfares. What is so surprising about the report is that these three measures, taken together, really supported neither of the heretofore dominant visions of the city's future. The *Major Traffic Street Plan* failed to match the ambitions of either local expert planners or downtown elites.

On the face of it, the consulting board's report seemed quite uncontroversial, concerned only with traditional, proven, technical traffic measures. Indeed, the first of its recommended provisions was a time-honored mainstay of the early city planning movement. The system of wide automotive boulevards radiating directly from the downtown district to the outlying sections of the metropolis that Bartholomew, Olmsted, and Cheney sought to introduce in Los Angeles was a standard feature of the City Beautiful plans of many cities. Clay McShane points this out in *Down the Asphalt Path:* "In most American cities, business leaders, likely motorists, turned to City Beautiful plans, featuring the geometric fantasies and massive rebuilding plans of Daniel Burnham and other architects. These plans encouraged automobility by building formal grand boulevards on the model of what Baron Georges Haussmann had done in Napoleon III's Paris. These ideas permeated the architects who dominated the early planning profession."[77] Thus, the Bartholomew, Olmsted, and Cheney plan's call for "Radial Thoroughfares from [the] Central Business District" was, by 1924, a quite traditional approach to city restructuring.

Yet such a proposal certainly could not have overjoyed indigenous garden city planners. The *Major Traffic Street Plan*'s matter-of-fact postulate—that it was a matter of extreme importance that "the central business district should be directly accessible from all parts of the city"[78]—ran directly against the priorities of local expert opinion. Not only was cutting new arteries through the very flesh of the city a crude sort of operation, contrary to the spirit of advance planning, but the specific remedy promised to exert a profoundly centralizing force upon the city. It was well known at the time that boulevards reinforced the symbolic and economic importance of the central business district: "Planners advocated them ['wide radial roads cut through gridirons'] for aesthetic reasons, noting that the roads provided incredibly long vistas, as a rule focused on the civic center or a major downtown monument."[79] Their clear display of civic organization and topographical order admirably suited radial boulevards to government seats and military centers—they cut a radial cross-section through a concentric city to display and reinforce the inherent structural hierarchy of social organization. This was not the technology of a decentralized region of autonomous garden cities. It was a tool for reinforcing the concentric structure of a traditional city.

Worse, the specific corridor that the *Major Traffic Street Plan* singled out as a major radial was one for which local planners already had plans. The Traffic Commission's experts chose Wilshire Boulevard to be expanded to eight full lanes of traffic, complete with off-street parking (see figure 18), thus making it the primary radial connecting the western suburbs to the core of the city.[80] Now, instead of being the backbone of the western communities, Wilshire was doomed to be another conduit for traffic to flow downtown. This only promised to encourage the ribbon development that planners were zoning to prevent and the cross-town commuting that they wished to root out altogether.

Combined with this web of potentially centralizing radials, though, the Bartholomew, Olmsted, and Cheney plan called for a new system of ring, or distributor, roads and a network of "interdistrict thoroughfares" to connect outlying regions. Both provisions were intended to reduce pressure on the downtown by allowing long-distance travel in the region to avoid the crush of traffic at the hub. The distributor streets would more efficiently parcel out traffic wishing to enter the central city, allowing those vehicles to approach the district at the point closest to their ultimate destination and thus avoid "milling around" in the congested area.[81] The

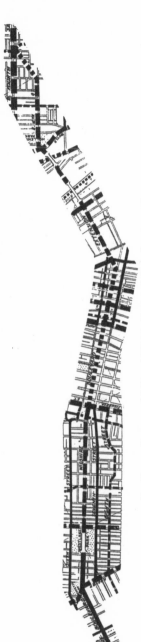

Map No. 14—Recommended Plan of Wilshire Boulevard Extension Across Town.

FIGURE 18. Wilshire would be the major east-west radial to result from the Bartholomew, Olmsted, and Cheney report, 1924. From Los Angeles Traffic Commission, *A Major Traffic Street Plan for Los Angeles* (Los Angeles: Traffic Commission, 1924), map 14.

interdistrict thoroughfares, on the other hand, were an ambitious initiative to extend Los Angeles's street grid throughout undeveloped county land, but again by encouraging traffic to bypass the downtown central business district. As the *Major Traffic Street Plan* put it, "There are few streets in Los Angeles today that afford direct and adequate communication between the various centers of importance other than the downtown business district. There should be as complete a system of direct, wide interdistrict thoroughfares of this character, doing a service similar to that of the radial thoroughfares connecting directly with the central business district."[82]

Not only would downtown be cut out of the circuit of urban travel but a collection of suburban "subcenters"—so-called centers of importance—would receive the same street access as the city's heart. This was not exactly what Los Angeles's business elite wished to hear. Reducing downtown traffic was critical, but not by taking potential consumers elsewhere. Already burgeoning new competing subcenters, such as Pasadena and Hollywood, had used the earlier parking ban as an opportunity to appeal to Angelenos through newspaper advertisements, attempting to lure them away from downtown. Now the Bartholomew, Olmsted, and Cheney plan seemed to encourage this business predation. In addition, although the *Major Traffic Street Plan* claimed to focus on the central district of the city, in practice it seemed to give that vital section short shrift. Under the heading "Business District Improvements" (after page 29), for example, this plan suggested ways of bypassing the congested district altogether. Even worse, in the body of the 1924 plan the city's core was dismissively referred to as "the congested district." Apparently, all that was important about the very heart of the metropolis was that it attracted excessive automotive traffic. If the opening and widening of major thoroughfares into the business district was a laudably centralizing element in the plan and might make life easier for commuters daily stuck in jams along these major radial thoroughfares, the plan did not offer to do anything about these throngs once they arrived in the congested district. Perhaps most importantly, though, the Traffic Commission offered no streetcar reform. When this crucial topic was addressed, on page 30 of the report, it was merely to say that little could be done until the local rail system could be rerouted. This complex task the Bartholomew, Olmsted, and Cheney plan renounced entirely, leaving the subject to another report, supposedly under development, which would specifically deal with the rapid transit future of the region.

What is so surprising about the Traffic Commission report, then, is that the *Major Traffic Street Plan* almost entirely failed to deliver the goods for either of the city's heretofore most vocal constituencies. The downtown traffic relief so ardently desired by local businessmen came about in large part through a program designed to direct vehicular traffic away from the central district (through the interdistrict thoroughfares and the distributor streets). This was hardly a solution Los Angeles's centralizing elites could warm to. Likewise, although the Bartholomew, Olmsted, and Cheney plan effectively diluted the importance of the downtown district—

which the garden city planners felt was absolutely necessary—it sought to link satellite subcenters to the main downtown area by a series of grandiose centralizing boulevards. Kept firmly in downtown Los Angeles's orbit, these subcenters looked very little like a cluster of autonomous garden cities. This was not the sort of decentralization local planning professionals had sought from a major civic plan. Clearly, the *Major Traffic Street Plan* envisioned a metropolis foreign to both planner and businessman.

RELEGATING VISIONS OF THE
URBAN FUTURE TO THE BACKSEAT

Los Angeles' greatest immediate need in solving its street traffic congestion problem is the development of an orderly and well-balanced system of thoroughfares throughout the city. . . . This is the purpose of the present study.

LOS ANGELES TRAFFIC COMMISSION, *A MAJOR TRAFFIC STREET PLAN* (16)

What distinguishes the Bartholomew, Olmsted, and Cheney report is that it is a thoroughgoing attempt to make the existing city come to terms with the flexibility inherent in automobility. The major provisions of the 1924 plan shared a common goal of facilitating increased automotive transport throughout the expanding city—and all three were taken almost verbatim from the earlier Auto Club plan. The consulting board acknowledged as much in their preface, admitting that "many of the recommendations contained in these reports [the Automobile Club report and the earlier Traffic Commission endorsement] have been incorporated in whole or in part in the present plan."[83] Perhaps another indicator of these priorities lay in the Traffic Commission's fourth outside expert, who was much less famous at the time. The commission had chosen as its chief traffic consultant Miller McClintock,[84] a young traffic engineering guru and graduate student at Harvard University who theorized that urban traffic ought to be thought of as "friction." The more frictions on a city's operation, the less efficiently the metropolis as a whole would function.[85] Although he would become far more influential nationally in the coming decade,[86] McClintock and his "efficient machine" theory of friction-free urban transportation must have influenced the consulting board to focus almost exclusively on a street widening program: "When choice is open, and when in doubt, it is the part of wisdom and of conservation to aim for greater thoroughfare capacity rather than for less."[87]

This was a plan designed from the first more to respond to public pressure about traffic congestion than to solve the region's long-term structural problems. Not surprisingly, the *Major Traffic Street Plan* immediately traced Los Angeles's traffic problems to the "unscientific width and arrangement of streets."[88] This structural flaw, the report emphasized, was not merely a problem in itself—outdated infrastructure in a supposedly modern city—but a product of the region's dependence on the private automobile, which was stifling the existing transit infrastructure: "Automobiles used exclusively for passenger transport occupy 14.3 times as much road way space per person carried (according to L.A. Railway figures) as do street cars in the Los Angeles business district."[89] Further, private car transport was a growing proportion of commuting traffic, as scattered suburban developments, increasingly far from existing interurban tracks, sprang up on the urban fringes.[90]

Like the earlier Auto Club plan, the Bartholomew, Olmsted, and Cheney report did not seek to rescue the city's streetcar system (the parking ban had so attempted, and it had failed). Instead, the consulting board merely sought to provide adequate road space for the new motorists, concluding that "the place of the automobile in the transportation problem of Los Angeles is far more important than in the cities of the East."[91] The 1924 plan went on to note that "Los Angeles is unique in the importance of its automobile traffic, in relation to its general transportation problem. The checks taken for purposes of study show that almost as many people daily enter the congested area of the city by automobile as enter it by all other means of transportation."[92] With this quantitative emphasis, the report fundamentally posed the traffic problem in Los Angeles as a simple one. The commission saw congestion primarily as a problem of hydraulics, not fundamental urban form. Consulting traffic expert McClintock lectured the City Club that "congestion is the 'retardation or obstruction to the normal flow of traffic.' High density of traffic does not make congestion if there is a high discharge factor. . . . Too slow a movement, too small an area, or too many vehicles for a given space makes congestion. Nothing else can."[93] Logically, then, given this diagnosis, the solution would be straightforward: either correct these flaws in street capacity to accommodate the increased flow or channel this pressure into new courses. Ultimately, by viewing their mission strictly in terms of increasing traffic volume, the consulting board members proved eager to implement any project that might expand capacity: "The economic gain of increasing the average scale of the street system as a whole would justify almost any amount of reconstruction by slashing through a major street system on a 'modern' scale of street width and of directness. That is the sort of reconstruction Paris did in the 18th and 19th centuries. Tokio and Canton are doing it now."[94] This willingness to engage in massive public works merely to allow better automobile access to the "congested district" clearly did not accord with the local planners' concern with reducing the traffic pressure at the source—that is, reducing the number of automobiles making long trips over the region's road network. Nor did this report consider supporting the existing rail network as a solution to the problem, as business leaders may have preferred. Clearly, this plan was designed from the start to make Los Angeles safe for long-distance automotive commuting, not to implement visions of proper urban structure.[95]

The *Major Traffic Street Plan* that emerged in 1924 was an ambitious, expensive, and wide-ranging infrastructure program, but it was also a remarkably conserva-

tive one. By the mid-1920s, most experts in the region agreed that serious structural changes would be necessary in Los Angeles if the city wished to do more than
merely treat the symptoms of its traffic problems. The long-term solution to automotive chaos would require radical modernization of the growing metropolis. Local elites differed dramatically about what form this modernization would take, but
all agreed that the *Major Traffic Street Plan* could never deliver it. The broad support the Traffic Commission's plan received in official circles reflects the fact that,
since the scheme avoided serious engagement with questions of urban form, it was
a program that offended no one. What's more, it was useful to everyone in city government, because it emerged in 1924 as the most clear and convincing proof that
city officials were responding to the public concern about traffic. What none of these
local elites probably fully realized was that the *Major Traffic Street Plan* would exert a profound and almost entirely unexpected influence on the basic structure of
the metropolis, thus changing the very ground of the fundamental disagreements
over city form that it seemed so neatly to avoid. Consequently, although long-sim-
mering splits within Southern California's civic leadership over the question of metropolitan form were sublimated into an uneasy coalition of planners and businessmen, allied in unanimous, if tepid, support of a traffic plan that belonged to
neither group, the repercussions of this very plan would, within a couple of years,
force this latent conflict into the open.

Despite the lack of enthusiasm shown for this program by businessmen and plan-
ers, one constituency in Southern California greeted the *Major Traffic Street Plan*
with enthusiasm. Ordinary Angelenos concerned about the mounting social costs
of traffic and congestion wholeheartedly applauded the Traffic Commission's suggestions. And in retrospect, well they should, for this was a plan that promised just
what the public demanded—more roads for motorists. In the time frame of the
1920s, most Angelenos were naïve enough to expect that increased street capacity
would result in direct and lasting traffic relief. Consequently, citizens rallied to the
cause of the anticongestion program and lobbied for immediate passage of the bond
measures associated with the *Major Traffic Street Plan*. Early on, the major newspapers of the city also signed on. A terse 1923 *Los Angeles Examiner* editorial transmits the spirit of the moment:

> Los Angeles needs wide streets, and lots of them.
>
> Los Angeles needs smooth streets, and lots of them.
>
> Los Angeles needs through streets, and lots of them.
>
> Los Angeles needs more streets, and lots of them.[96]

This enthusiasm was soon translated into popular action. In the election of 4 November 1924, city officials offered up two linked bond measures, Propositions A
and B, to fund the Traffic Commission's recommended construction program. Both

passed resoundingly, as public anxiety about traffic was so intense that the electorate was willing to abandon its habitual hostility toward expensive public works.

PLANNING DECENTRALIZATION

It is my contention that the present form of city growth which we may refer to as "centralized" is based more upon sound economics and logical social science than generally seems to be understood.

HARLAND BARTHOLOMEW, "A PROGRAM TO PREVENT ECONOMIC
DISINTEGRATION IN AMERICAN CITIES" (5)

By 1924 it was becoming clear to many in Southern California's community of civic leaders that the region was at a crossroads in its growth. As automobile-borne migrants flooded the narrow streets and bought up real estate farther and farther into the hinterland, the structure of the traditional small city of the 1910s was contorting and fracturing. Los Angeles had clearly and suddenly reached a point in its development where it was going to have to either reevaluate its stance on growth or rapidly and deliberately transform its infrastructure and form. Given its booster ambitions, there was simply no choice: Los Angeles needed to modernize.

But what course of modernization would the city's elites chart? The debates of the mid-1920s over traffic control in Southern California evoked conflicting visions of urban modernity. In fact, they represented radically different ways of bringing the twentieth-century American metropolis into clear view. Although these disagreements came into open conflict only in the campaign over the rapid transit plan of 1926, they pervaded the *Major Traffic Street Plan* as well. Whereas two years later the fight would be between local planners and downtown-oriented businessmen, in 1924 the conflict arose within a group that had thought itself in perfect agreement.

The official out-of-town planners of the Traffic Commission's consulting board had been chosen, as we have seen, not merely for their national stature in the profession but because they were openly committed to a philosophy of urban decentralization—a commitment that made them appear to be in perfect harmony with a local contingent of professional planners who were contemplating visions of radical urban deconcentration. These were, in other words, some of the nation's leading proponents of the concepts of urban modernization in favor among planners in Southern California. The plan these outside experts produced fell far short of delivering the sort of manifesto for garden city decentralization for which local experts must have been hoping. Yet was the *Major Traffic Street Plan* not an avowedly decentralizing plan? Shouldn't Los Angeles's planners have been pleased that their brethren on the consulting board had worked so hard to acknowledge and support urban development beyond the confines of the central district? Undoubtedly, Bartholomew, Olmsted, and Cheney felt they were responding directly to the concerns of their local peers in bestowing sustained attention on the development of regional subcenters in the metropolis.[97] In this respect, they surely felt, Los Angeles's *Major Traffic Street Plan* represented one of the most thorough decentralization programs yet contemplated for an American city. Nevertheless, this was clearly no program for local planners' notions of decentralization.

The 1924 plan was an entirely different scheme from that contemplated in the writings or published lectures of local experts. A clue to this difference lies in the *Major Traffic Street Plan*'s most decentralizing element: the provision to encourage new subcenters of development. In the Bartholomew, Olmsted, and Cheney report, it is clear that these peripheral precincts were to be considered extensions of the centralized structure of the current city, not as entirely new urban loci. Although some business activity would be delegated to these new business districts—"They are neighborhood centers for local shopping that the central business district cannot and should not continue to draw to itself at the cost of interfering with kinds of business which have a better right to a central location"[98]—they would essentially serve as secondary hubs in the existing concentric model. This was not the sort of clustered, quasi-autonomous development Los Angeles's planners had been contemplating. Indeed, these decentralizing consultants were talking about not the wholesale abandonment of metropolitan centralization implied in garden city plans but what they called the "specialization of centers."[99] The subsidiary centers would not be complete communities able to exist on their own, but merely locations of some distinct activity: "These centers are some of a local shopping character, some of an industrial character, and some even of an agricultural character, such as the San Fernando Valley."[100] For Bartholomew, Olmsted, and Cheney, decentralized business districts would supplement, not supplant, the metropolis's central core.

The *Major Traffic Street Plan* essentially treated these subcenters like it did the existing downtown core. As such, they threatened eventually to recapitulate all the problems and inefficiencies of the current downtown, such as overcentralization and consequent traffic congestion, at multiple points throughout the metropolitan region. Bartholomew, Olmsted, and Cheney acknowledged as much in their "Gist of the Report": "The traffic congestion in the area surrounding the central business district . . . will in the future find repetition in numerous sub-centers that are even less prepared to accommodate great growth. The present plan is frankly presented as a foundation upon which to erect a much broader structure of streets for the accommodation of the vast volume of traffic the future is bound to produce throughout the entire metropolitan district."[101] In the future, these new satellite subcenters would thus potentially fall victim to the same congestion problems currently endemic to downtown within the highly centralized city. The Bartholomew, Olmsted, and Cheney plan offered little hope that such a fate might be avoided, warning merely that programs of street restructuring would have to be repeated endlessly, at great expense, in the years to come. This was not the sort of advance planning local experts had envisioned.

Once again it seemed that the overriding pressure for traffic relief overwhelmed all efforts to remake the city. If local planners had hoped that the *Major Traffic Street Plan* would offer them a politically advantageous opportunity to write their vision of the future metropolis into civic policy, they were disappointed. Although local planners had long thought certain street adjustments were probably inevitable and undoubtedly necessary for future development, such improvements were certainly not their chief concern. They were more interested in subdivision control and the alignment of streets not already overcome by traffic. This sort of preparation should fall to city planning. As Whitnall put it in a speech to the City Club in 1919, "City Planning is the art of laying out cities to serve the business requirements, convenience, health and comfort of the public. It is guiding the growth of a city in conformity with a scientific design. It is adjusting the physical form of the city to the peculiar needs of its parts. Most cities look back at what COULD have been done. City Planning is for the purpose of looking forward to what CAN be done and cuts out the looking backward."[102] These experts wished to concern themselves primarily with the gradual, long-term task of shaping development to ensure that the Greater Los Angeles region could form itself harmoniously into a cluster of garden cities. To do that, local centers must not merely be zones of specialization for the larger metropolis or mirrors of the larger concentric urban structure; they would have to be the bases of autonomous, self-contained communities. Such truly independent centers would have to serve primarily their own neighborhoods and not just be cogs in the larger centralized metropolitan machinery. Indeed, Los Angeles's indigenous understanding of decentralization was premised on the notion that the region's many business districts should primarily serve local constituencies. Bartholomew, Olmsted, and Cheney's scheme of linking these local centers tightly to each other (through the interdistrict thoroughfares) and to a single dominant regional core (through the radial boulevards) would, by contrast, preclude their necessary self-contained autonomy.

These patterns of commuting, of traffic, were fundamentally important to planners. They were effectively a window onto the functional relationships of the modern city. For Los Angeles's planners, the garden city plan sought to restrict much of this movement to short-distance travel between residence and workplace or shopping district. Consequently, the independent communities should be interconnected by a road system, but not so effectively as to undermine the strict and foundational association between workplace and residence upon which their very promise of traffic reduction was premised. Autonomous communities were supposed to eliminate commuting altogether, providing all their residents would ordinarily need—jobs, shopping, entertainment—within a short drive, or even a stroll, of their homes. The expected observable decline in citywide traffic congestion would reveal that these localized subcenters were doing their jobs properly, that they were hosting the important activities of their adjacent communities.

The traffic patterns the 1924 plan envisioned—and worked to facilitate—would reflect an entirely different sort of urban organization. The Traffic Commission report emphasized particularly the need to tie its subcenters into the larger circuits of everyday regional automotive travel:

> Throughout the metropolitan district there are numerous centers of development within which traffic originates or terminates whose relation to the central business district is more or less remote. . . . A secondary structural element of the major street plan is composed of the thoroughfares connecting these various centers. . . . These are to be distinguished from the radial thoroughfares in that they afford inter-communication between parts of the community outside the central business district.[103]

The configuration of traffic projected and accommodated in the outside experts' report assumed (and provided for) continued long-distance automobile commuting. The new subcenters discussed in the Bartholomew, Olmsted, and Cheney plan were clearly never intended to serve as the localized cores of autonomous neighborhoods, but rather would be limited regional shopping districts, which might, like Hollywood or Pasadena, draw traffic from throughout the metropolis. The consequent patterns of automobile movement that could be expected to emerge from this report would betoken functional relationships in the larger topography quite unlike those envisioned and advocated by local decentralizers. Logically, given the meanings planners derived from traffic, the intended function of the subcenters can be inferred from the movements expected to emanate from them.

If these areas of business specialization were clearly not expected to be garden cities, what were they? As dependent localities, nevertheless drawing traffic from throughout the larger metropolitan region, these subcenters—the heart of Bartholomew, Olmsted, and Cheney's decentralization proposals—would have been quite familiar in 1920s America. They were not limited to professional planners' theories: they were suburbs. They were primarily residential districts on the urban outskirts, attached to small commercial districts of minor import or specialized function supplementing—but by no means supplanting—the central business district. Essentially, then, these outside planners saw decentralization as another term for suburbanization.

Here was a case not only of traffic hysteria hijacking momentum for more basic structural reforms, but of fundamental confusion about the very terms of such reform. During the 1920s, there was basic and unacknowledged disagreement about the meanings of key terms such as *decentralization*. Obviously, like Los Angeles's downtown businessmen, many eastern planning professionals thought of decentralization in far different terms than did the city's planning experts. Decentralization represented for many mainstream planners not a fundamental reorganization of the contemporary American city but a continuation of long-term trends toward suburban development. In the view of many professionals—Bartholomew, Olmsted, and Cheney obviously among them—cities had become too concentrated. Under proper supervision, these congested areas might be encouraged to spread out a bit, perhaps like they had when the streetcar reigned supreme.[104] At heart, then, these eastern planners still clung to the essentials of the concentric model of urbanism. As a consequence, though the consulting board urged in its report that some nonessential business activities be delegated to peripheral neighborhood commercial centers, it was fundamentally unwilling to cede the ultimate preeminence of the central business district. For these decentralizers, dealing with the traffic problem downtown was not merely a matter of preserving the growth and economy of the region; they felt they were rescuing the city itself—which for them was still synonymous with downtown: "The concentration of business, as previously indicated, is responsible for much present congestion. Concentration of business is more or less necessary and desirable."[105] In the eyes of the consulting board, although reducing population density was an admirable goal, a city without a healthy and discrete urban core would soon fall into confusion and chaos.

Obviously, this understanding was fundamentally different from that envisioned by Los Angeles's planners. The source of the confusion was a disjuncture in urban metaphorics: the groups envisioned different sorts of metropolises, but they did not fully recognize it at the time. They both sought urban legibility by instituting a clear diagrammatic order for the existing topography, but they had entirely different ideal conceptual maps in mind. Bartholomew, Olmsted, and Cheney held to the traditional map of urban form, which posed concentric circles of increasingly suburban development around a central core (figure 4). Southern Californian regional planners, by contrast, modeled their urban imagination and their visions of the ideal future metropolis on the famous diagrams offered by Ebenezer Howard of the garden city cluster (figure 7), which, although similarly circular, was by no means centralizing. The two maps defined very different notions of modern urban form, and they largely determined the sort of city that these divergent cadres of planners would attempt to construct. These maps formed the blueprints for the planners' work, and the two groups were essentially working from entirely different sets of plans.

Ultimately, although the outside planners were willing to contemplate under the philosophy of "decentralization" a mild decrease in overall urban density, they certainly had no intention of abandoning the concentric city altogether. In this respect, the planners were representative not only of the consensus within the profession but of the dominant mindset in American culture during the early twentieth century. In the end, these experts simply could not take seriously visions of garden cities. The maps in which Southern Californian planners saw the promise of radically deconcentrated ideal urban topographies were, in the eyes of these eastern experts, at best simply representations of abstract theory. At worst, the maps were pure fantasy. No real city could be constructed from that vision, and no conurbation designated to be constructed—or reconstructed—in accordance with such a model could ever be considered modern. In fact, the results of such a program of development might not even merit being called a city.

As responsible professionals, then, the Traffic Commission's consulting board of planners felt an obligation to assist Los Angeles, through its *Major Traffic Street Plan,* in developing not some sort of utopian mixture of urbanism and pastoralism but a real modern metropolis. And in the 1920s just about everyone in the country knew exactly what that meant.

3

Imagining the Metropolis in a Modern Age

In the 1920s most Americans shared a clearly defined and well-elaborated notion of modern urbanity that had nothing to do with pastoral garden cities and everything to do with steel, glass, and concrete. This common sense image of the contemporary city was defined in large part by the striking growth of traditional American metropolises during the period. These cities, most notably Chicago and New York, had undergone a series of transformations in the early twentieth century that seemed to point the way toward the urban future. Their example provided a coherent urban model—a hegemonic model to which the development of Los Angeles was directly opposed, in the eyes of many observers (including those eastern consultants brought in to draft the *Major Traffic Street Plan*).

If Los Angeles in the 1920s was desperately trying to become the city of the twentieth century, Chicago had already achieved recognition as a full-fledged modern metropolis. It was not that long ago, though, that Chicago had been more closely associated with the broad midwestern prairie than with modern urbanity. Especially prior to the 1871 fire, Chicago seemed like a natural extension of the farmland that anchored its economy: it had been (with disastrous consequences) predominantly a wooden city, constructed of the timber of the great Wisconsin forests; it had been a flat city, arrayed along the railroad lines that fed its industry; it had been a working-class city, building its wealth on commodity processing more than on financial manipulation. After the fire, however, Chicago's boosters—worthy rivals to their Southern Californian counterparts—had helped remake the metropolis in modern form, spawning innovations in the architecture of iron and structural steel and concentrating the city's commercial activity in a rebuilt downtown, known as "the Loop." This reinvention culminated in the Columbian Exposition of

1893, where Chicago announced itself as a world city and a metropolis of the future. Through the promise of the fair's "White City," Chicago offered a vision of urbanity without slums or decay, harmonious and balanced in its planning. Spawning the genesis of the tremendously influential City Beautiful movement, Chicago's exposition immediately imbued Chicago with the aura of futuristic urbanity.

MODERN CHICAGO

I have struck a city—a real city—and they call it Chicago.

RUDYARD KIPLING, *FROM SEA TO SEA* (2:139)

The White City represented Chicago's idyllic potential of gracious, composed, ordered urbanism, but the Loop signified the city's bustling and hectic reality. As the Chicago School sociologist Harvey W. Zorbaugh described it in his famous urban study, *The Gold Coast and the Slum,*

> In the [Chicago] river's southward bend lies the Loop, its skyline looming toward Lake Michigan. The Loop is the heart of Chicago, the knot in the steel arteries of elevated structure which pump in a ceaseless stream the three millions of population of the city into and out of its central business district. The canyon-like streets of the Loop rumble with the traffic of commerce. On its sidewalks throng people of every nation, pushing unseeingly past one another, into and out of office buildings, shops, theaters, hotels, and ultimately back to the north, south, and west "sides" from which they came.[1]

Whereas the marble columns and decorated façades of the Columbian Exposition suggested a nostalgic neoclassical renaissance, the industrial iron of the Loop delivered a very different, very contemporary urban grandeur. Massive fixed-rail transportation systems encircled this downtown district; the Loop was literally defined by its interurban infrastructure. These elevated trains held the city's suburbs in a tight embrace much as the freight railroad had long laid the great midwestern prairie at Chicago's doorstep. The hub of the interurban transit system thus precisely coincided with the hub of the metropolis's radial settlement—the Loop was the epicenter of the Chicago image of modern urbanity.

The huge metropolitan zone was rendered onto its central district not only by the rail transit but by a rigid grid system of streets. Born out of the Northwest Ordinance of 1787, as William Cronon tells us in his brilliant *Nature's Metropolis,* this elaborate system of subdividing land into precise and identical squares had proven a powerful technology for Chicago's dominance of its hinterland: "During Chicago's land craze of the 1830s, the grid turned the prairie into a commodity, and became the foundation for all subsequent land use."[2] This same system for ordering the landscape produced, by the beginning of the twentieth century, an imposing crosshatched system of roads emanating in three directions from the downtown hub, broken only by the waters of Lake Michigan. Just as the technology of the grid had facilitated Chicago's transformation of the prairie into property, and thus of the midwestern plains into the city's domain, so the gridiron street system organized peripheral settlement in relation to the Loop. And all Chicago existed in relation to this vital center, as Zorbaugh knew: "The city's conquest of the prairie has proceeded stride for stride with the development of transportation. The outskirts of the city have always been about forty-five minutes from the heart of the Loop."[3]

In contrast to Los Angeles's planners, Chicago's planning experts, who were given much authority after the success of the 1893 World's Fair, sought to create a highly centralized metropolis by ensuring the coherence and legibility of this downtown district. They were given broad authority to maintain the proper relationship between center and periphery in this growing metropolis. Consequently, the Loop came to anchor the entire urban region: "Apace with the expansion of the city has gone the ascendancy of the Loop. Every development in transportation, drawing increasing throngs of people into the central business district, has tended to centralize there not only commerce and finance, but all the vital activities of the city's life."[4] As a result of this centralizing impetus, the grid system of streets around the Loop eventually became highly congested, much as they had in Los Angeles by 1920. Also like the far western city, the midwestern metropolis took decisive steps to solve its traffic problem. Chicago's solution, however, was nothing like that being debated in Southern California at the time. This city thrived on its density and had little ambivalence about its centralized downtown district. Although the city had once been flat and pastoral, twentieth-century Chicago had no use for visions of idyllic garden cities. Consequently, Daniel Burnham's Chicago Plan envisioned a scheme of high-density thoroughfares capable of carrying all the traffic that should rightfully flow into the central business district. With faith in Chicago's industrial power and confidence that the Loop needed radical thinking to reconcile it with the automobile, the city's planners foresaw the need to construct a level for additional traffic raised on piers above these crosstown roads, similar to that being designed in bridges of the period. The obvious inspiration for the double-decking plan, though, was clearly the elevated railroads. The automobile would be treated similarly to the interurban train, as both served the same purpose: bringing the masses into central Chicago. As R. Stephen Sennott notes in "Chicago Architects and the Automobile, 1906–1926," the double-decked Wacker Drive was the epitome of modernity: "Completed in 1926 after designs by [Edward] Bennett, Wacker Drive replaced produce markets and a narrow South Water Street to form a major, new east-west thoroughfare."[5] Chicagoans were proud of their ingenuity in solving the traffic problem. In 1920, they seemed willing to approve the huge expenditures necessary to construct an elaborate system for bringing the automobile to the city's hub. In the course of the decade, city planners sought to develop new architectural structures to accommodate the vehicles. The chief of the City Plan Commission at the time, Eugene Taylor, described the way the city intended to manage streams of automobiles on the new roads to resolve the traffic problem: "Michigan Avenue and Wacker Drive—both two-level streets—were the first double-deck thoroughfares of which we know that were provided for the purpose of segregating conflicting streams of traffic and of separating on the same street rapid-moving, light vehicles from slow-moving, heavy, commercial vehicles."[6] Likewise, Sennott discusses the construction of several large downtown buildings designed with interior parking garage levels, conveniently integrated into the larger grid street system. Wacker Drive and the new Jewelers Building of 1926 were constructed in concert, with direct connections between the new thoroughfare and the building's interior automotive parking areas (served by an automobile-sized freight elevator).

The transportation infrastructure of this modern city was clearly visible, and it was unified. Multideck transit and multilevel buildings were integrated and woven together in the urban fabric of the Loop. The elevated roadway and the elevated interurban served to buttress the structural base of the downtown district and to intensify its built-up character. Both Wacker Drive and the railroad loop manifested urbanity in depth, reveling in the play of multiple levels and the use of the vertical plane in downtown development.

VERTICAL CHICAGO

By day the skyscraper looms in the smoke and sun and has a soul. Prairie and valley, streets of the city, pour people into it and they mingle among its twenty floors and are poured again back to the streets, prairies and valleys.
CARL SANDBURG, "SKYSCRAPER"

Verticality was consistent with the traditions of the indigenous Chicago School of architecture. From the 1890s, the city's builders—including Louis Sullivan, John Root, Dankmar Adler, and Daniel Burnham—had sought to construct taller and taller buildings to make the best use of the prestigious downtown real estate and equally to magnify the reputations of both their clients and their city (and incidentally themselves in this age of celebrity architects and builders). Revolutionary innovations like structural frames of steel and iron served to lift a building higher than was possible with load-bearing masonry walls. Indeed, as Cronon notes, "By the time of the World's Fair, Chicago had become famous for the height of its downtown office buildings."[7] This development continued in the city, and by 1920, Chicago's downtown was becoming more and more centralized, more and more built up (see figure 19). It seemed that every permutation of modern technology during the era contributed to the city's densely concentrated verticality: "The development of communication has further tightened the Loop's grip on the life of the city. The telephone has at once enormously increased the area over which the central business district can exert control and centralized that control. The newspaper, through the medium of advertising, has firmly established the supremacy of

FIGURE 19. Chicago's sublime Loop, 1930s. Courtesy of the International Historical Press Photo Collection of Sveriges Television (SVT) AB, Stockholm.

the Loop and, through the news, focused the attention of the city upon the Loop."[8] Instead of decentralizing, as some theorists expected, the new electrical devices of early twentieth-century society seem to have further concentrated the traditional metropolis. In effect, these technologies magnified the range and reach of the large city.

Zorbaugh is clear, though, that it is the tall building that serves as the definitive token of all this manifest modernity: "The skyscraper is the visible symbol of the Loop's domination of the city's life. . . . The skyscraper, thrusting the Loop skyward thirty, forty, fifty stories, has made possible an extraordinary centralization and articulation of the central business district of the modern city. Drawing thousands daily into the heart of the city, where the old type of building drew hundreds, the cluster of skyscrapers within the Loop has become the city's vortex."[9]

Fittingly, the decisive measure of Chicago's urban modernity arrived in 1922 not with the introduction of a new device but with a call to the imagination. The occasion was a contest sponsored by Chicago's leading newspaper: "The competition's programme was simple and enigmatic: 'To erect the most beautiful and distinguished office building in the world is the desire of *The Tribune.*'"[10] And this sky-scraper would be located right off Wacker Drive, in the heart of the Loop. As Paul Goldberger has observed, "The competition turned out to be one of the great architectural events of the early part of the century, something of a world's fair of skyscraper design."[11] Much public attention focused not only on the eventual victorious design, by John Mead Howells and Raymond Hood, but on the many and diverse runners-up, including the striking conception submitted by Eliel Saarinen, "which called for a stepped-back central tower, its masses soaring upward like mountains."[12] This competition was taken, both at the time and since, as a demonstration of the potential of modern construction technology. Beneath the dreams of Howells and Hood's neo-Gothic tower (complete with flying buttresses), Saarinen's futuristic streamlined form, and the dozens of other imaginative designs, lay the foundations of both a new architecture and a new urbanism. Represented in the competition was the range of state-of-the-art thinking about how to render verticality. The challenge of conceptualizing the proper representational form of great height was considerable and largely lacking in useful precedent, and it looked to be a blueprint for the future—an urban future that was decidedly vertical. By the 1920s, as the *Chicago Tribune* competition and the Loop both demonstrated, modern urbanity was inextricably linked in the mainstream imagination with the tall building. Clearly, the skyscraper was the material in which urban architects and builders sought to cast their notions of modernity.

LOOKING BACKWARD ON THE MODERN METROPOLIS

Simply glancing upward at the tall skyscrapers of the modern city filled many observers with awe. The superelevated tall buildings could seem nothing short of utopian. Indeed, the developed city of the era was very much the equal of the futuristic visions of previous years, at least in superficial physical appearance. And this appearance proved fundamental to the power of the urban vision during an age so enamored of the tall city. Yet how can we now capture the sense of wonder of urban observers when viewing the modern metropolis for the first time? As it happens, cultural representation of the period abounds with this experience. This theatrical display—the first vista of the urban skyline—became a much rehearsed, even archetypal, scene in narratives of urban representation. Let's for a moment look back at one of those narratives—Edward Bellamy's influential tract from the end of the nineteenth century—to trace the significance of that glimpsed skyline of the early twentieth.

Bellamy follows a grand tradition of presenting his utopian vision in the context of science fiction. He also participates in the convention of many utopian writers of his era of presenting future society through the encapsulating device of a particular metropolis of tomorrow, a city on the hill. Bellamy's protagonist, Julian West, awakes from a hypnotic sleep in the year 2000, 113 years after shutting his eyes. The trajectory of his coming into knowledge about the society into which he has emerged is significant and familiar. West awakes in a sleeping chamber of the future, but it does not reveal anything about this brave new world. Indeed, as is customary in this sort of narrative, the (time-)traveler is at first incredulous when informed of his present (temporal) location. Consequently, after receiving the peculiar news and "feeling partially dazed," he swiftly falls back asleep (after drinking a "cup of some sort of broth" offered by his twentieth-century host and tour guide, Dr. Leete). He awakes again, this time a mere twelve hours later, with a renewed suspicion that the previous night's revelations have all been "some elaborate practical joke."[13] West then looks in a mirror and finds himself unchanged—"The face I saw was a face to a hair and a line and not a day older than the one I had looked at as I tied my cravat . . . one hundred and thirteen years before"[14]—further fueling his doubt. What dispels this skepticism? What convinces the practical, rational, and scientific-minded traveler of his bizarre new context? As Dr. Leete confirms, it is only the urban visage that can prove what mere words cannot: "Since I cannot convince you, you shall convince yourself. Are you strong enough to follow me upstairs?" He is, and West follows as Dr. Leete "led the way up two flights of stairs and then up a shorter one, which landed us upon a belvedere on the house-top"—and for the first time West surveys the whole of the modern metropolis. Once exposed to this urban vista from the rooftop belvedere, he can no longer doubt the displacement: he is forced to recognize, to come to terms with, to convince himself of his new temporal position. The skeptical Julian West finally cannot maintain his (common sense) illusions "with the city beneath and around us."[15]

   Looking Backward effectively triangulates its protagonist to situate him in the narrative and in the changed social reality. First, it presents West's unchanged physical state (through the mirror); second, and most dramatically, it reveals the altered larger social structure through the view from the belvedere; and lastly, almost as a reassuring footnote, it affirms a familiar bourgeois domestic sphere of unchanged gender norms in Dr. Leete's "roomy apartment" ("Let us descend into the house; I want to introduce my wife and daughter to you").[16] Of the three locating or identifying coordinates, only the viewed city (Boston) has changed. That panoramic urban skyline stands in for the sweeping societal changes that Bellamy advocates and describes. The future is urban, and it is represented in the façade of the metropolis. The grand structure of the futuristic society is undeniably brought home by this brief visual survey of the metropolis; an entire social world is represented by the skyline of a single contemporary city. In other words, the essence of a society is embedded in its representative cityscape. Thus the significance of this representative scene: the revelation of Boston from the balcony both establishes West's physical location (geographical and temporal) and interpellates him into the new social order.[17] This act of fixing location is essentially visual; it occurs through the protagonist's (initially skeptical) gaze. It follows that Bellamy does not have West locate himself by going out and exploring his surroundings on foot. Instead, he and Dr. Leete sit in "easy chairs" on their elevated vantage and "take in" the city below, while the doctor didactically lays out the social structure in detail. In fact, an impromptu (and unguided) exploratory stroll around the streets of the metropolis the next day leaves West again confused and disoriented;[18] it is only by means of this comprehensive vista that the urban observer can properly and reassuringly situate himself in his world. Clearly, the dominant urban perceptual ideologies of the late nineteenth and early twentieth centuries ensure that the rational, totalizing gaze—whether of the scientific planner or the fantastic utopian tourist—is the privileged means of perceiving urban society.[19] Further, as I have suggested, Bellamy's definitive expository device—the revelation of the city from a vantage point—recurs in countless utopian and realistic narratives of the era. Tourists definitively locate themselves in time and in narrative reality by visually placing themselves in the city in relation to an exemplary skyline. In this logic, determinations of urban coordinates underwrite and guarantee larger temporal and perceptual determinations. The prominent skyline of the modern metropolis, as viewed from an elevated vantage point, presents to the traveler or observer self-evident proof of the reality of the utopian world, as well as a precise location in that world. The raised observation point thus allows simultaneously a comprehensive vision of the city and a full appreciation of the vertiginous interplay between the subjective disorientation of (implausible) time travel and the solid, fixed, unquestionable monumentality of the toweringly vertical better world of the future.

NEW YORK CITY AND REPRESENTATIONS
OF SKYSCRAPER URBANISM

> But one day, crossing the ferry
> With the great towers of Manhattan before me,
> Out at the prow with the sea wind blowing,
> I had been wearying many questions
> Which she had put on to try me:
> How shall I be a mirror to this modernity?
>
> WILLIAM CARLOS WILLIAMS, "THE WANDERER:
> A ROCOCO STUDY"

Bellamy's vision is part of a long and varied tradition of utopian urban representation, and as such, it is fairly representative of the genre—particularly in its revelation of the future city.[20] Yet *Looking Backward*'s utopian Boston is quite unusual in not being overwhelmingly dominated by skyscrapers; Bellamy's future is urban and his city is tall, but not as obsessively vertical as most.[21] By the early years of the twentieth century, an urban utopia would seem odd indeed if it were not composed of seemingly limitless towers. In the resolutely modern age of the 1920s, of Chicago's Loop and its paradigmatic towers, the city in popular representation became little more than a menagerie of skyscrapers. And this radically new landscape of towers prompted powerful flashes of recognition in urban observers of this period. This vista was, in combined effect, fully as powerful an image as that of the reconfigured Boston witnessed by Julian West.

Social critics of the time were fully aware of the novelty and power of the collective urban tableau.[22] Beginning in the 1890s, the term *skyline* came into increasing currency, conveying the cumulative and singular power of the massed forms of skyscrapers so characteristic of lower Manhattan by the end of the nineteenth century.[23] In fact, it was through this skyline that New York City came to dominate cultural representations of the metropolis: for all Chicago's enthusiasms and innovations, it was New York that redefined urbanism as resolutely vertical. As Paul Goldberger puts it,

> The notion of height was to become the overriding image of New York City in the years after 1900, and thus, by extension, the image of all American cities growing to maturity. The idea that a city is primarily an agglomeration of small- to medium-sized buildings, made urban by their closeness, was pushed aside by the coming of the skyscraper, and Americans began to define urbanity on the basis of size. A city showed its might by how many buildings it had and how many people were in it, and, more to the point, by how big these buildings could be made to be.[24]

By the end of the 1920s, New York had at least five times the number of tall buildings as did Chicago, its nearest rival in this regard.[25] Gradually, New York City became the symbol of modern urbanism; Manhattan became synecdochical for the entire metropolis, and its downtown skyline came to represent the essence of Manhattan.

Soon the image of the lower Manhattan skyline took on almost mystical properties. This representational trend held not just in utopian fiction but also in the visual arts. Art historian Merrill Schleier writes that "the New York skyline was perceived as among the most breathtaking of man-made wonders,"[26] adding that artists of the early twentieth century began to see the huge structures of the city as analogous to natural forms. Artist Joseph Pennell enthused that "the towering splendor of New York is one of the marvels of the world. The mind can only grope afterwards to express its proportions."[27] Schleier notes that in one painting the artist "situated the buildings among swirling, cataclysmic cloud formations, suggesting that their dramatic breadth was equal to the power of nature."[28] In this way, the painter sought to situate the modern skyline within the context of canonical representations of natural beauty and grandeur. Such twentieth-century representations of skyscrapers drew upon the work of nineteenth-century American landscape painters like Thomas Cole and Frederic Edwin Church. Likewise, a new school of urban artists—including the painter John Sloan, the architectural renderer Hugh Ferriss, and many artists not usually known as urban painters, such as Georgia O'Keeffe[29]—looked to nature for representational language, evoking a quasi-religious aura in their portrayals of the skyscraper city. Yet, as nostalgic and academic as these painters might be in contextualizing the skyscraper within the long tradition of American landscape art, they were celebrating structures that were unquestionably new. Although they relied upon long-established techniques of representing grandeur, these artists were obsessed with the modernity of their subjects. They sought to relate the modern and human-made to a classical tradition of representing the awe-inspiring.

A new school of urban photographers likewise reveled in portraying the monumentality of the skyscraper metropolis. As Thomas Bender has argued, these photographers strove to capture a shadow of the future in the "architecture of modern corporate power." Like that of the painters, theirs was primarily a "visual city," a monumental city, usually devoid of human presence. The sheer lines of the buildings and their massed forms drew photographers toward skewed lines of sight and expressionistic angles. Alfred Stieglitz, probably the most famous of the New York photographers of the age, pioneered such portrayals. His later pictures, like those of his contemporaries Edward Steichen and Lewis Hine (though it was certainly not his intention), reduced the skyscraper to an icon or symbol. In this way, the photographers, despite their use of very different technologies of image production, essentially joined the diverse group of painters in associating the urban skyline with the symbolic and mystical.[30] Indeed, as Robert Stern, Gregory Gilmartin, and Thomas Mellins argue in their monumental architectural history, *New York 1930*, "For Stieglitz, as for O'Keeffe, the city had come to represent the unification of nature and artifice, its skyscrapers looming like sheer cliffs above dark chasms."[31] The same representational logic—associating built forms with natural sights—animated all these self-consciously artistic portrayals of the vertical metropolis.

For all the cultural production presenting the tall building and the skyline as objects of high aesthetic and symbolic value, images of the skyscraper did not circulate only in museums. Indeed, visual representation of the tall urban structures provided a broad, often populist, shared discourse in the era. If, at least implicitly, painters and photographers presented the urban street as an art gallery and the skyscraper as a work of art, the images familiar to most urban residents were considerably less ambitiously or self-consciously artistic. In fact, the form of the modern skyscraper was most widely circulated in ostensibly objective urban depiction. In magazines, newspapers, and the increasingly ubiquitous picture postcards of the 1920s, the urban skyscraper predominated as the embodiment of modern progress.

Perhaps most striking in this respect were the famous *King's Views* of Manhattan and Brooklyn. Beginning back in 1891, Moses King began producing a series of tour guides depicting New York City, and later the United States as a whole. These "handbooks" were lavishly illustrated, furnished both with line drawings and, increasingly, with photographs. By 1896, King had spun these pictorial features of his guide books off into separate paperback collections of views of the modern city. As A. E. Santaniello notes in the preface to a recent reprinting of *King's Views,* these cheap and accessible picture books became an instant publishing sensation:

> The 1896 volume appeared at a most opportune time: the unparalleled growth of the new city [was] matched by the extraordinary interest in photography and the perfection of techniques that made rapid and inexpensive reproduction possible. The books sold in the hundreds of thousands because they could be cheaply produced in that quantity. King's formula for success was followed throughout the series, in the same folio-size format: hundreds of photographs with full captions explaining the vital (i.e., financial) statistics of the building and its function, views of single buildings and monuments juxtaposed with more animated portraits of city street scenes.[32]

Most New Yorkers and quite a few other Americans thought of Gotham in terms of these popular representations of iconic buildings.

The typical edition of *King's Views* begins with a series of vistas—usually two to the page, reproduced lengthwise across the oversized pages—of New York's skyline from different vantage points (see figure 20). In this way, the guides attempt both to give a cumulative overview of structures later pictured individually (somewhat in the form of an academic yearbook headed by a class picture) and to introduce the metropolis to the observer in a manner analogous to the way the tourist might ideally first sight the city. Following these expository metaphors, the guidebooks then proceed with a series of pages depicting New York's bridges, the notable ocean liners serving its docks, some of the river islands or quays, the Statue of Liberty, and a traditional "bird's-eye view" elevated-perspective map—all in an order that varied from edition to edition but preserved the essential elements. Through this progression of images, often spread over as many as ten pages, *King's Views* introduced the vicarious tourist to the city through its coastal structures; indeed, the *Views* portrayed the city *as* a network of structures. The metropolis could clearly only be depicted iconically, by the grandeur of its works of iron and steel.

The great majority of King's pages were, of course, dedicated to the representation of skyscrapers. A large, often full-page, image of a single building was the *Views'* standard presentation, the exemplary profile of the building accompanied only by a factual caption. In early editions, such as those of the 1890s, these captions were basic and brief, noting only the name and location of the depicted structure. In the later, more popular editions, though, the captions became more and more breathless, chock full of statistical data:

> WOOLWORTH BUILDING, Broadway, Barclay St. to Park Pl.; tallest building in the world, 55 stories, 792 ft. high; begun 1910, completed April, 1913; plot, 152 × 197 ft., cost $4,500,000; foundations, with caissons 19 ft. in diameter sunk to bed rock 110 to 130 ft. below sidewalk, cost $1,000,000; building, about $8,000,000; main building

FIGURE 20. New York's skyline, 1915. From Moses King, *King's Views of New York* (New York: Moses King, 1915), 35.

29 stories; tower, 86 × 84 ft., 36 stories above main building; light on top visible 96 miles at sea; stores and arcade on ground floor; Irving National Exchange Bank on first floor; built by F. W. Woolworth.[33]

Small notations above this caption and directly under the image noted the precise coordinates of the building by indicating adjacent points of reference in the picture: "Mail St. . . . Federal Building . . . Astor House . . . St. Paul's . . . Barclay St." and so forth. Also serving as reference points, ant-like street-level pedestrians at the base of the building testify to the height of the tower above. Indeed, although this particular image is a sketch—attributed to the Woolworth Company, and thus something of a publicity still—in about half of *King's Views* the building in question was actually photographed. In these photos, tiny passersby are often hand-painted into the image, if none was already present in the frame, to establish the building's superhuman scale.

The artifice of such crude visual manipulations—which are more subtle but still present in later editions of the guidebooks—testifies to the way *King's Views* continually straddle the representational boundaries between veridical depiction and artistic license. In these images, the referent is the solid and monumental building, its substance and authority legitimated both by the precise coordinates (i.e., its location within the indisputably real city) and by the numerical data of its structural dimensions, physical, temporal, and financial. Given the *Views'* abiding faith in the solidity and materiality of their subject matter, the books are free to play fast and loose with actual details of representation. Although photographs come fully into use in *King's Views* by the turn of the century, they never replaced sketches altogether. Although one might expect the new photographs to supplant older, less authoritative sketches, they assumed merely equivalent proportions within *King's Views* of the first two decades of the twentieth century. Throughout the books, sketches and photos are presented side by side, with no apparent distinction or notation—one would have to look closely to determine which was hand-drawn and which was "captured light." Clearly, the boundary between photo and sketch is fluid in these books of *Views,* especially when the photographs are often sketched on to elaborate or extend the images. And of course, the pictures are routinely framed and cropped to properly present the subject building. Often, in fact, the more important or famous buildings are drawn, not photographed, to more clearly depict the iconic form and accentuate the dominant verticality of the structure. In the representational logic operative here, the hand of the architectural renderer can produce a truer impression of the building's vital attributes and its grandeur than can a potentially deceptive photograph. The aesthetic of pure representation does not seem to apply in these *Views,* for there is no apparent effort to refrain from "doctoring" the photographs. These representational manipulations in effect accentuate the authority and materiality of the depicted structures.

King's Views' overriding priority in depicting New York's buildings is to properly present their verticality, immensity, and grandeur. A typical example of the representational logic at work here is the image of the Equitable Building in the 1915
edition (see figure 21). This picture demonstrates the lengths to which King's artists
went to compensate for an inherent problem in the book's format. In the *Views,*
buildings are presented in regularized picture-boxes, either one or two to the page.
This mode of representation effectively frames the iconic image and makes each
skyscraper fully recognizable, but in the process it elides a critical piece of information. In this depiction, it is impossible (short of counting stories) to tell at a glance
which buildings are taller in absolute terms. This lost relative scale is vital, as skyscrapers were generally esteemed, in the captions and layout of the book and among
observers generally, for their vertical height. Likewise, it is the difference in height—
with some more notable skyscrapers towering over more lowly buildings—that gives
the skyline views their drama. Yet, by presenting each building at the same size to
fill the standard frame, all sense of scale is lost. Each building seems to be pretty
much the same size.

This image of the Equitable Building reveals the books' solution to this problem. Using a set of representational manipulations and distortions, *King's Views*
manage to convey the exemplary height of the subject structure. First, the adjacent
buildings—the American Exchange National Bank on our left and the American
Surety Company on our right—are made much darker than the Equitable; in effect,
they seem to retreat in shadow. Indeed, whereas the Equitable Building is bathed
in light, even its cavernous interior court seemingly well lit, the neighboring buildings lurk in the skyscraper's shade. Even the sky around the cornice of the Equitable brightens, producing an aura, almost a halo, around the top of the tower—so
close to the divine is this building.

Second, the Equitable Building is set impossibly forward in the image; the perspective of the drawing is skewed so as to more "truthfully" convey the imposing
quality of the exemplary structure. Due to the combination of forced perspective
and strategic shadowing, the Equitable seems to leap ahead of its neighbors. Its
massed form dominates the scene principally by contrast to the neighboring buildings. The third trick of the image is the representation of the street scene. The bustle of active urban life unfolds at the skyscraper's foundations, but it is a strangely
sedate bustle. The portrayed people appear to be strolling, promenading, rather than
hurrying about their business. They are all well dressed (better than in contemporary photographed street scenes). Likewise, the streetcars and other street vehicles
occupy only a small fraction of the available street area, and they too are pristine.
Broadway is impossibly wide and empty in this depiction, its sidewalks much larger
than normal. The vantage point from which we observe the scene is similarly impossible—we are too far back. In actuality, another skyscraper would crowd the
scene, blocking this point of view. In this picture, though, the frontage space of the

FIGURE 21. The dignified and iconic Equitable Building, 1915. From Moses King, *King's Views of New York* (New York: Moses King, 1915), 35.

Equitable Building is free and clear. As a result, while this may seem a busy street, it is certainly not a crowded or hectic one. There is no traffic congestion in these streets, no press of the urban multitude on the sidewalks. The stately Equitable Building presides over a calm and controlled scene below, bringing light and gracious, if monumental, order to the entire tableau. This building does not merely tower over its neighbors, it presides over the block.

The array of representational manipulations served a primary end: *King's Views* presented the tall building as a sort of fetish. The commodity form of the view books mirrored the commoditized images contained within. Here, the skyscraper was effectively compacted for mass consumption—reduced to folio size, to two dimensions, to ink on pulp. The massive skyscraper became a miniature souvenir of itself. Like the popular picture postcards that advertised to the far reaches of the nation the tourist's appreciation for the massive structures, *King's Views* translated and circulated the urban tower as a convenient and portable image that could be admired and owned as an object of value, both conveying the grandeur of the original and serving as a little objet d'art. King's chapbooks trafficked in the currency of modern urbanism, allowing the consumer to possess a token of these edifices that were so fundamentally the product of massively coordinated labor and concentrated corporate capitalism. Through such representation, modern architecture appropriated connotations of the sacral (much as cathedrals and monuments long had done), endowing these structures of steel and glass with a personality that might at first glance seem antithetical to their mode of industrial, interchangeable mass construction.

In effect, representations such as those by modern painters, avant-garde photographers, and especially the best-selling *King's Views* did not just inflate the reputation of these tall buildings, advertising particular towers as exemplary forms and famous examples and thus making them instantly recognizable; it also—ironically enough—gave the form of the skyscraper an aura of originality through its mass circulation of mechanical representations. When visitors first witnessed a specific Manhattan skyscraper or the increasingly famous city skyline, they were not seeing the image for the first time. As a result of this ubiquitous visual discourse, an inevitable and characteristic flash of recognition filled local and tourist alike with a powerful sense of awe and an appreciation of the object's aura of grandeur.

The modern city's paradigmatic scene, the initial revelation of the massed skyscrapers as one approached the city, was repeated innumerable times in Jazz Age literature and became a primary trope in representations of travel to the great metropolis. Even such an irritable and cynical urban observer as the expatriate Henry James was struck, against his will, by the scene. As he tells it in *American Scene,* the skyline stands as an irreverent imitation of nature, a travesty of human ambition and impermanence: "You see the pin-cushion in profile, so to speak, on passing between Jersey City and Twenty-third Street, but you get it broadside on, this loose nosegay of architectural flowers, if you skirt the Battery, well out, and embrace the whole plantation. Then the 'American beauty,' the rose of interminable stem, becomes the token of the cluster at large. . . . They are simply the most piercing notes in that concert of the expensively provisional into which your supreme sense of New York resolves itself."[34] Soon, though, James begins to concede the strange, striking power of this exemplary skyline. These structures, although "grossly tall and grossly ugly" are indisputably modern: "The sky-scrapers and the league-long bridges, present and to come, marked the point where the age . . . had come out."[35] This produces in the writer a deep ambivalence and distrust, but also an uncontrollable, almost reflexive sense of wonder. The awesome modern vista defined the city and, as James himself recognized, could not be banished even from his own prose: "Yet was it after all that those monsters of the mere market, as I have called them, had more to say, on the question of 'effect,' than I had at first allowed?—since they are the element that looms largest for me through a particular impression, with remembered parts and pieces melting together rather richly now, of "down-town" seen and felt from the inside."[36] Here we can feel the allure of this paradigmatic moment of recognition, as well as the obviously irresistible pleasure evoked in its repetition, in recapitulating or reenacting that crystalline instant of first sighting the cityscape. Clearly, if Henry James could not resist being drawn to this image, there could certainly be no hope for the mass of tourists, who maintained less reserved detachment than he. Most enthusiastic visitors to the vertical city were simply overwhelmed by the grandeur they witnessed, immediate converts to what James terms derisively "the great religion of the Elevator."[37] Time and time again these urban observers struggled to put their emotions into words.

Although this discourse is ubiquitous, one more example should suffice to transmit the power of this compulsion to express the characteristic epiphany of visuality: "When a writer tackles such a big theme as New York he as a rule fetches a deep breath in the lower bay, steams as far as Staten Island, and then lets loose the floodgate of adjectives. How the city looks as you enter it is the conventional point of attack. . . . The first peep of lower Manhattan, with its craggy battlements, its spires splintering the very firmament."[38]

As James Huneker tells us in his New Cosmopolis of 1915, this descriptive discourse had by the early years of the twentieth century become clichéd. Nevertheless, he is forced, self-consciously, to reenact the ritual of revelation. Note here as well the close correlation between topography and typography. Huneker's illustrative prose is precisely situated in the cityscape. In particular, the exemplary rhetorical trope of urban description is tightly linked to a particular experience (that moment of recognition, the first glimpse of the skyline) and with a particular space in the metropolitan area (that spot outside the city but within its sphere of visuality—here, the harbor from which one can see the skyline). Huneker's point of entry into the trope of the city is the recapitulation, in narrative, of the physical entry into the city's domain. Metaphor then once more connects skyscraper to nature, with the skyline ultimately emerging transcendent—"splintering the very firmament."

THE MODERN SUBLIME

The fog has gone.
The city has popped back and sprawls triumphantly into space.
For a moment it seems as if the city had sprung up in an hour.
Then its sturdy walls and business windows begin to mock at the memory
of the fog in my mind.
"Fogs do not devour us," they say. "We are the ones who do the devouring.
We devour fogs and people and days."

BEN HECHT, *1001 AFTERNOONS IN CHICAGO*

It seems that the average urban citizen could hardly hope to avoid exposure to these ubiquitous representations. But why this obsession with the image of the skyscraper and the vertical metropolis? Why did such a rich cultural discourse revolve around this architectural form in the first decades of the century? Such questions of representation are inseparable from the practical question architectural critics and urban historians have been posing since the skyscraper boom began: why did the skyscraper emerge as an urban architectural form in the first place? Luckily, the answer to both the representational and the architectural question may lie in the same terrain and may allow us to understand the cultural power exercised in the era by this dominant form of modern urbanity.

For a long time it was argued that the skyscraper was a purely utilitarian structure, arising from clear and unambiguous economic motivations. According to this reasoning, as the power of the corporation was consolidated and intensified in the late nineteenth and early twentieth centuries, concentrations of income and wealth were also consolidated. The result was the concentration of more and more income and wealth into fewer and fewer large corporations, almost all of which were, by the turn of the century, headquartered in Manhattan. Given that the borough is a finite and restricted island, this intensive demand drove land values skyward. Thus it would seem that corporations acted rationally in making use of new technologies (the elevator, structural steel framing, electrical lighting, and air circulation) to maximize the value of their expensive downtown real estate by building upward. Unfortunately, this argument has been pretty thoroughly demolished in recent years. As Mark Girouard put it in his respected *Cities and People,* "The land-shortage theory is superficially attractive. In New York, Wall Street was at the tip of an island; the centre of Chicago was hemmed into a small area by the river and the railway yards. But it does not, in fact, bear looking into."[39] If land shortage alone justified vertical construction, observers have long asked, why is it that most European cities—dense and crowded as they are—are devoid of tall buildings? David Nye concludes that "the high costs of building higher were not justified by rents, and many areas of Manhattan and Chicago were comparatively undeveloped when the first skyscrapers went up. There was still abundant space for more modest structures. In short, traditional economic factors do not account for a penchant for tall buildings."[40]

Our question remains: why the tall buildings in twentieth-century American metropolises? Dutch architectural historian Thomas A. P. van Leeuwen offers a subtle explanation based on analysis of the development of clustered towers in the Italian town of San Gimignano.[41] That city-state, now a mere tourist side trip from Florence, has often been cited as an example of medieval precedents for skyscraper construction, as it featured in its heyday no fewer than forty-seven stone towers. Yet, as van Leeuwen points out, land was not scarce in that minor Tuscan town. Clearly, high real estate values were not the cause of the construction. However, competition for status and recognition was fierce, and it was of primary importance to the lords of the city-state (who controlled large portions of the ample surrounding countryside) to be close to their rivals and to the center of the (very Machiavellian) civic life. Consequently, a relatively concentrated section of this tiny city was crowded with fortress towers, one upon the other. It was not scarce land that drove this congestion, but rather desire for manifest status combined with a drive to be where the action was. Concentration was its own engine of development, operating entirely on an internal, self-sustaining logic. As van Leeuwen similarly concludes about turn-of-the-century Manhattan, "Speculation and land debt were entirely relative and had little to do with absolute quantities. What counted was proximity. It was the amount of available propinquity that was scarce, and a propinquity shortage could be created anywhere"—regardless of the amount of available land.[42] What New York City had was a shortage not of land (there was plenty of undeveloped real estate within a few miles of downtown) but of vacant land directly adjoining existing skyscrapers. Moreover, the importance of relative proximity, driven by status competition as much as by anything else, explains the production in New York City of the characteristic cumulative skyline: skyscrapers attract other skyscrapers. Once a few are built, others inevitably follow. The reason corporations would choose to build any skyscrapers at all lies, ironically enough, in our earlier discussion of how these tall buildings were artistically portrayed—and it is also why generations of art historians and travelers have flocked to San Gimignano. These towers became associated in the popular imagination, perhaps through the circulation of iconic representations (such as *King's Views*), with what generations of cultural critics have termed "the sublime."

Encompassing notions of grandeur and distance, the concept of the sublime expresses the contrast between the viewing subject and the object viewed. Often referred to in relation to an observer's perception of a huge geological formation—a mountain, a canyon, or a waterfall, for example—the idea is built upon differences in scale—for example, from the merely human to the geographical. As such, the sublime invokes a shift of context, a stark juxtaposition of previously self-contained measures, and this shift necessarily implicates the observing subject. The contrast between the observed/observing self (the human subject measured as relatively tall or short, a matter of inches) and the mountain (again measured as relatively tall or short, this time delineated in hundreds, or even thousands of feet) brings a shock of recognition. These relative scales are, although discrete and previously uncompared, nevertheless capable of comparison. They are both, in this case, matters of size, and therefore commensurable—and it is the latent but previously unrecognized difference in absolute magnitude that is so impressive. The subject is incomprehensibly reduced in relative size and, at the same time, placed in relation to the gigantic. Consequently, the observer is forced literally to expand his or her horizons, while at the same time recognizing his or her relative insignificance. Conversely, just as the individual is reduced in scale, he or she, as discrete object in one-to-one comparison with, say, a mountain, is thereby elevated in ontological stature. The contrast simultaneously denigrates the observer and enlarges her or his sense of self. Further, with almost inevitable connotations of the relation between human and deity, the term also implies a (pantheistic) religious notion of the individual's place in relation to the divine. Put this way, as it often was in American understandings of the concept, the sublime can be understood as the metaphorical bridge between a discrete and miniscule individual observer and an immensely grand but inherently commensurable divine. The observer looks at the mountain (perceiving at the same time him or herself in relation to that peak) and grasps—in a breathtaking jolt of recognition—a bit of the relation between the mortal self and transcendent, immortal natural forces.[43]

This notion of the sublime explains much of the power of the urban skyline during this period. Americans in the decades immediately before and after the turn of the century were swept up by an enthusiasm for what Joseph J. Corn and Brian Horrigan call the "technological sublime." In their 1984 *Yesterday's Tomorrows*, Corn and Horrigan compare the impact of renderings of futuristic buildings to " 'the sublime' of eighteenth- and nineteenth-century painting in which mere mortals stand awestruck before the splendor of nature."[44] David Nye offers the most detailed and sustained recent historiographical application of this technological version of the sublime in his *American Technological Sublime*. Nye argues that the skyscraper of the 1920s was an exemplary manifestation of a mode of the technological sublime he terms the "geometrical sublime"—the sense of the sublime arising from a contrast in purely physical scale. The tall buildings of the period were powerfully resonant in the public imagination precisely because they evoked strong feelings of awe in the (in comparison tiny) observer. Although Nye does not analytically pursue the exact nature of the sublimity inherent in these modern towers, *American Technological Sublime* makes perfectly clear the effect (and the broad circulation)

of this emotionally charged trope: "The geometrical sublime came to be a dominant way of seeing and understanding the city after the First World War. During
the 1920s a series of exhibitions, magazine articles, displays in department stores,
and works of art manifested a public enthusiasm for the new buildings that Merrill
Schleier calls 'skyscraper mania.'"[45]

For Nye, tall buildings were important because they helped connect this powerful sensation of awe to the contemporary practice of urban architecture, lending to
the concept of the "modern" a bit of the aura of the sublime. Combined with a contemporary association of inventive mechanical progress with societal evolution—
the technological sublime—cultural forms defined as modern came to be seen as
both progressive and great. Progress and modernity were thus seen not only as desirable or current but almost sacred—once more, utopian (almost eschatological)
hopes were embedded in the contemporary obsession with progress. The implicit
teleology of these concepts lent an air of 'manifest destiny' to the skyscraper. Indeed, as Lewis Mumford observed during the period, "There is, it is true, one universal and accepted symbol of our period in America: the skyscraper."[46]

The close association of the skyscraper with these powerful concepts of progress
and modernity—notions animated by the geometrical sublime evoked by these
buildings' great size—guaranteed that some of this aura would accrue to the institution (almost always a large corporation) that built or owned the tower. There was
a strong incentive for companies to build skyscrapers, as they advertised the power
and health of the concern. The leading historian of advertising, Roland Marchand,
emphasizes the importance of this association, arguing that corporations early on
began to reinforce the symbolism of the buildings through their own produced images: "By the mid-1920s, a picture of a skyscraper (along with an airplane and a dirigible) had become the artist's shorthand for the concept 'modern.'"[47] Artistic representation and commercial propaganda reflected and reinforced the connections
between these awe-inspiring buildings and their owners. Ultimately, everyone recognized that "skyscrapers had symbolic uses as landmarks and icons of progress,"
and that these uses justified the enormous expense of their construction.[48]

GLIMPSING THE FUTURE
IN THE MODERN SKYSCRAPER

*For [Europeans] a city is, above all, a past; to [Americans] it is mainly a fu-
ture; what they like in the city is everything it has not yet become and everything it can be.*

JEAN-PAUL SARTRE, "AMERICAN CITIES" (119)

The distinction between modernity and notions of a utopian future sometimes
blurred during the 1920s. At times, the progressive notion of the modern was so
powerful that some observers began to anticipate the imminent apotheosis of the

metropolis—recast entirely in skyscrapers, as it seemed it soon would be—to a eu-topic promised land. From the perspective of contemporary metropolitan enthu-siasts, urban progress, written in steel and glass and concrete, apparently knew no bounds. Even the most imaginative visionaries were unable to outpace the concrete development of the modern metropolis. The city seemed to have caught up with the future.

By the 1920s, what most struck observers of New York City's skyline was not the proliferation of tall buildings—that had been going on for decades already—but the look of the new buildings. By this time a qualitative as much as a quantitative change was underway. In the eyes of many skyscraper enthusiasts, the new structures were more and more closely approaching an ideal form. Early New York skyscrapers, such as the 1913 Municipal Building, were solid, weighty structures, capped with over-hanging cornices and marked linear divisions between floors, which served to ac-centuate the horizontal elements of the building. The edifice echoed the plane of the ground in its design elements; despite its height, the Municipal Building clearly owed its inspiration to the measured and modest classicism of the Beaux-Arts tra-dition. Other skyscrapers of the period, such as the iconic Woolworth Building of the same year, perched campanile-like towers upon more traditionally boxy lower substructures. Even the turret of the Woolworth Building, which jutted out of the cube below, seemed almost nostalgic, relying on Germanic gothic elements for its aesthetic inspiration, as if the tower was the lantern of a medieval cathedral. In con-trast, newer developments, such as the Equitable Building—which was, as we saw, a *King's Views* favorite and was completed only a few years later—were more resolutely and uniformly vertical.

By the time of the 1924 Shelton Hotel, architects seemed to have grasped the lessons of the *Chicago Tribune* competition, and particularly the impact of Eliel Saarinen's famed entry proposal, which envisioned modernism in terms of a lin-ear, unapologetically bare design. The new structures of the 1920s were stripped of their ornate claddings, the massive structures pared of detail and ornament. Sky-scrapers were becoming more self-consciously vertical, and that verticality seemed synonymous with modernity.

Although today we tend to think of modern skyscraper design in terms of the postwar International Style glass boxes that followed the 1952 Lever Building, and it is tempting to think of the developments of the 1920s as a first movement toward these ultimately pared and antiseptic designs, the tall buildings of the Jazz Age were clearly not trying to strip off ornament merely in order to reveal the skyscraper as a pure rectilinear solid. They instead attempted to harness design to an ideological purpose. As a group, they conveyed an aesthetic of verticality, of suspended, frozen vertical movement. These towers of the late 1920s seem as if they were striving for even greater heights but were cast into stone in the midst of their ascent.

The apotheosis of this architectural trend arrived at the very end of the decade, in the landmark Chrysler Building. Here modern materials, such as stainless steel cladding, sheathe windows cast as arrows pointing skyward. The skyscraper tapers at its peak, further accentuating the dominant impression of verticality. As it tapers, the waves of archlike cladding—each course's arch becoming increasingly steep as the layers approach the top—dissolve into a needle-like spire. This was clearly a structure designed with a sense of movement in mind, and it was definitely a structure that fully participated in the contemporary visual aesthetic of modern design.

This twenty-year evolution—from Municipal Building to Chrysler Building— reinforced the notion in the metropolis, and among urban observers farther afield, that the skyscraper was developing according to its own progressive design logic. The built form of the tall building appeared to be approaching a physical manifestation of fantastic and ethereal values of pure verticality. These structures, their shapes circulated throughout the world by the mechanisms of urban portrayal that we have seen, began to realize a new synthesis of sheer size or scale (the geometrical sublime) and the potential for movement celebrated in the ideologies of progress and modernism during the era.

In the 1920s, the hegemonic vision of modernity encapsulated in the Manhattan skyline fully bound itself up with the "vertical sublime," a specifically urban version of Nye's geometrical sublime. In the 1920s, modern urbanism was increasingly associated with this vertical sublime, which undergirded much contemporary architectural development and energized the idealistic power of urban representation. As a result, the aesthetic of the vertical sublime gave the metropolis much of the aura of awesome grandeur that characterized it at the time—the city's twentieth-century heyday. The Chrysler Building and its cousins seemed to manifest an urban future in the process of becoming. It was a pure case of the blurring of fantasy and architectural reality in the Jazz Age metropolis.

PLANNING THE FUTURE
OF THE VERTICAL METROPOLIS

The Chrysler Building merely hinted at the entanglement of serious architectural urban planning with the aesthetic of the vertical sublime. The fullest extent of the hegemony of this ideology of modernism was revealed through contemporary discourse on traffic and congestion, for by the mid-1920s New York City was grappling with a crisis of automotive commuting. Buildings such as the Chrysler, ever more capacious and towering, concentrated enormous numbers of office workers in a circumscribed geographical space. These workers flooded into interurban railways and, increasingly, private automobiles for their diurnal trip to and from their Manhattan offices. This was the familiar pattern of the concentric, concentrated metropolis, and it led to gridlock on the city's streets fully as serious as that which paralyzed Los Angeles at the time. Some urban experts began to fear for the future of a metropolis that was ever more vertical. Street traffic in New York in the 1920s was already a serious civic problem; the construction of taller and taller buildings—inevitable progress—would only increase the load on already overburdened Manhattan streets. Yet, in this quintessentially modern city, as in most of urbanized America at the time, planning for the sort of purposefully low-rise and low-density decentralization advocated by futurists in Southern California was unthinkable—it was apostasy in this vertical city. Such proposals were never even broached in New York, and although the decade witnessed some debate on the virtues of increased concentration, the consensus was that urban development dictated persistent, even intensified, vertical development—even in the midst of increasing traffic.

New York planners' response to this traffic crisis illustrates the power of the vertical sublime to shape imaginative urban possibilities in the era. As elsewhere, New York's planning discourse about traffic relied heavily upon organic metaphors and comparisons. Representative of New York planning experts was the noted architect Harvey Wiley Corbett, who argued in an influential 1927 *Architectural Forum* essay that the city, like any other living creature, had to grow or die: "Growth,—why is it both necessary and desirable? It is necessary because it is an essential element in the continued vitality of a city. The 'dead' portions of any city are those which are not growing—i.e., not increasing in number and bulk of buildings."[49] Here Corbett attributes to municipal manifest destiny the urgency of an ontogenetic imperative—grow (upward) or die. Modern urban expansion, understood explicitly and exclusively as the continual development and construction of ever-grander skyscrapers, was not merely desirable for notions of civic pride, it was absolutely essential for the survival of the organism. Here boosterism—channeled into the prevailing obsession with vertical modernity and filtered through a pervasive network of organic urban metaphors—takes on a life-or-death urgency in urban affairs. All this became the legitimate province of the expert planner: "I view city planning as the study of the city's proper growth."[50]

By the middle of the decade, many indigenous planners and business leaders (often the same people) felt that essential growth was threatened in New York by inexorably increasing traffic congestion. Corbett again:

> Movement of traffic is just as essential to the life of the city as the movement of the blood is to the life of the body. Thin traffic like thin blood represents an anæmic condition. Congested traffic, like excessive blood pressure, threatens the health of the body, that is to say, the normal and proper growth of the city. . . . Circulation,—why is it necessary for growth? It is necessary because lack of it has already shown, in many sections of New York, that growth will stop for lack of food,—people and freight,—and a locality once "dead" is difficult to revive. Growth in number of buildings in-

creases congestion in streets. Opening up the streets to relieve the congestion makes way for increased circulation and for increase in number and bulk of buildings, and what seems to be a "vicious circle" is created. Can some method be devised whereby growth and open circulation can both continue without the one operating against the other?[51]

Corbett recognized the bind of continual growth in the modern city—increasing density exacerbates already unmanageable traffic problems, and ameliorating these problems by adding street capacity merely encourages more high-density development. Corbett's solution to these interlinked problems of growth and circulation graphically illustrates the power and hegemony of the vertical sublime in conceptions of the modern metropolis.

For Southern Californian planners, the way out of the development/traffic bind was, of course, to bypass density altogether, relying on the potential of automotive transport to spread development out over a great geographical expanse. They sought to eliminate congestion by reducing concentration and attempting—not always successfully—to deintegrate the metropolitan area into discrete and relatively autonomous combined local business and residential centers—garden cities. For New York's planners, by contrast, the only reasonable path was to treat increasing transportation congestion in the same way they treated human concentration: displace it into vertical space. The proper answer to ever-increasing vehicular traffic was, like everything else, to make better use of the vertical dimension. If towering skyscrapers were causing problems by their intensive use of land, they also offered the logical resolution to those problems. The crisis was caused not by overcrowding per se but by congestion within a discrete, finite space—in the streets, in the case of automotive traffic. The solution was to multiply the available space for this circulation by separating traffic into different levels in the towering city: "In the congested centers of the city, at least, these three forms of traffic [foot, wheel, and rail] . . . do not belong on the same level."[52] Consequently, Corbett proposed constructing throughout Manhattan an intricate system of arcading above city streets to separate all traffic into discrete vertical strata. This plan was certainly ambitious, for it involved the gradual redesign of the entire city. Both utopian and practical urbanists of the era, though, thought this sort of urban redevelopment a relatively minor task, as the face of the city seemed to remake itself so frequently anyway. As Corbett put it in an earlier piece for *American Architect*, "The life of the average modern city building is not more than a generation. . . . There are very few modern buildings that are not pulled down to make way for more modern structures within thirty years, which is a long time in the rapid pace set by the metropolitan cities."[53] Each building in the reformed city would eventually share responsibility with its neighbors for setting aside space for Corbett's envisioned second-floor network of outdoor pedestrian arcades. They would share in the civic restructuring that would

FIGURE 22. Ferriss and Corbett's multilevel streets (*Regional Plan of New York and Its Environs,* 1924). Illustration by Hugh Ferriss; reprinted in Harvey Wiley Corbett, "Different Levels for Foot, Wheel and Rail," *American City* 31, no. 1 (1924): 1.

free the city's streets for uninterrupted automotive traffic flow (see figure 22). As Corbett put it,

> It seems rational, therefore, in any scheme proposing to divide traffic into its three natural divisions through a process of double or triple decking the streets, that we start by placing the wheel traffic, the largest and most rapidly growing, on the present street level, which is already there and requires neither to be dug out nor built up; that all rail traffic be placed underground, as subways; and that foot traffic be raised one story above the street level, carrying bridges across at all corners, and at one or two points in the long blocks as well, so that people can move uninterruptedly throughout as large

a district as is covered by the expansion of the double decking idea. Double decking, while difficult, is not impossible.[54]

Automobiles receive pride of place—on the root ground level—in this scheme, but are actually deemphasized by submerging them below the level of human habitation. People, in the form of pedestrian traffic, would partake of the elevated planes, promenading along stately cloisterlike arcades exclusively for their use.[55] Like the cars, rail transit would be removed from conflict with other types of traffic by being placed underground in subways or, as Corbett explains in a particularly fanciful passage, overhead on airy viaducts:

> Everyone agrees that rails could not remain on the streets or over them in elevated structures as at present, and they must go down, or else far up, as has been proposed and is now being seriously developed, in so-called "airways," i.e., light suspension bridges of open construction supported by pylon buildings at station points, the rail level being so high, 200 feet or more above the city, and the type of car so light, that none of the objectionable features of the present "elevateds" would be retained. The real point about rails is that they must "go out of the picture" as far as the visual aspect of the streets is concerned.[56]

Rail would find its own level—out of the way—in this vision of vertical urbanism. With so much new space open to urban planners, thanks to the example of the towering buildings, separate infrastructural streams could easily be located where they would not conflict. In the vertical city, the sky was not just the limit, it was a practically unlimited resource.

By separating all classes of traffic, the city would, in Corbett's vision, be free to turn the ground level over almost exclusively to automobiles, while allowing ever-higher skyscrapers (whose foundation requirements would presumably be minimal). Congestion would be met with increased circulatory potential, permitting virtually unchecked skyward development of the city. In essence, Corbett's solution to the street traffic crisis in New York was, appropriately enough, to look skyward—to fit the needs of the circulation problem to the dominant aesthetic of the modern metropolis. Making use of multiple vertical strata seemed the only logical answer for urban thinkers enraptured by the vertical sublime.

In this readiness to turn to multiple levels for traffic, Corbett was part of a much larger trend. Many visionaries of the era produced plans—often published in reputable "expert" city planning journals—for similar multiple-decked urban roadways. In 1927, for example, *The American City* produced a special issue exclusively concerned with contemporary plans for multiple-level roadways. The journal carried articles on Corbett's arcading proposals, as well as Dr. John A. Harriss's plan for a "multiple highway" through the very heart of Manhattan. This six-level highway—Harriss projected a system of these traversing greater Manhattan—would separate streams of automotive traffic much more elaborately than the single level suggested by Corbett. Here, all six decks would be open to motor transit:

> The upper level of the structure is for high-speed automobile traffic; the fifth level is for passenger cars; the fourth and third levels for one-way bus traffic; the second level for motor trucks; and the first or street level for local or mixed traffic. The four upper levels contain sidewalks or promenades—in addition, of course, to the sidewalks at the street level, on each side of the structure itself. . . . There are ramps to enable cars to move from one level to another, and moving stairways for pedestrians to do likewise.[57]

In Harriss's scheme, entire stretches of the city would be cleared for the construction of automobiles' multistory buildings. The technology of the skyscraper would be fitted for strictly automotive use, elevating the city street into a steel-framed building and thus multiplying the thoroughfare by raising it into the air. Like in Corbett's arcading plan, this multiple highway would solve the street congestion problem by finding abundant new street area in the previously unexploited territory of the air.

Amid the attention and respect given to these ambitious plans in mainstream planning and architectural circles of the 1920s, there were many more down-to-earth examples of the contemporary colonization and utilization of vertical urban space. One notable example was, of course, Chicago's reconstruction of Wacker Drive. Indeed, the notion of separating roadways by levels seemed to most urbanites in the era a logical extension of the development that led to the construction of the elevated railroads in Chicago, New York, and other American cities in the 1870s and 1880s and especially of New York's first (successful) subterranean railroads in 1900–20. Over the previous half-century, then, such staging of roadways in vertically discrete space seemed to go hand in hand with the other modern developments of the city, such as the iconic skyscraper or electric lighting.

Corbett's plans for integrating roadways and sidewalks into tall buildings was thus a fairly mainstream vision by 1920. Aside from the Chicago Jewelers Building, many buildings in the era were being constructed to house automobiles within their shells. Corbett's March 1927 *Architectural Forum* essay appeared in a special "reference" issue dedicated to descriptions of recently completed "automotive buildings," such as parking garages. Conversely, respected architect Raymond Hood (the winner of the *Chicago Tribune* competition and later designer of Rockefeller Center) presented in the *New York Times* in 1925 plans for a series of multiple-deck vehicular bridges across New York's rivers that would also feature space for permanent human habitation: "The moment one begins to speculate on the possibility of erecting apartment houses on our bridges, the thought comes that it is strange we have not always had them."[58]

Edgar Chambless famously proposed in 1910 the construction of a megastructural "roadtown," a quite radical integration of transport infrastructure and human habitation within the literal framework of a linear building that would stretch far out into America's rural expanses. By the time of the *American City* special issue, John K. Hencken had adapted Chambless's scheme. No longer was it to be a rural alternative to the vertical city; now the roadtown would be integrated into the very fabric of the modern metropolis. Hencken called for "a structure of 6 to 12 stories" combining several levels of roads with "shops, restaurants, offices, light manufacturing, wholesale businesses, apartments, hotels, and even schools, churches, and theaters." Termed by the magazine "an urban microcosm,"[59] this plan reproduced an entire city within the larger metropolis. For Hencken, the challenge of envisioning the modern city was not so much where the automobile and its roadways belonged in the urban fabric, but instead how urban elements might be integrated into the new landscape of automobility. Clearly, engineers and visionaries alike were hard at work in the 1920s figuring out how to locate the automobile in the built environment of the modern city.

These imaginative prospects sprang from a rich tradition of utopian urban representation. Indeed, if proven skyscraper builders such as Hood and Corbett were taken seriously in the local and national architectural community and their plans for multidecked thoroughfares and skyscrapers with roads running through them discussed widely and reprinted in professional journals, it was not because their schemes were particularly inventive or novel. Rather, they and their peers partook in a larger discourse about the future of the modern metropolis—a shared vision that was animated by pervasive conceptions of a modernity deeply enmeshed in the vertical sublime. For twenty years or more, the urban imagination had been shaped by an outpouring of images and descriptions of the inevitable city of the future. This visionary discourse was not only ubiquitous in early twentieth-century American cities, it was also fairly coherent. New York planners and architects of the 1920s were, in large measure, merely fitting their concrete expert proposals and plans to these preexisting vernacular fantasies.

VISIONS OF UTOPIAN URBANISM

As early as 1908, *King's Views* had elaborated its detailed depictions of iconic New York skyscrapers with equally detailed images of the city's projected utopian vertical future. These pictures, collectively titled *King's Dream of New York*, presented in vivid and technically precise specificity a utopian skyscraper metropolis of the future (see figure 23). Just as *King's Views* familiarized readers with the form and outlines of New York's modern buildings, *King's Dream* no less vividly acquainted New Yorkers with the utopian skyscraper future that would surely result from modern progress. The 1908 *King's Dream* was so popular among readers that King had his renderers produce a second version in 1911, and these now-famous images

FIGURE 23. King's dream of New York. From Moses King, *King's Views; New York, 1908, Four Hundred Illustrations* (New York: C. Francis Press, 1908); and *King's Views of New York, 1911, 1912; Four Hundred Illustrations* (New York: Moses King, 1911).

eventually assumed pride of place as the instantly recognizable cover pictures for King's books.

In both of King's projections, a long row of skyscrapers borders a long boulevard. This canyonlike street is filled with streetcars as well as crowds of pedestrians, and its sidewalks are raised two or three stories along elevated railway tracks. The boulevard is spanned at several places by narrow bridges. In the first of *King's Dreams*, drawn by Harry M. Pettit, these bridges and elevated sidewalks are crowded with pedestrians. Every cluster of buildings is connected to the next by small pedestrian bridges at various points. Crowded balconies near the tops of some buildings further demarcate this city's heights as an inhabited place—rooftop arcades and belvederes provide new public spaces for citizen gatherings. Above all hover swarms of airships, each labeled with an exotic destination: "Europe," "Panama Canal" (not yet opened in 1908), "Japan," and even "North Pole" and "South Pole." These dirigibles float in the domain of air and light at the crowded tops of the city's towers, and they define the metropolis as cosmopolitan—a worldly city, connected to the far reaches of the globe.

King's later image, first appearing in 1911 and drawn by Richard Rummell, substitutes bi- and tri-planes for airships and banishes the pedestrian masses from the lofty heights to the dark street below. Indeed, this later image elevates the street railways to the level of the towers, running train lines along the tops of buildings. No longer are the numerous bridges meant for pedestrians; now they are part of an expansive transit system that links the skyscraper towers. The 1911 image is darker than the 1908 utopian city and a bit more antiseptic, but it too bathes its buildings in sunlight, raising the heights of the city from the dark streets far below. Both images represent an apotheosis of the skyscraper, where the pinnacles and cupolas float in light and air, leaving the earthly ground-level city behind. These visions of the future city relocate new streets upon graceful bridges and arcades that span the heights, effectively merging the staple *King's Views* images of suspension bridges and skyscrapers. These bridges, though, are exclusively for trains or pedestrians. Although neither picture displays automobiles in the city of the future, they both lay the infrastructure for imagining a skyscraper city linked by elevated roadways and bridges, and later visionaries of the 1920s had no trouble adapting this image of the futuristic city to the modern age.

What exactly was it that made these images futuristic? What distinguished these drawings from the countless others in King's guidebooks? The pictures of *King's Dream* primarily differed from King's ordinary views in three ways: first, the city's skyscraper development was intensified—King's future was a city of nothing but skyscrapers, a wholly vertical city; second, these skyscrapers were linked, either thematically, through common design elements such as cornice lines or beaux-arts cupolas, or architecturally, mainly by bridges and elevated roadways; and third, the sky above these buildings was filled with airships—the bustle of street traffic was displaced from the dark roadways below to the new, light and airy rooftop space. All three of these elements would recur in countless visionary images of later years. *King's Dreams* also took part in a wider speculative tradition emerging with the mass circulation of pulp novels in the late years of the nineteenth century and continuing well into the twentieth. Pulp artists such as Frank R. Paul elaborated a science fiction future quite a bit like that presented by King's renderers. In countless such images, the ideal form of the metropolis achieved something of the status of canon (see figure 24). By the 1920s, most visions of the city of the future looked remarkably alike. It should come as no surprise that characteristic features of this mainstream urban future recurred in both visionary dreams and respectable plans. These details, such as arcaded streets and buildings linked by bridges, provided a language of transcendent urbanism defining the shape of the vertical future, and they were all based—like King's futuristic fantasies—on extrapolated understandings of modern New York City.

As most notions of the advancement of the modern metropolis coalesced around set images of a characteristic urban skyline, these ideas were enunciated through a common architectural vocabulary of utopian skyscraper urbanism. Fundamentally,

FIGURE 24. The grandeur of vertical modernity. Popular magazine fiction: William Robinson Leigh's "Visionary City," *Cosmopolitan*, 1908.

these images all shared an obsession with five primary elements. First, they all agreed that the city of the future would be constructed not of marble, wood, or brick, like Chicago's White City of 1893, but of "modern" materials, such as steel and glass. Stone or, better, concrete claddings would only serve to coat the façades of city buildings; the real substance of the new urbanism would be the same materials that composed the automobile and the airplane. These were artificial components, produced through industrial labor, unlike the "found" or natural materials of the traditional city.

The second ubiquitous constituent of the utopian city was density. The prospective metropolis would be increasingly concentrated and complex, piling level upon level, row upon row. All available space in the city would be taken by high-density development, displacing open space from ground level to more lofty planes. Parks and walkways would have to be moved onto raised surfaces because the land below would become too precious a resource. Despite this intensity of development, the city of the future would be orchestrated, not random. As crowded as images of the city seemed, they never featured the snaking Byzantine corridors of winding streets and buildings that characterized the European medieval town. Instead, the cosmopolis would concentrate legions of skyscrapers arrayed in neat rows along wide, deep street canyons. This development would be aligned to the rigid street grid, a defining feature of the Manhattan topography (above Greenwich Village, of course, and excluding Broadway). Streets in the utopian metropolis always meet at right angles, arranging the city's buildings in perpendicular columns that strictly regulate the urban expansion, constraining it to the vertical. The resulting quadrangular pattern of thoroughfares would channel the future city's growth into discrete towers instead of allowing a formless expanse. Thanks to the grid system, the urban fabric would be thick and dense, but it would be controlled. Likewise, the variation and individuality of these distinct urban structures would be tempered by a series of linking devices. Hence the importance of the elevated roads and walkways: these raised highways would mirror the effect of the street grid below, ordering the skyscrapers while linking them together (although not always in such a rigid grid; they were a bit more fanciful and "airy"). These twin systems of thoroughfares, elevated and ground-level, together served to connect and harmonize the disparate towers that dominated the skyline, allowing ever greater density of development without reducing the urban fabric to chaos.

The roads were intrinsic to a third common aspect of the envisioned skyscraper city: images of movement and speed predominated. Amid the solid towers, trains, airships, and often automobiles would zip by. Frequently, pedestrians would teem along streets, balconies, and elevated arcades. These various transportation systems projected the city not as a timeless monument or an uninhabited set-piece, but as a center of human activity and progress. If the beaux-arts designers of the period had eternal, dignified, and tranquil classical monuments in mind when they designed the civic buildings of Washington, D.C., or the Chicago World's Fair, urban visionaries in New York fixated on an ever-changing cityscape, bristling with activity and movement.

This constant motion did not, however, imply human toil. For all the hurly-burly of the imminent skyscraper metropolis, the common vision did not provide for representation of the infrastructure of labor that would make such a city run and give it purpose. In the midst of the spotless utopia, there was no space for workplaces or factories. It was perhaps this fourth facet of vernacular urban envisioning that seemed most fantastic at the time. As Harvey Corbett acknowledged in 1923, almost in passing, all such workplaces would inevitably be banished from gleaming Manhattan.[60] Consequently, although one can imagine that the antlike pedestrians often pictured scurrying about visionary street scenes are indeed commuting to and from work, the images never offer any concrete depiction of such necessary movement. Instead, the inhabitants of the skyscraper city often seem to do little more than gaze out appreciatively over their fantastic metropolis. While Bellamy's ideal future world described in great detail the great "industrial army" of the future, most early twentieth-century representations failed to depict such exigencies of daily existence. The dominant image is of a city caught up in progress, but its development seems to drive itself; it is as if progress were its own agent.[61]

The common denominator in these composite figures of the skyscraper utopia was, of course, dominant verticality. The vertical sublime transfixed urban futurists, and it energized their various representations of city form. The skyscraper was the backbone of the metropolis and the model for its future, not only because it was tall but because it served to situate and structure so many diverse vertical elements. The imminent metropolis reveled in the play of spatial layers, counterpoising rooftop with surface boulevard, elevated train tube or bridge with cornice line, raised pedestrian arcade with rows of oversized clerestory windows. Airships dominated the skies above these cities, as vehicles buzzed by on streets below. Most importantly, each skyscraper was constructed not as an unbroken upright line but as a series of perpendicular levels or strata. These parallel planes indicated the intricacy of the dominant verticality, accentuating the city's height by constantly offering suggestive visual cues or points of reference to the hypothetical observer. The vertical city was a stratiform city, staging multiple tiers along the general upward sense. Whether set-backs, terraces, shelves, or ornamental ledges, these stratified building elements constantly recurred in representations of the skyscraper metropolis, especially in the late 1920s. They served to break the monotonous linearity of the towers and highlight the depth and rich texture of the urban cityscape. The skyscraper city was envisioned, then, not simply as a uniformly elevated mass of architecture but as a multifarious landscape of successive vertical elements, arrayed in direct relation to one another. This was a towering skyline, but its verticality was subsumed to the demands of the vertical sublime. Consequently, each linear element, each mural façade, was set off against adjacent planar surfaces. The juxtaposition of these discrete upright segments served to draw attention to the mounting cumulative sense of verticality. Taken as a whole, the landscape of the skyscraper utopian city of the future represented an eclectic mix of exterior topographies, yet they collectively converged on the sky.

REALIZING VISIONS OF SKYSCRAPER UTOPIANISM

This vernacular dialect of the 1920s urban imagination swept up both fantasists and urban realists, shaping contemporary representations of the city's future. Respected architects produced countless plans for skyscraper blocks that clearly spoke the same language as those by Frank Paul or Moses King. In addition to the proposals by Raymond Hood and Harvey Corbett, more grandiose schemes were put forth by serious professionals, such as Mexico's Francisco Mujica. In 1929 Mujica produced a tabloid-sized massive *History of the Skyscraper* that extrapolated the "uniquely American" form of the tall building from Aztec and Mayan temples to modern Manhattan to "neo-American" structures of the future.[62] Here the obligatory connecting bridges and elevated arcades have been fully transformed into major interurban expressways, fixing the city's exemplary towers into regular city blocks. Each pyramidal building punctuates a cityscape dominated at surface level by automobiles.

Just as Mujica's vision of the metropolitan future sprang from ideas commonly circulating at the time, he was not alone in formalizing his envisioned city into neat rows of skyscrapers along massive urban roadways. Indeed, by the late 1920s, many plans for New York's future projected massive automotive corridors through the cosmopolis. By this time, the snaking elevated railways of earlier urban conceptions had mostly disappeared, replaced by schemes for integrating the private automobile into the city fabric. Following the influential work of Corbett and Ferriss in picturing this accommodation of the future city to the car, architects like Mujica assumed that their towering city would have to integrate broad roadways into the tableau. As a result, city planning in the Greater New York area during the decade fixated on ways to situate these oversized thoroughfares into the vertical skyline. In 1923, inspired by the publicity surrounding Corbett's early street arcading plans, the Regional Plan Association of New York and Its Environs, the city's expert planning body, formed an "Advisory Planning Group" to draw upon the ideas and inspirations of noted architects and builders. Here again Corbett—heading a panel on general traffic studies—"concluded with a sweeping predication that Manhattan a hundred years hence would be almost entirely a business district raised on platforms above ground level."[63] This staging scheme would leave the ground level open for automotive traffic. By 1929, when the Regional Plan Association published its final program, though, the engineers found more feasible a network of massive crosstown express highways, much like that pictured by Mujica around the same time. Their depiction of this urban future gave formal planning approval to the visionary utopian urbanism that had been circulating for generations. Once more, the plausible—even logical—and fantastic merged in 1920s New York under the heady influence of the vertical sublime and the shared vernacular understandings of modern urban progress that it inspired.

This reciprocal interaction of expert and vernacular visions of the future of the modern city played out most dramatically and most influentially on an international stage, in a series of motion pictures produced during the era. The 1930 film *Just Imagine* was explicitly modeled on the contemporary Regional Plan of New York, setting a rather flat vaudeville musical plot against the lofty heights of the towering metropolis of futuristic 1980. Much more successful cinematically was Fritz Lang's classic *Metropolis,* released four years earlier. Lang claimed his inspiration for the movie came after first sighting the New York skyline, and his evocation of the skyscraper utopia above ground certainly accords with the dominant model of envisioning the city's future. *Metropolis* is, however, one of few major works in this period to seriously probe the social basis of this prospective urbanity, if only as a pretext for more sweeping commentary about contemporary class struggle. The film defies the hegemonic mode of urban representation by revealing, in Dantesque allegory, the labor of the unseen working class. Indeed, in Lang's depiction, the utopia above is supported by the toil of countless proletarians far below the tower tops. Like *Just Imagine,* though, *Metropolis* was more admired in its day for its dazzling depiction of the future cityscape than for its (much more accomplished) storyline. Both movies, despite their very different ideological stances on the urban future, reinforced the dominant conceptions of modern urbanity that inspired them. Both presented the future in predominantly architectural terms, and both reveled in the urbanism that modern progress would surely bring. Although *Metropolis* suggested that not all urbanites would be free to share in this transcendent utopia, this film, no less than the ardent *Just Imagine,* presented this destiny as desirable and inevitable.

For all the wonder of the special effects in *Just Imagine* and *Metropolis,* these films circulated already familiar images of the future of the modern metropolis—images animated by a shared awe at the vertical sublime. From movies to pulp fiction to earnest professional plans, all were part of a moment in the late 1920s when utopianism and professional planning neatly coincided—when imaginative possibilities found fertile ground in the cityscape and were taken remarkably seriously. It may be hard to tell anymore what was fanciful and what was rational planning in this rich age of metropolitan hubris, modern enthusiasm, and unchecked faith in industrial and architectural progress. Today this pervasive utopian discourse seems ominously—and anachronistically—overshadowed by our common sense knowledge that the imminent Depression would cast a chill upon this sort of fervid imagining. Yet, even at the very precipice of economic collapse, enthusiasm for the urban future persevered.

THE SKYSCRAPER AS EPISTEMOLOGY

But ah! Manhattan's sights and sounds, her smells,
Her crowds, her throbbing force, the thrill that comes
From being of her a part, her subtle spells,
Her shining towers, her avenues, her slums—
O God! the stark, unutterable pity,
To be dead, and never again behold my city!

JAMES WELDON JOHNSON, "MY CITY"

In many ways the apotheosis of Jazz Age indulgence, as well as that era's dominant discourse of urbanism, was the iconic Empire State Building of 1931, for that monumental tower truly represented the culmination of 1920s trends. Begun under the shadow of mounting depression, the building's construction was advertised as both a crowning symbol of architectural might and a defiant mark of confidence in a rapidly failing economic system. That the construction project was attempted at all testifies to the bravado of the skyscraper builder—and to the disconnection between the ideology of the vertical sublime and the economic purposes for which such towers were ostensibly built, for the great building remained largely vacant throughout its first decade.[64] As a final symbol of the skyscraper age, however, the Empire State Building was a tremendous success. It was, first and foremost, the tallest building in the world. Further, it towered over relatively low-rise midtown Manhattan, literally defining that region's skyline for decades. Because of a lack of adjacent skyscraper competition, as well as its great height, the new tower commanded unbroken vistas from its vacant offices' windows, and it could be seen throughout the region.

In many ways, this building was a work of fantasy. Aside from its economic improbabilities, the Empire State Building represented a defining example of the new form of set-back architecture popularized by Hugh Ferriss half a decade earlier. It was also deeply tied into the skyscraper utopian vision of the modern metropolis, staging a subway station under its foundations and a dirigible mast on its tower. Most notably, the building was not constructed by a major corporation seeking the prestige and name recognition that such a tower would bring; it was a purely speculative venture. The Empire State Building was, in essence, a gigantic wager on its prospective reputation. As such, its builders were clearly hoping to cash in on the allure of the vertical sublime, seeking (in vain) to translate awe into office bookings.

Perhaps, though, the mark of the building's ultimate popular success, and a sign of its coming fame, was its use as a prop in what would turn out to be the vertical city's most successful filmic representation. For all the reverence to dreams of the urban utopia encapsulated in the set design of the futuristic *Just Imagine* and *Metropolis,* it was the 1933 *King Kong*—set definitively in the urban present of existing buildings—that best captured the passing era's enthusiasm for the modern skyscraper.

This filmic testament to the sublime grandeur of the tall building juxtaposed a titan of the natural world, the picture's eponymous colossal ape, with this ultimate expression of the technological and modern. The epic meeting between monkey and office building brought the wonder of the Darwinian tropical jungle to the scene of the Social Darwinian urban jungle. Appropriately enough, the king of nature heads directly, female human fetish firmly in hand, for the most evolved form in the modern metropolis. Of course, the Empire State Building easily bears the burden of Kong's ascent, staging the (literally) climactic final confrontation between ape and modern mechanized humanity, represented here by the fighter airplanes buzzing overhead. In the end, the champion of the primitive world is bested by the artifice of the modern, at this moment reproducing the staple set piece of the familiar skyscraper utopian fantasia, with airships swirling about the exemplary building's mooring mast. Ultimately—and perhaps a bit ambivalently—King Kong is definitively toppled from his presumptuous perch above the observation deck of the Empire State Building, falling to his death on the dark streets below.

The gratitude that Fay Wray might have felt for that observation deck, where the gorilla placed her in order to better swat at the harassing biplanes, was echoed by the many New Yorkers and out-of-town visitors who flocked to that eighty-sixth-floor belvedere after the skyscraper's construction. Shortly after its opening on 1 May 1931, the observation deck of the Empire State Building had become an important civic space in New York City. Although it was said that on a clear day the observer could see for eighty miles,[65] most eyes were fixed firmly on the city below and around. As the *New York Times* put it on opening day, "Few failed to exclaim at the smallness of man and his handiwork as seen from this great distance. They saw men and motor cars creeping like insects through the streets; they saw elevated trains that looked like toys."[66] The observation deck of the Empire State Building offered a new perspective on the surrounding metropolis, reducing the street-level jumble of the city to a scale model of itself.

This was the sort of view so critical to Bellamy's *Looking Backward*. The panoramic vista served in that novel to precisely locate the disoriented observer, revealing the dimensions of the surrounding city and establishing the spectator's coordinates within the revealed urban tableau. While few visitors to the skyscraper observation deck likely felt as bewildered as Julian West, thousands of urbanites found their understanding of the surrounding city reinforced by a view from that panoptic perspective. The Empire State Building's observatory, then, did for countless New Yorkers what Dr. Leete's rooftop belvedere did for the fictional traveler. Yet, for all its power as a tourist attraction, the observation deck offered vistas little different from those available from thousands of windows in that towering skyscraper. Moreover, although exemplary in its height, dozens of Manhattan buildings featured views hardly inferior to those visible through the windows of the Empire State Building. These ordinary urban vistas revealed themselves to tens of thousands of white-collar workers in the skyscraper city on a daily basis. For many denizens of the modern city, such elevated perspectives were part of everyday life. One could hardly venture anywhere in the towering city without at some point catching a glimpse from an elevated window. Through ordinary, unremarkable activity, a great number of urbanites were intimately familiar with the face of their city, as grasped from the perspective of a skyscraper.

And what did the city look like through those high windows? Obviously, the city as seen from a tall building looks quite a bit like a collection of other tall buildings. It was the ever-present skyline that the spectator saw. Indeed, every day the urbanite's gaze was matched, if rarely returned or acknowledged, by millions of anonymous unseen eyes peering through thousands of similar windows encasing hundreds of nearby towers.[67] This familiar urban vista was, of course, not very different from the vista available most anywhere in the modern city, on the ground or in a building; the skyline was everywhere, and it was everywhere apparent. As Nye notes, "The panoramic vision permits one not merely to view the city as a series of individual parts, but to read it as a total structure."[68] Consequently, most New Yorkers were intimately familiar with the outlines of their city, reading it at a glance, as a blind person's hand scans Braille; the raised outlines of the metropolis were utterly definitive, utterly distinctive. A quick look allowed most residents of the Jazz Age modern city to immediately triangulate their position in relation to these iconic forms. The tall buildings, the telltale signs of the city, were also characteristic landmarks by which urbanites every day set their sights. This system of urban navigation also explains the importance of exceptional buildings, such as the Empire State. Such distinctive, or particularly tall, structures quickly became indispensable points of reference, because they were immediately recognizable at a distance and their great height guaranteed that they would remain visible from the far reaches of the city. Whether from the window of another skyscraper or from the canyonlike streets far below, the perspectival configuration of the urban skyline told locals at a glance just where they were in the city.

Equally useful for urban location was the ordinary, lowly street grid. This much less flamboyant feature of the modern American city served as a primary technology of rational urban organization. Most obviously, the rigid quadrangular urban layout mimics at street level the ordering mechanism of a map, projecting the abstract rationale of the planner onto the urban topography. The grid precisely locates the urbanite in the cityscape: like the mathematical Cartesian coordinate system, all positions are simultaneously absolute and relative. The grid fixes the urban wanderer at a particular, fixed, and abstract point in the city (in close relation to the marked intersections of discretely ordered and unique streets). This location is also fixed by visual reference to a central, easily identifiable zero point, or origin: the cluster of ever-higher skyscrapers at the city's core. This was no coincidence. The regularity of midtown Manhattan's road network had long promoted the orderly and intensive building that marked the city. The quadrangular network of

FIGURE 25. The concentric model of urbanism correlates economic value and cultural prestige to centrality. Vividly portrayed in the iconic Manhattan skyline, this tangible effect of propinquity can just as easily be grasped in this photograph of a 1916 Pasadena exhibit on property values. Even in a small city, property values bear little relation to available land, instead reflecting the ideology of the vertical metropolis. From George A. Damon, "A 'Home-Made' City Planning Exhibit and Its Results," *American City* 15, no. 4 (October 1916): 374.

streets effectively served as a skeletal system for the skyscraper metropolis, encouraging structures to fill the available space between gridlines. Through the most fantastic visions of the utopian future, the fundamental outlines of the street grid remained in place. Ever-taller towers could be integrated into the unifying structure of this basic municipal element. Soon, in both fantasy and built reality, only the canyonlike streets separated and differentiated the resulting massive buildings. The orderly city block, with its characteristically dense construction, was in large part a product of this way of aligning the road network.

Because the city's tallest buildings tended to be concentrated in the financial or commercial sectors of the city during this period, the skyscraper and the street grid worked together to graph the economic and social structure of modern urbanity (see figure 25).[69] Reciprocally, the full impact of the grid as an ordering device only became apparent in the modern city when buildings began to rise from the ground level, offering an elevated perspective of the resulting urban landscape. From the heights of the skyscraper office window or observation deck, this grid system becomes perfectly clear, emerging out of the depths of the city in clearly demarcated canyons and corridors that were instantly recognizable.

In this way, the very high and the very low operate in concert to transmit information about the metropolis. The elevated panorama neatly transmits to anyone familiar with the workings of the city social, as well as strictly topographical, coordinates. Consequently, the structure of the metropolis became visible to the observer through its clearly linked hierarchy of vertical and horizontal correspondences. During the Jazz Age, the modern city stripped bare the dynamics of its own existence, unmistakably manifesting in clear and readable terms its social and geographical structure—and distinctly positioning the observer within this system of meaning.

The tall building was the preeminent symbol of the modern metropolis, and it provided the city with a convenient locus for cultural production. It served as a site and token of public discourse, and it animated representations of the city through the power of the vertical sublime. Yet, in the progress of everyday life for millions of denizens of the modern cosmopolis, the true importance of the skyscraper during this era was its role in the phenomenology of urban observation. The skyscraper helped make the exemplary modern city legible to its residents and comprehensible to its culture industry. It was an ever-present landmark and point of reference; it provided an elevated and privileged viewpoint from which to survey the metropolis. As such, the tall building served as both beacon and observation platform for countless urbanites. Ultimately, the skyscraper illustrates the intimate connection between modernity and legibility in the vertical sublime city—not just in making the form and future of the metropolis imaginable, but in providing epistemological tools to observe the modern city properly and comprehensively. In essence, the windows of the tall building provide for the ordinary urbanite what the map, survey, and comprehensive plan offer to the professional expert planner—a means of making sense of the urban landscape. For all the breathless enthusiasm shown for the tall building in this, its heyday, the Jazz Age skyscraper was not merely an icon or a metaphor; it was a tool to make the modern city comprehensible and legible to its residents and other everyday observers.

MAPPING SOCIAL ORDER
IN THE VERTICAL METROPOLIS

We were of the city, but somehow not in it.
ALFRED KAZIN, "A WALKER IN THE CITY" (11)

If the skyscraper was a mechanism and token of urban comprehension as well as capital accumulation, these exemplary structures—so often referred to as microcosms of the larger whole—also mirrored the city's exclusions. Revealing views of the skyline from within the metropolis were, for the most part, restricted to middle-class office workers and their bosses (as well as each skyscraper's army of low-paid janitorial and support personnel, at least surreptitiously). The office assistant or (usually female) secretary could occasionally look out the skyscraper window, but only the (usually male) corner-office executive could do so with a full sense of possession. In corporate practice, secretarial and clerical workspaces were usually situated in the bowels of the buildings, cut off from natural light and panoramic views. The epistemologically significant elevated gaze was defined not merely by what urban landmarks one could perceive but by one's position in the city's social hierarchy. The skyline view revealed the city to the privileged viewer, but it simultaneously revealed the privileged viewer to the city. Proper location in an elevated office building—the higher the better, the more central the better—was a clear sign of social status. Full access to skyscraper views was a conceptual franchise only open to a select class of Manhattanites. In a city where a panoramic perspective from a downtown skyscraper delivered a powerful sense of one's central position in an array of social hierarchies, full comprehension of the cityscape was a restricted commodity. One's ability to make sense of the full range of urban signs in this modern city—one's ability to achieve fluency in the various legible orders manifested in the concentric city's form—depended, at least in part, on one's position in those power structures. Although every New Yorker could read the basic marks of the metropolis and veteran urbanites could soon locate themselves within it, many city dwellers—and especially those relegated to the city's geographical, racial, and social peripheries—could really be sure only that the city did indeed have a clearly identifiable vital center and they were most certainly not in it.

By the 1920s, a bit over two million New Yorkers still lived in Manhattan. For all the rhetoric of living amid the clouds in towering apartment buildings, many fewer than in the past now lived in the exemplary central core of the borough.[70] The cluster of skyscrapers was an evacuated zone at night; workers could fill the structures by day, carrying out the vital economic tasks that were concentrated there, but they retreated to other sectors at night. This diurnal migration was perhaps the first sign of a larger, gradual erosion in the conceptual and social dominance of New York's urban core that would shake the wider discursive foundations of urban modernity in the aftermath of World War II, when decades of affluent and middle-class suburbanization finally began to sap the cultural capital of the great centralized metropolis. Even during the Jazz Age years, though, when the power of the modern vertical city was at its apogee, most urbanites in this metropolis lived at some remove from the city's core. In a fundamental sense, they observed "the City"— meaning, of course, Manhattan's skyline—from outside. Every time New Yorkers from the Bronx or Brooklyn or Newark, for that matter, looked up, they might spy the cluster of towers that marked the metropolitan epicenter. Such glimpses, in the passing routine of everyday life, reaffirmed entire neighborhoods' and communities' submission to the overwhelming logic of the towering metropolitan core. Evoked in that glance was a sense of manifest disenfranchisement, of dislocation, of being necessarily out of the center of things. For this was another function of the skyscraper in the vertical sublime metropolis: to make the residents of outlying parts of the region feel peripheral and marginal. In this simple way, the skyline graphically brought home to every part of the larger area the exemplary socio-economic structure of the concentric city.

As he later recalled, Alfred Kazin, growing up in Brooklyn in the 1920s, experienced his neighborhood "as the margin of the city"—"We were of the city, but somehow not in it":

> When I was a child I thought we lived at the end of the world. It was the eternity of the subway ride into the city that first gave me this idea. It took a long time getting to "New York"; it seemed longer getting back. Even the I.R.T. got tired by the time it came to us, and ran up into the open for a breath of air before it got locked into its terminus at New Lots. As the train left the tunnel to rattle along the elevated tracks, I felt I was being jostled on a camel past the last way stations in the desert.[71]

From any point within sight of those exemplary towers, residents could easily locate themselves—not just geographically but socially. Even when one was "within" the vertical metropolis, one was likely exterior to it. The radius of prized propinquity cut right through municipal boundaries, arraying the separate districts of the city—like the surrounding communities—in a system of centrality and marginality.

Of course, the conceptual logic of the skyscraper graphed wealth as well as locality. As height and centrality distinguished and privileged the exemplary towers, lowness and marginality debased the alleys and tenements far below. Jacob Riis perhaps most vividly illustrated this contrast at the end of the nineteenth century, but it remained sharp well into the twentieth: "Leaving the Elevated Railroad where it dives under the Brooklyn Bridge at Franklin Square, scarce a dozen steps will take us where we wish to go. With its rush and roar echoing yet in our ears, we have turned the corner from prosperity to poverty. We stand upon the domain of the tenement."[72]

Crowded and shadowed clusters of densely packed dwelling houses on narrow streets cowered in pointed juxtaposition to the tall buildings piercing the clouds into superelevated domains of light and air far above. As Kenneth Jackson observes, "In 1914, one-sixth of the city's total population still lived on the Lower East Side on only one-eighty-second of the city's land area."[73] For all the cultural enthusiasm for the dense and convoluted fabric of vertical construction, with its imbricated play of multiple interconnected levels, New Yorkers during the Jazz Age knew that congestion and crowding were marks not of modern progress but of backward and wretched privation. The vertical metropolis's slums, although by the 1920s increasingly displaced to a more proper (i.e., less visible) position on the fringes of the metropolitan region, testified to the socio-economic distances that overlay the other geographies of the cityscape.

Even for those not trapped in tenements on the Lower East Side, the manifest topographies of class in New York were ever-present. One scholar describes how slightly more affluent immigrants "moved often from one apartment to another, depending upon their changing fortunes. Thus, they learned how to interpret the view from the kitchen window as a measure of their class position."[74] Always living on the margins of the metropolis, whether on the edges of the Bronx, or Brooklyn, or the Lower East Side of Manhattan, these working-class New Yorkers judged their relative class status by constant reference to the city around them. In an autobiography from the 1950s, East Side novelist Anzia Yezierska, for instance, recounted a return to New York (she had been living in Hollywood for a time), where, although she was residing in ritzy central hotels, she felt constantly out of her proper place: "From the wide, sunny windows of my hotel apartment on Fifth Avenue, I could see the Hudson and East Rivers and the skyscrapers of downtown Manhattan. I had been living in my high-towered luxury for three years and still did not feel at home."[75] What she saw out of her apartment window connected her to an earlier time in her life. In a sense, her gaze was now displaced and reversed. Her eyes still situated Yezierska, if only in her memory, in a peripheral working-class neighborhood from which those skyscrapers were a world away: "An overwhelming nostalgia took me back to the East Side. . . . The same dark, irrational compulsion that makes a murderer risk his life to return to the scene of his crime pulled me back to this home that had never been home to me. The very forces that had driven me away drew me back."[76] Later in the autobiography, Yezierska drifts from a rich description of the ghetto's color and life to a recollection of its oppression and privation. She recounts her experiences working in a sweatshop, "in factories—sewing shirts, making artificial flowers, rolling cigars."[77] In this dense world of the Lower East Side she had felt not only peripheral but trapped. They went together. As a poor immigrant woman, she had felt no hope of movement within the static hierarchy of her social and geographical marginality. Her opportunity to escape finally came when she managed to talk herself into a job as a stenographer in a downtown office "on the twentieth floor of a Wall Street skyscraper. The sunlight, the air, the view all around New York introduced me to a life outside all my experience."[78] In the modern metropolis, escape is measured in terms of the latitude of relative centripetal and vertical movement.

During the 1920s, the only apparent exception to this concentric structure of the modern metropolis was an alternative city within the city. For African Americans in New York City, the uptown district of Harlem was the epicenter of urban experience in the Jazz Age (and for some time after). It was for blacks in America what Manhattan was for New York—a vital, organizing center. James Weldon Johnson expresses this reality in *Black Manhattan*: "Throughout colored America, from

Massachusetts to Mississippi and across the continent to Los Angeles and Seattle, its name, which has scarcely been heard, now stands for the Negro metropolis. Harlem is, indeed, the great Mecca for the sight-seer, the pleasure-seeker, the curious, the adventurous, the enterprising, the ambitious, and the talented of the Negro world; for the lure of it has reached down to every island of the Carib Sea and has penetrated even into Africa."[79] As Johnson makes clear in his descriptive travelogue, African American culture of the Jazz Age radiated from Harlem. If the modern metropolis is defined by its concentric structure, Harlem marks itself as the origin, the reckoning point, of local African American urban society. Perhaps Harlem denotes a parallel topography within Greater New York. This coordinate system of black urban modernity mirrors and coexists with—and but for a few miles, coincides with—that of white America. The overall structure of influence remains the same: Harlem exerts the same tyrannical and rigid dominance over African American experience as lower Manhattan does over other urbanites. Harlem is, then, a discrete metropolis within a metropolis; as Johnson says, it is a black cosmopolis.

This is the impression given by many African Americans upon arriving in New York. Perhaps most often cited in this respect is Langston Hughes, whose autobiographical *The Big Sea* lyrically transmits the author's deep, if vexed, affection for Harlem of the 1920s:

> I can never put on paper the thrill of that underground ride to Harlem. I had never been in a subway before and it fascinated me—the noise, the speed, the green lights ahead. At every station I kept watching for the sign: 135th street. When I saw it, I held my breath. I came out onto the platform with two heavy bags and looked around. It was still early morning and people were going to work. Hundreds of colored people! I wanted to shake hands with them, speak to them. I hadn't seen any colored people for so long—that is, any Negro colored people. I went up the steps and out into the bright September sunlight. Harlem! I stood there, dropped my bags, took a deep breath and felt happy again.[80]

This archetypal emergence scene repeats itself in countless African American arrivals to the great metropolis. Michael Brooks, among other critics, focuses on this first view of Harlem as a paradigmatic scene of African American urban observation: "Whites, remembering their first encounter with New York, describe skyscrapers rising out of the water or recall the great concourses of Penn Station or Grand Central. African Americans, by contrast, remember their arrival as a contrast between the noisy confinement of the subway and the sudden release of climbing the stairs into a Harlem where they could feel free."[81] A sense of being in the majority, or no longer being marginal, dominates these expressions of joy. The sight of active black bodies, self-confident and self-possessed, transfixes the freshly arrived African American migrant. Harlem promises an autonomy and freedom for which black Americans of the first decades of the century thirsted.

The joy is tangible and real, but, as many observers of the era remind us, Harlem has always been very much a part of New York City. Like every other point in this great concentric domain, Harlem is mapped in a rigid metropolitan order. Within this hierarchy, felt no less by the African American New Yorker than by the white, Harlem is not epicenter but periphery. "Harlem," in Ralph Ellison's phrase, "is nowhere": "To live in Harlem is to dwell in the very bowels of the city; it is to pass a labyrinthine existence among streets that explode monotonously skyward with the spires and crosses of churches and clutter under foot with garbage and decay. Harlem is a ruin."[82] Harlem was not only peripheral geographically (reaching down from the Bronx, Harlem was separated from downtown Manhattan by well over a hundred city blocks), it was also, by and large, poor. For all the glamour of Harlem clubs and speakeasies of the Jazz Age, the district was also the site of the endemic poverty and deprivation characteristic of a social order that discriminated against blacks. For all its cultural centrality, Harlem remained, in a whole range of important ways, caught within the dominating orbit of the skyscraper cluster to its south. In the end, this charmed enclave, like others in the stratified and heterogeneous modern city, could be easily located by all urbanites, both physically and socially, by its inferior relation to Manhattan's towering core.

Although it was written and set in the 1940s, Ralph Ellison's great masterpiece, *Invisible Man*, offers perhaps the best reinterpretation of these enduring psychosocial hierarchies in the vertical sublime modern city. When the novel's narrator first arrives in New York on a train, he is preoccupied, distracted, "daydreaming." He emerges into a train station devoid of definition, immersed immediately in a cityscape entirely lacking in topographical or narrative description. This first view of the city is a blank one, a missed recognition. Instead of expressing awe at the sight of the metropolis when he departs the train, the protagonist merely reveals his disorientation. He is forced to ask for directions to Harlem, is told, "That's easy . . . you just keep heading north,"[83] and then stumbles into the crowded and jostling subway. This subway trip is stripped of the thrill and excitement recounted so often in white observers' first encounters with cosmopolitan modern urbanity. He is simply crushed between a mass of intimately described passengers and vertiginously thrust down into the city's depths: "The train seemed to plunge downhill now, only to lunge to a stop that shot me out upon a platform feeling like something regurgitated from the belly of a frantic whale. Wrestling with my bags, I swept along with the crowd, up the stairs into the hot street" (158).

Here the narrator echoes generations of African Americans newly arrived in New York. The flash of recognition and revelatory excitement comes not at the sight of a vertical, modern city of skyscrapers but at a cosmopolitanism of an entirely different sort. It is not buildings and technology that impress Ellison's newcomer but the masses of "black people against a background of brick buildings, neon signs, plate glass and roaring traffic. . . . This really was Harlem, and now all the stories which I had heard of the city-within-a-city leaped alive in my mind" (158–59). It is the sight of Harlem from the subway steps that marks the moment of revelation—that first awed glimpse of the modern cityscape—for the African American tourist. Appropriately, the narrator is struck by the scene around him: "I moved wide-eyed, trying to take the bombardment of impressions" (159).

Yet, in this particular account, such cosmopolitanism is not merely another manifestation of the urban sublime, an African American variation on a universal theme of modern urbanity. The mood of reverie and appreciation is almost immediately shattered; an agitated crowd blocks the protagonist's progress along the avenue. A sidewalk speaker, "a short squat man [who] shouted angrily from a ladder to which were attached a collection of American flags," shatters the quiet spectatorial detachment of the urban observer: "It was ahead of me, angry and shrill, and upon hearing it I had a sensation of shock and fear such as I had felt as a child when surprised by my father's voice. An emptiness widened in my stomach" (159). This urban street is as threatening and disconcerting as it is awe-inspiring. Ellison's modern city, even supposedly nurturing Harlem, is a place of raw human emotion—a chaotic swirl of anger and violence: "The clash between the calm of the rest of the street and the passion of the voice gave the scene a strange out-of-joint quality" (160–61). Within a few steps, the traveler has again become disoriented and confused. His only recourse is once more to ask for directions—this time from a pair of bemused and casually intimidating white policemen. He is directed to the Men's House and admits he "would have to take Harlem a little at a time" (161). In the space of a page, *Invisible Man* twice deprives its protagonist of the expected moments of visual pleasure upon arriving in the modern metropolis. Likewise, the reader is denied the frisson by identification of these exemplary sights, these revelations of the city—these rhetorical tropes—so familiar and cherished in the literature of the late nineteenth and twentieth centuries.

Further, the narrator and reader soon find that in this particular African American version of New York, Harlem can never be a real, unambiguous space of possibility—the sheltering and self-contained alternative metropolis that it is for many other New York writers. Instead, in these initial Gotham sections of *Invisible Man*, still framed within a logic of capitalist ambition and hope, potential for success revolves around the (white) urban core of the city; as a consequence, for all its activity and energy, Harlem must remain resolutely marginal. Despite the attractive power of Harlem, for this migrant as for so many other Americans, it is ultimately downtown Manhattan that lies at the center of the urban orbit, as the envisioned ideal destination of the migratory circuit from rural southern poverty to urban northern promise.

The next day, Ellison's protagonist is determined to start off on a new foot with the city: "The next morning I took an early subway into the Wall Street district, selecting an address that carried me almost to the end of the island. It was dark with the tallness of the buildings and the narrow streets" (164). In search of a job and confident of his references, the newcomer finally encounters the archetypal skyscraper metropolis, like so many others before him: "I hurried to my address and was challenged with the sheer height of the white stone with its sculptured bronze façade. Men and women hurried inside, and after staring for a moment I followed, taking the elevator and being pushed to the back of the car. It rose like a rocket, creating a sensation in my crotch as though an important part of myself had been left below in the lobby" (165). Here at last is the moment of sublime, vividly physical, appreciation of the vertical metropolis. It is among these towers that New York's true economic center lies. This is no Horatio Alger tale, though. For the African American pilgrim, physical and social locations cannot so neatly coincide. The elevator ride is more disconcerting than thrilling, and in this building, the narrator finds not a fresh start but disappointment. He discovers he cannot get past the secretaries and receptionists, either in person or subsequently by telephone. He is forced to return to his little room in Harlem, a physical retreat from the towering skyscrapers commensurate to his economic hopes and aspirations.

Determined and ambitious, soon Ellison's narrator again ventures into the heart of white New York: "I felt better walking along. A feeling of confidence grew. Far down the island the skyscrapers rose tall and mysterious in the thin, pastel haze" (172). Once more he enters a towering building full of hope, only to meet rejection. Now, though, the disappointment is more profound, as he finds his references worthless. There is no ready ticket for the poor African American migrant to enter this world of wealth and power. He has been trespassing amid the towers; when the protagonist discovers that the advantageous job opportunity in New York City he had been promised was a ruse all along, the city's built architecture seems to conspire in his disappointment. "The elevator dropped me like a shot and I went out and walked along the street. The sun was very bright now and the people along the walk seemed far away. I stopped before a gray wall where high above me the headstones of a church graveyard arose like the tops of buildings" (193). The narrator, who so shortly before had ridden to the top of the world, is brought low. The shining cosmopolis of towers is now a mocking necropolis of gravestones.

In Ellison's depiction of the physical and psychological topography of power and privilege in the modern metropolis, the psychosocial hierarchy structures the cityscape both horizontally (concentrically, from downtown Manhattan outward) and vertically (from skyscraper pinnacle downwards). On his first failed pilgrimage to Wall Street, the narrator was spun back out to racially and geographically peripheral Harlem. This time, his trajectory combines an outward spiral with a continuous, vertiginous descent. Instead of retreating again to his uptown hostel, the protagonist takes a job offered in consolation at the Liberty paint factory, far out in the city's white periphery of Long Island (where, in accordance with the city's racial topography, they make Optic White paint—"It's the purest white that can be found"

[202]). Soon he is sent down to the boiler room far below the ground—"It was a deep basement. Three levels underground I pushed upon a heavy metal door marked 'Danger' and descended into a noisy, dimly lit room" (207)—and plunges into a surrealistic odyssey (or is this Orpheus's journey?) that ultimately takes him to the factory "hospital" and a course of shock therapy. Sometime later, the protagonist emerges dazed from the Long Island plant. Although he seems to have escaped the subterranean world, he continues to plunge downward:

> Along the walk the buildings rose, uniform and close together. It was day's end now and on top of every building the flags were fluttering and diving down, collapsing. And I felt that I would fall, had fallen, moved now as against a current sweeping swiftly against me. Out of the grounds and up the street I found the bridge by which I'd come, but the stairs leading back to the car that crossed the top were too dizzily steep to climb, swim or fly, and I found a subway instead. . . . The train plunged. I dropped through the roar, giddy and vacuum-minded, sucked under and out into late afternoon Harlem. (250–51)

His body battered, mind scrambled, hopes dashed, and faith in the order of society shattered, the migrant to the modern metropolis has already begun to understand the more subtle psychological dimensions of the city of towers—a place where one's precise coordinates are always manifestly clear. The legibility of the city of *Invisible Man* extends beyond mere physical location; it also comprehends topographic grids of class and race and hope.

In the end, of course, Ellison's African American protagonist finds "a home—or a hole in the ground, as you will. . . . My hole is warm and full of light. Yes, *full* of light. I doubt if there is a brighter spot in all New York than this hole of mine, and I do not exclude Broadway. Or the Empire State Building on a photographer's dream night. But that is taking advantage of you. Those two spots are among the darkest of our whole civilization" (6). Light and dark, high and low, central and marginal: the modern city is structured by oppositions—"contradictions," in the narrator's phrasing. Each pole in the city's exemplary topography is clearly demarcated, brilliantly comprehensible, and brutally impersonal. The entire social and structural force of the city serves this larger order through relentless processes of purification and segregation. Ellison's protagonist only begins to understand this modern metropolis, microcosm and center of a series of even more expansive worlds, when he recognizes his own invisibility in it. There is a hierarchy of visibility in the modern city as well: as those transcendent downtown buildings tower unavoidably and tangibly over the streets below, this marginalized individual fades into imperceptibility and obscurity. The rigid gridiron logic that makes skyscrapers visually and conceptually dominant reduces Ellison's African American migrant to virtual insignificance. Thus, although *Invisible Man* ends on a hopeful note of prospective reemergence, the dominant key of the represented urban world is set out by Louis Armstrong in the novel's first pages: "What did I do / To be so black / And blue?" (12). This gigantic Jazz Age—or Machine Age—urban mechanism is profoundly and inherently dehumanizing and brutalizing in its unyielding structures and systems of signification. For Ellison's African American New Yorker, the legible topography of the city may at first appear a clear centrifugal order of hope and promise, but in time it inevitably and inexorably reveals altogether more sinister geographies.

Ultimately, it is this play of posed contradictions—clear structure and partial comprehension, gridlike uniformity and great disparities of power and wealth, refinement and brutal exploitation, high and low, center and periphery—that characterizes the modern metropolis. Animated by the vertical sublime, as well as by raptures of transport and ordered stasis, this city proved a potent and alluring symbol of the Jazz Age. For most Americans, whether in New York, Chicago, or some other aspiring metropolis, or stuck out in the self-consciously peripheral rural "sticks," the skyscraper and its environment defined and exemplified the wonders of 1920s modernity. This was the transcendent modernity upon which Los Angeles of the mid-1920s dared to turn its back.

4

Modern Los Angeles

The two images are striking, if reassuringly familiar. One, a high-contrast photograph, features a lone woman casually surveying a modern urban landscape of tall buildings that seemingly stretches to the limits of vision (see figure 26). Her high perch (protruding, improbably, from outside the frame into the vertiginous image) affords her a royal perspective over all she observes and implies a viewing position elevated even above this cluster of towers. Her demeanor and stance convey the impression that she approves of the spectacle before her gaze. Is she evaluating this urban progress, or is she an allegorical figure, representing in attractive form and contemporary attire the very spirit of the modern metropolis around her?

The second image is far more futuristic and not ambiguous at all (see figure 27). In fact, this sketch is so finely delineated as to appear the work of a draftsman. Aside from the futuristic stylized glaring sun in the top right corner (and more vaguely—and improbably—a similar design in the bottom left), which could have come directly from the science fiction pulps of the era, this image conveys the full aspect of a serious technical schematic. In the center of the frame rises a single massive, roughly cruciform skyscraper, surmounted at its rooftop by a series of mooring masts for dirigibles, as well as airplane landing strips. Descriptive text boxes sketched into the drawing beside this towering structure direct the viewer's attention to notable features of the building. This graphic narration makes immediately clear that, at forty acres, this is no ordinary skyscraper. Instead, it purports to stretch "about 1,000 feet high with 15 times the floor area of the Woolworth Building." The tallest building of its age, this mammoth tower "would house about 150,000 people," a caption proclaims. Within this single megastructure would be situated an entire industrial complex, accompanied by thousands of elevated residential apartments honeycombed

FIGURE 26. Panorama of a dense conurbation. *Los Angeles Record*
anniversary edition cover, 1 January 1926.

into the crenellated central vertical shafts. Despite the density of habitation, each of
these myriad interior rooms offers an "unobstructed view of [the] surrounding country," also allowing a panoramic perspective over large portions of the many-branched
tower. Far below, a caption notes with an engineer's precision, the foundations of the
exemplary futuristic skyscraper rest on "caissons in a reservoir of liquid mud as protection from tornadoes, quakes, etc." This careful attention to architectural detail in
the utopian vision betokens the work of an expert delineator—an impression ver-
ified by the author's name drawn at the bottom of the frame: he is none other than
Lloyd Wright, son of the already legendary master builder and by this time himself
a notable (and usually quite serious) professional architect.[1]

Vivid but not particularly exceptional examples of the vertical sublime, these two
representative images—one confidently celebrating contemporary metropolitan

The labels within the figure read:

PASSENGER AND FREIGHT DIRIGIBLES AND AIRPLANES USING AIRPORTS ON ROOF OF BUILDING.

CITY OF FUTURE TO BE SINGLE UNIT OF REINFORCED CONCRETE FACED WITH BRONZE AND GLASS, ABOUT 1,000 FEET HIGH WITH 15 TIMES THE FLOOR AREA OF THE WOOLWORTH BUILDING. THIS STRUCTURE WOULD HOUSE ABOUT 150,000 PEOPLE.

BUILDING IN CENTER OF 20-MILE SQUARE METROPOLITAN DISTRICT, LAND BEING TAKEN UP WITH FARMS, FOREST AND PARKS. ALL EASILY ACCESSIBLE, WITHIN FIVE MINUTES' RUN FROM BUILDING.

ALL ROOMS HAVE UNOBSTRUCTED VIEW OF SURROUNDING COUNTRY, BEING COLUMNATED WITH BRONZE BUTTRESSED GLASS WINDOWS, REFLECTING LIGHT TO ALL PARTS OF STRUCTURE. BY MEANS OF SYSTEM OF BLINDS, LIGHT CAN BE SHUT OFF AT WILL

FORTY ACRE BUILDING ERECTED ON FLOATING FOUNDATION OF CAISSONS IN A RESERVOIR OF LIQUID MUD AS PROTECTION FROM TORNADOS, QUAKES, ETC.

DIRIGIBLE MASTS

AIRPLANE LANDING FIELDS

RESIDENTIAL, ADMINISTRATION, AND AMUSEMENTS

LANDING STATIONS AND DISTRIBUTION

INDUSTRIALS IN FOUNDATION AND LOWER STORIES.

LLOYD WRIGHT

FIGURE 27. Lloyd Wright's plan for a thousand-foot tower. *Los Angeles Examiner,* 26 November 1926. Courtesy of the kind permission of Eric Lloyd Wright.

progress, appropriately symbolized by a field of skyscrapers, the other packed with the imaginative detail of frenetic and enthusiastic urban utopianism—look like so many others emerging from the modern ebullience of Jazz Age New York or Chicago. The first image, though, was splashed across the cover of the working-class *Los Angeles Record*'s "Anniversary Edition," and the second appeared, also in 1926, in the solidly conservative *Los Angeles Examiner*.

VISIONS OF A VERTICAL LOS ANGELES

As we have seen, soon after 1910 an increasingly powerful cadre of planners in greater Los Angeles began formulating and adapting plans for a decentralized future Southern California modeled on the garden city concept. These experts contrasted their dream of a spread-out, sunny, and clearly demarcated cityscape to the congested, blighted, and chaotic cities they perceived in the East. They saw this truly new vision of the modern metropolitan region as ideally suited to the climate, topography, and culture of Los Angeles—more appropriate, in fact, than the existing built-up sections of the city. They fully intended to make those "congested districts" irrelevant to the lives of future Angelenos, who would hardly notice them gradually withering away, abandoned remnants of an obsolete urbanism.

Clearly, though, not all Angelenos agreed with this vision, nor with its explicit rejection of dominant models of urban modernity or of the existing urban core. Many established locals had no interest in utopian notions of scattered peripheral development, which looked to them like a renunciation of the central city's cherished municipal ambitions. Certainly, planners' reluctance to fully present their case for regional decentralization in the city's fora for public discourse—a reticence undoubtedly largely attributable to Progressive Era ideologies of detached professional expertise and disinterested political noninvolvement—was proving a serious mistake. These experts, who for a decade had claimed the exclusive privilege to "Dream dreams and see Visions" of the city's future, were instead visibly preoccupied with the seemingly irrelevant minutiae of zoning and subdivision regulation. It is no wonder, then, that many civic leaders in Greater Los Angeles, faced with mounting traffic chaos that planners appeared helpless to cure (the only promise of immediate relief being offered by outside consultants), began in the second half of the 1920s to openly promote radically divergent images of the future of the region.

Of course, the region's traditional booster coalition of businessmen, real estate promoters, and newspaper editors had for years been circulating their shared vision of Los Angeles as the great American metropolis of the Pacific—a city that would eclipse San Francisco, in particular, as the western outpost of modern urbanity. By the 1920s, despite its reputation for doughty traditionalism, that northern city had vigorously rebuilt after its earthquake and fire in resolutely ambitious form. Indeed, San Franciscans had erected their city's first skyscraper remarkably early, in the 1880s, in a project designed by none other than Chicago's pioneering architectural firm of Burnham and Root,[2] and had proceeded in the twentieth century to erect an ostentatiously fireproof core of respectable buildings both in the old central business district and along Market Street. Although in these decades the Northern Californian city had not gone as resolutely vertical as it would later in the twentieth century, it was clearly committed even at this point to a metropolitan future as a highly centralized, concentric urban metropolis. This is the path, of course, that Chicago had taken after its great fire, despite earlier utopian gestures toward the low-rise neoclassicism of the Columbian Exposition's White City. Chicago had become a famously vertical city; now San Francisco looked to be following the same course of urban modernization.

Los Angeles had had no great fire or earthquake. It already possessed a set of impressive downtown structures, and the overwhelming growth of the 1920s promised a new rush of central development. Signs of that expansion and intensification were already plain: the daily crush of traffic in the district unmistakably testified to the future of that thriving business zone. The only serious threat to prosperity downtown—aside, apparently, from the city's paid planning experts—was that very success, which might stifle commercial activity under a crush of automobiles, streetcars, and eager shoppers. Nevertheless, all other signs looked good for Jazz Age downtown Los Angeles, and in the wake of the overwhelming approval of the 1924 *Major Traffic Street Plan*, it seemed as if that one pressing crisis might eventually ease as well. Indeed, as Richard Longstreth points out in his important study of retail commerce in the region, *City Center to Regional Mall*, the downtown district was undergoing something of a boom in these years: "Despite ongoing traffic problems, downtown building construction continued at a fast pace during the 1920s. Sixteen buildings reaching the maximum allowable height limit stood downtown in 1918, seventy-two in 1925, one hundred three in 1929. At the decade's end, Los Angeles boasted one of the most extensive business cores of any American city, exceeded only by those few with larger populations."[3]

Skyscrapers, or the local height-limit version of them, were sprouting up all over the district, stretching the boundaries of commercial centralization far to the south and west. Certainly, if it were not for the novel growth of commerce in previously undeveloped or peripheral "subcenters" of the metropolis, this rapid building progress in the central business district would have received more historiographical attention over the past eighty years. Clearly, taken on its own terms, as an already highly developed urban core, downtown Los Angeles was not doing nearly as badly as city planners and other experts implied, nor as later historians have adjudged. By most measures, downtown was, at this point, not doing badly at all; the toll taken by outlying development and by the crushing traffic congestion appeared to many observers to hardly affect the vibrant district by the mid-1920s.

To most businessmen, it in fact seemed that Los Angeles's downtown was not

under siege—collapsing under the congestive weight of its functional overcentralization, as planners would have it—but rather overspilling its traditional bounds.
If far-off subcenters were growing, so too were areas of the city closer in. The eastern portion of Wilshire Boulevard, for instance, was attracting unprecedented commercial activity even in 1925, and that street was specifically selected in the *Major
Traffic Street Plan* to be a major radial boulevard connecting the western parts of
the city to the central business district. Preliminary work was already underway, at
this early stage, to put the plan into practice and cut the thoroughfare right through
Westlake Park, the previously solid buffer on the western edge of the downtown
core. It is not surprising, then, that some business leaders—again in alliance with
real estate interests (sometimes these were the same people)—saw Wilshire as the
future conduit for downtown expansion into the rapidly developing west side. They
envisioned the central district gradually extending to the west, as it had, to a smaller
degree, many times over the previous decades. The conceptual model here was
clearly Manhattan development, which had moved progressively uptown through
the previous half-century.

In this vein, an influential consortium of business leaders in the downtown area
did not just wish to extend the central district's influence westward; they planned
to orchestrate the development of the new Wilshire Boulevard corridor to modernize the entire metropolis. Logically, these men felt, downtown would need to
grow proportionately to the larger city. The growth in the west side, as well as the
region as a whole, which already exceeded all reasonable expectations, would eventually require a massive vertical and horizontal elaboration of the central district.
Although the city had grown chaotically during the 1920s, and particularly rapidly
at its most remote outskirts, businessmen could assume such a pattern of development to be merely the sloppy consequence of explosive growth—and perhaps of
mismanagement by the city's new planning bureaucracy. In fact, it was becoming
clear at this point that the vaunted city planning agencies did not intend to do anything to correct this fragmenting, scattershot development. It even seemed as though
planners were encouraging it to some degree, especially through zoning and other
regulatory support for outlying commercial subcenters. Nevertheless, all twentieth-
century urban experience taught that a city's inherent concentric pattern was sure
to reassert itself eventually. The entire regional transit infrastructure—and particularly the extensive streetcar system, although understandably overstressed at the
moment—would gradually funnel new Angelenos downtown for work and commerce, thus helping to restore the natural order of the metropolis. As this growth
was properly assimilated into the concentric structure of the city, the dense interior rings of that concentrated system would gradually expand outward, in larger
radii, while the inner core would expand upward. Ultimately, the proper development of Wilshire Boulevard would be central to both these inevitable, natural
processes of urban modernization.

It was gradually becoming clear by the middle of the decade that, beyond merely wishing to exploit the street's growing volume of traffic through ordinary roadside shops, these businessmen "harbored a much more ambitious program. Their vision of future development was thoroughly metropolitan in character. . . . Wilshire's destiny should entail not just an assemblage of fashionable shops but a skyscraper center of unparalleled dimensions."[4] As Longstreth explains, downtown leaders fully expected that Wilshire would be the first stage in an ambitious urban modernization program for the metropolis that would ultimately result in the revocation of the old restrictive height limit and the proper redevelopment of the downtown district as a region of vertical towers. These plans for Wilshire were most certainly not idle boosterism, nor was this the stuff of utopian impracticality. Many prominent and influential Angelenos firmly believed that such an ambitious "objective was attainable. Besides the redevelopment of Fifth Avenue in midtown Manhattan, which had been evolving since the late nineteenth century, precedent existed with North Michigan Avenue in Chicago, which, like Wilshire, was of recent vintage and was now rapidly becoming lined with tall buildings."[5] Freed from artificial restrictions—such as the height limit and, particularly galling, the planners' capricious designation through their new zoning powers of the entire Wilshire corridor as a low-density residential area—Los Angeles would surely follow the course of comparable cities of the era.

This was the dream of local booster Irving Hellman, "one of the city's prominent financiers and real estate investors."[6] In the mid-1920s, he edited and published in Los Angeles a journal aptly titled *The Skyscraper*. In the first issue, under the bold heading "The Skyscraper's Influence on Municipal Progress," Hellman declared that skyscrapers "express in the spirit of our city a challenge that invites us to time progress to the hour, to build on and on until we reach the full stature prescribed for the greater Los Angeles of the distant future."[7] The city, he implied, would be judged by Americans in terms of its vertical aspirations. If Los Angeles failed to commit to this preeminent symbol of modern urbanity, it would not only be shirking its destiny as a great metropolis but would be undermining its health. If urban observers secretly suspected that the old western cow town had simply outgrown itself, engorged by transitory migration, Angelenos' irrational refusal to modernize would surely confirm that damning assessment. The reputation and future growth of the city depended on keeping up with the times, and resplendent verticality was the obvious way to do this. This sort of rhetoric was commonplace in New York and other American cities at this time, but it was a challenge to the status quo—the common sense—prevalent in Los Angeles. Hellman's enthusiasm for the skyscraper and the vertical city form it implied, so typical in the larger national urban context, represented a radical, if growing, strand of visionary sentiment in Southern California of the 1920s (see figure 28).[8]

The views of Hellman and his peers were a direct challenge to the consensus built

Miss Los Angeles Contemplates a Brilliant Future

FIGURE 28. The allure of the vertical sublime. *Los Angeles Times,* 31 December 1928. Copyright 1928, *Los Angeles Times.* Reprinted with permission.

over the previous decade by Los Angeles's expert planning establishment. The influence of that "traditional" vision of modern urbanism, encapsulated so vividly in Manhattan's exemplary skyscraper skyline, threatened during its mid-1920s heyday to upset the carefully articulated utopian visions of the City Planning Commission. It is testimony to the cultural resonance and power of the vertical sublime during this time that decades of booster rhetoric about pastoral bungalow courts and undeveloped sweeps of verdantly citrus- and palm-covered countryside could be so blithely discarded by Los Angeles's business leaders. More pointedly, this discourse reveals a potential weakness in the planners' ability to transmit fully their visions and dreams to the community. In retrospect, it seems obvious that even during this period, when the garden city decentralizing vision seemed most overpowering in the city's collective imagination, powerful groups were skeptical about such a pastoral vision of the region's future. Downtown business leaders, who clearly questioned the modernity and monumentality of the low-density garden city plans, must have long harbored suspicions that such schemes were ultimately unworkable in a contemporary metropolis of the stature Los Angeles looked likely to assume during these boom years. With this sort of backing, it was probably inevitable that despite the best efforts of local planners, images of Los Angeles as a towering city of skyscrapers would remain a potent counterhegemonic force for years to come. Soon these divisions would explode into open conflict, spurring what one historian has termed "one of the bitterest campaigns in the history of the City of the Angels."[9]

GAINING PERSPECTIVE
ON A TROUBLED METROPOLIS

Discourse about skyscrapers and the vertical city reflected concerns not only about urban modernity perceived as a matter of style or about cosmopolitan boosterism and civic pride—as important as these may have been in an age of enthusiasm for and growth of the city—but about fundamental metropolitan comprehensibility. The emblematic skyscraper offered a privileged perspective on the concentric city, and it helped transmit that structural clarity to urban observers. If Los Angeles was already beginning to seem disturbingly illegible and disordered, with its traffic jams and barely controlled growth, perhaps that was because there was really no proper vantage point from which to make sense of it. Los Angeles's height-limit buildings, capped at 150 feet, offered no privileged perspective on such an expansive metropolis. These so-called skyscrapers, which stood at the base of Los Angeles's urban pretensions, were in truth more massive than they were tall. They were thick, squat, blocky forms, totally unlike the sleek pinnacled towers that captured the Jazz Age imagination of urban observers in Chicago, New York, and other cities fully committed to the vertical sublime. Without prominent skyscrapers, bridges, or other available observation posts, Southern California proffered few truly panoramic perspectives upon itself. Further, the views that were available in this period, such as the impressive vistas from Mount Lowe—located out past Pasadena and approachable only by a vertiginous four-hour round trip along a steep three-thousand-foot narrow-gauge railway—were neither readily accessible (and certainly not for everyday use) nor particularly well situated for observation of the city form (nor could they be easily spotted from down below).[10]

This paucity of usable sites for urban perspective was pressing enough that debate raged throughout the first half of the 1920s about the possibility of constructing a new city hall—plans for which had been bandied about from the early 1910s—which might serve as both an observation post upon the city and a landmark visible from the streets below. Squarely opposed to a proposed new towering civic center, though, was the city's height limit, generally recognized as the chief bulwark against Los Angeles following the developmental path taken by eastern metropolises. Would not, it was asked ominously, one tall building invite the wholesale transformation of the Pacific metropolis into a city of skyscrapers? Might not an elevated city hall betoken the end of Los Angeles's proud status as a city of low-slung bungalows and sunny streets? These were the stakes involved in the continuing debate over a new civic center, producing great confusion and uncertainty in the city of the mid-1920s. So powerful was the allure of modern urban models, of cities of spires and towers, and so insecure by this point was the still unrealized promise of a new sort of decentralized urban modernity, that for many Angelenos the construction of a single tall building threatened to decisively frame the future development of the entire metropolitan region.

Los Angeles was clearly at a crossroads, suffering from an unarticulated trepidation at the future. Coming at a moment of manifest civic popularity—demonstrated by a population explosion the likes of which even the most ardent booster could not have envisioned—this anxiety seems inexplicable. Yet Los Angeles was caught in a crisis of urban identity, stuck between visions of its future. Underneath this discourse lay a fundamental uncertainty about the city as it then was. Debate over the metropolis of tomorrow always implicitly revolved around blurry conceptions of the existing city—how it was structured, what gave it character or identity, what qualities were worth preserving or enhancing in the future. If Los Angeles had not many years before been an easily comprehensible place, it now seemed quite a bit less legible, its future less clear. And in an odd way, it was precisely the dramatic growth, this manifest endorsement of the Southern Californian lifestyle, that undermined civic confidence on a number of levels. In a sense, Los Angeles had overshot its immediate ambitions; the metropolis was suddenly facing a slew of big-city problems brought on by its explosive growth. No longer merely a city with enormous promise, Los Angeles now clearly had to reconcile the implications of its expansion within an existing environment. It had become, seemingly overnight, the fifth largest city in the country—with over a million people—and it was still growing.

In an age when urban growth restrictions were scarcely imaginable, it was taken as indisputable that development was a sign of urban health. Yet for the first time, civic leaders began to express some veiled concern about the repercussions of this breakneck growth. The *Examiner,* the city's leading newspaper, began to publicly consider the ramifications and responsibilities brought on by Los Angeles's expansion. In a box prominently demarcated with heavy leading and positioned at the top of every editorial page of the mid- and late 1920s, the paper declared ominously that "the second million population is on its way to Los Angeles." To prepare for this inevitable influx, the newspaper insisted, the city's infrastructure needed to be upgraded. On a daily basis, the editors offered a list of priorities, stressing the pressing need for basic utilities, such as water and power ("Boulder Canyon High Dam" and "Colorado River Aqueduct"), and especially traffic relief ("Major Traffic Highways" and "Rapid Transit System"). A city of this size was faced with new needs and new obligations. *"Get Ready, Los Angeles!"* the *Examiner* admonished.

This public notice was hardly necessary; everyone in Los Angeles could see by the mid-1920s that the explosion in the city's population was making a mess of the metropolis's infrastructure. Most visible, of course, was the vexing transportation crisis. Fanned by sensationalist newspaper coverage of grisly accidents and the failure of all deliberate measures, such as the implementation of the *Major Traffic Street Plan,* to immediately improve the daily commute, traffic discourse dominated local imagining. This crisis, tied as it was to recurrent moral panics about accident death tolls and the recklessness of speed, convinced many Angelenos that the city was failing to cope with its new size and status. Los Angeles seemed a juvenile delinquent among cities. The problem was not merely lagging infrastructural construction; the city was becoming disorganized and jumbled, blurring into an incoherent illegibility that threatened to make it the butt of a nation's hostile jokes. This critical discourse was taking an increasingly serious tone by the mid-1920s. For a city so invested in its image, a growing list of telltale urban inadequacies was serious indeed.

MAKING LOS ANGELES MODERN

Not lost on the elites of Southern California's business community, enviously eyeing eastern counterparts in their glassy towers, was the vertical city's promise to resolve many of these irksome problems once and for all. Chaotic and frustrating automotive traffic, swirling without discernable pattern or logic, seemed to this newly assertive contingent of would-be modernizers to be a plague visited upon the city as punishment for its rebellion against the prevailing trends in American urban development. By failing to properly build up its city core, these critics suggested, Los Angeles was being not simply inefficient or backward but self-destructive. A spread-out pattern of settlement might suit a provincial community, but it would bring disaster to a major metropolis of a million or more citizens. To support such a population, cities required intensive and elaborate infrastructure systems, making full use of multiple spatial planes. The modern large city required an array of stacked support systems, from subways to elevated roads to airplanes and skyscrapers. Only with this multilayered and dense infrastructure might cities expect to harmonize the potentially conflicting and virtually incalculable movements of so many individuals. This was the most attractive promise of the skyscraper city: to dissolve intractable essential urban frictions by partitioning them into a third dimension. By

making use of the practically unlimited frontiers of sky and earth, previously inevitable friction between streams of traffic, each vying for limited and precious surface area, could be made to literally vanish into thin air. The modern metropolis
offered the alluring possibility of delivering urbanites from vexing and contentious
strife over finite real estate, while offering an urban form that was entirely legible
and comprehensible, where proper boundaries could be policed and maintained.
Thus the trend toward the vertical was a matter not merely of aesthetics or style but
of efficiency and responsible necessity.

In the eyes of many of the city's business leaders, Los Angeles was going to become more vertical whether it wished to or not. In fact, the inevitability of the modernizing redevelopment of spread-out and low-rise Southern California had long
been acknowledged, surreptitiously, by engineers and other infrastructure experts.
Although isolated proposals for constructing elaborate urban infrastructure projects appeared throughout the first decades of the twentieth century in Los Angeles, by the 1920s such speculation began to find its way into official documents. In
arguing that the city's streets were too narrow, the Automobile Club suggested in
its influential 1922 traffic plan that "this can be corrected . . . by arcading or constructing sidewalks under the building fronts and setting the curbs back to the
present property lines."[11] The Los Angeles Traffic Commission's report of that year
dutifully repeated that "the width of the streets in the congested district might be
increased actually by arcading into buildings for a new sidewalk, moving the present
curb line then to the present building line and increasing the traffic way of the streets
by twice the width of the present sidewalk."[12] Mainly, the Traffic Commission was
interested only in increasing street width by claiming surface space from adjacent
buildings. In a vision that might have come directly from New York's Hugh Ferriss
and Harvey Corbett, though, the commissioners speculated at some length on the
possibility of making use of vertical space to accommodate downtown Los Angeles's crush of automotive and streetcar traffic. Instead of arcading sidewalks, they
raised the possibility of fully double-decking the city's downtown thoroughfares,
constructing elevated roadways right through the height-limit buildings: "The width
of streets in this congested district could also be increased by arcading back from
the street line a sufficient distance to provide a two-way auto drive at the second
floor level of all buildings, or at such level as would clear the trolley wires at street
crossings, extending this driveway across the streets on overhead structures, so as
to make them continuous."[13] Faced with the economic—and certainly, political—
cost of an elaborate urban reconstruction program that would require rebuilding
many of downtown's most valuable buildings, the Traffic Commission sensibly decided in the end to defer action on their vertical sublime flights of fancy: "The question of arcading for new sidewalks, second story auto driveways, and subways, in
and across the congested district, is one, however, that this Commission is not prepared, as yet, to make definite recommendations [on]."[14]

Despite the commission's unwillingness in 1922 to propose a full-scale urban modernization program, official speculation about such a reconstruction of Los Angeles did not fade away. The *Major Traffic Street Plan* of two years later returned to the topic, noting in a discussion of grade separations that "a still more intricate system might then be evolved, providing multi-story streets."[15] An appendix expanded upon this line of thinking, offering several drawings of possible elevated or submerged automotive roadways. Ultimately, however, the Traffic Commission was again unwilling to recommend such ambitious plans, concluding that although "under special conditions a continuous elevated roadway is worthy of thought," in general "this method of accelerating street traffic must be classed as an heroic measure to be adopted only when an impasse has been reached and the other usual means of relief prove inadequate."[16] Given the costs, full official sanction for vertical sublime solutions to Los Angeles's traffic problems would clearly have to wait.

However, the need for grade separations between intersecting forms of street traffic had become by the mid-1920s a matter of public urgency. Collisions resulting from the city's failure to remove streetcars and automobiles to discrete vertical levels were constant topics of media and public attention. As a planner skeptical of the growing discourse on the city's urban modernization put it, "The automobile now contests the surface of the street with the street car, and popular sentiment in many places demands that the street car give way and go underground or overhead."[17] Indeed, this was exactly what the *Major Traffic Street Plan* had assumed would eventually occur in the city, for, in the view of the Traffic Commission, this could be the only permanent solution to downtown's traffic woes: "The street car, owing to its economy of space and low cost of operation per passenger, must take precedence over other forms of vehicles in the congested area whenever the traffic capacity of the arteries approaches its limit, and prior to reduction in use of surface street cars by the still more intensive mass transportation offered by subways or elevated lines."[18] Despite this rhetoric of giving the public railways "precedence," the traffic commissioners were ultimately more interested in removing trains from the city's streets than in contemplating ambitious rapid transit construction programs. The problem of rapid transit was left to a future report specifically dealing with that subject. This would be the last mention of rapid transit in the *Major Traffic Street Plan*, the remainder of which was dedicated to lengthy discussion, which we have previously looked at, of a series of specific provisions for automobile transportation.[19] Given the potential construction costs of "this still more intensive mass transportation," Los Angeles's traffic planners were clearly unwilling to consider what appeared to be the most obvious solution for the downtown traffic crisis: making full use of vertical planes to separate and harmonize streams of traffic. Once more, substantial modernization programs for the city were raised in official discourse only to be deferred.

Although many of the city's engineers and experts were content to ponder the future necessity of such measures, one of the city's most powerful interests was willing to act. For the stalwart Pacific Electric Railway, the problem was a matter not of long-term inevitability but of urgent and immediate necessity. For the Pacific Electric, along with its sister, Los Angeles Railway, street traffic was no mere inconvenience; it was a threat to the company's very survival. Despite the remarkable prevalence of automobile ownership and automotive commuting, which was so obviously fouling up the city's traffic grid, the majority of Angelenos still relied on the streetcar to get around town. Yet the railway had suffered terribly throughout the decade from surface street congestion, and it was getting a bad reputation from the frequent grade-crossing collisions. By the mid-1920s, the traction companies' engineers began to express a note of desperation; major reorientations of the city's traffic infrastructure were absolutely essential if the transit system hoped to avoid total breakdown. After waiting fruitlessly for the city's leaders to act on the problem, the Pacific Electric decided in 1924 that it had to act on its own, and immediately. Thus the railway began excavations for what would become the city's first working subway, constructing its first link about "four-fifths of a mile from Hill Street between Fourth and Fifth Streets to a point near First Street and Glendale Boulevard,"[20] on the route toward the west side and Hollywood. Unlike the Traffic Commission, the notoriously stingy street railway system was clearly concerned enough about the severity and seriousness of the traffic problem that it was willing to take—and pay for—the first step in rebuilding the metropolis's transport infrastructure. Once again, the project of partitioning rail traffic into its own vertical plane was seen by engineers as the inevitable, exclusive, and necessary solution to a large city's transit problems. Consequently, the so-called Hollywood subway was presented quite explicitly as a step in the urban modernization of Los Angeles and was planned from the start as the first stage of a much larger system of elevated and submerged rail lines.

The Hollywood subway was seen by downtown interests as merely another step in the inevitable vertical development of their city. As important as the subway in this respect was the downtown station. The Pacific Electric's downtown terminal was situated at the foundations of a brand-new height-limit commercial building, where elevators could whisk "the commuter fortunate enough to be employed at an office in the structure" directly to his or her proper floor within seconds of alighting from the subway train.[21] This was exactly what skyscraper urban visionaries in Los Angeles were demanding.

The speed with which these plans were put into practice lent further encouragement to those enraptured by the promise of verticality. Begun in 1924, excavations on the new subway were finished on November 30, 1925, and the tube opened to great fanfare in 1926 (see figure 29).[22] Everything seemed to work; the "Subway Terminal Building itself was profitable" from the start, and "each train saved up to

FIGURE 29. Hollywood subway tunnel open for business, 1925. From Spencer Crump,
Ride the Big Red Cars: How Trolleys Helped Build Southern California (Los Angeles: Crest
Publications, 1962), 151. Courtesy of the kind permission of Pacific Railroad Publications.

fifteen minutes, thanks to the direct route and lack of interference from automobiles."[23] The prophets of a modern Los Angeles seemed vindicated. Yet, as soon as
the ceremonial bottle of ginger ale was smashed against the side of the first subway
train, all construction was halted on planned extensions to what officials had just
proclaimed would be "the seed of a vast subterranean system that would solve Los
Angeles' travel problems for all times" (see figure 30).[24] In 1924, critics of this vertical sublime dream had managed to draw to the attention of local politicians a city
charter provision requiring official approval of a full rapid transit plan before subway construction could progress.

This provision of the charter reflected the contemporary influence of the planning community, who insisted that no substantial construction program be allowed
to progress in the city without proper advance and comprehensive planning.[25] Al-

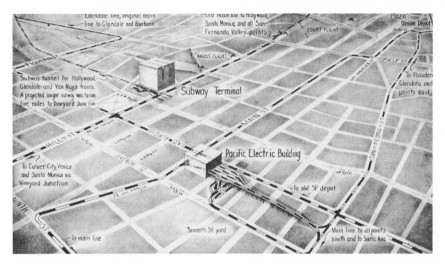

FIGURE 30. Extensive downtown network envisioned in the preempted Pacific Electric subway plan, 1925. Courtesy of the kind permission of Pacific Railroad Publications.

though this last-minute protest was not enough to halt construction on the Hollywood subway, which was already underway (and which proceeded using permits issued under special legal waivers), it did effectively hold up further work on the developing subway system.

A PROGRAM FOR A VERTICAL LOS ANGELES

In a sense, the businessmen who were more boldly advocating a large-scale urban modernization program—of which subway development would be merely one part—could view this enforced delay as something of an opportunity. After almost a decade of planners dominating civic discourse on the future of the metropolis with their visions of a decentralized Garden City paradise, downtown elites would now use this required rapid transit plan as an opportunity to put forth their own program for the city's prospective development. That the power of this centralizing group was on the rise was clearly demonstrated by the choice of engineers to draft the transit study. Once more, out-of-town experts were brought in; once more they brought a perspective at variance with that of the Los Angeles planning establishment. This time, though, downtown business leaders would get precisely the transportation advice they wanted. The city council retained the prestigious firm of Kelker, De Leuw, and Company from Chicago to plan a truly modern rapid transit system—and bring Los Angeles's rail infrastructure, as it were, into the twentieth century.

The plan these engineers submitted to the city in April 1925 could not have failed to delight the downtown interests who orchestrated the appointment. The report had as its primary goal the long-standing priority of grade crossing elimination,[26] a goal that was by now as commonplace in Los Angeles's civic consciousness as chatter about house prices and movie stars. Now perennial concern about traffic accidents was decisively recast as part of a discourse on verticality and modernity. The *Report and Recommendations on a Comprehensive Rapid Transit Plan for the City and County of Los Angeles* announced at the outset that the transit problems in Southern California stemmed from conflicts over the limited space of the existing street system, and that their solution required partitioning traffic into vertical urban space: "At the present time all classes of traffic move on the same plane (the street surface) and consequently there are frequent delays and interruptions. The segregation of traffic by providing separate planes is essential to permanent improvement and this best can be accomplished by the construction of rapid transit lines."[27] Grade crossing elimination required not merely the isolation of traffic streams at points of intersection but the wholesale segregation of rapid transit into its own level throughout the central city: "In the built-up sections of the city . . . the elevation or depression of the entire length of the track structure is necessary."[28] Only such radical reconstruction to exploit unused space could rescue the metropolis from its traffic blight. In fact, the report defined its very subject in terms of the use of vertical urban space: "Rapid transit operation requires the construction of railroad tracks either above or below the grade of streets."[29] There could be no transit without intensive urban modernization.

The Kelker De Leuw study delivered what the 1924 *Major Traffic Street Plan* would not. It concentrated its attentions on the central business area—what the earlier plan had termed "the congested district"—and attended to the city's outlying regions only in respect to their proper connections to that downtown core: "The focal point of the rapid transit system has been located at Seventh Street and Broadway in Los Angeles."[30] Given the centralizing focus, it was practically inevitable that the problems of the street railways finally would be given precedence and that such prioritization would spotlight the model of urban development (suburban periphery-vertical core) that downtown interests favored.[31] Once more, the 1925 plan delivered: "Horizontal street widening projects are essential and should be encouraged; however, vertical expansion of streets by the construction of subways, tunnels or elevated railroads will provide more relief from congestion in the central business district."[32] This program of "vertical expansion of streets" was exactly what the commercial interests in Los Angeles were calling for. The plan provided for a limited expansion of the new Pacific Electric subway, installation of "subsurface sidewalks, and the widespread construction of a network of elevated railway structures of modern design that would "provide for travel in natural light and open air and are particularly adapted to the climate of Los Angeles."[33]

That the plan of R. F. Kelker and Charles De Leuw delivered the sort of rapid transit program most favored by centralizers was no coincidence. In 1923, the year before they received their commission, that firm had published a *Report and Recommendations on a Physical Plan for a Unified Transportation System for the City of Chicago.* That transit study had called for the continued vertical development of the Chicago transit system, endorsing an expansion of the city's extensive use of elevated railroads knit into the dense fabric of the Loop. If Los Angeles's modernizers hoped their city would follow the developmental model of that protean midwestern metropolis, and if they wished to begin by emulating Chicago's modern transit infrastructure, Kelker De Leuw was the company to call upon. And these commercial elites got exactly what they wanted; declaring early on the similarities of the two metropolises—"In comparing Los Angeles with other large cities we find the closest analogy in the city of Chicago"[34]—the *Rapid Transit Plan for the City and County of Los Angeles* transposed the earlier Chicago report directly onto the topography of spread-out Southern California.

Kelker, De Leuw, and Company also explicitly endorsed the narrative of urban evolutionary development espoused by downtown boosters. Although the current transportation arrangements had been appropriate to Los Angeles when it was a low-density town of purely regional ambitions, the city would now have to take responsibility for its newfound stature and properly grow up: "Los Angeles, having passed through various stages of development, has become a metropolitan center and now requires rapid transit facilities in its urban area not only to meet present needs but to prepare the city for the growth of future years."[35] A proper city required proper infrastructure; trains and cars sharing surface streets with pedestrians was workable in a small city but unreasonably dangerous and slow in a real metropolis. Comparing the development of Philadelphia, Boston, Chicago, and New York, the *Rapid Transit Plan* insisted that these other cities had moved in the previous decades to get the streetcars out of the way of automobiles, by elevating one or both streams of traffic. Once more, the plan reinforced the notion that elimination of dangerous grade crossings—the old newspaper rallying cry in 1920s Los Angeles—fit right in with the larger discourse of vertical modernity.

If businessmen's persistent visions of a resurgent downtown of tall buildings, of a Wilshire Boulevard transformed into a grand corridor of skyscrapers, or of a towering and symbolic city hall could not by themselves shatter the preference for low-density development forged by a generation of city planners and civic boosters, perhaps the shared concern about traffic could. Indeed, faced with an intractable, incoherent, and intensifying transportation crisis, many of Los Angeles's civic leaders, perhaps for the first time in twenty years, were becoming unsure of their city's proper future. In the fight for rapid transit reform, the intensifying conflict between downtown business elites and decentralizing visionaries, which had simmered for a decade, was coming to the surface. Having clarified their collective resolve on this

issue, a significant core of downtown-based elites began to contemplate open re-
volt against the imaginative hegemony of the city's planners. These citizens, mostly
the same department store owners and bankers who had throughout the decade
been trying to bolster the place of the central business district in the spreading city,
clearly decided that decisive governmental action had to be taken to modernize Los
Angeles and halt its nascent decentralization. They would now throw their weight
behind Pacific Electric's subway efforts and the elevated rail proposals of the Kelker
De Leuw plan. Unlike earlier unresolved debates surrounding the downtown parking ban and the *Major Traffic Street Plan,* however, the resulting conflict would prove
decisive in shaping the course of the city in the decades to come.

THE POLITICS OF MODERNIZATION

The mounting tensions between garden city decentralizers and insurgent vertical
modernizers came to a head in early 1926. In that year, what had been a battle between groups of professional or elite visionaries about the theoretical future of the
metropolis suddenly became a matter of urgent public import. And it was not the
experts—engineers, planners, city officials—who ultimately ruled on these questions, but the voters of Los Angeles County. What is more, the cause of the actual
confrontation could hardly have been predicted. The spark that finally ignited the
conflict flared out of an obscure matter of public policy: a decade-long technical
legal battle of seemingly only peripheral interest to the populace at large. The case
stemmed from litigation brought before the State Railway Commission, starting in
the early 1910s. At that time, Angelenos had been served by three separate railroad
stations:

> They saw the Southern Pacific tracks for the trains from San Francisco curve around
> the river bed below Elysian Park and unite with the tracks for eastern trains on
> Alameda Street and proceed along Alameda to the old Arcade Depot. They saw the
> Santa Fe, with its eastern lines crossing the river under the old Buena Vista and Downey
> Avenue bridges, along the river bank to the La Grande Station and the lines from San
> Diego come up along the river from the south; the Union Pacific, with its lines along
> the east bank of the Los Angeles River, had its station fronting East First Street.[36]

By 1916, city attorneys were ready to try to compel the three carriers to make use
of a single Union Station to serve the city—to be built at public expense and located
next to the old Plaza. This new depot was supported by planning experts and was
intended to be open to all prospective rail companies, thus potentially breaking the
grip the three lines had on transport into and out of the metropolis.

Understandably, the existing carriers resisted these Union Station plans, hoping
to perpetuate their control over connections to the growing region. Consequently,

the fight lingered on for years, working its way from jurisdiction to jurisdiction, appellate level to appellate level, even (indecisively) reaching the federal Supreme Court in 1921. Generally, the city had been winning the cases, but it was having a difficult time finding an official agency with the power to force the railroads to submit. By 1925, the legal case was something of a civic institution, sinking into the obscurity of perpetual irresolution. Then, late in that year, a number of new developments transformed the ongoing debate, ultimately linking the issue to other contemporary conflicts. Beginning in December 1925, a series of prominent experts in the city began to propose compromise settlements. Soon the city council was faced with a bevy of competing plans to resolve the impasse.[37] The most important of these was proposed at the very end of the year.[38] This plan, put forth by the railways, fundamentally transformed the terms of the debate. Here the carriers proposed to themselves fund the construction of an elaborate system of interconnections between their existing terminals, creating a virtual Union Station.[39] What was so dramatic about this plan, however, was that the railroads would do this by building an expensive and modern system of elevated tracks between stations, indeed all the way to the riverbanks. This massive network of tracks would, according to the railroads, remove the bulky steam locomotives from the city's surface streets altogether. Even more notably, the carriers proposed allowing the Pacific Electric full access to their new elevated lines in the central city, removing countless interurban trains from the city's roads. The street railway would connect its existing facilities—including the new Hollywood subway, which opened for operation in early February 1926—to the railroads' elevated structures.[40] What the railways were offering Los Angeles was the foundation of a full-scale modern rapid transit network at no public expense.

This railroad proposal made quite an impact on the city bureaucracy, for it seemed to both resolve a costly and protracted legal impasse and provide the downtown rapid transit infrastructure commercial elites had long been demanding. The city council moved quickly to ratify the Kelker De Leuw plan—stripped of its specific route recommendations, which would now be replaced with those offered by the transcontinental railways—as the city's official transit plan.[41] Most of the city's newspapers enthusiastically endorsed this seemingly ideal solution.

Before this scheme could be approved by city officials, however, a number of Angelenos, led by the *Los Angeles Times*, moved to halt this so-called rush act, which promised to lead to intensive urban development in the downtown district.[42] Fearing the repercussions of a clash between the powerful coalition of planners and the *Times* on the one hand, and downtown interests and the other papers, on the other, the city council and mayor's office decided, after some dithering, to avoid the decision altogether. Instead, they made preparations to put the question to the voters in a nonbinding local ballot already scheduled for that April.

A REFERENDUM ON A VERTICAL LOS ANGELES

Worry and wear the needy who gather where rents are cheap,
Rob them of earth's first blessings, of quiet and rest and sleep.
HARRY BOWLING, "THE SONG OF THE 'L,'" *LOS ANGELES TIMES*,
29 APRIL 1926

Within weeks of the city council's decision, local politicians began movements to use the Progressive reform device of the referendum as a way to resolve a host of other pressing contemporary controversies.[43] In so doing, they transformed the April 1926 ballot into a significant public referendum on the future form of urbanism in Southern California. The disagreements between decentralizers and centralizers that had simmered since the 1920 parking ban now exploded upon the city at large. In a crowded ballot, a decade of polarizing positions crystallized around three aspects of urban modernization. Aside from two questions about the Plaza Union Station,[44] two measures tested proposals to lift zoning restrictions along large portions of Wilshire Boulevard in an effort to encourage that thoroughfare to develop into an intensive commercial strip of towers, and a third proposed waiving the city's height limit to permit the construction of the new city hall as a true skyscraper. Clearly, these three measures—which all bore upon attempts to make the city more vertical—were also tests of the power of professional planners to regulate urban development.

The Wilshire questions were particularly galling to local planning experts, because they directly challenged long-standing efforts to control that boulevard. The City Planning Commission had fixed on zoning as a means of limiting inappropriate (i.e., nonresidential) growth along the thoroughfare. Real estate developers, meanwhile, had vigorously challenged these efforts through the courts and the city council. Now these speculators were combining with downtown business interests to propose to the voters that the careful zoning of two major stretches of Wilshire be overturned. Clearly, this was an ambitious assault on planning control; no longer content with marginal tactics, development advocates now wished to strike down the vital regulation by popular fiat. As real estate mogul A. W. Ross put it in the *Times*, "It is only a question of time when it will be a tremendous business artery from the city to the sea. Already it is four-fifths open for business."[45]

These brazen claims raised the ire of a number of Angelenos during the campaign. Soon advertisements appeared in local newspapers attacking Ross and his fellow developers. A group billing itself the Wilshire Beautiful Association denounced the Wilshire Boulevard rezoning measure under the headline "Stop the Exploiter!"[46] "Are You going to help the Speculator Grab your last Great Boulevard?" an advertisement in the working-class *Record* asked. An editorial in the paper described rezoning as "the scheme of a handful of rich real estate speculators. They will make millions more by changing Wilshire Boulevard . . . into a congested business district."[47] Raising the specter of uncontrolled commercial development, opponents of rezoning called on the voters to "save Five Miles of Wilshire Boulevard from unrestricted erection of cheap buildings for any and All kinds of business." Recognizing the assault on visions of a harmoniously planned city, the Wilshire Beautiful Association also urged in the name of "all the people" that voters "sustain the City Planning Commission."[48]

Despite this enthusiasm for planning controls on Wilshire, opposition to the rezoning measure had less to do with the thoroughfare than with what rezoning might mean for the city as a whole. The true specter raised by the measure was that of the skyscraper and the intensive vertical development characteristic of eastern metropolises. The fears were not unfounded. During the campaign, many businessmen made it clear that they saw the Wilshire ballot question as a way to legitimate annexation of the street as a linear extension of the downtown business district. In particular, the new Wilshire Boulevard Development Association, composed almost exclusively of ambitious businessmen, launched a vocal campaign to "develop Wilshire Boulevard as the 'Fifth Avenue of the West.'"[49] Running a series of advertisements in local newspapers (see figure 31), the Wilshire developers circulated a number of images depicting the road as a high-class commercial corridor, "a stately thoroughfare, lined on either side with majestic skyscrapers," as the *Examiner* enthused.[50] So it was that businessmen hoped to extend the vertical sublime aspirations that their rapid transit plan portended for downtown to the west side district already being dubbed the "Miracle Mile."

The second locus of modernization efforts in the 1926 special election also revolved around visions of Los Angeles skyscrapers. This was the question of the new city hall, and once more a planning regulation was at stake in the debate. As with Wilshire Boulevard rezoning, objection to this question hinged on the notion that approval of the measure might allow the city to be transformed into a dense, towering metropolis.

Although the city hall project was endorsed by all the city's major newspapers, its supporters allowed a note of wariness to invade their enthusiastic public statements about the project. Invariably, backers of the measure stressed that this would be a one-time waiver of the local planning regulations. As the *Evening Express* put it, "Changing the charter so as to permit erection of the tall City Hall will have no effect on the height limit of 150 feet for other buildings. . . . That fact should be grasped by those who may fear that any exception to the terms of the charter restriction cannot be confined to the City Hall. . . . There will be no letting down of the bars, but commercial building will remain under the existing limitation of 150 feet in height."[51]

Editorialists felt it necessary to directly address fears that a waiver of the height limit would destroy the low-density character of local development. In a clear indication that opposition to a vertical Los Angeles was still intense during this period,

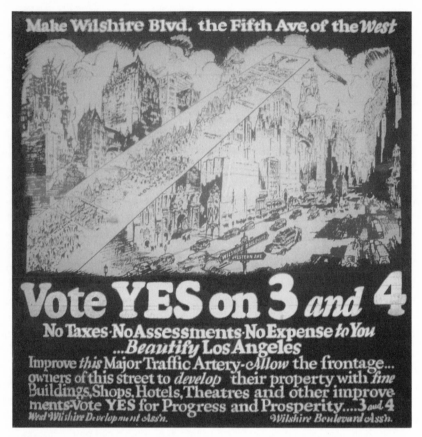

FIGURE 31. Advocates of Wilshire Boulevard development mobilized the vertical sublime. Advertisement for the Wilshire Boulevard Development Association, *Los Angeles Examiner*, 29 April 1926, 2:4.

city hall boosters constantly reassured their audiences about the skyscraper's benevolence. The architects were particularly outspoken in this respect, authoring a series of articles in local newspapers to reiterate their claim that "there is no danger that erection of the designed twenty-eight-story City Hall will weaken in any way the Los Angeles building height ordinance." As the *Times* summarized it, "Mr. Austin, who, with John Parkinson and Albert C. Martin, designed the proposed twenty-eight-story City Hall, declares that every possible objection to towering buildings was taken into consideration by the architects before submitting their plans."[52] These considerations included "provisions for garage space in the basement to care for more than 400 cars," since many local critics suspected the new city hall might increase downtown traffic snarls by concentrating so many city employees and thus aggravating the perennial parking crisis.[53]

Careful to avoid referring to the structure as a "skyscraper," promoters of the measure stressed the proposed new building's potential as a unique token of the city as a whole. As the *Evening Express* editorialized rapturously under the headline "City Hall a Symbol," "The new City Hall should not be a monument, but monumental, a grand example of the builders' art and symbolic of Los Angeles, a thing of beauty and utility." Such sentiments were echoed by prominent city councilman Boyle Workman, who argued along the same lines in the *Examiner,* emphasizing (peculiarly) "the value of the tower as an advertisement of the city. The single tower, rising approximately 450 feet, would be so dominant that the stranger entering Los Angeles would be compelled to overlook other less beautiful features."[54] Like these other advocates, Albert C. Martin, one of the building's architects, called attention to the proposed building as a "structure designed to stand out as the monumental symbol of the greatness of Los Angeles."[55] Martin went on to stress the tower's utility, particularly as an important unifying element for the city as a whole, pointing to the building's ability to offer the sort of panoramic perspective over the sprawling metropolis that was so sorely lacking: "It is intended to have the twenty-fifth floor of the tower fitted as a large hall surrounded by a balcony from which the city and environs can be viewed." Many city hall advocates came back to the prospect of such a prospect. Workman noted that "provision has been made for an observation balcony in the tower from which the whole of Los Angeles may be seen spread out in a beautiful panorama."[56]

This concern for urban legibility focused not solely on the observation deck, so much like that of Manhattan's skyscrapers, but on the building itself. Now the uniqueness of the building's ability to surmount the height limit was cast as an advantage, as the tower would tower over all other (height-limited) structures and thus restore proper epistemic order within the metropolis: "It should rise above surrounding buildings, looking out from its towering height upon the outspread city over which it would stand guard."[57] On the one hand, the new city hall would be visible from the far reaches of the region, drawing attention to the urban core. The exemplary skyscraper promised, by focusing civic attention on a downtown civic center, to aid in reemphasizing the concentric urban topography that had become obscured over the last decade. On the other hand, the building was ultimately cast as a necessary aberration. Although its backers made use of the rhetoric of the vertical sublime in stirring enthusiasm for the project, the tall city hall was tightly constrained by a web of guarantees that it would not beget a flood of imitators. A campaign that began in a rush of enthusiasm about the building's unusual height had soon settled into a project of soothing reassurance. Such was the tumult in local thinking on urbanism that the advocates of even this widely supported project were constantly on the defensive, caught in the continuing conflict between advocates of skyscraper modernism and partisans of low-rise decentralization.

In the end, no issue in the 1926 balloting was as divisive as the "straw poll" over the proposed Union Station. Opponents of the Plaza depot undoubtedly thought the contest would be a simple one. They were opposing a ready-made transit solution to seemingly esoteric arguments in favor of terminal unification. More important, they expected to capitalize on a decade of traffic discourse with a modern rapid transit program designed specifically to eliminate grade crossings. Whereas the Plaza site merely promised isolation of steam locomotives from local surface traffic (by channeling them in their own right of way along the Los Angeles River), the carriers' plan would achieve the same ends while guaranteeing the removal of almost 1,200 local streetcars from the way of the automobiles, amounting to an additional 18,000 crossings at grade avoided each day.[58] Further, the rapid transit plan, fully backed and bankrolled by the railways, could start construction immediately. The rail companies already retained on staff the necessary engineers and construction experts to bring their proposals rapidly to fruition. The president of Southern Pacific had confidently published a two-page spread in the five largest local papers detailing the many grade separations that the three railroads could put into place within eighteen months, if their plan received official endorsement.[59] Simply by dropping the fight for the Plaza terminal—which was opposed by four of the five newspapers anyway—the city could guarantee itself a multilevel rapid transit system making use of "overhead structures of modern design" in no time at all.[60]

The Southern Pacific, the Union Pacific, and the Santa Fe were unprepared for the ferocity of the onslaught launched almost immediately by the *Los Angeles Times* around the Plaza terminal question.[61] Further, they would never have predicted the particular line of argumentation and imagery along which the newspaper would concentrate its attack. Drawing on a long history of conflict between the railroads and the city (dating back to the battle over location of the city's port in the 1880s), the *Times* openly suggested that the carriers were concocting a willful and intricate conspiracy to cast dark shadows over the bucolic bungalows of sunny Southern California. In so doing, the *Times* managed a remarkable rhetorical coup. Almost immediately the newspaper launched into its assault, placing strongly worded articles on the first page under the punning but more than a little menacing heading "Keep the 'L' Out of Los Angeles" even before the ballot question was finalized.[62]

Combining a series of inflammatory political cartoons with hard-hitting "investigative" articles on the prospective rapid transit plan, Harry Chandler's broadsheet hammered home its message that elevated railroads were dark, noisy, unhealthy, and dangerously accident-prone. Throughout the two weeks leading up to the election, the *Times* featured illustrated reports from cities that were "cursed" by their elevated systems.[63] Chiaroscuro sketches suggesting how an elevated might blight Los Angeles reinforced high-contrast photographs of the darkened streets of eastern metropolises, as did dramatic shots of twisted and shattered steel cars hanging off bent structures in the aftermath of deadly collisions (see figure 32).[64]

KEEP THE 'L' OUT OF LOS ANGELES

The Railroad Commission and Interstate Commerce Commission, the people's engineers, have declared in favor of grade-crossing elimination in Los Angeles by means of a union depot in the Plaza area.

The railroads propose to eliminate grade crossing by building more than four miles of elevated "L" structures in our downtown area.

Vote "Yes" at April 30 special city election on union depot and Plaza site (Propositions 8 and 9) and keep the "L" out of Los Angeles.

The Railroads and Their Apologists Say Elevateds Are not Dangerous
This is a photograph of an "L" accident in Brooklyn where many were killed and injured when the cars fell off the high trestles to the street, thirty-five feet below. The accompanying article shows why elevateds are peculiarly liable to such accidents.

FIGURE 32. A menacing threat. *Los Angeles Times,* 29 March 1926, 1:1. Copyright 1926, *Los Angeles Times.* Reprinted with permission.

FIGURE 33. Visions of urban darkness. *Los Angeles Times,* 24 April 1926, 1:2. Copyright 1926, *Los Angeles Times.* Reprinted with permission.

Captions such as "Even California Sun Would Balk at This" warned readers that the dank scenes before their eyes could be repeated around Los Angeles (see figure 33).[65] A "Stygian gloom," correspondents testified, permeated the unhealthful atmosphere: "Under an elevated structure, even on the brightest day, it is as twilight. It is a cloud before the sun that never passes."[66]

Before long, rapid transit advocates were scrambling to respond to the *Times'* evocative and chilling images. A group calling itself the Business Men's Association of Los Angeles began placing large advertisements in local newspapers, including on occasion the *Times* itself, protesting the railroads' case. For the most part, these counterattacks tried to deflect Chandler's assaults, insisting for instance that "the railroads' plan does not contemplate elevated structures lengthwise of streets, but along a private right-of-way, and through an industrial district, where it would not be objectionable and where it would not result in property damage. It would not be street darkening since it would not run on the streets."[67] Evidently, the *Times* had established its discursive hegemony; advocates of rapid transit were forced to resort to claims that their "objectionable" and "darkening" structures would only cast shadows over private property. Faced with powerful images of blight ("places beloved of germs and microbes" that "defy cleanliness" in their "dark corners") and din (a "nerve-wracking roar," "a hollow rumble," "insomnia taking auditory form"), advocates of the el began to repudiate what had recently been their most cherished marks of urban modernity.[68]

Gamely, the railroads tried to steer the debate back toward the elimination of grade crossings. The powerful Hearst-controlled *Examiner* contended that "there is no question of elevateds. Those proposed, to be exclusively east of Main street in industrial districts, will cross streets over private rights of way. The issue is elimination of dangerous grade crossings and traffic betterment."[69] Despite these efforts, the *Times* seemed to have struck a popular nerve in its juxtaposition of Californian sun and air with eastern darkness, steel, and smoke. The newspaper was mobilizing Los Angeles's carefully constructed booster image—an image that organ had played no small part in creating—to wage a war over the future of the metropolis. Defending the low-density pastoralism of Southern California—a bucolic rurality that was, by this time, fading under a profusion of ticky-tacky tracts and subdivisions that the myth had inspired—the *Times* persistently returned in its public relations campaign to the specter of the darkening "L." Clearly, rapid transit plans were being subsumed into the discourse on the el, and the overhead railroads were being devoured in a hopeless contest between images of East and West. Dreams of vertical sublime modernity were being crushed by a powerful local rhetoric of pastoral Mediterraneanism.

In the end, the gambit that proved most effective for backers of the railroad plan was a particularly cynical one. Instead of attempting to put forward the advantages of their ambitious alternative project, rapid transit supporters began, by the late stages of the campaign, to repeatedly allude to the adjacent Chinese American and Mexican American ghettoes. Asking if the Plaza location offered an attractive and inviting first impression for visitors to the city, advertisements by the Business Men's Association played on local prejudices. As one spread put it, "The truth is that the so-called Plaza union station would face Chinatown, which lies between the Civic Center and the site proposed for the station."[70] In this way depot opponents mobilized the anxiety white Angelenos felt during this time about urban illegibility to suggest that properly hidden ethnic districts were now becoming prominent, and that the all-important boundaries defining racial order in this highly restrictive metropolis would be overturned by the Union Station plans. Before long, the *Examiner,* which was the most aggressive opponent of the Union Station proposal (probably because of the *Times'* support for it), began referring to the envisioned depot simply as the "Chinatown Terminal." "If there is ever to be a union station," the Hearst paper insisted, "let it at least not be located between Chinatown and 'Little Mexico.'"[71]

Continually calling attention to this "undesirable location next to Chinatown and Mexican settlements," the paper also (rather shamelessly) indignantly railed against the potential destruction of the "romantic atmosphere of [the] Plaza."[72] In the midst of this apparent contradiction, clearly a potent distinction was being made between the desirable mission mythology of the old church and the less picturesque actual inhabitants of the area.[73] While an actual urban neighborhood was assumed to be a sign of blight and decay, a cheerfully sanitized version of the Spanish-era pueblo was granted to be an urban asset, a sign of historical character and romance.

Ultimately, the discontinuity in racialist discourse on the part of Plaza opponents proved a rhetorical and political error. Backers of the Plaza site soon began to exploit these internal contradictions in a Machiavellian program to neutralize the *Examiner's* charges of racial blurring. One advertisement by the Citizens' Union Station Committee, for instance, claimed that "the Plaza Terminal will be a monumental gateway to Los Angeles, harmonizing with the Civic Center and historic old Plaza— creating in the minds of the newcomer [sic] an everlasting impression of beauty and civic achievement." Not only would the "historic Plaza" not be "destroyed in the building of a Union Depot," the ad reassured readers, "to the contrary, this landmark of old Los Angeles will be beautified and perpetuated."[74] Yet this co-opting of the mission myth was only the first, most benign aspect of the neutralization project. Indeed, if opponents of the Union Station measures had hoped to race-bait the *Times,* they soon found that the paper could also turn this trick. Thus, after starting with a flood of mission nostalgia of its own, seamlessly fitting the plaza site into a long tradition of booster rhetoric, Chandler's paper launched into a more serious strategy. Starting in mid-April 1926, the *Times* began to actively reposition its Plaza Union Station plans as a first step in a larger—and in retrospect, much more sinister—program of urban redevelopment. What the paper had in mind was clearly revealed under the heading "End of Chinatown." Here the newspaper recast the terminal as the first step in an ambitious program of ethnic cleansing:

> The Civic Center Plaza depot plans spell the passing of Chinatown and its rookeries into the dim history of early Los Angeles. The steam shovels are now at work in the opening of the new Spring street north of First street. Just as the old buildings are being torn down on Main and Spring streets near Temple street to make way for the new City Hall, so under the Civic Center-Plaza union depot plans the character of the entire district will be changed as more and more buildings are torn down to make way for new and widened streets, parkways and sites for the State, Federal and other city and county buildings. Chinatown is doomed by the march of the greater Los Angeles Civic Center and the Plaza union depot.[75]

Instantly, the *Times* figured out how to neutralize the racial associations Plaza opponents hoped to attach to the new Union Station location. There would be no taint from the Chinatown site because Chinatown would be leveled, wiped entirely from the map. Where the *Examiner* merely employed words, the *Times* was eager to put bulldozers to work. Under these plans, the buildings of this long-established urban community would be sacrificed in the name of civic progress, succumbing to a particularly brutal process of modernization: "Those opposed to a union station at the Plaza have stated that such an edifice would not be built in the midst of Los Angeles' Chinatown. . . . With the completion of the Civic Center and the union depot there will be no more Chinatown. In place of the dirty, ramshackle buildings of the present Chinatown will rise stately buildings of the city, county and Federal government."[76] If downtown supporters of a vertical sublime metropolis thought their rapid transit plans would restore urban legibility and order through a sophisticated and elaborate process of eastern-style urban modernization and concentration, they would discover in early spring 1926 that Angelenos had far blunter ideas about how best to reimpose proper boundaries in the metropolis.

Before long, other partisans began to present the Union Station ballot questions as matters of urban redevelopment and racial engineering. Clearing the old Chinese American community from the central city would not just remove a "slum," it would for the first time make a major portion of the city presentable to outsiders. This "passing of Chinatown"—as Marshall Stimson, "prominent Los Angeles attorney," put it in "addressing a meeting of the Los Angeles School Teachers' Association"[77]—would allow this historic portion of the city, long kept hidden from view, to become an important civic site: "It will form such a gateway to Los Angeles as no other city has and will be worth millions to the city for the 'first impression' it will give visitors. The Civic Center will forever do away with Chinatown and its environs."[78] Visitors to the Pacific metropolis, along with the city's residents, would be spared the sight of the community's sizable and growing ethnic diversity. Los Angeles's carefully crafted image as a "white" city, with clearly demarcated racial boundaries, would be reinforced—not weakened—by construction of this new urban "gateway" on the Plaza site.[79]

Looking back on the 1926 election campaign, it is easy to see that in the space of a couple of months the *Times* had engineered two dramatic discursive shifts. First, it had effectively transformed the rapid transit plans of its opponents from an optimistic Jazz Age modernization proposal into a scheme to darken Southern California's streets (and polity) with the hideous "L." Then the paper had turned the negative racial associations attributed to its own plans into a justification for wholesale ethnic realignment of entire districts of the city. Instead of being tainted by the racial connotations of its preferred Plaza site, the *Times* emerged as the champion of the cause of racial purity. In this pivotal campaign, which a number of historians have pointed to as a turning point in local thought on matters of rapid transit and downtown development,[80] the battle between visions of the urban future was fought almost exclusively upon the field of contemporary understandings of and anxieties about the existing city.

Ultimately, the 1926 campaign testifies not merely to the *Times*' considerable political weight in twentieth-century Los Angeles, as many have argued, but to the power of the mechanism by which the newspaper maintained its hegemony (despite having lower circulation than the *Examiner*). Simply put, the *Times* capitalized on its editors' sharp consciousness and effective mobilization of dominant understandings of the existing city, and particularly shared notions of the connections between urbanism and race. Time and again, these dynamics of white and black (and "yellow" and "brown"), light and dark, proved potent and resonant in local consciousness. In view of the explicit racialization of the rapid transit debate, we are justified in examining the discourse surrounding the rival plans with a bit of care, for by understanding how this broadsheet so influentially "read" the city and successfully mobilized that reading, we may be able to trace the ways Jazz Age Los Angeles was made legible—at least in the collective imagination of its dominant groups.

In the ideological context of 1920s Los Angeles, the vivid evocations of "blight" and "darkness" attending the prospective el were racially coded from the start. The prospect of transforming the "sunny" and "bright" city into a more shadowy, dim one—a particularly literal version of what Mike Davis famously referred to as "sunshine and noir"—played on Angelenos' contemporary anxieties about realignments in the city's previously relatively transparent and fixed social geography.[81] As we will see in the next chapter, the mid-1920s and 1930s witnessed a substantial revision of existing demographic boundaries. More critically, many middle-class white Angelenos felt during these years that stable lines of segregation were breaking down (an illusion to which no nonwhite citizen was likely to fall victim). In referencing the potential "darkening" of prominent parts of the metropolis, the *Times* editors certainly knew they would inflame shared fears about imminent spatial (and other) miscegenation in the city.

Although African Americans only constituted a tiny fraction of the Jazz Age Los Angeles population, blacks have always punched above their demographic weight in the metaphorics of dominant white racial imaginings. Dark streets would certainly suggest dark skins to most Angelenos in this racially hypersensitive era. The explicitly linked evocation of Latino and Asian American minority communities further collapsed this racist imagery into a ludicrously simple dynamic of paired oppositions: West (lily-white Turnerian individualism) versus East (immigration and racial mixture), white versus black, light versus dark, sun versus shadow, health versus disease, life versus death.

The parallel (and connected) specter of slum-like "blight" connoted, even more explicitly, a potential collapse of the city's precious booster image as a middle-class metropolis where inhabitants might live a carefree existence in their detached homes, with their private automobiles parked nearby. Despite the mythology, many Angelenos, even in this period of relative prosperity, were extraordinarily insecure in their class position (as reflected, of course, in the relative success of the city's radical movements during the 1910s). Contrary to the mythology, most locals did not at this time own their own cars, and many did indeed live in crowded apartment buildings. The alluring prospect of upward social mobility seemed endangered by the rapid transit "modernization" represented in the *Times*' scare pieces. The slums and tenements of eastern cities—blighted and darkened by looming overhead tracks so powerfully evoked in the newspaper coverage—quite simply frightened middle-class Angelenos. Whether these people feared that single-family homes would disappear and they would be forced into claustrophobic accommodations, or whether they merely felt threatened by the prospect of a visible urban underclass, such images indelibly and subversively linked rapid transit in the local imagination not with gleaming skyscrapers but with the depths of human misery.

This revised association was really not as difficult to engineer as might at first appear, given the era's fascination with the vertical sublime. As the automobile emerged as a viable transportation alternative for middle-class commuters, support for mass transit necessarily faded. Despite the still significant ridership numbers and the support of downtown elites (whose businesses dominated and relied on the hub system), the Red and Yellow Cars had fallen into wide disfavor, as Scott Bottles shows so well in *Los Angeles and the Automobile*. Even those forced to continue using this transit system resented it. Already in Southern California, rapid transit was beginning to symbolize not middle-class transport but the conveyance of the poor. A slow shift in popular imagining was recasting the once universal streetcar as not only a hindrance to traffic but a symbol of the poor and implicitly a threat to clear segregation in the city. Quite simply, mass transit gave the urban poor cheap mobility about town, and this potentially uncontrolled movement was disorienting for many middle-class Angelenos.

The trump card played in this allusive, excessive discourse, then, involved not simply race or class but urban legibility—which, as a product of an array of deeply held social and ideological core beliefs, pulled together and energized a panoply of charged and dangerous anxieties. In a city where systems of urban order fundamental to basic social and topographical comprehensibility were already unsettled, amid explosive and chaotic urban growth and seemingly random and destructive traffic, the prospect of further dislocation and disorientation was threatening indeed. Middle-class white Angelenos, at least those who voted, may have been consciously afraid that vertical modernization would bring with it contact with racial minorities and the rise of class conflict, but what must have been more frightening still was the prospect that the fabric of the city might become unclear and threatening. It is significant that these citizens' confidence in their own mastery over the urban landscape, and the intrinsic social relations embedded there, could by this point be easily shaken by such subtle, coded metaphorics as those mobilized in the rapid transit debate. Clearly, images of light and dark were tapping into deeper fears Angelenos had at this time about their changing metropolis.

In Jazz Age Southern California's ocular obsession, which played itself out in everything from the cultural influence of the moving pictures and the associated

FIGURE 34. Los Angeles Chinatown before the 1926 election and the same area after Chinatown was razed to make way for Union Station. California Historical Society / Title Insurance & Trust Co. Courtesy of kind permission of the University of Southern California, on behalf of the USC Special Collections (CHS-14531 & CHS-14530).

traffic spectacle to the relative attractions of different models of legible urban structure, the powerfully evoked image of the elevated's visual pollution inherently spot-
lighted an entire range of anxieties associated with early twentieth-century urban
modernization. The manifest visual disorder betokened in the transport rhetoric
ominously threatened to erase the boundaries considered essential, structural, and
inviolable, while revealing what should properly be kept hidden in any stable community. In many respects, then, the 1926 debate over seemingly esoteric rapid transit arrangements crystallized and mobilized the subterranean discourses that obsessed Angelenos, structuring their understanding of the city throughout the
decade. We will witness the specific deployments of a few of these exemplary cultural tropes—such as delinquency, eroding concepts of community, traffic chaos
and danger, imminent urban disorder, and the breakdown in perceptible lines of
segregation—in the next chapter. But, for the time being it is evident that, for the
most part, this was what modernization would mean to Angelenos in the mid-1920s:
not towering buildings or a dense urban core but ethnic purification and a transport system premised upon the automobile. Although many in Southern California were still taken by mainstream models of urban greatness during the Jazz Age,
the special election of 1926 guaranteed that Los Angeles would not soon reverse
course and turn toward a resoundingly vertical future.

In the end, the ballot returns confirmed what seemed clear in the campaign. The
efforts to rezone Wilshire as a skyscraper corridor were defeated.[82] The tall city hall
was approved, but only with such fervent reassurances about the limitations on its
waiver that the height limit remained sacrosanct for decades afterward. Finally, and
most importantly, the Kelker De Leuw rapid transit plan was doomed by the passage of the Union Station measures.[83] The voters confirmed what had become apparent in the course of the debate: in the Jazz Age, Los Angeles was not willing simply to emulate the dominant vertical model of urban modernity. Yet the election
discourse had other ramifications: within a decade Chinatown was razed to make
way for the new terminal (see figure 34), and the Plaza was "reconstructed" as the
controlled, sanitized Olvera Street tourist attraction.[84]

REJECTING THE VERTICAL METROPOLIS

*We shall work on our transit problem in our own way, but it will not be in the
New York way.*

LOS ANGELES CITY PLANNERS GEORGE DAMON AND GEORGE DUNLOP,
FROM A TALK BEFORE THE CITY CLUB, "RAPID TRANSIT SITUATION IN
LOS ANGELES" (3)

Local planners must certainly have been pleased by so clear a public ratification of
their vision of the metropolis. Equally reassuring must have been the *Times'* strong
defense of the low-density urbanism they were working so hard to preserve. And

indeed, in the wake of the election the planning community seemed more confident than ever in their ambitions for the region and for their profession. The greater part of this confidence, however, stemmed not from their victory at the polls but from the process leading up to the referenda. In the special election of 1926, the planners had not remained silent; they had taken the local challenges to their dreams as an opportunity to clarify their thought on urban decentralization. And they had done this in a particularly public manner, at last presenting much of their deliberations before local and national audiences.

During the rhetorical battle leading up to the 1926 ballot measures, planning director Gordon Whitnall waged a series of skirmishes in the local newspapers with various businessmen's groups. The conflict began with a series of addresses to the influential City Club, covered in detail in the *Times*. In the first of these, the Los Angeles planner, just returned from a national planning conference in the East, "cited as a 'horrible example' of the tendency of cities to centralize their population and interests" New York's contemporary skyscraper boom.[85] Declaring that the "further east he went the better Los Angeles had looked to him," Whitnall reiterated in another City Club speech ten days later the importance of the city's low height limit. Going still farther, "both Mr. [George] Damon and Mr. Whitnall urged immediate restrictions on Wilshire Boulevard," the latter calling for a six-story limit for the bulk of the city, including, specifically, along Wilshire Boulevard.[86]

In response to these pronouncements, ten days later a group of property owners of "the Wilshire and Westlake Park districts" met at the Ambassador Hotel to voice "indignant and forceful protests . . . against C. [*sic*] Gordon Whitnall, director-consultant of the Los Angeles City Planning Commission."[87] This ad-hoc association excoriated Whitnall's proposed height limit "as nothing short of confiscation of property rights, a whimsical idea, and one which even in its nascent state has already affected property development." The property owners drafted, unanimously adopted, and forwarded to city officials a strongly worded resolution condemning the planners' notions. They were even more blunt in rallying speeches; according to the *Times*, one speaker declared, "Let's get Mr. Whitnall's scalp!"

"Whitnall Hits Back at Critics," declared the newspaper's headline a week later, as it reported the planning chief's address before the Women's Political League ("meeting yesterday in the Windsor Tea Rooms for luncheon," the Women's Page was careful to note). "I am now a political issue," Whitnall declared, "referring to the petition now being circulated and signed by the heads of civic organizations to remove him from the commission."[88] Instead of shrinking from the controversy, the planner pushed forward his attacks. Having returned from another planning conference—this time in New York City—Whitnall declared that "New York is now paying tremendously for her mistake of high buildings where rents are enormously high and yet so great is overhead expense in operating and maintaining that rents are high enough to pay only in the top stories so foul is the air, so dark and so undesirable are the intermediate stories. . . . I would have this city avoid the mistake of New York." Declaring triumphantly before his audience of middle-class women that "we may be the greatest city in the world unless we blunder now," the planner reassured his listeners that he "had no intention of resigning." Finally, "speaking dispassionately," Whitnall promised, "I'll hold on forever, . . . I'm in the work for as long as I live—the work of making Los Angeles beautiful, desirable, sanitary for posterity, as well as now."

The Women's Political League seemed to take the planner's message to heart. Florence Kelley, also lately come from New York, "confirmed all that Mr. Whitnall said in regard" to that city: "New York continues with her folly which will be her ruination unless checked." Another warm reception greeted Whitnall's message at the Los Angeles Kiwanis Club luncheon at the downtown Biltmore Hotel six days later. There, continuing his barnstorming tour of the principal institutions of the city's civil society, the planning director once more attacked the "overcrowding" in New York City: "Business centered on the lower end [of Manhattan Island], and as it expanded the arteries leading to this center became more and more congested. Elevated railways provided a remedy for a time, then subways were installed. But with no limit to the height of business buildings congestion continued, until today there is no way out unless they discover a way of providing ingress and egress by air."[89] Against this bleak picture of "congested arteries," Whitnall reassured the Kiwanis members that "it is to prevent such conditions in Los Angeles that height-limit restrictions have been adopted here."

After engaging with popular opinion at women's clubs and other middle-class public fora, Whitnall and the other planners moved to take their case to the most important elite civic forum in Los Angeles: the City Club. In the half-year preceding April 1926, the City Club had often hosted discussions of rapid transit in Greater Los Angeles, often focusing on the potential ramifications of the Kelker De Leuw report.

By the early weeks of 1926, the City Club had come to something of a consensus, such that the club's committee on rapid transit was prepared at the end of January to issue a formal *Report on Rapid Transit* for public distribution. The committee was composed, with one exception, of city planners and those sympathetic to the aims of the planners. The report was a particularly clear expression of the collective opinion of these experts, and that opinion was a firm one: "A system of subways and elevated roads to provide rapid transit facilities for the population within the six-mile circle should not be considered at this time by Los Angeles."[90] The planners' verdict on the broader aims of the Kelker De Leuw study was as direct and definitive as was their rejection of its proposed implementation. The City Club report declared that the rapid transit plan proposed for Los Angeles was not only inappropriate but would, if enacted, make conditions far worse than they already were.

If it is, as is so often suggested, for the purpose of relieving congestion, the experience of other cities is unanimous that rapid transit systems as contemplated by Kelker and De Leuw will not relieve it but will rather increase congestion. Considering the results obtained in cities like New York, Boston, and Philadelphia, we may ask whether Los Angeles is justified in beginning the endless chain program of expenditures in subway and elevated structures which inevitably have tended to increase the congestion in those centers of population.[91]

If R. F. Kelker and Charles De Leuw intended to reduce congestion in Southern California, the planners insisted, this report would produce the exact opposite result.

At first glance, it would appear from this statement that these planners wished simply to shift the meaning of *congestion* from the commonly accepted "traffic congestion" to the more narrowly technical "congestion of population," thus highlighting what they saw as the greater evil. Actually, though, the City Club members did something more complex: they held the two meanings of *congestion* to be equivalent, to describe the same social fact. This double connotation is evidence of a larger shared body of belief, a collective agreement on the functioning of the contemporary metropolis. The question of rapid transit was only one small part of this larger understanding, albeit an important part. In the context of the twentieth-century city, they thought, transit could no longer be considered purely as a means of efficiently moving people. Rejecting the instrumentality of much thought on urban transport— that raising the capacity and speed of a particular mode of conveyance would move more people to a given set of destinations more quickly—Los Angeles planners believed that transit technology inevitably reshaped city form on a fundamental level. Indeed, in their view, transportation was constitutive of urban topography. Patterns of development in a given metropolis would strictly follow existing lines of communication and transportation.

Working from this premise, the men of the City Club came to the recognition that fixing the problem of traffic congestion in a given city could never merely be a matter of improving transport capacity. Adding ever more intensive infrastructures of conveyance would only multiply the existing problem. Conventional cities were caught in a vicious circle: rapid transit is installed to relieve (traffic) congestion, but as an effect of its operation, it encourages much greater density and intensity of urban development (i.e., people settle and locate their businesses along the new transit lines, which inevitably increases congestion of population), which serves in time to overwhelm that new transit infrastructure, once more producing congestion in the traffic system. Rapid transit could never be made so fast or of such high capacity that it could keep pace with the tendency of urbanites to use it. Demand would always eventually outstrip supply. As the City Club report put it, "Rapid transit in a metropolitan district inevitably increases the number of persons who use the downtown streets. Pedestrians and sidewalk congestion [are] its necessary result. This congestion in turn affects adversely the mobility of vehicular traffic and the choking of streets is thereby made more certain."[92] The logic here is paranoid, but it is compelling and transparent. What is more, such neo-Malthusianism coherently allowed planners in Los Angeles to pose eastern-style modernization as not merely undesirable but disastrous. The dense (vertical) city was, according to this teleology, ultimately destined for ever more intense development, with ever more tightly packed urban populations, until the infrastructural technology collapsed altogether. Far from emulating these modern metropolises with projects such as those proposed in the 1926 rapid transit study, then, Los Angeles had to find a way to escape the transit development paradox entirely.

It was this need to conceive of a way to escape the vicious circle of mass transit that led Los Angeles planners of the 1920s to react so strongly against the very structure of the twentieth-century concentric city. Writing in early summer 1926, City Club secretary C. A. Dykstra explained the thoughts of his peers to experts in other American cities in a notable article called "Congestion De Luxe—Do We Want It?" published in the *National Municipal Review*. There, Dykstra justified the club's refusal to support rapid transit of any sort in Los Angeles:

> The argument for this [the Kelker De Leuw plan] or some other comprehensive plan is conclusive to many minds. It runs as follows: we stand in street cars miserably crowded; streets are so choked that we could not use more cars if we had them; our streets are narrow and since it is too costly to widen them, let us create new streets under or over; we need comfort, speed and economy in transportation and we can get it by "mass transportation." From this point the argument becomes prophetic. . . .
> A careful study of this whole argument will show that it proceeds upon assumptions which many will question. Is it inevitable or basically sound or desirable that larger and larger crowds be brought into the city's center; do we want to stimulate housing congestion along subway lines and develop an intensive rather than an extensive city; will rapid transit spread the population anywhere except along the new right of way; is it ultimately desirable to have an area of abnormally high land values with its consequent demand for the removal of building height restriction; must all large business, professional and financial operations be conducted in a restricted area; must the worker be transported through the heart of the city to get to his work; as a matter of fact are not all of these assumptions, which were controlling in the past generation, being severely arraigned by thoughtful students?[93]

Advanced thought in the planning profession showed a preference for urban decentralization. Nevertheless, as Olmsted, Bartholomew, and Cheney demonstrated, many professional urban planners were reluctant to take this as anything more than an endorsement of the sort of suburbanization that had been ongoing for almost fifty years at this point. The city planners in Los Angeles, however, really did intend to apply the ideology of decentralization to urban problems, and they were willing to contemplate its full ramifications. As a result, these men were driven during this period toward legitimately radical programs of urban development and design. An example of this radicalism is, of course, their approach to congestion: by 1926 they had come to feel that the only rational alternative to ever-increasing congestion was simply to avoid urban concentration altogether. In the view of Dykstra and his colleagues, the traditional concentric city form was becoming increasingly untenable.

Ultimately, this was again a question of modernity: here, urban modernism was not about ever-increasing urban density or height, but rather depended on the potential of new technologies to transform patterns of human settlement. Like Henry Adams (or today's apostles of the Internet), these 1920s planners felt certain that the electric dynamo—along with the telephone and automobile—could deliver benefits that previously required highly localized heavy infrastructure. With such distributed and individualized mechanisms of communication, power, and transportation, urban density no longer served any purpose. Ultimately, Los Angeles planners reveled in the notion that they were, as the City Club rapid transit report put it, "entering upon an era of decentralization."[94]

This faith in "true," or radical, decentralization—abjuring urban centers altogether—remained strong amid the national cultural enthusiasm for the very concentrated cities these planners feared. Thus, despite the powerful and evocative poetics of the vertical sublime, Los Angeles's planners reaffirmed their earlier commitment to distributed, clustered development in Southern California. Instead of compelling the centralization of business by building transit infrastructures, Angelenos should continue to encourage urban decentralization. Indeed, Dykstra again emphasized that the City Club's "committee defended the outside business center idea as against the downtown theory. And it emphatically pointed out that there is no solution or cure for the rapid transit difficulty. Every attempt to cure brings on an aggravated case of the disease to be cured."[95] To escape the paradoxes of mass transportation and congestion, Los Angeles would be far wiser to adopt new, more modern patterns of development, patterns more adapted to the new possibilities inherent in the distributed technologies of the twentieth century than to the outmoded requirements of the nineteenth. Here local planners once more turned their thoughts to such things as "Satellite Sub-Centers," as George Damon put it in 1924: "The real answer to the problem, however, is not to build big cities, but to plan and create great living districts, made up of comparatively smaller centers of population and industry. Instead of producing tremendous land values at congested centers, our efforts should be directed toward spreading out these values over a large contiguous district."[96] In the end, this is exactly the program the City Club decided to endorse. The rapid transit committee's solution was not to build any sort of improved transit infrastructure in Southern California, but instead to continue ever more earnestly the larger changes local planners had been pushing so hard all decade. For these radical planning experts, the solution to the traffic problem remained the same as it had been all decade: "The great city of the future will be a harmoniously developed community of local centers and garden cities, a district in which the need for transportation over long distances at a rapid rate will be reduced to a minimum."[97]

From parking ban to *Major Traffic Street Plan* to rapid transit debate, the essential problems—and solutions—posed by planners remained constant. The only long-term way to eliminate congestion in the modern metropolis was to free citizens from their daily commutes, to eliminate the need for transportation. Again, this was not mere preference or ideal situation, but the tangible and realizable destiny of Southern California: "There can be developed in the Los Angeles area a great city population which for the most part lives near its work, has its individual lawns and gardens, finds its market and commercialized recreational facilities right around the corner and which because of these things can develop a neighborhood with all that it means."[98] Ideally, the neighborhood—"with all that it means"—could host and nurture all important human activities within the city, rendering unnecessary an intensive transit infrastructure. And once more, the oppositions of light and dark structure this conception of the ideal modern metropolis in Southern California: "Under such conditions city life will not only be tolerable but delightful—infinitely more desirable and wholesome than the sort induced and superinduced by the artificially stimulated population center which constantly must reach higher and higher into the air for light, air and a chance to see the sun."[99]

Paradise on earth this might appear to be, but through the application of a few simple regulations and principles, all this Greater Los Angeles could become. Such a radical program of urban restructuring was never intended to require major redevelopment of the built city. Growth would do the planners' work, and the outmoded portions of the existing metropolis would fade in relative importance. The key to this process of painless conversion of the region into clusters of garden cities is simple prevention. Merely by limiting—with the tools of subdivision control and zoning—dense, blighting urban development, planners would free the region to expand "naturally" and without undue urban congestion into a bright landscape of pleasant, interconnected but functionally independent communities. Ultimately, planners could deliver on the most ambitious dreams of a paradisiacal future simply "by zoning our residence districts against the intrusion of the factory and the apartment and by opening up additional subdivisions with suitable streets, parkways, boulevards, trading centers and recreational facilities."[100] Through these simple measures, as Dykstra proclaimed to the City Club in late 1925, "it will be possible for garden cities to take the place of slums and industrial congestion."[101]

In the contest over efforts to transform the city into a vertical metropolis, the vigorous public relations campaign by city planners, combined with the ongoing ideological campaign in the influential City Club, undoubtedly helped offset the tremendous logistical advantages held by the city's (largely pro-vertical-development) business leaders. In retrospect, given the outcome of the 1926 special election—and the withering away of the petition drive for Whitnall's removal from public office—it seems clear that the garden city planners achieved an ideological hegemony in favor of their vision of decentralization that was powerful and nimble enough to overcome even the concerted political efforts of the city's wealthiest and best-connected citizens. Clearly, the rhetorical battles of the mid-1920s drove a wedge between members of the city's previously united elite, as certain downtown institutions, particularly the *Times,* abandoned strongly held common sense ideas of modernity and civic progress in favor of the planners' vision of decentralized development. Oppositional conceptions of progress and growth intermingled with strongly evocative images of urban blight and decay. This combination ultimately proved powerful enough to overthrow established discursive and political alignments.

"WE DID JUST THE WRONG THING"

In the context of what Dykstra called "a centralization complex which thinks in terms of higher and higher land values, heavier sales volumes, pedestrian counts, bigger rentals and finally, in order to carry such values, bigger and better skyscrapers,"[102] Los Angeles's decentralizers were not alone in contemplating radical critiques of the vertical city (see figure 35). What local planners had preached at national planning gatherings all decade had finally, by the mid-1920s, begun to resonate in eastern planning circles as well. Most notably, some transportation theorists in those concentrated cities were now echoing similar, if less radical, sentiments about urban transit in their regions, as witnessed in a 1926 article titled "Is There a Vicious Circle of Transit Development and City Congestion?" Writing in the *National Municipal Review,* Daniel Turner, an engineer working for New York's Transit Commission, suggested that intensive transportation infrastructures in Manhattan were encouraging unhealthy densities of development: "The high speed furnished by the express service in the subway was the magnet. Because of it the people were actually induced to ride more than they had ever ridden before. . . . In other words, the new subway instead of relieving the congestion, accelerated the traffic increase and in a short time created a worst [*sic*] congestion than before."[103]

Although Turner, unlike the Los Angeles City Club, was not prepared to repudiate rapid transit altogether, he did feel that New York had made a serious mistake in failing to try to construct transit networks that might at least spread out the urban population. It was, Turner implied, perhaps already too late for his own city: "Instead of creating such decentralizing transit facilities, in order to take advantage of the fact that the population always follows rapid transit, and thus utilize the new lines to diffuse the population and thus relieve the congestion on the old lines, we did just the wrong thing."[104] Although critics such as Turner wished to decentralize existing metropolises, they were ultimately resigned to their cities' increasing congestion. It was simply too late to remake the traditional metropolis. Neverthe-

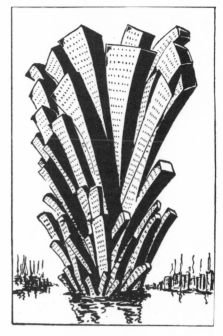

THE
S K Y-
SCRAPER
T A L L
I S   A
W O N D E R
T O A L L
A T H I N G
TOADMIRE
B E Y O N D
QUESTION

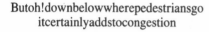
Butoh!downbelowwherepedestriansgo
itcertainlyaddstocongestion

FIGURE 35. Two examples of the mounting rhetoric against the skyscraper, even in the East. Left: Reprinted in Howard Mansfield, *Cosmopolis: Yesterday's Cities of the Future* (New Brunswick, NJ: Rutgers University Press, 1990). Right: "Top Heavy: Illustration," from Hendrik Willem van Loon, *Story of America*. Copyright 1927 by Boni & Liveright, Inc. Copyright renewed 1942 by Liveright Publishing Inc. Used by permission of Liveright Publishing Corporation.

less, such a tacit endorsement of alternative versions of urbanism would soon be carried much farther in the planning discourse of eastern metropolises.

Perhaps the most dramatic evidence that urban experts in the concentric cities of the East were having doubts about the direction of their continued development was a contentious battle between New Yorkers Henry Curran and Harvey Wiley Corbett. In an extended series of exchanges appearing one after another in many of the nation's most important planning journals, Curran and Corbett debated the future of the concentrated metropolis through much of 1926 and 1927. The conflict began in reaction to one of Corbett and Ferriss's ambitious vertical sublime visions of future New York, published in the *National Municipal Review* in June 1926. In a response to that piece, Henry Curran, a lawyer for New York's City Club, launched a direct attack upon the very cathedrals of the vertical sublime. As the *National Municipal Review,* sensing a fight, enthusiastically informed its professional readers, "The skyscraper, so generally considered as the hall-mark of a real city, is meeting serious opposition in the very metropolis in which it has attained its greatest development and fame."[105] Curran, whom the journal described as "leading the fight against the skyscraper in New York," declared in an accompanying article that "the worst enemy of the American city today is the skyscraper." He then offered a warning to unsuspecting officials in the nation's less developed cities: "It is true that in some cities this modern form of monster has not yet increased and multiplied to the point of peril. It is true that in some others, the blow has not yet fallen, though the danger is in sight. But it is also true that in still some other cities, the skyscraper has already become a plague that we may well range alongside our ancient city scourges of cholera, yellow fever, tuberculosis and slums."[106]

In this age when enthusiasm for tall buildings saturated the culture, such invective could not go unchallenged. Within a few weeks, Corbett responded with a reply in the *National Municipal Review*. Attacking first Daniel Turner's earlier pieces advocating planned suburbanization—"He thinks we might start subways from points where nobody is, and carry them out of the city to places where nobody wants to go"—Corbett admitted in the enthusiastically titled "Up with the Skyscraper" that New York was congested, but he insisted that it was not the fault of the skyscrapers: "Traffic is bad in New York, but it is worse in other cities where the average building height is far less. Detroit and Los Angeles, for instance."[107] Despite these pragmatic arguments, though, Corbett wanted to make a larger point about urbanity in general. He did this by turning on Henry Curran's biological arguments. The city, Corbett hypothesized, is a living thing, and in this stage of its lifecycle the tall building must be seen as a necessary feature of its natural anatomy: "You can't kill off the skyscraper, for it would be against nature and progress. . . . Growth is progress. The only way to stop a tree from growing is to kill it. A city is not just a mass of bricks, stones, streets, subways. It is an organic-growing thing, with its inhabitants flowing through its veins like the corpuscles in the blood."[108] The development of a city must be allowed to follow its own course, Corbett implied, and in Jazz Age America, that course was vertical.

Still undaunted, Curran fired back a final volley. Focusing on Harvey Corbett's metaphor, the skyscraper critic claimed that there was something deeply unnatural about the modern city: "We are still a nation of prairies and plains and far mountains—and yet Harvey would have us forego our freedom of motion, and tie ourselves up into a pulsing pretzel of interwoven moles, squirming under the overshadowing masses of his skyscraper brood."[109] Arguing that great concentration would only guarantee blighted living conditions, Curran rebelled against the notion that an entire city could be contained within sheaths of glass and steel. "Is," he asked, "Harvey really on the level with us when he spins this fairy tale about people being born, living, and dying all within the skyscrapers, each in his own predestined skyscraper?"[110] Curran concluded his assault on Corbett and the reigning discourses of verticality in the modern metropolis with a mournful plea to the city's unhappy souls to be saved from what he called the depths of "Harvey's Inferno," lying far below the heavenly cloud-piercing towers.[111]

Ultimately, for all Henry Curran's eloquence, most easterners would not be ready in this era to seriously consider abandoning their gleaming towers. At the same time, they would never feel so free after the mid-1920s to proclaim the sublime future of their towering and bustling metropolises. Instead, they would progressively resort to attempts to exert control over their urban landscape. In this project, eastern planners would find it necessary to turn to the techniques pioneered in Los Angeles. Curran, somewhat less strident, suggested such a course in 1927, in a brief aside from his debates with Harvey Corbett:

> Skyscrapers should be separated and spaced and kept within reasonable height limits so that human workaday population will be separated, scattered and decentralized, instead of all pulled into one small spot every morning and from every direction, and then being sprayed out from that same small spot again in the evening. . . . We need a law that will preserve the occasional beauty and the attempted utility of the skyscraper, but will save at the same time, the safety and comfort of the street below.[112]

In such conciliatory proclamations, Curran ultimately pointed the path to an uneasy resolution. The skyscraper would not be repudiated in the cities of its birth and growth, but neither would these exemplary modern metropolises fully develop into the vertical sublime fantasias that many urban observers felt were inevitable over time. Rather, as Curran suggested, regulatory compromises would be enacted to stabilize the skyscraper metropolis in its existing form. These regulations began to come into effect in New York City just about the same time that Los Angeles's voters turned against its downtown modernization plans. In this context, New York's famous setback zoning ordinances, the illustrations for which were eventually penned by none other than Hugh Ferriss, must be regarded as part of a larger national attack on the discourses of skyscraper urbanism. The cluttered, dense texture of urbanism presented over the years in such visions as King's Dreams would eventually be replaced by a new sparse, controlled verticality. Indeed, for skyscraper enthusiasts such as Ferriss, this new regulation promised to harmonize the mighty buildings that now competed with and crowded one another. The setback zoning laws of the era were explicitly intended, as many historians have observed, to protect the skyscrapers from themselves—they would thin out the skyline but at the same time protect it from more drastic public reaction. They would, it was hoped, also allow a modicum of sunlight to filter down to the darkened streets below.[113]

This was the legacy of the special election of 1926 for Los Angeles's decentralizers. With their eastern counterparts plunged into such divisive public disarray, and even skyscraper visionaries such as Corbett and Ferriss now reduced to advocating zoning regulation to mitigate the manifestly harmful effects of their creations, these western planners must have surely thought they had not just triumphed in local politics but were making headway on the larger philosophical questions as well. Many informed experts in the wider profession now seemed to take notions of garden city decentralization seriously. There could have been no better sign of the turning tide in the profession than when, in late April 1925, many of the nation's planning experts—including a delegation from Los Angeles—traveled to New York City to attend the International City and Regional Planning Conference. There an assembled audience of the nation's scientific planners heard no less an authority on the garden city ideal than Ebenezer Howard speak. Aging and a bit frail, Howard remained vigorous in the articulation of his beliefs. Reminding listeners that "I did look ahead myself, and pictured not only a garden city, but a group of garden cities," Howard suggested that it was now up to America to build on a large scale what he—"an uninfluential person like myself"—could not hope to back in England. It was undoubtedly with great attention, then, that the visiting contingent of Los Angeles's professional planners listened to the father of the garden city concept promise the influential body before him that "yes, there are possibilities ahead, possibilities of creating not only new towns, but new regions, of creating a new civilization which shall surpass ours as the civilization of our time surpasses the old."[114]

"AN AGE OF EARTH DWELLERS"

Throughout the 1920s, downtown businessmen and their allies had looked upon the pronouncements of local planners and urban theorists with benign skepticism. Against the dry and abstract discussions of those scientific professionals, men of commerce placed their faith in their city's continued growth. These businessmen had traditionally held the reins of power in the small but growing city—they felt it was properly their metropolis. After all, they had guided its growth, and they continually energized its bustling downtown. It was perfectly understandable that these magnates should wish to spur the future development of their city by propelling it along the path to modernization so brilliantly blazed by the great cities of the age. While planners expounded upon decentralization, regional governance, and the desirability of semiautonomous clusters of settlement, business leaders could only look at what their peers and rivals in eastern metropolises were doing and saying. As local planners crystallized their ideas about the future form of a distributed and clustered Southern California in lectures, conferences, and writings, downtown elites had collectively continued to dream dreams and see visions of an entirely different sort of urbanism.

The special election of 1926 was, in a profound sense, a rebuke to the ambitions of those who had traditionally led the city. Abandoned by many of their allies in the boosterish real estate community and, even worse, betrayed by their beloved *Times,* downtown elites were forced at last to recognize that, on some level at least, planning bureaucrats were more in sympathy with the sentiments of a majority of Angelenos than they were themselves. It seemed clear now that while downtown businessmen were refining and perfecting the metropolitan future of Los Angeles, planners had been quietly working to capture the imagination not only of the city's existing residents but also of the hordes of new citizens. The experts had thus, in some subtle and unnoticed manner, succeeded in selling those hundreds of thousands of recently arrived migrants who overfilled those countless bungalows in the western expanses of the city and daily clogged the remote thoroughfares in their automobile-bound wanderings, on what seemed a thoroughly antiurban vision of Southern California's destiny. Clearly, through the course of the explosive 1920s, the city had not merely grown but fundamentally changed as well. The city's center of gravity was shifting away from the downtown district and its formerly influential denizens, and toward the indeterminate peripheries of the region. With it the collective imagination of the majority of Angelenos had also shifted.

So it was that what ultimately emerged from the campaign of 1926 was a renewed confidence that Southern California's future would not follow the lines of eastern metropolises of the Jazz Age. The editorial section of the *Express*, generally a much more soft-spoken local newspaper than the *Times*, the *Examiner*, or the *Record*, was telling in this respect. On 5 April 1926, in the middle of the special election frenzy, that journal declared triumphantly at the top of its editorial page: "Los Angeles, City of Homes."[115] Declaring that "Los Angeles maintains its reputation as a city of homes," the *Express* championed the dominant single-family low-density style of local residential development. Below this self-congratulatory paean to the status quo was juxtaposed another descriptive editorial piece. Titled "The Future City," it presented a radically divergent picture of urban settlement: "Combination office and apartment buildings of 80 stories and more, linked together by aerial causeways, with airplane landings on the roofs. . . . To visit a neighbor the inhabitants of one building would step out onto a walk or causeway maybe several hundred feet up in the air, or, going to the roof of their own building, take an airplane and fly to the building they wished to visit." Here the skyscraper urbanism of the Jazz Age metropolis (the site of this vertical sublime vision was, not surprisingly, identified as New York) intruded into the tumult and conflict of a Los Angeles still poised at a crossroads between models of urban development. All along, though, the conclusion was preordained. Whether Angelenos fully understood the garden city ideal or not, they were full participants in the discourses engendered by it. Despite the concerted efforts of the city's business elite, the hegemony of low-density single-family development in the imagination of Angelenos remained ultimately unshaken. As the editors of the *Express* concluded thoughtfully in their account of this city of the future (and perhaps of the future of their own city, as envisioned by downtown modernizers), "This is no mere fanciful picture, but actually what men of affairs see for the future, and plan to create with their money. But it isn't inviting. It seems better to have lived in an age of earth dwellers."

5

Metropolis at a Crossroads

In the wake of the special election of 1926, Los Angeles's planners thought they had triumphed over all opposition, that the 1920s would be the decade when the principles of regional planning were finally demonstrated to the world. Before long, Southern California would be remade as a new sort of cityscape, a harmonious agglomeration of pleasant, manageable garden cities, where the bonds of community could be built and lived, and where residents could enjoy the economic, cultural, and technological advantages of the modern metropolis without the crushing poverty, alienation, and ugliness so characteristic of the great cities of the age. As C. A. Dykstra put it, "The natural reaction of a population anywhere is to spread out in sub-centers, to build up small communities and business districts, to get the advantages of the city without its very apparent disadvantages."[1] This was the ideal medium between country and city, the synthesis that brought the advantages of both while eliminating many of their curses. It would not—as a human society—be a perfect place, but this reshaped Southern California would be as paradisiacal as was realizable for mortal and fallible humans. Planners in Southern California were boosters too.

What actually took place, of course, was quite different. Indeed, the divergence between this utopian vision and what occurred is conveyed in vivid detail by Richard Neutra, in a reminiscence penned a bit more than a decade later. Neutra, by then an acclaimed architect, planner, and long-time Angeleno, recounted at the outset of World War II an incident from an earlier, more optimistic age of scientific rationality at the very beginning of the Great Depression. In 1931, "the International Congress for Modern Building in Brussels arranged an instructive exhibition of metropolitan maps illustrating several dozen of the world's largest population centers.

All maps were drawn on the same scale and with standard symbols expressing types of building use."[2] With this exhibit the professional city planning movement sought to use its classic ordering logic to create a common symbolic language for describing and categorizing the world's cities. The authoritative and standardized comprehensive maps thus produced would allow planners to systematically compare diverse metropolises and treat their endemic social ailments.

Yet, Neutra recounts, there was a problem at the exhibition, and it concerned the new topography of Los Angeles that had emerged in the five years since the 1926 election: "The scale and symbols were found well suited for practically all world-cities except Los Angeles. For this metropolis the chosen scale produced a monstrously oversized chart. The numerous section mounts necessary to compose the Los Angeles map filled huge walls of the exhibition hall, practically monopolizing the space." Even more troubling than the sheer size of the extended metropolitan area, though, was its manifest illegibility: "The required symbolic indications, such as of the location of workers' quarters, garden districts, cottage suburbs, multi-story apartments, slum and blighted areas, and business zones, quite easily noted on European or east American city maps, were shown to be almost ridiculously inapplicable when charting Los Angeles. A map produced according to this established set of rules became a huge and strange jungle of misunderstandings, not possible of interpretation even by connoisseurs and experts." Neutra describes the "puzzled amazement of European students" at the chaotic cityscape before them. Although there were indeed recognizable "cottage suburbs and satellite garden cities," these pleasant patches were engulfed by amorphous "business zones" that "seemed to stretch hundreds of miles along endless traffic boulevards which cut through unoccupied or agricultural areas." No one could quite come to terms with "this monster map," which dwarfed those of its more compact and traditional counterparts in the exhibition. Critical urban sectors were unidentifiable, simply missing. Perhaps the standardized symbols failed to comprehend the typologies of this possibly sinister urban zone. Yet, through the usual designators at least, slums and tenement blocks could not be found; suburb and city seemed to merge imperceptibly and seamlessly. The most basic urban relationships—between workplace and residence, industry and commerce, public and private space—seemingly followed no logical pattern. "Was this metropolis a paradise, or did there exist here a type of blight which fitted none of its classical descriptions?"

In the end, the experts on "modern building" were no less stumped than were Los Angeles's contemporary planning professionals. Even in 1931, it was not quite clear what this shapeless conurbation was all about, for the supposedly comprehensive map failed to deliver the promised comprehensibility. Instead, the application of scientific planning technologies to the spaces of Southern California merely "emphasized strikingly a uniqueness of layout, a type of very loose metropolitan aggregation and of habitational routine, hardly comparable and commensurable to anything else of the sort on the globe."[3] This incomprehensibility was baffling to the European experts. To local planners, it was dispiriting.

THE DISORDERED METROPOLIS

The last great experiment is the extension of zoning into the metropolitan district.

GORDON WHITNALL, "THE EXPERIENCE IN THE LOS ANGELES REGION," PRESENTED AT THE NATIONAL CONFERENCE ON CITY PLANNING (129)

What happened to the city in those five years between 1926, when prospects looked so bright for the controlled development of Greater Los Angeles, and the Belgian exhibition in 1931? Despite Harland Bartholomew's contention at the time that "the modern American city cannot be reorganized or reconstructed in any short space of time,"[4] this is, in effect, precisely what had happened in Southern California, although not according to anyone's plan or program. The incomprehensible landscape Neutra describes began to take form almost immediately after the special election of 1926. It came as a surprise to the confident planners who were so busy in that period making ambitious plans for the future development of the metropolis. In a sense, these experts who so prized comprehensive vision were blindsided by the events of the late 1920s. Perhaps this is because the first signs of trouble emerged from a political battle they were sure they had decisively won: the zoning of Wilshire Boulevard.

Given the results of the referenda, planners undoubtedly felt not only that they had been vindicated in their efforts of the previous six years but that they now clearly had the citizenry behind them in their larger zoning program. This Progressive Era faith in the democratic mandate, however, could not protect the newly professionalized City Planning Commission from the treacherous day-to-day operations of urban politics. Having failed to overturn zoning wholesale through the 1926 special election, real estate speculators turned to a new technique: what the voters would not do at once, city government could do by bits. In this way, and almost effortlessly, these developers effectively subverted what was then considered the most advanced and sophisticated zoning ordinance in the country.

The Los Angeles City Council retained the power throughout the 1920s to grant spot variances for specific parcels of land. Much to the chagrin of planners, the council granted a fair number of individual exceptions. Noted real estate entrepreneur A. W. Ross and his fellow speculators turned aggressively to expand these exceptions into the wholesale abrogation of zoning ordinances. As Ralph Hancock admiringly writes in *Fabulous Boulevard,*

> Ross then shrewdly conceived the idea of turning these same zoning restrictions into an asset. He determined to develop his tract one lot at a time, submitting to the planning commission complete plans and specifications in each instance and asking for a

zoning variance to permit that particular structure to go up; in other words, to proceed on what is known in Los Angeles as "spot zoning." . . . So, instead of opening the
entire strip for uncontrolled business, like other sections had been, it was possible to
control what went into the Miracle Mile and exclude undesirable structures.[5]

By usurping planners' power through these tactics, with the (supposedly) unknowing collusion of the city council, Ross now became the one exercising control over
development along Wilshire Boulevard. Instead of guaranteeing control over the urban landscape, zoning was merely plunging planners into messy case appeals and
city council debates. In a remarkably short time, real estate developers had managed
to detect and exploit a serious weakness in planners' primary strategy for rational
subdivision control.

As a result of this rezoning by exception, the Wilshire corridor no longer promised to anchor a string of semiautonomous garden style districts, but instead was
spreading the blight of inappropriate commercial ribbon development right through
the western portions of the metropolis. In fact, even in late 1926, it was evident that
retail space on the boulevard was expanding in scope and value: "Forty corners in
famed sector show average annual value increase of 744 percent," the *Los Angeles Examiner* enthused.[6] A couple of years later, a headline in the *Times* retrospectively raved,
"Wilshire Boulevard Business Growth in Five Year Period Declared Phenomenal."[7]
Clearly, this was not simply a matter of a few small neighborhood shops and gas stations, but much more serious—and unprecedented—business concentration.

Before the City Planning Commission could figure out just what was going on
along Wilshire and assemble the political coalition necessary to halt it, something
even more dramatic occurred in the Wilshire corridor. Fed up with city planners
in the aftermath of their defeat in the 1926 special election, downtown business elites
literally threw their lots in with the real estate speculators. Using the developers'
strategy of undermining zoning, businessmen could perhaps realize their ambitions
to make Wilshire the "Fifth Avenue of the West" after all. Leading his peers in this
regard was John Bullock, who, according to Richard Longstreth, "had contemplated
branch expansion for some time. In 1924, his company purchased land at Wilshire
and Vermont . . . to use for development once the area was rezoned."[8] Plans for this
subsidiary branch were risky for a businessman who a few years before "could see
neither rhyme nor reason for opening up business 'out in the sticks,'"[9] but it was
part of a larger project to develop at least the eastern portions of Wilshire into a
grand extension of the central district. Bullock, though, was no longer interested
merely in supplementing his downtown store with a small branch, but was contemplating something much more radical.

The store that John Bullock eventually built "on a bean field near Vermont Avenue" and opened to the public in 1929 was no mere suburban branch outlet. It was
an Art Deco palace, ornamented with "elegant interiors, including murals and sculp-

ture"[10] that depicted "a theme, the spirit of transportation—fast, streamlined, transportation, which shows up first in the magnificent painted ceiling of the south entrance's porte cochere; here are Mercury and ships and planes and even the *Graf Zeppelin*, all done in glowing, brilliant colors, with hard-edged Art Deco assertiveness and elegance."[11] *Vogue* and *Harper's Bazaar* called it "the most beautiful department store in the world."[12]

Bullock was not alone in his expansion scheme: Within months, Bullock's "archrival Tom May secured property across the street from Bullock's first site; Marshall Field officials were exploring the possibilities of having a store nearby."[13] These men, perennial stalwarts of the central district, moved surprisingly quickly. Soon there was not one large store on Wilshire but a swarm of them. What was so peculiar about this development, though, was that these businessmen were locating their new stores not in eligible suburban areas such as Hollywood or Pasadena but just about in the middle of nowhere: these department stores, traditionally the anchors and symbols of business concentration, were relocating to seemingly random points along the new boulevard. What is more, the new emporia were huge; they rivaled or even eclipsed the downtown flagship locations in size and lavish decor. By 1929, Wilshire was suddenly developing into a viable alternative to downtown as a center of commercial concentration.

Despite this success, the Wilshire Boulevard developments of 1927 and after no longer fit in with notions of turning the street into "a skyscraper corridor of unparalleled dimensions." The vertical sublime vision was clearly out of step with the Southern Californian mindset in this era. Instead, the dry goods magnates constructed imposing but low-slung buildings. Bullock's Wilshire has been described by architectural experts Charles Moore, Peter Becker, and Regula Campbell in their excellent *The City Observed* as "a five-story pile with a ten-story tower, both with lots of copper spilling over the parapets like a generous crème de menthe topping on a parfait, all green over the beige cast stone of the walls."[14] These were not mammoth towers; the buildings that were built along Wilshire did not even approach the existing height limit. Although this street was becoming a major commercial district, it was not doing so in the manner of a Michigan Boulevard or Fifth Avenue. Instead of forming a solid line of ritzy shop fronts, these new stores were often separated by miles of undeveloped or lightly developed land. A department store could easily sit next to an agricultural field or a fruit stand. It was becoming clear that Wilshire Boulevard was developing in a fashion no one had foreseen. This was certainly not what downtown elites had envisioned when they contemplated opening west side branch stores. Likewise, local planners did not approve of any one commercial district, downtown or on this new street, drawing shoppers from the whole metropolitan region. Neither a neighborhood business area nor a traditional clustered downtown, the Wilshire corridor became by the end of the 1920s a brandnew sort of major shopping district—one that stretched intermittently for miles.

FIGURE 36. Wilshire Boulevard defined a new, spread-out business district. Spence Air Photos. Courtesy of the Benjamin and Gladys Thomas Air Photo Archives, Department of Geography, UCLA.

Why this strange topography, unprecedented in American urban history? Unlike Los Angeles's traditional central commercial zone, this new boulevard business district was dedicated and adapted entirely to the private automobile. As Richard Longstreth observes in *City Center to Regional Mall,* "Wilshire became a magnet for commercial enterprises to serve the burgeoning populace close by and also the large, mobile, and affluent trade that lay beyond in several directions. The automobile transformed the corridor into a major spine of development by making access easy. Without streetcars, travel along Wilshire was far less cumbersome for the motorist than on most parallel arteries."[15] Wilshire's new store branches were designed to serve the automotive commuter in a way that the downtown stores never were. They presented bold and eye-catching façades toward the boulevard, while hiding spacious, free off-street parking lots, only accessible by side streets, directly behind themselves. When examined more closely, it became apparent that their main entrances faced the parking lot—the boulevard-side façades were mostly for show. What was evolving here was a new architecture suited to automobility.

This was also an architecture adapted to a fragmented and decentered urban geography. The department stores chose Wilshire for their stores precisely because it was so easily accessible from much of the western half of the metropolitan region. Thanks to the improvements of the *Major Traffic Street Plan,* and to the system of streets that planners had helped lay out, this thoroughfare stretching far into the new subdivisions was now more convenient for automobile-borne Angelenos than was the downtown district. For citizens living in the distant western districts of the city, the traditional central business district was annoyingly remote. The decentralized landscape of Greater Los Angeles thus proved fertile ground for this innovation in commerce (see figure 36).

Wilshire Boulevard was not a new commercial center serviced by a major thoroughfare, it was a major thoroughfare serving as a commercial center in its own right. As Longstreth puts it: "Between the late 1920s and the 1940s Wilshire became not only one of Los Angeles's most heavily traveled arteries but the city's most touted corridor of commerce, whose prestige challenged, and in some respects eclipsed, that of downtown."[16] Other historians echo this point. Robert Fishman observes that "downtown department stores hastened to establish elaborate branch stores on Wilshire Boulevard while letting their downtown stores run down."[17] In a year or two, the deemphasis of the central business district that some planners had been advocating for more than a decade was suddenly occurring—but not as they wished and through no conscious action of their own.

A NEW URBAN LANDSCAPE, A CRISIS IN URBAN LEGIBILITY

Wilshire was defining a new, entirely more serious sort of ribbon development that was threatening the primacy of Los Angeles's downtown.[18] As such, Wilshire demonstrated the divergence of boosterism and planning. The boulevard was the land speculator's paradise but the planner's perdition. This development jeopardized both the Traffic Commission's attempts through the *Major Traffic Street Plan* to reassert the functionality of the central business district and the City Planning Commission's dreams of decentralization through garden city development. Wilshire was not developing as a local commercial subcenter for a few communities on the west side; it was developing into another central business district, drawing traffic from all parts of the metropolis. In fact, this commercial activity was already beginning to congest and slow traffic over a large region. This irony—that the corridor planned to relieve downtown traffic was now usurping that district's role and thus producing its own congestion—did not at all amuse Los Angeles's planners or traffic engineers. Those downtown businessmen who had stayed with their old locations were frightened.

What was even more troubling, though, was that the Wilshire experience was not unique. Many of the region's other large thoroughfares were being transformed from traffic conduits into shopping destinations. By 1930 a full quarter of the commercial and professional activity in Los Angeles was carried out in places that were not supposed to be business districts at all, and this proportion continued to rise through the early 1930s.[19] Moreover, this phenomenon was not confined to Los Angeles retail. Robert Fishman notes in *Bourgeois Utopias* that increasingly "factory workers were automobile commuters, coming to their jobs from every section of the metropolis rather than from a single factory zone."[20] Local planners recognized the importance of these developments as they were happening, although the experts were at a loss about what to do about them. All they could do was watch. At a meeting of professional planners discussing ribbon development, for instance, Gordon Whitnall announced to his colleagues that what had happened to Wilshire Boulevard was now occurring elsewhere in Greater Los Angeles: "One street many miles long had for instance a transition overnight from a rather orderly residential section into a most extensively developed business shoe-string. I refer to Western Avenue. We have hundreds of Western Avenues now."[21] Writing in *Sunset,* Walter V. Woehlke vividly described this transformation, using it to synopsize for his readers all the strange happenings in Los Angeles in the mid-1920s: "Something new and unexpected happened. . . . When a broad north-and-south thoroughfare was opened on Western avenue and an ever increasing motor traffic poured over this street, it suddenly, almost overnight, blossomed out as a subsidiary business district and land values went up with a tremendous bang."[22]

The particular example of Western Avenue is significant not merely because it was another radial boulevard, like Wilshire, turning into a business strip, but precisely because this road was not like Wilshire Boulevard at all. Western ran perpendicular to Wilshire, intersecting that radial at a point more than two miles west of downtown. That outlying cross streets to the boulevard were now turning into commercial districts, and attracting a great deal of traffic, was particularly disturbing to informed observers. This was not merely a case of the business district extending along a major boulevard toward newer parts of town. Nor was it a case—peculiar enough in itself—of an entire business district migrating to one formerly peripheral boulevard. The developments of the late 1920s were the first signs of a dissolution of normal commercial concentration. In a remarkably short time, business was springing up chaotically throughout the western district of town, increasingly overflowing all identifiable business districts.

The repercussions for the city's traffic were immediately apparent to Angelenos; not only was the city's commercial infrastructure somehow changing, but its familiar flow of traffic was becoming unrecognizable. The city's street grid, even at points far from downtown, was being overwhelmed by the inevitable cross-traffic generated by the concurrence of so many new commercially intensive thoroughfares. Angelenos were suddenly commuting in an unprecedented crosshatched pattern, spreading the traffic congestion across a vast territory. Now, as motorists tried to make turns, and especially left turns, to and from crowded intersecting roads, they created what is today known as gridlock. Whereas the city, under its traditional concentric pattern of development and transit, had been mired in congestion from the sheer crush of inbound or outbound commuters, Greater Los Angeles was now bound by cross—as well as traditional linear—traffic from all over the region (see figure 37).[23]

Once more, Angelenos could only view this traffic snarl as a symptom of larger problems with their metropolis. And in a sense it did indeed signal radical change. As Fishman observes, "By the end of the 1920s a new urban structure was in place in Los Angeles. Crucial metropolitan functions had exploded over the landscape, their scattering supported by an extensive network of roads that permitted multi-dimensional travel."[24] Just as the course of traffic no longer followed a predictable, natural pattern, so too the city as a whole was becoming dislocated. Something new was developing, and it was profoundly disturbing to all Angelenos—frustrated motorists and puzzled planners alike.

For Los Angeles's professional planners, the events of the late 1920s were particularly disheartening. Instead of garden city decentralization, countless razor-thin congested "downtown" strips were proliferating across the landscape, jumbled against each other almost randomly. Previously, zoning had seemed to offer the sort of progressive urban restructuring that ordinary subdivision controls or expensive road construction plans would not deliver. Yet, by the end of the decade, most of Wilshire had been granted variances, making a mockery of zoning control. Several commentators have suggested that it was the inconsistent application of the zoning regulations, caused by a malleable city bureaucracy, that ultimately caused the failure of zoning along Wilshire Boulevard.[25] While this assessment is certainly correct, it is also clear that the fundamental problem went deeper than that. Behind the zoning efforts in Southern California lay a premise that was fundamentally flawed.

Los Angeles planners had felt that they could restore legibility and order to the city by clarifying and segregating identifiable urban elements. They soon discovered that producing a comprehensible urban landscape was not just a straightforward matter of inserting absent markers into the fabric of the metropolis. The categorizational logic that underwrote zoning was appropriate and revealing in the concentric city but fundamentally inapplicable and confusing in the new topography emerging in Southern California. In Los Angeles, these telltale signposts of urban location were missing not because of an oversight of development, as if in haste (or through fraud) they had been simply left out, but because they did not serve the same clear purpose in the novel sort of city Los Angeles was becoming. In a traditional American metropolis, the presence of low-density houses would unambiguously denote a peripheral residential district far from the center of urban activity, just as major department stores would necessarily imply a discrete business area. But these familiar indicators were present all over Greater Los Angeles, especially in the zones of most recent development, and they were all mixed together. Merely separating them in space, as zoning attempted to do, would not alter the underlying functional relationships between these urban elements, and in Los

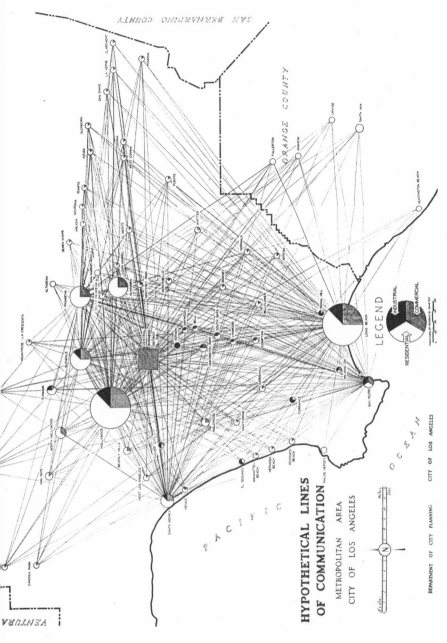

FIGURE 37. Potential traffic flows follow no clear pattern on the map. From *A Parkway Plan for the City of Los Angeles and the Metropolitan Area* (Los Angeles: City Planning Commission, 1941), 30.

Angeles these relationships were themselves confusing. In this new topography, distinctions between home and business no longer necessarily dictated particular commuting, shopping, or settlement patterns. In a sense, the increasingly "chaotic" traffic of the decade told the truth of a topographical structure that planners—accustomed to interpreting the city in terms of fixed, visibly identifiable elements set into diagrammatic order—could not even see. Ultimately, planners' claim to comprehensive vision—so central to their mission and sense of purpose—dissolved along with their zoning controls.

MAKING SENSE OF THE ILLEGIBLE METROPOLIS

If this was not the topography of the garden city or traditional suburbanization, what exactly was it? For years, historians have been describing what occurred in Greater Los Angeles during the 1920s simply as "decentralization," as if that term could adequately convey the unique nature of this new form of development. Here, for instance, Scott Bottles grapples with the problem in *Los Angeles and the Automobile:* "Suburbs had appeared in American cities as early as the nineteenth century, but the city center had remained the hub of the region. Los Angeles after 1920, however, began to develop several focal points. It was this transition from the centralized city to the multifocal urban structure that marked the arrival of the modern decentralized metropolis."[26] What was going on in Southern California at this time was indeed decentralization, but it was an entirely novel form of it—as different from garden city decentralization or suburban decentralization as those were from concentric centralization. Bottles's use of the term represents a third meaning of decentralization. Just as the two camps of planners were not fully aware that they were using the word to mean different things in the mid-1920s, so too later historians have too easily conflated this third discrete form of urban development with the others.[27]

In the last decade, a number of analysts have focused attention on what they identify as a new class of urban form, characteristic of such areas as contemporary Orange County, California, or the region around Fairfax County, Virginia. Marc Gottdiener and George Kephart describe this novel urban geography in a piece titled "The Multinucleated Metropolitan Region: A Comparative Analysis": "Because of the massive regional dispersal of population, industry, and commerce, we now have vast urbanized areas for which the concept of urban dominance is becoming obsolete. These areas constitute a settlement-space form that is polynucleated, functionally dispersed, culturally fragmented, yet hierarchically organized, and that extends for tens and even hundreds of miles."[28] Although discussed under various names by Joel Garreau, Robert Fishman, and Edward Soja, among others, this urban morphology is best described by Rob Kling, Spencer Olin, and Mark Poster as "postsuburbanization."[29]

Kling, Olin, and Poster's *Postsuburban California* traces the development of this "postsuburbia" during the last thirty years, but this new form of decentralization was in fact occurring throughout Southern California during the 1920s. In fact, the following description of 1990s Orange County could describe what so disturbed the expert planners of Greater Los Angeles more than sixty years earlier: "We note that Orange County is not simply decentralized, but . . . it is multicentered as well. It is organized around many distinct, specialized centers rather than a traditional city center surrounded by industrial and residential areas. A visitor who is used to traditional cities with central downtowns to house city halls, museums, churches, and major businesses may be bewildered by Orange County's spatial layout."[30] Both visitors to and residents of Los Angeles in the late 1920s often found the metropolis bewildering in its spatial organization. A few turbulent and explosive years had transformed Greater Los Angeles from a traditional, if somewhat spread out, concentric city into something utterly new: a dispersed, polynucleated, massively deconcentrated urban form. Indeed, this creation of a *greater* Los Angeles back in the Jazz Age introduced an urban form that is only now being adequately identified. During the 1920s, this new form—a regional metropolis spread across a vast landscape, with multiple subcenters but no single overriding downtown core—simply seemed like chaos.

Without previous exposure to this sort of urban topography, Angelenos lacked the conceptual tools to abstract their experience of the landscape into a stable and reliable understanding of the metropolitan region. The resultant disorientation affected everyone to some extent, but it hit planning experts particularly hard because of their occupational need to understand the metropolis in a comprehensive and detailed manner. The problem was not merely that planners and ordinary residents did not have the proper terminology to describe what was happening in Greater Los Angeles during the '20s, but lacking specific techniques to read the cityscape as a whole, they found it extremely difficult to integrate the cityscapes around them into a comprehensive urban vision. As Kling, Olin, and Poster observe, "The fundamentally decentralized spatial arrangement of postsuburban regions—in which a variety of commercial, recreational, shopping, arts, residential, and religious activities are conducted in different places, linked primarily by private automobile transportation—makes them complex, seemingly incoherent and disorienting."[31] Even today many Americans find postsuburban spaces hard to grasp comprehensively. For Southern Californians of the 1920s, merely finding one's way around was difficult at times. Although most Angelenos soon developed ways to orient themselves reliably within their familiar territory, conceptualizing the place as a whole remained quite daunting. Greater Los Angeles was evolving into a disconnected collection of experienced spaces that simply would not gel into any of the familiar urban models.

If today we can grasp the outlines of what was happening in Greater Los Angeles in the era as the clear consequence of the development of postsuburbanization, it is certain that no one at the time could quite put a finger on it. In fact, the confusion striking observers of Los Angeles in the '20s would linger far beyond the Belgian planning congress of 1931, and even beyond Richard Neutra's reborn urban planning movement of the 1940s. Yet, for all the efforts of later generations of Angelenos to come to terms with their city's landscape, it was during this early period that Angelenos first began to acknowledge the peculiarly transformed topography, and it was then that they first tried to respond to it.

In the Jazz Age, hope for a means of understanding the syncopated chaos of this Southern Californian sprawl seemed distant indeed. Yet, during the ensuing decades, as many American cities grappled with the challenges of integrating the urban and the modern, Angelenos also began work, not always consciously, on developing critical techniques for apprehending and making sense of their discordant postsuburban metropolis. At the time these changes were beginning, many Angelenos— and professional planners in particular—responded to the transformation of their metropolis with frustration and anger.

In the face of this growing uncertainty, another contingent of expert observers stepped into the breach. This new group of seers emerging in the late 1920s and early 1930s felt sure, as had planners a decade before, that they would be able to make sense of the exasperation and anomie in contemporary Los Angeles. These were the followers of the nascent academic discipline of urban sociology, and they almost immediately identified Los Angeles's chaotic cityscape and its increasingly disorienting social relations as a prime topic for research. Like the city's ambitious planners, these scholar-observers laid claim to a comprehensive vision of the city through their methodology. They also shared a Progressive Era faith in scientific and professional expertise. The community studies carried out by urban sociologists during this period were, like the planners' tool of zoning, in many ways responses to the perceived confusion of the urban landscape.

Moreover, the conservative planning tool and the crusading new social science fundamentally saw the city in similar terms, and they shared many of the same categorizational preoccupations. Both had been inspired by new formalist understandings of urban space and organization, particularly those most famously illustrated by the sociologist Ernest Burgess in "The Growth of the City," the second chapter of his, Robert Park, and Roderick McKenzie's extraordinarily influential book *The City*.[32] For both groups of experts, urban space was fundamentally visible—survey observation produced data that could then be abstracted, generalized, and quantified. In essence, everything that could be seen could be categorized, and these categories would then accurately and comprehensively reflect the underlying reality of city life. Furthermore, these urban typologies could be recombined into diagrams and maps, which would precisely and compactly reveal the necessary relationships between identified and categorized elements by displaying their basic geographical propinquity. Whereas planners sought to apply an ideal map to a landscape, sociologists sought to derive one from an observed social, demographic, and architectural topography. For both groups, however, the map and the city could ideally be brought into direct correspondence.

In addition to these shared notions of urban topography, these experts shared a conviction in the connections between the cityscape and the people living there. The two approaches fundamentally assumed in common that aberrations in social behaviors and topographical urban patterns must somehow be closely linked. Finally, and most importantly, despite a profound confidence that a rigorous process of expert analysis and intervention would restore proper visual and disciplinary order in the city, with a few notable exceptions, neither group ultimately managed to make much sense of the postsuburban landscape emerging in Southern California. Nevertheless, we can read these sociological texts today not so much as insightful explanations of what was happening in postsuburban Southern California, although there is some of that here, but more significantly as a measure of Angelenos' anxious contemporary responses to it. These urban observers chronicled the expressed fears, social dislocations, and tentative and localized reactions of those people whose city was, before their very eyes, becoming illegible, disordered, and even delinquent.

MAPPING A DISORDERED SOCIETY ONTO
A DISORDERED TOPOGRAPHY (AND VICE VERSA)

The speed-jazz mania of the day is sweeping youth into its vortex. To get a bigger and bigger thrill out of life, and to drive high-powered cars in the company of low-moraled girls, wrecks youth. The race is on: Will civilization wreck youth before youth wrecks civilization?

EMORY S. BOGARDUS, *THE CITY BOY AND HIS PROBLEMS* (143–44)

The growth of city planning as a profession in the early decades of the twentieth century is much indebted to the new discipline of urban sociology, for sociologists had already done much to elaborate understandings of the concentric structure of the city. The early work of the academics had served to institutionalize such structural readings of urban form as the Burgess diagram of the concentric city. Armed with these methodological tools, along with an obsession with detailed urban observation rivaling that of city planners, sociologists set out during the 1920s to explore the conditions of human existence in American cities. Motivated often by concern for the downtrodden, these sociologists often seemed more empathetic academic counterparts to the surveyors of the city planning profession. Beginning in Chicago, where the concentric urban model was first clarified, researchers sought to apply rigorous methods of analysis to their observation of urban social relations. By the middle of the decade, a school of inspired sociologists had established themselves in the metropolitan area of Los Angeles, centered at the University of Southern California. Led by students of the University of Chicago's Robert Park, such as the eminent Emory Bogardus (later author of a number of canonical sociological textbooks), these academic researchers witnessed in fragments a number of the profound social changes transforming the city during this tumultuous decade.

Bogardus's most important work on Los Angeles during the 1920s was an influential study of "boy life" in the city. The project report, published in 1926 with the aid of the Rotary Club in connection with an exhibition produced for public display at Los Angeles's downtown public library, identified a series of social causes and detrimental effects of (mostly male) juvenile delinquency in the growing metropolis. Like *traffic,* the word *delinquency* could easily evoke an array of social concerns for observers. Most predictable of the findings, perhaps, was that generational boundaries were increasingly transgressed in the chaotic modern city. Chronicling a perceived rash of "unruly" behavior among Los Angeles's youth, *The City Boy and His Problems* testified to breakdowns in family control, as observed by social workers, church and school authorities, city officials, and the boys themselves (ranging in age, for the purposes of the study, between about twelve and sixteen years).[33] As Bogardus gravely put it, "Nearly all our data show that large numbers of parents are failing in the training of boys and girls. Granting 'good heredity stock,' the unfitness still exists."[34] Beneath the expected concern about disorderly youths—not unique in the era—there is in the Bogardus study a fascinating glimpse of some dislocations affecting Los Angeles during the 1920s.

Perhaps most prevalent among the many threads in the discourse on delinquency is a persistent echo of anxiety about what the automobile was doing to the culture of the city. Boys used cars, the report suggested, to run amok in the city. When they had access to automobiles, all lines of propriety began to break down. Often discussions of such freedom mirrored broader worries about mass culture, public amusements, and a "promiscuous" intermingling of boys and girls. As one of Bogardus's respondents, a social worker, put it delicately, "The auto has been a very great contributing factor in creating the problem boy. When young people get out in autos they always want to go as fast as the car will go, and that gives an exhilarating effect upon the occupants and tends to break down the barriers that before existed."[35] Speed is an aphrodisiac in this account, and the prospect of cruising randomly around city streets allegedly seduced many a young lad into a life of debauchery.

Indeed, once more the automobile became the focal point for concern about excessive personal license: "The automobile is the undoing of many a boy. . . . With the automobile at his command, the boy easily speeds up beyond home control."[36] The delinquent becomes, as it were, a citizen of the city at large, abandoning his place as a creature of the domestic sphere. Instead of having his activities confined to proper realms—the homes, schools, churches, and institutional clubs that provide the basic sites of research in Bogardus's study—the boy equipped with an automobile could go just about anywhere in the metropolis. By facilitating this uncontrolled mobility, the automobile contributed to the chaos and confusion of the city at large. This consternation at the activities of Southern California's youth, as represented by the academic sociologists, betokened a parallel frustration with the disorder of the urban landscape. Both phenomena testified to the subtle erosion of those clear lines of separation and segregation of gender, race, and locality that had traditionally served to impart order and social legibility upon the metropolis.

Other sociologists—such as Bessie Averne McClenahan, a student of Bogardus's at USC—observed similar shifts in systems of racial or ethnic segregation at the time. Of course, by no means was the system of Los Angeles's racial restrictions fading. Indeed, these restrictions were as pervasive as ever, but the locations they marked changed continually through the 1920s and 1930s. Traditional enclaves moved and dispersed, areas previously restricted to African Americans, say, or to Mexican Americans, now contained a more diverse mix of nonwhites or of immigrant would-be whites. Moreover, the boundaries of these segregated zones were themselves shifting, virtually under the feet of the city's residents. White residents' anxiety about these transformations comes across strongly in McClenahan's study of a neighborhood near the university (unfortunately, she did not survey minority Angelenos to access their perspectives on this transformation). The sociologist, always particularly sensitive to urban boundaries—like the city planner—describes with great precision at the outset of her report the specific demarcations pertinent to her study—a recitation no doubt familiar in pattern to most urban dwellers during that period: "The area selected constitutes approximately three-quarters of a larger section of perhaps twenty-four or twenty-five blocks lying within two of the earlier additions to the city of Los Angeles. This larger square is hemmed in on two sides by business and street car lines, on the third side by a street of heavy traffic and some business activities, and on the fourth, by a railroad. All four of these boundaries are streets or boulevards of definite importance in connection with the transportation system of the city."[37] Just as significant as these transportation boundaries are the city's racial borders, and McClenahan continues her description by seamlessly moving from physical to social and ideological frontiers: "Across the northwest corner of the square may be drawn a racial boundary line which marks the extent of the invasion of Negroes and Japanese into the territory which previously had been occupied by whites. The area under scrutiny lies east and south of the racial boundary line." The lines of racial division—here, the "racial boundary line"—stand out in the survey no less clearly than formal lines of transportation and urban circulation. These demographic, or human, distinctions are set just as firmly into the ground of the city as are the streetcar tracks.

The lines revealed in the study, though, were moving even as they were being surveyed. The consequent threat of what the sociologists (rather prejudiciously) termed "invasion" occupied much local attention.

Fear was aroused and resentment stirred with the repetition of what was believed to be the slogan of the Negroes, "On to Vermont!" Previous to the circulation of this statement, the gradual movement of the Negroes across Normandie Avenue into the section had not been viewed with alarm. Gradually the white residents had given way, but there seemed to have arisen a sort of blind faith that the invasion would stop at Budlong, only two blocks west of Vermont Avenue. Therefore, the purchase by a Negro of a dwelling east of Budlong precipitated action.[38]

As McClenahan's research reveals, residents of Los Angeles retained a faith during the 1920s that although the familiar racial boundaries were shifting, there were stable urban divisions that would stand definitively. Yet, as the decade progressed and ethnic enclaves shifted as the city did, this faith eroded. A reactionary politics of boundary fixing intensified in the period as a consequence. McClenahan observes that "the northwest corner of the square is no longer in the hands of the Caucasians. The nearer approach of the Negroes, particularly, is prompting egress on the part of many residents of the area and the interviews give clues to some of the opinions current among them. The idea is frequently expressed that they should be kept in their places. The white residents do not want them as neighbors."[39] As a result of this anxiety, whites began to make distinctions among ethnic groups based on their perceived "shiftiness." For instance, according to the study, "preference for the Japanese is based on the belief that they keep up the appearance of their property better and 'keep their places.'"[40] Prejudicial attitudes among working and middle-class white Angelenos during this period, then, were finely tuned to the geography of the region. Those minority citizens who seemed more fixed in a particular place were inherently less disturbing and abhorrent than those who appeared to be transgressing visible borders and intruding into spaces that were not properly "theirs."

Clearly, a portion of the anxiety concerning racial transgression resulted from the growth of Southern California during its boom decade. The influx of migrants during the 1920s, though, was dominated by white midwesterners, and later analysts of Los Angeles's racial segregation have generally suggested that the pressure on the housing market made residential exclusion of minorities more severe during the period.[41] Furthermore, the decade was a prime one for the spread of restrictive covenants, as McClenahan's survey shows (in the course of her investigations, she interviews residents who are in the process of drafting such covenants for their neighborhood), which worked to halt the movement of minority Angelenos into lily-white districts. By any objective measure, the system of racial segregation in the metropolis was not breaking down (it would not be challenged for another two decades).

This system was, however, becoming less clearly legible.[42] Bogardus's study of delinquency once again reflects the discourse on this confusion, as he quotes a teacher citing interracial mixing as a source of intergenerational conflict: "I come in contact with the parents, who constantly come to me and tell me their troubles with their children. The greatest difficulty is the conflict of cultures. We find it present among all types, all classes, nations and races. The contacts the children make in school may alienate them from their parents."[43] The everyday "contacts" between heterogeneous children blur the proper boundaries of association; social contamination from these chaotic and mixed public spaces is then brought back into the heart of the most sacrosanct private ones. Even within the seemingly homogeneous family home, this teacher suggests, Angelenos could perceive a subversive racial "invasion."

Was there, however, really a greater degree of interracial contact as the '20s progressed? Although this seems empirically unlikely, given the skepticism of later historical accounts on this point as well as the intensity of restrictive efforts during the decade, it seems likely that once again the clear boundaries of racial regimentation became considerably less clear. They may have been as effective as previously in physically balkanizing the city, but they no longer presented a simple, comprehensible, and tidy cognitive map for residents. Remembered topographies of race had to be continually updated, revised, and modified to keep up with the shifting patterns of settlement and resettlement in this still racially conscious—if now somewhat confused—metropolis.

BREAKING THE BONDS OF AFFECTION
IN THE POSTSUBURBAN NEIGHBORHOOD

The auto is a very great benefit to man, but we do not know just how to use it. We get out and speed, going faster than the nervous system can stand. Almost every boy in this school has an auto at his disposal some time during the week, and he is going to get out in it and go. And it is a cinch he is not going alone. Then he has to go for miles before he can see anything but streets and streets and more streets.

A BOY, QUOTED IN *THE CITY BOY AND HIS PROBLEMS* (71)

Judging from the frenzied attempts by some Angelenos to reimpose clear order on the city and stabilize shifting boundaries of generation, sexuality, gender, and race, previously stable systems of urban legibility in Southern California could no longer be assumed to operate reliably by the late 1920s. The resulting uncertainties about the new postsuburban metropolis played themselves out in anxieties about the ontological status of the community itself. Angelenos of this period began to express concern about whether Los Angeles was any longer capable of nurturing expected sorts of urban relationships. These fears were animated by a suspicion that the community was subtly unraveling as a cohesive entity. Perhaps all that now held the place together was "streets and streets and more streets." Indeed, for all the descriptive vividness of the ground-level shifts in racial habitation within a Los Angeles neighborhood, the most powerful observation in McClenahan's monograph comes with her more theoretical conclusion, for here she observes some of the profound "psycho-social" changes taking place in the city.

McClenahan draws somewhat surprising conclusions from her investigation of this central Los Angeles neighborhood. She does not, as one might expect, focus her final thoughts on the changes wrought by the shifting racial lines within the community, with new residents moving in and older denizens fleeing for the new western subdivisions. In fact, these movements she takes for granted, as in themselves only tangentially significant. Instead, she argues that a more profound transformation was taking place in the neighborhood—more radical than mere demographic alterations. Although some residents were moving out, others moving in, and still others attempting futilely to resist these changes by instituting restrictive covenants, all were subtly and pervasively altering the ways they used the city itself.

If, as urban sociologists and others had suggested, patterns of urban human interaction in the American city were traditionally based in and organized around the neighborhood, in Los Angeles this connection between locality and community seemed to be breaking down.[44] Along with the novel and not always contiguous patterns of racial and physical geography, a new affiliational urban topography was being superimposed upon them in this period: "The social life of the city seems to be measurable in two dimensions: the territorial, on the basis of the actual space utilized; and the psychosocial, on the basis of a person's contact with other persons and their mutual inter-stimulation and response, i.e., on the basis of associations."[45] In general, these coordinates of urban life align closely, as most urbanites traditionally find community in close proximity to their homes. As McClenahan affirms, "There is a close relationship between these two dimensions: for instance, the psychosocial range of any person may be limited by the radius of a few blocks in a congested urban section" (2). This coincidence of interaction and propinquity reflects in part the structure of the American metropolis as a mosaic of tightly knit ethnically and economically homogeneous enclaves. In essence, the neighborhood circumscribes what is thought of as "home," and "home" describes the close proximity in which most social interaction occurs.

"However," the sociologist cautions, it is also possible that "these two definitions may not coincide," that physical and social closeness may not directly correspond. McClenahan proceeds to map these hypothetical divergent landscapes: "The person occupies a certain space; he has 'standing room.' His neighbor and he live on adjoining lots and both are affected by street conditions, traffic regulations, transportation conveniences, telephone service, tax rates, property values or rentals. Outside of these civic and general economic concerns, related to 'place,' the two men, although living next door to each other, may have nothing in common" (2–3).

The only connections some neighbors may have are those objective associations arising strictly from the condition of sharing a discrete "place." And these logical affiliations, in fact, may be entirely superficial; they may not reflect any real psychosocial "closeness" at all. Indeed, the two neighbors "may belong to different racial cultures and may not be governed by the same mores. Each has his own circle or circles of friends and fellow members of play group, lodge, church. These informal or more formal associations may spread across miles of space and have no relation to the place considered home" (2–3). It is precisely this theoretical disconnection between the perceived topographies of community and of geography that seems, most disturbingly, to arise out of the confused changes in postsuburban 1920s Southern California, McClenahan tells us.

The respondents in the sociologist's survey seemed to be finding community far from their local neighborhoods, often at the far reaches of the region. Using a transportation infrastructure that now supported long trips in multiple, centrifugal directions—and no longer merely between outlying district and downtown—these residents no longer looked to their immediate locality for friends and associates. Neighborhood no longer implied social connection, and proximity no longer guaranteed contact. The people McClenahan talked to continually echoed the same sentiments: "We know nothing about the neighbors. None of them has ever come in to see us nor do we see any of them. Our friends live in various parts of the city and in the small cities around Los Angeles" (68). These Angelenos sometimes regretted the loss of "neighborliness" and the sense that the community had lost its identity, but frequently they already seemed to be adapting to the new postsuburban affiliational geography.

In retrospect, the development of new patterns of association seems an inevitable response both to the restless and unsettled migrations in the exploding metropolis and to the shifting and confusing boundaries of racial settlement. In this sense, then, the rise of novel modes of human interaction in the city represents a new strategy for enforcing clear lines of associational order by rebuilding through social interaction those "proper" societal segregations that no longer seemed to operate legibly in urban space. Proximity now had little to do with relationships of any sort. As one respondent declared, "My friends are not my neighbors. I don't have anything to do with any of them. We have lived here for twelve years" (69). Clearly, the unwillingness to form close bonds with neighbors had little to do, at least in this case, with length of residency. This citizen was no recent migrant, and he or she was not motivated by the sort of restless wanderlust so frequently observed in Jazz Age Angelenos.

This resident did not wish to move but felt that the city was shifting around him or her: "I don't like the apartment house [next door]. We are not planning to move but we would sell if we could get our price from white people. We wouldn't be un-Christian enough to sell to 'niggers.' They are not any closer than they used to be but the neighborhood has changed with the building of apartment houses" (69).

Here, the shifting boundaries of race and class become interwoven and conflated, and reactive racism is clearly tied to territorial dislocation. An apartment house full (presumably) of white working-class tenants can immediately evoke African American neighborhood "invasion" in the mind (and discourse) of this respondent. In this example, as in many others, one can witness how Angelenos bluntly sought to mobilize the language of race and racism as a pervasive and brutal, if perhaps not fully conscious, strategy for actively bolstering the psychosocial distance between themselves and others. It is as if the interviewee wished to "push away" those undesired neighbors by casting them as abjectly "other." Unwanted white neighbors are recoded subtly as somehow allied with "blackness," thus recasting an uncomfortable lack of expected social interaction (after all, one should, properly, be neighborly with those living nearby) as a (proper) racial social segregation (one is, of course, expected to keep one's distance from racial others). The awkward disconnection between social and physical proximities, then, forces Angelenos to react by mobilizing anxieties of racial mixing even where such spatial miscegenation is not taking place.

The attempt to justify or legitimize the lack of basic neighborliness also reflects an effort to recompose fundamental urban legibility. As social connection becomes increasingly detached from physical contiguity, the concept of community starts to lose meaning. Southern Californians could no longer locate their own psychosocial territory in the district adjacent to their homes. The postsuburban topography of the region made it very difficult to read the structure of one's own neighborhood and very easy to find association elsewhere (thus multiplying the illegibility). Thanks to Los Angeles's new urban form and novel transportation infrastructure, and to its residents' reactionary responses to this mounting illegibility, it was now becoming easier to simply shirk all undesired social interaction. Quite simply, the city no longer compelled such contact. The implication was clear. Southern California did not, unlike other urban areas, work to encourage social juxtaposition; Los Angeles was becoming an anticosmopolitan city.

In a larger sense, McClenahan's study identifies more than a retreat from specific neighbors or specific groups of neighbors; it shows an outright rejection of proximity-based social contact. As the sociologist observed, "Among the renters as among the owners are frank expressions of their wish for non-participation with neighbors. A new definition of a 'friendly neighborhood' is apparent; it is one in which the 'neighbors tend to their own business'" (70). One respondent in the survey put it particularly bluntly: "We are renting and have been here six years. . . . We like to live here because of the conveniences, the local shops, and the junior high school. I don't want to neighbor and I do not know how people neighbor" (70). Another, sharing this strong view that neighborhood interaction ought to be avoided altogether, directly argued for the desirability of social distance: "We have rented here for two months. I know nothing about the neighborhood and I never did have anything to do with my neighbors. I lived in the N. apartments in S. for ten years and never spoke to a neighbor in the house. I find it best not to, you are much safer. Then no one knows your business and I don't care to know any one else's" (70).

Clearly some residents of Los Angeles were not only adapting to the new post-suburban urban form but melding it with their own ideologies and preferences. These people were choosing their place of residence in the city based on explicitly antineighborly and anticosmopolitan criteria. Driven by such sentiment, ground-level settlement patterns in Southern California were changing to reinforce larger postsuburban structural trends in the urban fabric.

McClenahan is at pains to stress that this decline of "neighboring" did not im-ply a more general breakdown in social interaction. Rather, she insists, it meant that Angelenos merely interacted with others of their own choosing, over far greater distances. Social and physical geographies simply no longer coincided: "Non-participation in his neighborhood may be correlated with association with companions none of whom has locus in the particular geographical area in which the activity occurs. The participants may come from a wide radius and may know each other only in that one relationship, as Mrs. W. explained in considerable de-tail: 'I have three different sets of friends.' These were met in different places and none of the groups had to do with the other groups nor did Mrs. W. meet her friends in any but the one connection" (99).

The "psycho-social" map of Los Angeles was, by this time, deviating from the spatial map in ways sociologists had not seen in other places. Physically coherent and proximate urban districts no longer seemed to correspond with social geogra-phies, and identifiable neighborhoods housed not the expected tight-knit and in-terdependent communities but instead a sort of consensual social indifference.

In retrospect, Bessie McClenahan's *The Changing Urban Neighborhood* seems to be a landmark in the urban observation of Southern California. Its interview methodology identified, in a way the surveys of other sociologists and planners could not, some of the most profound changes beginning to transform the post-suburban region. Although each of McClenahan's respondents keeps track of per-sonal connections and presumably could map them onto the landscape of the city, it is clear that no objective observer could ever hope to make sense of such discor-dant, subjective topographies as a comprehensive whole.

The growing inability of anyone in the sprawling metropolis to perceive the work-ings of the entire city, even in abstract form, has serious implications for any at-tempt to apply traditional conceptions of community or public space to this urban landscape. Indeed, the sociologist's final conclusions seem almost wistful. "In the early days," McClenahan reflects, "association covered a somewhat larger territory and was spatially limited to the district, largely because of inadequate transporta-tion facilities. Best friends often lived in the neighborhood, which was more ex-tensive than adjacent houses and seems to have covered several blocks" (75). This, of course, was the standard model of urbanism in the concentric metropolis of the late nineteenth and early twentieth centuries. In Greater Los Angeles, though, things had changed; locale no longer predicted association: "Social activities are not limited to the area. There are associations with relatives, with friends, and with club members at various places in the city" (72). Far from guaranteeing community, topographical proximity now seemed to actively militate against it. As McClenahan concludes, "But whatever the source of his associations, his relationship to the nighdwellers is limited even in its most complete expression by the wish for privacy and protection from associations unrelated to his social values and thrust upon him merely because of proximity within a common locus" (72). People in Los Angeles of the 1920s seemed to be forging new notions of community and new patterns of association in their daily lives, in the process eschewing neighborly interaction. For them, city life meant something different than it did for most Americans in the period. Indeed, implicit in McClenahan's survey of neighborhood in the nascent postsuburban metropolis is a comparison with more traditional notions of community—either urban understandings that were hegemonic in her chosen neighborhood or rural concepts inherited from and transmitted by the area's newcomers, many of whom were migrants from the Midwest. Clearly, neither model of human interaction applied in this strange new city.

McClenahan's study reveals that objective, measurable space no longer determined the lived reality of Los Angeles's citizens in this period. If this conclusion is accurate, the instrumental maps so important to urban observers might no longer accurately reflect the everyday experiences of Angelenos. The psychosocial geography of the postsuburban region might no longer be commensurable, ultimately, with the visible topography of the region—it might no longer even be theoretically possible to delineate these relationships in any simple and stable way, let alone establish a direct, one-to-one correspondence between the social and architectural geographies of the postsuburban metropolis. Plotted on a standard survey map, patterns of work, recreation, and association might seem as chaotic and jumbled as the region's traffic. In fact, that traffic might be the only visible manifestation of those intrinsic relationships. The basic functional operation of the city would be simply illegible to the expert gaze. The old maps still might accurately and precisely depict the outward tokens of urbanism—office buildings, streets, shops, houses, parks, and so on—but they would now connote nothing of the critical relationships between these visible manifestations. The superstructure of urban life might still be surveyed by planners and sociologists, but those markers would mean precious little if one had no real idea how the citizens used them, which citizens used them, or even if they did at all.

Because of this manifest breakdown in externally legible patterns of social interaction, patterns of interaction between Angelenos could no longer be either assumed from physical location or easily observed and charted by experts. Just because such patterns could not be effectively generalized, abstracted, or predicted, however, did not mean that local urbanites during this period of transformation were bereft of contacts and relationships. On the contrary, as McClenahan's survey reveals, Angelenos were learning to forge new sorts of affiliational connections appropriate to the postsuburban topography, but these bonds followed essentially individual and outwardly invisible, private paths. Ironically, then, although ordinary Angelenos appeared to be adapting to the new urban form, expert observers were having a much harder time of it. Sociologists found it difficult to generalize into quantifiable data and regularized patterns what some could apprehend anecdotally.[46] Obsessed with a vision of diagrammatic omniscience, planners found it extremely difficult to switch paradigms of urban conceptualization. They could observe the changing city, but could not adequately characterize these transformations or use them to generate appropriate new comprehensive and cohesive models.[47] Another group of urban observers—cultural critics and commentators—ultimately also proved unable to reconcile an illegible postsuburban community with common sense notions of cosmopolitan urbanity.

MODERN METROPOLIS OR OVERGROWN VILLAGE?

As one of the newcomers who came to Southern California in the great influx of the 'twenties, . . . I hated, as so many other people have hated, the big, sprawling, deformed character of the place. I loathed the crowds of dull and stupid people that milled around the downtown sections dawdling and staring, poking and pointing, like villagers visiting a city for the first time. I found nothing about Los Angeles to like and a great many things to detest.

CAREY MCWILLIAMS, *SOUTHERN CALIFORNIA: AN ISLAND ON THE LAND* (375)

If McClenahan was one of the few urban surveyors to cogently describe the social ramifications of the larger crisis in urban legibility brought on by emerging postsuburbanization, it is not as if these changes in patterns of community went unnoticed by other observers. McClenahan had been able, through her interview methodology, to conduct her analysis on the individual level, where—through frantic ad hoc boundary reconstruction and the creation of newly personal and private affiliational geographies—Angelenos were responding to the erosion in urban legibility in Greater Los Angeles. For most other urban critics, though, it often seemed that Los Angeles's very cosmopolitan urbanity was dissolving. Instead of detailed and specific analysis of ongoing ground-level social transformations, many urban observers of the region resorted to hyperbolic criticism. As Mike Davis most famously argued in *City of Quartz*, in the absence of "a scholarly municipal history," critics collapsed all ambivalence toward Southern California into "a robust fiction called *noir*," essentially a mirror image of the traditional sunny booster rhetoric.[48] In analyzing the dark side of this twinned dynamic of sunshine and *noir*, Davis identifies several scathing "attempts . . . to establish authentic epistemologies for Los Angeles," ranging from the reactions of a school of antibooster "debunkers" to the more sophisticated but even more caustic Frankfurt School "exiles."[49]

In the context of the late 1920s and 1930s, we can read in this larger framework a further axis of critique. Many of these divergent strands in the *noir* discourse channeled social critique into reflection on the spatial configuration of the metropolis. At first, this characteristic played itself out in indirect ways, as critics blamed a range of problems manifest in the city on the collective character of its residents. Here, the flaws in the city reflect the mindset of the citizenry, which was increasingly attributed to the influence of one particular subset of the populace, namely its newest immigrants. Many of these newcomers were former midwestern farmers who had retired along the Pacific. Collectively termed "the Iowans," these new Angelenos became the focal point for much sarcastic criticism. They—and thus the city as a whole—were alternately puritan or cultish (with particular reference on both sides to celebrity radio evangelist Aimee Semple McPherson), abstinent or decadent (an important theme in these Prohibition years), flighty and faddish or dull and unimaginative (as Carey McWilliams and Nathanael West saw them). The contradictions in these representations reflect the flexibility and incoherence of the larger criticism. It also hints, though, at how useful Iowans would be to the hyperbolic and inconsistent *noir* discourse as ciphers through which to link critique of disordered society to illegible urban form.

In fact, in the discourse of postsuburban decline and fragmentation, the trope of the midwesterner carried special weight. In Carey McWilliams's reminiscence, he insisted that the new provincial immigrants to the city were unable to recognize marks of urbanity when they saw them (and thus acted like lost tourists in their city's traditional downtown). The implication here, as in many similar critiques, was that these midwesterners would make their homes not in cosmopolitan settings but in inappropriate ruralized ones. Their discomfort in proper urban settings drove them to settle farther and farther afield during the 1920s. This impression was further elaborated by the sharp-tongued Morrow Mayo, who asserted at the beginning of the 1930s that "at the present moment this great town of Los Angeles—this huge collection of villages—may be appraised without much difficulty. Here is an artificial city which has been pumped up under forced draught, inflated like a balloon, stuffed with rural humanity like a goose with corn."[50] Once more, the city took on the ruralness of its inhabitants; it had become little more than an overgrown town. In this mode of *noir* critique, the booster propaganda of the famously "middle-class" city was turned on its head: Los Angeles was now an overly comfortable resort, a tacky oasis of phony luxury that catered only to uncultured former farmers, lower-class bumpkins whose only claim to wealth came from having sold everything they had back in Iowa for a chance to settle into Southern Californian indolence.

The provinciality of the region's new inhabitants reflected the failings of the local urban culture, for in this view, Los Angeles had become big without becoming a center of civilization: "Superficially and quantitatively Los Angeles is a city. It has street-cars, buildings, noise, traffic, theaters, restaurants, department stores, and hotels. Qualitatively, it cannot yet be placed in that category."[51] In comparison with traditional metropolises, which had been so effectively vilified only a few years before in the rhetoric surrounding the el, Southern California suddenly seemed deficient. Mayo offered a criterion for true urbanity that rested squarely upon cosmopolitanism, and Los Angeles appeared woefully inadequate: "What makes a city, properly so called, is not buildings, nor the number of people in the buildings, but what goes on inside the heads of the people in the buildings. What makes a place, large or small, actually a village or a city is the presence or lack of a spirit, an atmosphere, of urbanity" (328). Here, Mayo explicitly associates being urban with being "urbane," and suggests that Angelenos just don't fit the bill: " 'Urbane,' says the dictionary, 'is opposed to rustic'; and 'urbanity' is 'the character or quality of being urbane; strictly, the city quality, from the assumption that life in the city results in superior refinement.' Thus a community of a thousand urban people is far more of a city than a community of a hundred thousand rustics" (328). It is not skyscrapers, then, that define modern urbanism, but cosmopolitan temperament and a manifest shared sense of cultural attainment.

This city of traffic jams, afternoon matinees, and especially, Iowans can never aspire to true urban sophistication. After all, "if one were to take a hundred Middle Western towns of ten thousand population each and place them end to end in the prairie, would he have a great metropolis? He would not. He would have a huge country village of a million population, a remarkable sociological phenomenon; and that is precisely what Los Angeles is" (328). Ultimately, for Mayo, Los Angeles "has retained the manners, culture, and general outlook of a huge country village" (327). The city was incapable of transforming these midwestern farmers into true cosmopolites because it was itself not cosmopolitan. Likewise, as the product of these provincials, the city itself was provincial. This reciprocal relationship between inhabitants and culture was reflected most obviously in topographical form, for here the rural character of the supposed metropolis manifested itself most visibly. Unlike more traditional, compact cities, Los Angeles devoured the countryside, carelessly assimilating land. The implication here was that Southern California, like its inhabitants, lacked the restraint and discipline to develop true urban society. The topography of Los Angeles represented geographically the lack of rigor—the sloppiness— of its civic culture.

The local journalist and anecdotal historian Harry Carr, writing at about the same time, concurred with Mayo's critique, mourning that "spilled out over four hundred and fifty square miles, Los Angeles had too much room to grow."[52] Here geographical size reflects and explains a profound culture of sloppiness. "In cities like New York, where the area is restricted and there can be no spread, old buildings are torn to make way for new." In Los Angeles, on the other hand, easy land and easy lifestyles combine to eliminate this process of renewal, while leaving the entire metropolis fundamentally immature, its development stunted: "The growth of metropolitan Los Angeles was like a child biting a cookie and throwing it down half-eaten to run after another cookie. Each generation has picked up and moved farther out on the level plain." Within this discourse, Los Angeles's sprawling form was not the product of some unique and futuristic human geography but instead resulted from simple carelessness.

In Nathanael West's depictions of Los Angeles, particularly *The Day of the Locust*, the city is little more than façade. West likewise associates the denizens of Southern California, especially the Iowans, with the architectural and physical topography of the city. Both built and human environments are, for West, fundamentally phony. The collapse of appearance and experience into mere cinematic representation is in West's view the primary heresy of the Californian culture. From the legions of dim-witted extras wandering through the city to the fake arabesque and Camelot architecture of the houses, the spaces of Southern California are overrun with ostentatious simulation. The celebrated cinematic traffic mêlées and wild chases of the previous decade's popular amusement (and amazement) are recast as petty voyeurism and artificial spectacle. In West's Los Angeles, urban perception and filmic mise-en-scene are becoming inextricably entangled, leaving the city as little more than an oversized movie set. Further, although West's critique focuses primarily on the interface between cinema and urbanity, it is worth noting that *The Day of the Locust* personifies the fragmentation and anomie of the metropolis in its protagonist, Tod Hackett. "Despite his appearance, he was really a very complicated young man with a whole set of personalities, one inside the other like a nest of Chinese boxes," West writes, having first described "his large sprawling body."[53]

Finally, the notion that Los Angeles, for all its impressive growth, was still really a provincial backwater continued to inform a great deal of discourse on the city. In this view, Southern California had not really "earned" urbanity, it had merely fallen into it, or even stolen it. The inhabitants—Carr concludes his history of the region with a reference to the ubiquitous "little old schoolteacher from Dubuque" (392)—may have been deluded into thinking they were living in a city, but that is merely because they would not recognize a real metropolis if they saw one. This city—filled, as West famously put it, with the people who "had come to California to die" (60)—is simply a village suffering from gigantism. In Mayo's formulation, Los Angeles is a deformed circus "freak" among cities (328).

"THERE ISN'T ANY PLACE THAT IS LOS ANGELES"

Its profile was so illusive that in 1930 one magazine writer glanced at what he could see of the city's 450-square-mile sprawl and remarked, "There is no Los Angeles face!"

W. W. ROBINSON, *LOS ANGELES: A PROFILE* (18)

Whether freak or overgrown village, Los Angeles in the late 1920s and 1930s was subject to a frenzy of criticism that refracted its culture and society through the metaphorics of urban topography. Soon this entire *noir* discourse about the illegible metropolis began to be encapsulated into one word: *sprawl.* It was a term that efficiently described the region's great geographic spread, as well as the attendant sense of chaos in that expansion. With connotations of unplanned or lazy physical distribution, *sprawl* reflected the impression that Los Angeles's shape was not novel or modern but merely lazy. Encompassing popular anxieties about spatial confusion, topographical urban illegibility, and shifting boundaries of social segregation, *sprawl* touched on a wide range of concerns about Los Angeles in the 1920s. As the city drew more and more migrants, the word circulated widely through the discourse of local and visiting observers. By the time of Los Angeles's international exposure via the Olympic Games of 1932, *sprawl* was a primary token of the region for countless reporters and visitors to the western metropolis. It could denote the declining preeminence of downtown, the growth of multiple regional subcenters, the seemingly random pattern of development, or the jumbled street system. As Harry Carr put it in 1935, the term's currency reflected the ease with which it indicated the city's lack of an organizing totem, a symbolic center: "Fifth Avenue is New York. Market Street is San Francisco. Paris is the Champs. Berlin is looking through the Brandenberger Thor down the Linden. Shanghai is the Bund. Peking the Forbidden City. But there isn't any place that is Los Angeles. Approximately one thousand correspondents came here for the Olympic Games and they all felt a sacred duty to describe Los Angeles. They all said it was 'sprawling.' That adjective went sizzling over the cables in just about every language that can be put into words."[54]

Even in the late 1920s, it was difficult to find published commentary on the region that did not somewhere invoke the language of sprawl. Clearly, this repetition marked something more than a general inability to find one's way around the city. Much like the shared anxiety about "traffic" that had begun earlier in the decade, the concern with "sprawl" reflected real concerns about social changes only perceptible at the edges of one's field of vision—a sort of partial, not fully comprehended, peripheral apperception of a connected set of breakdowns in the societal order. As a discursive signifier, concern about "sprawl" keyed into larger significance, connoting misgivings about a chaos of complex social changes, in effect arraying these seemingly random changes onto a topographic field. Demographic disorder thus played out in the public discourse as anxiety about spatial disorder; shifting social relations produced criticism of the city's unfixed and anarchic geographical relationships. Sprawl discourse channeled not just uncertainty about the physical shape of Los Angeles, unprecedented and illegible as it was, but anxiety about an aggregate of subtle societal transformations not easily grasped as a whole. Some of these were peculiar to Southern California, including a number of dislocations caused by the rapid population growth, while others were broader, also affecting other cities during this same time period. Within Greater Los Angeles, though, these subtle distinctions dissolved, as sprawl seemed to represent everything that was uniquely wrong with the development of the metropolis.

Perhaps the most fascinating deployment of the discourse of sprawl lay in the soon-clichéd joke that the only thing Los Angeles lacked in urban amenities was the metropolis itself. As local real estate researcher and prolific historian W. W. Robinson recounted, "In the early 1920's, sardonic visitors to Southern California began describing Los Angeles as 'six suburbs in search of a city.' Later the number became ninety or one hundred."[55] Over the years, the variations on the saw were practically infinite, and it was frequently repeated in various forms. Perhaps this was such a lively trope because its implicit criticism went straight to the heart of the utopian dreams city planners had so long cherished for Southern California. Not only was Los Angeles represented as a formless sprawl of indistinguishable (and innumerable) suburbs, but it knew what it was missing. Angelenos had built the outskirts but, in their haste, had forgotten the centralized downtown-oriented city. The insinuation in this discourse, and in all sprawl discourse, was that Los Angeles was unplanned, the product of unsupervised and unguided development. The opposite was in fact the case. If anything, Los Angeles suffered from an overabundance of visionary, comprehensive, and—unfortunately—contradictory planning. The Southern California landscape was overdetermined by dreams and visions.

The development of Los Angeles in the 1920s might have fallen somewhat short of the regional planners' envisioned utopia, but Southern California had still avoided many of the "mistakes" of eastern cities as they saw them. The low-density multicentered character of the metropolitan area—the sprawl, this symptom of the alleged lack of planning—was the very aspect of Los Angeles's topography that planners thought had gone most right. What critics saw as sprawl Los Angeles planners saw as the successful fruit of their labors. In this instance, their plans had actually found solid form, albeit not entirely as they had envisioned it. Ironically, then, it was the very topography of interdependent but deconcentrated communities that was identified as unplanned sprawl. The form the planners considered to be their most tangible achievement had become the butt of the joke.

The thing Southern Californian planners had most sought to avoid—the congestion of crowded, dim downtown streets—Los Angeles was now thought to lack. It was on this point that the topography of the garden city and the trope of the midwesterner melded in dismissive critique. Los Angeles was flat. It was as flat as an Iowa farm. It might be massive, but that massed form was strictly horizontal. The sprawling city spilled settlement over the land, never rising to any distinguished height. It might creep up rises and down valleys, cling to hillsides and clutter the beaches, but it was—in the general impression—the land of the single-story bungalow. All was flattened out in a sort of leveled mediocrity: a seemingly classless (and therefore low-class) equality where no distinction was made between downtown and outskirts, center and periphery. The physical structure of the sprawling city mirrored the improper social topography, where mass culture triumphed over high culture and movie stars outranked commercial elites. There was a conviction implicit in sprawl discourse that cultural discipline and civic order could arise only through hierarchical concentration. Consequently, in the common sense of the era, Los Angeles could not be considered truly urban. Modernity and cosmopolitanism required something more than great physical size and massed human population; it required more than sunshine and midwestern retirees. In this pervasive view, Los Angeles's pretensions to greatness could never be more than boosterism so long as the region remained fundamentally scattered, disordered, and random.

So profoundly felt and deeply internalized was the region's epistemic crisis that these discursive assaults emanated primarily not from the unenlightened East but almost wholly from within the city itself. At the very pinnacle of the city's power as a magnet for migrants, contemplative locals subversively expressed their doubts about Los Angeles's status as a modern city. Morrow Mayo claimed in 1933 that he had once thought Los Angeles would mature into its predestined role as a "great, vibrant, world metropolis, worthy of the name,"[56] but he now thought the place perhaps doomed by its careless geography, its lulling climate, and its lazy culture. Clearly, even these Angelenos could not excuse, let alone ameliorate, the illegibility and incomprehensibility of their hometown. As Harry Carr derisively described it,

> The residence district is as much a crazy-quilt patchwork as the down-town district. If you ask a native to see the residence part, he will say: "Which residence district?" There are dozens—separated by miles. . . . It is impossible to understand Los Angeles unless you realize that it is not a town; it is a lot of towns. For a quarter of a century it has not been safe for the mother of any attractive village to leave it alone in the house; Los Angeles would kidnap it before she got back. The map of Los Angeles looks as though some one had dropped it and the pieces had scattered.[57]

Locals and visitors alike, despite their attraction to Los Angeles's sunshine and its freedom and amid the incessant—and increasingly, it seemed, shrill—boosterism, despaired by the late 1920s at the city's future. Regarded as a whole, the chaotic and confused metropolis—"this sprawling giant among cities"[58]—seemed fragmented to the point of dissolution, suburban to the point of rural pastoralism, and disordered to the point of anarchy.

Clearly, the discourse and rhetoric of sprawl was a charged one for Angelenos in the 1920s. For Carey McWilliams, *sprawl* connoted the oversized, "deformed" physical geography and the somehow linked anti-intellectual—"dull and stupid"—character of its gawking inhabitants, who could not understand the importance of a downtown district.[59] In the view of the experts on delinquency in Bogardus's survey or the wary and stand-offish neighbors of McClenahan's report, aimless automotive cruising and altered patterns of psychosocial association represented an erasure of the universally recognized and comprehended patterns of urban life. Still another mobilization of sprawl is represented in Neutra's reconstructed depiction, where the traffic confusion of the 1920s features prominently. In this discourse, the city's lack of traditional urban features, such as those sought by the "Modern Building" experts at the Belgian exposition (apartment blocks, subways, and such), proves that its postsuburban form is somehow incomplete. To Harry Carr, *sprawl* referred to the metropolis's lack of an exemplary center.[60] Discussions of sprawl expressed one's inability to comprehend Los Angeles as a whole or to get one's bearings within the city. For W. W. Robinson, California's sprawl brought to mind a certain urban anonymity, a sense—shared by Carr—that the place could never be fully perceived. Nathanael West felt that the sprawling city was too fixated on shallow appearances, on film-set pasteboard showiness. Finally, in Morrow Mayo's use of the term one detects a suspicion that Los Angeles is really nothing other than an overextended village, no more modern than the family farm, whose only claim to greatness is the false one of sheer size. For Mayo, this city's sprawl confirms that it is not only not modern but hardly a city at all.

What had become of this hopeful metropolis, which had for so long, as Mayo was the first to observe in 1935, been circulated and sold as a commodity?[61] It seems amazing, given this widespread concern, that a mere decade earlier, at the beginning of the 1920s, Los Angeles had been a fairly comprehensible place, not unlike other American cities in its size and shape. Settlement had been organized concentrically, around a bustling downtown business center. The residential suburbs arrayed themselves around this urban hub, connected by a state-of-the-art interurban railway system and a network of ordinary, if a bit underdeveloped, local streets and paved highways. Those charged with assessing this metropolis had felt they understood the structure and operation of their city. Likewise, newcomers to the city felt merely the same sort of urban disorientation as that affecting migrants to any American metropolis of the era; using tactics and knowledge gained by experience with other American cities, they soon came to terms with this particular metropolis. Now, though, the clear boundaries of social order were fading, washed out by the chaos of rapid growth and radical urban restructuring. Some influential Angelenos now circulated their own doubts about their city's evolution, mobilizing the caustically derisive discourse of sprawl in its many and varied manifestations to convey a range of anxieties about Southern California and its future. Through the popular circulation of this charged signifier, Angelenos and others asked, "What sort of city is this?" What had become of this modern metropolis, this city of the future? With the onset of nascent postsuburbanization and the experts' failure to do anything about it, observers of Greater Los Angeles would be forced to repeat these awkward questions throughout the ensuing decades.

6

Gardens and Cities

It was a simple determination but a professedly daunting one: "Long stretches of congested streets, through mile after mile of monotonous urban surroundings must be offset somehow."[1] Angelenos' everyday experience of their urban topography was, by the end of the 1920s, dangerously dispiriting: unbroken and disordered urbanism now stretched as far as the eye could ordinarily see. As one of Emory Bogardus's boys testified for the social researchers, Los Angeles had become a cold and alien place, where even someone with a car "has to go for miles before he can see anything but streets and streets and more streets."[2] By all accounts, the postsuburban topography of Southern California, far from cultivating a restful and balanced lifestyle, was instead becoming increasingly dreary and dull, alienating and disorienting.

Already in 1930, Los Angeles was clearly not the garden it once had been. As every Angeleno already knew, part of the problem was this vast and undifferentiated network of urban streets. Streets should have been the antidote to urban alienation; after all, advertising constantly emphasized the automobile's effortless ability to carry the urbanite out of town to a still and restful countryside. Instead, local roads stretched seemingly endlessly and aimlessly through the sprawling conurbation: "Traveling on congested roads, through longer, tedious stretches of unrefreshing, monotonously urbanized territory, is proving too great a waste of time and effort in proportion to the mileage of attractive country traversed."[3] The countryside, once a short hop from all parts of the sheltering basin, had now receded out of reach. Los Angeles, the admonition went, "is unique among populous metropolitan regions in the fact that the great mass of its people live in detached bungalows and cottages with a high proportion of open space on their lots. . . . The spread of private house blocks over a vast urban area tends to remove the open countryside to a far greater distance from the homes of most of the people than would denser types of development."[4] The reper-cussions of this alienating blight would only increase as the city continued its in-evitable expansion. More and more faceless urban tracts, cloistered by further miles of congested and barren streets, would further gird the region in the elemental ma-terials of modern alienation. If Los Angeles had apparently avoided the fate faced by other ambitious cities of the era, of developing into an inhumanly dense vertical skyscraper metropolis, it now looked liable to imprison its unsuspecting denizens in a less elevated, more dusty jacket of concrete and steel. As real estate developments devoured the countryside, sprawling over the landscape, contact with a rejuvenat-ing nature continued to ebb away: "With the growth of population the urban area is becoming greater; the large open spaces of the countryside are being pushed farther and farther from the center and are being made less and less accessible to the people."[5]

More and more, by the end of the 1920s, expert local observers were beginning to fear that in the absence of contact with nature, whether through open spaces or through urban parklands, the attractions of this peculiar modern metropolis, so long taken for granted, would be lost amid the jumble of faceless tracts, abandoned in an urban maze of "streets and streets and more streets."

VISION MADE MANIFEST

No scheme for beautifying the city can be complete that does not include a comprehensive plan for a metropolitan park system.

DANA BARTLETT, *THE BETTER CITY* (44)

Was all this nostalgia for a lost suburban pastoralism a byproduct of the anti–Los Angeles rhetorical backlash of the era? Was this merely another aspect of the sprawl vitriol that dominated national discourse about the exemplary western metropo-lis? To the contrary, these anguished introspections appeared in a germinal docu-ment released by Los Angeles's habitually boosterish planning establishment. It was titled *Parks, Playgrounds, and Beaches for the Los Angeles Region,* and it was a scathing critique of the existing topography of development in Southern Califor-nia at the end of the 1920s. The last remnants of primordial Los Angeles, bucolic land of orange groves and pleasant bungalows, were vanishing forever. Replaced by sprawling urban blight, the seemingly limitless and invulnerable charms of the once-pristine environment and landscape were manifestly at risk. The psychological costs of this destruction were dire, the report indicated, but the economic effects threat-ened to be even worse: "With the growth of a great metropolis here, the absence of parks will make living conditions less and less attractive, less and less wholesome, though parks have been easily dispensed with under the conditions of the past. In so far, therefore, as the people fail to show the understanding, courage, and orga-nizing ability necessary at this crisis, the growth of the region will tend to strangle itself."[6] The booster machinery of a continually growing metropolis could not, this document suggested, be trusted to keep pace with the spreading blight. The boom would sow the seeds of its own bust, taking with it the pristine natural landscape that had always been the region's primary asset.

Unlike contemporary sprawl discourse, this document did not just bemoan the present, it also pointed toward the future. Indeed, *Parks, Playgrounds, and Beaches* claimed that the natural charms of the Southern California region could be resurrected. The solution offered by planners was both bold and terribly expensive. How expensive? Calling for a massive eminent domain condemnation of private property throughout the already heavily developed metropolis, it would require an unprecedented expansion of the city's authority and budget. It was, essentially, a scheme very much in the tradition of twentieth-century Progressivism, laying out a vast public program of urban renewal and beautification under the auspices of a parks and recreation plan.

Envisioned in this report was a system of recreational areas that would surpass eastern urban parks in size and urban accessibility.[7] "The total area of this proposed regional system of parkways and large parks, including 16,000 acres of existing publicly owned parks, water lands, and similar areas," the plan proclaimed, "is approximately 70,000 acres, and the aggregate length of the proposed routes is 440 miles" (96). Incredibly, this amounted to more than a 400 percent expansion of what was—thanks to the grants composing the huge but concentrated and largely inaccessible Griffith Park—an already respectable quantity of local parkland, to be connected by a network of lushly landscaped parkways of the most modern type, which, if laid end to end, would stretch all the way from downtown Los Angeles to the San Francisco Bay.

Clearly, this was not a proposal for a scattering of neighborhood parks, nor a single vast preserve; it constituted a true interconnected usable network that Angelenos would experience every day—"a system of continuous parks and parkways inter-penetrating the Region and connecting it with the countryside" (12). As the report declared,

> *Experience elsewhere points clearly to one of the most urgent park needs of the Los Angeles Region—the need for a system of interconnected pleasureway parks, regional in scope.* Such a system should be so distributed that no home will be more than a few miles from some part of it; and should be so designed that, having reached any part of it, one may drive within the system for pleasure, and *with* pleasure, for many miles under thoroughly agreeable conditions and in pleasant surroundings. Freed from interruption of ordinary urban and suburban conditions, driving there may be either wholly for the pleasure of such a driving or, more generally, it may be over the pleasantest if not always the shortest route to some other recreational objective. (12–13)

Both a greenbelt buffer and a system of loosely linking corridors, these 54,000 acres of easily accessible parklands closely integrated into the urban fabric would give a clear and legible shape to the dangerously sprawling and incoherent conurbation. This was not only a park plan, it was a much more extensive proposal for the future shape of the entire metropolitan region. Simply put, *Parks, Playgrounds, and Beaches* was the manifesto of Los Angeles's advance planning community, the clear proposal for restructuring the metropolitan region that had so long been implicit, gestating—and deferred. This was, in the guise of a recreational facilities study, a meticulously detailed and self-confident blueprint to remake a developed urban area into a cluster of discrete communities, thus putting the garden back into the city.

THE GARDEN IN THE MACHINE

The parks are the lungs of London.

WILLIAM WINDHAM, FROM A SPEECH IN THE BRITISH HOUSE
OF COMMONS, 30 JUNE 1808

But why a park plan? Why did this great regional master plan take the form of a program for recreation and public access to nature? The reason for this particular rhetorical and institutional vehicle goes to the ideological core of the long-standing emphasis on the "garden" in the garden city mythos. It also touches on a complex and powerful set of quasi-agrarian notions that had informed popular and expert thought on American urbanism for quite some time. The roots of Southern California's park plan lie in larger American cultural traditions that date back well into the previous century, finding their footings in the established developments of the East. To discover the meaning of the plan's ambitious proposals and understand the ramifications of its embedding of urban renewal goals in a framework of park development, we must explore this context in depth. Behind the Los Angeles recreation plan of 1930 lay a network of ideological conceptions and common sense assumptions about urbanism, and about the relationship of parklands to urban developments, that had shaped the rhetoric of nature in Southern California for a decade. In essence, we must find the relation between garden and city in the intellectual tradition of the idealized American garden city.

From the conclusion of the Civil War through the 1920s—that is, the three-quarters of a century or more preceding the Los Angeles park plan—cities, although clearly in economic, social, and cultural ascendance, were viewed with considerable suspicion by those who stopped to think or at least write about them. Charged by an ancient and persistent Western European ambivalence toward the city and fed by the more contemporary and graphic horrors of the emerging industrial metropolis, this discourse consistently put city and country at odds, with the weight of moral rectitude and economic productivity (in a vaguely physiocratic sense) attributed to the latter. In the Jeffersonian agrarian tradition of American thought, as discussed by such notable scholars as Leo Marx, Jackson Lears, and Kenneth Jackson, the fruits of republican virtue sprang almost exclusively from tilled soil.[8] The Republic was truly at home only on the range. In this discourse, the manifest and profound disjuncture between city and country mapped onto similarly significant dichotomies between nature and artifice, productivity and consumption, purity and sin, fresh air and pollution, rhetoric and common sense, and many other familiar pairs.

At the heart of this series of oppositions lay a fundamental insistence that the two realms were properly discrete and independent. As massive and extensive American cities arose, especially in the second half of the nineteenth century, they increasingly blurred the sharp boundaries between urban and rural. As William Cronon so ably demonstrates for Chicago in *Nature's Metropolis*, the great metropolises always sent tentacles far into the supposedly innocent countryside. Furthermore, the cities transformed the hinterland, freely exchanging rural resource and urban commodity, often merely by applying cutting-edge information technology.[9] Through an elaborate transportation and communication network, courtesy of the railroad and telegraph, these imperial cities became central processing centers for vast expanses of outback. As the city required the constant input of its hinterland, so too did those more remote regions require the technology, markets, and capital of their urban counterparts. The interconnections between the two zones were profound and intricate. As Cronon insists, the sharp distinctions so frequently drawn between city and countryside had more of a cultural and ideological basis than a social or economic one, and in truth it rapidly became impossible—physically or analytically—to separate the two regions in any lived topography.

In this complex, interlinked conceptual context, any attempt to view the development of the American city in that period as simply cut off from or opposed to some abstract and (preferably untouched) "nature" is impossibly vexed. Even within the relatively purified realms of common sense ideology and the correspondingly constructed lived urban spaces of the era, cities have long been more than a little blurred at the edges. This held topographically as well; by the 1860s, cities tended to surround themselves with liminal, transitional zones. In a strict sense, all cities "sprawled"—the traditional "walking city" of a (seemingly always already) bygone age definitively vanished under the expansive horizontal and vertical growth of many commercial centers. The far reaches of town were increasingly inaccessible for most urbanites by the late nineteenth century, particularly in the absence of ready access to rapid transit. For this simple logistical reason, the outlying urban areas tended for most of the century to be exclusively upper-class, although they began to broaden their constituency in the 1880s as trolley lines reached them.[10] Indeed, as has been more than adequately described in countless urban historical monographs, many of the established wealthy eagerly relocated from the convenient urban centers to these more remote suburban residential retreats. The association of such places with pastoral values—they were commodiously suburban, halfway toward the rural, after all—allowed these leafy zones, so firmly fixed within the economic, cultural, and social orbit of the metropolis, to pose as agrarian outposts or antiurban retreats. Thus it was the well-to-do who most notably, in the historical literature at least, mobilized the Manichaean discourses of urban and rural to present their private homes as an escape from the worldly cares of the consumer capitalist world around them.

Although the story of the rise of the isolated suburban retreat is quite familiar by now, thanks to a great deal of thorough historiography over the past half-century, it is useful to reprise a few elements of this narrative that are relevant to our current discussion.[11] These suburbs were almost always situated in a lush, landscaped environment, ostensible refuges from the surrounding capitalist world that made them possible and necessary. Whereas the city was a hostile and aggressive site of Social Darwinian liberal competition, the domestic world preserved, frozen and stable, a benevolent and sheltering patriarchalism.[12] Although the private home, the "haven in a heartless world" (in the telling cliché) could be located anywhere in the metropolitan region—its womblike virtues were essentially internal, after all—it was best situated in an accommodating and exclusive suburb. The suburban community was both an extension to that domestic sphere, a sort of buffering expansion of the house's walls, and a pastoral retreat. In its verdant and growing milieu, the suburb counterpoised life against the city's lifelessness. Through a powerful series of associations, many of which influence us today, this "natural" environment was promoted as actively healthful and regenerative. The city, dark and cold, was sickly; the green suburbs were correspondingly invigorating and salubrious.[13] These discourses deployed all the cultural connotations of abstract Nature: the suburb was ultimately an archive of lively rurality, a preserve of pastoral virtue.

Of course, it is important to remember, before getting carried away by the alluring images, that these leafy groves were no less a product of industrial production than were the skyscrapers that served as equally powerful, diametrically opposed symbols of cosmopolitanism. The foliage so conspicuously displayed in suburbs was as modern and new as any other technological product. The plant matter in the typical American suburb was calculated and mass-manufactured—even in the nineteenth century, these flora were the hybridized, cross-bred, cultivated outcomes of complex agricultural engineering processes. Marketed and expertly selected, these vegetative commodities were almost exclusively long-distance imports, transplanted from diverse environmental contexts by the machinery of global exchange that they were intended to screen out. Further, before they were actually experienced by suburbanites, these plantings were carefully installed in meticulously prepared and landscaped earth according to cutting-edge scientific schemes. Ultimately, all this groundwork resulted in a style of landscaping, of simulacra (particularly in the later nineteenth century), that gently feigned an ideal of "wildness" and chance—a randomness fully as calculated as the gridiron street pattern of the adjacent metropolis.[14] Yet for all their cleverly deceptive characteristics, these suburban glades were eminently comfortable and unobtrusive. From the earliest developments, they were constructed with care and skill. Consequently, these suburbs generally succeeded in producing an amenable and restful pastoral setting. Combined with the ideological allure of the rurality they so expertly deployed, suburbs proved attractive indeed for late nineteenth-century upper-class urbanites. They quickly became essential elements in the concentric topography of American urbanism, forming the basis of Southern California's early and persistent Mediterranean self-image as a bucolic metropolis of bungalows and green private yards.[15]

The introduction of rurality in urban contexts was not confined to marginal and outlying suburbs. Just as the modern city's economy required a constant input of pastoral resource products, raw material that pervaded every corner of the larger metropolitan industrial complex, so too the less overtly utilitarian tokens of nature imbricated themselves in the most geographically central regions of the nineteenth- and early twentieth-century city. Although the planted and verdant character of many later twentieth-century metropolises is not found in this period in any but the most tentative forms—street trees, urban yards, and front gardens were rare in most American cities—many municipalities did experiment with large, centrally located planted zones.

The most prominent among these new urban parks was New York City's Central Park, constructed roughly from 1857 to the early 1870s. Created under the supervision of pioneering landscape architect Frederick Law Olmsted (along with Calvert Vaux), Central Park was planned to be a sort of interior suburb for Manhattan, as Olmsted made clear in an address to the American Social Science Association in 1870:

> We want the ground to which people may easily go after their day's work is done, and where they may stroll for an hour, seeing, hearing, and feeling nothing of the bustle and jar of the streets, where they shall, in effect, find the city put far away from them. We want the greatest possible contrast with the streets and the shops and the rooms of the town which will be consistent with convenience and the preservation of good order and neatness. We want, especially, the greatest possible contrast with the restraining and confining conditions of the town, those conditions which compel us to walk circumspectly, watchfully, jealously, which compel us to look closely upon others without sympathy. Practically, what we most want is a simple, broad, open space of clean greensward, with sufficient play of surface and a sufficient number of trees about it to supply a variety of light and shade. This we want as a central feature. We want depth of wood enough about it not only for comfort in hot weather, but to completely shut out the city from our landscapes.[16]

Here again was the suburban redoubt, screening urbanity from the eyes of the citizen, if only for a time.[17] This refuge, though, lay at the very heart of the city. Thus, if the suburban development was an extrinsic manifestation of the attempt to produce a pastoral retreat within the sphere of the great metropolis, the urban park was seen as its intrinsic counterpart.[18] Like the suburb, the urban park is an antidote to urbanism, a specific response to the derisive connotations long attached to city life.[19]

In their earliest days, however, these planted areas were not thought of in quite the populist egalitarian terms employed by Olmsted. Conceptions of urban preserves as important public spaces open to all citizens, although present in the 1860s and 1870s, were simply not realistic. In practice, those civic luminaries who promoted public parks viewed them far more readily as upper-class urban oases comparable to the newly developing suburbs. Like the suburbs, urban commons were not open to all comers. In the absence of cheap public transportation, these verdant spaces were more exclusive than Olmsted implies they should ideally be. In fact, urban parks in the mid- to late nineteenth century were for the most part only accessible by private carriage. Manhattanites were free to walk to Central Park, but it was quite a hike for most—the park was, we should remember, fairly far uptown in this era, and there was no subway until the first decades of the twentieth century. In practice, many of the park's users in these years were upper-class urbanites who could reach them by private transport.

In fact, so many of these wealthy commuters arrived at the park by carriage in its early years that Olmsted and the other park designers soon set out to invent ways for these carriages to play a part in the park experience. Many parts of the new parks were not planned to be experienced on foot—they were intended strictly as playgrounds for the surreys of the well-to-do. As urban historian Clay McShane recounts, "Drives on which the wealthy could promenade their outfits were important parts of large new parks. By 1890 the largest cities in the U.S. had built, on the average, twenty miles of park drives."[20] Indeed, McShane argues that Olmsted's parks, in particular, were designed with this sort of recreation in mind. Despite the egalitarian ideals of the landscape architect, the actual built space was notably exclusionary:

> New York's Central Park became the prototype of the new parks. . . . The main feature of the park was a series of drives reserved exclusively for private carriages. Olmsted banned omnibuses, hacks, and street railways from the park drives. To ensure uninterrupted riding Olmsted, himself a carriage lover, restricted this ordinary traffic to underpasses cut through the park. Non-elite riders lacked a view of the park, seeing only high stone walls as they passed through. Nor could passers-by on abutting streets see into the park in most places, because Olmsted isolated it with high walls along most of its periphery. The entire park appears to have been constructed with the end of providing a view from the carriage drives.[21]

There is no place here for the intermingling of people of all classes. Rather, many of the late nineteenth-century urban parks were strictly segregated by income (and, in places, by race or gender). Despite the utopian connotations of the public space and particularly Olmsted's own ideals, these central urban retreats tended to have much in common with the exclusive peripheral suburbs.

CROSSING THE DIVIDE:
THE PARKWAY AND THE AMERICAN METROPOLIS

The leafy suburb and the city park were important devices in the modern city, for they worked to bridge the ideological divides between city and country, making urbanity more palatable for Americans by softening it and offering respite from its most alienating aspects. In a sense, though, oases of rurality distracted from the thoroughgoing defoliation of metropolitan areas. Throughout the nineteenth century, cities intensified their urban development by eliminating existing trees, particularly the street trees that lined the roads of many smaller towns. In 1868, while designing Brooklyn's Prospect Park, Olmsted developed a mechanism intended to restore these lost bits of buffering vegetation. He envisioned offering urbanites a refreshing "change both of scene and of air" that they could experience in the course of their daily peregrinations about town. In formal parks, graceful roads lined with vegetation would serve urbanites as both recreational tracks and corridors for ordinary travel. Imagine, he implored, the city dweller's relief as he passed "into a street of this character after the trees have become stately and graceful."[22]

With proper advance planning and "if such streets were made still broader in some parts, with spacious malls," these planted corridors could be elaborated into something entirely different and more ambitious: a new type of route, which could serve as the main "trunk line of communication between two large districts of the town or the business centre and the suburbs." According to Olmsted, these paths "should be so planned and constructed as never to be noisy and seldom crowded, and so also that the straightforward movement of pleasure-car carriages need never be obstructed, unless at absolutely necessary crossings, by slow-going heavy vehicles used for commercial purposes."[23] These technical restrictions were intended not merely to expedite traffic but to encourage suburban commuters to use these convenient and efficient roads and maintain their relaxing and soothing characteristics. The principal point of the park streets was to deliver "some substantial recreative advantage," a brief pastoral reprieve, to urbanites "necessarily passing through them, whether in going to or from the park, or to and from business." Middle-class commuters, too busy on working days to make use of a full-scale park, would derive the benefits of the modern city without going out of their way. These "elongations of the park, varying say from two to five hundred feet in width, and radiating irregularly from it," Olmsted termed "formal Park-ways." Not just tree-lined avenues, these parkways were planned and landscaped strips of vegetation that would completely screen out the surrounding cityscape. This verdure would, in effect, swaddle the carriage road with a bucolic buffer. By the 1870s, these parkways became indispensable parts of any city plan. They were considered not as roads within city parks but as essential extensions to any municipal common. Parkways were, in essence, linear parks—narrow leafy corridors through the urban fabric.

By the late 1870s, most parkways were situated so as to connect large central parks with peripheral suburbs. As such, they extended the urban common to the countryside. This bridge connected interior and exterior bits of pastoral reserve in the modern cosmopolis. As Clay McShane argues, though, the parkway soon became a tool for the protection and isolation of suburbs: parkways controlled and regulated the growing city's connection to the exclusive communities that were, by later standards, really not far from the city core: "Olmsted hoped to create and preserve middle- and upper-class suburbia by a massive public-works investment in parkways. The prohibition of common carrier traffic assured class segregation, as well as preserving the appropriate 'natural' feel. Those who could not afford their own carriages could not visit the newly developed suburbs, let alone buy homes there, unless they walk long distances."[24] These parkways would not just screen out the adjacent urban landscape; they would actively block its intrusion into the suburban preserves. As with the Central Park drives, engineered to clearly separate ordinary commercial cross traffic from elite recreational riding, these parkways would scrupulously protect the suburbs they served from inappropriate intrusions.

To protect the parkways, Olmsted specified that "cross streets would only be cut through the new highway at infrequent intervals to minimize interference with carriage traffic."[25] As it happened, this sort of restrictive control over cross traffic was more difficult in the middle of the crowded and built-up city than in the midst of a large protected green. In practice, elite partisans of urban parkways had to contend with an inconvenient inheritance of English common law—that any owner of property adjacent to a road, as well as any other street tangential to that road, must have right of open connective access. In the formal parkway, however, aesthetics served an ingenious pragmatic purpose, as McShane explains: "The road included six rows of trees alongside the roadway, essentially making it a narrow, elongated park. Access streets to homes on the parkway would lie outside the strip of park land. The park strip was not just an amenity. It also served the legal purpose of preventing abutters from demanding access to the highway for other vehicles. Common-law granted abutters access to all streets, but in this case, they would abut, not on the street itself, but on the narrow strip of city owned park." By means of this limitation of access, elite users of these carriage paths could travel about town without entering the normal street system. In a sense, then, parkways allowed quasi-rural suburban enclaves to send protective planted shoots deep into the core of the nineteenth-century metropolis. This sort of insulation reduced, of course, elites' incentive to ameliorate existing conditions in cities—conditions that they took the lead in denouncing, in abstract and idealized terms, as corruptive and devitalizing. After all, with such effective buffers as protected parkways and exclusive suburbs, they had less and less contact with corrosive urbanity.

After a period of decline at the end of the nineteenth century, parkways experienced a resurgence with the popularization of the automobile in the early decades of the twentieth century.[26] Unlike the grand and quintessentially cosmopolitan city boulevard—a style championed most notably by Daniel Burnham—the interurban parkway powerfully deployed its rural aesthetic. These parkways preserved the land values of outlying suburbs, keeping them firmly within the radius of the larger metropolis. Soon this purpose overrode their original conception as mere extensions of central urban parks. They were now important park strips in their own right, existing autonomously, with no direct connection to the older commons. As one parkway planner observed, "Although their importance as connections between the various links in the park system is still recognized, the development of a comprehensive system of parkways today finds its justification primarily in the need of the community for rapid trafficways radiating from the center of the city to the suburbs, and connecting the various suburbs themselves with one another."[27] As more and more of the better-off residents of large American cities began to relocate to the new suburbs, leaving the core of the city to the poor and to towering and dense business developments, the need for centrally located park drives for elite recreation decreased. Now automotive parkways served the same purpose, while providing important commuter conduits. Americans, or at least influential and wealthy Americans, began to think of large urban gardens more in terms of radial park strips than centrally located pastoral fields. Certainly, these new conduits were more modern than the older commons, and they appealed by offering clear routes for the wealthy to exercise and display their new automobiles. Consequently, by the early twentieth century, much of the enthusiasm for separate large inner city parks had decreased among urban planners and their backers.

ILLUSIONS AND TRANSPORTS:
THE EXPERIENCE OF THE PARKWAY AESTHETIC

In some cities, planners began to speculate that automotive parkways might soon replace urban commons altogether: "We no longer stressed the necessity for the large park within the city as the means to this pleasure. The automobile and the state and county highways ramifying in all directions put the enjoyment of pastures, green fields and orchards within a few minutes' reach of the outskirts of every city."[28] In the early twentieth century, parkways were thought of as improved parks—green corridors that conveyed the urbanite into and through the undeveloped countryside. Instead of retreating to pseudo-rural suburbs, those with the means now had the possibility of regularly escaping the city altogether. Through the new individualist technology of the family automobile, citizens would be free to explore the great outdoors.

Once there, they got quite a surprise—one that ultimately would alter the way parks and parkways were conceived. The countryside, far from being the promised idyllic opposite of the modern metropolis, was upon examination far removed from virgin nature. For years, encroaching ribbon development had sent tendrils of urban development far into the countryside along roads and byways. Mirroring the city, rural areas were deeply interpenetrated by development and commercial construction. In the environs of the expansive early twentieth-century city, pastoral charms seemed more and more remote. Wilderness and open space within a few hours' radius of many major cities had become far from pristine.

Perhaps the best example of the use of a parkway to redeem a contaminated quasi-rural area was along the Bronx River valley, a long narrow strip of Westchester County that served mainly as the watershed for Greater New York City. By the turn of the twentieth century, this alluvial vale had become cluttered with refuse and industrial waste from New York City. Over the course of more than twenty years, city planners and engineers—spurred on by the New York Zoological Society, which had first focused public attention on ecological conditions in the valley—carefully designed and constructed a linked series of sculpted roadways that became known as the Bronx River Parkway. This was, as one of its designers attested, a true motor parkway: "The Bronx River Parkway was the first of the Westchester County parkways. It is some 16 miles long and 200 to 1,200 feet wide. The final section was opened in 1925. The roadway is, in general, located in the center of the right-of-way. Grades were at first separated on only a few of the principal cross-streets, but the remaining grade crossings proved so obstructive to traffic that most of them have since been eliminated."[29] These features mark the parkway as a pleasure road, a purely recreational zone.[30] This road was, its designers made clear, a real park; as such, it was never intended merely to convey automobiles efficiently. As a pleasure highway, the parkway was designed to be inefficient. It was intended not to expedite traffic but to allow it to flow in a controlled manner. As Sigfried Giedion observed ten years later, "The fundamental law of the parkway [is] that there must be an unobstructed freedom of movement, a flow of traffic maintained evenly at all points without interruption or interference."[31] With its grade separations and infrequent stops, the parkway had long been dedicated to the notion of constant and unrestricted movement. By the 1920s, though, cars were capable of speeds far beyond those previously possible. Parkway planners came to recognize the value of restraint: the slower the road—within certain limits, and so long as it was not hindered by aggravating jams and stops—the longer and more pleasant the drive. As another of its architects later recalled: "This parkway was not designed as an important arterial way, for during the first quarter of this century the speed of automobiles was generally limited to 25 miles per hour, and there was relatively little traffic. Rather, it was planned as a pleasant recreational drive connecting the system of parks in the Borough of the Bronx with the highways surrounding certain reservoirs of the New York City water supply system in Westchester County."[32] Overly fast movement would negate the benefits of the parkway's landscaping, for the motorist would be moving too quickly to take note of it. In fact, from the 1920s it was widely recognized in parkway design circles that the greater the velocity, the more constricted the driver's effective radius of vision. At high speeds, motorists would see nothing but roadway.[33] Restricted highway velocities were essential to any substantial perception of this linear park space—and the experience of nature was, of course, the whole rationale for the parkway.

This was a road dedicated to the experience of leisurely travel. It was no express route, although its designers did, of course, work to remove interferences to the flow of traffic. Rather, the parkway in general presented itself above all as the ideal means of appreciating the surrounding landscape. From the inlaid stone facing on the overpasses (which was quarried locally and specially chosen to be appropriate in appearance), to the pleasant rest stops and vista points, to the wrought iron drain grates and carefully painted curbs, the parkway conveyed a polished and tasteful appearance (see figure 38). Here nature was elegantly presented—the very epitome of rural balance and order. In every respect, the Bronx River Parkway was conceived of as a work of art. It was a recreational resource that had been carefully manicured and shaped to fit in with and accentuate the surrounding landscape. Intended to link a series of scenic reservoirs, preserves, and wildlife sanctuaries that the wealthy, ecologically minded inhabitants of Westchester County had worked to protect as suburban preserves over the preceding years, the parkway reassuringly cast these artifices as the very essence of rurality and nature.

Gradually, in Westchester and elsewhere, planners realized that motorists rarely left their cars to explore the scenic destinations. Tourists' entire experience of nature was mediated through the windshield of the automobile. These Sunday drivers were apparently perfectly satisfied perceiving only that countryside arrayed around the parkway concrete. Thus the need for elaborate and deeply (hence expensively) landscaped park sections alongside parkways seemed less and less pressing. As one Bronx River Parkway designer, Herbert Swan, observed in an *Architectural Record* article of 1931, the verges of motorways could not really practically be used for recreational purposes other than as scenery anyway. The parkway, once thought of as a mixed-use linear park—narrow, but a real park—was now recognized as something different. The trees, shrubs, grasses, and other plantings along the roadways really only served as backdrops, as in a diorama, for the scenic drive: "From the point of view of recreation, a central planting strip is not nearly so serviceable as a side planting strip. . . . As a rule, all strips, whether central or side strips, are undesirable for recreational use, even as promenades. The recreational value that accrues from their views should be appraised from the pleasure and relaxation they afford the motorist rather than the pedestrian. The pedestrian should, so far as practicable, be discouraged from utilizing the parkway and induced to seek his recreation elsewhere."[34] Clearly, by this period parkways were no longer seen as narrow versions of the parks that had been built since the 1860s. As Swan's comments reveal, urban planners had little sympathy for those unable to make use of the elab-

FIGURE 38. Parkways cultivated a refined image: Merritt Parkway, 1940. Library of Congress, Prints and Photographs Division, Historic American Engineering Record, HAER CONN,1-STAMF,12-2.

orate parkways. Although parkways did introduce urban denizens—or at least those who could afford to use them—to the virtues of abundant and refreshing vegetation, planners were fully willing to acknowledge that these new places could never fulfill Olmsted's second ambition of a half-century before: that urban park spaces should inculcate a sense of community and encourage social interaction. Parkways substituted shared sensory experience for communal contact.

The Bronx River Parkway, like the numerous twentieth-century motor parkways that came after it, deviated from the utopian aspirations associated with urban parks in the previous century, but they were nevertheless radically innovative, compelling attractions. In essence, the automotive parkway was a new sort of park; it was built to be not just a conduit—a piece of transportation technology—but something to be experienced in itself. The parkway became its own destination. It conveyed the rejuvenating experience of nature all by itself, without the need for the motorist to actually walk upon the land.

Perhaps the most powerful example of the parkway's mediation between rural and urban lay in the ways it effectively rendered its own contrivances invisible (see figure 39). This may have been a road form transplanted from the city, but it paid careful respect to the surrounding countryside, following the contour of the terrain and erasing all visible signs of radical earthworks (cuts and fills were particu-

FIGURE 39. Seamless installation of the parkway into the landscape: Taconic Parkway, 1933. Library of Congress, Prints and Photographs Division, Historic American Engineering Record, HAER NY,14-POKEP.V,1-103.

larly heavily replanted to suture the land back around the road as seamlessly as possible). Needless to say, through their control over the buffering park strips, these roads banned ribbon development, advertising (the billboard controls were frequently commented upon during the era), and overt signs of technology (such as flashy and distracting interchanges or access ramps). Beyond all this, it meticulously camouflaged its support systems: the parkway's service areas, for instance, such as rest stops, vista points, or even gas stations, were all carefully designed by parkway authorities to fit in with the surrounding countryside. The visible infrastructure of the parkway corridor was draped in appropriate local materials and uniformly indigenous architectural styles. The road was engineered to seem part of its setting.

Not only did the parkway effectively cleanse the countryside of its presence, but it also expunged potentially discordant traces of human artifice. In this respect, the parkway engineered its setting to appear as part of the roadway's rural aesthetic. It effectively made the pastoral more pastoral. Rural areas, especially so close to New York City, had accumulated centuries of built artifacts, the inevitable detritus of long habitation. Most of these markers—contemporary and archeological alike, buildings and well-beaten paths, fences and quarries—were meticulously removed from the field of the motorist's vision during parkway construction (see figure 40).

This is why parkways were such ambitious, expensive projects: they required a

A. Before. Buildings along river   B After. Buildings removed and land cleared

FIGURE 40. Rural renewal in parkway construction: Bronx River Valley. From Jay Downer, "The Bronx River Parkway," paper presented at the Proceedings of the National Conference on City Planning, New York, 7–9 May 1917.

far greater expanse of land and a much more intensive preparation process than was required by a simple automotive roadway. In fact, these roads were often sited in deep river valleys precisely because the surrounding hills cheaply occluded inappropriate views. A narrow ravine could be purified, visually controlled, far more easily than could an open meadow or, worse, a hilltop. The resultant parkway corridor provided motorists with a virtually unbroken vision of pastoralism—a bucolic rurality that contained no discordant traces of civilization.[35]

Through subtle landscaping and extensive engineering of local environments, these parkways presented nature as far as the eye could see—and not a yard farther. Thematically unified and consistent, without inappropriate visual elements to distract from the impression of being in the wild, the parkway corridor was a complete, hermetically insulated world.[36] This artifice was, as one noted architectural critic has observed, subtly hidden from the visitor: "Although the motorist undoubtedly realized that some landscaping had been carried out in parkway construction, he or she probably did not recognize the extent of this environmental engineering. In effect, then, the experience was virtually seamless—road and pastoral countryside merged imperceptibly, woven skillfully together. The parkway, as one noted critic has observed, 'was conceived as part of its surroundings, as a part of nature.'"[37] Great care had to be put into preparation, varying the effect in tune with the surrounding topography and ecology. It was of paramount importance to produce a convincing and immersive simulation of the natural landscape—or at least of what motorists might expect of that landscape.

Ultimately, the parkway was a hybrid zone, a middle ground that blurred the distinctions between urban and rural, nature and artifice, while simultaneously making a show of their differences. This mode of presentation, this performance of a pointedly novel and sublime "natural" landscape for thousands of the urban elite, might be termed a parkway aesthetic.

Parkway designers were well aware of the importance of this aesthetic. It was, after all, the main point of this sort of recreational road. These engineers honed their skills through successive projects, each time refining the details and mechanisms of the road's compelling and coherent stagecraft. Although they probably did not see their constructions as complex simulations, or even as theatrical devices, parkway designers were well aware of the effects they wished to produce. From practice and shared knowledge, they knew how to reproduce appropriate effects in a given road project, on a particular set of terrain features. One parkway designer, quoting from a statement he made in the 1930s, later recalled the importance of these subtle and site-specific elements of parkway fabrication: "It is desirable to plant slopes and other areas with native materials in a restrained manner so as to cause the [parkway] to be part of, and in character with, the surroundings; for example, a heavily planted greenbelt through the countryside of open pastures is to be deplored. . . . The motorway of the future will be measured largely by its aesthetic value."[38] Even the most quantitatively minded parkway engineer fully understood that this roadway corridor could never be considered in purely utilitarian terms. This flagrantly inefficient, indirect, speed-restricted route could not be evaluated by technical merits alone. All aspects of its construction, from the radii of its curves to the situation of its roadbed in the surrounding topography, had to be subordinated to larger aesthetic considerations. The design of a parkway was not so much highway engineering as landscape architecture. In every respect, form truly did follow function.

This function, like that of other parks of the era, was to mediate between city and country (see figure 41). By representing a tamed and comfortable nature—a pastoralism that could be fully appreciated by the eye from a moving automobile—the parkway both reinforced urbanites' idealizations about the world outside the city and served dialectically, like the metropolitan suburb or common, to bridge (and simultaneously reiterate) the traditional ideological division between urban and rural. This sophisticated technical mechanism extended the active sphere of urban influence—flooding city dwellers into the countryside every weekend on paved and expertly graded roads that, because of their grade separations and infrequent entry points, were useless to the surrounding farmland—while limiting and regulating that influence. At its essence, the parkway was a technology as much of exclusion as of access. The urbanite was invited into the country but restricted from experiencing it in any but the most controlled terms. Within the closed world of the parkway corridor, every discordant element was screened out; all inappropriate marks of civilization—and particularly city life—were carefully occluded. And of course, the most potent exclusion of all in the automotive parkway was a human one: by its very nature, it allowed only a well-off minority of citizens to enter its do-

FIGURE 41. Bucolic representation of nature on the Taconic Parkway, 1950. Note that landscaping by the side of the road was scaled not to the pedestrian but to the driver. Library of Congress, Prints and Photographs Division, Historic American Engineering Record, HAER NY,14-POKEP.V,129).

main. There was no way to experience the motor parkway by public transit. This was, by the 1930s, the most advanced and (deceptively) modern form of park design, but it was an art accessible only to those few with the income and free time to experience it.

MODERN PARKWAYS FOR MODERN CITIES

Utopia [can be] realized in the suburbs.

HOUSING REFORMER CAROL ARONOVICI, QUOTED IN CHRISTINE BOYER, *DREAMING THE RATIONAL CITY* (42)

Perhaps the person who understood the parkway's purposes best—and who most helped to crystallize its effects—was New York State's commissioner of parks, Robert Moses. He was also probably one of the first people to fully recognize the powerful appeal of the modern automotive parkway to the increasingly prosperous urban middle classes. The automobile parkway was a creature of the suburbs and rural areas; no parkway entered New York City before the late 1930s. A consummate operator in the city electoral machine, Moses fully realized the political weight of his exemplary towering metropolis. He saw that the key to popular favor in that dense city was, ironically, to provide an (imagined) potential escape for urbanites—to harness the surrounding countryside for the use of city residents. In this respect, he immediately saw the usefulness of the Bronx River Parkway. A network of roads modeled on the Bronx River Parkway might serve both to regulate exclusive access to vast new suburban developments for the relatively well-to-do and to allow ordinary city dwellers to feel as if they had full access to these new public preserves.

Through a complex combination of political maneuvering, mobilization of public opinion, and calculated overstepping of his legal and budgetary authority, Moses managed through the course of the late 1920s and 1930s to plan and construct a vast network of parkways throughout Long Island. As Robert Caro meticulously details in his monumental *The Power Broker: Robert Moses and the Fall of New York*, Moses managed to thread parallel parkway corridors—again, only as wide as necessary to maintain a seamless and unobstructed simulation of nature—between the country estates of some of New York's most wealthy landowners. Widely heralded as a triumph of the public welfare over arrogant privilege, these parkways secured Moses's progressive reputation among urban New Yorkers. Now every city dweller might freely (without tolls or stoplights) venture from the dense city to experience the bucolic landscapes that had so long been the exclusive preserve of the so-called rural "barons." Tied to these corridors were conveniently located amenities for those motorists who wished to get out of their cars. Lavish and scenic public facilities— such as the famous Jones Beach—had been prepared for the urbanite's free use. Seemingly, the entire expanse of Long Island was now laid at the feet of eager tenement dwellers.

These parkways were immediately seen as probing extensions of the city's hegemony—tools to harness the rural resources around New York City to serve its teeming population. The new roads were the radii of an ever-widening sphere of influence of this exemplary concentric city. As Marshall Berman, who grew up in awe of Moses and his projects, later put it, all these new parkways "helped, as Moses said, to 'weave together the loose strands and frayed edges of the New York metropolitan arterial tapestry,' and to give the enormously complex region a unity and coherence it had never had."[39] Both unifying and expanding, these parkways drew the countryside into the city's embrace, while simultaneously extending the benefits of this new pastoral landscape to all New Yorkers.

As Berman soon realized, though, these parkways were not really the mechanisms of social equality and universal access. Like all parkways, they were technologies of regulation and control. Few New Yorkers owned automobiles in this period (doing so was always a hassle, as well as an enormous and unsustainable expense, particularly in Manhattan and the denser parts of the outer boroughs), and the parkways were not open to pedestrians. This effective exclusion was not a co-incidence; as Caro explains, Moses had "restricted the use of state parks by poor and lower-middle-class families in the first place, by limiting access to the parks by rapid transit; he had vetoed the Long Island Rail Road's proposed construction of a branch spur to Jones Beach for this reason."[40] By the 1930s, Moses—in a sense fulfilling the legacy of Olmsted's original park roads—decided to engineer segre-gation right into the new roadways: "He began to limit access by busses; he instructed [engineer Sidney] Shapiro to build the bridges across his new parkways low—too low for busses to pass." Supposedly technical design decisions were dictated by social considerations, and the parkway once more served to regulate (or restrict) traffic. Clearly, Moses knew just whom he was serving with his plush and ornate corridors.[41] Like the suburbs and parks—and indeed, parkways—of Olmsted's day, Robert Moses's roads and resorts were planned for the wealthy. It was once more the captains of industry, along with their enervated middle-class paper pushers, who truly required the rejuvenation that ready contact with the pastoral might provide.

It was thus by a supreme act of political sleight-of-hand that Moses managed to convince the mass of urban dwellers that his public facilities really were intended for the public. Although in practice the masses could not directly experience these parkways or visit these beaches and preserves, they could take pride in ownership of them. Moreover, they could take comfort in the notion—the primary illusion implicit in any such park space—that the city was not so cold, so alienating now that its environs encompassed, only a short drive away, such vast stretches of pris-tine nature. This skillful orchestration of the ideologies of pastoralism and the con-temporary park movement mark many of Moses's projects of the prewar era. By the mid-1930s, he had managed—with wide and enthusiastic public support, particu-larly from within the metropolis—to construct the most extensive parkway system in the country.

Although constructed far out into the countryside, these parkways were always focused on New York City. They were marketed politically to the voters of the city and were designed to serve the ideological, if not recreational, needs of urbanites. Indeed, it became clear over time that Moses was obsessed with the relation of the city to its surroundings, and that he was fully aware of the parkways' utility in me-diating this connection. This attention to the metropolis was perhaps Moses's most profound modification of the parkway technology he inherited from the designers of the Bronx River Parkway (most of whose designers Moses hired to work for him). A particularly striking example of Moses's innovative use of the parkways to serve the modern skyscraper city was the design of the Long Island parkways' endpoints. These rural roads ended as they came to New York City, their final approaches to the metropolis carefully planned to mobilize the aesthetics of the vertical sublime in powerful and dramatic ways. Moses's parkways "created a series of spectacular new visual approaches to the city, displaying the grandeur of Manhattan from many new angles—from the Belt Parkway, the Grand Central, the upper West Side—and nourishing a whole new generation of urban fantasies."[42] At a certain point, not far from Manhattan, the motorist would suddenly catch a glimpse of the skyline. This stunning vista was then occluded, only to be more fully displayed again a few minutes later. This sort of stagecraft was built into the parkway's route, which made use of the topography to frame these memorable moments of perception. The series of images thus produced is analogous to what is referred to in filmmaking as the "reveal"—the sequence of shots that pays off by building suspense to visually present a vital detail of plot or character. If the rural parkway was intended to convey a vicarious experience of pastoral nature, the ever more elaborate and majestic parkway approaches to Manhattan were manifestly intended to immerse the motorist in a proper reverence for the vertical metropolis, as the limitless towers of this exemplary city were displayed to great effect from these roadways.[43]

Here, the parkway staged and presented, in a tableau more stunningly clear and grandiose than any other, the metropolitan skyline instead of a bucolic countryside. The aesthetic technology of this sophisticated representational form was now redirected to serve the modern city, setting these clustered towers as the sublime landscape to be taken in by the motorist. Berman describes his ambivalent amazement at Moses's work of transforming the outward face of the metropolis:

> The uptown Hudson riverfront, one of Moses' finest urban landscapes, is especially striking. . . . You cross the George Washington Bridge and dip down and around and slide into the gentle curve of the West Side Highway, and the lights and towers of Manhattan flash and glow before you, rising above the lush greenness of Riverside Park, and even the most embittered enemy of Robert Moses—or, for that matter, of New York—will be touched: you know you have come home again, and the city is there for you, and you can thank Moses for that.[44]

The ordinary New Yorker could appreciate the parkways for providing, at least in theory, a route to an inviting and pleasant countryside, as well as a clearer and more awe-inspiring panoramic view of the city itself. The parkway under Moses's direction served the dense vertical city, both by laying the surrounding countryside at its feet, and thus increasing the effective radius of its concentric structure, and by showcasing the metropolis. The parkway bridged the division between urban and rural—this time by applying its representational machinery alternately to exemplary views of each.

In his meticulous design of these parkway approaches, Moses fully comprehended the doubled significance of the parkway as a medium. It mediated between rural and urban—either softening or accentuating, as needed, the divisions between ideological poles—but it also presented to its users a set of carefully inscribed messages. Primarily in its resonant and powerful aesthetic, the parkway had a content.

Early on, Moses recognized that the parkway, if constructed properly, would produce in the motorist a coherent, reproducible experience—a powerful ensemble of impressions that they would understand and remember. By staging a simulation of rural topography, the parkway extended the traditional urban park into an immersive, compelling, and even didactic representational tool. Further, by continually directing the motorist's gaze—toward a visually attractive landscape element, a suddenly revealed vista, or the simple rise and fall of the roadway—the parkway designer could ensure that the tourist experienced a specific sequence of images. As architectural theorists Christopher Tunnard and Boris Pushkarev explain in their analysis of the parkway in *Man-Made America: Chaos or Control?* there is a logic to the well-designed parkway that could subtend a definite perceptual and aesthetic experience.[45] Although certainly not all tourists saw the same things in their peregrinations, or interpreted what they saw in the same ways, most motorists perceived an array of elements—many carefully arranged, others merely the consequence of contingent design choices or local conditions—that worked synchronously to produce a coherent parkway experience.

The automotive parkway and the motion picture spring from the same representational logic and the same understanding of human perception. Although they were products of the same era, reaching a classical formal fluency in the late years of the Jazz Age and the early 1930s, these twinned examples of modern engineering were at the time perceived in radically different ways by most Americans. The "movie" was quintessentially urban and technological, the parkway, through its ideology and its carefully designed aesthetic, ostensibly rural and natural. Yet both orchestrated controlled, regular movement to produce images that spectators were proficient at decoding. Both the filmgoer and the parkway motorist understood the fundamental rules of the road; they could by this time easily make sense out of the images they perceived, recognizing the narratives and settings portrayed—as well, as Robert Moses fully knew, as the *auteur* behind the camera. In a sense, then, the parkway and the motion picture both presented a sort of game to their spectators, one that rewarded attention and participation. Like the contour of the road, this complex perceptual play did not come naturally—although it often occurred so unconsciously as to appear so. Rather, viewers and designers alike learned elaborate and expertly developed techniques of continuity. Only through these consensual illusions could the apparatus be occluded, the technology sutured over, and the result made to seem uncontrived, guileless, and convincing.[46]

In both film and parkway, the pay-off for participating in the ludic play was simple: sensory pleasure. While the more complex ideological messages of the parkway certainly could be decoded and even evaluated by motorists, the less intellectual experience of driving a well-crafted parkway was more immediate. As Sigfried Giedion reveals in a rapturous representation of the experience of driving one of these advanced parkways in his seminal *Space, Time, and Architecture*, the allure of the parkway was not so much its expert stagecraft but the visceral sensation of sculpted, directed movement itself:

> Air views show the great sweep of these early highways, the beauty of their alignment, the graceful sequence of their curves, but only at the wheel of the automobile could one feel what they really meant—the liberation from unexpected light signals and cross traffic, and the freedom of uninterrupted forward motion, without the inhuman pressure of endlessly straight lines pushing one on to dangerous speeds. . . . Freedom was given to both the driver and car. Riding up and down the long sweeping grades produced an exhilarating dual feeling, one of being connected with the soil and yet of hovering just above it, a feeling like nothing else so much as sliding swiftly on skis through untouched snow down the sides of high mountains.[47]

These roads were instruments of feeling as well as intellect. They directed the libido as much as the eye. And this was perhaps also part of their appeal as instruments of the sublime—either that of the skyscraper metropolis or, in most cases, of the pastoral. For the most part, these parkways did not just present an image of enveloping and restful nature; rather they made motorists feel like they were flying through it. By mobilizing this powerful modern aesthetic—aviation had a particular hold on the imagination of many in the 1920s and 1930s, after all[48]—the parkway also served overt ideological purposes. Such graceful movement effectively accentuated the poetic and harmonious aspects of the rural landscape, greatly intensifying the allure of the pastoral ethos. As Giedion describes it, the parkway design aesthetic

> humanized the highway by carefully following and utilizing the terrain, rising and falling with the contours of the earth, merging it completely into the landscape. The road was laid into the countryside, grooved into it between gentle green slopes blending so naturally into the contiguous land that the eye cannot distinguish between what is nature and what the contribution of the landscape architect. In the middle, separating the opposing movements of traffic, are garden strips, widening and contracting as the course of the road required. Sometimes the traffic lanes flowed together in approaching a bridge, joined as they passed under, and then separated again, drawing apart to restore the landscaped spaced [sic] between them.[49]

With the evocation of such graceful and rapturous images associating the road with idyllic natural landscapes, it should be no surprise that many cities in the first decades of the twentieth century moved to remake their environs by way of the modern parkway. Indeed, just as the parkway came over time to displace the urban park as an exciting and modern civic feature, the parkway aesthetic also replaced many urbanites' immediate experience of the countryside.

Through these innovations in design and stagecraft, the Bronx River Parkway—as well as Robert Moses's Long Island projects of the 1920s and 1930s—set an influential example for urban planners. Without a doubt, the New York parkway system proved the most exciting model for urban recreational planning in the United States during the era.

PUTTING THE GARDEN BACK IN THE GARDEN CITY

The Los Angeles Region probably has a greater future need for parks, of certain kinds at least, than any other community of its size.

OLMSTED BROTHERS AND BARTHOLOMEW AND ASSOCIATES, *PARKS, PLAYGROUNDS, AND BEACHES FOR THE LOS ANGELES REGION* (5)

For the mass of Los Angeles's planners, long interested in notions of the garden city and seeking a new model of modern urbanity, contemporary developments in park design and thought must have seemed exciting indeed.[50] Potentially, a well-developed park system could minister to many of the postsuburban metropolis's ills. For sprawling Los Angeles, the technologies emerging from the modern park seemed particularly appropriate, and particularly necessary. In its rapid growth, little room had been set aside for open space, or even for useful recreational areas: "Due mainly to the improved transportation, especially to the wide use of the automobile, the population living in continuous Metropolitan urban and suburban conditions spreads over an area much greater than was formerly possible."[51] Garden city advocates were aware, of course, that Ebenezer Howard had stressed the importance of parks and large agricultural greenbelts to the community. It should have come as no surprise, then, that the planners' first blueprint for Southern California, finally making available for public review ideas so long in gestation, took the form of a park plan. The County Regional Planning Commission's chief engineer, William Fox, later attested in an oral history interview that *Parks, Playgrounds, and Beaches for the Los Angeles Region* "was the culmination of the entire concept of planning of this entire region. . . . And [Regional Planning Commission director] Hugh Pomeroy, in his great imagination, created the idea, and we drafted the plan in our drafting room under his direction and our drafting skills. It was a comprehensive parkway and park plan for the region. . . . It was a comprehensive plan, probably the best that will ever be made for this region."[52] An extensive system of parks promised to restore the diminished bucolic landscape to Greater Los Angeles, providing the perfect setting for a host of garden city communities. By reintroducing a natural ethos into the metropolis, parks would help situate new neighborhoods and restore the quality of life in existing sections of town—after all, parks were widely seen as the best means available to planners to counter the anomie and alienation so common in the modern metropolis. For all these reasons, a park plan, particularly one presented under the aegis of the Olmsted Brothers (sons of the great nineteenth-century park planner), provided just the sort of thoroughgoing infrastructural redevelopment that local planners felt was needed. Under the cover of such a tremendously ambitious recreational program, planners would not only redress Southern

California's lack of parks but produce a network of verdant public spaces—both carefully landscaped and more rustic open areas—that would transform every section of Los Angeles County.[53]

A further advantage of such a plan was its progressive use of the technology of the modern parkway. The parkway promised to soothe some inherent contradictions in the cherished garden city dream. Planners continually sought to promote both a larger regional perspective and a renewed focus on the local community. The parkway seemed, at least potentially, the perfect technology for mediation between these two poles. Although the greater metropolitan district would provide—not necessarily at a single physically central location—those more specialized and cosmopolitan services that marked a great city, for everyday tasks citizens would look closer to home.[54]

This pattern, planners felt, would hold not only for commerce and labor but for recreation as well. In their free time, many Angelenos would be able to find recreational opportunities in their own neighborhoods—and even in their own backyards, as the 1930 park plan insisted: "The great mass of [Los Angeles's] people live in detached bungalows and cottages with a high proportion of open space on their lots. . . . Private home yards of fair size partially satisfy the need for outdoor recreation, especially for little children and for old and inactive people."[55] Nevertheless, as with other parts of daily life, some pleasure activity would necessarily require use of the larger Southern California region, with its famous beaches and mountains. The parkway would provide easy access to the far reaches of the metropolitan district for occasional trips but would insulate autonomous neighborhoods. Thus, if the garden city cluster was intended to nurture the convenience and human environment of the neighborhood, while providing some of the efficiencies and scale of a larger metropolitan region, the parkway might serve the vital function of stabilizing and regulating these relations, just as it mediated between rural and urban values.

The lines of demarcation between these properly local and regional activities could be reinscribed by careful location of these roads. Planners had been shocked to discover that their efforts at metropolitan deconcentration did not so much promote clustered development as underwrite long commutes—often to locations that did not seem appropriate for any sort of development, let alone development drawing motorists from the entire region. A chief culprit in this random and unplanned emergence of multiple and misplaced business districts, everyone felt, was the favorable exposure of major thoroughfares to passing drivers. This is what had taken place, most famously, on Wilshire Boulevard: a traffic conduit had proven, by virtue of having so many people pass through it every day, to be a particularly attractive spot for businesses. The parkway promised to put an end to overgrown ribbon development. If planners could install protective park strips along some of the city's major routes, they could prevent inappropriate commercial development without having to engage in the messy and disappointing politics of zoning regulation. No business could make use of the attractive street frontage because it would be publicly owned open space. On a larger scale, the parkways would serve as park buffers. Only certain streets would be allowed to cross each parkway, thus creating numerous cul-de-sacs, which were inherently local in character. Existing ribbon development would be unlikely to spread beyond a few streets. Thus, although parkways could not replace every urban avenue, strategically located limited-access roads might effectively serve as firewalls to reduce the effects of scattered and seemingly random commercial development throughout the city.

The automotive parkway could be the perfect solution to many of Los Angeles's problems at the end of the 1920s. It was a modern contrivance, an intellectual product of the vertical metropolises of the East. It might restore to Southern California a bit of the feeling of futurism and innovation that had begun to erode under the withering vitriol about sprawl and "the Iowans." It would at the same time limit sprawl by containing future development, particularly on the outskirts of the metropolitan area where many of the parkways were to be located. Perhaps most importantly, though, the parkways, and the enhanced park system they were intended to link, would protect the remnants of the Southern Californian landscape from inappropriate development. A bit of the open countryside, so much of which had been gobbled up by housing tracts and commercial districts during the booming 1920s, would be protected and made accessible to motorists. It was this remaining pastoral reserve, after all, that underlay so many of the region's claims to the good life. *Parks, Playgrounds, and Beaches,* then, promised a decisive and comprehensive program to protect the values of Mediterraneanism and the garden ethos, allowing Greater Los Angeles to resume its vaunted position as leading American exemplar of the harmonious synthesis of urban and rural.

In a sense, the Olmsted and Bartholomew report reflects the contemporary state of expert planning in Southern California. Despite having won a series of battles to prevent Los Angeles from modernizing as a concentric vertical metropolis, the region was not developing according to plan. It sprawled seemingly randomly, and its proper boundaries and lines of order had become illegible and confused. By 1930, planners were willing to look for technological solutions to their urban problems— even solutions developed back east. Proposing a park and parkway plan was, at least tacitly, quite an admission: tools designed to mitigate or at least provide refuge from the most onerous blights of the dense modern metropolis were needed in the "better city." By this point it was clear that a decade of efforts had gone off track: a host of professional "scientific" planning methods, from subdivision control and street platting to zoning and legal restrictions, had all failed to prevent undesired development in Los Angeles. Every tool dedicated to shaping future growth and molding it in appropriate directions had come to naught. This park plan thus implied a concession that advance planning had failed. Finally, planners in Southern California were forced to admit that preemptive measures had failed and call upon Angelenos to enact what was essentially an ambitious, wide-ranging, and fantastically expensive urban redevelopment scheme.

Overtly participating in the fray of urban partisan politics was anathema to professional planners, for such involvement compromised their aura of professional, even scientific, objectivity and rationality. Although they worked to "educate" the populace about the importance of planning and its particular ends, experts felt that any but the most subtle and controlled involvement in open debates might taint their Progressive reputation for disinterested civil service. Yet how thin this line between publicity and politicking had always been (especially given their fervent and quasi-public efforts against the rapid transit plans of the mid-1920s in the City Club and other such fora) was revealed by the ready skill with which planning director Hugh Pomeroy took pains to line up city interests behind his park and parkway program. As regional planner William Fox recounts:

> He had all the way through his work this support of all those newspapers. He had Harry [C.] Chandler of the L.A. Times, who was alive. He had the support of William Randolph Hearst, who was also alive. The editor of the Examiner paper in Los Angeles, he was the spokesman for Harry Chandler and for Hearst—Hearst told him what to do. So Hugh worked right with them, and he had their backing. He also had the backing of the big powerful cement trusts, which were going to build all these freeways [sic], and that was a terrific influence in this city. The Griffith Company was doing most of the construction, and was in on the thing also, as were about three others. There were the big people. He had their backing.[56]

Clearly, Pomeroy and his cadre of professional planners were now fully willing to engage in the rough-and-tumble of urban politics to put their park plan into effect. As Greg Hise and William Deverell meticulously detail in Eden by Design, by the end of the 1920s a remarkable coalition of civic officials, public planners, and established business interests had been assembled behind this ambitious plan.

THE "WATERLOO" OF PLANNING IN SOUTHERN CALIFORNIA

We had the best opportunity. I think that time has passed.
WILLIAM FOX, "SEVEN DECADES OF PLANNING AND DEVELOPMENT IN THE LOS ANGELES REGION" (161)

What happened in 1929, when the planners finally submitted their ideas to public scrutiny, was dramatic. As the 1985 interview with Chief Engineer Fox undertaken by the UCLA Oral History Project vividly reveals, the planners found that their built consensus in favor of restructuring Southern California had suddenly dissolved. In the interview transcript, Edward Holden (also an engineer) asks Fox in passing about the 1930 plan: "Did the planning commission have something to do with thinking about some plan of Regional Parks?" "Yes," Fox replies.

> *Fox:* That's what was Pomeroy's Waterloo, really.
>
> *Holden:* Waterloo?
>
> *Fox:* Yes, that's what caused him to resign.[57]

According to Fox, the coalition behind the park plan abruptly collapsed, not because the scheme was itself flawed but because the planners simply failed to properly negotiate the political terrain. Regional Planning Commission chief Hugh Pomeroy was, according to Fox, a visionary: "Mr. Pomeroy, without a doubt, was a genius."[58] He failed to recognize, however, that urban politics revolved around not vision and dreams but basic instrumental calculations. By this latter measure, the 1930 park plan was completely unrealistic. It contemplated expenditures of almost a quarter of a billion [1930] dollars. The Olmsteds and Bartholomew had estimated that, if one excluded those flood-control facilities and highway improvements in the plan that were necessary anyway, the plan only really called for "$124,000,000 for which special financing is needed." *Parks, Playgrounds, and Beaches* outlined a fantastically exorbitant program, especially for a city coping with the costs of rapid growth and lacking an established industrial tax base. Nevertheless, the plan admitted that "this estimate . . . is a fair measure of the size of the problem that confronts this Region," and suggested that "it will take many years even to approach a completion of the program."[59]

Fox insists that he warned his boss that these figures were simply too high to meet with approval from elected officials, and the plan should therefore be revealed piecemeal. Divulging the full extent of the metropolitan reconstruction project, with its enormous disruptions and costs, would be political suicide. Pomeroy failed to heed the advice of his right-hand man: "Finally where he had made his big mistake—now, I don't want this on the record. Hugh Pomeroy gave them the whole works, and it frightened his backers and they bolted."[60] The political establishment in Los Angeles County could not reasonably contemplate such a gargantuan undertaking. Even the prospect of so many lucrative contracts, with potential profits trickling down through every inch of the tight-knit local business and political communities, could not justify a project of this magnitude. *Parks, Playgrounds, and Beaches* was effectively dead well before it was printed and circulated in the middle of 1930.[61]

The backlash against this expense inevitably hit the planners. The fate of this ambitious park plan, ironically enough, demonstrates the wisdom of the planners' traditional emphasis on foresight. Advance planning was intended to eliminate the necessity of such large and politically hazardous reconstruction programs. In this instance, experts had not perceived the postsuburban future of the American metropolis. Advance planning techniques had ultimately failed, forcing local experts to propose this drastic, and doomed, urban reorganization program. As a result of this failure of vision, the lead visionary, Hugh Pomeroy, paid a high price for the plan's impracticality. Pomeroy quit as head of the Regional Planning Commission in 1927 to more freely lobby for the park plan. That same year, he became executive secretary of the Citizens' Committee on Parks, Playgrounds, and Beaches. In the early 1930s, in the wake of the plan's failure, Pomeroy resigned from this position as well, never again to hold an official post in Southern California planning. But Pomeroy was not the only visionary planner to feel the consequences of the plan's rejection. In 1930, Gordon Whitnall left the City Planning Commission he had founded a decade before to become a private planning consultant to a number of peripheral communities. C. A. Dykstra and George Damon also left in this period. Most of the more visionary planners making up the influential and cohesive institutionalized establishment in Jazz Age Greater Los Angeles vacated their public roles at about this time. A heady era in urban planning in Southern California ended with none of the fanfare and confident public statements that had heralded its beginning.

So much for the dreamers, but what of their dreams? About the park plan, Fox is left to sadly recount, "I can say that probably it was just ahead of its time. And the public authorities and the business world just weren't ready for it. It was buried, and I think that most of the plan was chewed up." Worse, according to Fox (who would remain with the Regional Planning Commission for more than two decades), future plans in the region were "devoid of the recreation and beauty that would have produced real character for this county, real character that would have made it known all over the world as a California type of development that other counties wouldn't have imitated because of climate. We had the best opportunity. I think that time has passed."[62] The events of 1930 proved to be the Waterloo not just of Hugh Pomeroy and many of his fellow planning leaders but of professional planning in Southern California. For the first time since before 1920—and for at least a decade to come—visions of a better city of clustered garden communities were seen no more.

Yet we must ask about the context of this failure. Perhaps under different circumstances the planners' ambitious park and parkway proposal would have been more favorably received. After all, Pomeroy had clearly lobbied all the locally powerful interests. The planners could ordinarily exert a good deal of influence in Los Angeles's social and governmental circles during this period. The end of the 1920s was simply the worst time to release, at long last, an expensive and radical manifesto for urban restructuring. By the middle of 1930, when the park plan was finally released, ambitious new infrastructural projects were simply out of the question. The stock market had crashed the previous October, and local government was scrambling to react to the sudden change in circumstances. The impact of the economic crisis was felt everywhere, and the resulting austerity did not spare planning bureaucracies, as the City Planning Commission's 1931 annual report testifies:

"Owing to reductions in budget allowances, this Department has had to operate, during the past year, with reduced personnel, and at less cost than during either of the preceding two years. The routine work of the Department has increased to such an extent that it has become necessary to practically abandon certain important activities."[63]

Overall, the Depression devastated local planning agencies, and this condition did not quickly improve. *City Planning in Los Angeles,* the department's own account, testifies that "many years were to pass . . . before the Department would be provided with addition [*sic*] facilities and personnel to begin to meet the duties assigned to it."[64] A series of admissions in Depression-era planning publications are representative. For instance, the 1938 annual report (combining, "to effect an economy,"[65] the annual report for 1937 as well) featured yet another new director-manager of the City Planning Commission stating that, "forced to operate within a very limited budget," very little work could be done by the commission: "This is unfortunate but is the best that can be done with the small staff available."[66] The city bureaucracy in general had been gutted by the Depression, but professional planning in Greater Los Angeles was hit disproportionately hard. The institutional gains of the 1920s largely dissolved during these hard times; by the mid-1930s, for all intents and purposes, planning was no longer a priority in Southern California.

Looking back at the park plan, one wonders if the planners failed because they were fantastically unlucky—gestating a vision for years but finally putting forward large-scale plans to enact it at the worst imaginable time—or because they had begun to lose faith in their own dreams and visions. In any case, the failure of this plan, and of the larger utopian schemes so long cherished by local experts, had been developing for some time. The 1930 report's failure was not due purely to a lapse of political acumen or a lack of proper foresight. By the end of the 1920s, deep structural flaws pervaded local planning thought. One indicator of this larger weakness was a growing fissure in the once-cohesive planning community. Although many planners once on the city payroll were laid off during the Depression, many had already quit. Indeed, in 1930 Gordon Whitnall left the planning agencies he had worked so hard to bring into existence. According to William H. Mullins's *The Depression and the Urban West Coast, 1929–1933,* though, the severity of the economic crisis was not generally felt in western cities until early 1931, and deep budget cuts and layoffs were put off until 1932.[67] Whitnall left before the Depression truly began to make itself felt. Many others of that pioneering group also drifted away before the park plan met its demise.

Although it is difficult for any historian to know, at this remove, what exactly led to the exodus of planning talent at the end of the 1920s, it would be an easy supposition that disenchantment may have played a considerable part. As postsuburban sprawl refigured the region beginning in the second half of the decade, planning experts expressed great frustration at their inability to make sense either of the changes underway or the form of the metropolis. Many planners may have simply given up the ambitious task of planning the region, preferring instead to focus on more manageable municipal responsibilities; this may explain why so many former officials became professional consultants to the small communities scattered throughout the area. Other planners left Southern California entirely, opting to apply their expertise to more traditional eastern metropolises.

Perhaps this was not an abdication; maybe they believed their work in Greater Los Angeles to be essentially complete, and they now wished to spread the gospel of decentralization more broadly. Indeed, one possibility is that these men, far from viewing the developments of the late 1920s as a series of fiascos, may have seen planning in the region as a signal success. Although it had not turned out quite as expected, amid the sprawl and chaos, nevertheless the primary planning goal of metropolitan decentralization had obviously been met. This was not the sort of decentralization local planners favored, but Los Angeles's concentric urban structure had certainly been decisively deconcentrated. It is plausible that, looking back on the failure of the rapid transit plans of 1926, planners could feel that they not only had presided over the city's reconfiguration but had won the major philosophical arguments about urban form. Yet despite these surface successes, it is hard to believe that city planners could have seen their work in 1930 as any real success, let alone as substantially complete. Planners' anxiety at the emerging crisis in legibility and urban order during this period pervades their writings and recorded speeches and mitigates against any interpretation of this kind.

It seems more likely, especially in Whitnall's case, that planners simply began to lose faith in their cherished garden city model for the region. By the late 1920s, Whitnall in particular began to express the sentiment that plans for urban organization which relied too heavily on notions of community autonomy and self-sufficiency were no longer appropriate for the sprawling Southern Californian region. The developments of the second half of the 1920s had changed the ground on which planning might be carried out, and reform schemes suited to the concentric dense topography of the traditional city were no longer appropriate for a metropolis of the sort Greater Los Angeles was becoming. Although the notion of clustered garden cities had always provided for linking discrete communities so as to pool cultural and economic resources, it is likely that many Southern Californian planners began to feel that an even more thorough regional perspective might be necessary. Regional planning in Southern California had been inaugurated in a conference as far back as January 1922, when Whitnall had proclaimed his foundational "Declaration of Interdependence": "In the large metropolitan centers throughout the country there has been a growing consciousness of the interdependence of communities that together constitute the metropolitan district."[68] By the late 1920s, with life in Greater Los Angeles no longer dominated by the central city's dense downtown district, as it had been a few short years earlier, this interdependence must have seemed more than a slogan. By this time, it had become increasingly difficult to see any part of the larger region as autonomous. Boundaries throughout the city seemed under siege, if not actively and flagrantly transgressed. Thus, although the city of the era seems to later observers to be even more rigidly segregated than it would later become, in the context of the tumultuous 1920s it seemed as if no border could be trusted to hold fast. It was no wonder, then, if Whitnall and some of his peers had given up on the formal institutions of city planning when they did precisely because they felt the dreams to which these organizations had been committed all decade were no longer relevant in the transformed metropolis of the day.

CITY WITHOUT LIMITS: THE INFINITE METROPOLIS

We may be the greatest city in the world unless we blunder now.

GORDON WHITNALL, 1925, QUOTED IN MARTHA NYE, "WHITNALL HITS BACK AT CRITICS"

Perhaps a stronger and less speculative indicator of the internal collapse of the planning establishment of Greater Los Angeles lies in the plans themselves. *Parks, Playgrounds, and Beaches* has recently assumed a status among historians of Los Angeles as the final moment of an idyllic Southern California, "a window into a lost future," in the words of no less a hard-nosed debunker of booster rhetoric than Mike Davis.[69] This ignored blueprint for "the better city"—Greg Hise and William Deverell call it a "remarkable" and "compelling" document—was intended to expand the region's manifest amenities.[70] It is, these historians suggest, a plan that might have insulated Angelenos from many ecological liabilities while putting the city in a more balanced and harmonious relationship with its natural environment. Above all, *Parks, Playgrounds, and Beaches* could have actively forced Southern California to make good on its booster rhetoric by forever preserving the benefits of a bucolic Mediterraneanism. This ambitious park and open space plan would, in Davis's words, inculcate "a vigorous social democracy of beaches and playgrounds."[71] Ideally, this "heroic culmination of the City Beautiful era in American urban design" would open the assets of the region to all through a vast expanse of publicly accessible recreational space.[72] As Davis almost rapturously concludes in "How Eden Lost Its Garden," "If their proposals had been implemented, the results would have been virtually revolutionary. The existing hierarchy of public and private space in Los Angeles might have been overturned. A dramatically enlarged commons, not the private subdivision, might have become the commanding element in the Southern California landscape. Preserved natural ecosystems (Olmsted was a passionate champion of native flora) might have imposed clear boundaries on urbanization."[73] If enacted, this park and commons plan would have truly been, in Hise and Deverell's evocative phrase, "Eden by design."

Yet it is worth asking just how radical *Parks, Playgrounds, and Beaches* really was.

Although local planners had high hopes for the decentralized urbanism envisaged by the 1930 park plan, it seems unlikely that they held any illusions that this one project, massively expensive and ambitious as it was, might be able to bring about a topography of garden cities where a decade of protracted and painstaking efforts at traffic control, zoning, and subdivision control had time and again failed. Indeed, a close reading of the plan suggests strongly that *Parks, Playgrounds, and Beaches* was never expected to have the sort of revolutionary effects posthumously attributed to it. Despite their utopian aspirations and ambitions, local planners ultimately held hopes for their metropolis rather different than those of later critics. Even if the park plan had been fully implemented and it had succeeded beyond all reasonable expectation, it would never have created the sort of Eden later historians hoped for.

If, as Davis suggests, the plan would have imposed "clear boundaries on urbanization," it was because these park greenbelts were intended by planners to preserve the legibility and clear segregation of the settlements they would differentiate. These open spaces would effectively screen discrete communities from the incursions of nonresidents.[74] Though the plan promised "a dramatically enlarged commons," that space would not have made a dent in the cultural and topographical dominance of the private subdivision. By 1930, it was at least a generation too late to impede the momentum of the real estate developers. Finally, if the plan intended to overturn the "existing hierarchy of public and private space in Los Angeles," the delineation of several large quasi-rural preserves and a number of convenient neighborhood parks would not accomplish this revolutionary task. The city already possessed Griffith Park within its borders—granted to the city in 1896 but still largely inaccessible in the 1920s[75]—and had found its status as a metropolis of private homes little threatened by this subversive expanse of internal commons (already by far the largest of its kind in the nation). Even the park plan's most radical proposal, the expropriation of large swaths of beachfront property—which drew the greatest public controversy and media resistance upon the report's release—would not have seriously challenged the overall order of public and private within the city. *Parks, Playgrounds, and Beaches* was, above all, a belated mitigating response to the already accomplished private subdivision of Greater Los Angeles. Even the timid reforms envisioned in the report—which were never intended to transform the fundamental structure of the single-family subdivided region, but rather to better preserve it—proved ultimately to be well beyond the means of the heavily indebted metropolis.[76]

But the most important fact this historical discourse on the 1930 report fails to recognize is that this was not primarily a park plan at all. It was a parkway plan. Although the 1930 plan's "Specific Recommendations" section ostensibly touches on local playgrounds (ten pages), public beaches (twenty-one pages), regional athletic fields (three pages), and large rural preserves (eight pages), the entire report views

Southern California through the lens of the parkway and the recreational drive. *Parks, Playgrounds, and Beaches* devotes no fewer than forty-three pages to parkway planning (a greater number than the other park recommendations combined). Given this fascination with the parkway, it should come as no surprise that the Olmsted and Bartholomew report's final conclusion is that "the most extensive and possibly the most urgently needed class of park and recreation facilities recommended for the Los Angeles Region is that of parkways and related large parks."[77]

In a sense this is perfectly understandable. One might logically expect that, for planners searching—almost desperately—for some tool that might allow them to reassert control over the fractured landscape, the parkway would be promising indeed. The technology would underwrite a vast public works project that would restore some of the lost charm of the landscape, as well as supporting the development of a modern deconcentrated metropolitan region. Parkways could link garden communities into clusters; they could serve as rural buffers to prevent these properly autonomous neighborhoods from growing together into the sort of undifferentiated urban mass that the postsuburban city had become. In essence, parkways might allow Los Angeles's planners to correct their earlier errors and properly mediate the relationship between community and neighborhood, local and locale, common and commons.

Yet the plan expresses its aims in entirely different terms. Instead of establishing harmonious future development, parkways are described here merely as ways to counter the alienation faced by residents of the existing sprawling metropolis. They would serve the purpose the elder Olmsted had originally intended: providing a rural retreat to rejuvenate residents. Los Angeles was overwhelmingly a city of automobilists, the report declared, and driving was already an important local form of recreation: "By means of automobile travel a large portion of the population therefore seeks outdoor recreation to an enormous aggregate amount and over long distances both within the metropolitan area and by passing through it to the country beyond."[78] Given this existing predisposition to use the private car as the means to interact with restful nature, the parkway would be ideally suited to treating the psychosocial urban blights of metropolitan Southern California. Since, the report assumed, automobile ownership was near universal in the region,[79] the parkway might be transformed from a recreational drive for the elite few into a true mass medium:

> In the old days only a small percentage of the people could enjoy park scenery from moving vehicles, and even they would not often travel many miles through city streets for that pleasure. As to the mass of the people, an isolated park that gave opportunity to drive or walk a mile or two in pleasant park scenery by going only a short distance through the streets satisfied them well. Today, almost everybody can, and frequently does without hesitation, get into a car and go five or ten miles through uninteresting streets to get to what he considers a really pleasant route of pleasure travel, perhaps

in a park or public forest, but more likely just a region that isn't yet all built up. But the majority, when they get out of town, want to drive fifty or a hundred miles in pleasant surroundings, coming home by a different route. All this is more true of the Los Angeles Region than it is of any other great metropolis.[80]

Instead of having to drive many miles past dispiriting and ugly urban sprawl to find a chance undeveloped spot, Angelenos would have in the parkways ready access to a curative shelter from miles of unbroken urbanism. This plan, as its map indicates (see figure 42), would make most of Southern California a catch-basin of wide, sheltered parkway drives.

Ultimately, though, this plan expresses little genuine interest in offering Angelenos even the mild therapeutics of the traditional urban park. For all their sophistication, parkways offered far less to urbanites than did old-fashioned commons. Indeed, despite its many built social exclusions, the modern urban park was designed as an interactive, open device—a technology to soften the edges of urbanism by encouraging city dwellers to interact with a tamed, reassuring nature.

The parkway, by contrast, was designed from the start for a far more restricted range of uses. It offered, at its essence, a purely visceral experience of nature, strictly channeled through the windshield of the moving automobile. Social interaction, limited as it was in the typical American city park, was practically prohibited along the parkway corridor. Chance encounters at vista points and roadside gas stations could never substitute for real cultural interchange and shared activity. Social mixing was quite simply not the point of the parkway. Rather, as human involvement in the parkway was largely restricted to the particular, individual sensory experience of the automobilists, this landscaped environment effectively served only as backdrop to the internal, personal worlds sequestered within the confines of the private automobile. If the park is, in any sense, a public space, the parkway must be considered an insulated, elongated private sphere—a protected zone of individual, or at most familial, interaction. The 1930 plan for Greater Los Angeles, then, must be understood primarily as a plan for the enhancement of private, not public, space.

Recent historians of *Parks, Playgrounds, and Beaches* are certainly correct in seeing it as a powerful indictment of the sort of metropolis Greater Los Angeles was becoming, but they are wrong to pin their most progressive aspirations on this plan. As a matter of fact, this is not a hopeful plan at all. Even its most ambitious recommendations are more concerned with vividly recounting the horrors of the existing city than with sketching out the ideal promised future. Throughout, the 1930 park plan is marked by a pervasive and corroding disgust with the existing built topography of the Los Angeles region. Every description of the city betrays a palpable revulsion: "The beaches, which are pictured in the magazines to attract the eastern visitors, are suffering from the rapid encroachment of private use; the wild canyons are fast being subjected to subdivision and cheek-by-jowl cabin construction; ... the

PLATE 46. General plan for a complete system of parkways and large parks for the Los Angeles Region. (Base
map by courtesy of Automobile Club of Southern California.)

FIGURE 42. Los Angeles Parkway plan. Parkways are indicated in black. From Olmsted Brothers and Bartholomew and Associates, *Parks, Playgrounds, and Beaches for the Los Angeles Region* (Los Angeles: Citizens' Committee on Parks, Playgrounds, and Beaches, 1930), plate 46.

roadsides are more and more disfigured by signboards, shacks, garages, filling stations, destruction of trees, and multiplication of poles and wires" (23).

This is a blighted landscape, and it is everywhere. Indeed, such images are so onerous, the planners complain tellingly, that "driving for pleasure is often an exhausting and hazardous ordeal rather than a recreation" (23). The specter of visual pollution in the existing city haunts this report, and descriptions of this blight remain its most damning indictment and its most persistent theme. It is as if, in the view of these planners, Southern California's most pressing problem was that it did not look enough like it did in its own advertising.

This disappointment is framed by a ubiquitous internalization of contemporary cultural criticism of the city. Evidently, planners had become captivated by the potent critical discourses of sprawl. In fact, this discourse colors the authors' very ability to comprehensively see the city about them. Instead of viewing the metropolis, as they were professionally trained to do, as a collection of discrete but interacting components, an integrated network of individual systems—particular residential tracts, streets, sewers, business centers, and so on—planners cast the city in this report as a homogeneous and undifferentiated whole. It is not a city of distinctive (potentially quasi-autonomous) neighborhoods—the basis of individual communities and what Bessie McClenahan called the positive act of "neighboring"—but "miles of unbroken urbanism." This is the corrosive and totalizing language of sprawl, and it blinds the authors of *Parks, Playgrounds, and Beaches* to the specific landscapes of the city around them. The result is a park plan that reads more like a destructive urban renewal program than a city beautification scheme, let alone a visionary rebalancing of public and private. At every point where this plan should, logically, change in tone from condemnation of present conditions to rapturous celebration of the better city to come, the discourse bogs down in caustic rhetoric. Instead of selling its readership on a more harmonious potential city, this plan continually returns to a dominant thematics of blight and despair. In essence, the plan shows almost no enthusiasm for its own plans. For all its lauded potential, the 1930 park plan finds more utopianism in the past than in the future. At least implicitly, the plan continually hearkens back to an already lost Edenic Los Angeles—before the explosion of sprawl, when nature and urbanism were in balance—rather than looking forward to the better city it hopes to make.

Far from being a revolutionary manifesto, at its essence the 1930 plan was nostalgic, or even reactionary. In fact, it was an ambitiously reactionary manifesto. It overtly sought to reproduce in a bustling metropolitan area the very sort of quasi-rural landscape that Angelenos by this time surely felt had long passed away. Though Southern California was no longer the bucolic and pleasant land of orange groves and open fields that it had been only a few decades before, it could, with great effort, the plan seemed to suggest, be restored to its former pristine condition. This is not a vision of a new kind of city, but a yearning for a pastoralism that is no city at all.

And it was precisely this hope of reclamation, or redemption, that underlay the plan's obsession with parkways. Aside from their practical uses, parkways represented for planners of the era the prime contemporary example of large-scale landscape reconstruction and renewal. The lesson of the New York parkway program was that, with proper preparation and design, the most extreme transformations in the earth, including those on the very outskirts of a fully developed metropolis, might, within a very short time period, be hidden under a guise of undisturbed nature. The modern parkway proved that properly mobilized technology could enable engineers to impose the most modern, disruptive forms onto an existing terrain, then stitch the land back together such that visitors afterward would think that it had been that way all along. The cultural turmoil, political contests, and unprecedented growth of the 1920s had produced in Greater Los Angeles a postsuburban topography that was entirely unexpected and undesired. By 1930, planners in Southern California saw the sort of radical transformation carried out by eastern engineers as the only way to set back the clock to a time when the region could still be remade according to definite plans.

It is impossible to read this report without detecting, along with the palpable disdain for the urban environment, a note of despair as to the prospects for improvement. The enthusiasm for the parkway in this plan seems to spring less from hope that it might cure the city—either by restructuring its topography or by restoring its environment to an earlier, more pastoral state—than from its potential to artificially simulate an essential rural purity entirely alien to the existing metropolis. As a result, very little of the 1930 park plan actually aims to restore the charms of the lost commodious landscape. It is as if the plan were acknowledging that Los Angeles was already a lost cause; ultimately, this ambitious document cannot seriously contemplate any sort of real return to Eden. Instead, the 1930 park plan privileges vicarious visual pleasure over active use. There is something peculiar, and particularly telling, about the plan's evocation of this urban landscape. When discussing lack of public access to the coastline, for instance, the Olmsted and Bartholomew report expresses the problem in terms of "a practically continuous row of buildings, walls and planting between motorists and the seacoast of Los Angeles County" (23). The perceived problem is not public access to the ocean but wasted scenic potential from a car window.

Similarly, while discussing undeveloped preserves and open spaces, Olmsted and Bartholomew do not even mention actual use of these spaces. Instead, nearby recreational assets become mere backdrop:

> The mountains, which are dominant scenic assets, are slowly losing value because of the intensive urban growth. On the one hand such growth is steadily cutting off views of the mountains, views that can be effectively obtained only across open foregrounds sufficient in scale to complete and unify the landscape composition. The constant process of building upon open areas, the confinement of highways between rows of

dwellings, stores, advertising structures and other near-by obstructions is gradually eliminating enjoyment of the inspiring mountain scenery from the plains. This is a great loss which can be stopped only by a reservation of occasional public open fore-grounds. (23–24)

In this park plan, mountain ranges are purely "scenic assets," not nearby places to visit, and open parks in the basin below are "foregrounds" offering a pleasing sense of depth for the sublime vista in the background. Likewise, in discussing "outdoor enjoyment," the report complains that "the hills and sightly eminences in and around Los Angeles have never been properly worked into the expanding structure of the city in order to preserve their *landscape value* or save for public enjoyment the *magnificent views from their summits*" (23, 24, italics added). In suggesting remedies to this lack of appropriate scenic integration, the Olmsteds and Bartholomew recommend "projects similar to such famous and popular drives as the skyline boulevards of Oakland and San Francisco" (25). The implicit understanding here is telling: roads are intended to showcase naturally sublime vistas, and to do this properly these parkways must be carefully located in the topography. Good views require adequate foreground distance and contrast, and they must be posed from elevated points—both to provide scenic panoramas and, most important of all, to avoid obstruction by (axiomatically) unsightly urban elements (see figure 43).

Throughout the report, the appearance of the city is damning. The proof that the metropolis, so recently a locus of hope and concerted effort, had become delinquent and blighted was there for all to see. The disordered appearance of the built environment was evidence enough that planning efforts in the 1920s had gone awry. The failures of a city cluttered by inharmonious and conflicting developments, mired in an incomprehensible morass of traffic congestion, and far removed from the simple pastoralism of its recent past were manifest in the city's chaotic topography. Sprawl told spectators everything they needed to know about Los Angeles.

Unfortunately for these local planning professionals committed to the project of urban observation, clear vision had by the end of the decade overwhelmed all other priorities of regional planning. The outward signs of city structure had over-shadowed their referents. Easily observed surface clarity in the built environment became synonymous with efficiency of urban operation, and visible disorder in-trinsically connoted blight, decay, and malfunction. Whereas urban legibility was supposed to be a matter of stable boundaries and clear functional distinctions—between peoples, places, and uses—it had now become a simple matter of visual aesthetics. The imperceptible underlying markers of a city's true mechanical operation, to which planners were supposedly so attuned, faded in the face of manifest surface clutter and disorganization. While planners could not be sure from their technologies of observation whether their metropolis was devoid of blight or over-ridden with it, their eyes revealed no such ambiguity. Sprawling Los Angeles's very

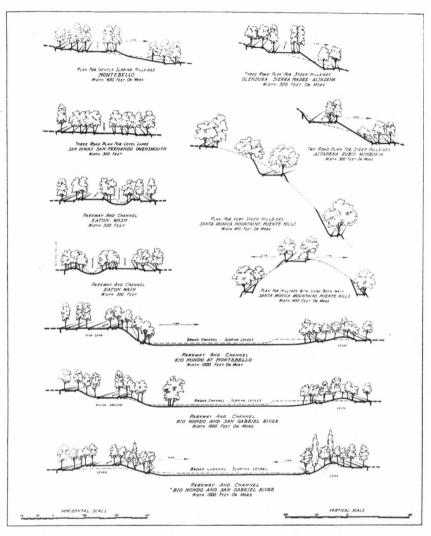

FIGURE 43. Diagram of an ideal parkway's integration into and use of topographical features to control views. From Olmsted Brothers and Bartholomew and Associates, *Parks, Playgrounds, and Beaches for the Los Angeles Region* (Los Angeles: Citizens' Committee on Parks, Playgrounds, and Beaches, 1930), plate 48.

appearance unimpeachably, and damningly, testified to its essential corruption. Now, instead of merely segregating undesired urban elements—architectural and human—planners wished to blot them from sight altogether. Within their visual obsession, such occlusion might effectively make these problems simply disappear.

This ocular obsession helps explain local planners' fascination with the modern parkway, for behind the automotive parkway of the 1920s and 1930s there was always an obsession with visuality. The parkway aesthetic was founded on an elaborate sequence of masks and screens, harmonious views and carefully framed vistas. Through its implication in an aesthetic of sight, *Parks, Playgrounds, and Beaches* is concerned not so much with providing refreshing outdoor recreation and activity, direct contact with a restoring nature, as presenting for public view posed and pristine natural settings in the ideological context of the sublime. In fact, all the urban recreational areas featured in the report—perhaps with the exception of the ball fields that are touched upon for a paragraph or two—are spots to be experienced vicariously, at a distance: "Enjoyment of *scenery* from an automobile, moving as fast as practicable, is much more possible with broad open *scenery* from high level roads where the nearby features are unimportant than in narrow canyons and intimate small scale landscape where the *scenes* are passed so rapidly that no really good *views* are possible. In general canyons should be protected from the rush of through travel, and main roads should be placed where possible on the *view-commanding* slopes and ridges" (88, italics added). A consequence of this visual bias is that the 1930 park plan seems to perceive Southern California as essentially a series of stage sets or a contiguous sequence of scenic film locations.

This conception of Los Angeles as potentially one great scenic drive pervades the entire discussion, and this, of course, also grounds the plan's use of parkways, for the automotive parkway is understood here, at least implicitly, as a piece of representational machinery: a mechanism to project citizens into a simulated, vicarious experience of nature.

The report's sketches of idealized parkway segments reveal the fantasy underlying the seemingly objective arguments and figures. These roads bear no trace of established urbanity; they revel in a rural innocence, owing more to the Hudson Valley School of landscape figuration than to any twentieth-century street scene. Indeed, these broad, expansive vistas dilute the illusory forward motion of the diminishing roadway (although the pavement envisioned here is so expansive, so broad, as to rob the lanes of any hint of linearity). These are planar, enveloping spaces pictured with all the motion of a diorama, and they seem to promise not a modern aesthetic of movement or frenzied human activity, but a calm bucolic stillness (see figure 44).

Clearly, for these planners, the parkway aesthetic dominates all analysis of the larger region. Or, inflected through a decade of motion picture experience, Los Angeles has collapsed into its own representational logic. The automotive parkway has

FIGURE 44. An ideal parkway, as envisioned in the Olmsted plan, conforms to the aesthetic, screening discordant elements from view. From Olmsted Brothers and Bartholomew and Associates, *Parks, Playgrounds, and Beaches for the Los Angeles Region* (Los Angeles: Citizens' Committee on Parks, Playgrounds, and Beaches, 1930), plate 57.

become, for the erstwhile planners/directors, an apparatus that allows all Angelenos to participate as spectators in an elaborate metropolitan mise-en-scene—a costume drama where the city itself masquerades as a rural idyll. In this sense, the aesthetic of the parkway, like that of the motion picture, merely offers respite from modern urban life, not actual reform. In essence, for all later historians' utopian investment in *Parks, Playgrounds, and Beaches,* this plan never really offered to harmonize and protect an Edenic region, but simply to provide the more well-to-do of its demoralized residents a bit of weekend recreation. And this was, after all, all the park plan ever claimed for itself.

Yet not only is this plan ultimately unconvincing as a radical proposal for urban restructuring, it is hardly even a realistic scheme for the amelioration of the worst aspects of urban sprawl. Instead, *Parks, Playgrounds, and Beaches* succumbs to its own subtle but pervasive disillusionment with the city itself. Ultimately, this plan only aims to hide from view a built environment far beyond saving.

Caught up in a sort of visual frenzy, planners began to perceive parkways not as tools for the betterment of urban life, for the careful mediation between city and country, but as veils to hide the surrounding city from its own residents—to protect Angelenos from what had become of Los Angeles. As the plan reminded its readers, these new roads "should be well screened from the urban and suburban surroundings through which they pass" (13). They should be shielded from the outward signs of a city gone terribly wrong.

THE PARKWAY VERSUS THE CITY

Implicit in *Parks, Playgrounds, and Beaches for the Los Angeles Region* is a much more drastic program for Greater Los Angeles than that of hiding the city from its residents. The parkway, as a park, was always in an ambivalent relationship with the city. Essentially, the parkway presents rural nature very much in opposition to the metropolis. In American urban ideology, preserves of nature can serve as an antidote to modern alienation and ugliness precisely because, and only because, nature is urbanism's antithesis, its diametrical and essential Manichaean opposite. Los Angeles's proposed parkways, though, were not to be located in some remote rural spot, or even on the city's outskirts, where the boundaries between these antipodes might be properly regulated and maintained. Instead, they would run right through the city itself. The bits of nature to which these roads provide access lie amid housing tracts and gas stations, small stores and telephone poles. As with any American city, it would be impossible to find in even deconcentrated Southern California stretches of land that remained pristine enough or could be redeveloped cheaply enough to provide the sort of setting a parkway project requires.

Thus, although the proposed parkways have subsequently been viewed as minor accoutrements of a city beautification plan, it is clear from the start that they were intended for far more ambitious, or drastic, purposes. As elaborate and well-developed technologies of modern engineering, by the 1920s parkways could never be conceived of simply as hedgerows that could be put in place by whim to provide a bit of park buffer as needed. If done properly, parkway construction required wholesale reconstruction of the earth and enforced purification and homogenization of the surrounding landscape.[81]

Moreover, implicit in the park movement, as well as in later parkway evolution, is an increasingly explicit rejection of modern urbanism. The parkway aesthetic was inevitably obsessive—it would captivate the would-be parkway planner, who would, merely by earnestly attempting to follow its design logic, almost inexorably become compulsively concerned with the ever more radical measures necessary to support the roadway's fundamental simulation. Any discordant urban feature, no matter how momentarily glimpsed, could disrupt the sustained gracious illusion of the parkway corridor, rending the simulation and jumbling the carefully orchestrated sequence of sensory images. Even in the design stage, the most distant visual distractions seem undesirable. Although the designer might begin contemplation of the siting process by trying to connect a few scenic spots, he or she would inevitably begin to think about closing the gaps, the breaks, in the flow of sublime beauty—

suturing the continuous diegesis. Soon, every inappropriate element appears distracting, jarringly interposing an interfering and ugly outside world in the hermetic space of the parkway corridor. This obsession leads, through a logical progression, to the desire to remake more and more of the surrounding countryside, until the entire region—or that visible from the roadway—can be brought into harmony with the landscaping.

Eventually, then, if they were fully carried out, parkway construction efforts would inevitably require wholesale destruction of much of the existing metropolis. No wonder this proposal would be so expensive—the drafters of *Parks, Playgrounds, and Beaches* knew full well that an urban parkway project, truly motivated by the parkway aesthetic, would require enormous governmental expenditures to purify, to visually insulate, these urban park strips. Shutting out all traces of an existing city of a million inhabitants from two hundred miles of relatively narrow park corridors was, of course, an impossible task. Such a grand project might be conceivable in a rural river valley, such as that of the Bronx River, or among the carefully landscaped and intentionally rustic estates of the Long Island gentry, but it would be ludicrously expensive and tremendously controversial in the heart of a developed urban area. It is for this reason that no true modern parkway was ever constructed within the built fabric of an American city during the twentieth century.

The 1930 parkway plan is pervaded by a half-conscious sense of its own impossibility. Even in this realm of visionary contemplation, planners are faced with insurmountable difficulties in trying to maintain their coherent and self-contained recreational simulation. Even in the ideal planning stage, too often views of the surrounding urbanity intrude into the imagined picture, or at least into the descriptive narrative. This is why the 1930 park plan so frequently bogs down in critical description of the blighted and alienating urban landscape of Southern California. As a result, the study is thick with dark recital of this random development. The plan reads less like a vision of a purified future than a dreary depiction of a jumbled present that can never measure up to an imagined ideal.

At its essence, *Parks, Playgrounds, and Beaches* takes for granted that urbanism is inherently ugly and blighting, that such visual impressions are authoritative, and that any passing glimpse of the surrounding city would therefore be necessarily distracting and dispiriting. Hence the obsession with the motorist's inability to get an unobstructed view of the sublime, whether in the form of mountains, beaches, or stands of trees. This obsession in turn reflects the planners' larger inability to envision a truly aesthetic urbanism. Repelled by images of the skyscraper metropolis— really a dense mass of tenements and claustrophobic office towers, in their view— planners can no longer see any alternative beauty in urban topography. For these visionary planners, there is no urban sublime; it is all the same—all ugly—to them.[82]

What was the real purpose of such an elaborate parkway system in this sprawling and unsightly urban topography? In the end, this plan does not try to remake

Los Angeles, but rather retreats from it. It does not try to locate usable parks within the city fabric to anchor new, more peaceful, less alienating developments, but attempts to remove Angelenos altogether from the sprawling metropolis. By and large, the utopianism of the 1920s—when a balanced and harmonious life might be situated amid a bucolic setting that was the city itself—is absent here. The city is no longer a locus of excitement, a modern and dynamic site of cosmopolitan activity. Rather, it is a prison, a vast and anonymous sea of built-up and cold artifice: "To people of today, how great would be the value of the home only a few miles from a parkway of ample road capacity and agreeable scenery, where one might drive through a chain of similar parkways to distant parts and enjoy the open country of Southern California! Contrast this with the far inferior worth of a home shut off from any considerable area of open land by twenty to fifty miles of practically uninterrupted cities and suburbs."[83] This report is a claustrophobic document. The landscape of decentralized urbanism continually emerges as a specter—"twenty to fifty miles of practically uninterrupted cities and suburbs"—and it is always posed against the promise of release. Indeed, *Parks, Playgrounds, and Beaches* is enraptured by prospects of urban transcendence, of liberation. Ultimately, this study reads less like a plan for urban renovation, or even a simple park plan, than an evacuation scheme.

It is as if *Parks, Playgrounds, and Beaches* wished it could restore an ideal mythic Southern California—but knows it cannot. Its recommended projects uniformly seek to reclaim a long-lost primal scene, a gracious and sublime vista long since obscured by billboards and ticky-tacky residential tracts, dust and automotive exhaust. But, as the plan's authors inherently recognize the impossibility of such regression, it is ultimately pervaded by despair: the once-beautiful city has become an eyesore—something from which to avert one's gaze. And since, in the logic of the park plan, recreation means recreational driving, the only hope left for Angelenos is to drive as far as possible from this sprawling, unsightly urbanity. *Parks, Playgrounds, and Beaches* would at least offer a possibility of escape.

By 1930, the long-repressed undercurrents of profound ambivalence toward urbanism in the garden city ideal were finally beginning to collapse into outright revulsion at the idea of the city. In retrospect, the garden city ideal was, like the park movement, an attempt to rescue the city from itself. It sought to transform the metropolis into a more humane environment, countering urban concentration with a notion of decentralization built on a smaller and more manageable community. After a decade of concerted reform effort supported by broad institutional and legal authority, this "better city" had emerged not as a commodious middle ground that would harmonize city and country, primitive and modern, rustic and urbane, but as what appeared even to the most sympathetic planners as faceless urban sprawl.

Ultimately, William Fox's reminiscence of Hugh Pomeroy as a man who failed because local authorities were too timid to accept his plans sounds a bit like an apology for a planning movement that was finally crushed not so much by resistance to its ambitions from a radically changing metropolis as by its members' failure of vision. This vision failed because their alternative to the concentric city—the only alternative they could imagine, which they stuck to through the entire decade—was a garden city dream that finally proved incompatible with large-scale twentieth-century urbanism. The planners' dreams proved too inflexible to keep pace with the changing landscape of Southern California.

The boosterism so cherished by planners and business elites alike had overwhelmed the schemes of both sets of civic leaders. By the mid 1920s, the city had changed too quickly and too radically for either envisioned program of planned modernization. The businessmen were defeated on the levels of discourse and politics. By the end of the decade, the planners were defeated by the internal contradictions of their own plans and by their inability to adapt to an evolving and ultimately incomprehensible postsuburban city form. By the end of the decade, faced with this illegible and chaotic sprawling urban landscape, which no longer even offered the potential of nurturing clustered autonomous garden communities, the city's dreamers perhaps (and perhaps subconsciously) lost hope.

It could be that the problem here was not just the planners' understandable inability to foresee the emergence of novel postsuburban patterns of development, but a chronic failure to see and dream in synchronicity with other Angelenos. Pomeroy, Whitnall, and their peers had begun the 1920s very much at the forefront of a wider consensus about the future of Greater Los Angeles. During this critical decade, however, the legible and stable order of the city began to degrade, partly as a result of urban deconcentration efforts carried out by those same experts. Angelenos' conception of their collective future began to diverge, although most citizens evidently rejected any notion of their home returning to the fold of traditional concentric cities. Planners, for their part, ultimately had no adequate response to postsuburbanization; by the end of the decade, they could not sustain any sense of clear comprehensibility within the sprawling city. While ordinary Americans continued to flood into Southern California, the experts were beginning to give up on it. After all this disillusionment, though, and even in a time of severe and paralyzing economic and epistemic crisis, these professionals could not bear to abandon their prerogative to "Dream dreams and see Visions." Indeed, as Fox, the nostalgia engineer, regretfully concludes about his boss, regional planning director Hugh Pomeroy, "He was a dreamer, and that's what planning needs. His dreams were so fantastic. He was way ahead of his time."[84]

Epilogue

A City That Moves

"'What Can We Do About This?' screamed a big placard in the Los Angeles Museum of History, Science and Art. It meant Los Angeles's own looks and lack of livability."[1] Thus declared *Time* under the heading "Dream City." "Los Angeles' gangling growth makes everybody happy except U.S. city planners," the magazine continued. In fact, the disdain for "the great, sprawling town" was so caustic that "if the city planners could burn Los Angeles down they would rebuild it very differently." This was the subject of "the biggest city planning show California had ever seen"—an exhibit intended to "show the public how city planners thought the ideal Los Angeles should look."

The potential Dream City took solid form in late October 1941, more than a decade after the demise of Los Angeles's ambitious park and parkway plan. Formally titled ". . . And Now We Plan," the public display at the County Museum at Exposition Park sought, in the words of its publicity material, to "awaken the public to the part that it can play in achieving a well-planned community."[2] This call for open democratic participation did not exactly jibe with the larger message of the exhibit, though, which emphasized not community input but expert foresight. Los Angeles's problems, the exhibit made clear, sprang not from a legacy of inadequate public debate over the disposition of the metropolis but from the fact that "it has grown without thoughtful planning."[3] Regrettably, "in the past altogether too little planning accompanied our development," resulting in a chaotic and random built environment where "the great city sprawls in every direction touching its satellite towns on every side."[4]

PLANNING POSTSUBURBIA

The remedy for Los Angeles's manifest legacy of unplanned development could only reside in the deliberate, coordinated exertions of experts, for "progress henceforth depends on the discovery of a way to plan and co-ordinate the development of housing, industries, recreation, communication, and transportation."[5] Through this concerted effort, this "articulate, collective determination," the sprawling, fragmented megalopolis—"the chaos of today"—might be brought into some sort of harmony, becoming a "healthy, happy, beautiful, orderly place" (27, 29). And this coordinated unanimity was clearly, according to these Angelenos, the only way to "bring about that integration of our community" which would restore proper order to the larger topography (8). "Citizens of the metropolis today," the exhibit declared on a prominent signboard, "are not satisfied with patchwork. They know the value of modern design."[6]

Despite this unifying concern with the face of the region, the exhibit made clear that the new holistic spirit of planning had to start at the neighborhood level. Too often in the past, communities were conceived as a "series of rectangular blocks" in close proximity. This topography was undifferentiated without being properly balanced and homogeneous. As a result, "seldom does a group of blocks have a definite character or boundary, or assume any significance as a neighborhood" (9). Without clear functional limits and unifying design, these Los Angeles developments produced not a sense of identity but an anxious anomie. This anxiety, moreover, was continually heightened by the random social and demographic changes that, in inevitable waves, quickly and repeatedly transformed the entire character of the area. Without proper planning, residents of the city could never be sure who their neighbors would be or what would become of their district. Consequently, "in such a neighborhood the sense of instability in itself prevents the development of community consciousness. There is little neighborly contact, but rather a continual and often irritating consciousness of neighbors" (9). In the present "heedless, planless community," continual migration simply jams together countless strangers without allowing evolution of "the ideal community life" (26). As the *Los Angeles Times'* Arthur Millier described it in the Sunday Magazine section,

> Here's the message which this large display presses home by a persuasive series of relief maps, stage sets, photo and painted murals, illuminated photographic transparencies, elaborate models, lantern slides, a time clock and a recorded voice: God gave this county a wonderful, primitive terrain. See what successive waves of immigrants and industries have done to it. Two million people, through bad planning, are slowly strangling the possibility of decent life in this metropolitan county. How, then, are the almost inevitable 5,000,000 to live, work and play here? "By planning now," say the makers of this exhibit.[7]

Without proper expert coordination of design and development, future growth in Southern California would merely repeat, and exacerbate, previous mistakes and blunders. The larger message here was that unless checked on the local level, Southern California's devouring sprawl—making the entire region, in Millier's words, "one vast, conglomerate metropolis"—would continue to undermine the basis of clear and legible public space and community life (12).

The manifest visual chaos of the sprawling metropolis fascinated these erstwhile planners. Throughout the exhibit, images of blight punctuated the larger message that contemporary Greater Los Angeles was not only deficient in "looks," as *Time* put it, but fundamentally disorganized. The perceptible confusion revealed in the graphic images was incontrovertible, mute testimony to the underlying social and functional conflations that undermined the proper operation of the community (perhaps simply, irrefutably assumed from outward appearances). Clearly, the visual discourses of sprawl and blight, which had echoed throughout local representation since the debate over the rapid transit plan in the mid-1920s, persisted as a powerful and persuasive rhetoric into the 1940s: "In a series of 12 large transparencies they show the benefits of privacy, spaciousness, sunlight, quiet and accessibility—which they term the desirable factors for planning—contrasted with crowding, airlessness, darkness, traffic congestion, and other effects of poor planning."[8] After all these years (and for many more to come), the metaphorics of light and dark, openness and closure, clarity and confusion still structured Southern Californian understandings of the built topography of postsuburbia. Now, though, it was "sprawling" Los Angeles, not the vertical cities of the East, that was shadowy and blighted, mirroring and inverting the earlier discourse.

The designers of ". . . And Now We Plan" felt that a fundamental reconfiguration of the urban topography was the only way Angelenos could begin to restore order not only in the sprawling landscape but in their fractured polity. Once more, the solution was based in the neighborhood. Only by attending to the small unit might the proper boundaries between urban spaces be restored and maintained. Indeed, the planners made clear, "the basis of the plan is a neighborhood with a living area one-half mile square" (26). Within this circumscribed zone could ideally arise "a reasonably homogeneous and harmonious development" that would encourage social interaction and a viable home life: "The desirable neighborhood is one developed as a community in which the concept of home extends beyond the individual house and lot to the neighborhood" (9). The connections between home and community would be made plain, emphasizing, as the *Los Angeles Daily News* put it, "garden design of residence property, which may be near the factory where the residents work" (see figure 45).[9]

The exhibit traced out a detailed picture of this new envisioned community structure: "The units comprising the living space are shopping center, recreational center, church, and grammar school. Dwellings all face toward the green areas.

FIGURE 45. The community commons: Ramona Gardens. From Los Angeles County Museum, . . . *And Now We Plan* (Los Angeles: Los Angeles County Museum, 1941), 11.

Working and living areas are properly separated by great belts of green. Similarly separated are the various units of the living area" (26). Here, the single-family home would remain the basis of good community life, but some provision would be made for a discrete section of "multiple dwellings which will have ready access to both shopping centers and transit and transportation centers."[10] Regardless of specific housing arrangements, the overriding priority was the harmony and coherence of the neighborhood unit: "The fostering of neighborhood unity is a vital part of the task of making a big city livable, amid the necessities for centralized economic and political functions" (12).

At essence, the concept of community structuring ". . . And Now We Plan" is topographical. Configurations of social relations mirror the underlying arrangement of urban spaces, situating desirable modes of interaction. A sense of community springs, the exhibit makes clear, from stable social boundaries and functions, and these superstructural relationships only arise from a proper arrangement of public space. The planners are quite explicit here: the ideal neighborhood requires provision for a shared common on the (idealized) New England village model, for there "a definite relationship existed between the plan of the village with church, school, shops, and houses clustered around a central green" (12). The schematic clarity of the Puritan township, where the orderly (and "pure") demarcation of spaces and obligations is visible to all, obviously appealed to these modern planners, whose avowedly progressive designs could be similarly encapsulated in a simple abstract diagram of community organization—which was displayed prominently at the exhibition (see figures 46 and 47).

Despite the reputed paucity of planning in the Los Angeles region over previous decades, the designers of the County Museum exhibit managed to almost perfectly recapitulate, both in language and in visual representation, the clustered garden city ideal advocated by Jazz Age professional planners. Without being fully aware of their influences and inspirations, a new generation of erstwhile planning revolutionaries had rediscovered ideas that had long structured planning thought in the region. The intellectuals behind ". . . And Now We Plan"—"extremely talented young men and women,"[11] "mostly between the ages of 25 and 35 years. Most of them are architects or architectural graduates. A few are active regional planners. There is a social worker or two,"[12] collectively calling themselves Telesis—were channeling the spirit of a now scattered and dissipated planning tradition. Clearly, the depredations of the Great Depression wiped out the memory of the proposals and personalities of the earlier formative era in local imagining, but did little to fundamentally alter the basic ideas.[13]

There is, however, one critical difference between the ideal future city envisioned by Telesis and that which had preoccupied the imagination of planners during the earlier era. As the neighborhood diagram makes clear, the autonomous subcenters of the 1940s are tightly linked to broad, direct "freeways" running throughout the

FIGURE 46. The ideal map on display at ". . . And Now We Plan." From ". . . Now We Plan," *California Arts and Architecture* 57, no. 11 (1941): 23.

metropolitan region. The exhibition catalogue reconfirms the centrality of these highways: "At the upper left of the photograph of the model is the high school campus containing a large athletic field, whose parking area serves a dual function—for athletic events and related community activities on weekends, and during the week for factory workers in the industrial section located beyond the campus on the other side of the freeway. Pedestrian tunnels under the freeway enable these workers to cross safely and easily from the parking area to the industrial plants" (26). These new freeways would allow long-distance movement and serve, like the parkways of the old 1930 plan, as buffers to segregate and order neighborhood development. This prescription, under the heading "Circulation," occupied a great portion of ". . . And Now We Plan" (both the catalog and museum display), and the Telesis planners placed great importance on the new transportation technology. As Millier described it in the *Times,* "Transportation is the key to decent living, working and playing in our automobile-minded county, so Telesis went to town in this section of the show, in its attempt to demonstrate good planning for getting where you want to go. . . . Motion is the essence of modern life" (14). This reborn planning movement sought not only to understand the city as an ensemble of static

FIGURE 47. Detail of model community diagram. From Los Angeles County Museum, . . . *And Now We Plan* (Los Angeles: Los Angeles County Museum, 1941), 26.

objects—where traffic is merely a visible, and often disturbing, manifestation of the underlying functional relationships between elements—but to integrate a sense of movement directly into the urban model.

Attention to highways is absolutely essential, the exhibit suggested, because a great deal of the blight in the existing city can be traced back to the urban street system's traffic, dangerous grade crossings, and pollution. The old-fashioned grid of automotive routes simply could not properly contain the excess of motion in the modern metropolis. The freeway promises to correct this situation by channeling movement into modern, strictly regulated, orderly corridors: "New types of highways are needed to replace the pattern of streets and roads designed for the slow moving vehicle. Freeways, such as the Arroyo Seco Parkway, with divided roadways, adequate lighting at night, no cross traffic, no business or residential frontage on the roadway, enable the motorist to save time with safety for himself and others" (21). The modern freeway represents a technology of interconnection and clear demarcation. As such, it also represents a fundamental structuring technology that relates the foundational part (the neighborhood) to the larger whole (the region). In the new planning discourse, the harmonious balance of urban elements and the clear segregation of their intrinsic spaces can only be realized through the careful use of freeways to protect new neighborhood developments.

FREEWAYS AND PARKWAYS

At this point we have to ask: is this new vision of 1941 merely a reprise of the faded dreams of 1929 and 1930? Is the promised freeway of this later era a rehash of the rejected parkways of the Jazz Age? To some degree, this second generation of Southern California planners had clearly resuscitated an old conception of the urban future, updating a few of the elements, clarifying others, and presenting the whole in a much more open and compelling manner than that attempted at the end of the Progressive Era. The novel mode of presentation structuring the exhibit was itself the product of a subtly changed understanding of the role of the highway (and traffic) in the ideal metropolis, representing the nascent development at the onset of the 1940s of a new apparatus of perceptual technology that promised to make the post-suburban topography more legible to its inhabitants.

Whereas the 1930 Los Angeles parkway plan had sought to situate an entirely inappropriate rural technology within the fabric of the city, a freeway plan would, in the context of its era, be something altogether different. Generally, the historiography of transportation has elided the differences between parkway and freeway—a conflation that the casual slippage between contemporary uses of the two terms implicitly supports. The standard account traces the early automotive parkways of the 1910s (primarily the Bronx River Parkway), by way of the Berlin AVUS, to the German autobahn (both acknowledged taking inspiration from the Westchester

County prototypes), and then, through the convenient intervention of General (and later President) Eisenhower, to the postwar interstate highway system. This tidy story is much too tidy, for it treats these road forms not as cultural products embedded in intrinsic ideological and social systems, but as technologically rational—and neutrally detached—artifices. Although there were certainly linkages in expertise and execution between the development of these road forms, they are quite distinct devices, arising out of divergent planning and engineering traditions and serving radically different purposes.[14]

Whereas the parkway was intimately tied to a natural aesthetic, the freeway was from the start designed to be an urban, openly technological creation—an engineering solution to facilitate mass automotive transportation. The roots of the freeway lie not in the antiurban park movement of the late nineteenth century but in the vertical sublime metropolitan enthusiasm of the 1920s. Many utopian visionaries had pictured broad, elevated automotive thoroughfares cutting right through the skyscraper city. This was not merely the stuff of utopian imagination. Often called "Express Highways" or "Superhighways" in that era, these modern artifices were seen as technical solutions to contemporary transportation problems. They did not seek to mediate the relation between country and city or hide their implication in the landscape; instead they were intended to be confined strictly within the fabric of a densely developed cityscape of towers and streets. As such, these early freeways were inspired more by the urban railroad's aesthetic of utilitarian (or ostentatious) technological infrastructure, particularly the iron trestles on which trains often entered the twentieth-century metropolis, than by some ideal of simulating undisturbed nature.

The Regional Plan of New York and Its Environs envisioned a full-scale freeway project as early as 1931, but the first serious consideration of the urban freeway predates those famous representations by at least five years. In 1926, the City of Detroit—much like Los Angeles in these years, both in population and in the striking novelty of its emergence as a major metropolis—proposed a detailed superhighway plan that sought to integrate the automobile (as popular in this city as in Southern California) into the built landscape of the city.[15] The high-capacity roads envisioned in the plan were explicitly intended "to speed up city traffic,"[16] as one contemporary newspaper report described it. Integrated with a high-speed rapid transit line, the new superhighway would be grade-separated, elevated in large portions, and divided into discrete lanes for express and local traffic. This last provision clearly reflected the influence of the train on the design of the roadway. This superhighway thus represented an attempt to adapt the technological forms of the urban railroad to the automobile.

Chicago contemplated similar road plans in 1929, and New York actually constructed several miles of an elevated express roadway along the western edge of Manhattan during the era, although it never quite measured up to the visionaries' ambitions. By this time these new highways had acquired the name "freeway," coined by Edward Bassett in an explicit attempt to differentiate them from the rural parkways. The freeway, Bassett proclaimed, was a roadway dedicated to orderly, rapid movement of automobiles and commercial trucks. Whereas the formal parkway was designed for recreational travel, restricting traffic to the private automobile, this new road form was intended to be utilitarian.[17] Consequently, roadside plantings and such amenities, so critical to the parkway's purpose, were considered unnecessary in freeway construction. This was to be a tool allowing the modern city to expedite the movement of traffic through its spaces, relieving congestion and preventing needless "frictions."

METROPOLIS OF STREETS

Although several Los Angeles newspapers carried reports on freeway design in eastern cities, planners in Southern California explicitly rejected any consideration of such projects in the 1920s and early 1930s. Although they worked hard, and ultimately unsuccessfully, to construct a system of parkways throughout the region, these Jazz Age planners stated repeatedly in professional contexts that freeway construction was not appropriate for Los Angeles: "Director Charles H. Diggs of the Los Angeles County Regional Planning Commission writes to state that this omission [of express roads from the Regional Plan of Highways] was not an oversight but the result of careful consideration."[18] As this report in the *National Municipal Review* implies, planners in other cities were surprised at any city that did not plan in 1930 for urban freeways.

So where did those freeways in "... And Now We Plan" come from? It was not local planners who raised public interest in express highways for the Los Angeles basin but, significantly, the Automobile Club of Southern California. As it had in 1922, the Auto Club initiated a broad debate over novel traffic solutions when it released in early 1938 what it termed a "traffic survey." This report—"prepared under the direction of E. E. East, chief engineer,"[19] in actuality a detailed construction program—received extensive local press coverage and inspired a great deal of public commentary. It was the first public plan in the region to attempt to come to terms with postsuburban social topography: "The analysis of these [traffic count] data indicate that the relation which formerly existed between the home and place of occupation has almost, if not completely, disappeared."[20] As a result of the chaotic "crisscrossing of traffic,"[21] new types of roadway would be required to convey Angelenos the long distances they regularly traveled, while avoiding, as much as possible, congestion, confusion, and friction.

Appropriately, the "survey" called for an interconnected system of what it called "motorways." The linguistic innovation was important, because it elided the fact that the Automobile Club plan attempted rather incongruously to combine elements

MOTORWAY
THROUGH A RESIDENTIAL DISTRICT

TRAFFIC SURVEY
LOS ANGELES METROPOLITAN AREA
1937
ENGINEERING DEPARTMENT
AUTOMOBILE CLUB OF SOUTHERN CALIFORNIA

FIGURE 48. Obsolete visions of urban parkways. Left: Motorway cuts a greenbelt swathe
through a suburb. Right: Echoing Hugh Ferriss's vertical sublime sketches of a decade
before, the Automobile Club portrays a motorway cutting through a downtown office
building's upper floor. From Automobile Club of Southern California (Engineering
Department), *Traffic Survey: Los Angeles Metropolitan Area* (Los Angeles: Automobile
Club of Southern California, 1937), 6. Courtesy of the kind permission of the Automobile
Club of Southern California Archives.

of the motor parkway, not all that different from that envisioned in *Parks, Playgrounds, and Beaches* of almost a decade before, with a vision of urban freeways
that might have come directly from the pen of Hugh Ferriss at the height of 1920s
skyscraper enthusiasm. In residential districts, these motorways would run on 360-
foot fully landscaped rights of way, but within the built-up sections of the city, they
would rest on elevated structures, confined in width to a mere hundred feet (see
figure 48). More dramatically, these urban roadways would be constructed to run
right through the third stories of substantial new "motorway buildings" in the downtown district, and "surface streets would be crossed on bridges connecting motorway buildings" (see figures 49 and 50).[22] The *Daily News* was enraptured by the vertical sublime prospect of "super motorways crossing downtown and other business
districts on upper-story levels, through specially designed parking and office build-

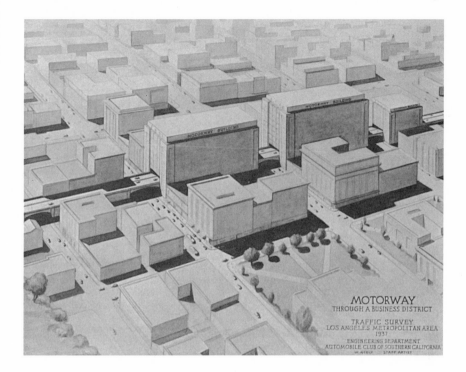

MOTORWAY
THROUGH A BUSINESS DISTRICT

TRAFFIC SURVEY
LOS ANGELES METROPOLITAN AREA
1937
ENGINEERING DEPARTMENT
AUTOMOBILE CLUB OF SOUTHERN CALIFORNIA
W. KELLY   STAFF ARTIST

ings and bridging ground-level streets!"[23] The *Times* described the plan equally enthusiastically: "Imagine driving your car on an exclusive express highway through the congested Los Angeles metropolitan region at a constant speed without a stop or hindrance!"[24]

Despite the newspapers' exclamations, many Angelenos greeted this utopian vision with skepticism or even derision. The rural portion of the plan was too reminiscent of the defeated 1930 parkway proposal, and the urban segment was clearly prohibitively expensive, the stuff of urban fantasy. For the Auto Club's E. B. Lefferts, writing in *The American City* the next year, however, the elevated motorway was simply the only available option: "Utilization of planes other than the surface plane for passage of traffic is submitted as the only other method of providing additional ways for traffic in heavily built-up areas."[25] Ultimately, though, the Auto Club could justify neither the fully vertical sublime exuberance of the business district superhighways nor the nostalgic romanticism of the residential district parkways. Although the survey had inspired great debate in the metropolis and effectively sparked public interest in this novel form of traffic relief, the hybridized motorway concept would not ultimately bring Southern California into the modern transportation era.

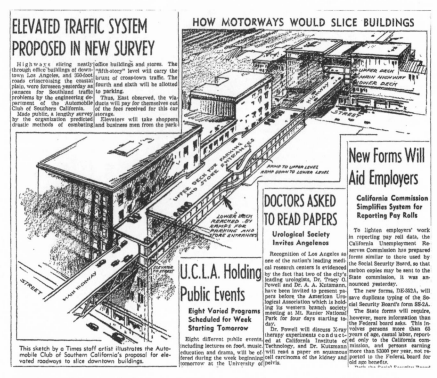

ELEVATED TRAFFIC SYSTEM PROPOSED IN NEW SURVEY

Highways slicing neatly through office buildings of downtown Los Angeles, and 350-foot roads crisscrossing the coastal plain, were foreseen yesterday as panacea for Southland traffic problems by the engineering department of the Automobile Club of Southern California.

Made public, a lengthy survey by the organization predicted drastic methods of combating office buildings and stores. The "fifth-story" level will carry the brunt of cross-town traffic. The fourth and sixth will be allotted to parking.

Thus, East observed, the viaducts will pay for themselves out of the fees received for this car storage.

Elevators will take shoppers and business men from the park-

HOW MOTORWAYS WOULD SLICE BUILDINGS

New Forms Will Aid Employers

California Commission Simplifies System for Reporting Pay Rolls

To lighten employers' work in reporting pay roll data, the California Unemployment Reserve Commission has prepared forms similar to those used by the Social Security Board, so that carbon copies may be sent to the State commission, it was announced yesterday.

The new forms, DE-352A, will save duplicate typing of the Social Security Board's form SS-2A.

The State forms will require, however, more information than the Federal board asks. This involves persons more than 65 years of age, casual labor, reported only to the California commission, and persons earning more than $3000 per year, not reported to the Federal board for old age benefits.

DOCTORS ASKED TO READ PAPERS

Urological Society Invites Angelenos

Recognition of Los Angeles as one of the nation's leading medical research centers is evidenced by the fact that two of the city's leading urologists, Dr. Tracy O. Powell and Dr. A. A. Kutzmann, have been invited to present papers before the American Urological Association which is holding its western branch society meeting at Mt. Ranier National Park for four days starting today.

Dr. Powell will discuss X-ray therapy experiments conducted at California Institute of Technology, and Dr. Kutzmann will read a paper on squamous cell carcinoma of the kidney and pelvis.

U.C.L.A. Holding Public Events

Eight Varied Programs Scheduled for Week Starting Tomorrow

Eight different public events, including lectures on food, music, education and drama, will be offered during the week beginning tomorrow at the University of

This sketch by a Times staff artist illustrates the Automobile Club of Southern California's proposal for elevated roadways to slice downtown buildings.

FIGURE 49. A *Los Angeles Times* staff artist interprets the Automobile Club's vertical sublime fantasia. *Los Angeles Times,* 27 July 1937. Copyright 1937, *Los Angeles Times.* Reprinted with permission.

Instead, the Auto Club's proposal was almost entirely superseded by a much more utilitarian document released in late 1939. This report, written by city engineer Lloyd Aldrich and circulated under the aegis of the newly formed Transportation Engineering Board, stripped the earlier survey of its more fantastic elements, replacing both sorts of motorway with simple, functional freeways. Pragmatism set the tone of this report, titled *A Transit Program for the Los Angeles Metropolitan Area:* "[The board] considers that the most effective measures will be those which will most radically change the overall speed of transit of private vehicles and mass transportation carriers in moving persons and property over the long distances which it is necessary to traverse in the Los Angeles Metropolitan Area."[26] Instead of cutting through the built-up downtown district, let alone its buildings, these freeways would skirt the area wherever possible, avoiding additional costly construction projects: "In general, motorway buildings and parking projects were considered to be more properly ventures for private enterprise."[27] Elevated sections would surmount cross streets,

FIGURE 50. Reminiscent of King's dreams: a doctored photo illus-
trates bridges connecting motorway buildings. From Automobile
Club of Southern California (Engineering Department), *Traffic Survey:
Los Angeles Metropolitan Area* (Los Angeles: Automobile Club of
Southern California, 1937), 34. Courtesy of the kind permission of
the Automobile Club of Southern California Archives.

FIGURE 51. Arroyo Seco Parkway, opening day, 1940. From California Department of Public Works, Division of Highways.

but the roadways were designed for efficiency, not dramatic effect, and would make use of elaborate and expensive grade separation structures only where necessary.

More importantly, although the report discussed the virtues of full parkway width and plantings, these roadways would generally lie on the same restricted rights of way in developed and undeveloped parts of the region. Landscaping costs would be reduced by depressing the roadway, wherever possible, and planting on the cuts, thus facilitating grade separations and reducing the need for additional noise buffers. Thus the plan largely abandons the formal parkways intrinsic to the earlier reports. The visions of planners and landscape architects had been replaced by the more calculated pragmatism of public engineers, and the relation of the roadway to the surrounding environment—so important to both the vertical sublime and the parkway aesthetic—was deemphasized as a design priority.

The effects of this transformation in thought were immediate and dramatic. The Arroyo Seco Parkway—which had been under construction since 1938, and for which plans had circulated since the Robinson Report of 1909—was, midway through, quietly redesigned as a freeway. Although it ran along the bed of a virtually undeveloped seasonal riverbed that had long been preserved for future park use, the road as constructed clearly emphasized speed of transit over scenic ameni-

FIGURE 52. Utilitarian urbanism: Cahuenga Freeway with Pacific Electric Red Car in center divider, 1948. Within a couple of years, the rapid transit right of way would be removed in favor of more lanes for automobiles. Courtesy of the kind permission of Pacific Railroad Publications.

ties (much of the surrounding landscape was not even visible, obscured by concrete retaining walls and culverts, as can be seen in figure 51). Although it retained its parkway title until the late 1940s, when it suddenly became the Arroyo Seco Freeway, it never conformed to the parkway aesthetic. Even more significant for freeway advocates was the so-called Cahuenga Parkway, which began construction in 1939. This roadway was intended from the design stages as an express route, cutting off the surrounding scenic hillsides with concrete embankments, and with a high-speed Pacific Electric interurban line down its center (see figure 52). Eventually extended to form a link in the Hollywood Parkway (which, by the time it was completed, was renamed the Hollywood Freeway), the new road resembled nothing so much as the Detroit and Chicago superhighway plans of the 1920s and early 1930s. These Southern California construction projects clearly inspired some of the enthusiasm in the 1941 Telesis show for future freeway plans—now understood in

Los Angeles not as utopian fantasies but as practical devices. The Arroyo Seco and Cahuenga Freeways ensured that any future planning vision for the metropolis would now include freeways as basic transport infrastructure.

MAGIC MOTORWAYS

The machine age is here to stay.

CLARENCE DYKSTRA, "THE FUTURE OF LOS ANGELES" (8)

Despite the evident enthusiasm for the nascent freeways in 1941 Los Angeles, the utility and scale of the contemporary freeway plans do not by themselves explain the prominence of these new roadways in the Telesis show. In fact, the direct inspiration for the vision of freeways in the exhibit and its accompanying publications, and for the reborn planning effort in Southern California, was once more a product of the exemplary vertical city to the east. In 1939 and 1940, New York City, to great national acclaim, presented the World's Fair. Probably the most famous display at that celebrated exhibition, and the most influential upon urban visionaries, was the General Motors Futurama exhibit produced by Norman Bel Geddes (see figure 53). Futurama, based on Bel Geddes's earlier explorations of the freeway concept, envisioned a city of "1960" reminiscent of Hugh Ferriss's drawings.[28]

Here freeways coursed between differentiated and well-spaced towers, while pedestrians (all visitors to the fair) promenaded on second-story arcades. Of course, the automobiles on display were all vintage 1939, this being the GM pavilion, but the rest of the presentation was uniformly futuristic. A powerful mythology of the Machine Age made such utopian modernity seem somehow inevitable. The overriding theme of the show—that the freeway would soon ensure both more harmonious urban life and easy access to the scenic and recreational potential of the countryside—impressed many visitors.

Perhaps even more influential than this overt message was the medium by which it was transmitted. Bel Geddes, best known up to this point as a noted stage set designer, was a master of compelling design, and the exhibit employed a series of innovative techniques to immerse the spectator in the representation. Most significantly, the viewer did not simply meander through the show space—in fact, he or she did not walk at all. Individual oversized chairs attached to a flexible track laid into the floor pulled the visitor through the display rooms at a steady, controlled pace.

As viewers were transported through the many rooms of the show, they passed by a series of elaborate and detailed models while a voice-over (with swelling musical accompaniment)—projected through speakers installed in the moving chair and keyed to its progress—described the action. Bel Geddes was impressed with the narrative power of film, and the entire exhibit can be thought of as an extended

FIGURE 53. Multilevel arcaded streets for Futurama visitors, 1939. From *To New Horizons* by General Motors (1940).

sequence of quasi-filmic representations. The exhibit was arranged in a logical serial manner, with a cohesive plot that traced the movement of the freeway through a series of American landscapes (or the viewer's progress, from the perspective of a small aircraft, over and along that roadway and through these settings). From countryside to the (supposedly midwestern) skyscraper city, the freeway traversed the topography of the heartland. As it entered the towering metropolis, the scale changed, zooming the viewer in, so to speak, on an even more impressively precise depiction of the road and its surroundings. Eventually, the scale resolved to that of real life, and the tourist departed the moving chair and emerged as a pedestrian on one of the arcaded second-story urban walkways.[29]

Surrounded by contemporary GM cars whizzing past, standing on a fully realized futuristic street corner, the tourist received the full impact of this directed immersion in the extended narrative. This new mode of presentation, which owes much to cinema and influenced the modern theme park, did not just vividly convey the larger messages of the exhibition. Rather it staged, even enacted, a particular way of perceiving the world. Although not consistently at freeway level, the sweeping, narrativized trip through the spaces of the attraction replicated some of the experience of driving on one of these envisioned motorways. In fact, it recapitulated, in more literal form, the illusion Sigfried Giedion identified in 1941 as the central impression derived from driving over a well-crafted modern parkway: the sensation of flying above the road surface.

By simulating an exciting and vertiginous motorway driving experience for the spectators, many of whom had undoubtedly never driven such a roadway (with the brief exception, perhaps, of those short parkway stretches Robert Moses had just constructed to link the suburban World's Fair to Manhattan), Futurama powerfully reinforced its intended message. In effect, the exhibit offered a preview of both the visceral sensory experience of driving a freeway and the way a freeway driver perceives a landscape. The ride portrayed the countryside and, especially, the city as if viewed through the window of a moving car, thus reinforcing the imminence and desirability of the motorway future. It actively modeled, in a pleasurable and recreational manner, the sensations of freeway driving and of seeing the city from the perspective of the urban motorway. In essence, this unusual mode of presentation— where the spectator does not consciously "read" the exhibit but instead "experiences" it from a vivid first-person perspective—served the ideological ends of the show particularly well.[30]

. . . AND NOW WE PLAN

In this fully established, industrial time, the far-stretching, formless city of Los Angeles has come into being. It is a metropolitan area of a thousand square miles and more. . . . It sprawls like a great puppy on the rug before the comfortable fire! . . . The need of our times, of our far-flung potential city, is a comprehensive master plan!

REMSEN D. BIRD, "METROPOLITAN SYMPHONY"

It was this experiential, linear, first-person diegetic technology and its connection to the freeway form that most impressed the Telesis group in their design of ". . . And Now We Plan." Although staging a presentation like Futurama was far beyond their means, they used some of the concepts from Futurama for their own ends. As *Westways,* the organ of the Automobile Club of Southern California, described it, the Telesis show was organized as an instructive trip through the region's history: "Scenes of the Los Angeles area, reproduced in miniature sets, typify the stages of development Los Angeles has passed through. And in other sets and charts, the rapid growth of the city is shown to be responsible for some of the illogical, haphazard developments. Highways, freeways, recreational areas and housing projects show the solution to growing congestion."[31] The logic of the show, taking the visitor from display to display, made the Progressive message seem inevitable, arising naturally from the juxtaposition of images and messages. The developments of the first four decades of the twentieth century in Southern California were effectively cast as a

FIGURE 54. Theatrical sets vividly present the blighted city. From ". . . Now We Plan,"
California Arts and Architecture 57, no. 11 (1941): 22.

series of tragic mistakes caused by the lack of proper urban planning—a legacy that
led inexorably to the contemporary city, with its disorganization, blight, and sprawl,
all of which could only be ameliorated by proper freeway planning.

But significantly, this linear series of "miniature sets" was not conceived or staged
in a normal museum exhibition space, where patrons are free to wander among displays. Instead, the exhibit had a rigid, deterministic logic to it, as the *Los Angeles
Times* admiringly attested: "Once you start into it, it's almost like entering the Fun
House. There is only one way to go, through curving spaces and corridors. You see
everything in sequence from start to finish. The show tells a complete story."[32] Like
Futurama, ". . . And Now We Plan" presented its sequential narrative in a deterministic fashion, allowing visitors only one way to experience the show (see figures
54 and 55).

The imitation of Futurama's novel mode of presentation was certainly intentional,
and Telesis accessed an impressive range of modern design talent in putting together
their show. As Arthur Millier informs us, "Architect Richard Neutra provided the
initial layout for the exhibit. . . . Industrial Designer Walter Baermann, one of the

FIGURE 55. Didactic corridors channel the flow of information. From ". . . Now We Plan," *California Arts and Architecture* 57, no. 11 (1941): 22.

pioneers in staging this type of controlled, special-built display, was technical advisor."[33] In addition to this local expertise, actual Futurama sets and technical advice were provided by none other than Norman Bel Geddes's consulting firm.[34]

Although certainly not as vivid and immersive—but making extensive use in its own right of projected images and synchronized recordings—the Telesis show duplicated something of the medium and message of the famous New York attraction. This mimesis also analogically replicated the experience of freeway driving. The (pedestrian) Los Angeles County Museum visitor and the (transported) Futurama tourist both experienced a focused narrative that not only sold the freeway as a necessary feature of daily life but recapitulated a bit of the experience of driving along one of these corridors.

Whereas ordinary urban automotive navigation of the era freely allowed the driver to stop, pull off the road, or entirely change direction quite frequently (at the end of each block, generally), the freeway severely constricts this range of possibilities. The road allows access and egress only at long intervals, even framing what the driver is able to see to some extent (although, in most cases, not in the calculated manner of a motor parkway), producing at times the illusion that the automobile and driver exist on a separate experiential, and not just spatial, plane from the surrounding topography. In perceiving this novel deployment of urban space, it often seems less as if one moves through the city, plotting definite courses, than as if the city instead moves around the driver, recomposing itself only when the car exits the immersive motorway environment.

"... And Now We Plan" provided Angelenos with a preview of life in an idyllic planned metropolis of freeways and clustered garden communities. It managed to meld generations of earlier urban imagining—its authors now apparently forgotten—with a strikingly contemporary vision of advanced transport infrastructures. In so doing, it was able for a time to resuscitate Ebenezer Howard's 1890s garden city model as a thoroughly modern form of urbanity. Presented through these new modes of publicity and representation, the exhibit promised, at last, to involve Angelenos in the planning project—at least as spectators, if not actual decision makers. The imagination of this new generation of planners would, to some extent, be openly shared with the region's citizens. In an era of Machine Age top-down central planning, this sort of public participation must have seemed progressive indeed.

On 7 December 1941, six weeks into the planned four-month run of the exhibit at the County Museum, the imagination and attention of Angelenos, along with other Americans', were suddenly jolted across the Pacific. In the tumult attending the onset of World War II, Telesis's work, which had for a brief time transfixed local media and culture, immediately faded into obscurity.[35] During the war, the city would be as substantially transformed as it had been during the tumultuous, explosive 1920s—a transformation that would eventually, after great struggle, fundamentally upset the clear order of racial, class, and gender segregation operative in the region. In the war's aftermath, freeways would be designed and built in Southern California, but not to anchor garden communities and not, in fact, by planners. The famous system of roads that gave Los Angeles so much of its postwar definition was implemented by professional state engineers at the California Division of Highways—who, especially in the early years, paid little heed to local urban contexts and visions. And of course, in the decades to come, new generations of Angelenos would periodically bemoan the unplanned, "sprawling" shape of the megalopolis, declaring, as if for the first time, "... And Now We Plan."

Conclusion

"To Dream Dreams and See Visions"

In the hopeful years of the early 1920s, before the metropolis spun away from its reassuring concentric form, Los Angeles's planners felt confident in their ability to plan their metropolis. They possessed powerful techniques and knowledge that would reveal the city to their comprehensive gaze, making the mysteries of the urban form fully apparent. This confidence was still at its height in the summer of 1924, when planning director-manager Gordon Whitnall addressed a national meeting of city planning experts. Here Whitnall assumed the mantle of the seer or the booster; where others only saw an existing metropolis, he foresaw the incipient city of tomorrow in the process of becoming. This, after all, had always been the promise of planning: to "Dream dreams and see Visions," to grasp the future of the city in advance and thus be able to prepare for that destiny. "We find ourselves in the peculiar position of being a community in its inception, and yet with a fair realization of what the future holds in store," Whitnall proclaimed.[1]

The future the confident planners of Southern California were charting for their metropolis was radical, for it departed from all existing precedent. These planners felt "an obligation to prevent the recurrence of those mistakes which have happened in the growth of metropolitan areas in the east."[2] As Whitnall declared to his peers, most of whom worked in metropolitan areas in the East, "We know too the mistakes that were made in the east and to a degree the things that contributed to those mistakes." Los Angeles would not follow their example. This place, "the better city," would not crowd its residents into congested and blighted tenement blocks or pack them into cold and sunless towers, but would instead set forth a new model of American urban life. As Whitnall acknowledged so defiantly before the assembled planners, "We still have our chance, if we live up to our opportunities of showing the right way of doing things. It will not be the west looking back to the east to learn how not to do it, but the east looking to the west to see how it should be done." "This," he concluded, "is our regional ambition for Southern California."[3]

REQUIEM FOR THE PLANNERS

The great distinction between the Los Angeles metropolitan district and any other such area is that our metropolis in embryo has recognized its future even before that future has been reached.

GORDON WHITNALL, "CITY AND REGIONAL PLANNING IN LOS ANGELES" (105)

By the mid-1930s, it had become abundantly clear that Southern California would not be exactly the paragon its ambitious planners intended. The region was by now a sprawling, jumbled mass of urbanity that seemed to evade all efforts at comprehension. It was also clear that the cherished future of clustered garden cities would not be the example Southern California would provide for the rest of the country. Two decades of garden city dreams had missed their real opportunity for realization, despite intermittent later revivals, as a result of a loss of vision, political failure, and economic depression. The time had passed. Planning had not ultimately turned Southern California into a new urban paradise. Now, that profession, far from shaping the fate of an entire region, seemed barely to survive at all.

Despite these defeats, though, Whitnall had been correct: Los Angeles had indeed been wrenched from its traditional concentric form. Because the planners' radical and ambitious schemes were not ultimately realized in Southern California, a number of historians have determined that the 1920s generation of regional planners failed in their aims. In a literal and real sense, this verdict is certainly correct. Some of these historians have suggested further that planning in Greater Los Angeles was an even greater failure because so much potential lay in the region and planners were so early aware of that great opportunity. This pronouncement too is largely accurate. The enthusiastic and confident rhetoric of so many planning professionals during the period testifies to the tangible disappointment many of them later felt at the seemingly chaotic pattern of actual development, but by the 1930s, the city had truly become quite unlike metropolises of the East. Those observers who have implied that these planners were ineffectual in the end—that despite their promise and efforts they were ultimately unable to affect the development of the growing metropolitan region—are simply wrong.[4]

Planners did not, in the end, remake the metropolis as they desired, but they did nevertheless remake it. By 1930, Los Angeles had broken the mold of American urbanity; it had become a large metropolis without being significantly centralized and concentrated. This sort of decentralization planners had valued above all else. Although sometimes seen as a curse today, urban disaggregation was seen at the time as a radical and utopian notion in an era of ever more densely packed tenements and skyscrapers. Southern Californian planners triumphantly oversaw the decline of concentric urbanism in Los Angeles, but their second, more visionary, goal of remaking Greater Los Angeles as a cluster of garden cities was at best only half successful. It is true that many elements of the imagined, intended city persisted through the twentieth century and that over time countless spots of planned garden city style development came to dot the map of the region. Nevertheless, Southern California became a postsuburban, sprawling megalopolis instead of a balanced and neighborly region of clustered garden communities. Here again, though, Whitnall was right in 1924: many other (often western) metropolises followed Los Angeles's lead in this respect over the ensuing decades.

Of course, those who had a voice in the development of Southern California during the 1920s—not just the various groups of expert planners but the real estate subdividers, the automobile commuters, the swarms of car-borne immigrants, the downtown political and business interests, the dreamers and boosters—never intended that Los Angeles should become a postsuburban region. Whether traditional centralized metropolis (including the spread-out suburban variations), pastoral Mediterranean resort, or idealized cluster of garden cities, the various dreams of a future Los Angeles never seemed to contemplate the sprawling, multicentered, fragmented city that was coming into being at the end of the 1920s. Southern California's strange postsuburban topography was not simply the result of isolated natural developments, specific technologies, prevailing ideologies, scientific plans, uncontrolled and random growth, but was a combination of all these intentionalities and coincidences in a short span of time. This first postsuburban metropolis arose out of the juxtaposition of many conflicting desires and programs. Indeed, contrary to conventional wisdom, Greater Los Angeles's urban form was planned; in fact, it was overdetermined by plans. In a sense, then, Greater Los Angeles was the product of a mélange of ideal, possible, imagined cities; its eventual shape was a product of divergent dreams, all acting on the same urban landscape. That in so short a period—a single decade—so many groups attempted to implement so many divergent visions and dreams in Los Angeles testifies to the practical impossibility of any single group being able to monopolize the right to comprehend and plan the metropolis.

Ultimately, for their part, Southern Californian planners had failed to unite this vast collection of local visionaries behind their garden city plan. For all their emphasis on vision, they proved unable to listen—and to explain—when necessary. Their efforts to guide the development of the region by scientific means, without public scrutiny, ended, like so many Progressive Era projects, mired in city politics and economics. Sticking to their plans despite growing evidence that the ideological consensus was eroding, planners displayed not merely a surprising lack of political judgment but a larger conceptual inflexibility. They seemed unable to adapt to changing topographical and cultural realities. And this fatal rigidity seems, in retrospect, to be a product of their cherished urban vision. These experts were unable to resist the tantalizing clarity of the garden city model, with its diagrammatic modes of representation. Planners assumed that the sort of abstract functional simplicity revealed in Ebenezer Howard's alluring, deceptively neat sketches would guarantee an efficient and harmonious community. The self-evident logic of the map overrode any potential reconsiderations of urban form derived from theoretical adjustment or empirical observation. The built city could never live up to the potential of the plan. Nevertheless, the garden city promised an absolute topographical orderliness that was just too attractive to give up, even as planners throughout the 1920s encountered mounting resistance from local elites and even more troublesome developments on the ground.

The fact that planners, in particular, failed to adapt their observational techniques to allow them to make sense of the new postsuburban topography must stand as the most damning indictment of those charged with clearly seeing the city around them. All along, these professionals had simply assumed that a rejection of the seemingly "autocratic" concentric mode of urban organization would force the city into a new structure based around the autonomous neighborhood unit and the locally preferred single-family home. Instead of either metaphoric pole, however, a new sort of community gradually emerged, one that preserved the larger urban community characteristic of traditional concentric urbanism but removed the central business district from its position of absolute dominance. A distributed and decentered form, this postsuburban topography tied more and more of the Southern Californian region into a unitary but heterogeneous whole. This new urban configuration conformed to no ideal map but was there nevertheless. Instead of properly identifying and cogently analyzing this nascent postsuburbanization, most local planners, like other observers, saw only chaotic and alienating sprawl. The resultant crisis in urban legibility was a significant failure for those who so recently had boldly claimed to "Dream dreams and see Visions" of a better city.

AN ARCHAEOLOGY OF LOST VISIONS

For all their manifest failures of comprehensive vision during the Jazz Age, Los Angeles's planners had not entirely failed in their attempts at perception. Indeed, perhaps the most profound and long-lasting effects of the planning tradition of the 1920s in Southern California were more in the realm of the imagination, of common sense ideology, than in a shifting and overdetermined urban topography. These experts were blinded by their own urban epistemologies—ways of seeing the city that proved particularly ill adapted to the new postsuburban topography. Nevertheless, an alternative set of possibilities lay implicit and largely unacknowledged in the history of urban perception in Jazz Age Los Angeles. Although never fully recognized at the time, these new ways of looking occasionally emerged, even in the mid-1920s, as musings or speculation in the discourse of leading planners. Crucially, although they were unable to act upon their insights, Southern Californian professional planners did manage, over the years, to hit upon a couple of entirely novel techniques for making sense of the disturbing new landscape of postsuburbia. Little noticed at the time, these new epistemic tools would eventually become commonplace, thereby helping Angelenos of later years make sense of their disordered cityscape. Subtly present in various forms in many writings, lectures, and presentations of Southern California planners during the decade, the new tools for perceiving the metropolis were expressed most clearly in a speech delivered by Gordon Whitnall in 1924, when planning in Southern California was still charged with potential and hope, naïveté and hubris.

Whitnall began that talk in Philadelphia not with bold declarations of Los Angeles's destiny (that was left for his conclusion) but with a personal story. It was an account of an afternoon in April 1923, when the planner had ascended above the tangled landscape of Greater Los Angeles in a small airplane: "The Regional Planning Commission, in connection with topographically mapping out [the] whole district, was instrumental in securing aerial photographs. . . . It was my privilege, preceding the taking of the picture, to have an opportunity of seeing Los Angeles from the altitude of 12,000 feet."[5] Whitnall then described to his audience at the national city planning conference what he had seen from that privileged position. In a doubled sense, Whitnall was prepared to share (albeit only with other planners) his expert perspective over the growing Southern California region as a whole—and what he saw in the mid-1920s would remain prescient over the decades that followed, despite the subsequent decline of the planning profession in the Greater Los Angeles area.

As a professional planner looking from 12,000 feet, Whitnall could make out patterns in the countryside below that were invisible to other Angelenos in their daily lives:

> From this elevation many people would only see GROUND, but I saw what appeared to be a whole section of rusty fly screen that somebody, in a fit of temper, had thrown to the ground, causing it to break into portions, the central portion remaining relatively intact and relatively large, with one portion of it on the corner almost detached and connected with a few strands of wire. That was the metropolitan street system. I never appreciated before how all but essentials were screened out from that elevation, and how easy it would be to analyze a particular thing because there was nothing else to analyze.[6]

Here the elevated vantage point affords the trained expert a comprehensive and panoramic perspective over the discontinuous and fragmented landscape below.

This was, of course, the promise of such a towering observation point, and Whitnall makes clear that from such a spot the countless warps and threads of the growing city's urban fabric—the people, buildings, neighborhoods, social relations and interactions, and the like—faded from sight. This "screening out" of such social detail left behind a clear and precise image of the sprawling metropolis. From this remove, the city neatly resolved into a sort of map of itself. Los Angeles achieved a clarity from the air invisible from the ground.

Was this sort of perspective the answer to Los Angeles's developing crisis of legibility, this lapse of urban comprehensibility that would, over the next few years, particularly stymie planners and ordinary Angelenos alike? Couldn't the powerful epistemological tools developed in the vertical cities of the East be applied here? Unfortunately, as it soon becomes clear from Whitnall's talk, this sort of perspective, available to easterners every day, really could not restore comprehensibility to the fragmented and deconcentrated landscape developing in Southern California. To reach a comprehensive perspective over this vast city—already in the mid-1920s beginning to sprawl chaotically, spreading in a fragmented and disordered fashion over the entire region—an observer would be required to ascend over two miles. Clearly, the privileged vantage point offered by an elevated spot centered over the core of the concentric city—the leverage supporting the skyscraper observation deck's panoramic perspective—was quite simply unavailable to observers of this sprawling metropolis.

Even Whitnall's survey airplane offered no real solution, for even if such travel became as ubiquitous as skyscraper utopians predicted, this transient point of observation could not be identified from the ground. In this case, the observation deck was but a speck buzzing among the clouds. Ultimately, a lone survey plane, on the mission of a single spring morning, could never serve as the same kind of meaningful orientation point as that offered by the clustered towers of the Chicago Loop or Manhattan. Even if the airplane delivered a comprehensive perspective, it could not fulfill the corresponding epistemological function of the observation deck of the modern skyscraper: a point from which to observe that could itself be easily seen and located.

Aside from the practical impossibility of constructing an accessible, permanent point this high—even the most exalted and lofty of modern skyscrapers did not reach one-tenth the height of Whitnall's survey plane—such an elevation would render the observed street grid below entirely unidentifiable; it was merely a "screen."[7] Inevitably, a fixed and identifiable spot lofty enough to panoramically take in such a vast expanse would require an elevation from which the urban landmarks below would fade into fuzzy obscurity. As a mechanism of panoramic and comprehensive clarity, then, the elevated perspective was simply inapplicable in Los Angeles. Obviously, the epistemic tools so powerful and available in vertical metropolises would prove entirely ineffective in this new horizontal city.

A NEW MODE OF PERCEPTION: THE MOBILE GAZE

Whitnall acknowledged in his talk that an altitude sufficient for taking in the entire expanse of the sprawling metropolis actually rendered the topography below indistinct and undifferentiated. After having established the frame from 12,000 feet, the director of planning had therefore ordered the plane to descend "down to an elevation of 6000 feet." From this height, insufficient to take in the entire sweep of settlement below, Whitnall recounted that he suddenly saw what was not visible from the comprehensive position above: "There entered into the picture elements of depth and color, and—you would think I am fanciful—an element of motion. I mean a motion of cities, the growing, flowing, advancing motion of the physical conditions of communities that in the expansion process are encroaching on each other." Previously, Whitnall had observed through the epistemic lens of the survey map, but now he sees through a different sort of filter. The landscape of Southern California, so often projected to the nation as movie set or a booster destination, now resolves itself though the eyes of the visionary planner, metaphorically. Greater Los Angeles was a motion picture: "It was really visible through power of reason, aided by the sense of sight. I could see the motion just as I have seen, through the expedient of the motion picture, motion come out of that which did not seem to move." This simile described the envisioned development of the land below: "I could understand that in the ordinary process of development this motion would continue and communities would continue to merge, so that finally they would be one."[8] Whitnall's metaphor expressed the planners' central observational mission—to project over time, to visualize the future development of the metropolis. Southern California was destined to be not a collection of discrete and self-contained communities but, for all intents and purposes, a single integrated metropolis.

Perhaps even more usefully, though, Whitnall's notion of Southern California as a motion picture mirrors the planner's sequence of narration and inspection; he had used his viewing apparatus, the airplane in this case, to gradually zoom in from the establishing shot of 12,000 feet to a relative close-up at half that distance. This latter shot could no longer frame the entire region, but instead took it in by stages, continually panning over the landscape. In this movement, Whitnall abandoned the planner's favored universal and comprehensive perspective for a new mode of perception that revealed the city more clearly. In so doing, Whitnall modeled a critical epistemic mode, a perceptual tool, that would become more and more important for Angelenos in the following decades. By reducing his elevation—zooming in—from the abstract perspective of the topographic map or the observation deck, Whitnall reflected that the urban witness could now detect both actual and virtual motion. The city is a moving thing, composed of moving people, and the airplane that revealed this movement was also in constant motion. Although the metropolis was already too large and disordered to be conceived as a whole, the movement of the survey airplane as it circled above the city produced a very different—and much more useful—image than that perceptible from a fixed observation point. This was a sequential image, a synthetic amalgam of discrete and partial snapshots linked serially by the action of a scanning, moving gaze. By traveling through urban space, by taking the city in serially instead of comprehensively, the aircraft reveals the city progressively, as a series of perceived sequences. These sequences compose themselves in the observer's mind as recognizable virtual corridors, familiar linear passages in space. This implicit recognition of the "path" (in Kevin Lynch's terminology) or the "route" (in that of Michel de Certeau) as a means of ordering and perceiving urban space was the first of the planner's two great unrecognized insights of the Jazz Age.

This mode of perception is, as Whitnall noted at the time, analogous to the type of perception at work in cinematic spectatorship during this period. As individual shots connect to produce narrative cinema, and as countless moving cameras traced seemingly random routes across the Los Angeles cityscape, these fragmented perceived snapshots of the city could be assembled in the active mind of the viewer (or resident) into a coherent and legible whole. Although neither Whitnall nor any other Angelenos fully realized it at the time, this mode of perception—which film theorist Anne Friedberg has termed the "virtualized mobile gaze"—is typical of the experience a motorist has driving through a landscape.[9]

Sigfried Giedion was probably the first person to make this perceptual mode fully explicit, when in 1941 he described what he took to be the fundamental importance of the modern automotive parkway: "As with many other creations born out of the spirit of this age, the meaning and beauty of the parkway cannot be grasped from a single point of observation, as was possible when from a window of the château of Versailles the whole expanse of nature could be embraced in one view. It can be revealed only by movement."[10] For Giedion, the parkway, which requires that a mobile gaze be perceived comprehensively, defines a new, more modern mode of perception. The fixed vantage point dominant in Western notions of perception since the Renaissance was now giving way, in Giedion's view, to a new observational epistemology. No longer was the fixed panoramic perspective privileged; exemplary contemporary spaces could never be fully perceived from one point of view, but only by the observer's movement through time and space.[11]

The mobile gaze was, in essence, a decentered perspective appropriate for a decentralized urban landscape. Perhaps if planners had realized the epistemological potential of the mobile gaze during this critical period, they might have proposed a parkway system for Southern California integrated into the surrounding urban topography rather than dedicated to occluding it. Planners of the 1920s never fully recognized the radical implications of that airplane survey, and thus remained devoted to deriving a fixed, diagrammatic comprehensive perspective over a metropolis that more and more evaded such totalistic perception. Planners during the 1920s and 1930s would ultimately fail to translate the epistemology of the mobile gaze into the built environment of Southern California. Yet, although this subtle epistemic insight, never fully realized or expressed, would have little immediate effect—Angelenos remained largely confused by their city's form during this period—it would eventually prove valuable in everyday practice.

In the years to come, with the aid of the postwar freeway system, Angelenos would increasingly find themselves able to link comprehensible and familiar urban landmarks into a network of known routes, a matrix of comfortable passageways within the larger cityscape. Touring the metropolis, deploying their mobile gazes, Angelenos could individually impose legible order upon the more familiar realms of their city. Without reference to any universal fixed locating point in this flat and expansive metropolis, citizens would be able to construct their own relative cognitive maps. Their individual movements would gradually offer Angelenos a way to make sense of their sprawling and discordant postsuburban topography. Although the metropolis as a whole would remain disturbingly blurred and vague, each resident might now at least make sense of familiar spaces within it. This was not a comprehensive schema that could necessarily be shared, and it certainly was not a universal order like that conveyed within the concentric metropolis, but it was a new epistemology of urban perception that would better allow Angelenos to make sense of their postsuburban cityscape.

A NEW MODERN SUBLIME:
THE HORIZONTAL METROPOLIS

From this new way of knowing urban topography would emerge an appropriate new aesthetics of urban form. One can detect traces of this new aesthetic—the planners' second foundational insight—in that same planning conference address of 1924. Gordon Whitnall admitted that he could not see much from 12,000 feet. The topography of the land—hills and valleys, tall business districts and low-slung housing developments—all merged into one indistinguishable mass of sprawling urbanity. Yet from this abstract, "screened" perspective the planner had an epiphany, as he recounted in his talk of 1924: "Just one more thought as to what really constitutes our regional district here in Southern California. Not until a year ago this month did the full realization come to me in striking form of its inherent unity."[12] Here, the planner says, he recognized the full extent of the region's growth; like so many others over the next decades, he saw Greater Los Angeles stretching beyond the horizon.

But instead of seeing this emerging geography as a chaotic and unhealthy development, as did so many later observers, Whitnall perceived in this far-flung urbanism a new manifest destiny for Southern California. This would never become a true vertical city of skyscrapers; instead it would be a horizontal metropolis. In his conference paper, Whitnall expresses awe at the sheer extent of this perceived potential horizontality, as yet only hinted at in the built topography below. This recognition convinced the planner that Los Angeles was destined to depart from the traditional model of urban development.[13] This future metropolis, Whitnall prophesied, would remain an expansive, planar place, devouring the surrounding countryside in its metropolitan embrace. What the rational expert in urban observation found at 12,000 feet was a new awe and appreciation for a novel mode of modern urbanity. This perceived cityscape now appeared not as ugly, chaotic sprawl but as a planar expanse that might even be impressive, or even—especially at night—beautiful. We might explain this sudden insight, this epiphany, as a recognition of a new modern urban grandeur. It was a horizontal sublime.[14]

What had looked random and disordered on a survey map now seemed progressive and modern, a new sort of better city. In the years after 1924, Whitnall began to consider, if only speculatively, metaphorically, and tentatively, new ways of conceptualizing, and appreciating, the potential of the horizontal metropolis of the future. It was central to this new imagination not to focus on the autonomous garden city, or even a cluster of loosely linked garden cities, but to think instead in terms of the entire metropolitan region—the vast expanse instead of the discrete unit. The planner began by reconsidering the proper relationship between part and whole in Greater Los Angeles: "Whatever the future holds in store for the metropolitan district must happen within the confines of the 800 square miles of the greater Los Angeles. The many municipal units which occupy this area are being rapidly filled in and are assuming a relationship to each other very much like the sections of an orange inside the skin. Daily the intervening territory between these urban units is becoming less and less until it is not difficult to prophesy the day when the whole 800 square miles will become largely urbanized."[15] As Whitnall surmised in another article published the same year, the future of Greater Los Angeles might be one not of municipal fragmentation but of practical unification: "The plastic communities here are rapidly crystallizing into a gigantic metropolis."[16] This was clearly an extension of his earlier "Declaration of Interdependence" among the region's separate cities, yet here the idea was developing into something much more powerful and ambitious.

Whitnall would go on to explain the ramifications of his insight in a series of papers presented to planning conferences over the next couple of years. In these talks, the planner laid out the beginnings of a coherent and useful way of conceiving the postsuburban metropolis to come. Indeed, in 1926, the year it became absolutely clear that Los Angeles would not become a predominantly vertical city, Whitnall began to speculate more boldly on how such a "gigantic metropolis" might actually function. In this task, the planner evoked as representative the image of a contrivance of steel and glass fully as modern as the skyscraper—the automobile. In an almost entirely inappropriate lecture before an audience of planners in central Florida, misleadingly titled "The Place of the East Coast in a State Plan for Florida," Whitnall expounded upon the exceptional regional structure of Southern California. Greater Los Angeles, he told his no-doubt puzzled peers, demonstrated a new way to envision the modern city:

> Let me take the modern, well-known mechanism known as a Ford. Every Ford has four wheels; that is, when it leaves the factory; it has an engine—they call it that; a carburetor, a transmission, a steering gear, and all of the other smaller incidental details which it must have in every detail before it can operate as a complete, independent mechanism. Now, the only differences between a Ford and a Rolls-Royce are price, color scheme, size, and other conditions of refinement, but basically they are identical. So that if you are dealing with an automobile, you must of necessity have a complete automobile, regardless of the model or regardless of the price.[17]

The contemporary metropolis, Whitnall conjectured, may appear to operate like an automobile—with clearly demarcated functions and mechanisms—but it did not have to be put together like an automobile:

> It is not necessary, in the case of communities, to have in each of them a carburetor and an engine and four wheels and a steering gear, and the other what-nots. One community may be composed wholly of an engine, and, if I may carry the simile to the extreme, another may consist wholly of upholstery.[18]

Each municipality, or part thereof, had always been thought of by planners as a more or less autonomous and discrete mechanism. Like an automobile, it would not function if it did not have all the necessary parts: a Ford without an engine or wheels would simply fail to move. This was the logic behind the overwhelming concentric metropolis, and it was the logic too of the autonomous garden city.

Whitnall now insisted that the analogy was flawed. Planners in Southern California were realizing that self-sufficiency and autonomy had no real purpose in a metropolitan region where residents could make full use not only of their own neighborhood, their own community, but of the surrounding communities: "We have already recognized that it is no longer necessary for one community, regardless of size, to have all of the component parts that we used to consider necessary to make a community."[19] The reigning common sense of planning assumed, Whitnall argued, that the basic unit of human community—whether village, town, or city—was necessarily a discrete entity. This assumption had led over the years to inefficiency in urban organization, as he argued a year later: "Where we have left each of these individual cities to its own devices it has attempted to become a complete Ford,—each one wanted its carburetor, its wheels, its upholstery, etc.,—but we find that that is economic waste."[20] Now, Whitnall suggested, it was desirable to streamline the region's structure by using the powers of county planning agencies to eliminate redundancies and duplications among urban forms: "By emphasizing the elements of regional zoning we are actually accomplishing a setting aside of whole communities for one type of activity." Each part could be taken in relation to the whole, and each town would be planned solely in light of "the best function of the community" to the larger region.[21] Southern California might remain a collection of discrete cities, each with its own character and polity, but they would be functionally integrated into a larger metropolitan structure. In terms of economic operation, Greater Los Angeles, stretching from the ocean to the desert and from Orange County to Ventura County, would be the only truly autonomous entity; every individual city within this vast collection would rely upon and feed into the larger whole.

Whitnall's tentative, metaphorical model of urban organization represents a potential third schematic type of metropolis. This would not be a centralized skyscraper metropolis, but neither would it be a cluster of autonomous garden cities. It was a dream of urban decentralization, but a new vision of deconcentration—a middle ground between the extreme poles of garden city autarky and anarchic sprawl. In the mid-1920s, Whitnall was unable to express his insight clearly. In these public talks, he could only hint at what he perceived. Perhaps one reason for the lack of clarity was that the planner got lost in his own poetic and allusive language; he got his metaphors inextricably bound together. Whitnall's reference to the Ford automobile, in particular, was hopelessly overdetermined. Although he appears not to realize his confusion, the planner is clearly thinking not only of the Ford but of Fordism as well. He points to the autonomous automobile (the Model-T) but refers inferentially to its exemplary mode of production (the assembly line process). This image is as much a representation of the mode of the Ford's production as of its individual and functional anatomy. The Southern California pictured here is one of interchangeable, reproducible parts, where exact location in the production process is less important than functional contribution to the ultimate outcome. Each part of the Ford could be produced independently, in almost any sequence. Only the final assembly—the most visible part of the Ford process, but certainly not the most important—was synchronous. The serial order dictated by the production line represented merely the exigencies of efficient assembly. There was little intrinsic necessity in the precise order of production; in fact, most essential work was carried out simultaneously at various stages along the chain of suppliers. It is this separation of production subprocesses, with interchangeable and standardized parts, that made the Ford mode of production famous, and it was this separation of functions that clearly provided the model for Whitnall's conception of urban organization.

Clearly, this vision of a cohesive and functionally integrated larger horizontal metropolis goes far beyond interdependence, or even municipal federalism. It is instead a vision of utilitarian consolidation, a metaphor of monopoly, where economies of scale would allow Southern California, while remaining a relatively legible and ordered landscape of individual communities, to function as one megalopolis. This is a conception fundamentally divergent from that of the garden city cluster, although it is clearly related to that form of urban organization. Here, each community would not be autonomous and self-contained, offering residents local employment, recreation, and commerce; instead, each community would be dedicated to a single unified function. Some districts would be bedroom suburbs (although certainly not orbiting a single downtown core), others would be industrial or commercial centers. No municipality would be complete in isolation from the surrounding region, and the region as a whole would rely upon these separate functional units for essential services and facilities needed by everyone. Greater Los Angeles would indeed be greater than the sum of its parts.

This was the urban model Los Angeles made famous after the Jazz Age. By the 1940s, a monumental technology appropriate to this new sort of city would find its ideal home in Southern California. The freeway could link these many component communities, mediating and integrating their separate functions. The freeway would bring the horizontal metropolis together, but in so doing it would develop an aesthetics of its own, prompting postwar generations of designers to adapt the form to ever more impressive ideals of heroic modernity. If the skyscraper was exemplar, symbol, and epistemological key for the vertical metropolis, the freeway would become the embodiment and icon of a new horizontal sublime. Like the tall building, it served to locate Angelenos within their sprawling landscapes, and it would fundamentally reconfigure existing notions of time and distance—and therefore of relative proximity—between postsuburban locations. The freeway would serve Angelenos both as exemplary landmark and spatial mediator for the decentralized urban topography. Eventually, it would allow residents to travel around the metropolitan region without appearing to move through it—and this would have profound epistemological and social effects. In essence, the freeway would help Angelenos make sense of their region, and would consequently develop into a primary embodiment of the new horizontal sublime.

Ultimately, the Jazz Age visionary could not truly envision any of these implications of the potent and rich metaphorics of decentralized horizontality he mobilized. More generally, Southern California planners over the remainder of the 1920s proved to be far too wedded to a utopian vision of garden city urbanism to develop such alternative conceptions of the workings of a flat, deconcentrated metropolis, where function no longer clearly and legibly followed form. Unlike the garden city, based on a cluster of self-sufficient small towns, or eastern skyscraper urbanism, which structured the metropolis around a dense towering central core, Greater Los Angeles would chart a future as a postsuburban metropolis. It would be fragmented, but not evenly. It would retain urban functions, but not in a centralized form. The entire metropolitan district could be seen as one amorphous, sprawling community, interconnected by automobile transportation networks and linked by a common interdependence.

The planners' inability to fully recognize the shape of their metropolis, to see it clearly and comprehensively, betokens a lack of flexibility that was truly unfortunate. The sort of tentative and experimental musing evinced by Gordon Whitnall in the mid-1920s, if further matured, might have at least freed local planners to continue imagining the future of their region. Instead, they seem in the second half of the 1920s, when Greater Los Angeles underwent its most dramatic transformation, to have lost faith and focus. Some men, including Whitnall, quit the bureaucracy; others stuck rigidly to the original scheme, even as it became increasingly impractical and inappropriate—or, by the 1930s, reactionary. Nevertheless, it is clear that a few planners had begun to move beyond the garden city by 1926 or 1927, and were thinking in larger, regional terms. This would remain a lasting legacy of local planners' vision; the ability to see in a sprawling horizontal landscape a modern urban grandeur most other Americans could only imagine in the context of a vertical, compact metropolis would persist in the coming decades, and it would inform the choices Angelenos made in responding to the region's manifest shortcomings.

Southern California would remain over the next decades a profoundly confusing place. The emerging anomie and alienation expressed during the 1920s would no longer be confined in coming years to countercultural voices and sociological studies, or sublimated into the hysteria of traffic discourse. Rather, they would pervade much of the metropolis's popular culture and common sense. Nevertheless, traffic discourse would remain a fixation for Angelenos, continuing to frame local choices about public space, community, social order, and metropolitan organization. Particularly with the massive freeway construction effort of the postwar years, residents of Southern California would continue to apply infrastructural and technical solutions to inherently philosophical and social problems—further dividing an already fragmented polity. In the end, although the insights of the 1920s generation of planners would not ultimately reinvigorate the local planning profession in this era or restore the metropolis to stable comprehensibility and order, Whitnall and his fellow planners had helped provide, if only allusively and tentatively, a set of basic tools for coming to terms with postsuburbia. They had, if only for a time, reclaimed their prerogative to "Dream dreams and see Visions."

INTRODUCTION

1. Kevin Lynch, *The Image of the City* (Cambridge, MA: MIT Press, 1960), 46.

2. Lynch, *The Image of the City*, 47.

3. Lynch, *The Image of the City*, 50.

4. Michel de Certeau, *The Practice of Everyday Life*, trans. Steven Rendall (Berkeley: University of California Press, 1984 [1974]), 119.

5. Kevin Lynch, "Reconsidering *The Image of the City*," in *Cities of the Mind: Images and Themes of the City in the Social Sciences*, ed. Lloyd Rodwin and Robert M. Hollister (New York: Plenum Press, 1984), 156.

6. The concept of legibility, which Kevin Lynch derived from, I believe, the ideologies of urban planning, is ultimately deeply confused. It conflates the ability of a given person or the community as a whole to make sense of their surroundings with a basic sense that inheres in some way within the built environment. Independent of its inhabitants, a place can, Lynch's theoretical model implies, be inherently legible or illegible. Thus, legibility is not a set of learned and transmitted strategies or tools for making sense of a given set of spaces, but rather some basic order that either does or does not already exist in the architecture and topography of the landscape. Thus, in "reading" the city, people are understood not to actively construct sense from a tabula rasa or, through daily experience and learned technique, slowly transform neutral material space into a rich fabric of remembered and evocative places. Instead, history and design embeds meaning into a city for the urbanite to discover simply and more or less readily. In a sense, though, this notion collapses a city into a stage set and elevates city planning to the most skilled form of stagecraft—a purposely representational, even didactic, art. There is surely some hubris to this conception of the planner's agency within the urban environment. What the epistemology of the path implies on the most basic level is that—unlike more maplike ways of viewing the city, which present the city omnisciently— meaning in a given metropolis, at any given time, from any given perspective, is highly con-

tingent and subjective. The significance of a given landmark, in this mode of urban observation, emerges from the goals and experiences of the observer or traveler, and does not simply inhere within the architectural or topographical features or relationships of the object itself.

7. Antonio Gramsci, *Selections from the Prison Notebooks,* trans. Quintin Hoare and Geoffrey Nowell Smith (New York: International Publishers, 1971), 419.

8. Lynch, *The Image of the City,* 46.

9. This epistemological incompatibility might explain why Lynch's three case-study cities—Boston, Jersey City, and Los Angeles, which were chosen for their topographical differences—elicited quite different sorts of significant elements from survey respondents. Lynch, *The Image of the City,* 14–15. Lynch attributes this difference, rather circularly, to the distinctiveness of the three cities (as these cities were taken from the start to be distinct from one another, any observed variation in the surveys might be simply and neatly attributed to that preconceived variation). I suggest that this variation might be just as attributable to different dominant modes of reading these topographies as to any actual difference in quantity and quality of discrete elements. In other words, *The Image of the City* cannot really determine, as Lynch assumes, that one environment is somehow "richer" in signification (or, to use his terms, higher in "imageability" or "character") than another merely by counting the number of paths, edges, districts, nodes, and landmarks cited by respondents. Lynch, *The Image of the City,* 32, 26.

10. Lynch, *The Image of the City,* 8.

11. Certeau, *The Practice of Everyday Life,* 115.

12. Lynch, *The Image of the City,* 4.

PROLOGUE

1. Quoted in John L. Chapman, *Incredible Los Angeles* (New York: Harper & Row, 1967), 4.

2. Dan Fowler, "Los Angeles: The World's Worst Growing Pains," *Look* 20, no. 5 (1956): 21.

3. Fowler, "Los Angeles," 21.

4. Charles Weltner, quoted in Chapman, *Incredible Los Angeles,* 4.

5. Thirteen stories amounted to about 150 feet in practice. Leonard Pitt and Dale Pitt, *Los Angeles, A to Z: An Encyclopedia of the City and County* (Berkeley: University of California Press, 1997), 63.

6. Bill Davidson and Frank D. Morris, "Traffic Nightmare—and a Promise of Dawn," *Collier's* 125 (1950): 26.

7. Los Angeles Traffic Commission, *A Major Traffic Street Plan for Los Angeles* (Los Angeles: Traffic Commission, 1924), 11. Significantly, there were already about 936,000 residents of the surrounding suburbs by 1920, according to David Gebhard and Harriette von Breton's *Los Angeles in the Thirties: 1931–1941* (Los Angeles: Hennessey & Ingalls, 1989 [1975]), 18.

8. The exact downtown commuting figures for 1923: 750,000 interurban commuters per day; 653,374 automobile commuters per day (Los Angeles Traffic Commission, *A Major Traffic Street Plan for Los Angeles,* 11).

9. According to the Olmsted, Bartholomew, and Cheney report of 1924, only 21 percent of the downtown business district was given over to roadway, as compared to more than 35 percent in such cities as San Francisco, Washington, D.C., and St. Louis. Ibid., 12.

10. Bruce Henstell, *Sunshine and Wealth: Los Angeles in the Twenties and Thirties* (San Francisco: Chronicle Books, 1984), 23.

11. Even in 1924, when the city's population was estimated at about a million people, there were 430,000 registered automobiles in the city. Los Angeles Traffic Commission, *A Major Traffic Street Plan for Los Angeles*, 11.

1. "LOS ANGELES IS NOT
THE CITY IT COULD HAVE BEEN"

1. See, among other works, David Gebhard and Harriette von Breton, *Los Angeles in the Thirties* (Los Angeles: Hennessey & Ingalls, 1989); Martin Wachs, "Autos, Transit, and the Sprawl of Los Angeles: The 1920s," *Journal of the American Planning Association* 50, no. 3 (1984); Mark Foster, "The Decentralization of Los Angeles during the 1920's" (Ph.D. diss., University of Southern California, 1971), "The Model-T, the Hard Sell, and Los Angeles's Urban Growth," *Pacific Historical Review* 44, no. 4 (1975), and *From Streetcar to Superhighway* (Philadelphia: Temple University Press, 1981); Scott Bottles, *Los Angeles and the Automobile* (Berkeley: University of California Press, 1987); and Robert Fogelson, *The Fragmented Metropolis* (Berkeley: University of California Press, 1967).

2. Fogelson, *The Fragmented Metropolis*, 275.

3. Greg Hise, *Magnetic Los Angeles: Planning the Twentieth-Century Metropolis* (Baltimore, MD: Johns Hopkins University Press, 1997), 4.

4. Hise's emphasis on the role of private developers is certainly well placed, as they collectively exerted tremendous influence on the topography of the region. Nevertheless, although subdividers certainly carried out extensive detail work in a large number of communities in Greater Los Angeles, particularly after the 1920s, few of them harbored any comprehensive vision of the metropolis. This was piecemeal planning, planning at the edges; it certainly did not fulfill the requirements and ambitions of the city planning profession of the 1920s and 1930s.

5. Gebhard and Breton, *Los Angeles in the Thirties*, 19. Local planners, ironically enough, actually had very little to do with the design of the freeway system.

6. Charles D. Clark, "Land Subdivision," in *Los Angeles: Preface to a Master Plan*, ed. George W. Robbins and L. Deming Tilton (Los Angeles: Pacific Southwest Academy / Ward Ritchie Press, 1941), 159.

7. Clark, "Land Subdivision," 169.

8. Clark, "Land Subdivision," 160.

9. L. Deming Tilton, "The Master Plan," in *Los Angeles: Preface to a Master Plan*, 255.

10. Dan Fowler, "Los Angeles: The World's Worst Growing Pains," *Look* 20, no. 5 (1956): 23.

11. Mike Davis, *City of Quartz: Excavating the Future in Los Angeles* (New York: Vintage Books, 1992 [1990]); and Kevin Starr, *Inventing the Dream: California through the Progressive Era* (New York: Oxford University Press, 1985), *Material Dreams: Southern California through the 1920s* (New York: Oxford University Press, 1990), and *Endangered Dreams: The Great Depression in California* (New York: Oxford University Press, 1996).

12. Dana W. Bartlett, *The Better City: A Sociological Study of a Modern City* (Los Angeles: Neuner Company Press, 1907), 29.

13. Bartlett, *The Better City,* 48.

14. Bartlett, *The Better City,* 48.

15. Robinson's plan was completed and distributed among interested city officials and citizens in December 1907, the same year as Bartlett's *The Better City* was published, but was not printed until two years later (Robert Lee Williams, "The City Planning Movement in Los Angeles, 1900–1920" [M.A. thesis, California State University, Long Beach, 1972], 23).

16. Charles Mulford Robinson, "Los Angeles, California: The City Beautiful" (Los Angeles: Municipal Arts Commission, 1909), 3.

17. Robinson, "The City Beautiful," 31.

18. The provision of a union passenger terminal would cause considerable controversy twenty years later. Efforts to enact this suggestion of the Robinson report gained momentum with the release of a transportation study carried out under the aegis of Chicago transportation planner Bion J. Arnold in 1911, but were mired in legal battles for more than twenty years. Bion J. Arnold, "The Transportation Problem of Los Angeles," *California Outlook* 11, no. 19 (1911): 1–20.

19. Mansel G. Blackford, *The Lost Dream: Businessmen and City Planning on the Pacific Coast, 1890–1920* (Columbus: Ohio State University Press, 1993), 88.

20. Robinson, "The City Beautiful," 3.

21. Bartlett attributes this phrase to "Señor Dominguez, of the great Dominguez rancho, [who] was the first dreamer of the Greater Los Angeles" in the 1870s (*The Better City,* 33).

22. Robinson, "The City Beautiful," 21.

23. Robinson, "The City Beautiful," 7.

24. Robinson, "The City Beautiful," 21.

25. Williams, "City Planning Movement," 27.

26. Blackford, *The Lost Dream,* 88.

27. John E. Lathrop, "City Planning Exhibit," *California Outlook* 16, no. 16 (1914): 14.

28. Williams, "City Planning Movement," 47.

29. Williams, "City Planning Movement," 47. Whitnall's background in radical Wisconsin also was deeply entwined with early planning efforts. In fact, his father, C. B. Whitnall, was a noted pioneer in Milwaukee city and recreation planning.

30. Williams, "City Planning Movement," 49.

31. Quoted in Fogelson, *The Fragmented Metropolis,* 249.

32. Quoted in Fogelson, *The Fragmented Metropolis,* 248–49.

33. G. Gordon Whitnall, "City and Regional Planning in Los Angeles" (paper presented at the National Conference on City Planning, Philadelphia, 7–10 April 1924), 106.

34. Whitnall's use of the phrase "the better city" is unlikely to be coincidental. Bartlett's *The Better City* was well enough known locally to guarantee that most Angelenos would understand the allusion and thus the claim to Bartlett's booster legacy.

35. M. Christine Boyer, *Dreaming the Rational City: The Myth of American City Planning* (Cambridge, MA: MIT Press, 1983), 16. Boyer here cites Robert A. Woods's article "Pittsburgh."

36. Boyer, *Dreaming the Rational City,* 60.

37. Boyer, *Dreaming the Rational City,* 3.

38. Through the shifts in circulating metaphors, planners expanded and altered their realm of authority. No longer was the moral condition of the populace the problematic at

stake; now, all primary concern must lie with the health of the city itself. Consequently, planners defined as urban "ailments" and problems to be treated those things that interfered with the city's flows and circulation, proper differentiation of tissues and organs, modes of growth, and the like. These would now be the city's real problems, and curing these ills would be, by definition, the planners' proper domain of action.

As Michel Foucault reminds us in *The History of Sexuality* (New York: Vintage Books, 1990), metaphoric language is not just colorful and vivid; such discourse produces specific objects of knowledge as being significant, and thus structures power relations in a society. In such metaphors lies the rationality that compels reasoned action. This new discourse of the profession of city planning would have a profound effect on the face of urban America.

39. Boyer, *Dreaming the Rational City*, 71.

40. Boyer, *Dreaming the Rational City*, 71.

41. Boyer, *Dreaming the Rational City*, 71.

42. The survey came into increasing use as city planning began to become professionalized between around 1907 and 1913, as Boyer points out (*Dreaming the Rational City*, 62).

43. Boyer, *Dreaming the Rational City*, 74.

44. Boyer, *Dreaming the Rational City*, 74–75.

45. For more detailed theoretical exposition of this mechanism of urban perception, see Michel de Certeau, *The Practice of Everyday Life* (Berkeley: University of California Press, 1984); and George Lipsitz, *Time Passages: Collective Memory and American Popular Culture* (Minneapolis: University of Minnesota Press, 1989).

46. Antonio Gramsci, *Selections from the Prison Notebooks,* trans. Quintin Hoare and Geoffrey Nowell Smith (New York: International Publishers, 1971), 419.

47. Bartlett, *The Better City*, 20.

48. James McFarline Ervin, "The Participation of the Negro in the Community Life of Los Angeles" (M.A. thesis, University of Southern California, 1931), 7. Ervin offers the 1920 census figure of 15,579 African Americans in the city, out of a total population of 576,673 (3.1 percent).

49. Foster, "The Decentralization of Los Angeles," 62. James Ervin describes six discrete African American districts in Southern California, all similarly located around the city's center ("The Participation of the Negro," 12–13).

50. Foster, "The Decentralization of Los Angeles," 61.

51. Lonnie G. Bunch III, *Black Angelenos: The Afro-American in Los Angeles, 1850–1950,* ed. Nancy McKinney (Los Angeles: California Afro-American Museum, 1988), 36.

52. J. Max Bond, "The Negro in Los Angeles" (Ph.D. diss., University of Southern California, 1972), 35.

53. Foster, "The Decentralization of Los Angeles," 61.

54. Foster, "The Decentralization of Los Angeles," 47–48.

55. Leonard Pitt and Dale Pitt, *Los Angeles, A to Z: An Encyclopedia of the City and County* (Berkeley: University of California Press, 1997), 413.

56. Foster, "The Decentralization of Los Angeles," 72. Of course, many of the African Americans in Pasadena, like Beverly Hills, were servants, restricted to their own domestic segregations.

57. Watts, an almost exclusively African American suburb located seven miles south of

downtown, was absorbed into Los Angeles proper in 1926, with the explicit backing of the Ku Klux Klan, to prevent the election of a black mayor (Pitt and Pitt, *Los Angeles, A to Z*, 537).

58. Foster, "The Decentralization of Los Angeles," 53.

59. Foster, "The Decentralization of Los Angeles," 57.

60. Foster, "The Decentralization of Los Angeles," 65–66.

61. Foster, "The Decentralization of Los Angeles," 65.

62. Boyle Heights was predominantly a community of Eastern European Jews during the period; Bartlett mentions the existence of a small "Italian Colony," as well as discrete neighborhoods of Russian and German immigrants (*The Better City*, 79).

63. For a sophisticated analysis of some of these boundaries in a later period, see Kyle Julien's "Sounding the City: Jazz, African American Nightlife, and the Articulation of Race in 1940s Los Angeles" (Ph.D. diss., University of California, Irvine, 2000).

64. Bunch, *Black Angelenos*, 34.

65. Pitt and Pitt, *Los Angeles, A to Z*, 209, 10.

66. Foster, "The Decentralization of Los Angeles," 60.

67. Bessie Averne McClenahan, *The Changing Urban Neighborhood: From Neighbor to Nigh-Dweller: A Sociological Study* (Los Angeles: University of Southern California, 1929), 91.

68. Margaret Marsh, *Suburban Lives* (New Brunswick, NJ: Rutgers University Press, 1990), 142.

69. As Kathy Peiss makes clear in her *Cheap Amusements: Working Women and Leisure in Turn-of-the-Century New York* (Philadelphia: Temple University Press, 1986), the rigid series of dichotomies that made up gender norms (suburban/urban-private/public-bourgeois/working class) tended to hold much more sway over suburban middle-class women than over female working-class urbanites. In fact, Peiss vividly describes the public amusements of which New York working women, often immigrants, partook. In so doing, these women continually stretched the boundaries of gender proscriptions. Likewise, the bourgeois suburban world of segregated Los Angeles certainly had its cracks and fissures, if not perhaps on the scale described by Peiss. Nevertheless, despite the resistance, the boundaries themselves remained manifestly in place throughout the period in Southern California. Resistance to such discourse, as Michel Foucault reminds us, operates from within that discourse, transcending its control—its common sense hegemony, to once more use Gramsci's terms—only during rare periods of discursive rupture (*The History of Sexuality*, 94–95).

70. Harry Carr, *Los Angeles: City of Dreams* (New York: Grosset & Dunlap, 1935), 253.

71. Robert Fishman, *Bourgeois Utopias: The Rise and Fall of Suburbia* (New York: Basic Books, 1987), 99.

72. Bartlett, *The Better City*, 74.

73. In the common sense of professional planners in this period, the term *segregation* can never be separated from its (present-day) racial connotations. Segregation of land use, or of housing, or even of traffic streams always evokes and recalls the segregation of racial and ethnic populations.

It is in this vein that we should read the unquestioned need for and bemoaned lack of proper segregation that lay behind housing reformers' dissatisfaction with the tenement. The tenement was thought to be not only dangerous and unsanitary but chaotic. These structures encouraged the "promiscuous" mixing of people. Race and gender were not properly segregated (although class was, of course) in these environments.

In Los Angeles, this antitenement sentiment drove a considerable amount of public discourse and policy. The single-family home was not merely a preferred architectural style, it was the city's bulwark against the tenement slums of the East. The revulsion against chaotic tenement structures went so far among some planners and social reformers that all multiple-family dwellings were tainted: "The people who live even in the palatial apartments are nevertheless living in tenements. An apartment is merely a tenement house with a college education, soon forgotten when the surroundings begin to go down." Andrew W. Crawford, quoted in H. M. Brinckerhoff, "The Effect of Transportation upon the Distribution of Population in Large Cities" (paper presented at the Annual Conference on City Planning, Pittsburgh, 9–11 May 1921), 67.

74. Occasionally, these boundaries were challenged in specific instances, including some of the racially restrictive covenants. Nevertheless, these deed restrictions were validated in courts repeatedly until a Supreme Court ruling in 1948 finally struck them down. Pitt and Pitt, Los Angeles, A to Z, 210.

75. Wachs, "Autos, Transit, and the Sprawl of Los Angeles," 306.

76. Foster, From Streetcar to Superhighway, 66–67. The planner Foster is talking about here is W. L. Pollard. Pollard's comment is from a paper presented before the California Planning Association in October 1932.

77. People tended, it was quickly discovered, to park as close as possible to their final destinations. This proximity meant that planners could eliminate, for automobilists, one great sampling blind spot that afflicted their traditional streetcar surveys: that crucial moment when the rider is recorded leaving the train and sets out on foot. At that moment, traffic counts totally lost track of the pedestrian. The obverse of the precision about parking spots as an indicator of destination was the even more exact information of automobile registrations. Surveyors could, in this period, freely examine the registrations of parked cars, and trace those automobiles to their (presumed) point of origin. These methodological benefits accruing to automobile traffic counts undoubtedly added to the private car's appeal to planning professionals. Quite simply, they could see automobilists far more clearly than they could streetcar patrons (who always remained, as a consequence, a bit fuzzy within planning discourse).

78. Charles Henry Cheney, "City Planning and Efficiency," California Outlook 16, no. 17 (1914): 18.

79. For the best monographic treatment of the Good Roads Movement, see Michael Berger, The Devil's Wagon in God's Country (Hamden, CT: Archon Books, 1979).

80. Fogelson, The Fragmented Metropolis, 252.

81. Fogelson, The Fragmented Metropolis, 252.

82. Edward Bellamy, Looking Backward: 2000–1887 (New York: Penguin, 1982 [1888]), 218.

83. Bellamy, Looking Backward, 55.

84. Stanley Buder notes in his Visionaries and Planners (New York: Oxford University Press, 1990) that Howard's logic was typical of English reformers in his day: "Dialectical reasoning to arrive at an ideal synthesis was common in communitarian thinking and writing" (caption to figure 2).

85. Ebenezer Howard, *Garden Cities of To-morrow* (London: Faber and Faber, 1945 [1898]), 145.

86. Howard, *Garden Cities of To-morrow,* 146.

87. Robert Fishman, *Urban Utopias in the Twentieth Century: Ebenezer Howard, Frank Lloyd Wright, and Le Corbusier* (Cambridge, MA: MIT Press, 1977), 37.

88. Stanley Buder argues in his "Ebenezer Howard: The Genesis of a Town Planning Movement" that the garden city model "offered a planned alternative to the alienation and disorder many identified with the growth of large cities, while enhancing, or at least leaving unimpaired, such basic values of Victorian society as individual freedom, importance of the family as a social unit, and the sanctity of property and free enterprise" (396).

89. It is worth noting that this disclaimer did not actually appear in the first editions of Howard's book, but only in those after 1902. Buder, *Visionaries and Planners,* caption to figure 5.

90. The sketch, in the natural simplicity of its precise draftsmanship, has appealed to many subsequent critics as well. It is almost invariably reprinted in histories of planning, urbanism, and even architecture.

91. Fishman, *Urban Utopias,* 42.

92. Lewis Mumford, "The Garden City Idea and Modern Planning," in Ebenezer Howard, *Garden Cities of To-morrow* (London: Faber and Faber, 1945), 35.

93. Mumford, "The Garden City Idea and Modern Planning," 34.

94. Mumford, "The Garden City Idea and Modern Planning," 36.

95. Howard, *Garden Cities of To-morrow,* 140.

96. Howard, *Garden Cities of To-morrow,* 142.

97. Howard, *Garden Cities of To-morrow,* 142.

98. Fishman, *Urban Utopias,* 40-41.

99. Mumford, "The Garden City Idea and Modern Planning," 29.

100. John L. Thomas, "Utopia for an Urban Age: Henry George, Henry Demarest Lloyd, Edward Bellamy," *Perspectives in American History* 6 (1972): 157.

101. Buder, *Visionaries and Planners,* 94.

102. Dana Bartlett, "City Planning Progress," *California Outlook* 11, no. 21 (1911): 15. For most professional planners, the reference to "English Town planning" alone would suggest garden city planning.

103. These "subcenters" are discussed in some detail in the Bion J. Arnold transportation report, which was written in part by future Los Angeles planner George Damon. Here, subcenters are described as the natural products of a community's proper growth, and are not so clearly posed as replacements for the downtown district. Arnold, "The Transportation Problem of Los Angeles," 16. By the mid-1920s, however, as the traffic congestion problems around the central business district worsened, planners such as Damon became quite explicit in their understanding that these subcenters should assume many of the functions previously carried out by Los Angeles's downtown. Take, for instance, Damon's address before the fourth national city planning conference, "Relation of the Motor Bus to Other Methods of Transportation" (paper presented at the National Conference on City Planning, Philadelphia, 7-10 April 1924), in which he goes so far as to argue for the gradual but total abandonment of the dominant interurban system in Southern California because of its dan-

gerous centralizing tendencies. This suggestion, although later to be enacted much as suggested, was quite extreme for the mid-1920s and reflects the evolution of planners' thought in Los Angeles toward more and more radical conceptions of decentralization. For more on the meaning of these subcenters, see chapter 2.

104. Fogelson, *The Fragmented Metropolis*, 252.

105. Fogelson, *The Fragmented Metropolis*, 205.

106. As we saw earlier, it was widely acknowledged that interurban streetcar systems tended to reinforce concentric patterns of urban development. Also, the planners were well aware that the Pacific Electric network in Los Angeles was already hard-pressed to keep up with present development. By promoting a gradual transition from fixed rail to flexible automotive transit, the planners felt they could encourage decentralization. Since new satellite garden communities would generally be unconnected to the existing rail system, residents would find it more difficult to travel to downtown Los Angeles for employment. Instead, they would find work within their own neighborhoods, at industries lured to the garden communities by planners and land developers. The locality would replace the large city or the metropolitan region as the sphere of daily travel, and the load upon the road system would decrease over time. In the context of a decentralized urban region, the planners believed, the automobile would become an agent not of traffic congestion but of modern and flexible self-sufficiency. Common travel distances would be reduced, and the fixed patterns of daily commuting would disappear.

2. PARADISE MISPLACED

1. "Tries to Kidnap Official's Wife," *Los Angeles Times*, 27 March 1921, 1:10.

2. "Traffic," *Los Angeles Times*, 18 December 1910.

3. Remi Nadeau, *California: The New Society* (Westport, CT: Greenwood Press, 1974 [1963]), 111. Nadeau was, of course, referring to Henry Huntington's Pacific Electric.

4. James Montgomery Flagg, *Boulevards All the Way—Maybe* (New York: George H. Doran, 1925), 149.

5. Mark Stewart Foster, "The Decentralization of Los Angeles during the 1920's" (Ph.D. diss., University of Southern California, 1971), 140.

6. The gendered bias of the ban was taken for granted by the newspapers in 1920, although it would perhaps be easier to see today the class dimension of an interdiction against automobile travel that left streetcars unhindered. Nevertheless, the papers reported almost exclusively on women as victims of parking ban enforcement, as the city's primary shoppers. See, for instance, "Martyr to Test No-Parking Law," *Los Angeles Examiner*, 13 April 1920, 1:4; "1 Woman Wins Probation; Scores Who Park Fined," *Los Angeles Examiner*, 15 April 1920, 2:1; "Talks to Club on New City Ordinances," *Los Angeles Examiner*, 11 April 1920, 8:18; "The No-Parking Cure for All Traffic Ills Goes into Effect," *Los Angeles Times*, 11 April 1920, 6:1; "To End Inroads of Parking Ban," *Los Angeles Times*, 21 April 1920, 2:1; Pauline Payne, "Star Brands It Non-Shopping Law; Not 'No-Parking,'" *Los Angeles Herald*, 22 April 1920; "The Perils of a Parkless Town," *Los Angeles Times*, 29 February 1920; Howard C. Kegley, "The Ballad of Parkless Town," *Los Angeles Times*, 24 April 1920; and "Arrest Hundreds as 'Parking' Violators," *Los Angeles Herald*, 10 April 1920, 1:1.

7. "Relief Pledged from Auto Ban," *Los Angeles Times*, 24 April 1920, 2:1.

8. The entry of women into previously forbidden urban public spaces during the first years of the twentieth century remained highly regulated in this era, despite women's increasing activism. Even among the most mobile minority of female urbanites, the city was riven by gender boundaries. Well into the 1920s, many working-class men, as Dana Frank notes in *Purchasing Power*, "believed women's place was in the home only," and therefore worked to restrict their wives from significant roles in the public spaces and politics of the city (Cambridge: Cambridge University Press, 1994), 123. Indeed, Alice Kessler-Harris ends her discussion of female workers before 1920 by concluding that "in the first two decades of the twentieth century, . . . traditional views of women prevailed." Instead of freedom to move as they wished about the city, even the relatively small group of female wage-earners found their range of occupations severely limited, their prospects stifled by protective legislation, and their latitude within the city correspondingly constricted. *Out to Work: A History of Wage-Earning Women in the United States* (Oxford: Oxford University Press, 1982), 213–14. Despite a feminist movement that drew women into public politics, particularly during the 1910s, and which championed the right of women to hold jobs outside the home, domesticity guaranteed that most women still spent a majority of their time in private homes (either as housewives or servants). Nancy F. Cott, *The Grounding of Modern Feminism* (New Haven: Yale University Press, 1987), 20–24, 119. Even Kathy Peiss argues in *Cheap Amusements* ([Philadelphia: Temple University Press, 1986], 32–33) that the increasing recreational freedom she attributes to some young working-class women in New York City was largely alien to most other female urbanites. For the most part, turn-of-the-century "women's participation in public and commercial forms of leisure was narrowly defined, their activities located instead in the home, streets, parks, and churches" of their neighborhoods.

Beyond the rigid nineteenth-century separation of domestic and public spheres lay other, increasingly more relevant, blunt gender segregations in place in the early twentieth century. As women began to venture into previously forbidden urban public spaces in their roles as workers, activists, and consumers, those new zones became internally segregated by gender. Department stores in central business districts, as Gunther Barth points out in *City People*, offered for the first time a cosmopolitan urban experience to respectable women of the late nineteenth century ([Oxford: Oxford University Press, 1980], 144–47). Yet these stores had defined themselves by the 1880s primarily as properly feminine realms. Such "protective" and appropriate spaces allowed unchaperoned women in unprecedented numbers to visit downtown spaces, while protecting female urbanites from urban dangers and excitement. As Susan Porter Benson, in *Counter Cultures: Saleswomen, Managers, and Customers in American Department Stores, 1890–1940* [(Urbana: University of Illinois Press, 1986), 94], and Elaine S. Abelson, in *When Ladies Go A-Thieving: Middle-Class Shoplifters in the Victorian Department Store* ([New York: Oxford University Press, 1989], 28–41), reveal in their respective studies, the large store, heavily policed and run exclusively by men, was persuasively cast as an extension of the domestic sphere—"a sanitized, safe environment"—where women could feel at home. Even though a sizable minority of urban women entered downtown districts on a regular basis by the 1900s, their movements in these public realms conformed to new alignments of urban gender restrictions. Indeed, as David Nasaw cautions in *Going Out*, whereas a few female urbanites had begun to gain access to downtown public amusements as far back as the 1890s, more generally "the dividing line between those who patronized the variety shows and those who remained outside was not social class, but gender and 'respectability'" ([New York: Basic Books, 1993], 14). Only venues specifically catering to female patrons were designated to be fully safe and proper. Again, as with the department stores, those few urban spaces open to female activity tended, on the whole, to remain highly segregated along gender lines throughout the first decades of the twentieth century. As Martin Wachs argues, the ideology of separate spheres was built right into the structure of the American city and its rail transportation system, ensuring that Americans even in the first decades of the twentieth century would recognize and, for the most part, respect the urban order ("Men, Women, and Urban Travel: The Persistence of Separate Spheres," in *The Car and the City: The Automobile, the Built Environment, and Daily Urban Life* [Ann Arbor: University of Michigan Press, 1992], 87, 90).

Overall, it was not until after World War I that women began to enter the public spheres of the city in large numbers on their own terms. The first mass point of entry of female urbanites into downtown recreations came in the late 1910s with the introduction of the motion picture. Nasaw, *Going Out*, 232. The appropriation of the new urban movie palaces by women in the Jazz Age allowed them a toehold within the public spaces of the traditional city, as Clara Kimball Young demonstrated. In these years, female filmgoers actively stretched the bounds of urban gender segregation, making a space for themselves in new areas of the city's central recreational district. Here, it is worth keeping in mind that, although by the 1930s Hollywood cinema was strongly associated with female spectatorship, this was something of a new development. Janice A. Radway, *Reading the Romance: Women, Patriarchy and Popular Literature* (Durham: University of North Carolina Press, 1984); Tania Modleski, *Loving with a Vengeance: Mass Produced Fantasies for Women* (New York: Methuen, 1984). Indeed, Nasaw notes that "only in the 1920s picture theaters and palaces did the women constitute a majority of the moviegoing audience" (*Going Out*, 233). The colonization of downtown streets for public movie-going, then, transpired remarkably suddenly and represented a notable expansion of the legitimate urban sphere open to women in Los Angeles and elsewhere. The cultural resonance of 1920s female protests against the parking ban, then, lay in the rising public consciousness that women were in fact now laying claim to a downtown district that had until very recently remained almost exclusively a male preserve.

9. "Relief Pledged from Auto Ban," 2:1.

10. "Relief Pledged from Auto Ban," 2:1.

11. On middle-class women's role in the parking ban protest, see "Plan Revision of Auto Law," *Los Angeles Examiner*, 23 April 1920, 1:4, and "No Parking Law to Be Flayed," *Record*, 1920.04.23, 1:2. Here, though, the commensurate right of female store employees to access the same spaces by streetcar failed to penetrate into the public debate. Although it was precisely this automotive congestion that was hindering the proper operation of those interurbans, the debate was cast in terms of a conflict, first, between department store magnates and their middle-class customers and, second, between city bureaucrats and the citizenry at large. The working-class employees and consumers, dependent upon the trolleys, went unheard.

12. It is both ironic and tragic that Young's career went into sharp decline by the late 1920s—a decline that culminated in her severe injury in an automobile collision the same

week as her possessions were auctioned off to pay overdue bills. "Ex-Star of Films Hurt in Traffic," *Los Angeles Times,* 7 June 1932, 2:2.

13. This discourse on women drivers is discussed in Virginia Scharff's excellent *Taking the Wheel* (New York: Free Press, 1991), 22–33; Michael Berger, "Women Drivers! The Emergence of Folklore and Stereotypic Opinions Concerning Feminine Automotive Behavior," *Women's Studies International Forum* 9, no. 3 (1986): 257–63; and Martin Wachs, "Men, Women, and Urban Travel: The Persistence of Separate Spheres," 96.

14. Betty McConnell Bowring, "Can Women Really Drive?" *Touring Topics* 18, no. 1 (1926): 24.

15. Bowring, "Can Women Really Drive?" 25.

16. "Auto Deaths Set New Record," *Los Angeles Times,* 23 February 1920, 2:1.

17. Daniel Smith Crowningshield, *The Jolly Eight: Coast to Coast and Back* (Boston: Richard G. Badger, 1929), 94.

18. The Yellow Car rerouting described by the police chief in the introduction and reflected in the editorial cartoon had in fact been an attempt "to aid the no-parking ordinance." "Car Revision Is Sweeping," *Los Angeles Times,* 31 March 1920, 2:1.

19. See for instance "Auto Deaths Set New Record," 2:1.

20. "Murderous Speed Maniacs," *Los Angeles Times,* 18 March 1920, 2:4.

21. "Five Killed in Auto Mishaps," *Los Angeles Times,* 12 April 1920, 2:1.

22. The papers continually emphasized the overall scale of the carnage. From July 1919 to February 1920, for instance, 981 Los Angeles pedestrians alone were hit by cars. "Auto Deaths Set New Record," 2:1.

23. "Traffic," *Los Angeles Times,* 18 November 1926, 2:4.

24. "Murderous Speed Maniacs," 2:4.

25. "Hits Those Who Make Streets Death-Traps," *Los Angeles Times,* 22 March 1920, 2:1.

26. The association of automobility, particularly among teenagers, and unrestrained sexuality ran strongly through the popular culture of the era. Often, sexual license, youth culture, and the movement of the automobiles were linked together through evocations of "jazz" or even "speed-jazz." This matrix of association even led to attempts by authorities to regulate youth sexuality through traffic regulation. In 1920, for instance, the *Los Angeles Times* ran a scathing indictment of "auto mashers" who cruised the streets of the city attempting to seduce young women. Young men "always driving a snappy-looking automobile drift about the city during the early part of the evening." "Rock Pile for Auto Mashers," *Los Angeles Times,* 9 January 1920, 2:1. Driving close to the curb, these delinquents would call out to female pedestrians, "'Come, honey, let's take a little spin.' Sometimes the girls get in, but more often they look around for help. In the latter case, when no men are near the mashers deliver themselves of a little Broadway wit and drive away looking for other victims." The paper reported, however, that the chief of police, recognizing the need for traffic regulation "after hundreds of complaints had come to his office and 'automobile mashing' on the downtown streets become one of the most popular outdoor sports, issued instructions to every police officer in the city to arrest on sight all men attempting to pick up girls on the streets." The *Times* gleefully observed, in reporting the arrest of four youths, that such delinquents would henceforth "'mash' rocks inside the Eastside Police stockade."

27. "Speed Murderers," 2:4.

28. "Murderous Speed Maniacs," 2:4.

29. "Speed Murderers," 2:4.

30. "Murderous Speed Maniacs," 2:4. Given that the paper had itself been bombed four years before, the *Los Angeles Times*' association of reckless drivers with anarchists conveys particularly strongly the fervor of its resentment against those subverting traffic laws.

31. "Murderous Speed Maniacs," 2:4.

32. "Autoists! Beware Vigilantes: Secret Organization Starts Work of 'Spotting' Reckless Auto Drivers in Los Angeles," *Los Angeles Herald*, 1 April 1920, 2:1. Vigilante "No. 1" was, according to the *Herald*, none other than Los Angeles mayor Snyder. "Martyr to Test No-Parking Law," 1:4."

33. "Speed Murderers," 2:4.

34. "Murderous Speed Maniacs," 2:4; "Speed Murderers," 2:4.

35. "Speed Murderers," 2:4.

36. Emory S. Bogardus, *The City Boy and His Problems: A Survey of Boy Life in Los Angeles* (Los Angeles: House of Ralston, 1926), 79.

37. Leonard Pitt and Dale Pitt, *Los Angeles, A to Z: An Encyclopedia of the City and County* (Berkeley: University of California Press, 1997), 297.

38. Nadeau, *California: The New Society,* 215.

39. William Wilcox Robinson, *The Key to Los Angeles* (Philadelphia: J. B. Lippincott, 1963), 108.

40. Ashleigh Brilliant, *The Great Car Craze: How Southern California Collided with the Automobile in the 1920's* (Santa Barbara: Woodbridge Press, 1989), 202.

41. Rayner Banham, *A Critic Writes,* ed. Mary Banham et al. (Berkeley: University of California Press, 1996), 174; Kevin Starr, *Material Dreams: Southern California through the 1920s* (New York: Oxford University Press, 1990), 210.

42. Nadeau, *California: The New Society,* 207.

43. Nadeau, *California: The New Society,* 210.

44. Nadeau, *California: The New Society,* 215.

45. Michel de Certeau, "Spatial Practices," in *The Practice of Everyday Life,* trans. Steven Rendall (Berkeley: University of California Press, 1984 [1974]).

46. Quoted in Robert M. Fogelson, *The Fragmented Metropolis: Los Angeles, 1850–1930* (Berkeley: University of California Press, 1967), 252.

47. Mel Scott, *American City Planning* (Berkeley: University of California Press, 1969), 207.

48. Scott, *American City Planning,* 208.

49. Mansel G. Blackford, *The Lost Dream: Businessmen and City Planning on the Pacific Coast, 1890–1920* (Columbus: Ohio State University Press, 1993), 92. Zoning had been introduced in California as early as the 1870s (see Warner's *The Urban Wilderness* [(Berkeley: University of California Press, 1995), 28–29] for an excellent brief summary of this early use); in the 1910s and 1920s, a new wave of "scientific" zoning hit America's cities. Los Angeles was a pioneer in this effort, as the first major city in the country to enact a zoning ordinance. According to Mel Scott's *Metropolitan Los Angeles: One Community* ([Los Angeles: John Randolph Haynes and Dora Haynes Foundation, 1949], 37), in 1908 the City of Los Angeles "adopted two ordinances dividing the city into residential and industrial zones, seeking

thereby to keep industry out of residential areas." Robert M. Glendinning cites the date of 1909 (most commonly identified by scholars) for the birth of zoning in the region. His article "Zoning: Past, Present and Future," in the influential 1941 planning manifesto *Los Angeles: Preface to a Master Plan* (George W. Robbins and L. Deming Tilton, eds. [Los Angeles: Pacific Southwest Academy / Ward Ritchie Press, 1941]), also notes that zoning efforts in the state of California date to 1861. Mark Foster, alone among historians, claims in his dissertation, "The Decentralization of Los Angeles during the 1920's," that Los Angeles's "City Council enacted the first zoning ordinance in 1904" (229). He gets this date, however, from the city's own planning history, *City Planning in Los Angeles: A History*, by Philip J. Ouellet (Los Angeles: Department of City Planning, 1964). Whatever the date of the city's first zoning attempts, it was clearly not until the 1920s that zoning in Southern California was enacted with the degree of precision, sophistication, and thoroughness for which professional expert planners called. After 1920, the Los Angeles City Planning Commission and the County Regional Planning Commission began programs of comprehensive city and regional zoning, modeled after the refined zoning ordinance enacted by New York City's planners in 1916 (Scott, *Metropolitan Los Angeles*, 86).

50. See Mansel Blackford's *The Lost Dream*, 3; see also chapter 3.

51. Ralph Hancock, *Fabulous Boulevard* (New York: Funk & Wagnalls, 1949), 159–60.

52. Richard Longstreth, *City Center to Regional Mall: Architecture, the Automobile, and Retailing in Los Angeles, 1920–1950* (Cambridge, MA: MIT Press, 1997), 104.

53. M. Christine Boyer, *Dreaming the Rational City: The Myth of American City Planning* (Cambridge, MA: MIT Press, 1983), 156.

54. George A. Damon, "Inter and Intra Urban Transit and Traffic as a Regional Planning Problem" (paper presented at the National Conference on City Planning, Baltimore, 30 April–2 May 1923), 53.

55. Warner, *The Urban Wilderness*, 31.

56. Boyer, *Dreaming the Rational City*, 153.

57. Warner, *The Urban Wilderness*, 32.

58. For the official city account of the formation of these various bodies, see Philip Ouellet's *City Planning in Los Angeles: A History*, produced for the Los Angeles Department of City Planning in 1964.

59. Representative here were the ominous conclusions drawn by the ever-influential *Los Angeles Times* in the aftermath of the ban fiasco: "No-Parking Law Proves Motor Cars Absolutely Essential," *Los Angeles Times*, 25 April 1920, 6:1.

60. G. Gordon Whitnall, "The Experience in the Los Angeles Region" (paper presented at the National Conference on City Planning, Philadelphia, 9–11 May 1927), 127.

61. Whitnall, "Experience," 128.

62. The immense scale of urban expansion in Southern California during the early years of the 1920s would leave even the most enthusiastic municipal cheerleader aghast. Writing in 1927, Whitnall reflected in awe: "During the last seven years the city of Los Angeles has been confronted with the practical problems of assimilating a population greater than the whole city of San Francisco" (ibid., 127). The note of pride in competition with a northern municipal rival might have been lost amid the turmoil of this uncontrollable growth.

63. G. Gordon Whitnall, "City and Regional Planning in Los Angeles" (paper presented at the National Conference on City Planning, Philadelphia, 7–10 April 1924), 106.

64. Automobile Club of Southern California, *The Los Angeles Traffic Problem,* 3.

65. Automobile Club of Southern California, *The Los Angeles Traffic Problem,* 20.

66. Ouellet, *City Planning in Los Angeles,* 3–8.

67. Automobile Club of Southern California, *The Los Angeles Traffic Problem.*

68. For an official history of this important local civic fixture, see J. Allen Davis's *The Friend to All Motorists* (Los Angeles: Anderson, Ritchie, & Simon, 1967), as well as Richard Mathison's somewhat less stiff *Three Cars in Every Garage* (Garden City, NY: Doubleday, 1968). The regional focus of the organization made the Automobile Club one of the first truly metropolitan institutions in Southern California (Mathison, *Three Cars in Every Garage,* 53).

69. Automobile Club of Southern California, *The Los Angeles Traffic Problem,* 29.

70. Los Angeles Traffic Commission, *The Los Angeles Plan* (Los Angeles: Los Angeles Traffic Commission, 1922), 4.

71. Los Angeles Traffic Commission, *The Los Angeles Plan,* 4.

72. Los Angeles Traffic Commission, *The Los Angeles Plan,* 4.

73. Los Angeles Traffic Commission, *The Los Angeles Plan,* 3.

74. Pitt and Pitt, *Los Angeles, A to Z,* 394.

75. Los Angeles Traffic Commission, *A Major Traffic Street Plan for Los Angeles* (Los Angeles: Traffic Commission, 1924), 5.

76. Traffic Commission, *A Major Traffic Street Plan,* 5.

77. Clay McShane, *Down the Asphalt Path: The Automobile and the American City* (New York: Columbia University Press, 1994), 209.

78. Traffic Commission, *A Major Traffic Street Plan,* 28.

79. McShane, *Down the Asphalt Path,* 211.

80. Traffic Commission, *A Major Traffic Street Plan,* 40.

81. Traffic Commission, *A Major Traffic Street Plan,* 27.

82. Traffic Commission, *A Major Traffic Street Plan,* 28.

83. Traffic Commission, *A Major Traffic Street Plan,* 7.

84. Traffic Commission, *A Major Traffic Street Plan,* 4.

85. Jeffrey L. Meikle, *Twentieth Century Limited: Industrial Design in America, 1925–1939* (Philadelphia: Temple University Press, 1979), 207.

86. Jeffrey Meikle notes that McClintock was "described by *Fortune* in 1936 as the 'No. 1 man' in the field" of traffic engineering (ibid., 206).

87. Traffic Commission, *A Major Traffic Street Plan,* 19.

88. Traffic Commission, *A Major Traffic Street Plan,* 12.

89. Traffic Commission, *A Major Traffic Street Plan,* 18.

90. Traffic Commission, *A Major Traffic Street Plan,* 11.

91. Traffic Commission, *A Major Traffic Street Plan,* 11.

92. Traffic Commission, *A Major Traffic Street Plan,* 16.

93. "The Traffic Crisis," *City Club Bulletin* 6, no. 364 (1924): 4.

94. Traffic Commission, *A Major Traffic Street Plan,* 18.

95. Their quantitative methods also determined how Bartholomew, Olmsted, and Cheney

would read the structure of the metropolis. They would perpetuate the existing structure of the city because that centralized character is what gave meaning to their statistical analysis of the traffic problem. The reason for this is simple: the use of and dependence upon downtown traffic counts. In the 1924 plan, the downtown "congested district" stands out because that was the only district in the entire metropolitan region for which the Traffic Commission had reliable, authoritative quantitative data. On 14 February 1924, approximately 1,250 Boy Scouts, "averaging about eleven years of age," under the direction of A. G. Seiler, local scout field executive, were sent out before 7 A.M. to establish a cordon around downtown and to count every automobile entering or exiting the cordoned district. Philip P. Sharples, "Traffic Counts by Boy Scouts in Los Angeles," *American City* 31 (1924): 198; Traffic Commission, *A Major Traffic Street Plan*, 67. The precise boundaries of this district were, of course, determined by planning directors. Sharples, "Traffic Counts by Boy Scouts in Los Angeles," 197. The street corners upon which the scouts were stationed, then, served in advance to demarcate the district's margins and the chief data points. Further, this artificial cordon thus produced, through the labor of the Boy Scouts, an array of quantitative data that could be mapped to the urban topography.

In so doing, the planners acted to construct the district as a unified, comprehensive, legible place, imposing a unity on this area, and further reinforcing the area's integrity in relation to outlying areas. The study of Los Angeles's traffic thus really produced survey data only for this limited area. The report's discussion of traffic in the central business district, then, is given the additional significance of quantitative detail, while the outlying areas remain fuzzy. Moreover, the exact stations of the scouts literally defined the central business district. This district was far different in size and shape by the time of this survey than it had been a decade before. The 1924 plan effectively reified the downtown into a fixed configuration, at the same time clearly setting its boundaries. By rigidly marking off this area from the adjacent urban fabric, borders and functional boundaries that had been fuzzy, indistinct, and fluid were now set with the solid authority of numerical precision. In so doing, the Traffic Commission locked their analysis to a certain urban model even before the survey work began: the establishment of a discrete cordon assumes a concentric model of urbanity and a distinct relationship between the space enclosed or created by the cordon and all external areas, which are thereby determined by definition to be subsidiary, suburban, and peripheral. Traffic Commission, "A Major Traffic Street Plan," 67–69.

96. *Los Angeles Examiner,* 20 July 1923, 1:16, quoted in Robert Fishman, *Bourgeois Utopias: The Rise and Fall of Suburbia* (New York: Basic Books, 1987), 165.

97. Not surprisingly, when Gordon Whitnall came before the City Club to state his support for the goals of the Traffic Commission, he concentrated on the provision for these new business centers: "We must encourage local and sub centers of business development, thus decreasing the average length of the average trip." "Congestion Cost to the Community," *City Club Bulletin* 3, no. 238 (1922): 2.

98. Traffic Commission, *A Major Traffic Street Plan*, 18.

99. Traffic Commission, *A Major Traffic Street Plan*, 18.

100. Traffic Commission, *A Major Traffic Street Plan*, 28.

101. Traffic Commission, *A Major Traffic Street Plan*, 9.

102. "Report on City Planning," *City Club Bulletin* 3, no. 122 (1919): 1.

103. Traffic Commission, *A Major Traffic Street Plan*, 28.

104. Boston was probably the urban model most admired by these regional planners. As Sam Bass Warner describes in his classic *Streetcar Suburbs* (New York: Atheneum, 1962), that city had in the 1890s arrayed a number of suburban business centers—such as Cambridge, Brookline, and Somerville—around the traditional downtown. These new subcenters effectively distributed population outside of the central district. What Bartholomew, Olmsted, and Cheney were envisioning when they discussed decentralization, then, was suburbanization.

105. Traffic Commission, *A Major Traffic Street Plan*, 18.

3. IMAGINING THE METROPOLIS IN A MODERN AGE

1. Harvey W. Zorbaugh, "The Shadow of the Skyscraper," in *The Social Fabric of the Metropolis: Contributions of the Chicago School of Urban Sociology*, ed. James F. Short, Jr. (Chicago: University of Chicago Press, 1929), 3.

2. William Cronon, *Nature's Metropolis: Chicago and the Great West* (New York: Norton, 1991), 102.

3. Zorbaugh, "The Shadow of the Skyscraper," 3–4.

4. Zorbaugh, "The Shadow of the Skyscraper," 4.

5. R. Stephen Sennott, "Chicago Architects and the Automobile, 1906–1926: Adaptations in Horizontal and Vertical Space," in *Roadside America: The Automobile in Design and Culture*, ed. Jan Jennings (Ames: Iowa State University Press, 1990), 164.

6. Eugene S. Taylor, "A Comprehensive System of Elevated Super-Highways," *City Planning* 7, no. 2 (1931): 118.

7. Cronon, *Nature's Metropolis*, 346.

8. Zorbaugh, "The Shadow of the Skyscraper," 4.

9. Zorbaugh, "The Shadow of the Skyscraper," 4.

10. Thomas A. P. van Leeuwen, *The Skyward Trend of Thought: The Metaphysics of the American Skyscraper* (Cambridge, MA: MIT Press, 1988), 16.

11. Paul Goldberger, *The Skyscraper* (New York: Alfred A. Knopf, 1982), 51.

12. Goldberger, *The Skyscraper*, 51.

13. Edward Bellamy, *Looking Backward: 2000–1887* (New York: Penguin, 1982 [1888]), 44.

14. Bellamy, *Looking Backward*, 47.

15. Bellamy, *Looking Backward*, 49.

16. Bellamy, *Looking Backward*, 50. Why the bracketed revelation in Bellamy's narrative? Why the doubled recognition by Julian West? Why, in other words, does the traveler have to explicitly recognize first the self, through the artifice of the mirror, and then the city, through the convention of the balcony view? Clearly, it is important that Julian West not be changed by his time travel, as this narrative is one of utopian social progress. For the purposes of the argument, it must be implicitly proven that it is not "man" that is changed to produce this better world, but merely the structure of social organization. Just as human nature is not to blame for contemporary problems of society, so no improvement in that nature will be necessary for society's twentieth-century ameliorations. Instead, it is simply the social structure—reflected in and encapsulated by a vista of the new Boston—that has been transformed in

the passage from flawed world to utopia. This pleasantly reassuring and conservative stance also, of course, accounts for Bellamy's similar refusal to envision radical changes in the structure of the nuclear family and its attendant gender spheres. Society's organization can be changed without having to change either the (male) individual or the cozy domestic life of patriarchy.

17. See Louis Althusser, "Ideology and Ideological State Apparatuses (Notes toward an Investigation)," in *Lenin and Philosophy* (New York: Monthly Review Press, 1969).

18. Bellamy, *Looking Backward*, 67–68.

19. Much critical debate in recent years has centered on the place of visuality in modern epistemic determination. Martin Jay suggests in *Downcast Eyes* that vision has been criticized in twentieth-century philosophy because it has been thought to be too much an objectifying sense, that the detached "gaze" (often conceived as a tool of the powerful, as in the work of Laura Mulvey) is implicated in oppressive regimes of power. Martin Jay, *Downcast Eyes: The Denigration of Vision in Twentieth-Century French Thought* (Berkeley: University of California Press, 1993); Laura Mulvey, "Visual Pleasure and Narrative Cinema," in *Visual and Other Pleasures* (Bloomington: University of Indiana Press, 1973). Yet this particular understanding of vision—where an observer can feel his or her (usually his, in this modality) perspective to be unreturnable and untraceable—may be a fairly recent and quite contingent conception. Jonathan Crary's *Techniques of the Observer: On Vision and Modernity in the Nineteenth Century* (Cambridge, MA: MIT Press, 1990) argues that a common trope in pre-nineteenth-century representation is the act of locating the observer within the portrayal. Perspective, in this logic, grounds all observation, and the point of view is therefore integral to the experience of viewing. The viewer is thereby fully implicated in the voyeuristic gaze. Crary identifies the camera obscura as a paradigmatic metaphor for the act of looking during the eighteenth century, as it is a technology that precisely locates the observer vis-à-vis the field of view. "What takes place from around 1810 to 1840," he argues, "is an uprooting of vision from the stable and fixed relations incarnated in the camera obscura" (14). By the mid-nineteenth century, the viewed object is no longer so resolutely fixed to the act of viewing and the definite position of the observer: "In a sense, what occurs is a new valuation of visual experience: it is given an unprecedented mobility and exchangeability, abstracted from any founding site or referent." Crary links this new, "modern" logic of seeing to a series of changes that began in the nineteenth century, all loosening the ties between reference and referent, and requiring a decentered, panoptic gaze (in this Crary cites the work of Michel Foucault).

Clearly, as Bellamy's narrative shows, this "obsolete" way of seeing, where the observer is located as surely as are the objects he or she observes, remains integral to this utopian novel. In this respect, the genre might serve as a particularly common, or paradigmatic, mode of modern perception in its own right, as utopian narratives proliferated in the late nineteenth and early twentieth centuries. Perhaps, contrary to Crary's argument, the understanding implicit in this mode of visuality—that the observer and observed are both involved in the act of seeing—has not been entirely erased. Indeed, more generally, within the phenomenology of vision there may in fact be a range of "privileged" modes operative in particular contexts. Whether or not one feels comfortable drawing such conclusions from the example of *Looking Backward*, it is certainly clear that Bellamy takes great pains to locate his observing traveler within the field of vision.

20. According to Frances Theresa Russell's *Touring Utopia* (New York: Dial Press, 1932), Bellamy's 1888 utopian narrative produced a torrent of imitation, rebuttal, and elaboration—in addition, of course, to the author's follow-up, *Equality* (New York: D. Appleton, 1897). Beginning with Arthur Vinton's 1890 *Looking Further Backward* (Albany, NY: Albany Book Company, 1890), the post-Bellamy discourse included four more would-be direct "sequels" published in various countries and languages in 1891 alone, followed by, on average, one a year over the next couple of decades. Clearly, the last decade of the nineteenth century and first two of the twentieth saw a veritable flood of post-Bellamy imagining. Including these variations on *Looking Backward,* there were no fewer than ninety-seven utopian novels published and circulated in America and Europe between 1890 and the mid-1920s. Russell, *Touring Utopia,* 27–34. Many of these utopias, particularly those classified by Howard Segal as "technological utopias," centered on a dramatically revealed city. *Technological Utopianism in American Culture* (Chicago: University of Chicago Press, 1985); "The Technological Utopians," in *Imagining Tomorrow: History, Technology, and the American Future,* ed. Joseph J. Corn (Cambridge, MA: MIT Press, 1987).

21. As Ann Douglas observes in *Terrible Honesty,* "New York and Chicago were competitors in [the] race for the air. (Boston, increasingly a noncontender in the megalopolis category, showed little interest in skyscrapers.)" *Terrible Honesty: Mongrel Manhattan in the 1920s* (New York: Farrar, Straus, and Giroux, 1995), 436.

22. This future dominated by skyscrapers raised the ire of the dyspeptic Lewis Mumford, who decries in *The Story of Utopias* what he sees as the antihumanist vision of these utopian novels. Mumford would, of course, become known by the 1930s for his denunciation of the skyscraper modern urbanism of contemporary Manhattan. Indeed, Merrill Schleier argues that a great deal of elite intellectual discourse on skyscrapers at the turn of the century was strongly negative from both social and architectural perspectives. *The Skyscraper in American Art, 1890–1931* (New York: Da Capo Press, 1986), 8–15. These responses to the skyscraper, at the very beginning of the period of its greatest cultural power and influence, resonate with what T. J. Jackson Lears reminds us was a strong antimodernist tradition in American intellectual culture. See *No Place of Grace: Antimodernism and the Transformation of American Culture, 1880–1920* (Chicago: University of Chicago Press, 1981). Eventually, these voices were largely lost amid the triumphant enthusiasm for towering cities of steel and glass. The artistic and intellectual leaders of American urban culture largely came over to the side of the skyscraper by the 1920s.

23. Merrill Schleier notes in *The Skyscraper in American Art, 1890–1931* that "by 1892, the picturesque potential of the 'skyline' was commented on," and from that point on artists came to focus their attentions on the massed form of the city's profile (28). Thomas A. P. van Leeuwen traces the origin of the term *skyline* to the mid-1870s, and argues that the phrase "'ever-changing skyline' was the standard code used to communicate prosperity and the accumulation of the city's collective wealth." *The Skyward Trend of Thought,* 85, 84. The word itself, then, came to be as much an iconic symbol as the vista to which it referred, conjuring up images of the city as a unitary object instead of a random aggregation of institutions and people.

24. Goldberger, *The Skyscraper,* 3–4.

25. Schleier, *The Skyscraper in American Art,* 68.

26. Schleier, *The Skyscraper in American Art,* 29.

27. Quoted in Schleier, *The Skyscraper in American Art,* 29.

28. Schleier, *The Skyscraper in American Art,* 29.

29. Schleier, *The Skyscraper in American Art,* 28–30.

30. Thomas Bender, untitled lecture, University of California, Irvine, 20 March 1995.

31. Robert Stern, Gregory Gilmartin, and Thomas Mellins, *New York 1930: Architecture between the Two World Wars* (New York: Rizzoli, 1987), 65.

32. Moses King, *King's Views of New York 1896–1915 & Brooklyn 1905* (New York: Benjamin Blom, 1974), vii.

33. King, *King's Views,* 1915: 39.

34. Henry James, *The American Scene* (Bloomington: Indiana University Press, 1968), 76.

35. James, *The American Scene,* 87, 79.

36. James, *The American Scene,* 80.

37. James, *The American Scene,* 186.

38. James Huneker, *New Cosmopolis: A Book of Images* (New York: Charles Scribner's Sons, 1915), 22.

39. Mark Girouard, *Cities and People: A Social and Architectural History* (New Haven, CT: Yale University Press, 1985), 320.

40. David E. Nye, *American Technological Sublime* (Cambridge, MA: MIT Press, 1994), 88.

41. Leeuwen, *The Skyward Trend of Thought,* 13.

42. Leeuwen, *The Skyward Trend of Thought,* 92.

43. The notion of the sublime has had considerable currency in historical scholarly discourse, ranging from Perry Miller's *The Life of the Mind in America* (New York: Harcourt, Brace, 1965) and Leo Marx's *The Machine in the Garden* (New York: Oxford University Press, 1964) to more recent work by John Kasson (*Civilizing the Machine* [New York: Penguin Books, 1976]) and John Sears (*Sacred Places: American Tourist Attractions in the Nineteenth Century* [New York: Oxford University Press, 1989]).

44. Joseph J. Corn and Brian Horrigan, *Yesterday's Tomorrows: Past Visions of the American Future* (New York: Summit Books / Smithsonian Institution, 1984), 43.

45. Nye, *American Technological Sublime,* 100.

46. Lewis Mumford, "American Architecture To-day," *Architecture* 58 (1928): 189. Mumford, of course, was no skyscraper enthusiast.

47. Roland Marchand, *Advertising the American Dream: Making Way for Modernity, 1920–1940* (Berkeley: University of California Press, 1985), 242.

48. Nye, *American Technological Sublime,* 89.

49. Harvey Wiley Corbett, "Up with the Skyscraper," *National Municipal Review* 16, no. 2 (1927): 202.

50. Corbett, "Up with the Skyscraper," 201.

51. Corbett, "Up with the Skyscraper," 201–2.

52. Corbett, "Up with the Skyscraper," 202.

53. Corbett, "Up with the Skyscraper," 149.

54. Corbett, "Up with the Skyscraper," 203.

55. My thanks to Liz Wiatr for the connection between Corbett's promenades, at least as rendered by Hugh Ferriss, and the cloisters of medieval monasteries.

56. Corbett, "Up with the Skyscraper," 203. Even in traditional metropolises such as New York, the elevated railway clearly had a derisive image by the mid-1920s.

57. "And This? Dr. John A. Harriss Proposes Six-Deck Streets," *American City* 36, no. 6 (1927): 803.

58. Orrick Johns, "Bridge Homes—A New Vision of the City," *New York Times*, 22 February 1925, 5.

59. "And How about This? The Henckenway—An Urban Microcosm," *American City* 36, no. 6 (1927): 802.

60. "Coming City of Set-Back Skyscrapers: Diminishing Terraces Stretching Indefinitely Upward," *New York Times,* 29 April 1923, 4:5.

61. Only in the exemplary later photographs of urban observers such as Lewis Hine—which emerged only during the 1930s, after the Great Depression had struck—was the actual physical labor that went into constructing the massive modern building at all apparent. In the heyday of the skyscraper craze in the 1920s, though, even this construction work generally escaped notice. Furthermore, once built, these skyscrapers appeared totally devoid of work, despite the tall building's ostensible economic purpose as concentrator of clerical and white-collar drudgery.

62. Francisco Mujica, *History of the Skyscraper* (Paris: Archaeology and Architecture Press, 1929).

63. David A. Johnson, *Planning the Great Metropolis: The 1929 Regional Plan of New York and Its Environs* (London: E & FN Spon / Chapman & Hall, 1996), 109.

64. Jonathan Goldman, *The Empire State Building Book* (New York: St. Martin's Press, 1980), 46.

65. Goldman, *The Empire State Building Book,* 75.

66. "Hoover Will Open Empire State Today," *New York Times,* 1 May 1931, 1:15.

67. A strange, and famous, inversion of this panoptic gaze occurs in *King Kong.* While the skyscraper's windows usually command unreciprocated views of the surrounding cityscape, Kong upsets the normal visual order when searching for Fay Wray. Indeed, he reaches right into a skyscraper apartment and grabs her. This disquieting scene explodes the security in anonymity characteristic of the modern city, in particular the tall building.

68. Nye, *American Technological Sublime,* 106.

69. Here, the grid defined an x and a y axis of urban location, while the skyscraper effectively determined the z (as well as the origin, thanks to the quality of propinquity). This three-dimensional coordinate system could surmount natural topography to definitively locate the city dweller.

70. According to Kenneth Jackson, in 1910 Manhattan's population reached its peak at about 2.3 million. "By 1940, it had declined to 1.9 million. . . . The outlying boroughs and suburbs exhibited a strong contrary pattern." "The Capital of Capitalism: The New York Metropolitan Region, 1890–1940," in *Metropolis, 1890–1940,* ed. Anthony Sutcliffe (London: Mansell, 1984), 328. Certainly, if not for the influx of African American migrants to Harlem during the 1910s and 1920s, Manhattan's population would have fallen far faster.

71. Alfred Kazin, *A Walker in the City* (New York: Harcourt, Brace, 1951), 10, 11, 8–9.

72. Jacob A. Riis, *How the Other Half Lives: Studies among the Tenements of New York* (New York: Hill and Wang, 1957 [1890]), 22.

73. Jackson, "The Capital of Capitalism," 326.

74. Deborah Dash Moore, "On the Fringes of the City: Jewish Neighborhoods in Three Boroughs," in *The Landscape of Modernity: Essays on New York City, 1900–1940,* ed. David Ward and Oliver Zunz (New York: Russell Sage Foundation, 1992), 253.

75. Anzia Yezierska, *Red Ribbon on a White Horse* (New York: Persea, 1981), 101.

76. Yezierska, *Red Ribbon on a White Horse,* 101–2.

77. Yezierska, *Red Ribbon on a White Horse,* 106.

78. Yezierska, *Red Ribbon on a White Horse,* 107.

79. James Weldon Johnson, *Black Manhattan* (New York: Da Capo Press, 1930), 3.

80. Langston Hughes, *The Big Sea* (New York: Persea Books, 1986 [1940]), 81.

81. Michael Brooks, *Subway City: Riding the Trains, Reading New York* (New Brunswick, NJ: Rutgers University Press, 1997), 185. Despite the frequency with which Hughes's account is used to illustrate this archetypal scene (Brooks places particular emphasis on Hughes's narrative in his argument), Hughes precedes his narrative of arriving in Harlem by subway with a parallel account that invokes the other great trope of urban revelation: "But, boy! At last! New York was pretty, rising out of the bay in the sunset—the thrill of those towers of Manhattan with their million golden eyes, growing slowly taller and taller above the green water, until they looked as if they could almost touch the sky! Then Brooklyn Bridge, gigantic in the dusk! Then the necklaces of lights, glowing everywhere around us, as we docked on the Brooklyn side. All this made me feel it was better to come to New York than to any other city in the world" (*The Big Sea,* 80).

Hughes and many other African Americans were just as taken with the grandeur of the New York skyline as were other urban observers. The appreciation in African American narratives, though, is inevitably tinged with a subtle but pervasive sense of exclusion. Those towers were manifestly foreign: they were the territory of the rich, the powerful, the white. Harlem, on the other hand, is taken on first sight as simultaneously cosmopolitan and welcoming.

82. Ralph Ellison, "Harlem Is Nowhere," in *Shadow and Act* (New York: Vintage, 1948), 295.

83. Ralph Ellison, *Invisible Man* (New York: Random House, 1952), 157.

4. MODERN LOS ANGELES

1. Best known for his Southern Californian residential architectural projects of later years, F. L. Wright, Jr., had extensive professional experience by 1926, not only through his own commissions but also from working for his father's firm and, interestingly, that of the Olmsteds. Charles Moore, Peter Becker, and Regula Campbell, *The City Observed, Los Angeles: A Guide to Its Architecture and Landscapes* (New York: Random House, 1984), 250.

2. Kevin Starr, *Inventing the Dream: California through the Progressive Era* (New York: Oxford University Press, 1985), 181.

3. Richard Longstreth, *City Center to Regional Mall: Architecture, the Automobile, and Retailing in Los Angeles, 1920–1950* (Cambridge MA: MIT Press, 1997), 20–21.

4. Longstreth, *City Center to Regional Mall,* 106.

5. Longstreth, *City Center to Regional Mall,* 106.

6. Longstreth, *City Center to Regional Mall,* 21.

7. Irving Hellman, "The Skyscraper's Influence on Municipal Progress," *Skyscraper* 1, no. 2 (1925): 6.

8. Richard Longstreth notes the power of the prevailing notion of urban modernity in his assessment of Hellman's statements. Longstreth, *City Center to Regional Mall,* 21–23.

9. Spencer Crump, *Ride the Big Red Cars: How Trolleys Helped Build Southern California* (Los Angeles: Crest Publications, 1962), 165.

10. Long a celebrated local tourist attraction, the Mount Lowe railroad was integrated into the far-reaching Pacific Electric system in 1900 and operated until 1937. Leonard Pitt and Dale Pitt, *Los Angeles, A to Z: An Encyclopedia of the City and County* (Berkeley: University of California Press, 1997), 334–35. For an immensely detailed and somewhat nostalgic look at this Southern Californian institution, see Charles Seims's *Mount Lowe: The Railway in the Clouds* (San Marino, CA: Golden West Books, 1976).

In the next decade, Angelenos would take to the new Griffith Observatory. This site, begun in the late 1920s and completed in 1935, did eventually offer one elevated perspective over the city that could "take in" the entire sweep of the metropolis: "On clear nights visitors gather on the terrace for a glorious panorama of the city lights sparkling below." Pitt and Pitt, *Los Angeles, A to Z,* 183. This observatory was geared as much for plumbing the depths of uncharted and mysterious urban space as it was for mapping the cosmos. In the 1930s the observatory offered views, if only for the brief duration of Angelenos' occasional visits, equivalent to those many New Yorkers enjoyed every day from their exemplary skyscrapers. Also like those skyscrapers, it was an urban spot that could be identified and located at a glance from many parts of the city, as well as in countless movies. Although in subsequent decades Griffith Observatory would become an important civic landmark for Angelenos, before its construction there was simply no way to take in a panoramic perspective of the city such as a middle-class New Yorker took for granted.

11. Automobile Club of Southern California, *The Los Angeles Traffic Problem: A Detailed Engineering Report* (Los Angeles: Automobile Club of Southern California, 1922), 18. Such a solution was also pondered in a report of the Los Angeles Municipal League the previous year. "Traffic Congestion and Regulation," *City Club Bulletin* 3, no. 230 (1921): 3. Within a couple of years, many officials were thinking more ambitiously. S. A. Jubb, prominent local transportation specialist, suggested at the "Traffic and Subway Problem of Los Angeles" forum at the City Club that "something further must be done such as the building of second-story streets in the middle of the block to provide automobile routes through the central part of the city." "Open Forum: The Traffic and Subway Problem of Los Angeles," *City Club Bulletin* 5, no. 308 (1923): 4. Jubb had already discussed such a measure before the City Club in 1922. "The Monday Evening Forum," *City Club Bulletin* 3, no. 241 (1922): 4. Although considered somewhat drastic due to their expense, such measures were well within the mainstream of contemporary traffic planning thought. The meticulously detailed visions of Hugh Ferriss and Harvey Corbett in New York had made such imagining respectable, even practical, during the era.

12. Los Angeles Traffic Commission. *The Los Angeles Plan* (Los Angeles: Traffic Commission, 1922), 12.

13. Los Angeles Traffic Commission. *The Los Angeles Plan,* 13–14.

14. Los Angeles Traffic Commission. *The Los Angeles Plan,* 13.

15. Los Angeles Traffic Commission, *A Major Traffic Street Plan for Los Angeles* (Los Angeles: Traffic Commission, 1924), 15.

16. Traffic Commission, *A Major Traffic Street Plan,* 53.

17. C. A. Dykstra, "Congestion De Luxe—Do We Want It?" *National Municipal Review* 15, no. 7 (1926): 395.

18. Traffic Commission, *A Major Traffic Street Plan,* 16.

19. Such was the perceived importance and power of automobilists, especially in the years after the failure of the downtown parking ban, that city engineers almost invariably focused on improving traffic conditions by improving conditions for cars. Consequently, the commission ultimately viewed its purview as only pertaining to automotive congestion, and its solutions were correspondingly limited to reorientations of the city's street system.

Scott Bottles casts this limitation in the political context of decentralization. He suggests that in conflicts between centralizers and decentralizers, catering to the needs of the automobile had support on all sides. *Los Angeles and the Automobile: The Making of the Modern City* (Berkeley: University of California Press, 1987), 173. Although this analysis is certainly accurate, the relative levels of support were not reciprocal. Downtown businessmen were far more committed to rapid transit as a solution to their problems than they were to road construction. Indeed, they were often ambivalent about road construction in narrow downtown streets, which would inevitably disrupt business. That is why they were willing in 1920 to ban the automobile from their district altogether during crucial business hours. The uproar that met this proposal points to a better explanation for Los Angeles's neglect of rapid transit in favor of the automobile: car owners were vociferous and visible. They formed a powerful and influential lobby within the city, and particularly among the wealthy. Rapid transit patrons, on the other hand, tended to be poorer and less vocal, except—as Bottles so ably points out—in their loud denunciations of the street railway system itself. In essence, local politicians undoubtedly attended more closely to the interests of the privileged minority of automobile enthusiasts than to the legions of working-class commuters who were anyhow cynically prone to view aid to rapid transit as handouts to the hated rail monopolies.

20. Crump, *Ride the Big Red Cars,* 151.

21. Crump, *Ride the Big Red Cars,* 152.

22. Crump, *Ride the Big Red Cars,* 151.

23. Crump, *Ride the Big Red Cars,* 152.

24. Crump, *Ride the Big Red Cars,* 151–52. A measure of the confidence in future subway expansion is the statement made by D. W. Pontius, president of Pacific Electric, at the opening of the Hollywood tunnel: "Los Angeles will have more subways. They are the logical answer to traffic congestion, rapid transit of passengers, grade crossing menaces and other problems which face transportation officials over the country. The bore of the Pacific Electric is the first in Los Angeles. Its use, ultimately, will become a habit. . . . Others are sure to come." "P.E. Subway Stimulates Commuter Travel," *Los Angeles Examiner,* 28 March 1926, 2:16.

Despite Pacific Electric's enthusiasm, it is always possible to judge the cultural importance of this sort of public event in Jazz Age Los Angeles by reference to the relative fame of the Hollywood celebrities brought out to legitimate the project. In 1920, automobilists enlisted Clara Kimball Young (who had been voted the most popular female actor in the motion pictures as recently as 1916). In the case of the Hollywood subway, Pacific Electric managed to recruit only Wallace Beery and Esther Ralston. "Hollywood Tube Service Opens Today," *Los Angeles Examiner*, 7 February 1926. Beery was a comedian of some repute in the 1910s. By the early 1920s he had attempted to remake himself as a character actor, with some slight success. By the time of the subway celebration of 1926, however, his reputation had faded considerably—he was relegated to playing supporting comic roles in undistinguished features. (His real claim to fame was that he had once, briefly, been the husband of silent screen diva Gloria Swanson.) Ralston was an even more minor star, appearing in these years in peripheral supporting ingenue roles. Daniel Blum, *A Pictorial History of the Silent Screen* (New York: Grosset & Dunlap, 1953), 56, 219, 67, 300. Judging from the contemporary status of these movie industry representatives, the relative cultural power of the street railway system clearly could not measure up to that of the automobilists.

25. Scott Bottles notes that "the Traffic Commission was a major proponent of this alteration." *Los Angeles and the Automobile*, 277n12.

26. R. F. Kelker, Jr., and C. F. De Leuw, *Report and Recommendations on a Comprehensive Rapid Transit Plan for the City and County of Los Angeles* (Chicago: Kelker, De Leuw and Company, 1925), 42.

27. Kelker and De Leuw, *Rapid Transit Plan*, 1.

28. Kelker and De Leuw, *Rapid Transit Plan*, 139.

29. Kelker and De Leuw, *Rapid Transit Plan*, 139.

30. Kelker and De Leuw, *Rapid Transit Plan*, 75. On the surface, it appears as if the *Rapid Transit Plan* would displease enthusiasts of skyscraper urbanism, as it endorses, at a number of points, the general philosophy of urban decentralization, particularly in its stated preference for single-family homes. Yet, in this view, residential "decentralization" would only reinforce the centrality of the built-up downtown district: "The principal factor in this decentralization was the operation of rapid transit lines which overcame distance with speed and enabled many workers to live in uncongested districts and work in the heart of the city." Ibid., 96. Once more, then, the ubiquitous language of "decentralization" conceals crucial differences between those who seek to preserve the basic structure of the concentric metropolis (such as Kelker and De Leuw) and those who prefer to dismantle it altogether.

31. See Kelker and De Leuw, *Rapid Transit Plan*, 3. For an opposing view, see also "Subways Boost Suburban Areas," *Los Angeles Examiner*, 28 February 1926, 4:13.

32. Kelker and De Leuw, *Rapid Transit Plan*, 38.

33. Kelker and De Leuw, *Rapid Transit Plan*, 105, 156, 7.

34. Kelker and De Leuw, *Rapid Transit Plan*, 25.

35. Kelker and De Leuw, *Rapid Transit Plan*, 89.

36. Marshall Stimson, "The Battle for a Union Station at Los Angeles," *Historical Society of Southern California Quarterly* 21, no. 1 (1939): 37.

37. Ultimately, these plans included schemes to build unified stations on bridges across the Los Angeles River at Sixth Street (the Noerenberg Plan) or between Seventh and Ninth Streets (the Maharg Plan), to construct a unified station on the east side of the river between Sixth and Seventh Streets (the Dunlap Plan) or between Seventh and Ninth Streets (the Daum

Plan). For the details of these proposals, see "Now There Are Six Plans for Station," *Los Angeles Record*, 15 March 1926, 10.

38. "C. of C. Fights Plaza Union Station: 4 Railroads Offer New Traffic Plan," *Los Angeles Examiner*, 30 December 1925, 1:1.

39. By this time, the Union Pacific had already abandoned its old station and was leasing space in Southern Pacific's Arcade Depot. The two railways therefore proposed to rebuild that station at the same spot, to accommodate both carriers.

40. "Subway Lines Opening Sunday," *Los Angeles Times*, 2 February 1926, 2:2.

41. Mayor George Cryer soon "suggested adoption of the Kelker-De Leuw report on a rapid transit system." "Beach Trade Chiefs Back 'L' Projects," *Los Angeles Examiner*, 22 January 1926, 2:1. A week later, as the *Examiner* noted in support of this solution, "Maj. R. F. Kelker, Jr. urged the adoption of an ordinance adopting the general plan as outlined in the Kelker-De Leuw report as the city's comprehensive plan." "Adoption of Kelker-De Leuw Rapid Transit Plan Urged," *Los Angeles Examiner*, 29 January 1926, 2:1. Likewise, Miller McClintock—who was the Traffic Commission's foremost expert, consulting for that body in the drafting of the *Major Traffic Street Plan*—told the city council at the same public hearing that, whichever union terminal was chosen, it was imperative to connect the station or stations to a modern rapid transit network.

42. "Warns against Rush Act," *Los Angeles Times*, 9 February 1926, 2:2.

43. In addition to five questions that collectively addressed the three urban modernization measures, the ballot also tested voters' minds on legalizing Sunday dancing at Venice, raising the pay for city police and firefighters, unifying the county's ports, ceding Dead Man's Island to the federal government as an immigration post, and constructing of a number of viaducts and automobile bridges over the Los Angeles River. These measures were widely supported by the local media (although the question of dancing at Venice, which originally impelled the special election, did draw some controversy). The *Los Angeles Examiner* took particularly strongly to the port unification question, making it an editorial priority. The question that all the newspapers advocated with the most unanimity, though, was that of the river bridge bonds (this topic was also played up in advertisements in those papers for prospective real estate tracts on the east side of the river).

44. Thanks to a series of clever maneuvers by Union Station proponents, the rapid transit question was not put directly to the voters for approval. Instead, transit advocates had to campaign for the defeat of two linked questions on the city's original plans—one testing the idea of a Union Station and the other asking if such a station should be located in the historic Plaza. Only by rejecting these paired measures could citizens register their endorsement of the alternate carriers' plan.

45. "Fabrications vs. Facts," *Los Angeles Times*, 28 April 1926, 2:3.

46. Wilshire Beautiful Association, "Stop the Exploiter! Save Wilshire Boulevard for All the People. Vote No on Propositions 3 and 4," *Los Angeles Record*, 28 April 1926, 8.

47. "Record Recommendations," *Los Angeles Record*, 29 April 1926, 9. The *Evening Express* also opposed the rezoning, fearing that business development might turn Wilshire Boulevard into a commercial slum. "Record Vote Is Expected in L.A. Tomorrow: Ten Questions on Ballot," *Los Angeles Evening Express*, 29 April 1926, 10. In general, other papers endorsed the proposed changes.

48. See "Save Wilshire Blvd. from Realestate Exploiters: Vote No on Propositions 3 and 4," *Los Angeles Herald*, 29 April 1926, 1:19.

49. Longstreth, *City Center to Regional Mall*, 105. The Wilshire Boulevard Association also compared the prospective development of their thoroughfare with Chicago's Michigan Avenue. See, for instance, "Urge Wilshire as L.A.'s Fifth Avenue," *Los Angeles Herald*, 6 April 1926, 1:13.

50. "Artery Seen as Busy Hub by Backers," *Los Angeles Examiner*, 25 April 1926. In a rare show of unanimity, the rival *Times* joined the *Examiner* in admiring speculations about the prospects for "imposing business and apartment buildings" along the boulevard. The *Times* was actually quoting Loren C. Barton of the Wilshire Boulevard Development Association. "Urges Yes Votes for Zone Plan," *Los Angeles Times*, 29 April 1926, 2:3.

51. "City Hall a Symbol," *Los Angeles Evening Express*, 23 April 1926, 18.

52. "Height-Limit Reason Given," *Los Angeles Times*, 25 April 1926, 5:4.

53. "Workman Asks High City Hall," *Los Angeles Examiner*, 7 April 1926, 2:8.

54. "Workman Asks High City Hall," 2:8.

55. Albert C. Martin, "New Hall Will Symbolize City," *Los Angeles Times*, 11 April 1926, 2:3.

56. "Workman Asks High City Hall," 2:8.

57. "City Hall a Symbol," 18.

58. William Sproule, "Every Dot a Grade Crossing," *Los Angeles Times*, 17 January 1926, 1:12.

59. This advertisement appeared in the newspapers on the following dates: *Los Angeles Record*, 16 January 1926, 6–7; *Los Angeles Times*, 17 January 1926, 1:12–13; *Los Angeles Examiner*, 17 January 1926, 1:6–7; *Los Angeles Herald*, 18 January 1926, 1:8–9.

60. Sproule, "Every Dot a Grade Crossing," 1:13.

61. A number of historians, including Spencer Crump and Scott Bottles, echo the *Times'* assertion that the newspaper stood alone against the other local dailies in its opposition to the carriers' rapid transit plan. See, for instance, "Straw Vote on Depot Question," *Los Angeles Times*, 26 February 1926, 2:2; as well as Crump, *Ride the Big Red Cars*, 165–66; Bottles, *Los Angeles and the Automobile*, 139. Actually, the situation was more complex. The *Examiner*, which had a greater circulation than its rivals, certainly opposed Chandler's *Times* at every step. The working-class *Record*, which denounced the Plaza site as "Harry's 'Onion' Station" or "Harry's 'Plaza' Scheme," nevertheless expressed considerable ambivalence about terminal unification. Although it made clear that it had no objection to a union station per se and went so far as to explicitly state its endorsement of such "beautification" efforts in principle, the *Record* certainly did not approve of the Plaza site, which it saw as a Chandler-inspired real estate speculation plot. The *Herald* was even more split, ultimately refusing to take any position on the Plaza question. The *Evening Express* ran a number of mildly critical articles about the Union Station plan, but at the time of the election it ran only timid and ambivalent editorials. Despite this variety of press opinion, all papers except the *Examiner* became less and less enthusiastic about the rapid transit plan as the election progressed; this undoubtedly reflects the effectiveness of the *Times'* vigorous opposition campaign. "Record Recommendations," 9.

62. These attacks were accompanied by advertisements (placed in all the major papers,

352 NOTES TO PAGE 188

but particularly in the *Times*) by an organization calling itself the Anti-Elevated Association of Los Angeles.

63. This series amounted to something of a travelogue, as the paper reported sequentially from Chicago, on 14–18 April: J. P. Gallagher, "Elevated Held Curse to Progress of Chicago," *Los Angeles Times*, 14 April 1926, 1:1+; J. P. Gallagher, "Chicago Takes Up Gage in Opposition to 'L' Railroad," *Los Angeles Times*, 15 April 1926, 1:1+; J. P. Gallagher, "Elevated Railroad Magnate Condemns Chicago 'L,' Joins in Fight to Provide Subway," *Los Angeles Times*, 16 April 1926, 1:1+; J. P. Gallagher, "Experts Call Building of 'L' Tragic Error," *Los Angeles Times*, 18 April 1926, 1:1+; followed by Boston, on 19–20 April: "Just What This 'L' Means," *Los Angeles Times*, 19 April 1926, 1:1+; "Values Fall Due to 'L,'" *Los Angeles Times*, 20 April 1926, 1:1+; New York City, on 21–25 April: W. A. Lyon, "New York Pays Piper for Dance That Opened 'L,'" *Los Angeles Times*, 21 April 1926, 1:1+; W. A. Lyon, "Property Values Soar when New York City Street Bans 'L,'" *Los Angeles Times*, 22 April 1926, 1:1–2; W. A. Lyon, "Foul Dirt, Darkness and Bedlam Curse of 'L,'" *Los Angeles Times*, 23 April 1926, 1:1–2; W. A. Lyon, "Effect of New York 'L' on Health Disastrous," *Los Angeles Times*, 24 April 1926, 1:1–2; W. A. Lyon, "City Warned by Expert of Menace in 'L' Plan," *Los Angeles Times*, 25 April 1926, 1:1–2; and finally Philadelphia, on 26 April: Carroll Shelton, "Philadelphia Bans 'L' as Dirty, Noisy, Inartistic," *Los Angeles Times*, 26 April 1926.

Inside the reports, local elevateds, in their "headlong swaying flight," were described as "dirty, noisy, inartistic," bringing "din, gloom, and property loss" and "foul dirt, darkness, and bedlam" to these "cursed" cities. Lyon, "Foul Dirt, Darkness and Bedlam Curse of 'L,'" 1:1. In each case, the reporters told how locals in these eastern metropolises were now fighting to remove their elevated railways, usually to replace them with subways (which the *Times* offered vaguely as a future alternative for Los Angeles, without actually proposing a new rapid transit plan). Easterners interviewed for these articles invariably warned the California city not to make the same "grave mistake" they did. Lyon, "City Warned by Expert of Menace in 'L' Plan," 1:1.

Often the articles directly challenged dominant thinking about modern urbanism in the era. The celebrated Chicago Loop, for instance, was described as an "iron jacket . . . an iron band of gloom and darkness . . . [which] fastened itself around the torso of Chicago. This iron band, supported in the air by unsightly stilts, and emitting almost constantly all the racket of a boiler factory in full blast, soon proved to be what its antagonists predicted: a steel corset retarding the natural growth of a great city." Gallagher, "Elevated Held Curse to Progress of Chicago," 1:3.

Without the curse of the elevated railroad, the *Times* argued—very much against the grain of conventional wisdom in the period—downtown Chicago would have prospered even more than it had during its boom years. The vertical bands of steel were not marks of technological and industrial progress but obsolete remnants of the world of tenements and blight. In this way, the paper not only critiqued elevated railroads and the proposed Los Angeles rapid transit plan, but the very vertical sublime that animated them. In a sense, this was a direct counterattack on Kelker, De Leuw, and Company, implicating that firm's plans for Southern California by ruthlessly attacking their implementation back home.

64. For a few examples of these train wrecks, see "Keep the 'L' Out of Los Angeles," *Los Angeles Times*, 29 March 1926, 1:1; Lyon, "City Warned by Expert of Menace in 'L' Plan," 1:2;

and Gallagher, "Experts Calls Building of 'L' Tragic Error." Occasionally, the paper would feature photos of elevated railway accidents around the nation without commentary—in the photogravure section, for instance, or as a simple dispatch—assuming that, by this point, readers would be able to connect these horrors to the contemporary campaign. See "Cause of Car Plunge Still Unfixed," *Los Angeles Times*, 23 March 1926, 1:8; and "Luckily, No One Was Killed . . . ," *Los Angeles Times*, 29 April 1926, 1:12.

65. Lyon, "Effect of New York 'L' on Health Disastrous," 1:2.

66. Lyon, "Foul Dirt, Darkness and Bedlam Curse of 'L,'" 1:1. Local celebrity radio evangelist Aimee Semple McPherson returned from a trip abroad during the campaign and was immediately recruited by the *Times* to spread the gospel of the anti-"el" crusade. Sermonizing that Los Angeles was "a place of refuge" for people seeking "peace, quiet and comfort," McPherson earnestly suggested that these refugees had fled to Southern California precisely to escape "the noise, dirt, unsightliness, gloom and danger of the elevateds." This city on a hill should not, she asserted, be defiled by the elevated, thereby "destroy[ing] the sacredness of the place" and turning it into a pit of "poisonous pestilence." "Evangelist Is Against Elevateds," *Los Angeles Times*, 29 April 1926, 2:1.

67. Business Men's Association of Los Angeles, "In the Spirit of Fair Play," *Los Angeles Record*, 12 March 1926, 13.

68. Lyon, "Foul Dirt, Darkness and Bedlam Curse of 'L,'" 1:1.

69. "These Issues Command Your Voting Interest," *Los Angeles Examiner*, 29 April 1926, 2:16. Efforts to refocus the discourse back onto traffic continued throughout the campaign: "The only proposition to be considered in the Plaza controversy . . . is 'What is the best way to eliminate grade crossings and to relieve traffic congestion in Los Angeles?'" Citizens' Union Station Committee, "Keep the Elevateds Out!" *Los Angeles Examiner*, 28 April 1926, 1:1+. The Business Men's Association, in particular, expressed shock and outrage over "misleading propaganda" that the railroads intended to build elevated structures along Los Angeles's boulevards, although that was precisely what the enabling Kelker and De Leuw plan had called for. In full retreat, a few days before the election, the presidents of the railroads published "signed statements" that they would never contemplate darkening the streets of Southern California with "longitudinal" elevateds. Business Men's Association of Los Angeles, "These Cartoons Misrepresent Facts," *Los Angeles Times*, 29 April 1926, 2:15. D. W. Pontius, president of Pacific Electric, chimed in with similar assurances: "The Pacific Electric Railway will never build an elevated line west of Main Street, and if elevateds are ever built, they will not be financed by the company. There is no man here who will live to see elevated railways in the residential district of Los Angeles." "Traffic Commission Hits Union Station," *Los Angeles Examiner*, 21 April 1926, 2:10. Even before the election took place, the notion of modern elevated railways through Southern California as the heart of a multilevel rapid transit scheme was dying. Clearly, by April 1926, the *Times* had succeeded in divorcing the Union Station and rapid transit issues, which the railroads had so skillfully linked only four months before.

70. "The Election Arguments," *Los Angeles Record*, 26 April 1926, 10.

71. "Plaza Depot," *Los Angeles Examiner*, 20 April 1926, 2:20. Some alternate shorthand references included "Depot in Chinese District" or simply "Chinatown site." "Depot in Chinese District, or No More Grade Crossings?," *Los Angeles Examiner*, 12 April 1926, 2:16; "Sane View of Plaza Plan by City's Traffic Experts," *Los Angeles Examiner*, 24 April 1926, 2:16. At

the same time, in an article in the same paper, city councilman Ralph Criswell also drew attention to earlier—rejected—efforts "to have the city accept a large area in the old Chinatown district as a site for a great passenger terminal." "Criswell Calls Plaza Terminal Unnecessary," *Los Angeles Examiner,* 29 March 1926, 1:5. Meanwhile, the Business Men's Association began referring to the Plaza terminal in the same way: as the "Chinatown property," as one advertisement put it. "Fabrications vs. Facts," 8. This was clearly a calculated campaign to solidify the association of the Union Station with the ethnic district.

72. "Plaza Plan, Ignoring P.E., Reveals Its Fatal Weakness," *Los Angeles Examiner,* 26 April 1926, 2:7.

73. Many opponents of the Union Station suggested in a similar vein that the Plaza site was no longer central to the city. It represented the metropolis's hazy past, whereas the city needed to put forward a more modern and dynamic impression of itself to visitors. See "Finance Head Raps Station on Plaza Site," *Los Angeles Examiner,* 21 January 1926, 1:6; "Expert Opposes Union Station at Plaza," *Los Angeles Examiner,* 21 February 1926, 2:15.

74. Citizens' Union Station Committee, "Keep The Elevateds Out!" 1:14.

75. "Magnificent Los Angeles Civic Center in the Making: Steam Shovels Clear Way for Downtown Beauty Spot," *Los Angeles Times,* 18 April 1926, 2:1.

76. "People vs. Railroads, Union Station Issue," *Los Angeles Times,* 20 April 1926, 2:2.

77. "Attorneys Support Union Station Plan," *Los Angeles Evening Express,* 21 April 1926, 29.

78. "Complete Our Civic Center by Voting 'Yes' on Propositions 8–9," *Los Angeles Times,* 28 April 1926, 2:1.

79. Many years later, Stimson helped repress official memory of this Chinese and Mexican American displacement in the construction of Union Station. In what remained for almost four decades the only published historical commentary about the battle over the Plaza site, his 1939 article in the *Southern California Quarterly,* "The Battle for a Union Station at Los Angeles," made no mention of the previous inhabitants of the land by then occupied by "the beautiful new Union Station, of which Los Angeles is now so proud" (43). The ethnic cleansing endorsed in the 1920s was itself cleansed from much of the historiography, although long-time residents surely remembered.

80. See, for example, Scott Bottles's *Los Angeles and the Automobile,* 281.

81. See Mike Davis, *City of Quartz* (New York: Vintage Books, 1992 [1990]), 15–98.

82. We will see what happened to Wilshire in the final years of the 1920s in the next chapter. It is worth noting here, though, that the boulevard would not become anything like a towering "Fifth Avenue of the West" for another forty years.

83. The Plaza location question squeaked by on a margin of 4,000 votes out of 190,000 cast. The small margin probably reflected the fear of ethnic boundary transgression among the predominantly white voters of Los Angeles, but the victory itself testified to the rhetorical skill of the *Times* in ultimately refocusing that anxiety. "The Election Results," *Los Angeles Times,* 2 May 1926,1:1.

84. Chinatown was cleared by 1933; Olvera Street opened in 1929. An excellent archaeological account of the destruction of Los Angeles's Chinatown is Roberta S. Greenwood, *Down by the Station: Los Angeles Chinatown, 1880–1933* (Los Angeles: Institute of Archaeology, University of California, Los Angeles, 1996). For an interpretation of the

efforts in the later 1920s to remake Olvera Street as a tourist attraction, and particularly of the efforts of Christine Sterling toward that end, see Phoebe Kropp's unpublished dissertation, "'All Our Yesterdays': The Spanish Fantasy Past and the Politics of Public Memory in Southern California, 1884–1939" (Ph.D. diss., University of California, San Diego, 1999), and *California Vieja: Culture and Memory in a Modern American Place* (Berkeley: University of California Press, 2006). In fact, this tourist-oriented reconstruction project was so successful that, by 1938, a newly disciplined (and much smaller) "fake chinoiserie" New Chinatown was opened at the northern edge of the downtown district. "New Chinatown," *Los Angeles Times*, 21 January 1938; Moore, Becker, and Campbell, *The City Observed*, 10.

85. "Far-Flung City Held Ideal Here," *Los Angeles Times*, 10 May 1925, 1:11.

86. "Low-Height Limitation Advocated," *Los Angeles Times*, 20 May 1925, 1:16.

87. "Height Limit Is Protested," *Los Angeles Times*, 30 May 1925, 1:5.

88. Myra Nye, "Whitnall Hits Back at Critics," *Los Angeles Times*, 5 June 1925, 2:6.

89. "Height Limit Commended," *Los Angeles Times*, 11 June 1925, 2:2.

90. C. A. Dykstra, "Report on Rapid Transit," *City Club Bulletin*, 30 January 1926, 10.

91. Dykstra, "Report on Rapid Transit," 9.

92. Dykstra, "Report on Rapid Transit," 4.

93. Dykstra, "Congestion De Luxe," 396–97.

94. Dykstra, "Report on Rapid Transit," 4.

95. Dykstra, "Congestion De Luxe," 398.

96. George A. Damon, "Relation of the Motor Bus to Other Methods of Transportation" (paper presented at the National Conference on City Planning, Philadelphia, 7–10 April 1924), 80.

97. Dykstra, "Report on Rapid Transit," 4.

98. Dykstra, "Congestion De Luxe," 398.

99. Dykstra, "Congestion De Luxe," 398.

100. George A. Damon, "Inter and Intra Urban Transit and Traffic as a Regional Planning Problem" (paper presented at the National Conference on City Planning, Baltimore, 30 April–2 May 1923), 53.

101. "The Open Forum," *City Club Bulletin* 8, no. 435 (1925): 4.

102. Dykstra, "Congestion De Luxe," 395.

103. Daniel L. Turner, "Is There a Vicious Circle of Transit Development and City Congestion?" *National Municipal Review* 15, no. 6 (1926): 321.

104. Turner, "Is There a Vicious Circle," 322.

105. "Is the Skyscraper Doomed?" *National Municipal Review* 15, no. 8 (1926): 438.

106. "The Skyscraper," *National Municipal Review* 16, no. 1 (1927): 1.

107. Harvey Wiley Corbett, "Up with the Skyscraper," *National Municipal Review* 16, no. 2 (1927): 101.

108. Corbett, "Up with the Skyscraper," 100–101.

109. Henry H. Curran, "The Skyscraper Does Cause Congestion: Major Curran Comes Back at Mr. Corbett," *National Municipal Review* 16, no. 4 (1927): 234.

110. Curran, "The Skyscraper Does Cause Congestion," 233.

111. Curran, "The Skyscraper Does Cause Congestion," 234.

112. Curran, "The Skyscraper Does Cause Congestion," 233.

113. For more on the New York zoning laws, see M. Christine Boyer, *Dreaming the Rational City* (Cambridge, MA: MIT Press, 1983), 161–70; Carol Willis, "Skyscraper Utopias: Visionary Urbanism in the 1920s," in *Imagining Tomorrow: History, Technology, and the American Future*, ed. Joseph J. Corn (Cambridge, MA: MIT Press, 1987), and her essay "Drawing towards Metropolis," in Hugh Ferriss, *The Metropolis of To-morrow*, reprint ed. (Princeton, NJ: Princeton Architectural Press, 1986), 157–60, 171; Thomas A. P. van Leeuwen, *The Skyward Trend of Thought* (Cambridge, MA: MIT Press, 1988 [1986]), 81; Joseph J. Corn and Brian Horrigan, *Yesterday's Tomorrows* (New York: Summit Books/Smithsonian Institution, 1984), 41–43; and Robert A. M. Stern, Gregory Gilmartin, and Thomas Mellins, *New York, 1930* (New York: Abrams, 1987), 31–39.

114. Ebenezer Howard, "Reply" (paper presented at the International City and Regional Planning Conference, Baltimore, 20–25 April 1925), 8–9.

115. "Los Angeles, City of Homes," *Los Angeles Evening Express*, 5 April 1926, 14.

5. METROPOLIS AT A CROSSROADS

1. C. A. Dykstra, "Congestion De Luxe—Do We Want It?" *National Municipal Review* 15, no. 7 (1926): 395.

2. Richard J. Neutra, "Homes and Housing," in *Los Angeles: Preface to a Master Plan*, ed. George W. Robbins and L. Deming Tilton (Los Angeles: Pacific Southwest Academy / Ward Ritchie Press, 1941), 189.

3. Neutra, "Homes and Housing," 190.

4. Harland Bartholomew, "A Program to Prevent Economic Disintegration in American Cities" (paper presented at the National Conference on City Planning, Philadelphia, 14–16 November 1932), 2.

5. Ralph Hancock, *Fabulous Boulevard* (New York: Funk & Wagnalls, 1949), 155.

6. Quoted in Hancock, *Fabulous Boulevard*, 160.

7. Quoted in Hancock, *Fabulous Boulevard*, 159.

8. Richard Longstreth, *City Center to Regional Mall: Architecture, the Automobile, and Retailing in Los Angeles, 1920–1950* (Cambridge, MA: MIT Press, 1997), 112.

9. Hancock, *Fabulous Boulevard*, 154–55.

10. Leonard Pitt and Dale Pitt, *Los Angeles, A to Z: An Encyclopedia of the City and County* (Berkeley: University of California Press, 1997), 64.

11. Charles Moore, Peter Becker, and Regula Campbell, *The City Observed, Los Angeles: A Guide to Its Architecture and Landscapes* (New York: Random House, 1984), 147.

12. Quoted in Hancock, *Fabulous Boulevard*, 270.

13. Longstreth, *City Center to Regional Mall*, 112.

14. Moore, Becker, and Campbell, *The City Observed*, 147.

15. Longstreth, *City Center to Regional Mall*, 105.

16. Longstreth, *City Center to Regional Mall*, 103.

17. Robert Fishman, *Bourgeois Utopias: The Rise and Fall of Suburbia* (New York: Basic Books, 1987), 171.

18. Where once Angelenos flocked to the central district for both work and entertainment, now they tended to go off in what seemed like a million directions. W. W. Robinson's reminiscence conveys a bit of the sense of loss and alienation many residents felt over downtown's decline: "Los Angeles, spread-eagling in all directions, gradually ceased having a day-and-night center in a single, active, downtown district. . . . Prior to the 1920's, this area had been alive during the day and evening hours with people, shops, stores, excellent restaurants, theaters, and churches. Saloons were numerous and heavily patronized. . . . Such was the 'central city' of the early 1900's—the place Angelenos and visitors went for business and fun." *Los Angeles: A Profile* (Norman: University of Oklahoma Press, 1968), 27–28. According to Robinson, downtown had been a primary site of communal interaction. In this sense, the central district served as a metonym for the city: it was the place that encapsulated urbanity for Angelenos.

Nevertheless, the authority attributed to such "public space"—i.e., the ethos of eidetic representation—has always played into the hands of dominant power structures in those cities. Only those who had "business" in these "public" spaces appeared there. The many social, cultural, and economic groups that were underrepresented in that significant district—that "space of appearance," in Hannah Arendt's phrase—were occluded in Angelenos' vision of the city. This zone was one of exclusion just as surely as was any other purportedly common space of the metropolis during the era, from the segregated beaches to the Hollywood Bowl. By contrast, downtown was a place of peculiar inclusion. A fascinating example of this facet of the district's representational machinery is Olvera Street, the "original" pueblo of the city, reconstructed in 1930 under the guidance of nostalgist Christine Sterling in connection with the Plaza Union Station development. Like the midway exhibits of a world's fair, this theatrical "ethnic" zone was more concerned with presenting an exotic image to visiting tourists than in providing an inclusive space for cultural exchange. If W. W. Robinson had fond memories of downtown Los Angeles, they were of a place where public space was not always open to the public.

19. Howard J. Nelson, *The Los Angeles Metropolis* (Dubuque, IA: Kendall/Hunt, 1981), 193.

20. Fishman, *Bourgeois Utopias,* 170.

21. G. Gordon Whitnall, "The Place of the East Coast in a State Plan for Florida" (paper presented at the National Conference on City Planning, Philadelphia, 29 March–1 April 1926), 43.

22. Walter V. Woehlke, "Roots of Los Angeles' Astonishing Growth," *Sunset* (1924): 195.

23. As a later report by the Automobile Club of Southern California (Engineering Department) put it, "The 1937 survey discloses a distinct change in the directional movement of traffic. A rectangular traffic movement has been super-imposed upon the original and greatly augmented radial movement, resulting in a crisscrossing of traffic and a street and highway congestion and hazard without parallel." *Traffic Survey: Los Angeles Metropolitan Area* (Los Angeles: Automobile Club of Southern California, 1937), 21.

24. Fishman, *Bourgeois Utopias,* 171. For further examples of this Southern Californian spatial innovation, the importance of which has received wide consensus among urban historians, see Scott L. Bottles, *Los Angeles and the Automobile: The Making of the Modern City* (Berkeley: University of California Press, 1987), 203–10; Mark Stewart Foster, "The Decen-

tralization of Los Angeles during the 1920's" (Ph.D. diss., University of Southern California, 1971), 155–57, 259–66; and Sam Bass Warner, Jr., *The Urban Wilderness: A History of the American City* (Berkeley: University of California Press, 1995 [1972]), 113–49.

25. See Robert Fogelson, *Fragmented Metropolis* (Berkeley: University of California Press, 1967); Hancock, *Fabulous Boulevard;* and Foster, "The Decentralization of Los Angeles during the 1920's."

26. Bottles, *Los Angeles and the Automobile,* 206–7.

27. Bottles was understating the situation, for his description could imply that downtown was simply superseded by Pasadena or Hollywood. Southern California in 1930, though, was not merely multifocal but virtually unfocused, or dispersed. Greater Los Angeles was not totally distributed to the point of homogeneous dispersal, but it was closer to that extreme than to a landscape composed of a small number of discrete subcenters.

In 1933, Los Angeles's downtown hosted a bit more than 30 percent of the region's retail commerce, and the fifteen largest subcenters collectively handled about 45 percent. Even more impressively, though, the remaining 25 percent (almost equal to downtown, and it would grow much larger in ensuing decades) took place in no proper business district at all—in hundreds of scattered strips, clusters, or isolated individual shops and offices (proportions calculated from raw data printed in Los Angeles County Regional Planning Commission, *Business Districts* [Los Angeles: Los Angeles County Regional Planning Commission, 1944], 29). The relative proportions for 1929 and 1939, which involve very similar absolute numbers, reveal the subsequent decline of downtown particularly sharply, as well as the early date at which outlying business districts overtook the Los Angeles central business district in retail activity: 37, 43, and 20 percent for 1929, versus 21, 51, and 30 percent for 1939. These calculations only reflect retail sales, of course. Wholesale figures might favor the downtown district, but measurements of residential dispersal or recreational activity would certainly highlight even more dramatically the decline of discrete centers of all kinds.

The following table may help illustrate the differences in understanding *decentralization* floating through historical and historiographical discourses on Southern California:

Suburbanization	= *Decentralization* =	Moderate shift in density of residential settlement from center to outer rings of concentric system
Garden City Cluster	= *Decentralization* =	Concentric system replaced by recentralization around autonomous and discrete subcenters
Postsuburbanization	= *Decentralization* =	Concentric system replaced by massive, decentered dispersal over the entire region

I use the term *postsuburbanization* for what Bottles calls *decentralization.*

28. M. Gottdiener and George Kephart, "The Multinucleated Metropolitan Region: A Comparative Analysis," in *Postsuburban California: The Transformation of Orange County*

since World War II, ed. Rob Kling, Spencer Olin, and Mark Poster (Berkeley: University of California Press, 1991), 33–34.

29. The term *postsuburban* implies a troubling teleology, which derives, thanks in part to the influence of the work of Robert Fishman on suburbia, from its authors' focus on Orange County through a developmental model: "We label this 'new city' a *postsuburban* spatial formation because it evolves from the spatial organization of a low-density suburban region." Rob Kling, Spencer Olin, and Mark Poster, "The Emergence of Postsuburbia: An Introduction," in *Postsuburban California: The Transformation of Orange County since World War II,* ed. Rob Kling, Spencer Olin, and Mark Poster (Berkeley: University of California Press, 1995), 6. Although in both Orange County and 1920s Greater Los Angeles postsuburbia developed out of a previously suburbanized area, that course of development should not necessarily be considered inevitable. Moreover, the evolutionary model implicit in the narrative distorts the potential for historical variation and subtly suggests that postsuburbia might in some way be a more "advanced" urban form than others—or at least that such development patterns might be the wave of the future more generally. The fact that exemplary contemporary postsuburban regions such as Orange County have grown to national prominence relatively recently (since World War II, for the most part) implies that postsuburbia is just now emerging as a spatial and societal formation and will soon likely become ubiquitous.

If, as I have argued here, Greater Los Angeles developed its postsuburban form at the end of the 1920s, then postsuburbia begins to seem a bit less futuristic. As Los Angeles was becoming postsuburban, after all, most of urban America was suburbanizing or constructing traditional urbanity. Such patterns of development, then, must be considered the products of contingent historical and ideological contexts, and do not follow any teleology. Despite this weakness in the neologism, *postsuburbanization* is a relatively compact term (at least compared to alternatives such as Gottdiener and Kephart's *multinucleated metropolitan region*). For a more complete understanding of this influential school of contemporary urban analysis, see Joel Garreau, *Edge City: Life on the New Frontier* (New York: Anchor Books / Doubleday, 1991); and Fishman, *Bourgeois Utopias.* Gottdiener and Kephart, "The Multinucleated Metropolitan Region," appears as the second chapter of Kling, Olin, and Poster's collection. Also worth looking at is M. Gottdiener, *The Social Production of Urban Space* (Austin: University of Texas Press, 1994 [1985]).

30. Kling, Olin, and Poster, "The Emergence of Postsuburbia," 6.

31. Rob Kling, Spencer Olin, and Mark Poster, "Beyond the Edge: The Dynamism of Postsuburban Regions," in *Postsuburban California: The Transformation of Orange County since World War II,* ed. Rob Kling, Spencer Olin, and Mark Poster (Berkeley: University of California Press, 1995), viii.

32. Ernest W. Burgess, "The Growth of the City: An Introduction to a Research Project," in *The City,* ed. Robert Park, Ernest W. Burgess, and Roderick D. McKenzie (Chicago: University of Chicago Press, 1925).

33. Emory S. Bogardus, *The City Boy and His Problems: A Survey of Boy Life in Los Angeles* (Los Angeles: House of Ralston, 1926), 10.

34. Bogardus, *The City Boy and His Problems,* 13.

35. Bogardus, *The City Boy and His Problems,* 75.

36. Bogardus, *The City Boy and His Problems,* 69.

37. Bessie Averne McClenahan, *The Changing Urban Neighborhood: From Neighbor to Nigh-Dweller: A Sociological Study* (Los Angeles: University of Southern California, 1929), 5.

38. McClenahan, *The Changing Urban Neighborhood*, 90–91.

39. McClenahan, *The Changing Urban Neighborhood*, 84.

40. McClenahan, *The Changing Urban Neighborhood*, 85.

41. Mark S. Foster, for one, argues this in his dissertation, "The Decentralization of Los Angeles during the 1920's."

42. An indication of the increasing confusion about these all-important boundaries during the period is the divergence among contemporary sociological sources, as well as later historians, as to the specific locations of various ethnic groups. Locations given by J. Max Bond, James Findlay, Mark S. Foster, George Sanchez, Bessie McClenahan, and others differ considerably, although a few prominent sections of the region did remain fairly stable. J. Max Bond, "The Negro in Los Angeles" (Ph.D. diss., University of Southern California, 1972); James Clifford Findley, "The Economic Boom of the 'Twenties in Los Angeles" (Ph.D. diss., Claremont Graduate School, 1958); Foster, "The Decentralization of Los Angeles"; George J. Sanchez, *Becoming Mexican American: Ethnicity, Culture, and Identity in Chicano Los Angeles, 1900–1945* (New York: Oxford University Press, 1993); McClenahan, *The Changing Urban Neighborhood*.

43. Bogardus, *The City Boy and His Problems*, 38.

44. Numerous studies during the 1920s reinforced the importance of neighborhood-based social circles. Among these, the most famous was undoubtedly that carried out by Robert and Helen Lynd in Muncie, Indiana (a.k.a. "Middletown"). Although much challenged over the course of the century, not least by the automobile, as the Lynds point out, these patterns of close-knit interaction persisted, as Herbert Gans showed as late as 1962, in many American cities and even suburbs (observations echoed, although somewhat differently, by Jane Jacobs in the same time period). See the Lynds' *Middletown: A Study in Modern American Culture* (New York: Harcourt, Brace, 1929); Gans's *The Urban Villagers: Group and Class in the Life of Italian-Americans* (New York: Free Press, 1962) and *The Levittowners* (New York: Random House, 1967); and Jacobs's *The Death and Life of Great American Cities* (New York: Vintage, 1992 [1961]). A late Chicago School attempt to theorize—and cast doubt on—just this sort of interaction is Louis Wirth's 1938 analysis of cosmopolitanism, "Urbanism as a Way of Life," *American Journal of Sociology* 44, no. 1 (1938).

45. McClenahan, *The Changing Urban Neighborhood*, 2.

46. McClenahan's study ends on a rather drastic note, essentially arguing that the thing she had come to study—the urban neighborhood—no longer existed as such in Los Angeles. McClenahan, *The Changing Urban Neighborhood*, 107–9.

47. This understanding of the planners' dilemma—the inability to repudiate an existing model in the absence of a ready replacement—follows the schema laid out by Thomas Kuhn in his influential *Structure of Scientific Revolutions* (Chicago: University of Chicago Press, 1970).

48. Mike Davis, *City of Quartz: Excavating the Future in Los Angeles* (New York: Vintage Books, 1992 [1990]), 36.

49. Davis, *City of Quartz*, 23.

50. Morrow Mayo, *Los Angeles* (New York: Alfred A. Knopf, 1933), 327.

51. Mayo, *Los Angeles,* 328.

52. Harry Carr, *Los Angeles: City of Dreams* (New York: Grosset & Dunlap, 1935), 251.

53. Nathanael West, *The Day of the Locust* (New York: New Directions, 1962 [1933]), 60.

54. Carr, *Los Angeles,* 251.

55. Robinson, *Los Angeles: A Profile,* 27.

56. Mayo, *Los Angeles,* 329.

57. Carr, *Los Angeles,* 256.

58. Freeman Tilden, "Los Angeles," *World's Work* 60, no. 5 (1931): 1.

59. Of course, by the late 1930s, McWilliams had reevaluated his earlier vivid impressions, coming to distrust the "hoary superstition" that Los Angeles was somehow provincial, "wholly lacking in those manifestations of 'civilization' with which San Francisco is so richly endowed." As a champion of Southern California's rich cultural—and racial—heterogeneity, the older McWilliams reflected that it had in fact taken him years to come to terms with both the climate and the culture of the sprawling metropolis. Carey McWilliams, "Tides West: What Is California? & Urbane S.F. vs. Rustic L.A.," *Westways* 29, no. 5 (1937): 4.

60. The notion of the exemplary center—the recognizable symbolic node at the heart of a culture—comes from the work of Clifford Geertz, particularly *Negara: The Theatre State in Nineteenth-Century Bali* (Princeton, NJ: Princeton University Press, 1980).

61. "Los Angeles, it should be understood, is not a mere city. On the contrary, it is, and has been since 1888, a commodity; something to be advertised and sold to the people of the United States like automobiles, cigarettes, and mouthwashes." Mayo, *Los Angeles,* 319.

6. GARDENS AND CITIES

1. Olmsted Brothers and Bartholomew and Associates, *Parks, Playgrounds, and Beaches for the Los Angeles Region* (Los Angeles: Citizens' Committee on Parks, Playgrounds, and Beaches, 1930), 3.

2. Emory S. Bogardus, *The City Boy and His Problems: A Survey of Boy Life in Los Angeles* (Los Angeles: House of Ralston, 1926), 71. This survey is discussed in chapter 5.

3. Olmsted Brothers, *Parks, Playgrounds, and Beaches,* 12.

4. Olmsted Brothers, *Parks, Playgrounds, and Beaches,* 20–21.

5. Olmsted Brothers, *Parks, Playgrounds, and Beaches,* 19. Implicit in this critique is a conviction that the effects of postsuburbanization had become apparent not only to expert planners and sociologists but to other Angelenos as well. Even if the resulting urban anomie might remain confined for a time—in this age of psychoanalysis and fascination with the unconscious—to the hidden and private psyches of a million urbanites, each separately assuming in his or her isolated private home that the experience of desperation and depression was strictly personal and individual, eventually Angelenos would have to express their shared frustration and seek some sort of release. Perhaps this was already happening; perhaps sprawl discourse was merely the first signs of a collective exasperation with the postsuburban metropolis. What would happen when, inevitably, the environmental rejuvenation that the masses of Angelenos over the years had been led to expect from this famed

garden spot was no longer available for ready deliverance? Already, *"the people are volun-
tarily spending millions of dollars every year for such recreation under conditions which are
growing more and more imperfect and unsatisfactory. . . .* The immense value to the people
of this kind of recreation is absolutely doomed to disappear. Urban growth will fill in one
after another of the open spaces, and expand continuously for score after score of miles."
Olmsted Brothers, *Parks, Playgrounds, and Beaches,* 13–14. The repercussions of removing
the safety valve of pastoral retreat would certainly have not only continued hidden and subtle psychological implications but severe and manifest economic and social ones.

6. Olmsted Brothers, *Parks, Playgrounds, and Beaches,* 1.

7. See Olmsted Brothers, *Parks, Playgrounds, and Beaches,* 44.

8. See Leo Marx, *The Machine in the Garden* (London: Oxford University Press, 1964);
T. J. Jackson Lears, *No Place of Grace* (Chicago: University of Chicago Press, 1981), and *Fa-
bles of Abundance* (New York: Basic Books, 1994); and Kenneth Jackson, *Crabgrass Frontier*
(New York: Oxford University Press, 1985).

9. This process is the reverse of the transformation of environment into resource, a process
later described by Martin Heidegger as "enframing." See "The Question Concerning Technology," in *The Question Concerning Technology, and Other Essays* (New York: Harper & Row, 1977).

10. See Sam Bass Warner, Jr., *Streetcar Suburbs* (New York: Atheneum, 1962).

11. See especially Margaret Marsh, *Suburban Lives* (New Brunswick, NJ: Rutgers Uni-
versity Press, 1990); Kenneth Jackson, *Crabgrass Frontier;* Mary Ryan, *Cradle of the Middle
Class* (Cambridge: Cambridge University Press, 1981); Robert Fishman, *Bourgeois Utopias*
(New York: Basic Books, 1987); and Sam Bass Warner, Jr., *Streetcar Suburbs* and *The Urban
Wilderness* (Berkeley: University of California Press, 1995), among many others.

12. There was a growing consensus in the early years of the twentieth century that the
very topography of the modern metropolis concentrated not just economic resources and
environmental contaminants but a host of more subtle stresses. As Frederick Law Olmsted
put it, "Whenever we walk through the denser part of a town, to merely avoid collision with
those we meet and pass upon the sidewalks, we have constantly to watch, to foresee, and to
guard against their movements. This involves a consideration of their intentions, a calcula-
tion of their strength and weakness, which is not so much for their benefit as our own. Our
minds are thus brought into close dealings with other minds without any friendly flowing
toward them, but rather a drawing from them. Much of the intercourse between men when
engaged in the pursuits of commerce has the same tendency—the tendency to regard others
in a hard if not always hardening way." "Public Parks and the Enlargement of Towns" (Boston:
American Social Science Association, 1870), 338.

Social interaction in these circumstances produces a feeling not of community or common interest but rather of social intrusion. Each passerby thus trespasses upon one's own
sense of personal space, upon one's own consciousness. The urban pedestrian is thereby aware
of his or her peers only through competition—rivalry for space on the sidewalk, for attention, for air to breathe. The social relations of the industrial metropolis, in Olmsted's view,
internalize a Social Darwinian struggle for survival within each individual, forcing strangers
passing on a street to engage, on a low level at least, in a stressful contest for subsistence or
advantage.

13. It was widely believed as far back as the late nineteenth century that vegetation could

counteract the increasing environmental pollution of the industrial metropolis. From the factories and workshops of the city came soot and smoke that made the air difficult to breathe, and foul waterborne contamination that made lakes and rivers impossible to drink from. Only trees and grasses could effectively filter out the pollution and restore some sort of atmospheric balance: parks would be, in Pitt's words, the "lungs" of the city. As Olmsted put it, "Air is disinfected by sunlight and foliage. Foliage also acts mechanically to purify the air by screening it." "Public Parks and the Enlargement of Towns," 339.

14. For the Southern California context, see Douglas Cazaux Sackman, *Orange Empire: California and the Fruits of Eden* (Berkeley: University of California Press, 2005); and Kevin Starr, *Americans and the California Dream, 1850–1915* (New York: Oxford University Press, 1973).

15. If this soothing psychological effect was beneficial to adults as a break from the exhaustion and alienation of the (industrialized, micromanaged, capitalist) workaday world, it could be absolutely essential for their children. This effect goes back to Emory Bogardus's boys. "Streets and streets and more streets" leave no proper playtime outlet for the impressionable urban youth: "The boy, like others, is often a victim of our jazz-made amusements"— "amusements of the nervous stimuli type." *The City Boy and His Problems,* 67. Forced to find entertainment among every variety of other children on the cold streets, it is no wonder that so many of these children end up the subject of sociological surveys, the object of the attentions of so many social workers and policemen. It was taken as axiomatic that there were no "juvenile delinquents" in the country. Only by bringing the wholesome recreative opportunities afforded by open spaces to the very heart of the metropolis could city children have a shot at proper moral and physical development.

Such thinking lay at the root not just of the neighborhood park movement in the late nineteenth and early twentieth centuries, but also of the more pragmatic American playground movement. As Bogardus concluded in Los Angeles in 1926, "The playground was one of the boys' first welfare agencies. . . . The rudimentary psychology of the playground is that it keeps boys busy. It keeps them doing something wholesome during their leisure hours. It keeps them from 'ganging,' destroying property, and developing predatory habits." *The City Boy and His Problems,* 110.

If the city corrupts children, trains them early on in the hardness that Olmsted described, these green and open public spaces can soften their dispositions and prevent them from falling into a depressive anomie or a pointless life of crime and violence. This is not merely a matter of aesthetics and beauty; it is about the health and safety of the city and its inhabitants.

16. Olmsted, "Public Parks and the Enlargement of Towns," 343.

17. Even more important than the supposed atmospheric benefits of these fugitive bits of rurality was their potential social value. These verdant spots, so deep, as it were, behind enemy lines, actively combated the increasingly apparent psychological blight afflicting urban Americans in this era. Olmsted is one of a number of nineteenth-century East Coast social critics to observe the dispiriting effects of modern metropolitan life on urbanites, particularly newcomers. Obviously, for all the anxiety expressed in and about Southern California in the 1920s and 1930s, distress about the urban environment was by no means unique to that era and place. Although residents of sprawling Los Angeles experienced a particular and troubling disorientation in their postsuburban metropolis, urban alienation was nothing new.

Instead, the alienation in Southern California was so deeply and widely felt because no one at the time possessed appropriate epistemological or therapeutic tools to cope with, to make sense of, the region's novel and confusing physical and social topography.

18. For Olmsted, as for many other thinkers of the late nineteenth and early twentieth centuries, parks counteract in two principal ways the alienation and anomie felt by urbanites. First, like the suburb, they shelter the citizen from the bustle of competitive life. Second, unlike the private sanctum of the suburban retreat, the urban park serves as a communal space, a place where people can interact. As Olmsted makes clear, if the first purpose describes a topographical transformation—the park provides a change of scenery, an improvement of the individual's physical environment—the second has even more ambitious aims: it seeks to transform the individuals themselves. Within the shared space of the park, the urbanite sheds the hard and hostile shell of ordinary modern city life, altering his or her own personality and disposition to take on a more generous, cooperative, and outgoing self.

19. As was so common in American culture, toward the turn of the century these garden zones were frequently cast in terms made famous by Frederick Jackson Turner. In some small way, then, these parks and suburbs were encapsulations of the formative American frontier, spaces of refuge where the citizen might escape the corrupting influences of modern life and where character could be forged through contact with nature. See Turner's "The Significance of the Frontier in American History," in *The Frontier in American History* (Tucson: University of Arizona Press, 1986); and Kenneth Jackson's *Crabgrass Frontier*. For the less charitable (or more politically radical), these places where capitalist alienation could be abeyed for a time functioned as distracting opiates of the (impressionable and all too easily co-optable) masses.

20. Clay McShane, *Down the Asphalt Path: The Automobile and the American City* (New York: Columbia University Press, 1994), 31.

21. McShane, *Down the Asphalt Path*, 33.

22. Olmsted, "Public Parks and the Enlargement of Towns," 340.

23. Olmsted, "Public Parks and the Enlargement of Towns," 343.

24. McShane, *Down the Asphalt Path*, 35.

25. McShane, *Down the Asphalt Path*, 34.

26. Given the hysteria around traffic accidents and grade crossings, it is no wonder that these controlled-access routes were built once more in the 1910s and 1920s (although, significantly, not in Los Angeles, which had none in this period).

27. Herbert S. Swan, "The Parkway as Traffic Artery [Part I]," *American City* 45, no. 4 (1931): 84.

28. Swan, "The Parkway as Traffic Artery [Part I]," 84.

29. Herbert S. Swan, "The Parkway as Traffic Artery [Part II]," *American City* 45, no. 5 (1931): 73.

30. Recreational use was part of the parkway's generally recognized definition: "The parkway differs [from other road types] in that it does not ordinarily admit commercial traffic. The parkway is regarded as a recreational highway along which publicly owned strips of land of considerable width have been reserved for landscaping, picnic grounds, and other public recreational purposes." Gilmore D. Clarke, "The Parkway Idea," in *The Highway and*

the Landscape, ed. William Brewster Snow (New Brunswick, NJ: Rutgers University Press, 1959), 43.

31. Sigfried Giedion, *Space, Time and Architecture: The Growth of a New Tradition* (Cambridge, MA: Harvard University Press, 1967 [1941]), 824.

32. Clarke, "The Parkway Idea," 38-39.

33. This dynamic is explained in some depth in a section entitled "Vision in Motion" in Christopher Tunnard and Boris Pushkarev's influential *Man-Made America: Chaos or Control?* (New Haven, CT: Yale University Press, 1963), 171-77.

34. Swan, "The Parkway as Traffic Artery [Part I]," 75.

35. Several of the Westchester County parkways of the era passed through, or very close to, fair-sized towns. In every case, the parkway was engineered such that these settlements, despite their expanse and proximity to the roadway, were almost entirely invisible to passing motorists. Suburban and even urban zones, highly developed, appeared to those on the parkways as undisturbed nature.

36. The exception to this visual homogeneity, of course, was the automobile. As the vehicle of perception and the enabling technology, this supreme instrument of mise-en-scene could effectively be expected to vanish from one's consciousness. This crucial apparatus was simply taken for granted.

37. Giedion, *Space, Time and Architecture,* 832.

38. Clarke, "The Parkway Idea," 48.

39. Marshall Berman, *All That Is Solid Melts into Air: The Experience of Modernity* (New York: Penguin, 1988 [1982]), 301.

40. Robert A. Caro, *The Power Broker: Robert Moses and the Fall of New York* (New York: Vintage Books, 1974), 318-19.

41. Caro's account of parkway and park segregation reveals the extent of Moses's nefarious use of architectural and bureaucratic control to enforce class and race segregation. For African Americans, Caro reminds us, "there were further measures. Buses needed permits to enter state parks; buses chartered by Negro groups found it very difficult to obtain permits, particularly to Moses' beloved Jones Beach; most were shunted to parks many miles further out on Long Island. And even in these parks, buses carrying Negro groups were discouraged from using 'white' beach areas—the best beaches—by a system Shapiro calls 'flagging'; the handful of Negro lifeguards (there were only a handful of Negro employees among the thousands employed by the Long Island State Park Commission) were all stationed at distant, least developed beaches." *The Power Broker,* 318-19.

A good part of the impact *The Power Broker* made on its readership in 1974 must be traced to these revelatory passages about Moses's more blatant efforts at "protecting" "his" parks and parkways. Yet Caro always casts this critique in terms of a single man gone bad. As we have seen, many historians argue that urban parks and parkways have had a long history of segregation.

Nevertheless, for Caro, Moses is an inventive genius—the "fall" of New York City results from a corresponding "fall" of Moses himself, from brilliant public servant to "power broker." This personalization—filtering as it does complex social processes through the ego (large though it may be) of this influential individual—forces Caro to contextualize the parkway bridges and beach restrictions not as part of a larger urban schema (of race- and class-segregated tenements and ghettoes in the concentric modern metropolis, from which bucolic beaches and lush parkways must have seemed enticing but far off indeed), but as part of one man's personal moral trajectory.

42. Berman, *All That Is Solid Melts into Air,* 301–2.

43. The reason, Moses realized, that the parkway would show off the vertical city so well was that the rural parkway was essentially a technology that emphasized horizontality. Unlike the urban park, the trees along a parkway did not convey the impression of a sheltering, deep, and quiet reserve—a seclusion defined by the shadows of the overhanging branches. Instead, trees merely added depth and definition to a landscape of gently rolling hills and river valleys (and of course, the neatly finished roadway). The movement of the automobile accentuated the seemingly flattened character of the surrounding countryside—this transit through space diminished the perceived dimensionality of the topography. After experiencing hours of such horizontal vistas, the returning tourist would be powerfully affected by the shocking verticality of Manhattan. The rural technology of the parkway, then, reaffirmed the striking urbanity of the modern metropolitan skyline.

44. Berman, *All That Is Solid Melts into Air,* 301–2.

45. Tunnard and Pushkarev, *Man-Made America,* 177–212.

46. Contemporary film theory has done much to explain how this process works in cinema. As the parkway is an essentially cinematic technology, developed during the heyday of the classical Hollywood narrative, this theoretical work may be useful in helping us understand the parkway's workings. This chapter makes particular use of Kaja Silverman's notion of "suture," or the work done to ensure that a particular representation maintains a continuous illusion. See "Suture," in *Narrative, Apparatus, Ideology: A Film Theory Reader,* ed. Philip Rosen (New York: Columbia University Press, 1986). In the case of the motor parkway, the purpose of this elaborate visual suture is to help (or force) the viewer to collaborate with the illusory representation inherent in the roadway corridor's design and landscaping.

In film theory, the question of this "suspension of disbelief" has been a vexed one. Traditionally, film spectatorship has been described in rigid structural terms, as a matter of indoctrination. The canonical spectatorship models of the 1970s, such as those offered by Laura Mulvey, Christian Metz, and Jean-Louis Baudry, generally represent the spectator as caught up in a play of illusion, where he (always he) merges his subjectivity with that projected in the movie. This model ranges from Mulvey's notion of identification, where the (male) viewer identifies with the male protagonist of the film and joins that "hero" in persecuting, investigating, or just plain gazing at the female object of the narrative—this is best explicated in her groundbreaking "Visual Pleasure and Narrative Cinema," in *Visual and Other Pleasures* (Bloomington: University of Indiana Press, 1973)—to Metz's (also psychoanalytic) identification with the camera (see *The Imaginary Signifier: Psychoanalysis and the Cinema* [Bloomington: University of Indiana Press, 1977]), to Baudry's metaphor of Plato's Cave, where the helpless and passive spectator (unlike the philosopher or, presumably, the film theorist) is duped by the illusion of shadow projections (see "Ideological Effects of the Basic Cinematographic Apparatus," in *Narrative, Apparatus, Ideology,* ed. Philip Rosen [New York: Columbia University Press, 1986]).

More recently, theories of representation have moved away from a simple determinist model of spectatorship. Indeed, Mulvey's more contemporary work casts the relationship between film and filmgoer in dialogical terms, drawing on the work of Mikhail Bakhtin, particularly that collected in *The Dialogic Imagination* (Austin: University of Texas Press, 1981); see some of the later essays in *Visual and Other Pleasures,* such as "Changes: Thoughts on Myth, Narrative, and Historical Experience." These new theories posit a viewer who is aware not only of the illusion of the representation, but also of his or her complicity in it. Among those who have explored film more as a text to be read than as an epistemological trap is Thomas Leitch, who has pointed to game theory in order to argue that audiences consciously "play along" with the representations they view rather than being duped by them (see *Find the Director and Other Hitchcock Games* [Athens: University of Georgia Press, 1991]; and Edward Branigan, *Point of View in the Cinema: A Theory of Narration and Subjectivity in Classical Film* [Berlin: Mouton, 1984], and *Narrative Comprehension and Film* [London: Routledge, 1992]). In all these contemporary theories, the ability to properly and consciously decode the semiotics of the form enables the viewer—as much of the modern parkway as of the classical Hollywood narrative—to make sense of the intended representation.

47. Giedion, *Space, Time and Architecture,* 825.

48. Ann Douglas discusses this "airmindedness" in her *Terrible Honesty: Mongrel Manhattan in the 1920s* (New York: Farrar, Straus, and Giroux, 1995), 434–61.

49. Giedion, *Space, Time and Architecture,* 825.

50. The Olmsted Brothers and Bartholomew and Associates continually make clear in their report that the Greater New York park system was both inspiration and challenge for Southern California. In a series of striking comparative metropolitan maps (particularly in the report's plate 44), Olmsted and Bartholomew overlay the Westchester County park system on the topography of Greater Los Angeles, making clear just how perfectly such a network of open spaces fits in the context of the western metropolis. Although their plan pays particular attention to the peculiar and individual landscape of Southern California, the manifest ambition here is to project the example of that model park network onto Los Angeles.

51. Olmsted Brothers, *Parks, Playgrounds, and Beaches,* 12.

52. William J. Fox, "Seven Decades of Planning and Development in the Los Angeles Region" (typescript), 1985, Oral History Program, University of California, Los Angeles, 161.

53. Although the prestigious Olmsted and Bartholomew firms were brought in to formally conduct the study, the plan seems to have been mainly the product of local planners. Unlike the *Major Traffic Street Plan* of 1924, and although Harland Bartholomew was once again brought in as an expert consultant and a group of local worthies (the Citizens' Committee on Parks, Playgrounds, and Beaches) authorized the project, this report would be a clear expression of indigenous planning sentiment. William Fox was trained as an engineer and had come to the Regional Planning Commission only a few years earlier. Nevertheless, he had been fully converted over the previous years to the true faith of planning and—by his account—had become something of a disciple of the professional planners. By this point (1930), Hugh Pomeroy, one of the original regional planners, had taken the helm of the county planning organization. Fox became his right-hand man, serving in later years as a forceful advocate of their shared efforts. Pomeroy, in his role as executive secretary of the Citizens' Committee, managed to overcome the planners' habitual reticence about engaging in direct political activity. The committee, for its part, was something of a front organization for the planners, according to Fox. Its members included Cecil B. DeMille, Samuel Goldwyn, Dou-

glas Fairbanks, Carl Laemmle, Mary Pickford (also a member of its Executive Committee), and a host of less cinematic civic-minded notables. William J. Fox, "Seven Decades of Planning and Development in the Los Angeles Region," 161.

Greg Hise and William Deverell, in *Eden by Design: The 1930 Olmsted-Bartholomew Plan for the Los Angeles Region* (Berkeley: University of California Press, 2000), 57n22, 56n2, argue forcefully that Olmsted's firm was indeed instrumental in the drafting of that report. They base their assertion on research at the Olmsteds' Massachusetts headquarters and in the Los Angeles Chamber of Commerce records (held at the University of Southern California). The latter source also grounds their argument that the Citizen's Committee was a front not for local planners but for the Chamber of Commerce. This research does not easily jibe with Fox's oral account. Clearly, there is a contradiction in the sources as to the precise provenance of the 1930 park plan. Nevertheless, it appears certain that a large—and fragile—coalition lay behind the ambitious scheme, involving local planners, outside consultants, businessmen, politicians, and interested citizens. Given the specific recommendations of *Parks, Playgrounds, and Beaches,* however, it seems undeniable that its most fundamental influences emerge from the twin planning spheres of eastern parkway design and Southern Californian garden city decentralization and metropolitan administrative consolidation. This study discusses the park plan as the product primarily of the local planning establishment, and regional planning chief Hugh Pomeroy in particular. Despite this choice of attribution, it now seems clear, thanks to the industrious research of Hise and Deverell, that the contributory influence of business interests and the Olmsted consulting firm was also significant—at least in the specific formulations used in the text of the plan.

54. Oddly, throughout the 1920s, experts were more worried about the potential for municipal reconcentration than about the existing postsuburban development. Many of them were certain that Angelenos would soon tire of their long trips. Indeed, for years planners feared that Los Angeles might after all collapse back into a dense concentric form as motorists, fed up with the traffic and the distances, moved to apartments in more central parts of the city. In the only passage—an anomalous single paragraph—to overtly discuss the urban structural purposes of parkways in strictly utilitarian terms, the Olmsted and Bartholomew report referred to this danger as the "evils of the 'friction of distance.'" Olmsted Brothers, *Parks, Playgrounds, and Beaches,* 21. Parkways would prevent the recentralization of the city by reducing this "friction of distance," and thus preserve the low-density structure of the region.

In retrospect, and in light of the postsuburbanization of the Southern California region in the years after the 1920s, recentralization seems like it should have been the least of the planners' worries. But this fear was legitimate—it expresses their recognition of just how radical the deconcentration effort was during this age of the dense vertical metropolis. Most planners had thought for years that concentration was natural and inevitable, the product of inherent structural forces in urbanity. Like the monopoly in business, the centralized metropolis would overwhelm all competition by its efficiencies, its economies of scale, and its powers of market dominance. The fact that Los Angeles was decentralized relatively easily no doubt greatly surprised local planners.

55. Olmsted Brothers, *Parks, Playgrounds, and Beaches,* 20.

56. Fox, "Seven Decades," 159.

57. Fox, "Seven Decades," 158.

58. Fox, "Seven Decades," 66.

59. Olmsted Brothers, *Parks, Playgrounds, and Beaches*, 37.

60. Fox, "Seven Decades," 159.

61. Greg Hise and William Deverell argue persuasively that the business consensus behind the park plan had dissolved by early 1929, well before the final release of the report. Drawing extensively on chamber of commerce records, Hise and Deverell show how that organization's fragile coalition of businessmen supporting such major planning initiatives had eroded over the previous year. The final indication of the chamber's division, according to Hise and Deverell, came when John Treanor, chairman of the sponsoring Citizens' Committee on Parks, Playgrounds, and Beaches and "wealthy cement company executive," failed to convince his chamber of commerce peers "to go on record" supporting a public referendum on the park and parkway plan (*Eden by Design*, 37). Thereafter, the business community's support for the expensive project could not be counted on, and most local officials felt they could not seriously propose such massive city bond burdens without such support.

Mike Davis argues, in "How Eden Lost Its Garden," in *The City: Los Angeles and Urban Theory at the End of the Twentieth Century*, ed. Allen J. Scott and Edward W. Soja (Berkeley: University of California Press, 1996), 164, that the *Los Angeles Times* played an important role in forcing apart the coalition backing the 1930 park plan. In the 1996 version of this essay, Davis suggests that the chamber of commerce was also wary of the more radical proposals in *Parks, Playgrounds, and Beaches:* "The Chamber of Commerce (which originally sponsored the 1930 report), as well as leading members of the Citizens' Committee, also took their distance from Olmsted and Bartholomew's bolder planks." In his 1998 revision, Davis places the blame squarely on the *Times:* "Under pressure from the *Times*, 27 prominent members of the Citizens' Committee withdrew their support from the park legislation, thus killing the Olmsted plan before the final report had reached the printer." *Ecology of Fear: Los Angeles and the Imagination of Disaster* (New York: Henry Holt, 1998), 68, citing "Take 'Bugs' Out of Park Bill," *Los Angeles Times*, 12 March 1929, and *Los Angeles Times*, 14 March 1929.

62. Fox, "Seven Decades," 161.

63. Board of City Planning Commissioners, *Annual Report* (Los Angeles: Board of City Planning Commissioners, 1931), 5.

64. Philip J. Ouellet, *City Planning in Los Angeles: A History* (Los Angeles: Department of City Planning, 1964), 19.

65. Board of City Planning Commissioners, *Annual Report* (Los Angeles: Board of City Planning Commissioners, 1938), 4.

66. "Annual Report" (1938), 10.

67. William H. Mullins, *The Depression and the Urban West Coast, 1929–1933* (Bloomington: Indiana University Press, 1991), 48, 95.

68. "First Regional Plan Conference," *City Club Bulletin* 3, no. 235 (1922): 4. Similar in tone and even more radical in substance was G. Gordon Whitnall, "City and County Consolidation for Los Angeles," *National Municipal Review* 10, no. 1 (1921): 7.

69. Davis, *Ecology of Fear*, 67.

70. Hise and Deverell, *Eden by Design*, vii, 52.

71. Davis, *Ecology of Fear*, 68.

72. Davis, *Ecology of Fear,* 67.

73. Davis, *Ecology of Fear,* 68.

74. Davis reads these strips of public land as "greenbelts" but then parenthetically notes that the plan refers to them as " 'pleasureway parks,' in their slightly awkward terminology" (*Ecology of Fear,* 67). The terminology is indeed awkward, but the meaning would have been clear to most Americans at the time (and it is made explicit in the report itself): These "greenbelts" were in fact the proposed automotive parkways. As such, although they were ostensibly intended to be, in Davis's term, "multipurpose," they would almost certainly in practice be off-limits to pedestrian use (67). Indeed, these "pleasureway parks" were generally planned to be only three hundred to four hundred feet wide, including their dense screening plantings. Olmsted Brothers, *Parks, Playgrounds, and Beaches,* 99, plate 48. This narrow provision would not have left much room for activities other than recreational driving.

75. Leonard Pitt and Dale Pitt, *Los Angeles, A to Z* (Berkeley: University of California Press, 1997), 184; Hise and Deverell, *Eden by Design,* 18.

76. In the revised version of "How Eden Lost Its Garden," Davis argues that the *Los Angeles Times* helped kill the 1930 park plan precisely because of the provisions for public ownership of the region's beaches. *Ecology of Fear,* 68. Of course, during the 1960s, under the administration of Pat Brown, this property was conveyed into the public trust by an act of the state government. This expropriation also ranks as one of the greatest achievements of the state government during this largely progressive period. Nevertheless, as Davis himself so memorably and powerfully makes clear, this ambitious rebalancing of public and private did little to slow the development of "fortress L.A." as a bastion of restrictive gated communities and inhospitable commons in the years thereafter. *City of Quartz: Excavating the Future in Los Angeles* (New York: Vintage Books, 1992), 221–64.

77. Olmsted Brothers, *Parks, Playgrounds, and Beaches,* 95. The true nature of this plan was, of course, embedded in the report's impressive array of financial data. According to the table of projected costs printed as the final item on the final page of the report's main text, the proposed "Connecting Parkways" amount to 37 percent of the total cost of the 1930 report, which is almost twice the amount dedicated to any other project.

Nevertheless, these numbers do not tell the whole story. This 37 percent proportion refers only to those portions of the proposed parkways that connect the other park projects (i.e., those parkways that would lie between other elements of the plan). Many of those other planned preserves (presumably with the exception of the athletic fields and playgrounds) would contain stretches of fully developed parkway running through them. The parkway costs of the roadways running along the shore, through large preserves, or through newly designated drainage basins were not included in the calculated proportion for the "connecting" parkways.

The master list of projects on pages 100–102 of the report, though, identifies how many miles of parkway do indeed lie in these other proposed reservations. Given that connecting parkways are estimated in the plan to cost about $53 million for 214 miles, or $247,000 per mile (for land acquisition and all improvements, calculating from the table on page 138), we can fairly conservatively calculate the proportion of the total plan costs intended to go toward all automotive parkway construction in Southern California: 62 percent—again, a clear majority—of the plan, according to my rough calculations produced below.

	Internal Parkway Mileage	Percentage of Total Plan Costs of the Project	Estimated Percentage of Project Costs from Internal Parkways	Portion of Project for Parkways as Percentage of Total Plan Costs
Shorefront roads and park areas	35	18	33	6
Large upland reservations	45	20	38	8
Large drainage basin reservations	9	8	19	2
Narrower drainage basin reservations	52	11	80	9
Connecting parkways	214	37	100	37
Athletic fields and playgrounds	0	5	0	0
Total				62

78. Olmsted Brothers, *Parks, Playgrounds, and Beaches,* 12.

79. The automobile was far from universal in Southern California. The majority of Angelenos relied exclusively on public transit well into the 1940s. See, in particular, Donald Baker, *A Rapid Transit Plan for Los Angeles, California* (Los Angeles: Central Business District Association, 1933); and Michael F. Shannon, *Transit Study 1944: Los Angeles Metropolitan Area* (Los Angeles: Central Business District Association, 1944). Nevertheless, automobile ownership was proportionately high in Los Angeles, and perhaps more importantly, automobility seemed to carry a cultural weight in Southern California unparalleled in other cities of the era.

80. Olmsted Brothers, *Parks, Playgrounds, and Beaches,* 13.

81. Some part of this purifying ambition persisted into the period after World War II, when new "freeways" (which were quite different from parkways) were used as urban "renewal" devices to justify annihilating entire (working-class and ethnic) neighborhoods.

82. This failure of imagination explains why, despite Davis's assertion to the contrary (*Ecology of Fear,* 67), the 1930 Los Angeles park plan could never be considered part of the City Beautiful tradition in American urban design. It was, rather, the product of a later, more chastened age, when urbanism was viewed only as a necessary evil—or on its own terms, according to an entirely different conception of the sublime.

83. Olmsted Brothers, *Parks, Playgrounds, and Beaches,* 14.

84. Fox, "Seven Decades," 66.

EPILOGUE

1. "Dream City," *Time* 38 (1941): 45.

2. Los Angeles Telesis, ". . . Now We Plan" (promotional materials) (Los Angeles: Telesis, 1941), 11.

3. Los Angeles County Museum, . . . *And Now We Plan* (Los Angeles: Los Angeles County Museum, 1941), 8.

4. Los Angeles County Museum, . . . *And Now We Plan.* As L. Demming Tilton explained in his contribution to a dense volume released by the Pacific Southwest Academy, *Los An-*

geles: Preface to a Master Plan (Los Angeles: Pacific Southwest Academy / Ward Ritchie Press, 1941), published with the assistance of the Haynes Foundation and intended to coordinate with the County Museum exhibition, this legacy of unplanned growth could not help but strike even the most casual observer of the metropolis: "The city-dweller steels himself with difficulty against the various types of irritations encountered in a badly organized urban area. He suffers from the noise and fumes of heavy traffic, the friction and conflicts of congested dwellings and residential areas. He views with shame the profuse and garish displays of commercialism, the unkempt vacant land along main arteries, the sordid slums. He misses the positive values in convenient, soothing rest spots, in spacious tree-bordered plazas, inspiring vistas, wide, well-planned scenic drives, impressive architectural compositions. Los Angeles is not the city it could have been, because no agency was responsible in its earlier days for the production of the plans and specifications from which a truly great metropolitan center could have been built" ("The Master Plan," 255).

Of course, ". . . And Now We Plan" did not claim to perform the crucial work of urban planning but sought merely to inspire others to take up the challenge. The exhibit was therefore itself a "preface" to comprehensive planning in the region.

5. Los Angeles County Museum, . . . *And Now We Plan,* 29.

6. Los Angeles County Museum, . . . *And Now We Plan,* quoting from Tilton, "The Master Plan," 265.

7. Arthur Millier, "Now We Plan," *Los Angeles Times Home Magazine* (19 October 1941): 3.

8. Ibid.

9. "A Future for L.A. County," *Los Angeles Daily News,* 27 October 1941.

10. Los Angeles County Museum, . . . *And Now We Plan,* 26. ". . . And Now We Plan" was clear in its preference for the traditional Los Angeles bungalow. In describing the decline of existing urban neighborhoods, the exhibit warned that "flats or apartments may invade the area, for, though single family homes predominate in the Los Angeles region, only a sixth of the city area is zoned for the single family residence" (9). Oddly, many of the exemplary projects mentioned in the exhibit and its accompanying materials, such as Ramona Gardens and the Wyvernwood development, featured communal living arrangements. Large pictures of the public spaces connected to these apartment blocks punctuated the display, providing visible proof that orderly development in the region was indeed possible. See . . . *And Now We Plan,* 3, 6, 10, among others. Thus, this disjuncture between imagery and text reveals Telesis's profound reluctance to envision a metropolis composed of anything but single-family homes.

11. ". . . Now We Plan," *California Arts and Architecture* 57, no. 11 (1941): 21.

12. Millier, "Now We Plan," 12.

13. Los Angeles's Telesis—its name helpfully defined for us in various publications, via Webster's, as "progress intelligently planned and directed; the attainment of desired ends by the application of intelligent human effort to the means"—was a group inspired by an organization of the same name operating in the San Francisco Bay Area. (". . . Now We Plan," *California Arts and Architecture,* 11.) One of the Bay Area members, Mel Scott, later to become one of the nation's foremost authorities on the planning profession, joined the Southern California offshoot, but in general the two groups were separate. Several noted figures

assisted the Los Angeles Telesis effort, including, most notably, famous architect and visionary Richard J. Neutra (whose Rush City Reformed makes a useful comparison to the garden city visions of ". . . And Now We Plan"). It may also be significant that women constituted about a fourth of Telesis's membership, whereas the previous (professional) cadre of urban planners had been uniformly male (and middle-class and white).

14. One should be skeptical of a too-easy elision of the ideological basis of the Nazi autobahn, the cultural semantics of which have been so well traced by Edward Dimendberg in "The Will to Motorization: Cinema, Highways, and Modernity," October 73 (1995), and Wolfgang Sachs in For Love of the Automobile: Looking Back into the History of Our Desires (Berkeley: University of California Press, 1992). Such abstraction of the technology from its social context also removes the interstate system from its essential cold war context and overlooks the absolutely foundational importance of what I have termed the "parkway aesthetic" in the planning and construction of the automotive parkway of the 1920s and 1930s.

Reducing these devices to their technical specifications, and their purposes to the simple movement of traffic, inherently replaces their historical interconnections—a complex and reciprocal play of influences, ideas, and personnel—with a simple causality of technological evolution. The standard narrative thus implies that the interstate highway is a more advanced and refined mechanism than the autobahn (having supposedly developed directly from it), in the same way as the autobahn is necessarily an improvement upon the primitive parkway. Here the slow speed capacities of the parkway provide ready evidence of its preterite technological apparatus. As we have seen, though, constraining the speeds of motorists was one of the parkway's design goals, as a stately, steady pace would best serve the crucial ideological and representational ends of the project. Indeed, the parkway, autobahn, and interstate highway are all equally refined forms, particularly when judged by their best exemplars. Although early versions of each of these roadways reveal design flaws, which were later corrected, there is certainly no evolutionary continuum among the three media. Each can boast fully developed, effective instances, and each followed its own historical course of internal refinement in accordance with its own underlying social and cultural priorities.

15. Detroit's Wider Woodward Avenue, a sixteen-mile improved roadway, was the first road of this type. Constructed of two parallel pavements "separated by a 40-foot electric railway right-of-way," it was renamed the Detroit-Pontiac Superhighway. Wyatt B. Brummitt, "The Superhighway," American City 40, no. 1 (1929): 86.

16. "204-ft. Roads to Speed Up City Traffic," Los Angeles Examiner, 7 March 1926, 7:3.

17. According to Edward Bassett, the difference between the parkway and his new freeway was not a matter of engineering specifications so much as fundamental purpose. The parkway was not intended for movement—this, again, is why the speed limits were so low and the situation of the roadbed in the topography so indirect. The freeway, conversely, was never thought of as a form of recreation—hence the abandonment of landscaping and other such amenities in many built freeways. Latham C. Squire and Edward M. Bassett, "A New Type of Thoroughfare: The 'Freeway,'" American City 47 (1932): 64.

18. "No Express Highways in Los Angeles Regional Plan," National Municipal Review 19, no. 9 (1930): 581.

19. "System of Super Highways Proposed for Los Angeles," Western Construction News 13, no. 4 (1938): 115.

20. Automobile Club of Southern California (Engineering Department), *Traffic Survey: Los Angeles Metropolitan Area* (Los Angeles: Automobile Club of Southern California, 1937), 20.

21. Automobile Club, *Traffic Survey,* 21.

22. Automobile Club, *Traffic Survey,* 32.

23. "Elevated Highway Network Proposed: Super Motorways through Buildings, over Streets Urged for L.A. District," *Los Angeles Daily News,* 16 February 1938, 1:10.

24. "Motorways Plan Ready," *Los Angeles Times,* 16 February 1938, 2:1.

25. E. B. Lefferts, "Correcting Los Angeles Traffic Snarls," *American City* 54 (1939): 101.

26. Transportation Engineering Board, *A Transit Program for the Los Angeles Metropolitan Area* (Los Angeles: Transportation Engineering Board, 1939), 1.

27. Ibid., 6.

28. Some of this earlier imagining was published in his *Horizons* (Boston: Little, Brown, 1932). A great deal of it was published in Bel Geddes's *Magic Motorways* (New York: Random House, 1940)—itself released to coincide with the publicity arising from the success of the fair.

29. For a detailed description of these presentation technologies, which presaged the modern theme park, see Jeffrey Meikle's insightful *Twentieth Century Limited* (Philadelphia: Temple University Press, 1979). Also useful is Robert Coombs's "Norman Bel Geddes: Highways and Horizons," *Perspecta* 13/14 (1971): 11–27, which reprints (but without credit) two fascinating files from Bel Geddes's papers at the University of Texas.

30. Wolfgang Schivelbusch, in his brilliant *The Railway Journey* (Berkeley: University of California Press, 1986, 64), connects the nineteenth-century fascination with the panorama to the contemporary spread of railroad travel. He argues that the train was the first technology to demonstrate the link between movement and perception, producing a panoramic mode of seeing: "Panoramic perception no longer belonged to the same space as the perceived objects: the traveler saw the objects, landscapes, etc. *through* the apparatus which moved him through the world. That machine and the motion it created became integrated into his visual perception: thus he could only see things in motion." The automobile, then, was not the first technology to produce this mediated sort of perception, although it did allow ordinary citizens to direct the mise-en-scene for themselves (and their passengers).

Similarly, Edward Dimendberg connects this same modality of mobilized vision to the twentieth-century innovation of cinema. He argues that the German autobahn of the 1930s was closely integrated in a number of ways into Nazi practices of filmmaking. The autobahn was explicitly designed "as a labor of representation"—like the contemporary American parkway. Dimendberg also connects this understanding of the technology directly to Bel Geddes's Futurama ("The Will to Motorization," 115).

31. Henry Berrey, "In January: '... And Now We Plan,'" *Westways* 34, no. 1 (1942): 4.

32. Millier, "Now We Plan," 12.

33. Millier, "Now We Plan," 12.

34. Los Angeles County Museum, ... *And Now We Plan,* 34; Millier, "Now We Plan," 3–4.

35. According to an article in the *Los Angeles Times,* the show was designed to remain

on display through the middle of the following January ("Planning Display to Show Growth," *Los Angeles Times,* 22 October 1941, 2:2). After the raid on Pearl Harbor, no mention seems to have been made of it in the local media (which had previously given it fairly extensive coverage), nor does there seem to be any significant institutional memory, in the city's many bureaucracies, of that once-celebrated show.

CONCLUSION

1. G. Gordon Whitnall, "City and Regional Planning in Los Angeles" (paper presented at the National Conference on City Planning, Philadelphia, 7–10 April 1924), 107.

2. Whitnall, "City and Regional Planning in Los Angeles," 110.

3. Whitnall, "City and Regional Planning in Los Angeles," 110.

4. This view has been expressed, in various forms, by such insightful critics as Robert Fogelson, in *The Fragmented Metropolis: Los Angeles, 1850–1930* (Berkeley: University of California Press, 1967), and Greg Hise, in "Home Building and Industrial Decentralization in Los Angeles: The Origins of Peripheral Urbanism, 1935–47" (paper presented at the National Conference on American Planning History, Richmond, VA, 10 November 1991).

5. Whitnall, "City and Regional Planning in Los Angeles," 109.

6. Whitnall, "City and Regional Planning in Los Angeles," 109.

7. Los Angeles's city hall, not yet constructed at this point, would reach only 454 feet, less than 4 percent of Whitnall's altitude. Likewise, the views from the Hollywood Hills and Griffith Observatory, although potentially more comprehensive, could not take in the sweep of the city (especially amid the smog that would obscure the view by the late 1930s). These latter sites did become famous for their views, but mostly for the abstract light show they revealed after dark.

8. Whitnall, "City and Regional Planning in Los Angeles," 109–10.

9. Anne Friedberg, *Window Shopping: Cinema and the Postmodern* (University of California Press, 1993), 15–38. On another level, one might think of this as the process that connects individual filmic frames into an illusion of continuous motion. Glimpses of individual urban locations could therefore be elided together into coherent and comprehensible spatial relationships by the simple act of moving from point to point about the city. Thus, a sort of urban "persistence of vision" would produce, if not exactly an illusion of seamless contiguity, a sense of related propinquity between discrete and spatially discontinuous urban sites.

10. Sigfried Giedion, *Space, Time and Architecture: The Growth of a New Tradition* (Cambridge, MA: Harvard University Press, 1967 [1941]), 826.

11. Again, as with film—which produces meaning out of the temporal variation of images (twenty-four discrete ones per second)—Giedion conceives of the mobile gaze in terms of change over time. As a series of consecutive, temporally progressive impressions (i.e., images unfolding over a span of time), this mode of perception expresses the Einsteinian connection between space and time ("Space-Time," as Giedion more properly calls it). Attributing contemporary consciousness of this characteristic mode of perception to a number of twentieth-century experimental artistic schools (such as the Cubists, with their attempts to fragment and juxtapose simultaneously coexisting points of view), Giedion sees this new mode of perception as being as fundamentally significant for modern epistemology as was the Cartesian Renaissance perspective against which it rebels (436).

12. Whitnall, "City and Regional Planning in Los Angeles," 109.

13. If he had taken his own insight into what we might term "the grandeur of sprawl" a bit more seriously, Whitnall might have realized at this early point that any attempt to refocus the region on the individual autonomous neighborhood would necessarily fail. He might have begun to come to terms with the nascent postsuburbanity that would fully appear years later. Thus, although the planner glimpsed the future, he failed to fully appreciate its implications—to shape his project to the developing topography, to take into account the actual terrain on which he worked.

14. Here, the valuable skills of expert observation come not from the trusted technical devices, such as the survey, the map, or the master plan, but from the imagination. Ultimately, from this elevation the planner achieved not mere veridical perception but a more profound clarity of "vision." This abstract altitude freed the planner to think, to dream. Without the distractions of the specific urban features below, the form and future development of the entire region could be properly envisioned, if only by the trained professional seer.

There appears to be something therapeutic for the planner about this perspective. Aside from mirroring his profession's prized epistemic technology, such elevation offers the harried planner an equally prized respite from the constant pressure from politicians and ordinary citizens alike to deliver the metropolis from its paralyzing transportation crisis. Indeed, from 12,000 feet, Whitnall could at last, if only illusorily, see the streets of metropolitan Los Angeles free from chaotic and aggravating automotive traffic.

15. Whitnall, "City and Regional Planning in Los Angeles," 105.

16. "Regional Planning Conference," *City Club Bulletin* 7, no. 384 (1924): 3.

17. G. Gordon Whitnall, "The Place of the East Coast in a State Plan for Florida" (paper presented at the National Conference on City Planning, Philadelphia, 29 March–1 April 1926), 205.

18. Whitnall, "The Place of the East Coast," 205.

19. Whitnall, "The Place of the East Coast," 204.

20. G. Gordon Whitnall, "The Experience in the Los Angeles Region" (paper presented at the National Conference on City Planning, Philadelphia, 9–11 May 1927), 131.

21. Whitnall, "Experience," 131.

BIBLIOGRAPHY

Abelson, Elaine S. *When Ladies Go A-Thieving: Middle-Class Shoplifters in the Victorian Department Store.* New York: Oxford University Press, 1989.

Adams, Thomas. "An American Garden City." *National Municipal Review* 10, no. 1 (1921): 31–38.

Althusser, Louis. "Ideology and Ideological State Apparatuses (Notes toward an Investigation)." In *Lenin and Philosophy,* 127–88. New York: Monthly Review Press, 1969.

"And How about This? The Henckenway—An Urban Microcosm." *American City* 36, no. 6 (1927): 802–3.

"And This? Dr. John A. Harriss Proposes Six-Deck Streets." *American City* 36, no. 6 (1927): 803–5.

Arnold, Bion J. "The Transportation Problem of Los Angeles." *California Outlook* 11, no. 19 (1911): 1–20.

Automobile Club of Southern California. *The Los Angeles Traffic Problem: A Detailed Engineering Report.* Los Angeles: Automobile Club of Southern California, 1922.

Automobile Club of Southern California (Engineering Department). *Traffic Survey: Los Angeles Metropolitan Area.* Los Angeles: Automobile Club of Southern California, 1937.

Axelrod, Jeremiah Borenstein. "Is the Freeway a Public Space? Tracing the Politics of Urban Topography in Modern America." Paper presented at "History and Theory" conference, University of California, Irvine, 1997.

Baker, Donald M. *A Rapid Transit System for Los Angeles, California.* Los Angeles: Central Business District Association, 1933.

Bakhtin, Mikhail. *The Dialogic Imagination.* Translated by Caryl Emerson and Michael Holquist. Austin: University of Texas Press, 1981.

Banham, Rayner. *A Critic Writes.* Edited by Mary Banham, Paul Barker, Sutherland Lyall, and Cedric Price. Berkeley: University of California Press, 1996.

Barth, Gunther. *City People: The Rise of Modern City Culture in Nineteenth-Century America*. Oxford: Oxford University Press, 1980.

Bartholomew, Harland. "A Program to Prevent Economic Disintegration in American Cities." Paper presented at the Twenty-Fourth National Conference on City Planning, Philadelphia, 14–16 November 1932.

Bartlett, Dana W. *The Better City: A Sociological Study of a Modern City*. Los Angeles: Neuner Company Press, 1907.

———. "City Planning Progress." *California Outlook* 11, no. 21 (1911): 19–20.

Baudry, Jean-Louis. "Ideological Effects of the Basic Cinematographic Apparatus." In *Narrative, Apparatus, Ideology: A Film Theory Reader*, edited by Philip Rosen, 286–98. New York: Columbia University Press, 1986.

Bel Geddes, Norman. *Horizons*. Boston: Little, Brown, 1932.

———. *Magic Motorways*. New York: Random House, 1940.

Bellamy, Edward. *Equality*. New York: D. Appleton, 1897.

———. *Looking Backward: 2000–1887*. New York: Penguin, 1982 [1888].

Bender, Thomas. Untitled lecture, University of California, Irvine, 20 March 1995.

Benjamin, Walter. "The Work of Art in the Age of Mechanical Reproduction." In *Illuminations*, edited by Hannah Arendt, 217–52. New York: Schocken Books, 1936.

Benson, Susan Porter. *Counter Cultures: Saleswomen, Managers, and Customers in American Department Stores, 1890–1940*. Urbana: University of Illinois Press, 1986.

Berger, Michael L. *The Devil's Wagon in God's Country: The Automobile and Social Change in Rural America, 1893–1929*. Hamden, CT: Archon Books, 1979.

———. "Women Drivers! The Emergence of Folklore and Stereotypic Opinions Concerning Feminine Automotive Behavior." *Women's Studies International Forum* 9, no. 3 (1986): 257–63.

Berman, Marshall. *All That Is Solid Melts into Air: The Experience of Modernity*. New York: Penguin, 1988 [1982].

Berrey, Henry. "In January: '. . . And Now We Plan.'" *Westways* 34, no. 1 (1942): 4.

Bird, Remsen D. "Metropolitan Symphony." *Western City* 15, no. 2 (1939): 20.

Blackford, Mansel G. *The Lost Dream: Businessmen and City Planning on the Pacific Coast, 1890–1920*. Columbus: Ohio State University Press, 1993.

Blum, Daniel. *A Pictorial History of the Silent Screen*. New York: Grosset and Dunlap, 1953.

Board of City Planning Commissioners. *Annual Report*. Los Angeles: Board of City Planning Commissioners, 1931.

———. *Annual Report*. Los Angeles: Board of City Planning Commissioners, 1938.

Bogardus, Emory S. *The City Boy and His Problems: A Survey of Boy Life in Los Angeles*. Los Angeles: House of Ralston, 1926.

Bond, J. Max. "The Negro in Los Angeles." Ph.D. diss., University of Southern California, 1972.

Bottles, Scott L. *Los Angeles and the Automobile: The Making of the Modern City*. Berkeley: University of California Press, 1987.

Bowling, Harry. "The Song of the 'L.'" *Los Angeles Times*, 29 April 1926, 2:4.

Bowring, Betty McConnell. "Can Women Really Drive?" *Touring Topics* 18, no. 1 (1926): 24–25.

Boyer, M. Christine. *Dreaming the Rational City: The Myth of American City Planning.* Cambridge, MA: MIT Press, 1983.

Bradley, Bill, ed. *Commercial Los Angeles, 1925–1947.* Glendale, CA: Interurban Press, 1981.

Branigan, Edward. *Narrative Comprehension and Film.* London: Routledge, 1992.

———. *Point of View in the Cinema: A Theory of Narration and Subjectivity in Classical Film.* Berlin: Mouton, 1984.

Brilliant, Ashleigh. *The Great Car Craze: How Southern California Collided with the Automobile in the 1920's.* Santa Barbara: Woodbridge Press, 1989.

Brinckerhoff, H. M. "The Effect of Transportation upon the Distribution of Population in Large Cities." Paper presented at the Annual Conference on City Planning, Pittsburgh, PA, 9–11 May 1921.

Brooks, Michael. *Subway City: Riding the Trains, Reading New York.* New Brunswick, NJ: Rutgers University Press, 1997.

Brummitt, Wyatt B. "The Superhighway." *American City* 40, no. 1 (1929): 85–88.

Buder, Stanley. "Ebenezer Howard: The Genesis of a Town Planning Movement." *Journal of the American Institute of Planners* 35, no. 6 (1969): 390–98.

———. *Visionaries and Planners: The Garden City Movement and the Modern Community.* New York: Oxford University Press, 1990.

Bunch, Lonnie G., III. *Black Angelenos: The Afro-American in Los Angeles, 1850–1950.* Edited by Nancy McKinney. Los Angeles: California Afro-American Museum, 1988.

Burgess, Ernest W. "The Growth of the City: An Introduction to a Research Project." In *The City*, edited by Robert Park, Ernest W. Burgess, and Roderick D. McKenzie. Chicago: University of Chicago Press, 1925.

Business Men's Association of Los Angeles. "Don't Jam the Streets with Traffic." *Los Angeles Evening Express*, 20 April 1926, 1:2.

———. "In the Spirit of Fair Play." *Los Angeles Record*, 12 March 1926, 1:13.

———. "These Cartoons Misrepresent Facts." *Los Angeles Times*, 29 April 1926, 1:9.

———. "Voters and Tax Payers of Los Angeles." *Los Angeles Times*, 29 April 1926, 2:15.

Caro, Robert A. *The Power Broker: Robert Moses and the Fall of New York.* New York: Vintage Books, 1974.

Carr, Harry. *Los Angeles: City of Dreams.* New York: Grosset & Dunlap, 1935.

Central Business District Association. *Parkway Transit Lines in the Central Business District.* Los Angeles: Central Business District Association, 1944.

Certeau, Michel de. *The Practice of Everyday Life.* Translated by Steven Rendall. Berkeley: University of California Press, 1984.

Chapman, John L. *Incredible Los Angeles.* New York: Harper & Row, 1967.

Cheney, Charles Henry. "City Planning and Efficiency." *California Outlook* 16, no. 17 (1914): 18–19.

Citizens' Union Station Committee. "Keep The Elevateds Out!" *Los Angeles Examiner*, 28 April 1926, 1:14.

"The City Plan." *City Club Bulletin* 6, no. 349 (1924): 2.

Clark, Charles D. "Land Subdivision." In *Los Angeles: Preface to a Master Plan*, edited by George W. Robbins and L. Deming Tilton, 159–72. Los Angeles: Pacific Southwest Academy / Ward Ritchie Press, 1941.

Clarke, Gilmore D. "Modern Motor Arteries." Paper presented at the National Conference on City Planning, Philadelphia, 23–26 June 1930.

———. "The Parkway Idea." In *The Highway and the Landscape,* edited by William Brewster Snow, 33–55. New Brunswick, NJ: Rutgers University Press, 1959.

Clymber, Floyd. *Cars of the Stars and Movie Memories.* Los Angeles: Floyd Clymer, 1955.

"Congestion Cost to the Community." *City Club Bulletin* 3, no. 238 (1922): 2.

Corbett, Harvey Wiley. "Different Levels for Foot, Wheel and Rail." *American City* 31, no. 1 (1924): 1–6.

———. "The Problem of Traffic Congestion, and a Solution." *Architectural Forum* 46, no. 3 (1927): 201–8.

———. "Up with the Skyscraper." *National Municipal Review* 16, no. 2 (1927): 95–101.

———. "What the Architect Thinks of Zoning." *American Architect* 125 (1924): 149–50.

Corn, Joseph J., ed. *Imagining Tomorrow: History, Technology, and the American Future.* Cambridge, MA: MIT Press, 1986.

Corn, Joseph J., and Brian Horrigan. *Yesterday's Tomorrows: Past Visions of the American Future.* New York: Summit Books/Smithsonian Institution, 1984.

Cott, Nancy F. *The Grounding of Modern Feminism.* New Haven, CT: Yale University Press, 1987.

Crary, Jonathan. *Techniques of the Observer: On Vision and Modernity in the Nineteenth Century.* Cambridge, MA: MIT Press, 1990.

Crinella, Marino. "Closing the Suburban Frontier" (photocopy). Department of History, University of California, Irvine, 1994.

Cronon, William. *Nature's Metropolis: Chicago and the Great West.* New York: Norton, 1991.

Crowningshield, Daniel Smith. *The Jolly Eight: Coast to Coast and Back.* Boston: Richard G. Badger, 1929.

Crump, Spencer. *Ride the Big Red Cars: How Trolleys Helped Build Southern California.* Los Angeles: Crest Publications, 1962.

"The Cure for Traffic Congestion." *City Club Bulletin* 3, no. 235 (1922): 2.

Curran, Henry H. "The Skyscraper Does Cause Congestion: Major Curran Comes Back at Mr. Corbett." *National Municipal Review* 16, no. 4 (1927): 229–34.

Damon, George A. "A 'Home-Made' City Planning Exhibit and Its Results." *American City* 15, no. 4 (1916): 369–78.

———. "Inter and Intra Urban Transit and Traffic as a Regional Planning Problem." Paper presented at the National Conference on City Planning, Baltimore, MD, 30 April–2 May 1923.

———. "Relation of the Motor Bus to Other Methods of Transportation." Paper presented at the National Conference on City Planning, Philadelphia, 7–10 April 1924.

Davidson, Bill, and Frank D. Morris. "Traffic Nightmare—and a Promise of Dawn." *Collier's* 125 (1950): 26–27+.

Davis, J. Allen. *The Friend to All Motorists: The Story of the Automobile Club of Southern California through 65 Years, 1900–1965.* Los Angeles: Anderson, Ritchie, & Simon, 1967.

Davis, Mike. *City of Quartz: Excavating the Future in Los Angeles.* New York: Vintage Books, 1992 [1990].

———. *Ecology of Fear: Los Angeles and the Imagination of Disaster.* New York: Henry Holt, 1998.

———. "How Eden Lost Its Garden: A Political History of the Los Angeles Landscape." In *The City: Los Angeles and Urban Theory at the End of the Twentieth Century,* edited by Allen J. Scott and Edward W. Soja, 160–85. Berkeley: University of California Press, 1996.

Dimendberg, Edward. "The Will to Motorization: Cinema, Highways, and Modernity." *October* 73 (1995): 91–137.

Douglas, Ann. *Terrible Honesty: Mongrel Manhattan in the 1920s.* New York: Farrar, Straus, and Giroux, 1995.

Downer, Jay. "The Bronx River Parkway." Paper presented at the National Conference on City Planning, New York, 7–9 May 1917.

"Dream City." *Time* 38 (1941): 45.

Dykstra, C. A. "Congestion De Luxe—Do We Want It?" *National Municipal Review* 15, no. 7 (1926): 394–98.

———. "The Future of Los Angeles." In *Los Angeles: Preface to a Master Plan,* edited by George W. Robbins and L. Deming Tilton, 3–12. Los Angeles: Pacific Southwest Academy / Ward Ritchie Press, 1941.

———. "Report on Rapid Transit." *City Club Bulletin,* 30 January 1926, 1–19.

East, E. E. "The Traffic Squeeze . . . A New Menace to Metropolitan Los Angeles." *Westways* 29, no. 9 (1937): 20–21.

Ellison, Ralph. "Harlem Is Nowhere." In *Shadow and Act,* 294–302. New York: Vintage, 1948.

———. *Invisible Man.* New York: Random House, 1952.

Ervin, James McFarline. "The Participation of the Negro in the Community Life of Los Angeles." M.A. thesis, University of Southern California, 1931.

Esse, Earl, and Simon Eisner. *Freeways for the Region.* Edited by Tom D. Cooke. Los Angeles: County Regional Planning Commission, 1943.

Findley, James Clifford. "The Economic Boom of the 'Twenties in Los Angeles." Ph.D. diss., Claremont Graduate School, 1958.

"First Regional Plan Conference." *City Club Bulletin* 3, no. 235 (1922): 4.

Fisher, Colin. "Frontiers of Leisure: Nature, Memory, and Nationalism in American Parks, 1850–1930." Ph.D. diss., University of California, Irvine, 1999.

Fishman, Robert. *Bourgeois Utopias: The Rise and Fall of Suburbia.* New York: Basic Books, 1987.

———. *Urban Utopias in the Twentieth Century: Ebenezer Howard, Frank Lloyd Wright, and Le Corbusier.* Cambridge, MA: MIT Press, 1977.

Fitzgerald, F. Scott. "My Lost City." In *The Crack-Up,* 23–33. New York: New Directions, 1932.

Flagg, James Montgomery. *Boulevards All the Way—Maybe.* New York: George H. Doran, 1925.

Fogelson, Robert M. *The Fragmented Metropolis: Los Angeles, 1850–1930.* Berkeley: University of California Press, 1967.

Foster, Mark S. "The Decentralization of Los Angeles during the 1920's." Ph.D. diss., University of Southern California, 1971.

———. *From Streetcar to Superhighway: American City Planners and Urban Transportation, 1900–1940.* Philadelphia: Temple University Press, 1981.

———. "The Model-T, the Hard Sell, and Los Angeles's Urban Growth: The Decentralization of Los Angeles during the 1920s." *Pacific Historical Review* 44, no. 4 (1975): 459–84.

Foucault, Michel. *The History of Sexuality: I: An Introduction.* Translated by Robert Hurley. New York: Vintage Books, 1990 [1976].

Fowler, Dan. "Los Angeles: The World's Worst Growing Pains." *Look* 20, no. 5 (1956): 21–25.

Fox, William J. "Seven Decades of Planning and Development in the Los Angeles Region" (typescript). Oral History Program, University of California, Los Angeles, 1985.

Frank, Dana. *Purchasing Power: Consumer Organizing, Gender, and the Seattle Labor Movement, 1919–1929.* Cambridge: Cambridge University Press, 1994.

Friedberg, Anne. *Window Shopping: Cinema and the Postmodern.* Berkeley: University of California Press, 1993.

Gallagher, J. P. "Chicago Takes Up Gage in Opposition to 'L' Railroad." *Los Angeles Times,* 15 April 1926, 1:1+.

———. "Elevated Held Curse to Progress of Chicago." *Los Angeles Times,* 14 April 1926, 1:1+.

———. "Elevated Railroad Magnate Condemns Chicago 'L', Joins in Fight to Provide Subway." *Los Angeles Times,* 16 April 1926, 1:1+.

———. "Experts Call Building of 'L' Tragic Error." *Los Angeles Times,* 18 April 1926, 1:1+.

———. "Union Depot Marks Era." *Los Angeles Times,* 27 April 1926, 1:1+.

Gans, Herbert J. *The Levittowners: Ways of Life and Politics in a New Suburban Community.* New York: Random House, 1967.

———. *The Urban Villagers: Group and Class in the Life of Italian-Americans.* New York: Free Press, 1962.

Garreau, Joel. *Edge City: Life on the New Frontier.* New York: Anchor Books / Doubleday, 1991.

Gebhard, David. "Introduction." In *California Crazy: Roadside Vernacular Architecture,* edited by Jim Heimann and Rip Georges, 11–25. San Francisco: Chronicle Books, 1980.

Gebhard, David, and Harriette von Breton. *Los Angeles in the Thirties, 1931–1941.* Los Angeles: Hennessey & Ingalls, 1989 [1975].

Geertz, Clifford. *Negara: The Theatre State in Nineteenth-Century Bali.* Princeton, NJ: Princeton University Press, 1980.

Giedion, Sigfried. *Space, Time and Architecture: The Growth of a New Tradition.* Cambridge, MA: Harvard University Press, 1967 [1941].

Girouard, Mark. *Cities and People: A Social and Architectural History.* New Haven, CT: Yale University Press, 1985.

"Give Los Angeles More Streets and Better Streets." *City Club Bulletin* 6, no. 378 (1924): 4.

Glendinning, Robert M. "Zoning: Past, Present and Future." In *Los Angeles: Preface to a Master Plan,* edited by George W. Robbins and L. Deming Tilton, 173–88. Los Angeles: Pacific Southwest Academy / Ward Ritchie Press, 1941.

Goldberger, Paul. *The Skyscraper.* New York: Alfred A. Knopf, 1982.

Goldman, Jonathan. *The Empire State Building Book.* New York: St. Martin's Press, 1980.

Gottdiener, M. *The Social Production of Urban Space.* Austin: University of Texas Press, 1994 [1985].

Gottdiener, M., and George Kephart. "The Multinucleated Metropolitan Region: A Comparative Analysis." In *Postsuburban California: The Transformation of Orange County since World War II,* edited by Rob Kling, Spencer Olin, and Mark Poster, 31–54. Berkeley: University of California Press, 1991.

Gramsci, Antonio. *Selections from the Prison Notebooks*. Translated by Quintin Hoare and Geoffrey Nowell Smith. New York: International Publishers, 1971.

Greenwood, Roberta S. *Down by the Station: Los Angeles Chinatown, 1880–1933*. Los Angeles: Institute of Archaeology, University of California, Los Angeles, 1996.

Hall, Peter. *Cities of Tomorrow: An Intellectual History of Urban Planning and Design in the Twentieth Century*. Oxford: Blackwell, 1988.

Hancock, Ralph. *Fabulous Boulevard*. New York: Funk & Wagnalls, 1949.

Hartman, Edward T. "Causes of Congestion in Boston." Paper presented at the National Conference on City Planning and the Problems of Congestion, Boston, 2–4 May 1910.

Hecht, Ben. *1001 Afternoons in Chicago*. Chicago: University of Chicago Press, 1992 [1921].

Heidegger, Martin. "The Question Concerning Technology." In *The Question Concerning Technology, and Other Essays*, 3–35. New York: Harper & Row, 1977.

Hellman, Irving. "The Skyscraper's Influence on Municipal Progress." *Skyscraper* 1, no. 2 (1925): 6.

Henstell, Bruce. *Sunshine and Wealth: Los Angeles in the Twenties and Thirties*. San Francisco: Chronicle Books, 1984.

Hines, Thomas S. *Burnham of Chicago: Architect and Planner*. Chicago: University of Chicago Press, 1979 [1974].

Hise, Greg. "Home Building and Industrial Decentralization in Los Angeles: The Origins of Peripheral Urbanism, 1935–47." Paper presented at the National Conference on American Planning History, Richmond, VA, 10 November 1991.

———. *Magnetic Los Angeles: Planning the Twentieth-Century Metropolis*. Baltimore, MD: Johns Hopkins University Press, 1997.

Hise, Greg, and William Deverell. *Eden by Design: The 1930 Olmsted-Bartholomew Plan for the Los Angeles Region*. Berkeley: University of California Press, 2000.

Howard, Ebenezer. *Garden Cities of To-morrow*. London: Faber and Faber, 1945 [1898].

———. "Reply." Paper presented at the International City and Regional Planning Conference, Baltimore, 20–25 April 1925.

Howells, William Dean. *Letters of an Altrurian Traveler*, 1893.

Hughes, Langston. *The Big Sea*. New York: Persea Books, 1986 [1940].

Huneker, James. *New Cosmopolis: A Book of Images*. New York: Charles Scribner's Sons, 1915.

Hyams, Edward. *A History of Gardens and Gardening*. New York: Praeger, 1971.

"The Intolerable City." *City Club Bulletin* 8, no. 445 (1926): 2.

"Is Super-Congestion Inevitable?" *American City* 36, no. 6 (1927): 800.

"Is the Skyscraper Doomed?" *National Municipal Review* 15, no. 8 (1926): 438–39.

Jackson, Kenneth T. "The Capital of Capitalism: The New York Metropolitan Region, 1890–1940." In *Metropolis, 1890–1940*, edited by Anthony Sutcliffe, 319–53. London: Mansell, 1984.

———. *Crabgrass Frontier: The Suburbanization of the United States*. New York: Oxford University Press, 1985.

Jacobs, Jane. *The Death and Life of Great American Cities*. New York: Vintage, 1992 [1961].

James, Henry. *The American Scene*. Bloomington: Indiana University Press, 1968.

Jay, Martin. *Downcast Eyes: The Denigration of Vision in Twentieth-Century French Thought*. Berkeley: University of California Press, 1993.

Johns, Orrick. "Architects Dream of a Pinnacle City." *New York Times*, 28 December 1924, 10.

———. "Bridge Homes—A New Vision of the City." *New York Times*, 22 February 1925, 4:5.

Johnson, David A. *Planning the Great Metropolis: The 1929 Regional Plan of New York and Its Environs*. London: E & FN Spon / Chapman & Hall, 1996.

Johnson, James Weldon. *Black Manhattan*. New York: Da Capo Press, 1930.

———. "My City." In *The Book of American Negro Poetry*, edited by James Weldon Johnson, 125. New York: Harcourt, Brace, 1931.

———. *Saint Peter Relates an Incident: Selected Poems*. New York: Viking, 1974 [1935].

Julien, Kyle. "Sounding the City: Jazz, African American Nightlife, and the Articulation of Race in 1940s Los Angeles." Ph.D. diss., University of California, Irvine, 2000.

———. "Transplanting the Heartland" (photocopy). Department of History, University of California, Irvine, 1994.

Kasson, John F. *Civilizing the Machine: Technology and Republican Values in America, 1776–1900*. New York: Penguin Books, 1976.

Kazin, Alfred. *A Walker in the City*. New York: Harcourt, Brace, 1951.

Kegley, Howard C. "The Ballad of Parkless Town." *Los Angeles Times*, 24 April 1920, 1.

Kelker, R. F., Jr., and C. F. De Leuw. *Report and Recommendations on a Comprehensive Rapid Transit Plan for the City and County of Los Angeles*. Chicago: Kelker, De Leuw & Company, 1925.

Kellogg, Paul U. *The Pittsburgh Survey*. New York: Russell Sage Foundation, 1914.

Kessler-Harris, Alice. *Out to Work: A History of Wage-Earning Women in the United States*. Oxford: Oxford University Press, 1982.

King, Moses. *King's Views of New York 1896–1915 & Brooklyn 1905*. New York: Benjamin Blom, 1974 [1915].

Kipling, Rudyard. *From Sea to Sea*. 2 vols. New York: Doubleday & McClure, 1899.

Kling, Rob, Spencer Olin, and Mark Poster. "Beyond the Edge: The Dynamism of Postsuburban Regions." In *Postsuburban California: The Transformation of Orange County since World War II*, edited by Rob Kling, Spencer Olin, and Mark Poster, vii–xx. Berkeley: University of California Press, 1995.

———. "The Emergence of Postsuburbia: An Introduction." In *Postsuburban California: The Transformation of Orange County since World War II*, edited by Rob Kling, Spencer Olin, and Mark Poster, 1–30. Berkeley: University of California Press, 1995.

Kropp, Phoebe. "'All Our Yesterdays': The Spanish Fantasy Past and the Politics of Public Memory in Southern California, 1884–1939." Ph.D. diss., University of California, San Diego, 1999.

———. *California Vieja: Culture and Memory in a Modern American Place*. Berkeley: University of California, 2006.

Kuhn, Thomas S. *The Structure of Scientific Revolutions*. Chicago: University of Chicago Press, 1970.

Larsen, Nella. "Quicksand." In *Quicksand and Passing*, 1–142. New Brunswick, NJ: Rutgers University Press, 1986.

Lathrop, John E. "City Planning Exhibit." *California Outlook* 16, no. 16 (1914): 14.

Lears, T. J. Jackson. *Fables of Abundance: A Cultural History of Advertising in America*. New York: Basic Books, 1994.

———. *No Place of Grace: Antimodernism and the Transformation of American Culture, 1880–1920*. Chicago: University of Chicago Press, 1981.

Leeuwen, Thomas A. P. van. *The Skyward Trend of Thought: The Metaphysics of the American Skyscraper*. Cambridge, MA: MIT Press, 1988 [1986].

Lefferts, E. B. "Correcting Los Angeles Traffic Snarls." *American City* 54 (1939): 99–101.

Leitch, Thomas. *Find the Director and Other Hitchcock Games*. Athens: University of Georgia Press, 1991.

Lipsitz, George. *Time Passages: Collective Memory and American Popular Culture*. Minneapolis: University of Minnesota Press, 1989.

Longstreth, Richard. *City Center to Regional Mall: Architecture, the Automobile, and Retailing in Los Angeles, 1920–1950*. Cambridge, MA: MIT Press, 1997.

———. *The Drive-In, The Supermarket, and the Transformation of Commercial Space in Los Angeles, 1914–1941*. Cambridge, MA: MIT Press, 1999.

Loon, Hendrik Van. *America*. New York: Boni & Liveright, 1927.

Los Angeles Central Business District Association. *Los Angeles Parkway and Transit System*. Los Angeles: Los Angeles Central Business District Association, 1946.

Los Angeles County Museum. . . . *And Now We Plan*. Edited by Roland McKinney. Los Angeles: Los Angeles County Museum, 1941.

Los Angeles Daily News. "Elevated Highway Network Proposed: Super Motorways through Buildings, over Streets Urged for L.A. District." 16 February 1938, 1:10.

———. "A Future for L.A. County." 27 October 1941, 1:14.

Los Angeles Evening Express. "Attorneys Support Union Station Plan." 21 April 1926, 29.

———. "City Hall a Symbol." 23 April 1926, 18.

———. "Los Angeles, City of Homes." 5 April 1926, 1:14.

———. "Record Vote Is Expected in L.A. Tomorrow: Ten Questions on Ballot." 29 April 1926, 3+.

Los Angeles Evening Herald. "Attorney Raps Plaza Site for Station." 18 January 1926, 1:12.

Los Angeles Examiner. "Adoption of Kelker-De Leuw Rapid Transit Plan Urged." 29 January 1926, 2:1.

———. "Artery Seen as Busy Hub by Backers." 25 April 1926, 4:3.

———. "Beach Trade Chiefs Back 'L' Projects." 22 January 1926, 1:11.

———. "C. of C. Fights Plaza Union Station: 4 Railroads Offer New Traffic Plan." 30 December 1925, 1:1.

———. "Criswell Calls Plaza Terminal Unnecessary." 29 March 1926, 1:5.

———. "Depot in Chinese District, or No More Grade Crossings?" 12 April 1926, 2:16.

———. "Expert Opposes Union Station at Plaza." 21 February 1926, 2:1.

———. "Finance Head Raps Station on Plaza Site." 21 January 1926, 1:6.

———. "Hollywood Tube Service Opens Today." 7 February 1926, 3:18.

———. "Martyr to Test No-Parking Law." 13 April 1920, 1:4.

———. "1 Woman Wins Probation; Scores Who Park Fined." 15 April 1920.

———. "P.E. Subway Stimulates Commuter Travel." 28 March 1926, 2:16.

————. "Plaza Depot." 20 April 1926, 2:20.

————. "Plaza Plan, Ignoring P.E., Reveals Its Fatal Weakness." 26 April 1926, 2:16.

————. "Sane View of Plaza Plan by City's Traffic Experts." 24 April 1926, 2:16.

————. "Subways Boost Suburban Areas." 28 February 1926, 4:13.

————. "Talks to Club on New City Ordinances." 11 April 1920, 8:18.

————. "These Issues Command Your Voting Interest." 29 April 1926, 2:16.

————. "Three Demolishing Smashes at Plaza Terminal Project." 20 April 1926, 2:20.

————. "Traffic Commission Hits Union Station." 21 April 1926, 2:1+.

————. "204-ft. Roads to Speed Up City Traffic." 7 March 1926, 7:3.

————. "Wm. Sproule Clears Plaza Site Issues." 17 January 1926, 1:15.

————. "Workman Asks High City Hall." 7 April 1926, 2:8.

Los Angeles Herald. "Arrest Hundreds as 'Parking' Violators." 10 April 1920, 1.

————. "Autoists! Beware Vigilantes: Secret Organization Starts Work of 'Spotting' Reckless Auto Drivers in Los Angeles." 1 April 1920, 1.

————. "Save Wilshire Blvd. from Realestate Exploiters: Vote No on Propositions 3 and 4."
29 April 1926, 1:19.

————. "Urge Wilshire as L.A.'s Fifth Avenue." 6 April 1926, 1:13.

Los Angeles Record, Editorial, 18 July 1923, 8.

————. "The Election Arguments." 26 April 1926, 1:4.

————. "Now There Are Six Plans for Station." 15 March 1926, 10.

————. "Record Recommendations." 29 April 1926, 1:1+.

Los Angeles Regional Planning Commission. Business Districts. Edited by Arthur H. Adams.
Los Angeles: Los Angeles Regional Planning Commission, 1944.

————. A Comprehensive Report on the Master Plan of Highways. I: The Plan and Its Preparation. Los Angeles: Los Angeles Regional Planning Commission, 1941.

————. Report of a Highway Traffic Survey in the County of Los Angeles. Los Angeles: Los
Angeles Regional Planning Commission, 1937.

Los Angeles Telesis. ". . . Now We Plan" (promotional materials). Los Angeles: Los Angeles
Telesis, 1941.

Los Angeles Times. "Auto Deaths Set New Record." 23 February 1920, 2:1.

————. "Car Revision Is Sweeping." 31 March 1920, 2:1+.

————. "Cause of Car Plunge Still Unfixed." 3 March 1926, 1:8.

————. "Civic Center Designers Indorse Plaza Union Depot Plan." 25 April 1926, 2:1–2.

————. "Clara Kimball Young." 25 April 1920, 3:15.

————. "Complete Our Civic Center by Voting 'Yes' on Propositions 8–9." 28 April 1926,
2:12.

————. "The Election Results." 2 May 1926, 2:4.

————. "Evangelist Is Against Elevateds." 29 April 1926, 2:1.

————. "Experts Favor Plaza Site for Union Railway Station." 12 April 1920, 2:1.

————. "Ex-Star of Films Hurt in Traffic." 7 June 1932, 2:2.

————. "Fabrications vs. Facts." 28 April 1926, 2:1.

————. "Fact and Comment: No-Parking Effects." 14 March 1920, 1.

————. "Far-Flung City Held Ideal Here." 10 May 1925, 1:11.

————. "Five-Cent Fares and Crowded Street Cars." 24 March 1920, 2:4.

————. "Five Killed in Auto Mishaps." 12 April 1920, 2:1–2.

————. "For Wider Streets." 25 April 1920, 1.

————. "Grauman's Rialto." 25 April 1920, 3:13.

————. "Half a Million Dollars to Beat Union Depot." 12 April 1920, 2:1–2.

————. "Height Limit Commended." 11 June 1925, 2:2.

————. "Height Limit Is Protested." 30 May 1925, 1:5.

————. "Height-Limit Reason Given." 25 April 1926, 5:4.

————. "Hits Those Who Make Streets Death-Traps." 22 March 1920, 2:1.

————. "Just What This 'L' Means." 19 April 1926, 1:1.

————. "Keep the 'L' Out of Los Angeles." 29 March 1926, 1:1–2.

————. "Low-Height Limitation Advocated." 20 May 1925, 1:16.

————. "Luckily, No One Was Killed. . . ." 29 April 1926, 1:12.

————. "Magnificent Los Angeles Civic Center in the Making: Steam Shovels Clear Way for Downtown Beauty Spot." 18 April 1926, 2:1–2.

————. "Milton Wins Beverly Sprints." 29 March 1920, 2:1.

————. "Motorways Plan Ready." 16 February 1938, 2:1.

————. "Murderous Speed Maniacs." 18 March 1920, 2:4.

————. "New Chinatown." 21 January 1938, 2:4.

————. "The No-Parking Cure for All Traffic Ills Goes into Effect." 11 April 1920, 6:1.

————. "No-Parking Law Proves Motor Cars Absolutely Essential." 25 April 1920, 6:1+.

————. "People vs. Railroads, Union Station Issue." 20 April 1926, 2:1–2.

————. "The Perils of a Parkless Town." 29 February 1920, 2:1+.

————. "Planning Display to Show Growth." 22 October 1941, 2:2.

————. "Public vs. Private Interest." 9 February 1926, 2:1–2.

————. "Railroads vs. the People." 29 April 1926, 2:1.

————. "Relief Pledged from Auto Ban." 24 April 1920, 2:1.

————. "Rock Pile for Auto Mashers." 9 January 1920, 2:1.

————. "Says Railroads Should Be Forced to Obey." 21 February 1926, 2:2.

————. "Secret of City Plan Revealed." 8 October 1929, 2:11.

————. "Speed Murderers." 8 March 1920, 2:4.

————. "Straw Vote on Depot Question." 26 February 1926, 2:1–2.

————. "Subway Lines Opening Sunday." 2 February 1926, 2:1–2.

————. "Take 'Bugs' Out of Park Bill." 12 March 1929, 2:1–2.

————. "To End Inroads of Parking Ban." 21 April 1920, 2:1+.

————. "To Round Up Speed Maniacs." 8 March 1920, 2:1.

————. "Traffic." 18 December 1910, 2:4.

————. "Traffic." 18 November 1926, 2:4.

————. "Traffic." 1 July 1928, 5:8.

————. "Tries to Kidnap Official's Wife." 27 March 1921, 1:10.

————. "Two Die in Auto Crash." 29 March 1920, 2:1.

————. "Urges Yes Votes for Zone Plan." 29 April 1926, 2:3.

————. "Values Fall Due to 'L.'" 20 April 1926, 1:1+.

————. "Vigilantes to Curb Autoists." 6 March 1920, 2:1.

————. "Warns against Rush Act." 9 February 1926, 2:1–2.

————. "Whitnall Quits City Plan Board." 14 February 1930, 2:2.
————. "Whitnall Will be President of City Planners." 15 June 1930, 2:3.
Los Angeles Traffic Commission. *The Los Angeles Plan*. Los Angeles: Los Angeles Traffic Commission, 1922.
————. *A Major Traffic Street Plan for Los Angeles*. Los Angeles: Los Angeles Traffic Commission, 1924.
————. *President's Annual Report*. Los Angeles: Los Angeles Traffic Commission, 1927.
Lynch, Kevin. *The Image of the City*. Cambridge, MA: MIT Press, 1960.
————. "Reconsidering *The Image of the City*." In *Cities of the Mind: Images and Themes of the City in the Social Sciences*, edited by Lloyd Rodwin and Robert M. Hollister, 151–61. New York: Plenum Press, 1984.
Lynd, Robert S., and Helen Merrell Lynd. *Middletown: A Study in Modern American Culture*. New York: Harcourt, Brace, 1929.
Lyon, W. A. "City Warned by Expert of Menace in 'L' Plan." *Los Angeles Times*, 25 April 1926, 1:1.
————. "Effect of New York 'L' on Health Disastrous." *Los Angeles Times*, 24 April 1926, 1:1+.
————. "Foul Dirt, Darkness and Bedlam Curse of 'L.'" *Los Angeles Times*, 23 April 1926, 1:1–2.
————. "New York Pays Piper for Dance that Opened 'L.'" *Los Angeles Times*, 21 April 1926, 1:1+.
————. "Property Values Soar When New York City Street Bans 'L.'" *Los Angeles Times*, 22 April 1926, 1:1–2.
"The Major Traffic Street Plan." *City Club Bulletin* 6, no. 365 (1924): 2.
Marchand, Roland. *Advertising the American Dream: Making Way for Modernity, 1920–1940*. Berkeley: University of California Press, 1985.
Marling, Karal Ann. *The Colossus of Roads: Myth and Symbol along the American Highway*. Minneapolis: University of Minnesota Press, 1984.
Marsh, Margaret. *Suburban Lives*. New Brunswick, NJ: Rutgers University Press, 1990.
Martin, Albert C. "New Hall Will Symbolize City." *Los Angeles Times*, 11 April 1926, 2:3.
Marx, Karl. *Capital*. Translated by Samuel Moore and Edward Aveling. Volume 1. New York: International Publishers, 1867.
Marx, Leo. *The Machine in the Garden: Technology and the Pastoral Ideal in America*. New York: Oxford University Press, 1964.
Mathison, Richard R. *Three Cars in Every Garage: A Motorist's History of the Automobile and the Automobile Club in Southern California*. Garden City, NY: Doubleday, 1968.
Mayo, Morrow. *Los Angeles*. New York: Alfred A. Knopf, 1933.
McCarthy, Thomas M. "The Arrogance of Wealth: Woodrow Wilson and Early Mass Automobility in America." Staunton, VA: Woodrow Wilson Birthplace Foundation, 2000.
McClenahan, Bessie Averne. *The Changing Urban Neighborhood: From Neighbor to Nigh-Dweller: A Sociological Study*. Los Angeles: University of Southern California, 1929.
McShane, Clay. *Down the Asphalt Path: The Automobile and the American City*. New York: Columbia University Press, 1994.
McWilliams, Carey. *Southern California: An Island on the Land*. Santa Barbara, CA: Peregrine Smith, 1979 [1946].

————. "Tides West: What Is California? & Urbane S.F. vs. Rustic L.A." *Westways* 29, no. 5 (1937): 4.

"The Meaning of the Zoning Decision." *City Club Bulletin* 6, no. 336 (1924): 3.

Meikle, Jeffrey L. *Twentieth Century Limited: Industrial Design in America, 1925–1939.* Philadelphia: Temple University Press, 1979.

"Metropolitan District Study." *City Club Bulletin* 3, no. 283 (1923): 3.

"Metropolitan Government." *City Club Bulletin* 6, no. 380 (1924): 3–4.

Metz, Christian. *The Imaginary Signifier: Psychoanalysis and the Cinema.* Bloomington: University of Indiana Press, 1977.

Miller, Perry. *The Life of the Mind in America, from the Revolution to the Civil War.* New York: Harcourt, Brace, 1965.

Millier, Arthur. "Now We Plan." *Los Angeles Times Home Magazine* (1941): 3–4+.

Modleski, Tania. *Loving with a Vengeance: Mass Produced Fantasies for Women.* New York: Methuen, 1984.

"The Monday Evening Forum." *City Club Bulletin* 3, no. 241 (1922): 4.

Moore, Charles, Peter Becker, and Regula Campbell. *The City Observed, Los Angeles: A Guide to Its Architecture and Landscapes.* New York: Random House, 1984.

Moore, Deborah Dash. "On the Fringes of the City: Jewish Neighborhoods in Three Boroughs." In *The Landscape of Modernity: Essays on New York City, 1900–1940,* edited by David Ward and Oliver Zunz, 252–72. New York: Russell Sage Foundation, 1992.

Mujica, Francisco. *History of the Skyscraper.* Paris: Archaeology and Architecture Press, 1929.

Mullins, William H. *The Depression and the Urban West Coast, 1929–1933.* Bloomington: Indiana University Press, 1991.

Mulvey, Laura. "Changes: Thoughts on Myth, Narrative, and Historical Experience." In *Visual and Other Pleasures,* 159–76. Bloomington: Indiana University Press, 1989 [1987].

————. "Visual Pleasure and Narrative Cinema." In *Visual and Other Pleasures,* 14–28. Bloomington: Indiana University Press, 1989 [1973].

Mumford, Lewis. "American Architecture To-day." *Architecture* 58 (1928).

————. *The Culture of Cities.* San Diego: Harcourt Brace Jovanovich, 1938.

————. "The Garden City Idea and Modern Planning." In *Garden Cities of To-morrow,* by Ebenezer Howard, 29–40. London: Faber and Faber, 1945.

————. *The Lewis Mumford Reader.* Edited by Donald L. Miller. New York: Pantheon Books, 1986.

————. "The Next Twenty Years in City Planning." Paper presented at the Planning Problems of Town, City, and Region: Nineteenth National Conference on City Planning, Philadelphia, 9–11 May 1927.

————. *The Story of Utopias.* New York: Viking Press, 1922.

"Must We Come To This?" *American City* 36, no. 6 (1927): 801.

Nadeau, Remi. *California: The New Society.* Westport, CT: Greenwood Press, 1974 [1963].

Nasaw, David. *Going Out: The Rise and Fall of Public Amusements.* New York: Basic Books, 1993.

Nelson, Howard J. *The Los Angeles Metropolis.* Dubuque, IA: Kendall/Hunt, 1981.

Nettlefold, J. S. "Town Planning." In *Town Planning in Theory and Practice* (London: Garden City Association, 1908).

Neutra, Richard J. "Homes and Housing." In *Los Angeles: Preface to a Master Plan,* edited by George W. Robbins and L. Deming Tilton, 189–202. Los Angeles: Pacific Southwest Academy / Ward Ritchie Press, 1941.

New York Times. "Coming City of Set-Back Skyscrapers: Diminishing Terraces Stretching Indefinitely Upward." 29 April 1923, 4:5.

———. "Hoover Will Open Empire State Today." 1 May 1931, 1:15.

"No Express Highways in Los Angeles Regional Plan." *National Municipal Review* 19, no. 9 (1930): 581.

Novak, Barbara. *Nature and Culture: American Landscape and Painting, 1825–1875.* New York: Oxford University Press, 1980.

". . . Now We Plan." *California Arts and Architecture* 57, no. 11 (1941): 21–23.

Nye, David E. *American Technological Sublime.* Cambridge, MA: MIT Press, 1994.

Nye, Myra. "Whitnall Hits Back at Critics." *Los Angeles Times,* 5 June 1925, 2:6.

Olmsted, Frederick Law. *The Papers of Frederick Law Olmsted.* Baltimore, MD: Johns Hopkins University Press, 1997.

———. "Public Parks and the Enlargement of Towns." Boston: American Social Science Association, 1870.

Olmsted Brothers and Bartholomew and Associates. *Parks, Playgrounds, and Beaches for the Los Angeles Region.* Los Angeles: Citizens' Committee on Parks, Playgrounds, and Beaches, 1930.

"The Open Forum." *City Club Bulletin* 8, no. 435 (1925): 4.

"Open Forum: Pershing Square and the Pacific Electric." *City Club Bulletin* 5, no. 297 (1923): 4.

"Open Forum: The Traffic and Subway Problem of Los Angeles." *City Club Bulletin* 5, no. 308 (1923): 4.

Ouellet, Philip J. *City Planning in Los Angeles: A History.* Los Angeles: Department of City Planning, 1964.

Park, Robert, Ernest W. Burgess, and Roderick D. McKenzie. *The City.* Chicago: University of Chicago Press, 1925.

Payne, Pauline. "Star Brands It Non-Shopping Law; Not 'No-Parking.'" *Los Angeles Herald,* 22 April 1920, 1+.

Peiss, Kathy. *Cheap Amusements: Working Women and Leisure in Turn-of-the-Century New York.* Philadelphia: Temple University Press, 1986.

Peterson, William. "The Ideological Origins of Britain's New Towns." *Journal of the American Institute of Planners* 34, no. 3 (1968).

Pitt, Leonard, and Dale Pitt. *Los Angeles, A to Z: An Encyclopedia of the City and County.* Berkeley: University of California Press, 1997.

Pomeroy, Hugh R. "Regional Planning in Practice." Paper presented at the National Conference on City Planning, Philadelphia, 7–10 April 1924.

Preminger, Alex, and T. V. F. Brogan, eds. *The New Princeton Encyclopedia of Poetry and Poetics.* Princeton, NJ: Princeton University Press, 1993.

Radde, Bruce. *The Merritt Parkway.* New Haven, CT: Yale University Press, 1993.

Radway, Janice A. *Reading the Romance: Women, Patriarchy and Popular Literature.* Durham: University of North Carolina Press, 1984.

"Rapid Transit Situation in Los Angeles." *City Club Bulletin* 9, no. 635 (1929): 3.

"Regional Planning Conference." *City Club Bulletin* 7, no. 384 (1924): 3.

"Regional Planning Is Not Just Rural Planning." *Western City* 15, no. 3 (1939): 13.

"Regional Plan of New York and Its Environs." New York: Regional Plan of New York and Its Environs, 1929.

"Report on City Planning." *City Club Bulletin* 3, no. 122 (1919): 1–2.

Riis, Jacob A. *How the Other Half Lives: Studies among the Tenements of New York.* New York: Hill and Wang, 1957 [1890].

Robbins, George W., and L. Deming Tilton, eds. *Los Angeles: Preface to a Master Plan.* Los Angeles: Pacific Southwest Academy, 1941.

Robinson, Charles Mulford. *Los Angeles, California: The City Beautiful.* Los Angeles: Municipal Arts Commission, 1909.

Robinson, William. *The Wild Garden: Or, our groves and gardens made beautiful by the naturalisation of hardy exotic plants; being one way onwards from the dark ages of flower gardening, with suggestions for the regeneration of the bare borders of the London Parks.* London: Garden Office, 1881.

Robinson, W. W. *Los Angeles: A Profile.* Norman: University of Oklahoma Press, 1968.

Robinson, William Wilcox. *The Key to Los Angeles.* Philadelphia: J. B. Lippincott, 1963.

Russell, Frances Theresa. *Touring Utopia: The Realm of Constructive Humanism.* New York: Dial Press, 1932.

Ryan, Mary. *Cradle of the Middle Class: The Family in Oneida County, New York, 1790–1865.* Cambridge: Cambridge University Press, 1981.

Sachs, Wolfgang. *For Love of the Automobile: Looking Back into the History of Our Desires.* Translated by Don Reneau. Berkeley: University of California Press, 1992.

Sackman, Douglas Cazaux. *Orange Empire: California and the Fruits of Eden.* Berkeley: University of California Press, 2005.

Sanchez, George J. *Becoming Mexican American: Ethnicity, Culture, and Identity in Chicano Los Angeles, 1900–1945.* New York: Oxford University Press, 1993.

Sandburg, Carl. "Skyscraper." In *The Complete Poems of Carl Sandburg,* 31–32. New York: Harcourt Brace Jovanovich, 1970.

Sartre, Jean-Paul. "American Cities." In *Literary and Philosophical Essays,* 114–25. New York: Collier Books, 1962.

Scharff, Virginia. *Taking the Wheel: Women and the Coming of the Motor Age.* New York: Free Press, 1991.

Schivelbusch, Wolfgang. *The Railway Journey: The Industrialization of Time and Space in the Nineteenth Century.* Berkeley: University of California Press, 1986.

Schleier, Merrill. *The Skyscraper in American Art, 1890–1931.* New York: Da Capo Press, 1986.

Scott, Allen J., and Edward W. Soja, eds. *The City: Los Angeles and Urban Theory at the End of the Twentieth Century.* Berkeley: University of California Press, 1996.

Scott, Mel. *American City Planning.* Berkeley: University of California Press, 1969.

———. *Metropolitan Los Angeles: One Community.* Los Angeles: John Randolph Haynes and Dora Haynes Foundation, 1949.

Sears, John F. *Sacred Places: American Tourist Attractions in the Nineteenth Century.* New York: Oxford University Press, 1989.

Segal, Howard P. *Technological Utopianism in American Culture.* Chicago: University of Chicago Press, 1985.

———. "The Technological Utopians." In *Imagining Tomorrow: History, Technology, and the American Future,* edited by Joseph J. Corn, 119–36. Cambridge, MA: MIT Press, 1987.

Seims, Charles. *Mount Lowe: The Railway in the Clouds.* San Marino, CA: Golden West Books, 1976.

Sennott, R. Stephen. "Chicago Architects and the Automobile, 1906–1926: Adaptations in Horizontal and Vertical Space." In *Roadside America: The Automobile in Design and Culture,* edited by Jan Jennings, 157–69. Ames: Iowa State University Press, 1990.

Shannon, Michael F. *Transit Study 1944: Los Angeles Metropolitan Area.* Los Angeles: Central Business District Association, 1944.

Sharples, Philip P. "Traffic Counts by Boy Scouts in Los Angeles." *American City* 31 (1924): 197–200.

Shelton, Carroll. "Philadelphia Bans 'L' as Dirty, Noisy, Inartistic." *Los Angeles Times,* 26 April 1926, 1:1.

Sibley, Hy. "Our Cosmopolitan Motor Parade." *Touring Topics* 17, no. 12 (1925): 22+.

Silverman, Kaja. "Suture." In *Narrative, Apparatus, Ideology: A Film Theory Reader,* edited by Philip Rosen, 219–35. New York: Columbia University Press, 1986.

"The Skyscraper." *National Municipal Review* 16, no. 1 (1927): 1.

Soja, Edward W. *Postmodern Geographies.* London: Verso, 1989.

Sproule, William. "Every Dot a Grade Crossing." *Los Angeles Times,* 17 January 1926, 1:12–13.

Squire, Latham C., and Howard M. Bassett. "A New Type of Thoroughfare: The 'Freeway.'" *American City* 47 (1932): 64–66.

Stansell, Christine. *City of Women: Sex and Class in New York, 1789–1860.* Urbana: University of Illinois Press, 1986 [1982].

Starr, Kevin. *Americans and the California Dream, 1850–1915.* New York: Oxford University Press, 1973.

———. *Endangered Dreams: The Great Depression in California.* New York: Oxford University Press, 1996.

———. *Inventing the Dream: California through the Progressive Era.* New York: Oxford University Press, 1985.

———. *Material Dreams: Southern California through the 1920s.* New York: Oxford University Press, 1990.

Stern, Robert, Gregory Gilmartin, and Thomas Mellins. *New York, 1930: Architecture between the Two World Wars.* New York: Abrams, 1987.

Stimson, Marshall. "The Battle for a Union Station at Los Angeles." *Historical Society of Southern California Quarterly* 21, no. 1 (1939): 36–44.

Sutcliffe, Anthony. "The Metropolis in the Cinema." In *Metropolis, 1890–1940,* 147–71. London: Mansell, 1984.

Swan, Herbert S. "The Parkway as Traffic Artery [Part I]." *American City* 45, no. 4 (1931): 84–86.

———. "The Parkway as Traffic Artery [Part II]." *American City* 45, no. 5 (1931): 73–76.

"System of Super Highways Proposed for Los Angeles." *Western Construction News* 13, no. 4 (1938): 115–16.

Taylor, Eugene S. "Chicago's Superhighway Plan." *National Municipal Review* 18, no. 6 (1929): 371–76.

———. "A Comprehensive System of Elevated Super-Highways." *City Planning* 7, no. 2 (1931): 118–20.

Thomas, John L. "Utopia for an Urban Age: Henry George, Henry Demarest Lloyd, Edward Bellamy." *Perspectives in American History* 6 (1972): 135–63.

Tilden, Freeman. "Los Angeles." *World's Work* 60, no. 5 (1931).

Tilton, L. Deming. "The Master Plan." In *Los Angeles: Preface to a Master Plan,* edited by George W. Robbins and L. Deming Tilton, 253–66. Los Angeles: Pacific Southwest Academy / Ward Ritchie Press, 1941.

"Traffic Congestion and Regulation." *City Club Bulletin* 3, no. 230 (1921): 3.

"The Traffic Crisis." *City Club Bulletin* 6, no. 364 (1924): 4.

Transportation Engineering Board. *A Transit Program for the Los Angeles Metropolitan Area.* Los Angeles: Transportation Engineering Board, 1939.

Tunnard, Christopher, and Boris Pushkarev. *Man-Made America: Chaos or Control?* New Haven, CT: Yale University Press, 1963.

Turner, Daniel L. "Is There a Vicious Circle of Transit Development and City Congestion?" *National Municipal Review* 15, no. 6 (1926): 321–26.

Turner, Frederick Jackson. "The Significance of the Frontier in American History." In *The Frontier in American History,* 1–38. Tucson: University of Arizona Press, 1986.

Veiller, Lawrence. "Slumless America." Paper presented at the National Conference on City Planning, Philadelphia, 1920.

Venturi, Robert, Denise Scott Brown, and Steven Izenour. *Learning from Las Vegas: The Forgotten Symbolism of Architectural Form.* Cambridge, MA: MIT Press, 1977.

Vinton, Arthur. *Looking Further Backward. Being a Series of Lectures Delivered to the Freshman Class at Shawmut College, by Professor Won Lung Li (Successor of Prof. Julian West).* Albany, NY: Albany Book Company, 1890.

Wachs, Martin. "Autos, Transit, and the Sprawl of Los Angeles: The 1920s." *Journal of the American Planning Association* 50, no. 3 (1984): 297–310.

———. "Men, Women, and Urban Travel: The Persistence of Separate Spheres." In *The Car and the City: The Automobile, the Built Environment, and Daily Urban Life,* 86–100. Ann Arbor: University of Michigan Press, 1992.

Warner, Sam Bass, Jr. "Slums and Skyscrapers: Urban Images, Symbols, and Ideology." In *Cities of the Mind: Images and Themes of the City in the Social Sciences,* edited by Lloyd Rodwin and Robert M. Hollister, 181–95. New York: Plenum Press, 1984.

———. *Streetcar Suburbs: The Process of Growth in Boston, 1870–1900.* New York: Atheneum, 1962.

———. *The Urban Wilderness: A History of the American City.* Berkeley: University of California Press, 1995 [1972].

West, Nathanael. *The Day of the Locust.* New York: New Directions, 1962 [1933].

Whitnall, G. Gordon. "Beauty in City Planning." *City Club Bulletin* 8, no. 421 (1925): 4.

————. "City and County Consolidation for Los Angeles." *National Municipal Review* 10, no. 1 (1921): 7–9.

————. "City and Regional Planning in Los Angeles." Paper presented at the National Conference on City Planning, Philadelphia, 7–10 April 1924.

————. "Civic Periscope." *City Club Bulletin* 3, no. 192 (1921): 3.

————. "A Comment on the 'Lakewood Plan.'" *American City* 70, no. 5 (1955): 135.

————. "The Experience in the Los Angeles Region." Paper presented at the National Conference on City Planning, Philadelphia, 9–11 May 1927.

————. "Importance of Broad City Planning." *Southern California Business* 1, no. 1 (1922): 8+.

————. "League News and Notes." *Western City* 8, no. 4 (1932): 20.

————. "Metropolitan Planning: 'Civic Laboratory of the Country' Creates New Unit of Government to Make Most of Its Area." *Los Angeles Times*, 1 January 1925, Midwinter: 10.

————. "The Place of the East Coast in a State Plan for Florida." Paper presented at the National Conference on City Planning, Philadelphia, 29 March–1 April 1926.

————. "Regional Planning in Los Angeles." *National Municipal Review* 12, no. 6 (1923): 333.

————. "Regional Planning Progress in the Los Angeles District." *American City* 29, no. 6 (1923): 578–79.

————. "Saving Money in Street Widening." *American City* 40, no. 2 (1929): 122–23.

Williams, Robert Lee. "The City Planning Movement in Los Angeles, 1900–1920." M.A. thesis, California State University, Long Beach, 1972.

Williams, William Carlos. "The Wanderer: A Rococo Study." In *Selected Poems of William Carlos Williams*, 108. New York: New Directions, 1986.

Willis, Carol. "Drawing towards Metropolis." In Hugh Ferriss, *The Metropolis of To-morrow*, 148–84. Princeton, NJ: Princeton Architectural Press, 1986.

————. "Skyscraper Utopias: Visionary Urbanism in the 1920s." In *Imagining Tomorrow: History, Technology, and the American Future*, edited by Joseph J. Corn, 164–87. Cambridge, MA: MIT Press, 1987.

————. "The Titan City: Forgotten Episodes in American Architecture." *Skyline* (1982): 26–27.

————. "Zoning and *Zeitgeist*: The Skyscraper City in the 1920s." *Journal of the Society of Architectural Historians* 45, no. 1 (1986): 47–59.

Wilshire Beautiful Association. "Stop the Exploiter! Save Wilshire Boulevard for All the People. Vote No on Propositions 3 and 4." *Los Angeles Record*, 28 April 1926, 1:8.

Wirth, Louis. "Urbanism as a Way of Life." *American Journal of Sociology* 44, no. 1 (1938): 1–24.

Woehlke, Walter V. "Roots of Los Angeles' Astonishing Growth." *Sunset* (1924).

Wurts, Richard, and Stanley Appelbaum. *The New York World's Fair 1939/1940 in 155 Photographs*. New York: Dover, 1977.

Yezierska, Anzia. *Red Ribbon on a White Horse*. New York: Persea, 1981 [1950].

Zorbaugh, Harvey W. "The Shadow of the Skyscraper." In *The Social Fabric of the Metropolis: Contributions of the Chicago School of Urban Sociology*, edited by James F. Short, Jr., 3–14. Chicago: University of Chicago Press, 1929.

INDEX

Note: *All institutional entries may be assumed to pertain to Southern California unless otherwise specified. Page numbers in italics indicate illustrations.*

Abelson, Elaine S., 334–35n8
Adams, Henry, 202
Adler, Dankmar, 117
African Americans (black Americans), 33–37, 40, 157–63, 194, 225, 230, 329nn48,49,56,57, 330n63, 345n70, 346n81, 365n41
Aldrich, Lloyd, 300
Arendt, Hannah, 357n18
Armstrong, Louis, 162
Arnold, Bion J., 328n18, 332n103
Arroyo Seco Parkway, 295, 302–4, *302*
Asian Americans, 34–36, 86, 191, 194, 225, 353–54n71, 354n79. See also Chinatown
autobahns, 295, 373n14, 374n30
Automobile Club, 70, 77, 82, 96–98, 105–6, 175, 297, *298–301*, 299–301, 306, 339n68, 357n23. See also *The Los Angeles Traffic Problem; Touring Topics; Traffic Survey: Los Angeles Metropolitan Region*
automobiles, 3, 11, 12, 16–19, 23, 42–46, 59–84, *76, 80*, 87, 90–108, 111, 116–17, 127, 136–42, 144–48, 168, 174–77, 181, 186, 188, 194–97, 202, 209, 215–20, 224–25, 242, 251–60, 263–67, 275–76, 282, 286, 293, 295–97, 303–9, 312, 317–22, 326n8, 327n11, 331n77, 333nn106,6, 335n26, 337n30, 339–40n95, 347n11, 348n19, 350n43, 360n44,

361n61, 365n36, 366n43, 371n79, 374n30
AVUS (*Automobil-Verkehrs- und Übungs-Straße*, Germany), 295

Baermann, Walter, 307
Bakhtin, Mikhail, 366–67n46
Banham, Reyner, 79
Barth, Gunther, 334–35n8
Bartholomew, Harland, 100–12, 201, 212, 267, 269, 275, 279–83, 326n9, 339–40n95, 341n104, 367n50, 367–68n53, 368n54, 369n61. See also *A Major Traffic Street Plan for Los Angeles; Parks, Playgrounds, and Beaches for the Los Angeles Region*
Bartholomew and Associates. See Bartholomew, Harland
Bartlett, Dana W., 22, 24, 27, 33, 38, 328nn15,21,34, 330n62
Barton, Loren C., 351n50
Bassett, Edward M., 297, 373n17
Baudry, Jean-Louis, 366n46
Becker, Peter, 214
Beery, Wallace, 348–49n24
Bel Geddes, Norman, 304, 308, 374n28
Bellamy, Edward, 48–49, 119–22, 147, 151, 341–42n16, 342n19, 343n20

Bender, Thomas, 123
Bennett, Edward, 116
Benson, Susan Porter, 334–35n8
Berger, Michael, 336n13
Berlin, 237, 295
Berman, Marshall, 260–62
Beverly Hills, 34, 87, 329
Bogardus, Emory S., 34, 224–26, 240–42, 363n15
Bond, J. Max, 34, 329, 360n42
boosterism and civic promotion, 2–3, 13–14, 16, 22–23, 33, 35, 39, 41, 43–44, 47, 64, 75, 79, 86, 91, 93, 95–96, 108, 114, 137, 167, 170–73, 181, 186, 191–94, 208–9, 210, 216, 234, 239, 243, 273, 287, 310, 312, 316, 328
Bottles, Scott, 20, 195, 220, 327, 348n19, 351n61, 358n27
Boyer, M. Christine, 27–30, 88, 329n42
Branigan, Edward, 366–67n46
Briegieb, Gusav A., 75
Brilliant, Ashleigh, 79
Bronx River Parkway (NY), 253–55, 257, 260–61, 264, 285, 295
Brooks, Michael, 158, 346n81
Buder, Stanley, 57, 331n84, 332n89
Bullock, John, 213–14
Burgess, Ernest, 45, 222–23
Burnham, Daniel, 102, 116–17, 168, 252
Business Men's Association, 190–91, 353n69, 354n71

Cahuenga Pass (Hollywood) Freeway, 303, 303–4
Campbell, Regula, 214
Caro, Robert, 260–61, 365n41
Carr, Harry, 38, 235–40
Carr, James, 14
Central Avenue, 33–34
Central Park (NY), 248–49, 251
Chambless, Edgar, 141–42
Chandler, Harry, 99, 188–92, 268, 351n61
Cheney, Charles Henry, 100–12, 201, 326n9, 339–40n95, 341n104. See also A Major Traffic Street Plan for Los Angeles
Chicago, 45, 45–47, 58, 93, 114–18, 118, 122, 131–32, 135, 141, 146, 163, 167–68, 170, 172, 179, 181, 223–24, 246, 296, 303, 315, 328n18, 343n21, 351n49, 352n63
Chinatown, 35, 191–97, 196, 353n71, 354n79, 354–35n84

Chinese Americans. See Asian Americans
Chrysler Building (New York City), 136
Citizens' Committee on Parks, Playgrounds, and Beaches, 270, 277, 281, 283, 367n53, 369n61. See also Parks, Playgrounds, and Beaches for the Los Angeles Region
City Club, 57, 106, 110, 198–205, 268, 340n97, 347n11
City Council, 25, 99, 212, 337n49
City Hall, 33, 35, 185–87, 192
City Planning Commission, 20, 25, 25–26, 41, 47, 60, 85–87, 90, 98–101, 171, 184–85, 198, 212–13, 270–71, 338n49
Clark, Charles D., 21
Corbett, Harvey Wiley, 137–42, 139, 147–48, 175, 205–7, 345n55, 347n11
Corn, Joseph J., 133
Cott, Nancy F., 334–35n8
Crary, Jonathan, 342–43n19
Criswell, Ralph, 353–54n71
Cronon, William, 115, 117, 246
Crump, Spencer, 178, 347, 351n61
Cryer, George, 350n41
Curran, Henry, 205–7

Damon, George A., 26, 88, 153, 198, 202, 270, 332n103
Davis, J. Allen, 339n68
Davis, Mike, 22, 194, 233–34, 273–74, 369n61, 370nn74,76,82
decentralization, 17, 18, 49–59, 87, 91–113, 118, 137, 167, 172–74, 181–82, 184, 187, 198–208, 216–23, 272–74, 286, 311, 321–22, 358n27. See also garden cities; post-suburbia
de Certeau, Michel, 6, 10, 31, 317
De Leuw, Charles. See Kelker, De Leuw, and Company
delinquency, 62–63, 78, 174, 197, 223–27, 240, 242, 336n26, 363n15
Detroit, 19, 206, 296, 303, 373n15
Deverell, William, 268, 327n3, 367–68n53, 369n61
Diggs, Charles H., 297
Dimendberg, Edward, 373n14, 374n30
Douglas, Ann, 343n21, 367n48
Downer, Jay, 257
downtown Los Angeles, 2, 14, 16–20, 18, 24, 26, 33, 35, 39, 41–46, 42, 58–59, 64–68, 74, 81, 85, 87, 91–105, 108–17, 122,

131–32, 155, 157, 159–62, 168–77, 175–87, 193, 195, 199–200, 202, 204, 207–9, 213–18, 221, 224, 229, 233–34, 237–40, 244, 272, 298, 300, 312, 322, 326n9, 330n7, 332n103, 333n106, 336n26, 339–40n95, 348n19, 349n30, 355n84, 357n18, 358n27
Dykstra, C. A., 201–4, 210, 270

East, E. E., 90, 297
elevated railroads, 16, 115–17, 141, 143, 148, 151, 156, 176–77, 180–200, *189–90*, 341, 345n56, 351–52n63, 352–53n64, 353nn66,69
Ellison, Ralph, 159–63
Empire State Building (New York City), 150–52, 162
Equitable Building (New York City), 127–29, *128*, 135
Ervin, James McFarline, 329nn48,49
European Americans (white Americans), 34–37, 40, 158–61, 191, 193–95, 225–26, 229–30, 346n81, 354n83, 365n41, 373n13

Federal Housing Administration, 21
Ferriss, Hugh, 122, *139*, 148–50, 175, 205, 207, 298, 304, 345n55, 347n11
Fishman, Robert, 50–51, 56, 216–18, 220, 359n29
Fogelson, Robert, 20, 46, 58, 375n4
Foster, Mark Stewart, 20, 33, 35–36, 41, 64, 337–38n49, 360n41
Foucault, Michel, 328–29n38, 330n69, 342–43n19
Fowler, Don, *15*, 21
Fox, William, 265, 268–70, 286–87, 367–68n53
Frank, Dana, 334n8
freeways, 292–309, *294*, *298–300*, *302–3*, 373nn14,17, 374n30. *See also* autobahns; parkways
Friedberg, Anne, 317
Futurama, 304–8, *305*, 374n30

Gale, Edward, *69*, *72*, *76*
Gans, Herbert, 360n44
garden cities, 49–61, *52–53*, *55*, 79, 85–94, 108–13, 202–4, 332n88, 358–59n27, 367–68n53, 373n13
Garreau, Joel, 220
Gebhard, David, 20–21, 326n7
Geertz, Clifford, 361n60
gender, 27, 37–39, 62–71, 74–75, 120, 155–57,

164, 330n69, 330–31n73, 333n6, 334–35n8, 335n11, 336n26, 341–42n16, 366n46, 372–73n13
Giedion, Sigfried, 253, 263–64, 306, 317, 375n11
Girouard, Mark, 131
Glendale, 34
Glendinning, Robert M., 337–38n50
Goldberger, Paul, 119, 122
Good Roads Movement, 97, 331n79
Gottdiener, M., 220, 359n29
Gramsci, Antonio, 7, 32, 330n69
Greenwood, Roberta S., 354–55n84

Hancock, Ralph, 87, 212
Harriss, John A., 140–41
Hecht, Ben, 131
Heidegger, Martin, 362n9
Helman, Irving, 170
Hencken, John K., 142
Hine, Lewis, 123, 345n61
Hise, Greg, 20, 268, 273, 327n3, 367–68n53, 369n61, 375n4
Holden, Edward, 268–69
Hollywood, 13, 62, 68, 78–81, 104, 111, 157, 177–79, 183, 214, 303, 334–35n8, 348–49n24, 357n18, 358n27, 366–67n46, 375n7
homeowners associations, 36–40, 225–27
Hood, Raymond, 119, 141–42, 148
Horrigan, Brian, 133
Howard, Ebenezer, 49–59, 61, 112, 208, 265, 309, 313, 331n84, 332n89
Howells, John Mead, 119
Hughes, Langston, 158, 346–47n81
Huneker, James, 130

Inglewood, 34

Jackson, Kenneth, 44, 156, 345n70
Jacobs, Jane, 360n44
James, Henry, 129–30
Japanese Americans. *See* Asian Americans
Jay, Martin, 342n19
jazz, 223, 330n63, 336n26, 363n15
Johnson, Ernest C., 74–75
Johnson, James Weldon, 157–85
Jubb, S. A., 347n11
Julien, Kyle, 330n63
Just Imagine (1930), 149–50

Kasson, John, 344n43
Kazin, Alfred, 156
Kelker, De Leuw, and Company, 179–83, 197–201, 349n30, 350n41, 351–52n63, 353n69. See also *Report and Recommendations on a Comprehensive Rapid Transit Plan for the City and County of Los Angeles*
Kelker, R. F. *See* Kelker, De Leuw, and Company
Kelley, Florence, 199
Kephart, George, 220, 359n29
Kessler-Harris, Alice, 334–35n8
Keystone Cops, 80. *See also* Sennett, Mack
King, Moses, 123–24, 126–29, *128*, 132, 135, 142–44, *143*, 148, 207, *301*
King Kong (1931), 150–51, 345n67
Kling, Rob, 220–21, 359n29
Kropp, Phoebe, 354–55n84
Kuhn, Thomas, 360n47

Lang, Fritz, 149
Laurel and Hardy, 79
Lears, Jackson, 245, 343n22
Lefferts, E. B., 299
legibility and urban comprehensibility, 1–13, 29–32, 36, 39–44, 49–51, 54, 59, 72–74, *72*, 81–83, 89–91, 112, 116, 151–58, 162–63, 172–75, 187, 191–97, 211–12, 217–40, *219*, 245, 267, 272, 274, 280, 290–92, 295, 313–23, 325n6, 347n10, 375n7
Leigh, William Robinson, 145, *145*
Leitch, Thomas, 366–67n46
Lipsitz, George, 31
London, 57, 245
Long Beach, 34
Long Island (NY), 161–62, 260–62, 261, 264, 285, 365n41
Longstreth, Richard, 88, 168, 170, 213, 215–16, 347n8
Los Angeles *Daily News*, 290, 298
Los Angeles *Examiner*, 77, 99, 107, 166, 166–67, 173–74, 185–87, 191–92, 194, 209, 213, 268, 350nn41,43, 351nn50,61
Los Angeles *Express*, 99, 185, 187, 209, 296, 351n61
Los Angeles *Herald*, 66, 77, 99, 351n61
The Los Angeles Plan, 98–99, 175. *See also* Traffic Commission
Los Angeles Railway (Yellow Cars), 106, 177, 195, 336n18
Los Angeles *Record*, 99, 167, 184, 209, 351n61

Los Angeles *Times*, 18, 63, 65, 68–77, 99, *171*, 183–98, 213, 268, 289, 293, 299–300, 336n26, 337n30, 338n59, 351nn50,61, 351–52n62, 352n63, 353nn66,69, 354n83, 369n61, 370n76
The Los Angeles Traffic Problem, 95–98, 175. *See also* Automobile Club
Lynch, Kevin, 4–11, 317, 325n6, 326n9
Lynd, Robert, and Helen Lynd, 360n44

A Major Traffic Street Plan for Los Angeles, 100–14, *103*, 168–69, 174, 176, 180, 182, 203, 215–16, 326–27, 340n95, 350n41, 367n53. *See also* Traffic Commission
Marchand, Roland, 134
Marsh, Margaret, 37
Martin, Albert C., 186–87
Marx, Leo, 245, 344n43
Mathison, Richard, 339n68
Mayo, Morrow, 234–36, 239–40
McClenahan, Bessie Averne, 37, 225–33, 240, 278, 360n46
McClintock, Miller, 105–6, 339n86, 350n41
McDowell, James, 70
McPherson, Aimee Semple, 234, 353n66
McShane, Clay, 101, 249, 251
McWilliams, Carey, 234, 240, 361n59
Meikle, Jeffrey L., 339n86, 374n29
Mellins, Thomas, 123
Merritt Parkway (CT), *255*
Metz, Christian, 366–67n45
Mexican Americans (Latinos), 34–35, 191, 194, 225, 354n79
Miller, Perry, 344n43
Millier, Arthur, 289–90, 293, 307
Miracle Mile, 185, 213–16. *See also* Wilshire Boulevard
Modleski, Tania, 285
Moore, Charles, 214
Moses, Robert, 259–64, 306, 365–66n41, 366n43
motion pictures, 2, 17, 65–68, *67*, 77–82, *80*, 149, 180, 236, 239, 263, 305, 316–17, 334–35n8, 347n10, 348–49n24, 366–67n46, 374n30, 375n9
Mujica, Francisco, 148
Mullins, William H., 271
Mulvey, Laura, 342n19, 366n46
Mumford, Lewis, 52–53, 56, 134, 343n22, 344n46
Municipal Building (New York City), 135–36

Nadeau, Remy, 63, 80

Nasaw, David, 334–35n8

Neutra, Richard J., 210–12, 222, 240, 307, 372–73n14

New York City, 9, 24, 46, 64, 86, 122–63, *125, 128, 143,* 197–200, 204–9, 236–37, 248–49, 253, 259–64, 296, 304, 330n69, 334n8, 337–38n49, 346n81, 347nn10,11, 365–66n41

New York *Times,* 141, 151

New York World's Fair (1939). *See* Futurama

"Now We Plan" exhibition. *See* Telesis

Nye, David, 131, 133–34, 136, 152

O'Keeffe, Georgia, 123

Olin, Spencer, 220–21, 359n29

Olmsted, Frederick Law, Jr., 100–12, 201, 265, 267, 269, 273–83, 326n9, 339–40n95, 341n104, 362n12, 367n50, 367–68n53, 367n54, 369n61. See also *A Major Traffic Street Plan for Los Angeles; Parks, Playgrounds, and Beaches for the Los Angeles Region*

Olmsted, Frederick Law, Sr., 248–51, 255, 261, 362–63n13, 363nn15,17, 364n18

Olmsted Brothers. *See* Olmsted, Frederick Law, Jr.

Ouellet, Philip J., 338n58

Pacific Electric (Red Cars), 44, 46, *72,* 167, 173, 177–83, *179,* 188, 193, 234, 303, *303,* 309, 333n106, 347n10, 348–49n24, 363n69

Park, Robert, 222

parking ban (downtown Los Angeles, 1920), 17–18, *18,* 41, 63–70, *66, 69,* 92–95, 100, 104, 106, 182, 184, 203, 333n6, 334–35n8, 335n11, 348n19

Parkinson, John, 186

Parks, Playgrounds, and Beaches for the Los Angeles Region, 265, 267, 269, 273–83, *277, 281, 283,* 361n5, 368nn53,54, 369n61, 370nn74,76,77. *See also* Bartholomew, Harland; Citizens' Committee on Parks, Playgrounds, and Beaches; Olmsted, Frederick Law, Jr.

parkways, 250–87, *255–57, 259, 277, 283,* 295, 364–65, 368, 370–71

Pasadena, 24, 34, 35, 96, 104, 111, 153, *153,* 172, 214, 329n56, 358n27

Paul, Frank R., 144, 148

Peiss, Kathy, 330n69, 334–35n8

Pennell, Joseph, 122

Pettit, Harry M., 143

Pitt, Dale, and Leonard Pitt, 78

Pitt, William, 363–64n13

the Plaza, 14, 182, 191–93, 197, 350n44, 351n61, 353n69, 353–54n71, 354nn73,79,83, 357n18

Pollard, W. L., 331n76

Pomeroy, Hugh, 26, 265, 268–70, 286–87, 367–68n53

Pontius, D. W., 348n24, 353n69

Poster, Mark, 220–21, 359n29

postsuburbia, 220–41, 359n29. *See also* decentralization

propinquity, 132, 153, 156, 223, 228, 345n69, 375n10

public or rapid transit. *See* elevated railroads; Los Angeles Railway; Pacific Electric; subways

Pushkarev, Boris, 263, 365n33

race and ethnicity, 33–37, 40, 86, 89, 157–63, 191–97, 225–30, 329nn48,49,56,57, 330nn63,73, 345n70, 346n81, 353–54n71, 354n79, 365n41

Ralston, Esther, 348–49n24

Regional Planning Commission, 92, 265, 269, 270, 297, 314, 338n49, 358n27, 367n53

Report and Recommendations on a Comprehensive Rapid Transit Plan for the City and County of Los Angeles, 95, 179–83, 197–201, 349n30, 350nn41,44, 353n69. *See also* Kelker, De Leuw, and Company

restrictive deed covenants, 36, 40, 226, 228, 331n74. *See also* segregation

Riis, Jacob, 156

Robinson, Charles Mulford, 22–24, 27, 302, 328nn15,18

Robinson, William Wilcox, 79, 238, 240, 357n18

Root, John, 117, 168

Rummell, Richard, 143

Russell, Frances Theresa, 343n20

Saarinen, Eliel, 119, 135

Sackman, Douglas Cazaux, 363n14

Sandburg, Carl, 117

San Fernando Valley, 5, 109

San Francisco, 22, 167, 168, 182, 237, 280, 361n59, 372n13

San Gimignano (Italy), 132

Santa Monica, 80

Sartre, Jean-Paul, 134

Scharff, Virginia, 336n13

Schivelbusch, Wolfgang, 374n30
Schleier, Merrill, 122, 134, 343nn22,23
Scott, Mel, 86, 337n49, 372n13
Segal, Howard, 343n20
segregation, 10, 32–41, 54, 59, 69–71, 89, 117,
    162, 180, 194–97, 218, 225–33, 248–51,
    261, 273–74, 282, 293–95, 309, 329n56,
    330–31n73, 334–35n8, 357n18, 365n41.
    See also restrictive deed covenants
Seims, Charles, 347n10
Sennett, Mack, 80. See also Keystone Cops
Sennott, R. Stephen, 116–17
Silverman, Kaja, 366n46
skyscrapers, 2, 9, 16, 46–50, 117–87, 118, 125,
    128, 139, 143, 145, 165, 170, 186, 195–98,
    205–9, 262, 298, 304–5, 343nn21,22,23,
    344n46, 345nn61,63,69, 347n10, 349n30
Sloan, John, 122
Soja, Edward, 220
sprawl, 12, 14–15, 15, 51–52, 58, 233, 236–46,
    265–67, 275–78, 288–90, 306–7, 361–62n5,
    376n13
Starr, Kevin, 22, 79
Steichen, Edward, 123
Sterling, Christine, 354–55n84, 357n18
Stern, Robert A. M., 123
Stieglitz, Alfred, 123
Stimson, Marshall, 193, 354n79
the sublime, 9, 90, 118, 125, 128, 131–66, 143,
    145, 165–66, 170–72, 171, 175, 185–87, 186,
    205–9, 258–64, 282–87, 297–306, 318–23,
    344n43, 352n63
suburbs, 2–3, 18, 22, 34–39, 43–45, 45, 50–53,
    58–61, 101–6, 111–13, 206, 211, 220–23,
    238–52, 326n7, 329–30n57, 330n69, 339–
    40n95, 341n104, 345n70, 357–58n27,
    359n29, 364nn18,19, 365n35
subways, 16, 139, 140, 150, 156–62, 174–83, 178,
    199–201, 204, 206, 240, 249, 346n81, 348–
    49n24, 352n63
Sullivan, Louis, 117
Swan, Herbert S., 254

Taconic State Parkway (NY), 256, 259
Taylor, Eugene S., 116
Telesis, 288–99, 291, 293–94, 303–9, 307–8,
    371n4, 371–72n11, 372nn10,12, 372–73n13
Thomas, John L., 56
Tilton, L. Demming, 21, 371–72n4
Touring Topics, 70, 83. See also Automobile
    Club

traffic and congestion, 12, 15–19, 21, 24, 28,
    41–47, 42, 59–65, 60, 68–113, 83–84, 136–
    48, 167–81, 199–205, 216–20, 219, 235–37,
    249–54, 289–90, 295–97, 323, 330n73,
    340n77, 347n103, 348n106, 357n23,
    364nn26,30, 368n54, 371–72n4, 373n14,
    376n14
Traffic Commission, 98–101, 104–5, 107–8,
    111, 113, 175–77, 216, 339–40n95, 340n97,
    349n25, 350n41. See also The Los Angeles Plan;
    A Major Traffic Street Plan for Los Angeles
Traffic Survey: Los Angeles Metropolitan Region,
    297–300, 298–301, 357n23. See also
    Automobile Club
Transportation Engineering Board, 300
Treanor, John, 369n61
Tribune Tower Competition (Chicago), 119,
    135, 141
Tunnard, Christopher, 263, 365n33
Turner, Daniel L., 204, 206
Turner, Frederick Jackson, 194, 364n19

Union Station, 182–84, 188–97, 350n44, 351n61,
    353n69, 353–54n71, 354nn73,79, 357n18

van Leeuwen, Thomas A. P., 132, 341, 343n23
Vaux, Calvert, 248
Vinton, Arthur, 343n20
visuality, 1–13, 29–32, 41–44, 48, 58–61, 82,
    118–63, 172–74, 187–97, 220–23, 252–59,
    279–87, 304–9, 314–23, 342n19, 345n67,
    365n36, 366–67n46, 374n30
von Breton, Harriette, 20–21, 326n7

Wachs, Martin, 20, 41, 334–35n8
Warner, Sam Bass, 88–89, 337n49, 341n104
Watts, 329n57
West, Nathanael, 234–40
Wheeler, Fredrick C., 25–26
Whitnall, C. B., 328n29
Whitnall, G. Gordon, 24–27, 25, 62–63, 84–85,
    95–96, 100, 110, 198–99, 217, 270–73, 310–
    23, 328nn29,34, 338n62, 340n97, 375n7,
    376n14
Wiatr, Liz, 345n55
Williams, Robert Lee, 25, 328
Williams, William Carlos, 121
Willis, Carol, 356n113
Wilshire Boulevard, 87–90, 102, 103, 169–70, 181,
    184–86, 186, 197–98, 212–18, 215, 266, 350n47,
    351n49, 354n82. See also Miracle Mile

Wirth, Louis, 360n44
women's clubs, 27, 57, 199
Woolworth Building (New York City), 126, 135, 164
Workman, Boyle, 187
World's Columbian Exposition (Chicago, 1893), 114–15, 168
Wright, Lloyd, 165, *166*, 346n1

Yezierska, Anzia, 157
Young, Clara Kimball, 17, 65–68, *67, 69*, 334–35n8, 335n12, 348–49n24

zoning, 21, 41, 86–90, 102, 167–85, 203, 207, 212–13, 218–22, 320, 337–38n49, 350n47, 356n113
Zorbaugh, Harvey W., 115–16, 118

TEXT

10/12.5 Minion Pro

DISPLAY

Minion Pro

COMPOSITOR

Integrated Composition Systems

PRINTER AND BINDER

Thomson-Shore, Inc.